BOOKS BY *H·L·MENCKEN*

‹‹‹‹‹‹‹‹›››››››

THE AMERICAN LANGUAGE

THE AMERICAN LANGUAGE: Supplement I

THE AMERICAN LANGUAGE: Supplement II

HAPPY DAYS ⎫
NEWSPAPER DAYS ⎬ which, taken together, constitute *The Days of H. L. Mencken*
HEATHEN DAYS ⎭

A NEW DICTIONARY OF QUOTATIONS

TREATISE ON THE GODS

CHRISTMAS STORY

A MENCKEN CHRESTOMATHY (with selections from
the *Prejudices* series, *A Book of Burlesques, In Defense of
Women, Notes on Democracy, Making a President, A Book
of Calumny, Treatise on Right and Wrong,* with pieces from
the *American Mercury, Smart Set,* and the Baltimore *Evening Sun,* and some previously unpublished notes)

MINORITY REPORT: H. L. MENCKEN'S NOTEBOOKS

THE BATHTUB HOAX and Other Blasts and Bravos from
the *Chicago Tribune*

LETTERS OF H. L. MENCKEN, selected and annotated
by Guy J. Forgue

H. L. MENCKEN ON MUSIC, edited by Louis Cheslock

THE AMERICAN LANGUAGE: The Fourth Edition and
the Two Supplements, abridged, with annotations and new
material, by Raven I. McDavid, Jr., with the assistance of
David W. Maurer

H. L. MENCKEN: THE AMERICAN SCENE, A
READER, selected and edited, with an introduction and commentary, by Huntington Cairns

These are BORZOI BOOKS, *published by* ALFRED A. KNOPF *in New York*

H. L. MENCKEN

The American Scene

A READER

H·L·MENCKEN

The American Scene

A READER

SELECTED AND EDITED, AND

WITH AN INTRODUCTION AND COMMENTARY, BY

HUNTINGTON CAIRNS

New York : Alfred·A·Knopf

1 9 6 5

L. C. catalog card number: 65–11127

THIS IS A BORZOI BOOK,
PUBLISHED BY ALFRED A. KNOPF, INC.

FIRST EDITION

CONTENTS

❀ · ❀ · ❀ · ❀ · ❀

(v)

Contents

Contents

INTRODUCTION

by Huntington Cairns

❁ · ❁ · ❁ · ❁ · ❁

WHEN H. L. MENCKEN came on the scene at the beginning of this century, there had been an eruption in the European intellectual community, typified not by Comte and Mill but by Nietzsche and Wagner. The ideas in the air were still in a confused state. In the process of sorting them, Mencken made himself the most provocative writer of his day in the United States. He summed up more than anyone else the dissatisfactions of the period, and by resolutely rejecting the values of his time he succeeded in transforming some of them. Although he was a journalist, his concern went deeper. It is this concern, coupled with the whirlwind force of his personality, which gives his writings their enduring appeal.

Mencken went to work for the Baltimore *Sun* in 1906, and remained there, although not continuously, for the rest of his life. He had become a reporter on the Baltimore *Morning Herald* in 1899, at the age of eighteen, and had mastered his trade with astonishing rapidity. Six years later, having held most of the positions on the news side of the *Herald,* from police-court reporter to managing editor, he was made editor-in-chief at the age of twenty-five. Then, through no fault of his, the paper suspended publication in June 1906. Offers came from numerous papers, including *The New York Times,* but in the end Mencken elected to stay in Baltimore and accepted a proposal from the Baltimore *Sun.* Meanwhile he was writing light verse for the popular magazines, later collected into his first book, and also some forty short stories for the same outlets. Not much of this writing was distinguished, but along with the usual hackwork of an energetic newspaperman (brochures for local business enterprises and ghost writing), it brought in needed income. His journalism was another matter. Competent members of the craft recognized its merits almost immediately. Within a month of his employment by the *Sun*, Colonel Henry Watterson, the nationally known editor of the Louisville *Courier-Journal*, wrote: "Think of it! The staid old Baltimore *Sun* has got itself a Whangdoodle. Nor is it one of those bogus Whangdoodles which we sometimes encounter in the sideshow business —merely a double-cross between a Gin-Rickey and a Guyascutus —but a genuine, guaranteed, imported direct from the mountains of Hepsidam." Eventually Mencken was to become the Supreme Whangdoodle.

When he went to the Baltimore *Sun*, he was not yet twenty-six years old, and was at the threshold of the career that brought him to national prominence. By his middle twenties his famous prose style had been largely formed. It possessed a vividness and a vitality, a discipline and a rollicksomeness that mark it as distinctly his own. He could never conceal from the proprietors of the *Sun* that occasionally he wrote anonymously elsewhere to make some extra money. In his youth he studied Huxley's prose with care. It was an excellent model, and from it he learned to combine a vigorous, controversial style with the graces of humor. As a newspaperman he knew the importance of the lead sentence, and his own were developed with precision. There were artifices in his writing—the "Prof. Drs.," the catalogues of incongruous idiocies—but at bottom it was as honest as the painting of Mary Cassatt. Its secret is still something of a mystery to students of prose, and to one of the chief of them, Bonamy Dobrée, it has something of the movement of Sir Thomas Browne's. But Browne had a European intellectuality which no American has ever approximated, and which was reflected in his prose. It was extremely self-conscious, the opposite of Mencken's writing. Browne's balances were not as studied as Samuel Johnson's, but they are there. In Mencken they are altogether missing. Browne's intolerance of the prevalent notions of his day was perhaps as deeply felt as Mencken's, but it was much more guarded. In any event, by the time of the publication of Mencken's book on Shaw in 1905, his first prose volume, the famous style was almost full-blown. Writing of *Man and Superman* he said:

> Like a full-rigged ship before a spanking breeze, it cleaves deep into the waves, sending ripples far to port and starboard, and its giant canvases rise half way to the clouds, with resplendent jibs, skysails, staysails and studding sails standing out like quills upon the fretful porcupine. It has a preface as long as a campaign speech; an interlude in three scenes, with music and red fire; and a complete digest of the German philosophers as an appendix. With all its rings and satellites it fills a tome of 281 closely-printed pages. Its epigrams, quips, jests, and quirks are multitudinous; it preaches treason to all the schools; its hero has one speech of 350 words. No one but a circus press agent could rise to an adequate description of its innumerable marvels. It is a three-ring circus, with Ibsen doing running high jumps; Schopenhauer playing the calliope and Nietzsche selling peanuts in the reserved seats.

In 1908, in his twenty-eighth year, Mencken made his first serious bid for national attention. He published *The Philosophy of Friedrich Nietzsche*, an early exposition of the philosopher's life and thought, and one still cited with approval by competent Nietzsche scholars. He also inaugurated his monthly department of book notices in the *Smart Set*, an enterprise that was to continue for fifteen years. In the end the bid was successful, but the novitiate was long. He did not publish his next important work— *A Book of Prefaces*—until 1917. Not until his early forties, at the close of World War I, when the men began to write who were to count in the succeeding years, men such as Edmund Wilson and Aldous Huxley, did he get the intelligent consideration he sought. Meanwhile he had assumed the editorship of the *Smart Set* in 1914 with George Jean Nathan; he was widely known in the United States and abroad; Vincent O'Sullivan in a mention of *A Book of Prefaces* in the *Mercure de France* had greeted him as the first American critic since Poe; and in 1919 he had published the first edition of *The American Language*. But the important critics of the period—Irving Babbitt and Paul Elmer More—for the most part ignored him. His support, when it arrived, came from the younger men, and not too many of them. Before him were the older critics, Babbitt and More, with their following in the academic world, and behind him were the coming men, T. S. Eliot, I. A. Richards, Conrad Aiken, and the New Critics, Ransom, Tate, Brooks, Blackmur, and others, most of them strongly influenced by academic traditions. These writers gave Mencken no support; they either attacked him or passed him by. His champions, apart from the scholars of the philological world, came from the ranks of the free-lance critics of the liberal weeklies and the daily press. They were a strong group, and although their power in large part was to pass eventually to the New Critics, and to the sociological critics of the thirties, they helped materially in the enhancement of Mencken's reputation. Perhaps just as important as his public notices was the word-of-mouth support he had from influential writers and teachers. Morris Cohen and other teachers of broad interest would call the attention of their classes to Mencken's work, and Joseph Conrad, writing to a friend in 1923, found his "vigor . . . astonishing. It is like an electric current . . . a sense of enormous hidden power . . . who could quarrel with such generosity, such vibrating sympathy, and with a mind so intensely alive." It was in sources such as these, until well into his middle years, when his writings began to appear in textbooks and the English faculties took notice of him, that Mencken found his backers.

Early in life he reached a view of the nature of things which he never found reason to modify. The world appeared to him meaningless and possessed of no inherent organization; it was not something to admire or to despise, it just was. Man's life in it was essentially tragic, a brief episode in a purposeless and irrational muddle. There was no solace religion could give a sensible man; religions were essentially absurd. Art, and particularly poetry, were slight aids in the alleviation of man's condition; they were at best anodynes, worthless as guides. This had been Goethe's conclusion in his old age. Poetry, he said, can accompany us through life, it cannot guide us. Mencken's general outlook was skeptical and positivist; it was the latter attitude which gave him the stance from which he conducted his assault upon the American scene. Although he was frequently charged by his enemies with a complete skepticism, or at the best with standards of the most trivial sort, he nevertheless held basic convictions which, even in a technical sense, amounted to a philosophy. If he had believed nothing, he would have been hopelessly at sea.

His belief was in knowledge, and by knowledge he meant the verifiable facts of science. He thought there was an irreconcilable conflict between philosophy and science, and he was irrevocably on the side of science. In the time of the ancient Greeks (a people he thought greatly overrated), philosophy, as he saw it, occupied almost the whole field of knowledge. Since that time the expansion of science, he believed, had forced philosophy's back to the wall, for philosophy occupied an area in which truth could never be known, and if it were known, it would be of no significance to the inhabitants of this earth. As philosophy retreated, science advanced, and philosophy soon would have nothing left with which to concern itself except mystical speculation. He thought the only possible world view was one grounded on science. He would accept as the truth only the results vouched for by science; all the rest of man's so-called knowledge was mere predilection and prejudice. However, even in science there were limits he would not overstep. His veneration of scientific knowledge was for the kind that predicts eclipses, permits bridges to be built, discovers medical specifics, and improves the electric light bulb. When scientists turned philosophers and attempted to explain the meaning of their discoveries, he would dismiss the enterprises as forays into theology.

This view, which appears to follow from the enormous successes of science in the last three hundred years, has been popular in contemporary times. In its essentials its merits have been proclaimed by Spencer and Comte in the nineteenth century, by Dewey and Russell in the twentieth. Although the position has had powerful opponents, it is widely accepted. Its chief defect lies in the circumstance that the results of scientific investigation, even when there is an attempt to synthesize them, are inadequate to account for the world. At that point philosophy attempts to supply the missing elements. But this is not a satisfactory answer to many minds, even those with an interest in the nature of the world, including Mencken's.

His confidence in science was at the root of his political thinking. The theory of democracy to him was completely untenable, and he argued against it from his first important book to his last. William Graham Sumner had said that the subject had become so sacrosanct that it could not be studied with candor and sincerity, and that no one dared analyze it as he would aristocracy or autocracy. Such admonitions meant little to Mencken. He attacked the idea with his incomparable invective in his routine journalistic writings and in his more considered essays. In his middle years he summed up his whole case in the volume *Notes on Democracy,* the last work of its kind in American thought. His critics have found the sources of his antipathy to the democratic idea in the Germanic middle-class atmosphere of Baltimore in the eighties, and in his early studies of Nietzsche. There is no evidence now available to resolve the issue, but it is a mistake to underestimate the extent of Mencken's reading. The influences his critics have emphasized may have played a role, although it should be noted that his chapter on the subject in his Nietzsche volume is more an exposition of his own views than of Nietzsche's. In addition, he knew the English tradition, exemplified by Carlyle, and continuing with Spencer, Arnold, Maine, and Lecky, and reflected even earlier in Scott's novels, which was hostile to the democratic notion. With the exception of Carlyle, whom he did not study until he was thirty-five, the works of these men were familiar to him before he wrote the Nietzsche volume; and since he uses their arguments they were perhaps a factor in forming his views. Through the writings of Huxley, which he read with care, and his other reading, he was led back to the ancient Greeks, democracy's first critics.

His basic objection to democratic theory, as with the writers who may have given him sustenance, was the belief that few men are competent to be entrusted with political power. This idea had been put forward in the famous allegory of the Ship of State by Plato in the *Republic,* a work which Huxley described as "noble" and which Mencken admired as a work of art. Huxley himself used the allegory in his essay "On the Natural Inequality of Men." Plato compares politicians to a mutinous crew of sailors who have made the none-too-bright owner (the demos) of the ship drunk, have taken possession of the ship, and are enjoying its food and wine while attempting to navigate it with no knowledge of the science of navigation; in fact, they even deny there is such a science, since if they admitted its existence they would have to confess they have no authority to command. Such ideas appealed to Mencken, but in his early writings he was without the support of science to sustain them. He could go no further than to say that "this natural incompetence of the masses is an actual fact," it has been "observed by a hundred philosophers . . . and fresh proofs of it are spread copiously before the world every day." But the army mental tests which came into vogue in World War I gave him the ammunition he needed. They seemed to show that 65.5 per cent of the population had the mental level of a thirteen-year-old. At first he attacked the tests as inherently non-sensical. In the end he accepted them, and thought it safe, nine times out of ten, to give them credence. Few things gave him greater pleasure than the discovery that his assaults on democracy had a basis in the apparent findings of empirical science.

In spite of his distaste for democratic theory and its consequences, he was happy to live under a democratic form of government. He had no preference for any other known kind, and he was vehemently opposed to authoritarianism, whether in its democratic or other varieties. He had no remedy for the defects he described in the democratic organization. His business, he said, was pathology, not therapeutics. In all democratic theory he could find only three elements that were logically sound and valuable: equality before the law, the limitation of government, and free speech. His so-called constructive proposals were nine-tenths buffooneries: that defeated candidates for the presidency should be hanged forthwith on the ground that otherwise they remained an intolerable nuisance the rest of their lives; that the punishment of recreant public officials by any citizen, from pummeling to lynching, be legalized, with penalties provided to the extent that the punishment exceeded the official's desserts; or that a simple cure for all the sorrows of the world, including war, would be to keep the human race gently stewed, possibly through the impregnation of the air with alcohol. Very occasionally he put forward serious proposals. He urged the abolition of the constitutional rule that a legislator must be an inhabitant of the state he represents. He thought the English system, which permitted the election of a Morley from some remote constituency, much preferable. He wrote out a modern Civil Rights Act and arranged for its consideration in Congress. He drafted a new constitution for the state of Maryland which included some Mencken specialties—the sterilization of criminals, unrestricted divorce after the third year of marriage, political disabilities for clergymen, lobbyists, and lunatics. His ideal government was a hierarchical form which he never spelled out in detail. Ernest Barker once remarked that the man of letters is by nature a Platonist in politics. Mencken might object to being so classified, but Barker's insight in his case is essentially sound.

With this background, Mencken set up shop in the *Smart Set* in November 1908, as a literary critic on a national scale. Thereafter, without intermission, he wrote a monthly article of about five thousand words for one hundred and eighty-two successive months, or a total of more than nine hundred thousand words. The task came to an end in December 1923. The following month, he launched the *American Mercury* with George Jean Nathan. His monthly articles continued in the *Mercury*, but by this time his major interest was no longer limited to literary criticism, but extended to the American scene in its widest aspect. He estimated that altogether he had passed judgment in the *Smart Set* on two thousand books. Looking back, he only regretted that he had been unduly tolerant. Too often he had overpraised books and authors. As for those with whom he dealt harshly, he could not remember a criticism, with one exception, that was excessive or unjust. He thought the books deserved the slatings he gave them, and even worse. This was his verdict on the fifteen years of what he called his critical episcopate. There is no question that on the whole the estimate is a fair one. But there are exceptions. Robert Frost was dismissed as a "Whittier without the whiskers," and Henry James was unduly denigrated, notwithstanding the now current critical effort in the same direction. But this is merely to say that his critical judgment, like Poe's and Hazlitt's, to name two stars in this firmament, was not absolute. To Mencken's credit, he never pretended that it was. His criticism should be taken as the recoil of an extraordinarily well-stocked, predisposed mind of acute discernment, tempered by an unmatched humor, and quickened by an urge to do execution upon the counterfeit. He wrote during one of the important transitional periods in the history of American letters; and that a mind so constituted was in a position to be a major force in giving that history the form it assumed after World War I can only be set down as a happy occurrence.

The immediate influences on his critical writing were Percival Pollard, Vance Thompson, and Huneker; from them all he learned the same lesson—a strong hospitality to the contemporary. Pollard, who belonged to the New York reviewing world at the turn of the century, is now not undeservedly forgotten; both his criticism and his prose left much to be desired. But his main interest lay in promoting the quality of American literature. He was liberal, but selective, in his welcome to new and neglected authors. As a young man in his teens, Mencken absorbed Pollard's writings. Vance Thompson was the editor of *M'lle New York*, a wit, a promoter of European literature, and a follower of Nietzsche. Huneker opened Mencken's eyes to the current European world of letters. His debt to both Pollard and Huneker was a large one, and he freely acknowledged it. He saw Huneker as much the abler man, but when he came to determine his own course he followed the path Pollard had marked out. Huneker's interest lay in the European ferment in art and letters. Mencken did not neglect that area, but his knowledge of the field could not compete with Huneker's. Like Pollard, he had an intense desire to see the development of a strong American literature, one worthy of a place on the world scene. It was in this direction that he threw the bulk of his energies, notwithstanding the fact that his first critical work was on Shaw and the second on Nietzsche. During the years in which criticism was his main concern he made himself the chief spokesman for the new currents that had begun to flow into the national scene. He was well-equipped for the task. He saw American literature as a whole, including the crannies in which it had lost itself; he had read widely and closely; he had a passion for his subject; and he was absolutely fearless in the expression of his opinions.

Against these real assets there are some deductions to be made, and some deductions to be canceled out which have been made, but which ought not to have been. Of the former, there was his disinclination to take poetry seriously. He thought of it as "a comforting piece of fiction set to more or less lascivious music." No doubt the constant stream of thin volumes of verse which crossed his desk each month were largely worthless. It has taken criticism forty or fifty years to sort out their contents, and much that was highly regarded during Mencken's reigning years has now perished. Once every year or so he would give the poets a hearing. Although he would make an honest effort at judiciousness, his sense of the comic would prevail; he therefore missed some of the permanent poetry of the time. When he came upon the lines

> *O the moon shone bright on Mrs. Porter*
> *And on her daughter*
> *They wash their feet in soda water*

in the most acclaimed poem of the period, he could conclude only that somebody's leg was being pulled. Nevertheless, as is customary, Mencken's attitude to poetry should not be dismissed as Philistine. Keats too at times held a similar view: "I am sometimes so very sceptical as to think Poetry itself a mere Jack a lanthern to amuse whoever may chance to be struck with its brilliance." But the circumstance remains that this conception of poetry will not fit the facts, as Keats knew.

Of his other impediments as a critic, only one demands notice. He resolutely refused to write on the standard subjects of his craft. He never tested his critical powers on the great names of the past, a practice which no critic of standing has ever forsworn. A Hazlitt might stop reading altogether, but he never ceased writing about the important men who had preceded him. Eliot, too, it is well to observe, has followed this course. The past, much more than the present, has been the subject of his criticism. Mencken's concern was with the contemporary, where he had a significant task to perform. He thought that studies of standard authors were academic essays in futility, as in truth many of them are. But the critic who does not keep these writers under review in his own writings runs the risk we all run in any field when we turn our backs on the past.

For the deductions to be canceled, the charges that he was ill-informed, that his ear was defective, that he had no literary scale of values, that he lacked "the sentiment of reverence," are either false or silly, as a reading of the *Smart Set* files will demonstrate. Even Babbitt, an academician of the first water, a learned man, who had been Mencken's target for many years, grudgingly in the end granted him certain "genuine critical virtues." In truth, he was better than that. A great deal of what he wrote he knew would not survive the critical eye of later days. He wrote too much and too often, but at the conclusion of the whole affair he had achieved what he set out to do. The American writer was free to function in a literary atmosphere completely different from that which prevailed in November 1908, when Mencken's national career began.

With the appearance of the *American Mercury* in 1924, Mencken's activity as a literary critic largely came to an end. He would review the important new literary works from time to time, including even poetry, but he deliberately set himself the task of covering a much wider field. He sought out particularly books which illuminated some aspect of the American scene, and he made excursions too into philosophy, art, science, history, and religion. This shift in the emphasis of his interests was deliberate and had been announced in the blurb he wrote for *Prejudices: Third Series*, published in 1922. Thereafter, he said, he would be more concerned with "general ideas" than with literary criticism, a resolution to which he adhered for the rest of his life. He was also aware that criticism was becoming increasingly self-conscious, or in his view, academic, a path he had no impulse to follow, nor was it a sound one for the *Mercury* as he saw its aims.

Mencken kept abreast of the work of the important critics of the new generation. There was occasional sniping from both sides, but he never came to grips with the writings of the chief of them, T. S. Eliot. Much later, in Mencken's sixty-eighth year, the occasion arose for him to meet some of the most representative of the group. He was reluctant on the ground that they were all opposed to his writings. Years earlier he had declined to meet Stuart P. Sherman, who had attacked his literary criticism in World War I as pro-German in character. Mencken's remark was:

"He is a dirty fighter." Mencken did not object to Sherman's attacks on himself; he resented Sherman's efforts during the war to write off the critically beleaguered Dreiser novels as worthless on the ground that Dreiser was of German descent and hence unpatriotic. But Mencken recognized that he had no such case against the younger critics and derived considerable pleasure from the meeting. If his attitude, so far as his writing went, was generally one of aloofness toward the critics of the 1920's, the case was otherwise with the so-called sociological critics of the 1930's. He gave them a fair, if Menckenesque, hearing in the *Mercury,* even when their books denounced him vigorously. The task, in his eyes, was an easy one, for he was on old and familiar ground, dating back to at least 1910, when he published in *Men Versus the Man* his debate with the socialist Robert Rives La Monte. Actually, Mencken's general abandonment of literary criticism for the role of critic of American life was not as radical as Huneker's shifts from musical criticism to dramatic criticism to art criticism, all of which involved laborious preparation on his part. As an editorial writer and journalist, Mencken had been occupied with American life for his entire writing career. At forty-four he merely concluded that his task in the literary field was done, and that he had little more to say in that area.

Thereafter, until the Depression of 1929 and its aftermaths, he was the most powerful critic of American life that it had known. He had no equal in controversial skill, his humor was unmatched, he had the journalist's sense of the significant, he had forged a colorful and distinctive prose, and his point of view was deeply individualistic. In general he was against government interference in both the economic and the political spheres. Primarily he was influenced in this respect by Herbert Spencer, but he rarely went as far as Spencer, who wanted even the operation of lighthouses to remain in private hands. He recognized the necessity of some governmental regulation, even the excursion by government into some areas of business that might be maintained by private enterprise, but it all should be kept to the strictest minimum. His thinking began always with the individual, never with the group, and with the premise that the good of the individual was to be realized in the discharge of a necessary function in a hierarchical state order. How, he demanded, would the place of the individual in that order be determined? Certainly not by the judgment of the bureaucracy, for, in all probability, the members of the bureaucracy are not the wisest of men. The only solution, as he saw it, was to let the forces of nature operate as they will. Inevitably, there will be a caste society, and it will be made by nature, not by man. In a well-run world the man at the top will be the individual who has added measurably to the world's store of knowledge; truth-seeking will take the place of money-making and military success as the standard of value. In his general thinking he went no further than these notions. He never attempted to work out a political theory in the classical systematic sense. The pitfalls into which Spencer fell when he essayed the task were perhaps a warning to him. Ultimately, the position he took was the one put forward in 1882 by Jevons, whose book *The State in Relation to Labour* he read in preparation for the La Monte debate. Abstract principles were useless for the determination of actual cases. Each proposal should be judged on the basis of the arguments for and against it. Most, or more likely all, political and social theories in Mencken's view were at best no more than probable guesses. It appealed to his conception of science to disregard theory and to look at each case on its own merits in the light of such evidence as might be available.

For a dozen years following the establishment of the *Mercury,* he was on the public stage as a commentator on American life, and for two thirds of that time he had the largest following ever had by a publicist in that position. At the peak of this phase of his career, *The New York Times* editorialized that he was the most powerful private citizen in the United States. There was no phase of American life of general interest upon which he failed to comment. What he saw usually displeased him. The country's rulers for the most part were charlatans; its poets and writers, with the exception of Dreiser, Sinclair Lewis, Scott Fitzgerald, and a few others, were unimportant; its colleges and universities were a disgrace; its clergy was a menace to civilized life; its newspapers were largely manned by incompetents; and its citizens were of such a low level of intelligence that they deserved what they got. It was a harsh indictment, probably the most severe ever put forward by a native American. He felt passionately about the future of America, and many of the objects of his attacks were highly vulnerable. They were, in fact, also under criticism from other quarters, particularly in the pages of the weeklies of the period, but the energy of Mencken's prose and his deep sense of the comic left him no real competitors. Moreover, other critics made the mistake, in Mencken's view, of proposing alternative plans to improve the country. Their ideal pictures of the best possible world seemed to him pictures of the worst possible world, based, as he remarked, on "a magnificent faith in incredible evidence."

At the same time, while his following was a large one, as such audiences go, he became the most denounced man in the United States. The bulk of the criticism was at the vituperative level and of no importance. He was labeled a weasel, a buzzard, a toad, a dog, a polecat, a howling hyena, and so on. In 1928 he published selected specimens in a little volume in which he noted that, in one year, more than five hundred separate editorials had been printed about him, at least four fifths of which were unfavorable. He fared no better in the world of letters. A Conrad might praise him in a letter to a friend; a Robert Bridges, to the consternation of the academic world, might declare upon arriving in New York that Mencken was the only person he was interested in meeting in the United States; but Mencken's support from that level was meager. Edmund Wilson and Walter Lippmann wrote about him with intelligence and detachment, but for the most part the serious essays on him were self-defeating because they were tendentious or patronizing—he was not a sound democrat, not a Marxist, not a Christian, he lacked a social sense, or he did not admire the proper literary figures. At the height of Mencken's fame, T. S. Eliot announced from his London aerie that Mencken was a destructive, not a constructive, critic. Mencken would have welcomed support, and perceptive understanding from men he respected, but as a hardened controversialist he did not expect it. Around men in his position, he wrote, "are enemies, and where he stands there is no friend. He can hope for little help from these men of his own kind, for they have battles of their own to fight." He now has a place in the anthologies; and the histories of his period, literary and otherwise, treat him at length and with respect. He would have been pleased to have this happen while he was alive, but it was not forthcoming.

With the Depression and the coming of the New Deal he lost his popular following. In his fatal illness his physician remarked that he had never known a patient who could see himself with such objectivity. He was equally detached in his view of himself as a publicist. In 1927 he stopped the publication of the *Prejudices* series with volume six when he concluded that the public had lost interest. He retired from the *Mercury* at the close of 1933, and with the outbreak of World War II he abandoned his weekly article for the Baltimore Sunday *Sun,* although he remained on the board of directors and was a news consultant until his death. But his friends in Baltimore knew him as the hardest-working man they had ever encountered. He labored continuously day and night, except Saturday evening, which he gave over to musical sessions with friends. Since the role of national publicist was denied him, he turned to other fields. He published three volumes of autobiography, perhaps as far from the self-revelatory Rousseau tradition as it is possible to get, but at the same time nostalgic and characteristically Mencken. The publication of many of the chapters of the autobiography in *The New Yorker* brought him a new and affectionate audience. He completely revised *The American Language* and ended with a three-volume work running to 2,166 pages, excluding the indices. He edited, under the title *A Mencken Chrestomathy,* a one-volume selection of his writings drawn from newspapers, magazine articles, and out-of-print books. He was an excellent self-critic, and his editorial work on the book gives evidence of pruning and rewriting. Some time after his stroke a book, put together from unpublished notes, was discovered among his papers, complete even to a preface. It was published in 1956 under the title *Minority Report: H. L. Mencken's Notebooks.* To many reviewers it brought back memories of great days in the newspaper and literary worlds.

Mencken's grandfather, who emigrated to Baltimore from Saxony in 1848, became the head of a prosperous wholesale tobacco business; but Mencken was a throwback to the scholarly professional tradition of his family extending to the seventeenth century. He was born on September 12, 1880, and learned the rudiments of education and the German language in a grammar school run by a conservative old German. His later training in the Baltimore Polytechnic Institute, a high school, gave him a large dose of mathematics and engineering; but it was not here that his interest lay. He was a born journalist and apparently was also born with that roving curiosity without which no one is educated, however many degrees he may acquire. Although he was not opposed to college education (in later life he would argue its advantages), he believed that he was capable of acquiring, through his own efforts and without an instructor, the knowledge he needed. Immediately after high school, he studied the classical English writers, from Chaucer to the present time, under the guidance of one of his former high-school teachers. For good technical criticism of his earliest writings he turned to the services of a competent correspondence school; here he learned to avoid long and pompous words and to write with simplicity and directness.

His attachment to Baltimore was so complete and persistent that the economic and professional lures of New York, though powerful, were repeatedly rejected. In his great days, offers from the important metropolitan papers of New York and the national newspaper chains were numerous; they kept up almost to his final incapacitating illness. When he was well into his sixties, a newspaper chain tempted him with a staggering annual salary, but it meant leaving Baltimore and he turned it down. From his house on Hollins Street he performed the difficult feat of editing the *Smart Set*, the *American Mercury*, and other magazines, by correspondence, supplemented with a well-planned commuting schedule to New York. No enticement that ever came his way, and none that he could imagine, could detach him from Baltimore.

On many occasions in his long writing career, he tried with all the skill of a journalist—but unsuccessfully—to make outsiders understand the charm of living in Baltimore. Native Baltimoreans knew, but Baltimore's special quality could not be conveyed to strangers. To non-Baltimoreans its white doorsteps, its cobblestones, its narrow streets and colorful markets, even its smelly harbor, were something for progress and urban renewal to iron away. But Mencken, like most Baltimoreans, loved it as it was. He was happy that Cathedral Street had a cathedral, he liked the promenade from the Cardinal's house on Charles Street hill down to Lexington Street in the center of the city, he was pleased that Baltimore was the only North American city in which a Prince of the church walked red-hatted, spare, and other-worldly among his people. The food, too, when properly cooked, delighted him— jowl and sprouts, pawnhoss from the sausage vats of Frederick County, the Chesapeake Bay soft-crab surrounded by a sliver of country bacon, the York cabbage, and the local strawberries. Above all, he relished the home life of Baltimore, the simplicity of its citizens with their attachments to their own opinions, dignities, and class. In his younger days something of the tradition of the colonial planter lingered on, and his natural Toryism was attracted by the patrician element in the city's life. But his love for Baltimore was not blind. He saw that Baltimore was not really a Cathedral town, scarcely even a Catholic one, and the ceremonials of the old world Cathedral cities were totally absent. The city was basically Puritan, governed by a system of Blue Laws dating back to 1723. But he loved it.

To the surprise of nearly everyone, he married in his fiftieth year. He had written many words, even a whole book, on women and the relations of the sexes, but always from the bantering point of view of the dedicated bachelor. "Love," he had declared early in life, "is the delusion that one woman differs from another." Nevertheless, women found him the most polite and agreeable of companions, and he maintained cordial relations with some of the exceptional women of his time. His bride was the Alabama short-story writer and novelist Sara Haardt, eighteen years his junior, and an instructor at Goucher College when they first met. It was a successful marriage marked by deep respect and affection on both sides. Sara managed his home with tact, falling easily into the circle of his friendships. Inasmuch as both were professional writers, they worked at their tasks in their separate studies until late afternoon, when they would meet in what Mencken called the "public rooms" to see friends and otherwise relax before an early dinner. It was Sara's practice not to meet him at breakfast, on the ground that no one had anything to say of interest at that hour.

But tragedy lingered over the marriage from the beginning. Sara was plagued by a succession of illnesses, and finally succumbed to meningitis after five years of married life. Notwithstanding her recurrent illnesses, she remained in Mencken's memory as a person of tremendous vitality. He said that he had never met anyone with more patience or more gallantry. When Mencken was faced with friendly or hostile biographers, he was the most generous of men and gave them all possible help. He had an absolute rule that they were free to write whatever they wished, no matter how critical. But for their chapters on Sara they found themselves in a more formidable atmosphere. He would not permit the slightest departure from his view of her.

His circle of acquaintances was enormous, but in his close friendships he followed the old injunction that they should be few in number. He also held the view that even close friendships should be reexamined from time to time, and those that had grown stale should be expunged. Nevertheless, the pattern of his life as a whole seems in this respect much like that of other men of his degree of complexity. He had his lifelong friendships, he had his differences with old friends, some patched up and some irretrievably lost. At bottom he valued most of them, and when some eventually wore themselves out it made him uneasy.

From the point of view of American letters, the most notable of all his connections was his literary partnership with George Jean Nathan, which extended from 1908 to 1925. Nathan's chief interest was the drama, a field in which as critic he eventually achieved a dominant voice. Mencken cultivated a number of domains, but public affairs was the overriding one. Nathan had no interest whatsoever in public matters or in politicians. America's entry into World War I enraged Mencken, but Nathan chose to ignore the whole business. "I do not care a tinker's damn," he wrote, "whether Germany invades Belgium or Belgium Germany, whether Ireland is free or not free, whether the Stock Exchange is bombed or not bombed, or whether the nations of the earth arm, disarm, or conclude to fight their wars by limiting their armies to biting one another." He explained that this was not a pose, it was the way he was made. In spite of this deep cleavage in their outlooks, the two men shared enough other views to maintain a working literary companionship of extraordinary length. They were clever men who enjoyed each other's company; they were both opposed to many of the manifestations of the American literary scene; and they saw that by working in partnership they might develop an influential public for their own ideas. They were successful in the latter enterprise, but in the end the partnership foundered as Mencken became more and more occupied with politics and Nathan refused to budge from his interest in drama.

It was a more mellow and a more learned Mencken who came before the public in his later writings; but he had not changed. The set of ideas with which he began his writing career he still embraced at the end, as the interviews he gave from time to time made clear, and as *Minority Report* proved. His personality was constant, and it had been tried in the fire of many a combat. He liked to think that because his notions had endured such tests they therefore possessed a measure of soundness. He remarked that his prose was of such a character that it was impossible for anyone to mistake exactly where he stood. His outlook at no time was popular with the general public, but he had made it his own, and it was supported by a long tradition. In attacking the cure-alls proposed in his day he stepped on many toes, and the rejoinders are still coming in; but the problems he discussed are genuine ones, they are still with us; and their solution is as urgent in our day as in his. He was sometimes mistaken, and he was sometimes harsh; nevertheless, when all his qualities are sifted, he emerges as one of the consequential men of his day. Throughout his life he insisted that in all he did he should be judged as a journalist. But he was a journalist of genius.

In 1948 he was incapacitated for further writing by a cerebral thrombosis. The approximately eight years that followed until his death on January 29, 1956, were years of boredom, alleviated to the extent possible by the unremitting devotion and attention of his brother August, a retired civil engineer and the author of several books. Although the stroke affected his speech, Mencken still saw friends at luncheon and at other times. He was fully aware of his condition, and would predict his own death with considerable buoyancy of spirits. He remarked that if he had been mistaken about the likelihood of an afterlife, he would make the only amend possible within his power. He would advance toward the Throne and say: "Gentlemen, I was wrong." He had deposited a sealed envelope in a strong box at the *Sunpapers,* to be opened immediately upon his death. It contained the injunction: Don't overplay it.

I

<<<<<<<<<<<<<<<<>>>>>>>>>>>>>>

The Critic
of American Life

Mencken was many things, a newspaperman specializing in political journalism, a literary critic, a magazine editor, an authority on American speech, a humorist of a high order, a writer of a unique and powerful prose. But foremost he was a critic of American life. He was, in fact, the most powerful critic American institutions and practices have known. The critical tradition that preceded him, represented chiefly by Cooper, Thoreau, and Henry Adams in a direct line, and indirectly by novelists such as James, Melville, and Dreiser, was notable. But attack was the mainspring of Mencken's writing; it was never relaxed from his earliest days to his last. In an interview on public affairs with Roger Butterfield for Life *a year before Mencken's stroke, the slightly exasperated Mr. Butterfield, after an hour's exposure to a characteristic philippic, at length asked: "Mr. Mencken, which would you rather be called, 'The Sage of Baltimore' or 'The Man Who Hates Everything'?" "I don't care a damn what you or anyone else calls me," he answered, "just so long as you don't call me an old dodo sneaked out of the dissecting room. In the present case it is a little inaccurate to say that I hate everything. I am strongly in favor of common sense, common honesty, and common decency. This makes me forever ineligible to any public office of trust or profit in the Republic."*

Deeper than his antipathy to any government except the least bureaucratic, to all attempts except the most neccessary to regulate the lives of individuals, to the humbug he found in much of the political, business, ecclesiastical, and professional worlds, was the position from which he saw the American scene itself in its common denominator. Mencken's early critics, following his own lead, imagined that he looked on the scene as a circus parade, a mixture of ordinary and strange animals, which provided him with an endless supply of amus-

(3)

ing copy. But Edmund Wilson more than forty years ago, in the first significant appraisal of Mencken, recognized that his point of view was more radical. Wilson juxtaposed the following poem by Whitman with a prose poem from Mencken:

> The pure contralto sings in the organ loft,
> The carpenter dresses his plank, the tongue of his foreplane whistles its wild ascending lisp,
> The married and unmarried children ride home to their Thanksgiving dinner,
> The pilot seizes the king-pin, he heaves down with a strong arm,
> The mate stands braced in the whale-boat, lance and harpoon are ready,
> The duck-shooter walks by silent and cautious stretches,
> The deacons are ordain'd with cross'd hands at the altar,
> The spinning-girl retreats and advances to the hum of the big wheel,
> The farmer stops by the bars as he walks on a First-day loafe and looks at the oats and rye, . . .
> The young fellow drives the express-wagon, (I love him, though I do not know him;)
> The half-breed straps on his light boots to compete in the race, . . .
> The Wolverine sets traps on the creek that helps fill the Huron, . . .
> The clean-hair'd Yankee girl works with her sewing-machine or in the factory or mill, . . .
> The Missourian crosses the plains toting his wares and his cattle, . . .

Mencken's vision was different:

> Pale druggists in remote towns of the Epworth League and flannel nightgown belts, endlessly wrapping up bottles of Peruna. . . . Women hidden away in the damp kitchens of unpainted houses along the railroad tracks, frying tough beefsteaks. . . . Lime and cement dealers being initiated into the Knights of Pythias, the Red Men or the Woodmen of the World. . . . Watchmen at lonely railroad crossings in Iowa, hoping that they'll be able to get off to hear the United Brethren evangelist preach. . . . Ticket-sellers in the subway, breathing sweat in its gaseous form. . . . Farmers plowing sterile fields behind sad meditative horses, both suffering from the bites of insects. . . . Grocery-clerks trying

to make assignations with soapy servant-girls. . . . Women confined for the ninth or tenth time, wondering helplessly what it is all about. . . . Methodist preachers retired after forty years of service in the trenches of God, upon pensions of $600 a year. . . . Wives and daughters of Middle Western country bankers, marooned in Los Angeles, going tremblingly to swami séances in dark, smelly rooms. . . . Decayed and hopeless men writing editorials at midnight for leading papers in Mississippi, Arkansas and Alabama. . . .

Something had happened to America between the middle years of the nineteenth century and Mencken's time; it was this shift in focus that was at the core of Mencken's dissatisfaction. The dream of the carefree world of the common man had given way to the realities of political and economic frustration that follow from such dreams. When Mencken encountered novels or the writings of taxi drivers, or convicts, which saw the world in his own manner, he was drawn to them. He once told Dreiser that the most valuable baggage Dreiser carried was his capacity for seeing the world from this standpoint; it was responsible for all his talent for evoking feeling.

Although few men ever labored with greater doggedness to set things in their proper light, Mencken steadfastly refused to entertain the slightest hope that conditions would improve, and formally predicted that the United States would blow up in a hundred years.

On Being an American

<<<<<<<<<<<<<<<<<<<<<<<<<<<<<<<<<<<>>>>>>>>>>>>>>>>>>>>>>>>>>>>>>>>>

• I •

A PPARENTLY there are those who begin to find it disagreeable
—nay, impossible. Their anguish fills the Liberal weeklies and every ship that puts out from New York carries
a groaning cargo of them, bound for Paris, London, Munich, Rome
and way points—anywhere to escape the great curses and atrocities that make life intolerable for them at home. Let me say at
once that I find little to cavil at in their basic complaints. In more
than one direction, indeed, I probably go a great deal further than
even the Young Intellectuals. It is, for example, one of my firmest
and most sacred beliefs, reached after an inquiry extending over
a score of years and supported by incessant prayer and meditation,
that the government of the United States, in both its legislative
arm and its executive arm, is ignorant, incompetent, corrupt, and
disgusting—and from this judgment I except no more than twenty
living lawmakers and no more than twenty executioners of their
laws. It is a belief no less piously cherished that the administration
of justice in the Republic is stupid, dishonest, and against all
reason and equity—and from this judgment I except no more than
thirty judges, including two upon the bench of the Supreme Court
of the United States. It is another that the foreign policy of the
United States—its habitual manner of dealing with other nations,
whether friend or foe—is hypocritical, disingenuous, knavish, and
dishonorable—and from this judgment I consent to no exceptions

whatever, either recent or long past. And it is my fourth (and, to avoid too depressing a bill, final) conviction that the American people, taking one with another, constitute the most timorous, sniveling, poltroonish, ignominious mob of serfs and goose-steppers ever gathered under one flag in Christendom since the end of the Middle Ages, and that they grow more timorous, more sniveling, more poltroonish, more ignominious every day.

So far I go with the fugitive Young Intellectuals—and into the Bad Lands beyond. Such, in brief, are the cardinal articles of my political faith, held passionately since my admission to citizenship and now growing stronger and stronger as I gradually disintegrate into my component carbon, oxygen, hydrogen, phosphorus, calcium, sodium, nitrogen and iron. This is what I believe and preach, *in nomine Domini*, Amen. Yet I remain on the dock, wrapped in the flag, when the Young Intellectuals set sail. Yet here I stand, unshaken and undespairing, a loyal and devoted Americano, even a chauvinist, paying taxes without complaint, obeying all laws that are physiologically obeyable, accepting all the searching duties and responsibilities of citizenship unprotestingly, investing the sparse usufructs of my miserable toil in the obligations of the nation, avoiding all commerce with men sworn to overthrow the government, contributing my mite toward the glory of the national arts and sciences, enriching and embellishing the native language, spurning all lures (and even all invitations) to get out and stay out—here am I, a bachelor of easy means, forty-two years old, unhampered by debts or issue, able to go wherever I please and to stay as long as I please—here am I, contentedly and even smugly basking beneath the Stars and Stripes, a better citizen, I daresay, and certainly a less murmurous and exigent one, than thousands who put the Hon. Warren Gamaliel Harding beside Friedrich Barbarossa and Charlemagne, and hold the Supreme Court to be directly inspired by the Holy Spirit, and belong ardently to every Rotary Club, Ku Klux Klan, and Anti-Saloon League, and choke with emotion when the band plays "The Star-Spangled Banner," and believe with the faith of little children that one of Our Boys, taken at random, could dispose in a fair fight of ten Englishmen, twenty Germans, thirty Frogs, forty Wops, fifty Japs, or a hundred Bolsheviki.

Well, then, why am I still here? Why am I so complacent (perhaps even to the point of offensiveness), so free from bile, so little fretting and indignant, so curiously happy? Why did I answer only with a few academic "Hear, Hears" when Henry James, Ezra Pound, Harold Stearns and the *émigrés* of Greenwich Village issued their successive calls to the corn-fed *intelligentsia* to flee the shambles, escape to fairer lands, throw off the curse forever? The answer, of course, is to be sought in the nature of happiness, which tempts to metaphysics. But let me keep upon the ground. To me, at least (and I can only follow my own nose), happiness presents itself in an aspect that is tripartite. To be happy (reducing the thing to its elementals) I must be:

a. Well-fed, unhounded by sordid cares, at ease in Zion.
b. Full of a comfortable feeling of superiority to the masses of my fellow-men.
c. Delicately and unceasingly amused according to my taste.

It is my contention that, if this definition be accepted, there is no country on the face of the earth wherein a man roughly constituted as I am—a man of my general weaknesses, vanities, appetites, prejudices, and aversions—can be so happy, or even one-half so happy, as he can be in these free and independent states. Going further, I lay down the proposition that it is a sheer physical impossibility for such a man to live in These States and *not* be happy—that it is as impossible to him as it would be to a schoolboy to weep over the burning down of his schoolhouse. If he says that he isn't happy here, then he either lies or is insane. Here the business of getting a living, particularly since the war brought the loot of all Europe to the national strong-box, is enormously easier than it is in any other Christian land—so easy, in fact, that an educated and forehanded man who fails at it must actually make deliberate efforts to that end. Here the general average of intelligence, of knowledge, of competence, of integrity, of self-respect, of honor is so low that any man who knows his trade, does not fear ghosts, has read fifty good books, and practices the common decencies stands out as brilliantly as a wart on a bald head, and is thrown willy-nilly into a meager and exclusive aristocracy. And here, more than anywhere else that I know of or have heard of, the daily panorama of human existence, of private and communal folly—the unending procession of governmental extortions and chicaneries, of commercial brigandages and throat-slittings, of theological buffooneries, of aesthetic ribaldries, of legal swindles and harlotries, of miscellaneous rogueries, villainies, imbecilities, grotesqueries, and extravagances—is so inordinately gross and preposterous, so perfectly brought up to the highest conceivable amperage, so steadily enriched with an almost fabulous daring and originality, that only the man who was born with a petrified diaphragm can fail to laugh himself to sleep every night, and to awake every morning with all the eager, unflagging expectation of a Sunday-school superintendent touring the Paris peep-shows.

A certain sough of rhetoric may be here. Perhaps I yield to words as a chautauqua lecturer yields to them, belaboring and fermenting the hinds with his Message from the New Jerusalem. But fundamentally I am quite as sincere as he is. For example, in the matter of attaining to ease in Zion, of getting a fair share of the national swag, now piled so mountainously high. It seems to me, sunk in my Egyptian night, that the man who fails to do this in the United States today is a man who is somehow stupid—maybe not on the surface, but certainly deep down. Either he is one who cripples himself unduly, say by setting up a family before he can care for it, or by making a bad bargain for the sale of his wares, or by concerning himself too much about the affairs of other men; or he is one who endeavors fatuously to sell something that no normal American wants. Whenever I hear a professor of philosophy complain that his wife has eloped with some moving-picture actor or bootlegger who can at least feed and clothe her, my natural sympathy for the man is greatly corrupted by contempt for his lack of sense. Would it be regarded as sane and laudable for a man to travel the Soudan trying to sell fountain pens, or Greenland offering to teach double-entry bookkeeping or counter-point? Coming closer, would the judicious pity or laugh at a man who opened a shop for the sale of incunabula in Little Rock, Ark., or who demanded a living in McKeesport, Pa., on the ground that he could read Sumerian? In precisely the same way it seems to me to be nonsensical for a man to offer generally some commodity that only a few rare and dubious Americans want, and then weep and beat his breast because he is not patronized. One seeking to make a living in a country must pay due regard to the needs and tastes of that country. Here in the United States we have no jobs for grand dukes, and none for *Wirkliche Geheimräte,* and none for palace eunuchs, and none for masters of the buck-hounds, and none (any more) for brewery *Todsäufer*—and very few for oboe-players, metaphysicians, astrophysicists, assyriologists, watercolorists, stylites and epic poets. There was a time when the *Todsäufer* served a public need and got an adequate reward, but it is no more. There may come a time when the composer of string quartettes is paid as much as a railway conductor, but it is not yet. Then why practice such trades—that is, as trades? The man of independent means may venture into them prudently; when he does so, he is seldom molested; it may even be argued that he performs a public service by adopting them. But the man who has a living to make is simply silly if he goes into them; he is like a soldier going over the top with a coffin strapped to his back. Let him abandon such puerile vanities, and take to the uplift instead, as, indeed, thousands of other victims of the industrial system have already done. Let him bear in mind that, whatever its neglect of the humanities and their monks, the Republic has never got half enough bond salesmen, quack doctors, ward leaders, phrenologists, Methodist evangelists, circus clowns, magicians, soldiers, farmers, popular song writers, moonshine distillers, forgers of gin labels, mine guards, detectives, spies, snoopers, and *agents provacateurs.* The rules are set by Omnipotence; the discreet man observes them. Observing them, he is safe beneath the starry bed-tick, in fair weather or foul. The *boobus Americanus* is a bird that knows no closed season—and if he won't come down to Texas oil stock, or one-night cancer cures, or building lots in Swampshurst, he will always come down to Inspiration and Optimism, whether political, theological, pedagogical, literary, or economic.

The doctrine that it is *infra digitatem* for an educated man to take a hand in the snaring of this goose is one in which I see nothing convincing. It is a doctrine chiefly voiced, I believe, by those who have tried the business and failed. They take refuge behind the childish notion that there is something honorable about poverty *per se*—the Greenwich Village complex. This is nonsense. Poverty may be an unescapable misfortune, but that no more makes it honorable than a cocked eye is made honorable by the same cause. Do I advocate, then, the ceaseless, senseless hogging of money? I do not. All I advocate—and praise as virtuous—is the hogging of enough to provide security and ease. Despite all the romantic superstitions to the contrary, the artist cannot do his best work when he is oppressed by unsatisfied wants. Nor can the philosopher. Nor can the man of science. The best and clearest thinking of the world is done and the finest art is produced, not by men who are hungry, ragged and harassed, but by men who are well-fed, warm and easy in mind. It is the artist's first duty to his art to achieve that tranquility for himself. Shakespeare tried to achieve it; so did Beethoven, Wagner, Brahms, Ibsen and Balzac. Goethe, Schopenhauer, Schumann and Mendelssohn were born to it. Joseph Conrad, Richard Strauss and Anatole France have got it for themselves in our own day. In the older countries, where competence is far more general and competition is thus more sharp, the thing is often cruelly difficult, and sometimes almost impossible. But in the United States it is absurdly easy, given ordinary luck. Any man with a superior air, the intelligence of a stockbroker, and the resolution of a hat-check girl—in brief, any man who believes in himself enough, and with sufficient cause, to be called a journeyman—can cadge enough money, in this glorious commonwealth of morons, to make life soft for him.

And if a lining for the purse is thus facilely obtainable, given a reasonable prudence and resourcefulness, then balm for the ego is just as unlaboriously got, given ordinary dignity and decency. Simply to exist, indeed, on the plane of a civilized man is to attain, in the Republic, to a distinction that should be enough for all save the most vain; it is even likely to be too much, as the frequent challenges of the Ku Klux Klan, the American Legion, the Anti-Saloon League, and other such vigilance committees of the majority testify. Here is a country in which all political thought and activity are concentrated upon the scramble for jobs—in which the normal politician, whether he be a President or a village road supervisor, is willing to renounce any principle, however precious to him, and to adopt any lunacy, however offensive to him, in order to keep his place at the trough. Go into politics, then, without seeking or wanting office, and at once you are as conspicuous as a red-haired blackamoor—in fact, a great deal more conspicuous, for red-haired blackamoors have been seen, but who has ever seen or heard of an American politician, Democrat or Republican, Socialist or Liberal, Whig or Tory, who did not itch for a job? Again, here is a country in which it is an axiom that a business man shall be a member of a Chamber of Commerce, an admirer of Charles M. Schwab, a reader of the *Saturday Evening Post*, a golfer—in brief, a vegetable. Spend your hours of escape from *Geschäft* reading Remy de Gourmont or practicing the violoncello, and the local Sunday newspaper will infallibly find you out and hymn the marvel—nay, your banker will summon you to discuss your notes, and your rivals will spread the report (probably truthful) that you were pro-German during the war. Yet again, here is a land in which women rule and men are slaves. Train your women to get your slippers for you, and your ill fame will match Galileo's or Darwin's. Once more, here is the Paradise of back-slappers, of democrats, of mixers, of go-getters. Maintain ordinary reserve, and you will arrest instant attention—and have your hand kissed by multitudes who, despite democracy, have all the inferior man's unquenchable desire to grovel and admire.

Nowhere else in the world is superiority more easily attained or more eagerly admitted. The chief business of the nation, as a nation, is the setting up of heroes, mainly bogus. It admired the literary style of the late Woodrow; it respects the theological passion of Bryan; it venerates J. Pierpont Morgan; it takes Congress seriously; it would be unutterably shocked by the proposition (with proof) that a majority of its judges are ignoramuses, and that a respectable minority of them are scoundrels. The manufacture of artificial *Durchlauchten, k.k. Hoheiten* and even gods goes on feverishly and incessantly; the will to worship never flags. Ten iron-molders meet in the back-room of a near-beer saloon, organize a lodge of the Noble and Mystic Order of American Rosicrucians, and elect a wheelwright Supreme Worthy Whimwham; a month later they send a notice to the local newspaper that they have been greatly honored by an official visit from that Whimwham, and that they plan to give him a jeweled fob for his watch-chain. The chief national heroes—Lincoln, Lee, and so on—cannot remain mere men. The mysticism of the medieval peasantry gets into the communal view of them, and they begin to sprout haloes and wings. As I say, no intrinsic merit—at least, none commensurate with the mob estimate—is needed to come to such august dignities. Everything American is a bit amateurish and childish, even the national gods. The most conspicuous and respected American in nearly every field of endeavor, saving only the purely commercial (I exclude even the financial) is a man who would attract little attention in any other country. The leading American critic of literature, after twenty years of diligent exposition of his ideas, has yet to make it clear what he is in favor of, and why. The queen of the *haut monde,* in almost every American city, is a woman who regards Lord Reading as an aristocrat and her superior, and whose grandfather slept in his underclothes. The leading American musical director, if he went to Leipzig, would be put to polishing trombones and copying drum parts. The chief living American military man—the national heir to Frederick, Marlborough, Wellington, Washington and Prince Eugene—is a member of the Elks, and proud of it. The leading American philosopher (now dead, with no successor known to the average pedagogue) spent a lifetime erecting an epistemological defense for the national aesthetic maxim: "I don't know nothing about music, but I know what I like." The most eminent statesman the United States has produced since Lincoln was fooled by Arthur James Balfour, and miscalculated his public support by more than 5,000,000 votes. And the current Chief Magistrate of the nation— its defiant substitute for czar and kaiser—is a small-town printer who, when he wishes to enjoy himself in the Executive Mansion, invites in a homeopathic doctor, a Seventh-Day Adventist evangelist, and a couple of moving-picture actresses.

· 2 ·

All of which may be boiled down to this: that the United States is essentially a commonwealth of third-rate men—that distinction is easy here because the general level of culture, of information, of taste and judgment, of ordinary competence is so low. No sane man, employing an American plumber to repair a leaky drain, would expect him to do it at the first trial, and in precisely the same way no sane man, observing an American Secretary of State in negotiation with Englishmen and Japs, would expect him to come off better than second best. Third-rate men, of course, exist in all countries, but it is only here that they are in full control of the state, and with it of all the national standards. The land was peopled, not by the hardy adventurers of legend, but simply by incompetents who could not get on at home, and the lavishness of nature that they found here, the vast ease with which they could get livings, confirmed and augmented their native incompetence. No American colonist, even in the worst days of the Indian wars, ever had to face such hardships as ground down the peasants of Central Europe during the Hundred Years' War, nor even such hardships as oppressed the English lower classes during the century before the Reform Bill of 1832. In most of the colonies, indeed, he seldom saw any Indians at all: the one thing that made life difficult for him was his congenital dunderheadedness. The winning of the West, so rhetorically celebrated in American romance, cost the lives of fewer men than the single battle of Tannenberg, and the victory was much easier and surer. The immigrants who have come in since those early days have been, if anything, of even lower grade than their forerunners. The old notion that the United States is peopled by the offspring of brave, idealistic and liberty-loving minorities, who revolted against injustice, bigotry and medievalism at home—this notion is fast succumbing to the alarmed study that has been given of late to the immigration of recent years. The truth is that the majority of non-Anglo-Saxon immigrants since the Revolution, like the majority of Anglo-Saxon immigrants before the Revolution, have been, not the superior men of their native lands, but the botched and unfit: Irishmen starving to death in Ireland, Germans unable to weather the *Sturm und Drang* of the post-Napoleonic reorganization, Italians weed-grown on exhausted soil, Scandinavians run to all bone and no brain, Jews too incompetent to swindle even the barbarous peasants of Russia, Poland and Rumania. Here and there among the immigrants, of course, there may be a bravo, or even a superman—*e.g.,* the ancestors of Volstead, Ponzi, Jack Dempsey, Schwab, Daugherty, Debs, Pershing—but the average newcomer is, and always has been simply a poor fish.

Nor is there much soundness in the common assumption, so beloved of professional idealists and wind-machines, that the people of America constitute "the youngest of the great peoples." The phrase turns up endlessly; the average newspaper editorial writer would be hamstrung if the post office suddenly interdicted it, as it interdicted "the right to rebel" during the war. What gives it a certain specious plausibility is the fact that the American Republic, compared to a few other existing governments, is relatively young. But the American Republic is not necessarily identical with the American people; they might overturn it tomorrow and set up a monarchy, and still remain the same people. The truth is that, as a distinct nation, they go back fully three hundred years, and that even their government is older than that of most other nations, *e.g.,* France, Italy, Germany, Russia. Moreover, it is absurd to say that there is anything properly describable as youthfulness in the American outlook. It is not that of young men, but that of old men. All the characteristics of senescence are in it: a great distrust of ideas, an habitual timorousness, a harsh fidelity to a few fixed beliefs, a touch of mysticism. The average American is a prude and a Methodist under his skin, and the fact is never more evident than when he is trying to disprove it. His vices are not those of a healthy boy, but those of an ancient paralytic escaped from the *Greisenheim.* If you would penetrate to the causes thereof, simply go down to Ellis Island and look at the next shipload of immigrants. You will not find the spring of youth in their step; you will find the shuffling of exhausted men. From such exhausted men the American stock has sprung. It was easier for them to survive here than it was where they came from, but that ease, though it made them feel stronger, did not actually strengthen them. It left them what they were when they came: weary peasants, eager only for the comfortable security of a pig in a sty. Out of that eagerness has issued many of the noblest manifestations of American *Kultur:* the national hatred of war, the pervasive suspicion of the aims and intents of all other nations, the short way with heretics and disturbers of the peace, the unshakable belief in devils, the implacable hostility to every novel idea and point of view.

All these ways of thinking are the marks of the peasant—more, of the peasant long ground into the mud of his wallow, and determined at last to stay there—the peasant who has definitely renounced any lewd desire he may have ever had to gape at the stars. The habits of mind of this dull, sempiternal *fellah*—the oldest man in Christendom—are, with a few modifications, the habits of mind of the American people. The peasant has a great practical cunning, but he is unable to see any further than the next farm. He likes money and knows how to amass property, but his cultural development is but little above that of the domestic animals. He is intensely and cocksurely moral, but his morality and his self-interest are crudely identical. He is emotional and easy to scare, but his imagination cannot grasp an abstraction. He is a violent nationalist and patriot, but he admires rogues in office and always beats the tax-collector if he can. He has immovable opinions about all the great affairs of state, but nine-tenths of them are sheer imbecilities. He is violently jealous of what he conceives to be his rights, but brutally disregardful of the other fellow's. He is religious, but his religion is wholly devoid of beauty and dignity. This man, whether city or country bred, is the normal Americano—the 100 per cent Methodist, Odd Fellow, Ku Kluxer, and Know-Nothing. He exists in all countries, but here alone he rules—here alone his anthropoid fears and rages are accepted gravely as logical ideas, and dissent from them is punished as a sort of public offense. Around every one of his principal delusions—of the sacredness of democracy, of the feasibility of sumptuary law, of the incurable sinfulness of all other peoples, of the menace of ideas, of the corruption lying in all the arts—there is thrown a barrier of taboos, and woe to the anarchist who seeks to break it down!

The multiplication of such taboos is obviously not characteristic of a culture that is moving from a lower plane to a higher—that is, of a culture still in the full glow of its youth. It is a sign, rather, of a culture that is slipping downhill—one that is reverting to the most primitive standards and ways of thought. The taboo, indeed, is the trade-mark of the savage, and wherever it exists it is a relentless and effective enemy of civilized enlightenment. The savage is the most meticulously moral of men; there is scarcely an act of his daily life that is not conditioned by unyielding prohibitions and obligations, most of them logically unintelligible. The mob-man, a savage set amid civilization, cherishes a code of the same draconian kind. He believes firmly that right and wrong are immovable things—that they have an actual and unchangeable existence, and that any challenge of them, by word or act, is a crime against society. And with the concept of wrongness, of course, he always confuses the concept of mere differentness—to him the two are indistinguishable. Anything strange is to be combatted; it is of the Devil. The mob-man cannot grasp ideas in their native nakedness. They must be dramatized and personalized for him, and provided with either white wings or forked tails. All discussion of them, to interest him, must take the form of a pursuit and scotching of demons. He cannot think of a heresy without thinking of a heretic to be caught, condemned, and burned.

The Fathers of the Republic, I am convinced, had a great deal more prevision than even their most romantic worshipers give them credit for. They not only sought to create a governmental machine that would be safe from attack without; they also sought to create one that would be safe from attack within. They invented very ingenious devices for holding the mob in check, for protecting the national polity against its transient and illogical rages, for securing the determination of all the larger matters of state to a concealed but none the less real aristocracy. Nothing could have been further from the intent of Washington, Hamilton and even Jefferson than that the official doctrines of the nation, in the year 1922, should be identical with the nonsense heard in the chautauqua, from the evangelical pulpit, and on the stump. But Jackson and his merry men broke through the barbed wires thus so carefully strung, and ever since 1825 *vox populi* has been the true voice of the nation. Today there is no longer any question of statesmanship, in any real sense, in our politics. The only way to success in American public life lies in flattering and kowtowing to the mob. A candidate for office, even the highest, must either adopt its current manias *en bloc,* or convince it hypocritically that he has done so, while cherishing reservations *in petto.* The result is that only two sorts of men stand any chance whatever of getting into actual control of affairs—first, glorified mob-men who genuinely believe what the mob believes, and secondly, shrewd fellows who are willing to make any sacrifice of conviction and self-respect in order to hold their jobs. One finds perfect examples of the first class in Jackson and Bryan. One finds hundreds of specimens of the second among the politicians who got themselves so affectingly converted to Prohibition, and who voted and blubbered for it with flasks in their pockets. Even on the highest planes our politics seems to be incurably mounte-bankish. The same Senators who raised such raucous alarms against the League of Nations voted for the Disarmament Treaty —a far more obvious surrender to English hegemony. And the same Senators who pleaded for the League on the ground that its failure would break the heart of the world were eloquently against the treaty. The few men who maintained a consistent course in both cases, voting either for or against both League and treaty, were denounced by the newspapers as deliberate marplots, and found their constituents rising against them. To such an extent had the public become accustomed to buncombe that simple honesty was incomprehensible to it, and hence abhorrent!

As I have pointed out in a previous work, this dominance of mob ways of thinking, this pollution of the whole intellectual life of the country by the prejudices and emotions of the rabble, goes unchallenged because the old landed aristocracy of the colonial era has been engulfed and almost obliterated by the rise of the industrial system, and no new aristocracy has arisen to take its place, and discharge its highly necessary functions. An upper class, of course, exists, and of late it has tended to increase in power, but it is culturally almost indistinguishable from the mob: it lacks absolutely anything even remotely resembling an aristo-cratic point of view. One searches in vain for any sign of the true *Junker* spirit in the Vanderbilts, Astors, Morgans, Garys, and other such earls and dukes of the plutocracy; their culture, like their aspiration, remains that of the pawnshop. One searches in vain, too, for the aloof air of the don in the official *intelligentsia* of the

American universities; they are timorous and orthodox, and constitute a reptile Congregatio de Propaganda Fide to match Bismarck's *Reptilienpresse*. Everywhere else on earth, despite the rise
of democracy, an organized minority of aristocrats survives from a
more spacious day, and if its personnel has degenerated and its
legal powers have decayed it has at least maintained some vestige
of its old independence of spirit, and jealously guarded its old
right to be heard without risk of penalty. Even in England, where
the peerage has been debauched to the level of a political baptismal fount for Jewish moneylenders and Wesleyan soap-boilers,
there is sanctuary for the old order in the two ancient universities, and a lingering respect for it in the peasantry. But in the
United States it was paralyzed by Jackson and got its death blow
from Grant, and since then no successor to it has been evolved.
Thus there is no organized force to oppose the irrational vagaries
of the mob. The legislative and executive arms of the government
yield to them without resistance; the judicial arm has begun to
yield almost as supinely, particularly when they take the form of
witch-hunts; outside the official circle there is no opposition that
is even dependably articulate. The worst excesses go almost without challenge. Discussion, when it is heard at all, is feeble and
superficial, and girt about by the taboos that I have mentioned.
The clatter about the so-called Ku Klux Klan, two or three years
ago, was typical. The astounding program of this organization was
discussed in the newspapers for months on end, and a committee
of Congress sat in solemn state to investigate it, and yet not a
single newspaper or Congressman, so far as I am aware, so much
as mentioned the most patent and important fact about it, to wit,
that the Ku Klux was, to all intents and purposes, simply the
secular arm of the Methodist Church, and that its methods were
no more than physical projections of the familiar extravagances of
the Anti-Saloon League. The intimate relations between church
and Klan, amounting almost to identity, must have been plain
to every intelligent American, and yet the taboo upon the realistic
consideration of ecclesiastical matters was sufficient to make every
public soothsayer disregard it completely.

I often wonder, indeed, if there would be any intellectual life
at all in the United States if it were not for the steady importation

in bulk of ideas from abroad, and particularly, in late years, from England. What would become of the average American scholar if he could not borrow wholesale from English scholars? How could an inquisitive youth get beneath the surface of our politics if it were not for such anatomists as Bryce? Who would show our statesmen the dotted lines for their signatures if there were no Balfours and Lloyd Georges? How could our young professors formulate esthetic judgments, especially in the field of letters, if it were not for such gifted English mentors as Robertson Nicoll, Squire and Clutton-Brock? By what process, finally, would the true style of a visiting card be determined, and the *höflich* manner of eating artichokes, if there were no reports from Mayfair? On certain levels this naïve subservience must needs irritate every self-respecting American, and even dismay him. When he recalls the amazing feats of the English war propagandists between 1914 and 1917—and their even more amazing confessions of method since—he is apt to ask himself quite gravely if he belongs to a free nation or to a crown colony. The thing was done openly, shamelessly, contemptuously, cynically, and yet it was a gigantic success. The office of the American Secretary of State, from the end of Bryan's grotesque incumbency to the end of the Wilson administration, was little more than an antechamber of the British Foreign Office. Dr. Wilson himself, in the conduct of his policy, differed only legally from such colonial premiers as Hughes and Smuts. Even after the United States got into the war it was more swagger for a Young American blood to wear the British uniform than the American uniform. No American ever seriously questions an Englishman or Englishwoman of official or even merely fashionable position at home. Lord Birkenhead was accepted as a gentleman everywhere in the United States; Mrs. Asquith's almost unbelievable imbecilities were heard with hushed fascination; even Lady Astor, an American married to an expatriate German-American turned English viscount, was greeted with solemn effusiveness. During the latter part of 1917, when New York swarmed with British military missions, I observed in *Town Topics* a polite protest against a very significant habit of certain of their gallant members: that of going to dances wearing spurs, and so macerating the frocks and heels of the fawning fair. The protest, it appears, was not voiced by the hosts and hostesses of these singular officers: they would have welcomed their guests in trench boots. It was left to a dubious weekly, and it was made very gingerly.

The spectacle, as I say, has a way of irking the American touched by nationalistic weakness. Ever since the day of Lowell— even since the day of Cooper and Irving—there have been denunciations of it. But however unpleasant it may be, there is no denying that a chain of logical causes lies behind it, and that they are not to be disposed of by objecting to them. The average American of the Anglo-Saxon majority, in truth, is simply a second-rate Englishman, and so it is no wonder that he is spontaneously servile, despite all his democratic denial of superiorities, to what he conceives to be first-rate Englishmen. He corresponds, roughly, to an English Nonconformist of the better-fed variety, and he shows all the familiar characters of the breed. He is truculent and cocksure, and yet he knows how to take off his hat when a bishop of the Establishment passes. He is hot against the dukes, and yet the notice of a concrete duke is a singing in his heart. It seems to me that this inferior Anglo-Saxon is losing his old dominance in the United States—that is, biologically. But he will keep his cultural primacy for a long, long while, in spite of the overwhelming inrush of men of other races, if only because those newcomers are even more clearly inferior than he is. Nine-tenths of the Italians, for example, who have come to these shores in late years have brought no more of the essential culture of Italy with them than so many horned cattle would have brought. If they become civilized at all, settling here, it is the civilization of the Anglo-Saxon majority that they acquire, which is to say, the civilization of the English second table. So with the Germans, the Scandinavians, and even the Jews and Irish. The Germans, taking one with another, are on the cultural level of greengrocers. I have come into contact with a great many of them since 1914, some of them of considerable wealth and even of fashionable pretensions. In the whole lot I can think of but a score or two who could name offhand the principal works of Thomas Mann, Otto Julius Bierbaum, Ludwig Thoma or Hugo von Hofmannsthal. They know much more about Mutt and Jeff than they know about

Nationalistic weakness

Goethe. The Scandinavians are even worse. The majority of them are mere clods, and they are sucked into the Knights of Pythias, the chautauqua and the Methodist Church almost as soon as they land; it is by no means a mere accident that the national Prohibition Enforcement Act bears the name of a man theoretically of the blood of Gustavus Vasa, Svend of the Forked Beard, and Eric the Red. The Irish in the United States are scarcely touched by the revival of Irish culture, despite their melodramatic concern with Irish politics. During the war they supplied diligent and dependable agents to the Anglo-Saxon White Terror, and at all times they are very susceptible to political and social bribery. As for the Jews, they change their names to Burton, Thompson and Cecil in order to qualify as true Americans, and when they are accepted and rewarded in the national coin they renounce Moses altogether and get themselves baptized in St. Bartholomew's Church.

Whenever ideas enter the United States from without they come by way of England. What the London *Times* says today, about Ukranian politics, the revolt in India, a change of ministry in Italy, the character of the King of Norway, the oil situation in Mesopotamia, will be said week after next by the *Times* of New York, and a month or two later by all the other American newspapers. The extent of this control of American opinion by English news mongers is but little appreciated in the United States, even by professional journalists. Fully four-fifths of all the foreign news that comes to the American newspapers comes through London, and most of the rest is supplied either by Englishmen or by Jews (often American-born) who maintain close relations with the English. During the years 1914–1917 so many English agents got into Germany in the guise of American correspondents—sometimes with the full knowledge of their Anglomaniac American employers—that the Germans, just before the United States entered the war, were considering barring American correspondents from their country altogether. I was in Copenhagen and Basel in 1917, and found both towns—each an important source of war news—full of Jews representing American journals as a side-line to more delicate and confidential work for the English department of press propaganda. Even today a very considerable proportion of the American correspondents in Europe are strongly under

English influences, and in the Far East the proportion is probably still larger. But these men seldom handle really important news. All that is handled from London, and by trustworthy Britons. Such of it as is not cabled directly to the American newspapers and press associations is later clipped from English newspapers, and printed as bogus letters or cablegrams.

The American papers accept such very dubious stuff, not chiefly because they are hopelessly stupid or Anglomaniac, but because they find it impossible to engage competent American correspondents. If the native journalists who discuss our domestic politics avoid the fundamentals timorously, then those who venture to discuss foreign politics are scarcely aware of the fundamentals at all. We have simply developed no class of experts in such matters. No man comparable, say to Dr. Dillon, Wickham Steed, Count zu Reventlow or Wilfrid Scawen Blunt exists in the United States. When, in the summer of 1920, the editors of the Baltimore *Sun* undertook plans to cover the approaching Disarmament Conference at Washington in a comprehensive and intelligent manner, they were forced, willy-nilly, into employing Englishmen to do the work. Such men as Brailsford and Bywater, writing from London, three thousand miles away, were actually better able to interpret the work of the conference than American correspondents on the spot, few of whom were capable of anything beyond the most trivial gossip. During the whole period of the conference not a professional Washington correspondent—the flower of American political journalism—wrote a single article upon the proceedings that got further than their surface aspects. Before the end of the sessions this enforced dependence upon English opinion had an unexpected and significant result. Facing the English and the Japs in an unyielding alliance, the French turned to the American delegation for assistance. The issue specifically before the conference was one on which American self-interest was obviously identical with French self-interest. Nevertheless, the English had such firm grip upon the machinery of news distribution that they were able, in less than a week, to turn American public opinion against the French, and even to set up an active Francophobia. No American, not even any of the American delegates, was able to cope with their propaganda. They not only dominated the conference and pushed through a set of treaties that were extravagantly favorable to England; they even established the doctrine that all opposition to those treaties was immoral!

When Continental ideas, whether in politics, in metaphysics or in the fine arts, penetrate to the United States they nearly always travel by way of England. Emerson did not read Goethe; he read Carlyle. The American people, from the end of 1914 to the end of 1918, did not read first-handed statements of the German case; they read English interpretations of those statements. In London is the clearing house and transformer station. There the latest notions from the mainland are sifted out, carefully diluted with English water, and put into neat packages for the Yankee trade. The English not only get a chance to ameliorate or embellish; they also determine very largely what ideas Americans are to hear of at all. Whatever fails to interest them, or is in any way obnoxious to them, is not likely to cross the ocean. This explains why it is that most literate Americans are so densely ignorant of many Continentals who have been celebrated at home for years, for example, Huysmans, Hartleben, Vaihinger, Merezhkovsky, Keyserling, Snoilsky, Mauthner, Altenberg, Heidenstam, Alfred Kerr. It also explains why they so grossly overestimate various third-raters, laughed at at home, for example, Brieux. These fellows simply happen to interest the English *intelligentsia,* and are thus palmed off upon the gaping colonists of Yankeedom. In the case of Brieux the hocus-pocus was achieved by one man, George Bernard Shaw, a Scotch blue-nose disguised as an Irish patriot and English soothsayer. Shaw, at bottom, has the ideas of a Presbyterian elder, and so the moral frenzy of Brieux enchanted him. Whereupon he retired to his chamber, wrote a flaming Brieuxiad for the American trade, and founded the late vogue of the French Dr. Sylvanus Stall on this side of the ocean.

This wholesale import and export business in Continental fancies is of no little benefit, of course, to the generality of Americans. If it did not exist they would probably never hear of many of the salient Continentals at all, for the obvious incompetence of most of the native and resident introducers of intellectual ambassadors makes them suspicious even of those who, like Boyd and Nathan, are thoroughly competent. To this day there is no American translation of the plays of Ibsen; we use the William Archer Scotch-English translations, most of them atrociously bad, but still better than nothing. So with the works of Nietzsche, Anatole France, Georg Brandes, Turgeniev, Dostoevsky, Tolstoi, and other moderns after their kind. I can think of but one important exception: the work of Gerhart Hauptmann, done into English by and under the supervision of Ludwig Lewisohn. But even here Lewisohn used a number of English translations of single plays: the English were still ahead of him, though they stopped half way. He is, in any case, a very extraordinary American, and the Department of Justice kept an eye on him during the war. The average American professor is far too dull a fellow to undertake so difficult an enterprise. Even when he sports a German Ph.D. one usually finds on examination that all he knows about modern German literature is that a *Mass* of Hofbräu in Munich used to cost 27 *Pfennig* downstairs and 32 *Pfennig* upstairs. The German universities were formerly very tolerant of foreigners. Many an American, in preparation for professing at Harvard, spent a couple of years roaming from one to the other of them without picking up enough German to read the *Berliner Tageblatt*. Such frauds swarm in all our lesser universities, and many of them, during the war, became eminent authorities upon the crimes of Nietzsche and the errors of Treitschke.

· 3 ·

In rainy weather, when my old wounds ache and the four humors do battle in my spleen, I often find myself speculating sourly as to the future of the Republic. Native opinion, of course, is to the effect that it will be secure and glorious; the superstition that progress must always be upward and onward will not down; in virulence and popularity it matches the superstition that money can accomplish anything. But this view is not shared by most reflective foreigners, as any one may find out by looking into such a book as Ferdinand Kürnberger's "Der Amerikamüde," Sholom Asch's "America," Ernest von Wolzogen's "Ein Dichter in

Dollarica," W. L. George's "Hail, Columbia!," Annalise Schmidt's "Der Amerikanische Mensch" or "Sienkiewicz's "After Bread," or by hearkening unto the confidences, if obtainable, of such returned immigrants as Georges Clemenceau, Knut Hamsun, George Santayana, Clemens von Pirquet, John Masefield and Maxim Gorky, and, via the ouija board, Antonin Dvořák, Frank Wedekind and Edwin Klebs. The American Republic, as nations go, has led a safe and easy life, with no serious enemies to menace it, either within or without, and no grim struggle with want. Getting a living here has always been easier than anywhere else in Christendom; getting a secure foothold has been possible to whole classes of men who would have remained submerged in Europe, as the character of our plutocracy, and no less of our *intelligentsia* so brilliantly shows. The American people have never had to face such titanic assaults as those suffered by the people of Holland, Poland and half a dozen other little countries; they have not lived with a ring of powerful and unconscionable enemies about them, as the Germans have lived since the Middle Ages; they have not been torn by class wars, as the French, the Spaniards and the Russians have been torn; they have not thrown their strength into far-flung and exhausting colonial enterprises, like the English. All their foreign wars have been fought with foes either too weak to resist them or too heavily engaged elsewhere to make more than a half-hearted attempt. The combats with Mexico and Spain were not wars; they were simply lynchings. Even the Civil War, compared to the larger European conflicts since the invention of gunpowder, was trivial in its character and transient in its effects. The population of the United States, when it began, was about 31,500,000—say 10 per cent under the population of France in 1914. But after four years of struggle, the number of men killed in action or dead of wounds, in the two armies, came to but 200,000—probably little more than a sixth of the total losses of France between 1914 and 1918. Nor was there any very extensive destruction of property. In all save a small area in the North there was none at all, and even in the South only a few towns of any importance were destroyed. The average Northerner passed through the four years scarcely aware, save by report, that a war was going on. In the South the breath of Mars blew more hotly, but even there large numbers of men escaped service, and the general hardship everywhere fell a great deal short of the hardships suffered by the Belgians, the French of the North, the Germans of East Prussia, and the Serbians and Rumanians in the world war. The agonies of the South have been much exaggerated in popular romance; they were probably more severe during Reconstruction, when they were chiefly psychical, than they were during the actual war. Certainly General Robert E. Lee was in a favorable position to estimate the military achievement of the Confederacy. Well, Lee was of the opinion that his army was very badly supported by the civil population, and that its final disaster was largely due to that ineffective support.

Coming down to the time of the world war, one finds precious few signs that the American people, facing an antagonist of equal strength and with both hands free, could be relied upon to give a creditable account of themselves. The American share in that great struggle, in fact, was marked by poltroonery almost as conspicuously as it was marked by knavery. Let us consider briefly what the nation did. For a few months it viewed the struggle idly and unintelligently, as a yokel might stare at a sword-swallower at a county fair. Then, seeing a chance to profit, it undertook with sudden alacrity the ghoulish office of *Kriegslieferant*. One of the contestants being debarred, by the chances of war, from buying, it devoted its whole energies, for two years, to purveying to the other. Meanwhile, it made every effort to aid its customer by lending him the cloak of its neutrality—that is, by demanding all the privileges of a neutral and yet carrying on a stupendous wholesale effort to promote the war. On the official side, this neutrality was fraudulent from the start, as the revelations of Mr. Tumulty have since demonstrated; popularly it became more and more fraudulent as the debts of the customer contestant piled up, and it became more and more apparent—a fact diligently made known by his partisans—that they would be worthless if he failed to win. Then, in the end, covert aid was transformed into overt aid. And under what gallant conditions! In brief, there stood a nation of 65,000,000 people, which, without effective allies, had just closed two and a half years of homeric conflict by completely defeating an enemy state of 135,000,000 and two lesser ones of more than 10,000,000 together, and now stood at bay before a combination of at least 140,000,000. Upon this battle-scarred and war-weary foe the Republic of 100,000,000 freemen now flung itself, so lifting the odds to 4 to 1. And after a year and a half more of struggle it emerged triumphant—a knightly victor surely!

There is no need to rehearse the astounding and unprecedented swinishness that accompanied this glorious business—the colossal waste of public money, the savage persecution of all opponents and critics of the war, the open bribery of labor, the half-insane reviling of the enemy, the manufacture of false news, the knavish robbery of enemy civilians, the incessant spy hunts, the floating of public loans by a process of blackmail, the degradation of the Red Cross to partisan uses, the complete abandonment of all decency, decorum and self-respect. The facts must be remembered with shame by every civilized American; lest they be forgotten by the generations of the future I am even now engaged with collaborators upon an exhaustive record of them, in twenty volumes folio. More important to the present purpose are two things that are apt to be overlooked, the first of which is the capital fact that the war was "sold" to the American people, as the phrase has it, not by appealing to their courage, but by appealing to their cowardice—in brief, by adopting the assumption that they were not warlike at all, and certainly not gallant and chivalrous, but merely craven and fearful. The first selling point of the proponents of American participation was the contention that the Germans, with gigantic wars still raging on both fronts, were preparing to invade the United States, burn down all the towns, murder all the men, and carry off all the women— that their victory would bring staggering and irresistible reprisals for the American violation of the duties of a neutral. The second selling point was that the entrance of the United States would end the war almost instantly—that the Germans would be so overwhelmingly outnumbered, in men and guns, that it would be impossible for them to make any effective defense—above all, that it would be impossible for them to inflict any serious damage upon their new foes. Neither argument, it must be plain, showed the slightest belief in the warlike skill and courage of the American people. Both were grounded upon the frank theory that the only way to make the mob fight was to scare it half to death, and then show it a way to fight without risk, to stab a helpless antagonist in the back. And both were mellowed and reenforced by the hint that such a noble assault, beside being safe, would also be extremely profitable—that it would convert very dubious debts into very good debts, and dispose forever of a diligent and dangerous competitor for trade, especially in Latin America. All the idealist nonsense emitted by Dr. Wilson and company was simply icing on the cake. Most of it was abandoned as soon as the bullets began to fly, and the rest consisted simply of meaningless words—the idiotic babbling of a Presbyterian evangelist turned prophet and seer.

The other thing that needs to be remembered is the permanent effect of so dishonest and cowardly a business upon the national character, already far too much inclined toward easy ventures and long odds. Somewhere in his diaries Wilfrid Scawen Blunt speaks of the marked debasement that showed itself in the English spirit after the brutal robbery and assassination of the South African Republics. The heroes that the mob followed after Mafeking Day were far inferior to the heroes that it had followed in the days before the war. The English gentleman began to disappear from public life, and in his place appeared a rabble-rousing bounder obviously almost identical with the American professional politician—the Lloyd George, Chamberlain, F. E. Smith, Isaacs-Reading, Churchill, Bottomley, Northcliffe type. Worse, old ideals went with old heroes. Personal freedom and strict legality, says Blunt, vanished from the English tables of the law, and there was a shift of the social and political center of gravity to a lower plane. Precisely the same effect is now visible in the United States. The overwhelming majority of conscripts went into the army unwillingly, and once there they were debauched by the twin forces of the official propaganda that I have mentioned and a harsh, unintelligent discipline. The first made them almost incapable of soldierly thought and conduct; the second converted them into cringing goose-steppers. The consequences display themselves in the amazing activities of the American Legion, and in the rise of such correlative organizations as the Ku Klux Klan. It is impossible to fit any reasonable concept of the soldierly into the familiar proceedings of the Legion. Its members conduct themselves like a gang of Methodist vice-crusaders on the loose, or a Southern lynching party. They are forever discovering preposterous burglars under the national bed, and they advance to the attack, not gallantly and at fair odds, but cravenly and in overwhelming force. Some of their enterprises, to be set forth at length in the record I have mentioned, have been of almost unbelievable baseness—the mobbing of harmless Socialists, the prohibition of concerts by musicians of enemy nationality, the mutilation of cows designed for shipment abroad to feed starving children, the roughing of women, service as strike-breakers, the persecution of helpless foreigners, regardless of nationality.

During the last few months of the war, when stories of the tyrannical ill-usage of conscripts began to filter back to the United States, it was predicted that they would demand the punishment of the guilty when they got home, and that if it was not promptly forthcoming they would take it into their own hands. It was predicted, too, that they would array themselves against the excesses of Palmer, Burleson and company, and insist upon a restoration of that democratic freedom for which they had theoretically fought. But they actually did none of these things. So far as I know, not a single martinet of a lieutenant or captain has been manhandled by his late victims; the most they have done has been to appeal to Congress for revenge and damages. Nor have they thrown their influence against the medieval despotism which grew up at home during the war; on the contrary, they have supported it actively, and if it has lessened since 1919 the change has been wrought without their aid and in spite of their opposition. In sum, they show all the stigmata of inferior men whose natural inferiority has been made worse by oppression. Their chief organization is dominated by shrewd ex-officers who operate it to their own ends—politicians in search of jobs, Chamber of Commerce witch-hunters, and other such vermin. It seems to be wholly devoid of patriotism, courage, or sense. Nothing quite resembling it existed in the country before the war, not even in the South. There is nothing like it anywhere else on earth. It is a typical product of two years of heroic effort to arouse and capitalize the worst instincts of the mob, and it symbolizes very dramatically the ill effects of that effort upon the general American character.

Would men so degraded in gallantry and honor, so completely purged of all the military virtues, so submerged in baseness of spirit—would such pitiful caricatures of soldiers offer the necessary resistance to a public enemy who was equal, or perhaps superior in men and resources, and who came on with confidence, daring and resolution—say England supported by Germany as *Kriegslieferant* and with her inevitable swarms of Continental allies, or Japan with the Asiatic hordes behind her? Against the best opinion of the chautauquas, of Congress and of the patriotic press I presume to doubt it. It seems to me quite certain, indeed, that an American army fairly representing the American people, if it ever meets another army of anything remotely resembling like strength, will be defeated, and that defeat will be indistinguishable from rout. I believe that, at any odds less than two to one, even the exhausted German army of 1918 would have defeated it, and in this view, I think, I am joined by many men whose military judgment is far better than mine— particularly by many French officers. The changes in the American character since the Civil War, due partly to the wearing out of the old Anglo-Saxon stock, inferior to begin with, and partly to the infusion of the worst elements of other stocks, have surely not made for the fostering of the military virtues. The old cool head is gone, and the old dogged way with difficulties. The typical American of today has lost all the love of liberty that his forefathers had, and all their distrust of emotion, and pride in self-reliance. He is led no longer by Davy Crocketts; he is led by cheer leaders, press agents, word-mongers, up-lifters. I do not believe that such a faint-hearted and inflammatory fellow, shoved into a war demanding every resource of courage, ingenuity and pertinacity, would give a good account of himself. He is fit for lynching-bees and heretic-hunts, but he is not fit for tight corners and desperate odds.

Nevertheless, his docility and pusillanimity may be overestimated, and sometimes I think that they *are* overestimated by his present masters. They assume that there is absolutely no limit to his capacity for being put on and knocked about—that he will submit to any invasion of his freedom and dignity, however outrageous, so long as it is depicted in melodious terms. He permitted the late war to be "sold" to him by the methods of the grind-shop auctioneer. He submitted to conscription without any of the resistance shown by his brother democrats of Canada and Australia. He got no further than academic protests against the brutal usage he had to face in the army. He came home and found Prohibition foisted on him, and contented himself with a few feeble objurgations. He is a pliant slave of capitalism, and ever ready to help it put down fellow-slaves who venture to revolt. But this very weakness, this very credulity and poverty of spirit, on some easily conceivable tomorrow, may convert him into a rebel of a peculiarly insane kind, and so beset the Republic from within with difficulties quite as formidable as those which threaten to afflict it from without. What Mr. James N. Wood calls the corsair of democracy—that is, the professional mob-master, the merchant of delusions, the pumper-up of popular fears and rages —is still content to work for capitalism, and capitalism knows how to reward him to his taste. He is the eloquent statesman, the patriotic editor, the fount of inspiration, the prancing milch-cow of optimism. He becomes public leader, Governor, Senator, President. He is Billy Sunday, Cyrus K. Curtis, Dr. Frank Crane, Charles E. Hughes, Taft, Wilson, Cal Coolidge, General Wood, Harding. His, perhaps, is the best of trades under democracy—but it has its temptations! Let us try to picture a master corsair, thoroughly adept at pulling the mob nose, who suddenly bethought himself of that Pepin the Short who found himself mayor of the palace and made himself King of the Franks. There were lightnings along that horizon in the days of Roosevelt; there were thunder growls when Bryan emerged from the Nebraska steppes. On some great day of fate, as yet unrevealed by the gods, such a professor of the central democratic science may throw off his employers and set up a business for himself. When that day comes there will be plenty of excuse for black type on the front pages of the newspapers.

I incline to think that military disaster will give him his inspiration and his opportunity—that he will take the form, so dear to democracies, of a man on horseback. The chances are bad today simply because the mob is relatively comfortable—because capitalism has been able to give it relative ease and plenty of food in return for its docility. Genuine poverty is very rare in the United States, and actual hardship is almost unknown. There are times when the proletariat is short of phonograph records, silk shirts and movie tickets, but there are very few times when it is short of nourishment. Even during the most severe business depression, with hundreds of thousands out of work, most of these apparent sufferers, if they are willing, are able to get livings outside their trades. The cities may be choked with idle men, but the country is nearly always short of labor. And if all other resources fail, there are always public agencies to feed the hungry: capitalism is careful to keep them from despair. No American knows what it means to live as millions of Europeans lived during the war and have lived, in some places, since: with the loaves of the baker reduced to half size and no meat at all in the meat-shop. But the time may come and it may not be far off. A national military disaster would disorganize all industry in the United States, already sufficiently wasteful and chaotic, and introduce the American people, for the first time in their history, to genuine want—and capital would be unable to relieve them. The day of such disaster will bring the savior foreordained. The slaves will follow him, their eyes fixed ecstatically upon the newest New Jerusalem. Men bred to respond automatically to shibboleths will respond to this worst and most insane one. Bolshevism, said General Foch, is a disease of defeated nations.

But do not misunderstand me: I predict no revolution in the grand manner, no melodramatic collapse of capitalism, no repetition of what has gone on in Russia. The American proletarian is not brave and romantic enough for that; to do him simple justice, he is not silly enough. Capitalism, in the long run, will win in the United States, if only for the reason that every American hopes to be a capitalist before he dies. Its roots go down to the deepest, darkest levels of the national soil; in all its characters, and particularly in its antipathy to the dreams of man, it is thoroughly American. Today it seems to be immovably secure, given continued peace and plenty, and not all the demagogues in the land, consecrating themselves desperately to the one holy purpose, could shake it. Only a cataclysm will ever do that. But is a cataclysm conceivable? Isn't the United States the richest nation ever heard of in history, and isn't it a fact that modern wars are won by money? It is not a fact. Wars are won today, as in Napoleon's day, by the largest battalions, and the largest battalions, in the next great struggle, may not be on the side of the Republic. The usurious profits it wrung from the last war are as tempting as negotiable securities hung on the wash-line, as pre-Prohibition Scotch stored in open cellars. Its knavish ways with friends and foes alike have left it only foes. It is plunging ill-equipped into a competition for a living in the world that will be to the death. And the late Disarmament Conference left it almost hamstrung. Before the conference it had the Pacific in its grip, and with the Pacific in its grip it might have parleyed for a fair half of the Atlantic. But when the Japs and the English had finished their operations upon the Feather Duster, Popinjay Lodge, Master-Mind Root, Vacuum Underwood, young Teddy Roosevelt and the rest of their so willing dupes there was apparent a baleful change. The Republic is extremely insecure today on both fronts, and it will be more insecure tomorrow. And it has no friends.

However, as I say, I do not fear for capitalism. It will weather the storm, and no doubt it will be the stronger for it afterward. The inferior man hates it, but there is too much envy mixed with his hatred, in the land of the theoretically free, for him to want to destroy it utterly, or even to wound it incurably. He struggles against it now, but always wistfully, always with a sneaking respect. On the day of Armageddon he may attempt a more violent onslaught. But in the long run he will be beaten. In the long run the corsairs will sell him out, and hand him over to his enemy. Perhaps—who knows?—the combat may raise that enemy to genuine strength and dignity. Out of it may come the superman.

· 4 ·

All the while I have been forgetting the third of my reasons for remaining so faithful a citizen of the Federation, despite all

the lascivious inducements from expatriates to follow them beyond
the seas, and all the surly suggestions from patriots that I succumb.
It is the reason which grows out of my medieval but unashamed
taste for the bizarre and indelicate, my congenital weakness for
comedy of the grosser varieties. The United States, to my eye, is incomparably the greatest show on earth. It is a show which avoids
diligently all the kinds of clowning which tire me most quickly—
for example, royal ceremonials, the tedious hocus-pocus of *haute
politique*, the taking of politics seriously—and lays chief stress
upon the kinds which delight me unceasingly—for example, the
ribald combats of demagogues, the exquisitely ingenious operations of master rogues, the pursuit of witches and heretics, the
desperate struggles of inferior men to claw their way into Heaven.
We have clowns in constant practice among us who are as far
above the clowns of any great state as a Jack Dempsey is above
a paralytic—and not a few dozen or score of them, but whole
droves and herds. Human enterprises which, in all other Christian
countries, are resigned despairingly to an incurable dullness—
things that seem devoid of exhilarating amusement by their very
nature—are here lifted to such vast heights of buffoonery that
contemplating them strains the midriff almost to breaking. I cite
an example: the worship of God. Everywhere else on earth it is
carried on in a solemn and dispiriting manner; in England, of
course, the bishops are obscene, but the average man seldom gets
a fair chance to laugh at them and enjoy them. Now come home.
Here we not only have bishops who are enormously more obscene
then even the most gifted of the English bishops; we have also a
huge force of lesser specialists in ecclesiastical mountebankery—
tin-horn Loyolas, Savonarolas and Xaviers of a hundred fantastic
rites, each performing untiringly and each full of a grotesque and
illimitable whimsicality. Every American town, however small,
has one of its own: a holy clerk with so fine a talent for introducing the arts of jazz into the salvation of the damned that his performance takes on all the gaudiness of a four-ring circus, and the
bald announcement that he will raid Hell on such and such a
night is enough to empty all the town blind-pigs and bordellos and
pack his sanctuary to the doors. And to aid him and inspire him
there are traveling experts to whom he stands in the relation of a

wart to the Matterhorn—stupendous masters of theological im-
becility, contrivers of doctrines utterly preposterous, heirs to the
Joseph Smith, Mother Eddy and John Alexander Dowie tradition
—Bryan, Sunday, and their like. These are the eminences of the
American Sacred College. I delight in them. Their proceedings
make me a happier American.

Turn, now, to politics. Consider, for example, a campaign for
the Presidency. Would it be possible to imagine anything more
uproariously idiotic—a deafening, nerve-wracking battle to the
death between Tweedledum and Tweedledee, Harlequin and
Sganarelle, Gobbo and Dr. Cook—the unspeakable, with fearful
snorts, gradually swallowing the inconceivable? I defy any one to
match it elsewhere on this earth. In other lands, at worst, there
are at least intelligible issues, coherent ideas, salient personalities.
Somebody says something, and somebody replies. But what did
Harding say in 1920, and what did Cox reply? Who was Harding,
anyhow, and who was Cox? Here, having perfected democracy,
we lift the whole combat to symbolism, to transcendentalism, to
metaphysics. Here we load a pair of palpably tin cannon with
blank cartridges charged with talcum powder, and so let fly. Here
one may howl over the show without any uneasy reminder that
it is serious, and that some one may be hurt. I hold that this eleva-
tion of politics to the plane of undiluted comedy is peculiarly
American, that nowhere else on this disreputable ball has the
art of the sham-battle been developed to such fineness. Two experiences are in point. During the Harding-Cox combat of blad-
ders an article of mine, dealing with some of its more melodramatic
phases, was translated into German and reprinted by a Berlin
paper. At the head of it the editor was careful to insert a preface
explaining to his readers, but recently delivered to democracy,
that such contests were not taken seriously by intelligent Americans, and warning them solemnly against getting into sweats over
politics. At about the same time I had dinner with an Englishman.
From cocktails to Bromo-Seltzer he bewailed the political lassi-
tude of the English populace—its growing indifference to the
whole partisan harlequinade. Here were two typical foreign attitudes: the Germans were in danger of making politics too harsh
and implacable, and the English were in danger of forgetting

politics altogether. Both attitudes, it must be plain, make for bad shows. Observing a German campaign, one is uncomfortably harassed and stirred up; observing an English campaign (at least in times of peace), one falls asleep. In the United States the thing is done better. Here politics is purged of all menace, all sinister quality, all genuine significance, and stuffed with such gorgeous humors, such inordinate farce that one comes to the end of a campaign with one's ribs loose, and ready for "King Lear," or a hanging, or a course of medical journals.

But feeling better for the laugh. *Ridi si sapis*, said Martial. Mirth is necessary to wisdom, to comfort, above all, to happiness. Well, here is the land of mirth, as Germany is the land of metaphysics and France is the land of fornication. Here the buffoonery never stops. What could be more delightful than the endless struggle of the Puritan to make the joy of the minority unlawful and impossible? The effort is itself a greater joy to one standing on the sidelines than any or all of the carnal joys that it combats. Always, when I contemplate an uplifter at his hopeless business, I recall a scene in an old-time burlesque show, witnessed for hire in my days as a dramatic critic. A chorus girl executed a fall upon the stage, and Rudolph Krausemeyer, the Swiss comedian, rushed to her aid. As he stooped painfully to succor her, Irving Rabinovitz, the Zionist comedian, fetched him a fearful clout across the cofferdam with a slap-stick. So the uplifter, the soul-saver, the Americanizer, striving to make the Republic fit for the Y. M. C. A. secretaries. He is the eternal American, ever moved by the best of intentions, ever running *à la* Krausemeyer to the rescue of virtue, and ever getting his pantaloons fanned by the Devil. I am naturally sinful, and such spectacles caress me. If the slap-stick were a sash-weight the show would be cruel, and I'd probably complain to the *Polizei*. As it is, I know that the uplifter is not really hurt, but simply shocked. The blow, in fact, does him good, for it helps to get him into Heaven, as exegetes prove from Matthew v, 11: *Heureux serez-vous, lorsqu'on vous outragera, qu'on vous persécutera,* and so on. As for me, it makes me a more contented man, and hence a better citizen. One man prefers the Republic because it pays better wages than Bulgaria. Another because it has laws to keep him sober and his daughter chaste. Another because the Woolworth Building is higher than the cathedral at Chartres. Another because, living here, he can read the New York *Evening Journal.* Another because there is a warrant out for him somewhere else. Me, I like it because it amuses me to my taste. I never get tired of the show. It is worth every cent it costs.

That cost, it seems to me, is very moderate. Taxes in the United States are not actually high. I figure, for example, that my private share of the expense of maintaining the Hon. Mr. Harding in the White House this year will work out to less than 80 cents. Try to think of better sport for the money: in New York it has been estimated that it costs $8 to get comfortably tight, and $17.50, on an average, to pinch a girl's arm. The United States Senate will cost me perhaps $11 for the year, but against that expense set the subscription price of the *Congressional Record,* about $15, which, as a journalist, I receive for nothing. For $4 less than nothing I am thus entertained as Solomon never was by his hooch dancers. Col. George Brinton McClellan Harvey costs me but 25 cents a year; I get Nicholas Murray Butler free. Finally, there is young Teddy Roosevelt, the naval expert. Teddy costs me, as I work it out, about 11 cents a year, or less than a cent a month. More, he entertains me doubly for the money, first as naval expert, and secondly as a walking *attentat* upon democracy, a devastating proof that there is nothing, after all, in that superstition. We Americans subscribe to the doctrine of human equality —and the Rooseveltii reduce it to an absurdity as brilliantly as the sons of Veit Bach. Where is your equal opportunity now? Here in this Eden of clowns, with the highest rewards of clowning theoretically open to every poor boy—here in the very citadel of democracy we found and cherish a clown *dynasty!*

The Husbandman

‹‹‹‹‹‹‹‹‹‹‹‹‹‹‹‹‹‹‹‹‹‹‹‹‹‹‹‹‹‹‹‹›››››››››››››››››››››››››››››

A READER for years of the *Congressional Record,* I have encountered in its dense and pregnant columns denunciations of almost every human act or idea that is imaginable
to political pathology, from adultery to Zionism, and of all classes
of men whose crimes the legislative mind can grasp, from atheists
to Zoroastrians, but never once, so far as I can recall, has that
great journal shown the slightest insolence, direct or indirect, to
the humble husbandman, the lonely companion of *Bos taurus,* the
sweating and persecuted farmer. He is, on the contrary, the pet
above all other pets, the enchantment and delight, the saint and
archangel of all the unearthly Sganarelles and Scaramouches who
roar in the two houses of Congress. He is more to them, day in
and day out, than whole herds of Honest Workingmen, Gallant
Jack Tars and Heroic Miners; he is more, even, than a platoon of
Unknown Soldiers. There are days when one or another of these
totems of the statesman is bathed with such devotion that it would
make the Gracchi blush, but there is never a day that the farmer,
too, doesn't get his share, and there is many a day when he gets
ten times his share—when, indeed, he is completely submerged
in rhetorical vaseline, so that it is hard to tell which end of him
is made in the image of God and which is mere hoof. No session
ever begins without a grand assault at all arms upon his hereditary
foes, from the boll-weevil and the San Jose scale to Wall Street
and the Interstate Commerce Commission. And no session comes
to an end without a huge grist of new laws to save him from

them—laws embodying the most subtle statecraft of the most daring and ingenious body of lawmakers ever assembled under one roof on the habitable globe. One might almost argue that the chief, and perhaps even only aim of legislation in These States is to succor and secure the farmer. If, while the bombs of goose-grease and rockets of pomade are going off in the two Chambers, certain evil men meet in the basement and hook *banderillas* into him—say, by inserting jokers into the chemical schedule of a new tariff bill, or by getting the long-haul rules changed, or by manipulating the loans of the Federal Reserve Banks—then the crime is not against him alone; it is against the whole American people, the common decency of Christendom, and the Holy Ghost. Horn a farmer, and you stand in contumacy to the platforms of all known parties, to the devout faith of all known statesmen, and to God. *Laborantem agricolam oportet primum de fructibus percipere.*

Paul wrote to the Bishop of Ephesus, at the latest, in the year 65 A.D.; the doctrine that I have thus ascribed to the Mesmers and Grimaldis of our politics is therefore not a novelty of their contrivance. Nor is it, indeed, their monopoly, for it seems to be shared by all Americans who are articulate and devote themselves to political metaphysics and good works. The farmer is praised by all who mention him at all, from archbishops to zoologists, day in and day out. He is praised for his industry, his frugality, his patriotism, his altruistic passion. He is praised for staying on the farm, for laboriously wringing our bread and meat from the reluctant soil, for renouncing Babylon to guard the horned cattle on the hills. He is praised for his patient fidelity to the oldest of learned professions, and the most honorable, and the most necessary to all of us. He takes on, in political speeches and newspaper editorials, a sort of mystical character. He is no longer a mundane laborer, scratching for the dollar, full of staphylococci, smelling heavily of sweat and dung; he is a high priest in a rustic temple, pouring out his heart's blood upon the altar of Ceres. The farmer, thus depicted, grows heroic, lyrical, pathetic, affecting. To murmur against him becomes a sort of sacrilege, like murmuring against the Constitution, Human Freedom, the Cause of Democracy. . . . Nevertheless, being already doomed, I herewith and hereby presume to do it. More, my murmur is scored in the manner of Berlioz, for ten thousand trombones *fortissimo*, with harsh, cacophonous chords for bombardons and ophicleides in the bass clef. Let the farmer, so far as I am concerned, be damned forevermore! To hell with him, and bad luck to him! He is, unless I err, no hero at all, and no priest, and no altruist, but simply a tedious fraud and ignoramus, a cheap rogue and hypocrite, the eternal Jack of the human pack. He deserves all that he suffers under our economic system, and more. Any city man, not insane, who sheds tears for him is shedding tears of the crocodile.

No more grasping, selfish and dishonest mammal, indeed, is known to students of the Anthropoidea. When the going is good for him he robs the rest of us up to the extreme limit of our endurance; when the going is bad he comes bawling for help out of the public till. Has anyone ever heard of a farmer making any sacrifice of his own interests, however slight, to the common good? Has anyone ever heard of a farmer practising or advocating any political idea that was not absolutely self-seeking—that was not, in fact, deliberately designed to loot the rest of us to his gain? Greenbackism, free silver, government guarantee of prices, all the complex fiscal imbecilities of the cow state John Baptists— these are the contributions of the virtuous husbandmen to American political theory. There has never been a time, in good seasons or bad, when his hands were not itching for more; there has never been a time when he was not ready to support any charlatan, however grotesque, who promised to get it for him. Why, indeed, are politicians so polite to him—before election, so romantically amorous? For the plain and simple reason that only one issue ever interests or fetches him, and that is the issue of his own profit. He must be promised something definite and valuable, to be paid to him alone, or he is off after some other mountebank. He simply cannot imagine himself as a citizen of a commonwealth, in duty bound to give as well as take; he can imagine himself only as getting all and giving nothing.

Yet we are asked to venerate this prehensile moron as the *Ur*-burgher, the citizen *par excellence*, the foundation-stone of the state! And why? Because he produces something that all of us must have—that we must get somehow on penalty of death. And how do we get it from him? By submitting helplessly to his unconscionable blackmailing—by paying him, not under any rule of reason, but in proportion to his roguery and incompetence, and hence to the direness of our need. I doubt that the human race, as a whole, would submit to that sort of high-jacking, year in and year out, from any other necessary class of men. When the American railroad workman attempted it, in 1916, there was instant indignation; when a certain small squad of the *Polizei* tried it, a few years later, there was such universal horror that a politician who denounced the crime became President of the United States. But the farmers do it over and over again, without challenge or reprisal, and the only thing that keeps them from reducing us, at intervals, to actual famine is their own imbecile knavery. They are all willing and eager to pillage us by starving us, but they can't do it because they can't resist attempts to swindle each other. Recall, for example, the case of the cotton-growers in the South. They agreed among themselves to cut down the cotton acreage in order to inflate the price—and instantly every party to the agreement began planting *more* cotton in order to profit by the abstinence of his neighbors. That abstinence being wholly imaginary, the price of cotton fell instead of going up—and then the entire pack of scoundrels began demanding assistance from the national treasury—in brief, began demanding that the rest of us indemnify them for the failure of their plot to blackmail us!

The same demand is made almost annually by the wheat farmers of the Middle West. It is the theory of the zanies who perform at Washington that a grower of wheat devotes himself to that banal art in a philanthropic and patriotic spirit—that he plants and harvests his crop in order that the folks of the cities may not go without bread. It is the plain fact that he raises wheat because it takes less labor than any other crop—because it enables him, after working sixty days a year, to loaf the rest of the twelve months. If wheat-raising could be taken out of the hands of such lazy *fellahin* and organized as the production of iron or cement is organized, the price might be reduced by a half, and still leave a large profit for *entrepreneurs*. It vacillates dangerously today, not because speculators manipulate it, but because the crop is irregular and undependable—that is to say, because those who make it are incompetent. The worst speculators, as everyone knows, are the farmers themselves. They hold their wheat as long as they can, borrowing our money from the country banks and hoping prayerfully for a rise. If it goes up, then we pay them an extra and unearned profit. If it goes down, then they demand legislation to prevent it going down next time. Sixty days a year they work; the rest of the time they gamble with our bellies. It is probably the safest gambling ever heard of. Now and then, true enough, a yokel who plunges too heavily comes to grief, and is ingested by the county-town mortgage-shark; now and then a whole county, or state or even larger area goes bankrupt, and the financial dominoes begin falling down all along the line from Saleratus Center to New York. But such catastrophes are rare, and they leave no scars. When a speculator goes broke in Wall Street it is a scandalous matter, and if he happens to have rooked anybody of importance he is railroaded to jail. But when a speculator goes broke in the great open spaces, there is a great rush of political leucocytes to the scene, and presently it is made known that the sin was not the speculator's at all, but his projected victims', and that it is the prime duty of the latter, by lawful order upon the Treasurer of the United States, to reimburse him his losses and set him up for a new trial.

The notion that wheat would be much cheaper and the supply far more dependable if it were grown, not by a motley horde of such puerile loafers and gamblers, but by competent men intelligently organized is not mine; I borrow it from Henry Ford, a busted seer. Since he betrayed them to Dr. Coolidge for a mess of pottage, the poor Liberals, once so enamored of his sagacity, denounce Ford as an idiot and a villain; nevertheless, the fact remains that his discussion of the wastefulness of our present system of wheat-growing, in the autobiography which he didn't write, is full of a powerful plausibility. Ford was born and brought up on a farm—and it was a farm, as farms go, that was very competently managed. But he knows very well that even the most competent farmer is but seldom more adept than a chimpanzee playing the violin. The Liberals, indeed, cannot controvert his judgment; they have been thrown back upon belaboring his political morals. What he proposes, they argue, is simply the enslavement of the present farmer, now so gloriously free. With capitalism gradually absorbing his fields, he would have to go to work as a wage-slave. Well, why not? For one, I surely offer no objection. All the rubber we use today is raised by slave labor; so is all the morphine consumed at Hollywood. Our children are taught in school by slaves; our newspapers are edited by slaves. Wheat raised by slave labor would be just as nutritious as wheat raised by men earning $10,000 a year, and a great deal cheaper. If the business showed a good profit, the political clowns at Washington would launch schemes to confiscate it, as they now launch schemes to make good the losses of the farmers. In any case, why bother about the fate of the farmer? If wheat went to $10 a bushel tomorrow, and all the workmen of the cities became slaves in name as well as in fact, no farmer in this grand land of freedom would consent voluntarily to a reduction of as much as ⅛ of a cent a bushel. "The greatest wolves," says E. W. Howe, another graduate of the farm, "are the farmers who bring produce to town to sell." Wolves? Let us not insult *Canis lupus*. I move the substitution of *Hyaena hyaena*.

Meanwhile, how much truth is in the common theory that the husbandman is harassed and looted by our economic system, that the men of the cities prey upon him—specifically, that he is the chronic victim of such devices as the tariff, railroad regulation, and the banking system? So far as I can make out, there is none whatever. The net effect of our present banking system, as I have already said, is that the money accumulated by the cities is used to finance the farmers, and that they employ it to blackmail the cities. As for the tariff, is it a fact that it damages the farmer, or benefits him? Let us turn for light to the worst Tariff Act ever heard of in human history: that of 1922. It put a duty of 30 cents a bushel on wheat, and so barred out Canadian wheat, and gave the American farmer a vast and unfair advantage. For months running the difference in the price of wheat on the two sides of the American-Canadian border—wheat raised on farms not a mile apart—ran from 25 to 30 cents a bushel. Danish butter was barred out by a duty of 8 cents a pound—and the American farmer pocketed the 8 cents. Potatoes carried a duty of 50 cents a hundredweight—and the potato growers of Maine, eager, as the phrase has it, to mop up, raised such an enormous crop that the market was glutted, and they went bankrupt, and began bawling for government aid. High duties were put, too, upon meats, upon cheese, upon wool—in brief, upon practically everything that the farmer produced. But his profits were taken from him by even higher duties upon manufactured goods, and by high freight rates? Were they, indeed? There was, in fact, no duty at all upon many of the things he consumed. There was no duty, for example, upon shoes. The duty upon woolen goods gave a smaller advantage to the manufacturer than the duty on wool gave to the farmer. So with the duty on cotton goods. Automobiles were cheaper in the United States than anywhere else on earth. So were all agricultural implements. So were groceries. So were fertilizers.

But here I come to the brink of an abyss of statistics, and had better haul up. The enlightened reader is invited to investigate them for himself; they will bring him, I believe, some surprises, particularly if he has been reading the *Congressional Record* and accepting it gravely. They by no means exhaust the case against the consecrated husbandman. I have said that the only political idea he can grasp is one which promises him a direct profit. It is, alas, not quite true: he can also grasp one which has the sole effect of annoying and damaging his enemy, the city man. The same mountebanks who get to Washington by promising to augment his gains and make good his losses devote whatever time is left over from that enterprise to saddling the rest of us with oppressive and idiotic laws, all hatched on the farm. There, where the cows low through the still night, and the jug of Peruna stands behind the stove, and bathing begins, as at Biarritz, with the vernal equinox—there is the reservoir of all the nonsensical legislation which now makes the United States a buffoon among the great nations. It was among country Methodists, practitioners of a theology degraded almost to the level of voodooism, that Prohibition was invented, and it was by country Methodists, nine-tenths of them actual followers of the plow, that it was fastened upon the rest of us, to the damage of our bank accounts, our dignity and our ease. What lies under it, and under all the other crazy enactments of its category, is no more and no less than the yokel's congenital and incurable hatred of the city man—his simian rage against everyone who, as he sees it, is having a better time than he is.

That this malice is at the bottom of Prohibition, and not any

altruistic yearning to put down the evils of drink, is shown clearly
by the fact that most of the state enforcement acts—and even the
Volstead Act, as it is interpreted at Washington—permit the
farmer himself to make cider as in the past, and that every effort
to deprive him of that astounding immunity has met with the
opposition of his representatives. In other words, the thing he is
against is not the use of alcohol *per se*, but simply the use of
alcohol in its more charming and romantic forms. Prohibition, as
everyone knows, has not materially diminished the consumption
of alcohol in the cities, but it has obviously forced the city man
to drink decoctions that he would have spurned in the old days—
that is, it has forced him to drink such dreadful stuff as the farmer
has always drunk. The farmer is thus content with it: it brings
his enemy down to his own level. The same animus is visible
in innumerable other moral statutes, all ardently supported by the
peasantry. For example, the Mann Act. The aim of this amazing
law, of course, is not to put down adultery; it is simply to put down
that variety of adultery which is most agreeable. What got it
upon the books was simply the constant gabble in the rural newspapers about the byzantine debaucheries of urban Antinomians
—rich stockbrokers who frequented Atlantic City from Friday to
Monday, vaudeville actors who traveled about the country with
beautiful mistresses, and so on. Such aphrodisiacal tales, read beside the kitchen stove by hinds condemned to monogamous misery
with stupid, unclean and ill-natured wives, naturally aroused in
them a vast detestation of errant cockneys, and this detestation
eventually rolled up enough force to attract the attention of the
quacks who make laws at Washington. The result was the Mann
Act. Since then a number of the cow states have passed Mann
Acts of their own, usually forbidding the use of automobiles "for
immoral purposes." But there is nowhere a law forbidding the use
of barns, cow-stables, hay-ricks and other such familiar rustic
ateliers of sin. That is to say, there is nowhere a law forbidding
yokels to drag virgins into infamy by the technic practiced since
Tertiary times on the farms; there are only laws forbidding city
youths to do it according to the technic of the great municipali-
ties.

Here we come to the limits of bucolic moral endeavor. It

never prohibits acts that are common on the farms; it only prohibits acts that are common in the cities. In many of the Middle
Western states there are statutes forbidding the smoking of cigarettes, for cigarette-smoking, to the louts of those wastes, bears
the aspect of a citified and levantine vice, and if they attempted
it themselves they would be derided by their fellows and perhaps
divorced by their wives, just as they would be derided and divorced if they bathed every day, or dressed for dinner, or attempted to play the piano. But chewing tobacco, whether in
public or in private, is nowhere forbidden by law, for the plain
reason that nine-tenths of all husbandmen practice it, as they
practice the drinking of raw corn liquor. The act not only lies
within their tastes; it also lies within their means, and hence within
their *mores*. As a consequence the inhabitants of the towns in
those remote marches are free to chew tobacco all they please,
even at divine service, but are clapped into jail the instant they
light cigarettes. The same consideration gets into comstockery,
which is chiefly supported, like Prohibition, by farmers and chiefly
aimed at city men. The Comstock Act is very seldom invoked
against newspapers, for the matter printed in newspapers lies
within the comprehension of the peasantry, and hence within
their sphere of enjoyment. Nor is it often invoked against cheap
books of a frankly pornographic character—such things as "Night
Life in Chicago," "Adventures on a Pullman Sleeper" and "The
Confessions of an ex-Nun"—for when yokels read at all, it is commonly such garbage that they prefer. But they are hot against the
infinitely less gross naughtiness of serious books, including the so-
called classics, for these books they simply cannot read. In consequence the force of comstockery is chiefly directed against such
literature. For one actually vile book that it suppresses it attempts
to suppress at least a dozen good ones.

Now the pious husbandman shows signs of an itch to proceed
further. Not content with assaulting us with his degraded and
abominable ethics, he begins trying to force upon us his still worse
theology. On the steppes Methodism has got itself all the estate
and dignity of a state religion; it becomes a criminal offense to
teach any doctrine in contempt of it. No civilized man, to be sure,
is yet actually in jail for the crime; civilized men simply keep out

of such bleak parking spaces for human Fords, as they keep out of Congress and Franz Josef Land. But the long arm of the Wesleyan revelation now begins to stretch forth toward Nineveh. The mountebank, Bryan, after years of preying upon the rustics on the promise that he would show them how to loot the cities by wholesale and *à outrance,* now reverses his collar and proposes to lead them in a *jehad* against what remains of American intelligence, already beleaguered in a few walled towns. We are not only to abandon the social customs of civilization at the behest of a rabble of peasants who sleep in their underclothes; we are now to give up all the basic ideas of civilization and adopt the gross superstitions of the same mob. Is this fanciful? Is the menace remote, and to be disregarded? My apologies for suggesting that perhaps you are one of the multitude who thought that way about Prohibition, and only half a dozen years ago. Bryan is a protean harlequin, and more favored by God than is commonly assumed. He lost with free silver but he won with Prohibition. The chances, if my mathematics do not fail, are thus 1 to 1 that he will win, if he keeps his health, with Fundamentalism—in his own phrase, that God will be put into the Constitution. If he does, then *Eoanthropus* will triumph finally over *Homo sapiens.* If he does, then the humble swineherd will drive us all into his pen.

Not much gift for Vision is needed to imagine the main outlines of the ensuing *Kultur.* The city man, as now, will bear nine-tenths of the tax burden; the rural total immersionist will make all the laws. With Genesis firmly lodged in the Testament of the Fathers he will be ten times as potent as he is now and a hundred times as assiduous. No constitutional impediment will remain to cripple his moral fancy. The Wesleyan code of Kansas and Mississippi, Vermont and Minnesota will be forced upon all of us by the full military and naval power of the United States. Civilization will gradually become felonious everywhere in the Republic, as it already is in Arkansas. What I sing, I suppose, is a sort of Utopia. But it is not the Utopia of bawdy poets and metaphysicians; it is not the familiar Utopia of the books. It is a Utopia dreamed by simpler and more virtuous men—by seven millions of Christian bumpkins, far-flung in forty-eight sovereign states. They dream it on their long journeys down the twelve billion furrows of their seven million farms, up hill and down dale in the heat of the day. They dream it behind the egg-stove on winter nights, their boots off and their socks scorching, Holy Writ in their hands. They dream it as they commune with *Bos taurus, Sus scrofa, Mephitis mephitis*, the Methodist pastor, the Ford agent. It floats before their eyes as they scan the Sears-Roebuck catalogue for horse liniment, porous plasters and Bordeaux mixture; it rises before them when they assemble in their Little Bethels to be instructed in the word of God, the plots of the Pope, the crimes of the atheists and Jews; it transfigures the chautauquan who looms before them with his Great Message. This Utopia haunts and tortures them; they long to make it real. They have tried prayer, and it has failed; now they turn to the secular arm. The dung-fork glitters in the sun as the host prepares to march. . . .

Well, these are the sweet-smelling and altruistic agronomists whose sorrows are the *leit-motif* of our politics, whose votes keep us supplied with Bryans and Bleases, whose welfare is alleged to be the chief end of democratic statecraft, whose patriotism is the so-called bulwark of this so-called Republic!

I I

<<<<<<<<<<<<<>>>>>>>>>>>>>

American Letters

❀ · ❀ · ❀ · ❀ · ❀

Mencken's critical writings are to be found for the most part in the files of the Smart Set, *in the various* Prejudices, *particularly the first three, and in* A Book of Prefaces. *The latter volume, the only one he published devoted wholly to literature, contained studies of Conrad, Dreiser, Huneker, and "Puritanism as a Literary Force." As originally planned, it was intended to give accounts of some Continental writers. A book with such a table of contents would have put him too much in the Huneker circle, and since he was determined to stand on his own feet he altered its structure. When he abandoned the* Smart Set *in 1923 to launch the* American Mercury, *he was at the top of his career as a critic, the closest embodiment of the Johnsonian type of literary dictatorship the United States had known.*

In his role as a critic, Mencken was always concerned with the primary question whether the work was good or bad. The problem of criticism itself interested him, and he advanced two different, but not contradictory, theories to account for his own practices. The first, which he labeled the "Croce-Spingarn-Carlyle-Goethe theory," appeared under the title "Criticism of Criticism of Criticism" as the famous lead article in Prejudices: First Series, *published in 1919. It had first been printed in a briefer version in the New York* Evening Mail *in 1918, and the substance of it had been published in the* Smart Set *in 1917. In an aside, Goethe had remarked that the critic, when face to face with a work of art, should ask: "What has the writer proposed to himself to do, and how well has he succeeded in carrying out his own plan?" Carlyle had expanded the statement in his essay on Goethe, and J. E. Spingarn used both the Goethe and the Carlyle passages in an attempt to clarify Croce's position. Mencken seized upon the doctrine*

(53)

and gave it wide currency. He took it to mean exactly what it says, an interpretation which was to bring a rejoinder from Professor Springarn. The doctrine was not to be understood literally, said Spingarn. What the artist "intends" is as irrelevant to criticism as the color of his hair. As Milton's nephew observed, every poet intends to write a good poem. According to Professor Spingarn, the doctrine correctly understood, meant that the poet's intention was to be found, not in his ambition, but in the work of art which he produces. The poem is his intention, said Spingarn.

Whether his understanding of Goethe's remark was correct or not, Mencken concluded with the gloss that the critic was a catalytic agent who mediated between the work of art and the reader or spectator. T. S. Eliot in a notable essay, "Tradition and the Individual Talent," independently employed the same image. However, Mencken shortly changed his opinion.

In a fresh effort to unravel the mystery of criticism, he concluded that the critic, when he operated at the higher levels, was as much an artist as the man whose work he was considering. The critic's writings were either works of art, or they were nothing. A book or a poem would serve as a text for a point of departure, but it was the critic's task to get himself and his own ideas into his essays, otherwise he remained a mere reviewer, "as hollow as a jug." This account of the critical process does not touch the issue of impressionism or objectivity in criticism. Without exception, the great critics have been men of large ideas who were able to see the book or poem in perspective; in their estimates they managed to say something of importance of their own. Lives of the English Poets is a classic instance. Johnson was commissioned to write "a concise account of the life of each author." But the subject, as Boswell observed, "swelled" to such an extent that, as he remarked, if Johnson's observations were collected in a systematic form by a modern Aristotle or Longinus, the result would be a critical document of the topmost order.

In practice Mencken carried out his own principle. In his appraisals of the work of other men the essence is always the special angle from which Mencken saw the world. That angle was of such luminous interest on its own account that it gave his critical writings enduring power and import.

The National Letters

▰▰▰

· I ·

Prophets and Their Visions

IT is convenient to begin, like the gentlemen of God, with a glance at a text or two. The first, a short one, is from Ralph Waldo Emerson's celebrated oration,"The American Scholar," delivered before the Phi Beta Kappa Society at Cambridge on August 31st, 1837. Emerson was then thirty-four years old and almost unknown in his own country, though he had already published "Nature" and established his first contacts with Landor and Carlyle. But "The American Scholar" brought him into instant notice at home, partly as man of letters but more importantly as seer and prophet, and the fame thus founded has endured without much diminution, at all events in New England, to this day. Oliver Wendell Holmes, giving words to what was undoubtedly the common feeling, hailed the address as the intellectual declaration of independence of the American people, and that judgment, amiably passed on by three generations of pedagogues, still survives in the literature books. I quote from the first paragraph:

> Our day of dependence, our long apprenticeship to the learning of other lands, draws to a close. . . . Events, actions arise, that must be sung, that will sing themselves. Who can doubt that poetry will revive and lead in a new age, as the star in the constel-

lation Harp, which now flames in our zenith, astronomers announce, shall one day be the pole-star for a thousand years?

This, as I say, was in 1837. Thirty-three years later, in 1870, Walt Whitman echoed the prophecy in his even more famous "Democratic Vistas." What he saw in his vision and put into his gnarled and gasping prose was

> a class of native authors, literatuses, far different, far higher in grade, than any yet known, sacerdotal, modern, fit to cope with our occasions, lands, permeating the whole mass of American morality, taste, belief, breathing into it a new breath of life, giving it decision, affecting politics far more than the popular superficial suffrage, with results inside and underneath the elections of Presidents or Congress—radiating, begetting appropriate teachers, schools, manners, and, as its grandest result, accomplishing, (what neither the schools nor the churches and their clergy have hitherto accomplished, and without which this nation will no more stand, permanently, soundly, than a house will stand without a substratum,) a religious and moral character beneath the political and productive and intellectual bases of the States.

And out of the vision straightway came the prognostication:

> The promulgation and belief in such a class or order—a new and greater literatus order—its possibility, (nay, certainty,) underlies these entire speculations. . . . Above all previous lands, a great original literature is sure to become the justification and reliance, (in some respects the sole reliance,) of American democracy.

Thus Whitman in 1870, the time of the first draft of "Democratic Vistas." He was of the same mind, and said so, in 1888, four years before his death. I could bring up texts of like tenor in great number, from the years before 1837, from those after 1888, and from every decade between. The dream of Emerson, though the eloquence of its statement was new and arresting, embodied no novel projection of the fancy; it merely gave a sonorous *Waldhorn* tone to what had been dreamed and said before. You will find almost the same high hope, the same exuberant confidence in the essays of the elder Channing and in the "Lectures on American Literature" of Samuel Lorenzo Knapp, LL.D., the first native critic of beautiful letters—the primordial tadpole of all our later Mores, Brownells, Phelpses, Mabies, Brander Matthewses and

other such grave and glittering fish. Knapp believed, like Whitman long after him, that the sheer physical grandeur of the New
World would inflame a race of bards to unprecedented utterance.
"What are the Tibers and Scamanders," he demanded, "measured
by the Missouri and the Amazon? Or what the loveliness of
Illysus or Avon by the Connecticut or the Potomack? Whenever
a nation wills it, prodigies are born." That is to say, prodigies
literary and ineffable as well as purely material—prodigies aimed,
in his own words, at "the olympick crown" as well as at mere rail-
roads, ships, wheat-fields, droves of hogs, factories and money.
Nor were Channing and Knapp the first of the haruspices. Noah
Webster, the lexicographer, who "taught millions to spell but not
one to sin," had seen the early starlight of the same Golden Age
so early as 1789, as the curious will find by examining his "Dissertations on the English Language," a work fallen long since
into undeserved oblivion. Nor was Whitman, taking sober second
thought exactly a century later, the last of them. Out of many
brethren of our own day, extravagantly articulate in print and
among the chautauquas, I choose one—not because his hope is
of purest water, but precisely because, like Emerson, he dilutes
it with various discreet whereases. He is Van Wyck Brooks, a
young man far more intelligent, penetrating and hospitable to
fact than any of the reigning professors—a critic who is sharply
differentiated from them, indeed, by the simple circumstance
that he has information and sense. Yet this extraordinary Mr.
Brooks, in his "Letters and Leadership," published in 1918, re-
writes "The American Scholar" in terms borrowed almost bodily
from "Democratic Vistas"—that is to say, he prophesies with
Emerson and exults with Whitman. First there is the Emersonian
doctrine of the soaring individual made articulate by freedom
and realizing "the responsibility that lies upon us, each in the
measure of his own gift." And then there is Whitman's vision of a
self-interpretative democracy, forced into high literary adventures
by Joseph Conrad's "obscure inner necessity," and so achieving a
"new synthesis adaptable to the unique conditions of our life."
And finally there is the specific prediction, the grandiose, Adam
Forepaugh mirage: "We shall become a luminous people, dwell-
ing in the light and sharing our light." . . .

As I say, the roll of such soothsayers might be almost endlessly lengthened. There is, in truth, scarcely a formal discourse upon the national letters (forgetting, perhaps, Barrett Wendell's sour threnody upon the New England *Aufklärung*) that is without some touch of this previsional exultation, this confident hymning of glories to come, this fine assurance that American literature, in some future always ready to dawn, will burst into so grand a flowering that history will cherish its loveliest blooms even above such salient American gifts to culture as the moving-picture, the phonograph, the New Thought and the bichloride tablet. If there was ever a dissenter from the national optimism, in this as in other departments, it was surely Edgar Allan Poe—without question the bravest and most original, if perhaps also the least orderly and judicious, of all the critics that we have produced. And yet even Poe, despite his general habit of disgust and dismay, caught a flash or two of that engaging picture—even Poe, for an instant, in 1846, thought that he saw the beginnings of a solid and autonomous native literature, its roots deep in the soil of the republic— as you will discover by turning to his forgotten essay on J. G. C. Brainard, a thrice-forgotten doggereleer of Jackson's time. Poe, of course, was too cautious to let his imagination proceed to details; one feels that a certain doubt, a saving peradventure or two, played about the unaccustomed vision as he beheld it. But, nevertheless, he unquestionably beheld it. . . .

• 2 •

The Answering Fact

Now for the answering fact. How has the issue replied to these visionaries? It has replied in a way that is manifestly to the discomfiture of Emerson as a prophet, to the dismay of Poe as a pessimist disarmed by transient optimism, and to the utter collapse of Whitman. We have, as every one knows, produced no such "new and greater literatus order" as that announced by old Walt. We have given a gaping world no books that "radiate," and surely none intelligibly comparable to stars and constellations. We have achieved no prodigies of the first class, and very few of the second class, and not many of the third and fourth classes. Our literature, despite several false starts that promised much, is chiefly remarkable, now as always, for its respectable mediocrity. Its typical great man, in our own time, has been Howells, as its typical great man a generation ago was Lowell, and two generations ago, Irving. Viewed largely, its salient character appears as a sort of timorous flaccidity, an amiable hollowness. In bulk it grows more and more formidable, in ease and decorum it makes undoubted progress, and on the side of mere technic, of the bald capacity to write, it shows an ever-widening competence. But when one proceeds from such agencies and externals to the intrinsic substance, to the creative passion within, that substance quickly reveals itself as thin and watery, and that passion fades to something almost puerile. In all that mass of suave and often highly diverting writing there is no visible movement toward a distinguished and singular excellence, a signal national quality, a ripe and stimulating flavor, or, indeed, toward any other describable goal. What one sees is simply a general irresolution, a pervasive superficiality. There is no sober grappling with fundamentals, but only a shy sporting on the surface; there is not even any serious approach, such as Whitman dreamed of, to the special experiences and emergencies of the American people. When one turns to any other national literature—to Russian literature, say, or French, or German or Scandinavian—one is conscious immediately of a definite attitude toward the primary mysteries of existence, the unsolved and ever-fascinating problems at the bottom of human life, and of a definite preoccupation with some of them, and a definite way of translating their challenge into drama. These attitudes and preoccupations raise a literature above mere poetizing and tale-telling; they give it dignity and importance; above all, they give it national character. But it is precisely here that the literature of America, and especially the later literature, is most colorless and inconsequential. As if paralyzed by the national fear of ideas, the democratic distrust of whatever strikes beneath the prevailing platitudes, it evades all resolute and honest dealing with what, after all, must be every healthy literature's elementary materials. One is conscious of no brave and noble earnestness in it, of no generalized passion for intellectual and spiritual adventure, of no organized determination to think things out. What is there is a highly self-conscious and insipid correctness, a bloodless respectability, a submergence of matter in manner—in brief, what is there is the feeble, uninspiring quality of German painting and English music.

It was so in the great days and it is so today. There has always been hope and there has always been failure. Even the most optimistic prophets of future glories have been united, at all times, in their discontent with the here and now. "The mind of this country," said Emerson, speaking of what was currently visible in 1837, "is taught to aim at low objects. . . . There is no work for any but the decorous and the complaisant. . . . Books are written . . . by men of talent . . . who start wrong, who set out from accepted dogmas, not from their own sight of principles." And then, turning to the way out: "The office of the scholar (*i.e.*, of Whitman's 'literatus') is to cheer, to raise and to guide men by showing them *facts amid appearances*." Whitman himself, a full generation later, found that office still unfilled. "Our fundamental want today in the United States," he said, "with closest, amplest reference to present conditions, and to the future, is of a class, and the clear idea of a class, of native authors, literatuses, far different, far higher in grade, than any yet known"—and so on, as I have already quoted him. And finally, to make an end of the prophets, there is Brooks, with nine-tenths of his book given over, not to his prophecy—it is crowded, indeed, into the last few pages—but to a somewhat heavy mourning over the actual scene before him. On the side of letters, the aesthetic side, the side of ideas, we present to the world at large, he says, "the spectacle of a vast, undifferentiated herd of good-humored animals"—Knights of Pythias, Presbyterians, standard model Ph.D.'s, readers of the *Saturday Evening Post*, admirers of Richard Harding Davis and O. Henry, devotees of Hamilton Wright Mabie's "white list" of books, members of the Y.M.C.A. or the Drama League, weepers at chautauquas, wearers of badges, 100 per cent patriots, children of God. Poe I pass over; I shall turn to him again later on. Nor shall I repeat the parrotings of Emerson and Whitman in the jeremiads of their innumerable heirs and assigns. What they all establish is what is already obvious: that American thinking, when it concerns itself with beautiful letters as when it concerns itself with religious dogma or political theory, is extraordinarily timid and superficial —that it evades the genuinely serious problems of life and art as if they were stringently taboo—that the outward virtues it undoubtedly shows are always the virtues, not of profundity, not of courage, not of originality, but merely those of an emasculated and often very trashy dilettantism.

· 3 ·

The Ashes of New England

The current scene is surely depressing enough. What one observes is a literature in three layers, and each inordinately doughy and uninspiring—each almost without flavor or savor. It is hard to say, with much critical plausibility, which layer deserves to be called the upper, but for decorum's sake the choice may be fixed upon that which meets with the approval of the reigning Lessings. This is the layer of the novels of the late Howells, Judge Grant, Alice Brown and the rest of the dwindling survivors of New England *Kultur,* of the brittle, academic poetry of Woodberry and the elder Johnson, of the tea-party essays of Crothers, Miss Repplier and company, and of the solemn, highly judicial, coroner's inquest criticism of More, Brownell, Babbitt and their imitators. Here we have manner, undoubtedly. The thing is correctly done; it is never crude or gross; there is in it a faint perfume of college-town society. But when this highly refined and attenuated manner is allowed for what remains is next to nothing. One never remembers a character in the novels of these aloof and de-Americanized Americans; one never encounters an idea in their essays; one never carries away a line out of their poetry. It is literature as an academic exercise for talented grammarians, almost as a genteel recreation for ladies and gentlemen of fashion—the exact equivalent, in the field of letters, of eighteenth century painting and German *Augenmusik.*

What ails it, intrinsically, is a dearth of intellectual audacity and of aesthetic passion. Running through it, and characterizing the work of almost every man and woman producing it, there is an unescapable suggestion of the old Puritan suspicion of the fine arts as such—of the doctrine that they offer fit asylum for good citizens only when some ulterior and superior purpose is carried into them. This purpose, naturally enough, most commonly shows a moral tinge. The aim of poetry, it appears, is to fill the mind with lofty thoughts—not to give it joy, but to give it a grand and somewhat gaudy sense of virtue. The essay is a weapon against the degenerate tendencies of the age. The novel, properly conceived, is a means of uplifting the spirit; its aim is to inspire, not merely to satisfy the low curiosity of man in man. The Puritan, of course, is not entirely devoid of aesthetic feeling. He has a taste for good form; he responds to style; he is even capable of something approaching a purely aesthetic emotion. But he fears this aesthetic emotion as an insinuating distraction from his chief business in life: the sober consideration of the all-important problem of conduct. Art is a temptation, a seduction, a Lorelei, and the Good Man may safely have traffic with it only when it is broken to moral uses—in other words, when its innocence is pumped out of it, and it is purged of gusto. It is precisely this gusto that one misses in all the work of the New England school, and in all the work of the formal schools that derive from it. One observes in such a fellow as Dr. Henry Van Dyke an excellent specimen of the whole clan. He is, in his way, a genuine artist. He has a hand for pretty verses. He wields a facile rhetoric. He shows, in indiscreet moments, a touch of imagination. But all the while he remains a sound Presbyterian, with one eye on the devil. He is a Presbyterian first and an artist second, which is just as comfortable as trying to be a Presbyterian first and a chorus girl second. To such a man it must inevitably appear that a Molière, a Wagner, a Goethe or a Shakespeare was more than a little bawdy.

The criticism that supports this decaying caste of literary Brahmins is grounded almost entirely upon ethical criteria. You will spend a long while going through the works of such typical professors as More, Phelps, Boynton, Burton, Perry, Brownell and Babbitt before ever you encounter a purely aesthetic judgment upon an aesthetic question. It is almost as if a man estimating daffodils should do it in terms of artichokes. Phelps' whole body

of "we church-goers" criticism—the most catholic and tolerant,
it may be said in passing, that the faculty can show—consists
chiefly of a plea for correctness, and particularly for moral correctness; he never gets very far from "the axiom of the moral law."
Brownell argues eloquently for standards that would bind an
imaginative author as tightly as a Sunday-school superintendent
is bound by the Ten Commandments and the Mann Act. Sherman
tries to save Shakespeare for the right-thinking by proving that he
was an Iowa Methodist—a member of his local Chamber of Commerce, a contemner of Reds, an advocate of democracy and the
League of Nations, a patriotic dollar-a-year-man during the
Armada scare. Elmer More devotes himself, year in and year out,
to denouncing the Romantic movement, *i.e.*, the effort to emanci-
pate the artist from formulae and categories, and so make him
free to dance with arms and legs. And Babbitt, to make an end,
gives over his days and his nights to deploring Rousseau's anarchistic abrogation of "the veto power" over the imagination, leading to such "wrongness" in both art and life that it threatens "to
wreck civilization." In brief, the alarms of schoolmasters. Not
many of them deal specifically with the literature that is in being.
It is too near to be quite nice. To More or Babbitt only death can
atone for the primary offense of the artist. But what they preach
nevertheless has its echoes contemporaneously, and those echoes,
in the main, are woefully falsetto. I often wonder what sort of
picture of These States is conjured up by foreigners who read,
say, Crothers, Van Dyke, Babbitt, the later Winston Churchill,
and the old maids of the Freudian suppression school. How can
such a foreigner, moving in those damp, asthmatic mists, imagine
such phenomena as Roosevelt, Billy Sunday, Bryan, the Becker
case, the I. W. W., Newport, Palm Beach, the University of Chicago, Chicago itself—the whole, gross, glittering, excessively
dynamic, infinitely grotesque, incredibly stupendous drama of
American life?

As I have said, it is not often that the *ordentlichen Professoren*
deign to notice contemporary writers, even of their own austere
kidney. In all the Shelburne Essays there is none on Howells, or
on Churchill, or on Mrs. Wharton; More seems to think of American literature as expiring with Longfellow and Donald G. Mitchell.

He has himself hinted that in the department of criticism of criticism there enters into the matter something beyond mere aloof ignorance. "I soon learned (as editor of the pre-Bolshevik *Nation*)," he says, "that it was virtually impossible to get fair consideration for a book written by a scholar not connected with a university from a reviewer so connected." This class consciousness, however, should not apply to artists, who are admittedly inferior to professors, and it surely does not show itself in such men as Phelps and Spingarn, who seem to be very eager to prove that they are not professorial. Yet Phelps, in the course of a long work on the novel, pointedly omits all mention of such men as Dreiser, and Spingarn, as the aforesaid Brooks has said, "appears to be less inclined even than the critics with whom he is theoretically at war to play an active, public part in the secular conflict of darkness and light." When one comes to the *Privat-Dozenten* there is less remoteness, but what takes the place of it is almost as saddening. To Sherman and Percy Boynton the one aim of criticism seems to be the enforcement of correctness—in Emerson's phrase, the upholding of "some great decorum, some fetish of a government, some ephemeral trade, or war, or man"—*e.g.*, Puritanism, democracy, monogamy, the League of Nations, the Wilsonian piffle. Even among the critics who escape the worst of this schoolmastering frenzy there is some touch of the heavy "culture" of the provincial schoolma'm. For example, consider Clayton Hamilton, M.A., vice-president of the National Institute of Arts and Letters. Here are the tests he proposes for dramatic critics, *i.e.*, for gentlemen chiefly employed in reviewing such characteristic American compositions as the Ziegfeld Follies, "Up in Mabel's Room," "Ben-Hur" and "The Witching Hour":

1. Have you ever stood bareheaded in the nave of Amiens?
2. Have you ever climbed to the Acropolis by moonlight?
3. Have you ever walked with whispers into the hushed presence of the Frari Madonna of Bellini?

What could more brilliantly evoke an image of the eternal Miss Birch, blue veil flying and Baedeker in hand, plodding along faithfully through the interminable corridors and catacombs of the Louvre, the while bands are playing across the river, and young bucks in three-gallon hats are sparking the gals, and the Jews and harlots uphold the traditions of French *hig leef* at Longchamps, and American deacons are frisked and debauched up on martyrs' hill? The banality of it is really too exquisite to be borne; the lack of humor is almost that of a Fifth Avenue divine. One seldom finds in the pronunciamentoes of these dogged professors, indeed, any trace of either Attic or Gallic salt. When they essay to be jocose, the result is usually simply an elephantine whimsicality, by the chautauqua out of the *Atlantic Monthly*. Their satire is mere ill-nature. One finds it difficult to believe that they have ever read Lewes, or Hazlitt, or, above all, Saintsbury. I often wonder, in fact, how Saintsbury would fare, an unknown man, at the hands of, say, Brownell or More. What of his iconoclastic gayety, his boyish weakness for tweaking noses and pulling whiskers, his obscene delight in slang? . . .

· 4 ·

The Ferment Underground

So much for the top layer. The bottom layer is given over to the literature of Greenwich Village, and by Greenwich Village, of course, I mean the whole of the advanced wing in letters, whatever the scene of its solemn declarations of independence and forlorn hopes. Miss Amy Lowell is herself a fully-equipped and automobile Greenwich Village, domiciled in Boston amid the crumbling gravestones of the New England *intelligentsia*, but often in waspish joy-ride through the hinterland. Vachel Lindsay, with his pilgrim's staff, is another. There is a third in Chicago, with *Poetry: A Magazine of Verse* as its Exhibit A; it is, in fact, the senior of the Village fornenst Washington Square. Others you will find in far-flung factory towns, wherever there is a Little Theater, and a couple of local Synges and Chekovs to supply its stage. St. Louis, before Zoë Akins took flight, had the busiest of all these Greenwiches, and the most interesting. What lies under the whole movement is the natural revolt of youth against the pedagogical Prussianism of the professors. The oppression is extreme, and so the rebellion is extreme. Imagine a sentimental young man of the provinces, awaking one morning to the somewhat startling discovery that he is full of the divine afflatus, and nominated by the hierarchy of hell to enrich the literature of his fatherland. He seeks counsel and aid. He finds, on consulting the official treatises on that literature, that its greatest poet was Longfellow. He is warned, reading More and Babbitt, that the literatus who lets feeling get into his compositions is a psychic fornicator, and under German influences. He has formal notice from Sherman that Puritanism is the lawful philosophy of the country, and that any dissent from it is treason. He gets the news, plowing through the New York *Times Book Review,* the *Nation* (so far to the left in its politics, but hugging the right so desperately in letters!) the *Bookman,* the *Atlantic* and the rest, that the salient artists of the living generation are such masters as Robert Underwood Johnson, Owen Wister, James Lane Allen, George E. Woodberry, Hamlin Garland, William Roscoe Thayer and Augustus Thomas, with polite bows to Margaret Deland, Mary Johnston and Ellen Glasgow. It slowly dawns upon him that Robert W. Chambers is an academician and Theodore Dreiser isn't, that Brian Hooker is and George Sterling isn't, that Henry Sydnor Harrison is and James Branch Cabell isn't, that "Chimmie Fadden" Townsend is and Sherwood Anderson isn't.

Is it any wonder that such a young fellow, after one or two sniffs of that prep-school fog, swings so vastly backward that one finds him presently in corduroy trousers and a velvet jacket, hammering furiously upon a pine table in a Macdougal Street cellar, his mind full of malicious animal magnetism against even so amiable an old maid as Howells, and his discourse full of insane hair-splittings about *vers libre,* futurism, spectrism, vorticism, *Expressionismus, héliogabalisme?* The thing, in truth, is in the course of nature. The Spaniards who were outraged by the Palmerism of Torquemada did not become members of the Church of England; they became atheists. The American colonists, in revolt against a bad king, did not set up a good king; they set up a democracy, and so gave every honest man a chance to become a rogue on his own occount. Thus the young literatus, emerging from the vacuum of Ohio or Arkansas. An early success, as we shall see, tends to halt and moderate him. He finds that, after all, there is still a place for him, a sort of asylum for such as he, not over-populated or very warmly heated, but nevertheless quite real. But if his sledding at the start is hard, if the corrective birch finds him while he is still tender, then he goes, as Andrew Jackson would say, the whole hog, and another voice is added to the raucous bellowing of the literary Reds.

I confess that the spectacle gives me some joy, despite the fact that the actual output of the Village is seldom worth noticing. What commonly engulfs and spoils the Villagers is their concern with mere technique. Among them, it goes without saying, are a great many frauds—poets whose yearning to write is unaccompanied by anything properly describable as capacity, dramatists whose dramas are simply Schnitzler and well-water, workers in prose fiction who gravitate swiftly and inevitably to the machine-made merchandise of the cheap magazines—in brief, American equivalents of the bogus painters of the Boul' Mich'. These pretenders, having no ideas, naturally try to make the most of forms. Half the wars in the Village are over form; content is taken for granted, or forgotten altogether. The extreme leftists, in fact, descend to a meaningless gibberish, both in prose and in verse; it is their last defiance to intellectualism. This childish concentration upon externals unfortunately tends to debauch the small minority that is of more or less genuine parts; the good are pulled in by the bad. As a result, the Village produces nothing that justifies all the noise it makes. I have yet to hear of a first-rate book coming out of it, or a short story of arresting quality, or even a poem of any solid distinction. As one of the editors of a magazine which specializes in the work of new authors I am in an exceptional position to report. Probably nine-tenths of the stuff written in the dark dens and alleys south of the arch comes to my desk soon or late, and I go through all of it faithfully. It is, in the overwhelming main, jejune and imitative. The prose is quite without distinction, either in matter or in manner. The verse seldom gets beyond a hollow audaciousness, not unlike that of cubist painting. It is not often, indeed, that even personality is in it; all of the Villagers seem to write alike. "Unless one is an expert in some detective method," said a recent writer in *Poetry*, "one is at a loss to assign correctly the ownership of much free verse—that is, if one plays fairly and refuses to look at the signature until one has ventured a guess. It is difficult, for instance, to know whether Miss Lowell is writing Mr. Bynner's verse, or whether he is writing hers." Moreover, this monotony keeps to a very low level. There is no poet in the movement who has produced anything even remotely approaching the fine lyrics of Miss Reese, Miss Teasdale and John McClure, and for all its war upon the *cliché* it can show nothing to equal the *cliché*-free beauty of Robert Loveman's "Rain Song." In the drama the Village has gone further. In Eugene O'Neill, Rita Wellman and Zoë Akins it offers dramatists who are obviously many cuts above the well-professored mechanicians who pour out of Prof. Dr. Baker's *Ibsenfabrik* at Cambridge. But here we must probably give the credit, not to any influence residing within the movement itself, but to mere acts of God. Such pieces as O'Neill's one-acters, Miss Wellman's "The Gentile Wife" and Miss Akins' extraordinary "Papa" lie quite outside the Village scheme of things. There is no sign of formal revolt in them. They are simply first-rate work, done miraculously in a third-rate land.

But if the rebellion is thus sterile of direct results, and, in more than one aspect, fraudulent and riduculous, it is at all events an evidence of something not to be disregarded, and that something is the gradual formulation of a challenge to the accepted canons in letters and to the accepted canon lawyers. The first hoots come from a tatterdemalion horde of rogues and vagabonds without the gates, but soon or late, let us hope, they will be echoed in more decorous quarters, and with much greater effect. The Village, in brief, is an earnest that somewhere or other new seeds are germinating. Between the young tutor who launches into letters with imitations of his seminary chief's imitations of Agnes Repplier's imitations of Charles Lamb, and the young peasant who tries to get his honest exultations into free verse there can be no hesitant choice: the peasant is, by long odds, the sounder artist, and, what is more, the sounder American artist. Even the shy and somewhat stagey carnality that characterizes the Village has its high symbolism and its profound uses. It proves that, despite repressions unmatched in civilization in modern times, there is still a sturdy animality in American youth, and hence good health. The poet hugging his Sonia in a Washington Square beanery, and so giving notice to all his world that he is a devil of a fellow, is at least a better man than the emasculated stripling in a Y.M.C.A. gospel-mill, pumped dry of all his natural appetites and the vacuum filled with double-entry bookkeeping, business economics and auto-erotism. In so foul a nest of imprisoned and fermenting sex as the United States, plain fornication becomes a mark of relative decency.

· 5 ·

In the Literary Abattoir

But the theme is letters, not wickedness. The upper and lower layers have been surveyed. There remains the middle layer, the thickest and perhaps the most significant of the three. By the middle layer I mean the literature that fills the magazines and burdens the book-counters in the department stores—the literature adorned by such artists as Richard Harding Davis, Rex Beach, Emerson Hough, O. Henry, James Whitcomb Riley, Augustus Thomas, Robert W. Chambers, Henry Sydnor Harrison, Owen Johnson, Cyrus Townsend Brady, Irvin Cobb and Mary Roberts Rinehart—in brief, the literature that pays like a bucket-shop or a soap-factory, and is thus thoroughly American. At the bottom this literature touches such depths of banality that it would be difficult to match it in any other country. The "inspirational" and patriotic essays of Dr. Frank Crane, Orison Sweet Marden, Porter Emerson Browne, Gerald Stanley Lee, E. S. Martin, Ella Wheeler Wilcox and the Rev. Dr. Newell Dwight Hillis, the novels of Harold Bell Wright, Eleanor H. Porter and Gene Stratton Porter, and the mechanical sentimentalities in prose and verse that fill the cheap fiction magazines—this stuff has a native quality that is as unmistakable as that of Mother's Day, Billy-Sundayism or the Junior Order of United American Mechanics. It is the natural outpouring of a naïve and yet half barbarous people, full of delight in a few childish and inaccurate ideas. But it would be a grave error to assume that the whole of the literature of the middle layer is of the same infantile quality. On the contrary, a great deal of it—for example, the work of Mrs. Rinehart, and that of Corra Harris, Gouverneur Morris, Harold MacGrath and the late O. Henry—shows an unmistakably technical excellence, and even a certain civilized sophistication in point of view. Moreover, this literature is constantly graduating adept professors into something finer, as witness Booth Tarkington, Zona Gale, Ring W. Lardner and Montague Glass. S. L. Clemens came out of forty years ago. Nevertheless, its general tendency is distinctly in the other direction. It seduces by the power of money, and by the power of great acclaim no less. One constantly observes the collapse and surrender of writers who started out with aims far above that of the magazine nabob. I could draw up a long, long list of such victims: Henry Milner Rideout, Jack London, Owen Johnson, Chester Bailey Fernald, Hamlin Garland, Will Levington Comfort, Stephen French Whitman, James Hopper, Harry Leon Wilson, and so on. They had their forerunner, in the last generation, in Bret Harte. It is, indeed, a characteristic American phenomenon for a young writer to score a success with novel and meritorious work, and then to yield himself to the best-seller fever, and so disappear down the sewers. Even the man who struggles to emerge again is commonly hauled back. For example, Louis Joseph Vance, Rupert Hughes, George Bronson-Howard, and, to go back a few years, David Graham Phillips and Elbert Hubbard—all men flustered by high aspiration, and yet all pulled down by the temptations below. Even Frank Norris showed signs of yielding. The pull is genuinely powerful. Above lies not only isolation, but also a dogged and malignant sort of opposition. Below, as Morris has frankly admitted, there is the place at Aiken, the motor-car, babies, money in the bank, and the dignity of an important man.

It is a commonplace of the envious to put all the blame upon the *Saturday Evening Post*, for in its pages many of the Magdalens of letters are to be found, and out of its bulging coffers comes much of the lure. But this is simply blaming the bull for the sins of all the cows. The *Post*, as a matter of fact, is a good deal less guilty than such magazines as the *Cosmopolitan, Hearst's, Mc-Clure's* and the *Metropolitan,* not to mention the larger women's magazines. In the *Post* one often discerns an effort to rise above the level of shoe-drummer fiction. It is edited by a man who, almost alone among editors of the great periodicals of the country, is himself a writer of respectable skill. It has brought out (after lesser publications unearthed them) a number of authors of very solid talents, notably Glass, Lardner and E. W. Howe. It has been extremely hospitable to men not immediately comprehensible to the mob, for example, Dreiser and Hergesheimer. Most of all, it has avoided the Barnum-like exploitation of such native bosh-mongers as Crane, Hillis and Ella Wheeler Wilcox, and of such exotic mountebanks as D'Annunzio, Hall Caine and Maeterlinck. In brief, the *Post* is a great deal better than ever Greenwich Village and the Cambridge campus are disposed to admit. It is the largest of all the literary Hog Islands, but it is by no means the worst. Appealing primarily to the great masses of right-thinking and unintelligent Americans, it must necessarily print a great deal of preposterous tosh, but it flavors the mess with not a few things of a far higher quality, and at its worst it is seldom downright idiotic. In many of the other great magazines one finds stuff that it would be difficult to describe in any other words. It is gaudily romantic, furtively sexual, and full of rubber-stamp situations and personages—a sort of amalgam of the worst drivel of Marie Corelli, Elinor Glyn, E. Phillips Oppenheim, William Le Quex and Hall Caine. This is the literature of the middle layer—the product of the national Rockefellers and Duponts of letters. This is the sort of thing that the young author of facile pen is encouraged to manufacture. This is the material of the best-sellers and the movies.

Of late it is the movies that have chiefly provoked its composition: the rewards they offer are even greater than those held out by the commercial book-publishers and the train-boy magazines. The point of view of an author responsive to such rewards was recently set forth very naïvely in the *Authors' League Bulletin.* This author undertook, in a short article, to refute the fallacies of an unknown who ventured to protest against the movies on the ground that they called only for bald plots, elementary and generally absurd, and that all the rest of a sound writer's equipment— "the artistry of his style, the felicity of his apt expression, his subtlety and thoroughness of observation and comprehension and sympathy, the illuminating quality of his analysis of motive and character, even the fundamental skillful development of the bare plot"—was disdained by the Selznicks, Goldfishes, Zukors and other such *entrepreneurs,* and by the overwhelming majority of their customers. I quote from the reply:

> There are some conspicuous word merchants who deal in the English language, but the general public doesn't clamor for their wares. They write for the "thinking class." The élite, the discriminating. As a rule, they scorn the crass commercialism of the magazines and movies and such catch-penny devices. However, literary masterpieces live because they have been and will be read, not by the few, but by the many. That was true in the time of Homer, and even to-day the first move made by an editor when he receives a manuscript, or a gentle reader when he buys a book, or a T. B. M. when he sinks into an orchestra chair is to look around for John Henry Plot. If Mr. Plot is too long delayed in arriving or doesn't come at all, the editor usually sends regrets, the reader yawns and the tired business man falls asleep. It's a sad state of affairs and awful tough on art, but it can't be helped.

Observe the lofty scorn of mere literature—the superior irony at the expense of everything beyond the bumping of boobs. Note the sound judgment as to the function and fate of literary masterpieces, *e.g.,* "Endymion," "The Canterbury Tales," "Faust," "Typhoon." Give your eye to the chaste diction—"John Henry Plot," "T. B. M.," "awful tough," and so on. No doubt you will at once assume that this curious counterblast to literature was written by some former bartender now engaged in composing scenarios for Pearl White and Theda Bara. But it was not. It was written and signed by the president of the Authors' League of America.

Here we have, unconsciously revealed, the secret of the depressing badness of what may be called the staple fiction of the country—the sort of stuff that is done by the Richard Harding Davises, Rex Beaches, Houghs, McCutcheons, and their like, male and female. The worst of it is not that it is addressed primarily to shoe-drummers and shop-girls; the worst of it is that it is written by authors who *are,* to all intellectual intents and purposes, shoe-drummers and shop-girls. American literature, even on its higher levels, seldom comes out of the small and lonesome upper classes of the people. An American author with traditions behind him and an environment about him comparable to those, say, of George Moore, or Hugh Walpole, or E. F. Benson is and always has been relatively rare. On this side of the water the arts, like politics and religion, are chiefly in the keeping of persons of obscure origin, defective education and elemental tastes. Even some of the most violent upholders of the New England superstition are aliens to the actual New England heritage; one discovers, searching "Who's Who in America," that they are recent fugitives from the six-day sock and saleratus *Kultur* of the cow and hog states. The artistic merchandise produced by liberated yokels of that sort is bound to show its intellectual newness, which is to say, its deficiency in civilized culture and sophistication. It is, on the plane of letters, precisely what evangelical Christianity is on the plane of religion, to wit, the product of ill-informed, emotional and more or less pushing and oafish folk. Life, to such Harvardized peasants, is not a mystery; it is something absurdly simple, to be described with surety and in a few words. If they set up as critics their criticism is all a matter of facile labeling, chiefly ethical; find the pigeon-hole, and the rest is easy. If they presume to discuss the great problems of human society, they are equally ready with their answers: draw up and pass a harsh enough statute, and the corruptible will straightway put on incorruption. And if, fanned by the soft breath of beauty, they go into practice as creative artists, as poets, as dramatists, as novelists, then one learns from them that we inhabit a country that is the model and despair of other states, that its culture is coextensive with human culture and enlightenment, and that every failure to find happiness under that culture is the result of sin.

· 6 ·

Underlying Causes

Here is one of the fundamental defects of American fiction— perhaps the one character that sets it off sharply from all other known kinds of contemporary fiction. It habitually exhibits, not a man of delicate organization in revolt against the inexplicable tragedy of existence, but a man of low sensibilities and elemental desires yielding himself gladly to his environment, and so achieving what, under a third-rate civilization, passes for success. To get on: this is the aim. To weigh and reflect, to doubt and rebel: this is the thing to be avoided. I describe the optimistic, the inspirational, the Authors' League, the popular magazine, the peculiarly American school. In character creation its masterpiece is the advertising agent who, by devising some new and super-imbecile boob-trap, puts his hook-and-eye factory "on the map," ruins all other factories, marries the daughter of his boss, and so ends as an eminent man. Obviously, the drama underlying such fiction— what Mr. Beach would call its John Henry Plot—is false drama, Sunday-school drama, puerile and disgusting drama. It is the sort of thing that awakens a response only in men who are essentially unimaginative, timorous and degraded—in brief, in democrats, bagmen, yahoos. The man of reflective habit cannot conceivably take any passionate interest in the conflicts it deals with. He doesn't want to marry the daughter of the owner of the hook-and-eye factory; he would probably burn down the factory itself if it ever come into his hands. What interests this man is the far more poignant and significant conflict between a salient individual and the harsh and meaningless fiats of destiny, the unintelligible mandates and vagaries of God. His hero is not one who yields and wins, but one who resists and fails.

Most of these conflicts, of course, are internal, and hence do not make themselves visible in the overt melodrama of the Beaches, Davises and Chamberses. A superior man's struggle in the world is not with exterior lions, trusts, margraves, policemen, rivals in love, German spies, radicals and tornadoes, but with the obscure, atavistic impulses within him—the impulses, weaknesses and limitations that war with his notion of what life should be. Nine times out of ten he succumbs. Nine times out of ten he must yield to the dead hand. Nine times out of ten his aspiration is almost infinitely above his achievement. The result is that we see him sliding downhill—his ideals breaking up, his hope petering out, his character in decay. Character in decay is thus the theme of the great bulk of superior fiction. One has it in Dostoevsky, in

Balzac, in Hardy, in Conrad, in Flaubert, in Zola, in Turgeniev, in Goethe, in Sudermann, in Bennett, and, to come home in Dreiser. In nearly all first-rate novels the hero is defeated. In perhaps a majority he is completely destroyed. The hero of the inferior—*i.e.,* the typically American—novel engages in no such doomed and fateful combat. His conflict is not with the inexplicable ukases of destiny, the limitations of his own strength, the dead hand upon him, but simply with the superficial desires of his elemental fellow men. He thus has a fair chance of winning—and in bad fiction that chance is always converted into a certainty. So he marries the daughter of the owner of the factory and eventually gobbles the factory itself. His success gives thrills to persons who can imagine no higher aspiration. He embodies their optimism, as the other hero embodies the pessimism of more introspective and idealistic men. He is the protagonist of that great majority which is so inferior that it is quite unconscious of its inferiority.

It is this superficiality of the inferior man, it seems to me, that is the chief hallmark of the American novel. Whenever one encounters a novel that rises superior to it the thing takes on a subtle but unmistakable air of foreignness—for example, Frank Norris' "Vandover and the Brute," Hergesheimer's "The Lay Anthony" and Miss Cather's "My Antonía," or, to drop to short stories, Stephen Crane's "The Blue Hotel" and Mrs. Wharton's "Ethan Frome." The short story is commonly regarded, at least by American critics, as a preeminently American form; there are even patriots who argue that Bret Harte invented it. It meets very accurately, in fact, certain characteristic demands of the American temperament: it is simple, economical and brilliantly effective. Yet the same hollowness that marks the American novel also marks the American short story. Its great masters, in late years, have been such cheese-mongers as Davis, with his servant-girl romanticism, and O. Henry, with his smoke-room and variety-show smartness. In the whole canon of O. Henry's work you will not find a single recognizable human character; his people are unanimously marionettes; he makes Mexican brigands, Texas cow-men and New York cracksmen talk the same highly ornate Broadwayese. The successive volumes of Edward J. O'Brien's "Best Short-Story" series throw a vivid light upon the feeble estate of the art in the land. O'Brien, though his esthetic judgments are ludicrous, at least selects stories that are thoroughly representative; his books are trade successes because the crowd is undoubtedly with him. He has yet to discover a single story that even the most naïve professor would venture to mention in the same breath with Joseph Conrad's "Heart of Darkness," or Andrieff's "Silence," or Sudermann's "Das Sterbelied," or the least considerable tale by Anatole France. In many of the current American makers of magazine short stories—for example, Gouverneur Morris—one observes, as I have said, a truly admirable technical skill. They have mastered the externals of the form. They know how to get their effects. But in content their work is as hollow as a jug. Such stuff has no imaginable relation to life as men live it in the world. It is as artificial as the heroic strut and romantic eyes of a moving-picture actor.

I have spoken of the air of foreignness that clings to certain exceptional American compositions. In part it is based upon a psychological trick—upon the surprise which must inevitably seize upon any one who encounters a decent piece of writing in so vast a desert of mere literacy. But in part it is grounded soundly enough on the facts. The native author of any genuine force and originality is almost invariably found to be under strong foreign influences, either English or Continental. It was so in the earliest days. Freneau, the poet of the Revolution, was thoroughly French in blood and traditions. Irving, as H. R. Haweis has said, "took to England as a duck takes to water," and was in exile seventeen years. Cooper, with the great success of "The Last of the Mohicans" behind him, left the country in disgust and was gone for seven years. Emerson, Bryant, Lowell, Hawthorne and even Longfellow kept their eyes turned across the water; Emerson, in fact, was little more than an importer and popularizer of German and French ideas. Bancroft studied in Germany; Prescott, like Irving, was enchanted by Spain. Poe, unable to follow the fashion, invented mythical travels to save his face—to France, to Germany, to the Greek Isles. The Civil War revived the national consciousness enormously, but it did not halt the movement of *émigrés*. Henry James, in the seventies, went to England, Bierce and Bret Harte followed him, and even Mark Twain, absolutely American though he was, was forever pulling up stakes and setting out for

Vienna, Florence or London. Only poverty tied Whitman to the soil; his audience, for many years, was chiefly beyond the water, and there, too, he often longed to be. This distaste for the national scene is often based upon a genuine alienness. The more, indeed, one investigates the ancestry of Americans who have won distinction in the fine arts, the more one discovers tempting game for the critical Know-Nothings. Whitman was half Dutch, Harte was half Jew, Poe was partly German, James had an Irish grandfather, Howells was largely Irish and German, Dreiser is German and Hergesheimer is Pennsylvania Dutch. Fully a half of the painters discussed in John C. van Dyke's "American Painting and its Tradition" were of mixed blood, with the Anglo-Saxon plainly recessive. And of the five poets singled out for encomium by Miss Lowell in "Tendencies in Modern American Poetry" one is a Swede, two are partly German, one was educated in the German language, and three of the five exiled themselves to England as soon as they got out of their nonage. The exiles are of all sorts: Frank Harris, Vincent O'Sullivan, Ezra Pound, Herman Scheffauer, T. S. Eliot, Henry B. Fuller, Stuart Merrill, Edith Wharton. They go to England, France, Germany, Italy—anywhere to escape. Even at home the literatus is perceptibly foreign in his mien. If he lies under the New England tradition he is furiously colonial—more English than the English. It he turns to revolt, he is apt to put on a French hat and a Russian red blouse. *The Little Review*, the organ of the extreme wing of *révoltés*, is so violently exotic that several years ago, during the plupatriotic days of the war, some of its readers protested. With characteristic lack of humor it replied with an American number—and two of the stars of that number bore the fine old Anglo-Saxon names of Ben Hecht and Elsa von Freytag-Loringhoven.

This tendency of American literature, the moment it begins to show enterprise, novelty and significance, to radiate an alien smell is not an isolated phenomenon. The same smell accompanies practically all other sorts of intellectual activity in the republic. Whenever one hears that a new political theory is in circulation, or a scientific heresy, or a movement toward rationalism in religion, it is always safe to guess that some discontented stranger or other has a hand in it. In the newspapers and on the floor of Congress a new heterodoxy is always denounced forthwith as a product of foreign plotting, and here public opinion undoubtedly supports both the press and the politicians, and with good reason. The native culture of the country—that is, the culture of the low caste Anglo-Saxons who preserve the national tradition—is almost completely incapable of producing ideas. It is a culture that roughly corresponds to what the culture of England would be if there were no universities over there, and no caste of intellectual individualists and no landed aristocracy—in other words, if the tone of the national thinking were set by the non-conformist industrials, the camorra of Welsh and Scotch political scoundrels, and the town and country mobs. As we shall see, the United States has not yet produced anything properly describable as an aristocracy, and so there is no impediment to the domination of the inferior orders. Worse, the Anglo-Saxon strain, second-rate at the start, has tended to degenerate steadily to lower levels—in New England, very markedly. The result is that there is not only a great dearth of ideas in the land, but also an active and relentless hostility to ideas. The chronic suspiciousness of the inferior man here has full play; never in modern history has there been another civilization showing so vast a body of prohibitions and repressions, in both conduct and thought. The second result is that intellectual experimentation is chiefly left to the immigrants of the later migrations, and to the small sections of the native population that have been enriched with their blood. For such a pure Anglo-Saxon as Cabell to disport himself in the field of ideas is a rarity in the United States—and no exception to the rule that I have just mentioned, for Cabell belongs to an aristocracy that is now almost extinct, and has no more in common with the general population than a Baltic baron has with the indigenous herd of Letts and Esthonians. All the arts in America are thoroughly exotic. Music is almost wholly German or Italian, painting is French, literature may be anything from English to Russian, architecture (save when it becomes a mere branch of engineering) is a maddening phantasmagoria of borrowings. Even so elemental an art as that of cookery shows no native development, and is greatly disesteemed by Americans of the Anglo-Saxon majority; any decent restaurant that one blunders upon in the land is likely to be French, and if not French, then Italian or German or Chinese. So with the sciences: they have scarcely any native development. Organized scientific research began in the country with the founding of the Johns Hopkins University, a bald imitation of the German universities, and long held suspect by native opinion. Even after its great success, indeed, there was rancorous hostility to its scheme of things on chauvinistic grounds, and some years ago efforts were begun to Americanize it, with the result that it is now sunk to the level of Princeton, Amherst and other such glorified high schools, and is dominated by native savants who would be laughed at in any Continental university. Science, oppressed by such assaults from below, moves out of the academic grove into the freer air of the great foundations, where the pursuit of the shy fact is uncontaminated by football and social pushing. The greatest of these foundations is the Rockefeller Institute. Its salient men are such investigators as Flexner, Loeb and Carrel—all of them Continental Jews.

Thus the battle of ideas in the United States is largely carried on under strange flags, and even the stray natives on the side of free inquiry have to sacrifice some of their nationality when they enlist. The effects of this curious condition of affairs are both good and evil. The good ones are easily apparent. The racial division gives the struggle a certain desperate earnestness, and even bitterness, and so makes it the more inviting to lively minds. It was a benefit to the late D. C. Gilman rather than a disadvantage that national opinion opposed his traffic with Huxley and the German professors in the early days of the Johns Hopkins; the stupidity of the opposition stimulated him, and made him resolute, and his resolution, in the long run, was of inestimable cultural value. Scientific research in America, indeed, was thus set securely upon its legs precisely because the great majority of right-thinking Americans were violently opposed to it. In the same way it must be obvious that Dreiser got something valuable out of the grotesque war that was carried on against him during the greater war overseas because of his German name—a *jehad* fundamentally responsible for the suppression of "The 'Genius.'" The chief danger that he ran six or seven years ago was the danger that he might be accepted, explained away, and so seduced downward

(79)

to the common level. The attack of professional patriots saved him from that calamity. More, it filled him with a keen sense of his isolation, and stirred up the vanity that was in him as it is in all of us, and so made him cling with new tenacity to the very peculiarities that differentiate him from his inferiors. Finally, it is not to be forgotten that, without this rebellion of immigrant iconoclasts, the whole body of the national literature would tend to sink to the 100% American level of such patriotic literary business men as the president of the Authors' League. In other words, we must put up with the aesthetic Bolshevism of the Europeans and Asiatics who rage in the land, for without them we might not have any literature at all.

But the evils of the situation are not to be gainsaid. One of them I have already alluded to: the tendency of the beginning literatus, once he becomes fully conscious of his foreign affiliations, to desert the Republic forthwith, and thereafter view it from afar, and as an actual foreigner. More solid and various cultures lure him; he finds himself uncomfortable at home. Sometimes, as in the case of Henry James, he becomes a downright expatriate, and a more or less active agent of anti-American feeling; more often, he goes over to the outlanders without yielding up his theoretical citizenship, as in the cases of Irving, Harris, Pound and O'Sullivan. But all this, of course, works relatively light damage, for not many native authors are footloose enough to indulge in any such physical desertion of the soil. Of much more evil importance is the tendency of the cultural alienism that I have described to fortify the uncontaminated native in his bilious suspicion of all the arts, and particularly of all artists. The news that the latest poet to flutter the dovecotes is a Jew, or that the last novelist mauled by comstockery has a German or Scandinavian or Russian name, or that the critic newly taken in sacrilege is a partisan of Viennese farce or of the French moral code or of English literary theory—this news, among a people so ill-informed, so horribly well-trained in flight from bugaboos, and so savagely suspicious of the unfamiliar in ideas, has the inevitable effect of stirring up opposition that quickly ceases to be purely aesthetic objection, and so becomes increasingly difficult to combat. If Dreiser's name were Tompkins or Simpson, there is no doubt whatever that he would affright the professors a good deal less, and appear less of a hobgoblin to the *intelligentsia* of the women's clubs. If Oppenheim were less palpably levantine, he would come much nearer to the popularity of Edwin Markham and Walt Mason. And if Cabell kept to the patriotic business of a Southern gentleman, to wit, the praise of General Robert E. Lee, instead of prowling the strange and terrible fields of mediaeval Provençe, it is a safe wager that he would be sold openly over the counter instead of stealthily behind the door.

In a previous work I have discussed this tendency in America to estimate the artist in terms of his secular character. During the war, when all of the national defects in intelligence were enormously accentuated, it went to ludicrous lengths. There were then only authors who were vociferous patriots and thus geniuses, and authors who kept their dignity and were thus suspect and without virtue. By this gauge Chambers became the superior of Dreiser and Cabell, and Joyce Kilmer and Amy Lowell were set above Sandburg and Oppenheim. The test was even extended to foreigners: by it H. G. Wells took precedence of Shaw, and Blasco Ibáñez became a greater artist than Romain Roland. But the thing is not peculiar to war times; when peace is densest it is to be observed. The man of letters, pure and simple, is a rarity in America. Almost always he is something else—and that something else commonly determines his public eminence. Mark Twain, with only his books to recommend him, would probably have passed into obscurity in middle age; it was in the character of a public entertainer, not unrelated to Coxey, Dr. Mary Walker and Citizen George Francis Train, that he wooed and won his country. The official criticism of the land denied him any solid literary virtue to the day of his death, and even today the campus critics and their journalistic valets stand aghast before "The Mysterious Stranger" and "What Is Man?" Emerson passed through almost the same experience. It was not as a man of letters that he was chiefly thought of in his time, but as the prophet of a new cult, half religious, half philosophical, and wholly unintelligible to nine-tenths of those who discussed it. The first author of a handbook of American literature to sweep away the codfish Moses and expose the literary artist was the Polish Jew, Leon Kellner, of Czernowitz. So with Whitman and Poe—both hobgoblins far more than artists. So, even, with Howells: it was as the exponent of a dying culture that he was venerated, not as the practitioner of an art. Few actually read his books. His celebrity, of course, was real enough, but it somehow differed materially from that of a pure man of letters—say Shelley, Conrad, Hauptmann, Hardy or Synge. That he was himself keenly aware of the national tendency to judge an artist in terms of the citizen was made plain at the time of the Gorky scandal, when he joined Clemens in an ignominious desertion of Gorky, scared out of his wits by the danger of being manhandled for a violation of the national pecksniffery. Howells also refused to sign the Dreiser Protest. The case of Frank Harris is one eloquently in point. Harris has written, among other books, perhaps the best biography ever done by an American. Yet his politics keep him in a sort of Coventry and the average American critic would no more think of praising him than of granting Treitschke any merit as an historian.

· 7 ·

The Lonesome Artist

Thus falsely judged by standards that have no intelligible appositeness when applied to an artist, however accurately they may weigh a stockbroker or a Presbyterian elder, and forced to meet not only the hunkerous indifference of the dominant mob but also the bitter and disingenuous opposition of the classes to which he might look reasonably for understanding and support, the American author is forced into a sort of social and intellectual vacuum, and lives out his days, as Henry James said of Hawthorne, "an alien everywhere, an aesthetic solitary."

The wonder is that, in the face of so metallic and unyielding a front, any genuine artists in letters come to the front at all. But they constantly emerge; the first gestures are always on show; the prodigal and gorgeous life of the country simply forces a sensitive minority to make some attempt at representation and interpretation, and out of many trying there often appears one who can. The phenomenon of Dreiser is not unique. He had his forerunners in

Fuller and Frank Norris and he has his *compagnons du voyage* in Anderson, Charles G. Norris and more than one other. But the fact only throws up his curious isolation in a stronger light. It would be difficult to imagine an artist of his sober purpose and high accomplishment, in any civilized country, standing so neglected. The prevailing criticism, when it cannot dispose of him by denying that he exists—in the two chief handbooks of latter-day literature by professors he is not even mentioned!—seeks to dispose of him by arraying the shoddy fury of the mob against him. When he was under attack by the Comstocks, more than one American critic gave covert aid to the common enemy, and it was with difficulty that the weight of the Authors' League was held upon his side. More help for him, in fact, came from England, and quite voluntarily, than could be drummed up for him at home. No public sense of the menace that the attack offered to free speech and free art was visible; it would have made a nine-days' sensation for any layman of public influence to have gone to his rescue, as would have certainly happened in France, England or Germany. As for the newspaper-reading mob, it probably went unaware of the business altogether. When Arnold Bennett, landing in New York some time previously, told the reporters that Dreiser was the American he most desired to meet, the news was quite unintelligible to perhaps nine readers out of ten: they had no more heard of Dreiser than their fathers had heard of Whitman in 1875.

So with all the rest. I have mentioned Harris. It would be difficult to imagine Rolland meeting such a fate in France or Shaw in England as he has met in the United States. O'Sullivan, during the war, came home with "A Good Girl" in his pocket. The book was republished here—and got vastly less notice than the latest piece of trade-goods by Kathleen Norris. Fuller, early in his career, gave it up as hopeless. Norris died vainly battling for the young Dreiser. An Abraham Cahan goes unnoticed. Miss Cather, with four sound books behind her, lingers in the twilight of an esoteric reputation. Cabell, comstocked, is apprehended by his country only as a novelist to be bought by stealth and read in private. When Hugh Walpole came to America a year or two ago he favored the newspapers, like Bennett before him, with a piece of critical news that must have puzzled all readers save a very small minority. Discussing the living American novelists worth heeding, he nominated three—and of them only one was familiar to the general run of novel-buyers, or had ever been mentioned by a native critic of the apostolic succession. Only the poets of the land seem to attract the notice of the professors, and no doubt this is largely because most of the more salient of them—notably Miss Lowell and Lindsay—are primarily press-agents. Even so, the attention that they get is seldom serious. The only professor that I know of who has discussed the matter in precise terms holds that Alfred Noyes is the superior of all of them. Moreover, the present extraordinary interest in poetry stops short with a few poets, and one of its conspicuous phenomena is its lack of concern with the poets outside the movement, some of them unquestionably superior to any within.

Nor is this isolation of the artist in America new. The contemporary view of Poe and Whitman was almost precisely like the current view of Dreiser and Cabell. Both were neglected by the Brahmins of their time, and both were regarded hostilely by the great body of right-thinking citizens. Poe, indeed, was the victim of a furious attack by Rufus W. Griswold, the Hamilton Wright Mabie of the time, and it set the tone of native criticism for years. Whitman, living, narrowly escaped going to jail as a public nuisance. One thinks of Hawthorne and Emerson as writers decently appreciated by their contemporaries, but it is not to be forgotten that the official criticism of the era saw no essential difference between Hawthorne and Cooper, and that Emerson's reputation, to the end of his life, was far more that of a theological prophet and ethical platitudinarian, comparable to Lyman Abbott or Frank Crane, than that of a literary artist, comparable to Tennyson or Matthew Arnold. Perhaps Carlyle understood him, but who in America understood him? To this day he is the victim of gross misrepresentation by enthusiasts who read into him all sorts of flatulent bombast, as Puritanism is read into the New Testament by Methodists. As for Hawthorne, his extraordinary physical isolation during his lifetime was but the symbol of a complete isolation of the spirit, still surviving. If his preference for the internal conflict as opposed to the external act were not sufficient to set him off from the main stream of American speculation, there would always be his profound ethical skepticism —a state of mind quite impossible to the normal American, at least of Anglo-Saxon blood. Hawthorne, so far as I know, has never had a single professed follower in his own country. Even his son, attempting to carry on his craft, yielded neither to his meticulous method nor to his detached point of view. In the third generation, with infinite irony, there is a granddaughter who is a reviewer of books for the New York *Times,* which is almost as if Wagner should have a granddaughter singing in the operas of Massenet.

Of the four indubitable masters thus named, Hawthorne, Emerson, Whitman and Poe, only the last two have been sufficiently taken into the consciousness of the country to have any effect upon its literature, and even here that influence has been exerted only at second-hand, and against very definite adverse pressure. It would certainly seem reasonable for a man of so forceful a habit of mind as Poe, and of such prodigal and arresting originality, to have founded a school, but a glance at the record shows that he did nothing of the sort. Immediately he was dead, the shadows of the Irving tradition closed around his tomb, and for nearly thirty years thereafter all of his chief ideas went disregarded in his own country. If, as the literature books argue, Poe was the father of the American short story, then it was a posthumous child, and had step-fathers who did their best to conceal its true parentage. When it actually entered upon the vigorous life that we know today Poe had been dead for a generation. Its father, at the time of its belated adolescence, seemed to be Bret Harte—and Harte's debt to Dickens was vastly more apparent, first and last, than his debt to Poe. What he got from Poe was essential; it was the inner structure of the modern short story, the fundamental devices whereby a mere glimpse at events could be made to yield brilliant and seemingly complete images. But he himself was probably largely unaware of this indebtedness. A man little given to critical analysis, and incompetent for it when his own work was under examination, he saw its externals much more clearly than he saw its intrinsic organization, and these externals bore the plain marks of Dickens. It remained for one of his successors, Ambrose Bierce, to bridge belatedly the space separating him from Poe, and so show the route that he had come. And it remained for foreign criticism, and particularly for French criticism, to lift Poe himself to the secure place that he now holds. It is true enough that he enjoyed, during his lifetime, a certain popular reputation, and that he was praised by such men as N. P. Willis and James Russell Lowell, but that reputation was considerably less than the fame of men who were much his inferiors, and that praise, especially in Lowell's case, was much corrupted by reservations. Not many native critics of respectable position, during the 50's and 60's, would have ranked him clearly above, say, Irving or Cooper, or even above Longfellow, his old enemy. A few partisans argued for him, but in the main, as Saintsbury has said, he was the victim of "extreme and almost incomprehensible injustice" at the hands of his countrymen. It is surely not without significance that it took ten years to raise money enough to put a cheap and hideous tombstone upon his neglected grave, that it was not actually set up until he had been dead twenty-six years, that no contemporary American writer took any part in furthering the project, and that the only one who attended the final ceremony was Whitman.

It was Baudelaire's French translation of the prose tales and Mallarmé's translation of the poems that brought Poe to Valhalla. The former, first printed in 1856, founded the Poe cult in France, and during the two decades following it flourished amazingly, and gradually extended to England and Germany. It was one of the well-springs, in fact, of the whole so-called decadent movement. If Baudelaire, the father of that movement, "cultivated hysteria with delight and terror," he was simply doing what Poe had done before him. Both, reacting against the false concept of beauty as a mere handmaiden of logical ideas, sought its springs in those deep feelings and inner experiences which lie beyond the range of ideas and are to be interpreted only as intuitions. Emerson started upon the same quest, but was turned off into mazes of contradiction and unintelligibility by his ethical obsession—the unescapable burden of his Puritan heritage. But Poe never wandered from the path. You will find in "The Poetic Principle" what is perhaps the clearest statement of this new and sounder concept of beauty that has ever been made—certainly it is clearer than any ever made by a Frenchman. But it was not until Frenchmen had watered the seed out of grotesque and vari-colored pots that it began to sprout. The tide of Poe's ideas, set in motion in France early in the second half of the century, did not wash England until the last decade, and in America, save for a few dashes of spray, it has yet to show itself. There is no American writer who displays the influence of this most potent and original of Americans so clearly as whole groups of Frenchmen display it, and whole groups of Germans, and even a good many Englishmen. What we have from Poe at first hand is simply a body of obvious yokel-shocking in the *Black Cat* manner, with the tales of Ambrose Bierce as its finest flower—in brief, an imitation of Poe's externals without any comprehension whatever of his underlying aims and notions. What we have from him at second-hand is a somewhat childish Maeterlinckism, a further dilution of Poe-and-water. This Maeterlinckism, some time ago, got itself intermingled with the Whitmanic stream flowing back to America through the channel of French Imagism, with results destructive to the sanity of earnest critics and fatal to the gravity of those less austere. It is significant that the critical writing of Poe, in which there lies most that was best in him, has not come back; no normal American ever thinks of him as a critic, but only as a poet, as a raiser of goose-flesh, or as an immoral fellow. The cause thereof is plain enough. The French, instead of borrowing his critical theory directly, deduced it afresh from his applications of it; it became criticism *of* him rather than *by* him. Thus his own speculations have lacked the authority of foreign approval, and have consequently made no impression. The weight of native opinion is naturally against them, for they are at odds, not only with its fundamental theories, but also with its practical doctrine that no criticism can be profound and respectable which is not also dull.

"Poe," says Arthur Ransome, in his capital study of the man and the artist, "was like a wolf chained by the leg among a lot of domestic dogs." The simile here is somewhat startling, and Ransome, in a footnote, tries to ameliorate it: the "domestic dogs" it refers to were magnificoes of no less bulk than Longfellow, Whittier, Holmes and Emerson. In the case of Whitman, the wolf was not only chained, but also muzzled. Nothing, indeed, could be more amazing than the hostility that surrounded him at home until the very end of his long life. True enough, it was broken by certain feeble mitigations. Emerson, in 1855, praised him—though later very eager to forget it and desert him, as Clemens and Howells, years afterward, deserted Gorky. Alcott, Thoreau, Lowell and even Bryant, during his brief Bohemian days, were polite to him. A group of miscellaneous enthusiasts gradually gathered about him, and out of this group emerged at least one man of some distinction, John Burroughs. Young adventurers of letters—for example, Huneker—went to see him and hear him, half drawn by genuine admiration and half by mere deviltry. But the general tone of the opinion that beat upon him, the attitude of domestic criticism, was unbrokenly inimical; he was opposed by misrepresentation and neglect. "The prevailing range of criticism on my book," he wrote in "A Backward Glance on My Own Road" in 1884, "has been either mockery or denunciation—and . . . I have been the marked object of two or three (to me pretty serious) official buffetings." "After thirty years of trial," he wrote in "My Book and I," three years later, "public criticism on the book and myself as author of it shows marked anger and contempt more than anything else." That is, at home. Abroad he was making headway all the while, and long years afterward, by way of France and England, he began to force his way into the consciousness of his countrymen. What could have been more ironical than the solemn celebrations of Whitman's centenary that were carried off in various American universities in 1919? One can picture the old boy rolling with homeric mirth in hell. Imagine the fate of a university don of 1860, or 1870, or 1880, or even 1890 who had ventured to commend "Leaves of Grass" to the young gentlemen of his seminary! He would have come to grief as swiftly as that Detroit pedagogue of day before yesterday who brought down the Mothers' Legion upon him by commending "Jurgen."

· 8 ·

The Cultural Background

So far, the disease. As to the cause, I have delivered a few hints. I now describe it particularly. It is, in brief, a defect in the general culture of the country—one reflected, not only in the national literature, but also in the national political theory, the national attitude toward religion and morals, the national habit in all departments of thinking. It is the lack of a civilized aristocracy, secure in its position, animated by an intelligent curiosity, skeptical of all facile generalizations, superior to the sentimentality of the mob, and delighting in the battle of ideas for its own sake.

The word I use, despite the qualifying adjective, has got itself meanings, of course, that I by no means intend to convey. Any mention of an aristocracy, to a public fed upon democratic fustian, is bound to bring up images of stockbrokers' wives lolling obscenely in opera boxes, or of haughty Englishmen slaughtering whole generations of grouse in an inordinate and incomprehensible manner, or of Junkers with tight waists elbowing American schoolmarms off the sidewalks of German beer towns, or of perfumed Italians coming over to work their abominable magic upon the daughters of breakfast-food and bathtub kings. Part of this misconception, I suppose, has its roots in the gaudy imbecilities of the yellow press, but there is also a part that belongs to the general American tradition, along with the oppression of minorities and the belief in political panaceas. Its depth and extent are constantly revealed by the naïve assumption that the so-called fashionable folk of the large cities—chiefly wealthy industrials in the interior-decorator and country-club stage of culture—constitute an aristocracy, and by the scarcely less remarkable assumption that the peerage of England is identical with the gentry—that is, that such men as Lord Northcliffe, Lord Iveagh and even Lord Reading are English gentlemen, and of the ancient line of the Percys.

Here, as always, the worshiper is the father of the gods, and no less when they are evil than when they are benign. The inferior man must find himself superiors, that he may marvel at his political equality with them, and in the absence of recognizable superiors *de facto* he creates superiors *de jure*. The sublime principle of one man, one vote must be translated into terms of dollars, diamonds, fashionable intelligence; the equality of all men before the law must have clear and dramatic proofs. Sometimes, perhaps, the thing goes further and is more subtle. The inferior man needs an aristocracy to demonstrate, not only his mere equality, but also his actual superiority. The society columns in the newspapers may have some such origin: they may visualize once more the accomplished journalist's understanding of the mob mind that he plays upon so skillfully, as upon some immense and cacophonous organ, always going *fortissimo*. What the inferior man and his wife see in the sinister revels of those amazing first families, I suspect, is often a massive witness to their own higher rectitude—to their relative innocence of cigarette-smoking, poodle-coddling, child-farming and the more abstruse branches of adultery—in brief, to their firmer grasp upon the immutable axioms of Christian virtue, the one sound boast of the nether nine-tenths of humanity in every land under the cross.

But this bugaboo aristocracy, as I hint, is actually bogus, and the evidence of its bogusness lies in the fact that it is insecure. One gets into it only onerously, but out of it very easily. Entrance is effected by dint of a long and bitter struggle, and the chief incidents of that struggle are almost intolerable humiliations. The aspirant must school and steel himself to sniffs and sneers; he must see the door slammed upon him a hundred times before ever it is thrown open to him. To get in at all he must show a talent for abasement—and abasement makes him timorous. Worse, that timorousness is not cured when he succeeds at last. On the contrary, it is made even more tremulous, for what he faces within the gates is a scheme of things made up almost wholly of harsh and often unintelligible taboos, and the penalty for violating even the least of them is swift and disastrous. He must exhibit exactly the right social habits, appetites and prejudices, public and private. He must harbor exactly the right political enthusiasms and indignations. He must have a hearty taste for exactly the right sports. His attitude toward the fine arts must be properly tolerant and yet not a shade too eager. He must read and like exactly the right books, pamphlets and public journals. He must put up at the right hotels when he travels. His wife must patronize the right milliners. He himself must stick to the right haberdashery. He must live in the right neighborhood. He must even embrace the right doctrines of religion. It would ruin him, for all opera box and society column purposes, to set up a plea for justice to the Bolsheviki, or even for ordinary decency. It would ruin him equally

to wear celluloid collars, or to move to Union Hill, N.J., or to serve
ham and cabbage at his table. And it would ruin him, too, to drink
coffee from his saucer, or to marry a chambermaid with a gold
tooth, or to join the Seventh-Day Adventists. Within the bound-
aries of his curious order he is worse fettered than a monk in a cell.
Its obscure conception of propriety, its nebulous notion that this
or that is honorable, hampers him in every direction, and very narrowly. What he resigns when he enters, even when he makes his
first deprecating knock at the door, is every right to attack the
ideas that happen to prevail within. Such as they are, he must
accept them without question. And as they shift and change in
response to great instinctive movements (or perhaps, now and
then, to the punished but not to be forgotten revolts of extraordinary rebels) he must shift and change with them, silently and
quickly. To hang back, to challenge and dispute, to preach reforms
and revolutions—these are crimes against the brummagem Holy
Ghost of the order.

Obviously, that order cannot constitute a genuine aristocracy,
in any rational sense. A genuine aristocracy is grounded upon very
much different principles. Its first and most salient character is its
interior security, and the chief visible evidence of that security is
the freedom that goes with it—not only freedom in act, the divine
right of the aristocrat to do what he jolly well pleases, so long as
he does not violate the primary guarantees and obligations of his
class, but also and more importantly freedom in thought, the
liberty to try and err, the right to be his own man. It is the instinct
of a true aristocracy, not to punish eccentricity by expulsion, but
to throw a mantle of protection about it—to safeguard it from the
suspicions and resentments of the lower orders. Those lower
orders are inert, timid, inhospitable to ideas, hostile to changes,
faithful to a few maudlin superstitions. All progress goes on on the
higher levels. It is there that salient personalities, made secure by
artificial immunities, may oscillate most widely from the normal
track. It is within that entrenched fold, out of reach of the immemorial certainties of the mob, that extraordinary men of the
lower orders may find their city of refuge, and breathe a clear
air. This, indeed, is at once the hallmark and the justification of an
aristocracy—that it is beyond responsibility to the general masses

of men, and hence superior to both their degraded longings and their no less degraded aversions. It is nothing if it is not autonomous, curious, venturesome, courageous, and everything if it is. It is the custodian of the qualities that make for change and experiment; it is the class that organizes danger to the service of the race; it pays for its high prerogatives by standing in the forefront of the fray.

No such aristocracy, it must be plain, is now on view in the United States. The makings of one were visible in the Virginia of the later eighteenth century, but with Jefferson and Washington the promise died. In New England, it seems to me, there was never any aristocracy, either in being or in nascency: there was only a theocracy that degenerated very quickly into a plutocracy on the one hand and a caste of sterile *Gelehrten* on the other—the passion for God splitting into a lust for dollars and a weakness for mere words. Despite the common notion to the contrary—a notion generated by confusing literacy with intelligence—New England has never shown the slightest sign of a genuine enthusiasm for ideas. It began its history as a slaughter-house of ideas, and it is today not easily distinguishable from a cold-storage plant. Its celebrated adventures in mysticism, once apparently so bold and significant, are now seen to have been little more than an elaborate hocus-pocus—respectable Unitarians shocking the peasantry and scaring the horned cattle in the fields by masquerading in the robes of Rosicrucians. The ideas that it embraced in those austere and far-off days were stale, and when it had finished with them they were dead: today one hears of Jakob Böhme almost as rarely as one hears of Allen G. Thurman. So in politics. Its glory is Abolition —an English invention, long under the interdict of the native plutocracy. Since the Civil War its six states have produced fewer political ideas, as political ideas run in the Republic, than any average county in Kansas or Nebraska. Appomattox seemed to be a victory for New England idealism. It was actually a victory for the New England plutocracy, and that plutocracy has dominated thought above the Housatonic ever since. The sect of professional idealists has so far dwindled that it has ceased to be of any importance, even as an opposition. When the plutocracy is challenged now, it is challenged by the proletariat.

Well, what is on view in New England is on view in all other parts of the nation, sometimes with ameliorations, but usually with the colors merely exaggerated. What one beholds, sweeping the eye over the land, is a culture that, like the national literature, is in three layers—the plutocracy on top, a vast mass of undifferentiated human blanks at the bottom, and a forlorn *intelligentsia* gasping out a precarious life between. I need not set out at any length, I hope, the intellectual deficiencies of the plutocracy—its utter failure to show anything even remotely resembling the makings of an aristocracy. It is badly educated, it is stupid, it is full of low-caste superstitions and indignations, it is without decent traditions or informing vision; above all, it is extraordinarily lacking in the most elemental independence and courage. Out of this class comes the grotesque fashionable society of our big towns, already described. Imagine a horde of peasants incredibly enriched and with almost infinite power thrust into their hands, and you will have a fair picture of its habitual state of mind. It shows all the stigmata of inferiority—moral certainty, cruelty, suspicion of ideas, fear. Never did it function more revealingly than in the late *pogrom* against the so-called Reds, *i.e.*, against humorless idealists who, like Andrew Jackson, took the platitudes of democracy quite seriously. The machinery brought to bear upon these feeble and scattered fanatics would have almost sufficed to repel an invasion by the united powers of Europe. They were hunted out of their sweat-shops and coffee-houses as if they were so many Carranzas or Ludendorffs, dragged to jail to the tooting of horns, arraigned before quaking judges on unintelligible charges, condemned to deportation without the slightest chance to defend themselves, torn from their dependent families, herded into prison-ships, and then finally dumped in a snow waste, to be rescued and fed by the Bolsheviki. And what was the theory at the bottom of all these astounding proceedings? So far as it can be reduced to comprehensible terms it was much less a theory than a fear—a shivering, idiotic, discreditable fear of a mere banshee—an overpowering, paralyzing dread that some extra-eloquent Red, permitted to emit his balderdash unwhipped, might eventually convert a couple of courageous men, and that the courageous men, filled with indignation against the plutocracy, might take to the highroad, burn down a nail-factory or two, and slit the throat of some virtuous profiteer. In order to lay this fear, in order to ease the jangled nerves of the American successors to the Hapsburgs and Hohenzollerns, all the constitutional guarantees of the citizen were suspended, the statute-books were burdened with laws that surpass anything heard of in the Austria of Maria Theresa, the country was handed over to a frenzied mob of detectives, informers and *agents provocateurs*—and the Reds departed laughing loudly, and were hailed by the Bolsheviki as innocents escaped from an asylum for the criminally insane.

Obviously, it is out of reason to look for any hospitality to ideas in a class so extravagantly fearful of even the most palpably absurd of them. Its philosophy is firmly grounded upon the thesis that the existing order must stand forever free from attack, and not only from attack, but also from mere academic criticism, and its ethics are as firmly grounded upon the thesis that every attempt at any such criticism is a proof of moral turpitude. Within its own ranks, protected by what may be regarded as the privilege of the order, there is nothing to take the place of this criticism. A few feeble platitudes by Andrew Carnegie and a book of moderate merit by John D. Rockefeller's press-agent constitute almost the whole of the interior literature of ideas. In other countries the plutocracy has often produced men of reflective and analytical habit, eager to rationalize its instincts and to bring it into some sort of relationship to the main streams of human thought. The case of David Ricardo at once comes to mind. There have been many others: John Bright, Richard Cobden, George Grote, and, in our own time, Walther von Rathenau. But in the United States no such phenomenon has been visible. There was a day, not long ago, when certain young men of wealth gave signs of an unaccustomed interest in ideas on the political side, but the most they managed to achieve was a banal sort of Socialism, and even this was abandoned in sudden terror when the war came, and Socialism fell under suspicion of being genuinely international—in brief, of being honest under the skin. Nor has the plutocracy of the country ever fostered an inquiring spirit among its intellectual valets and footmen, which is to say, among the gentlemen who compose headlines and leading articles for its newspapers. What chiefly distinguishes the daily press of the United States from the press of all other countries pretending to culture is not its lack of truthfulness or even its lack of dignity and honor, for these deficiencies are common to the newspapers everywhere, but its incurable fear of ideas, its constant effort to evade the discussion of fundamentals by translating all issues into a few elemental fears, its incessant reduction of all reflection to mere emotion. It is, in the true sense, never well-informed. It is seldom intelligent, save in the arts of the mob-master. It is never courageously honest. Held harshly to a rigid correctness of opinion by the plutocracy that controls it with less and less attempt at disguise, and menaced on all sides by censorships that it dare not flout, it sinks rapidly into formalism and feebleness. Its yellow section is perhaps its most respectable section, for there the only vestige of the old free journalist survives. In the more conservative papers one finds only a timid and petulant animosity to all questioning of the existing order, however urbane and sincere—a pervasive and ill-concealed dread that the mob now heated up against the orthodox hobgoblins may suddenly begin to unearth hobgoblins of its own, and so run amok. For it is upon the emotions of the mob, of course, that the whole comedy is played. Theoretically the mob is the repository of all political wisdom and virtue; actually it is the ultimate source of all political power. Even the plutocracy cannot make war upon it openly, or forget the least of its weaknesses. The business of keeping it in order must be done discreetly, warily, with delicate technique. In the main that business consists of keeping alive its deep-seated fears—of strange faces, of unfamiliar ideas, of unhackneyed gestures, of untested liberties and responsibilities. The one permanent emotion of the inferior man, as of all the simpler mammals, is fear—fear of the unknown, the complex, the inexplicable. What he wants beyond everything else is safety. His instincts incline him toward a society so organized that it will protect him at all hazards, and not only against perils to his hide but also against assaults upon his mind—against the need to grapple with unaccustomed problems, to weigh ideas, to think things out for himself, to scrutinize the platitudes upon which his everyday thinking is based. Content under kaiserism so long as it functions efficiently, he turns, when kaiserism falls, to some other and perhaps worse form of paternalism, bringing to its benign tyranny only the docile tribute of his pathetic allegiance. In

America it is the newspaper that is his boss. From it he gets support for his elemental illusions. In it he sees a visible embodiment of his own wisdom and consequence. Out of it he draws fuel for his simple moral passion, his congenital suspicion of heresy, his dread of the unknown. And behind the newspaper stands the plutocracy, ignorant, unimaginative and timorous.

Thus at the top and at the bottom. Obviously, there is no aristocracy here. One finds only one of the necessary elements, and that only in the plutocracy, to wit, a truculent egoism. But where is intelligence? Where are ease and surety of manner? Where are enterprise and curiosity? Where, above all, is courage, and in particular, moral courage—the capacity for independent thinking, for difficult problems, for what Nietzsche called the joys of the labyrinth? As well look for these things in a society of half-wits. Democracy, obliterating the old aristocracy, has left only a vacuum in its place; in a century and a half it has failed either to lift up the mob to intellectual autonomy and dignity or to purge the plutocracy of its inherent stupidity and swinishness. It is precisely here, the first and favorite scene of the Great Experiment, that the culture of the individual has been reduced to the most rigid and absurd regimentation. It is precisely here, of all civilized countries, that eccentricity in demeanor and opinion has come to bear the heaviest penalties. The whole drift of our law is toward the absolute prohibition of all ideas that diverge in the slightest from the accepted platitudes, and behind that drift of law there is a far more potent force of growing custom, and under that custom there is a national philosophy which erects conformity into the noblest of virtues and the free functioning of personality into a capital crime against society.

· 9 ·

Under the Campus Pump

But there remain the *intelligentsia*, the free spirits in the middle ground, neither as anesthetic to ideas as the plutocracy on the one hand nor as much the slaves of emotion as the proletariat on the other. Have I forgotten them? I have not. But what actually reveals itself when this small brotherhood of the superior is carefully examined? What reveals itself, it seems to me, is a gigantic disappointment. Superficially, there are all the marks of a caste of learned and sagacious men—a great book-knowledge, a laudable diligence, a certain fine reserve and sniffish-ness, a plain consciousness of intellectual superiority, not a few gestures that suggest the aristocratic. But under the surface one quickly discovers that the whole thing is little more than play-acting, and not always very skillful. Learning is there, but not curiosity. A heavy dignity is there, but not much genuine self-respect. Pretentiousness is there, but not a trace of courage. Squeezed between the plutocracy on one side and the mob on the other, the *intelligentsia* face the eternal national problem of main-taining their position, of guarding themselves against challenge and attack, of keeping down suspicion. They have all the attributes of knowledge save the sense of power. They have all the quali-ties of an aristocracy save the capital qualities that arise out of a feeling of security, of complete independence, of absolute im-munity to onslaught from above and below. In brief, the old bogusness hangs about them, as about the fashionable aristocrats of the society columns. They are safe so long as they are good, which is to say, so long as they neither aggrieve the plutocracy nor startle the proletariat. Immediately they fall into either misde-meanor all their apparent dignity vanishes, and with it all of their influence, and they become simply somewhat ridiculous rebels against a social order that has no genuine need of them and is dis-posed to tolerate them only when they are not obtrusive.

For various reasons this shadowy caste is largely made up of men who have official stamps upon their learning—that is, of professors, of doctors of philosophy; outside of academic circles it tends to shade off very rapidly into a half-world of isolated an-archists. One of those reasons is plain enough: the old democratic veneration for mere schooling, inherited from the Puritans of New England, is still in being, and the mob, always eager for short cuts in thinking, is disposed to accept a schoolmaster without looking beyond his degree. Another reason lies in the fact that the higher education is still rather a novelty in the country, and there have yet to be developed any devices for utilizing learned men in any trade save teaching. Yet other reasons will suggest themselves. Whatever the ramification of causes, the fact is plain that the pedagogues have almost a monopoly of what passes for the higher thinking in the land. Not only do they reign unchallenged in their own chaste grove; they also penetrate to all other fields of ratiocination, to the almost complete exclusion of unshrived rivals. They dominate the weeklies of opinion; they are to the fore in every review; they write nine-tenths of the serious books of the country; they begin to invade the newspapers; they instruct and exhort the yokelry from the stump; they have even begun to penetrate into the government. One cannot turn in the United States without encountering a professor. There is one on every municipal commission. There is one in every bureau of the federal government. There is one at the head of every intellectual movement. There is one to explain every new mystery. Professors appraise all works of art, whether graphic, tonal or literary. Professors supply the brain power for agriculture, diplomacy, the control of dependencies and the distribution of commodities. A professor was until lately sovereign of the country, and pope of the state church.

So much for their opportunity. What, now, of their achievement? I answer as one who has had thrown upon him, by the impenetrable operations of fate, the rather thankless duties of a specialist in the ways of pedagogues, a sort of professor of professors. The job has got me enemies. I have been accused of carrying on a defamatory *jehad* against virtuous and laborious men; I have even been charged with doing it in the interest of the Wilhelmstrasse, the White Slave Trust and the ghost of Friedrich Wilhelm Nietzsche. Nothing could be more absurd. All my instincts are on the side of the professors. I esteem a man who devotes himself to a subject with hard diligence; I esteem even more a man who puts poverty and a shelf of books above profiteering and evenings of jazz; I am naturally monkish. Moreover, there are more Ph.D.'s on my family tree than even a Boston bluestocking can boast; there was a whole century when even the most ignorant of my house was at least *Juris utriusque Doctor*. But such predispositions should not be permitted to color sober researches. What I have found, after long and arduous labors, is a state of things that is surely not

altogether flattering to the *Gelehrten* under examination. What I
have found, in brief, is that pedagogy turned to general public
uses is almost as timid and flatulent as journalism—that the professor, menaced by the timid dogmatism of the plutocracy above
him and the incurable suspiciousness of the mob beneath him,
is almost invariably inclined to seek his own security in a mellifluous inanity—that, far from being a courageous spokesman of
ideas and an apostle of their free dissemination, in politics, in the
fine arts, in practical ethics, he comes close to being the most
prudent and skittish of all men concerned with them—in brief,
that he yields to the prevailing correctness of thought in all departments, north, east, south and west, and is, in fact, the chief
exponent among us of the democratic doctrine that heresy is not
only a mistake, but also a crime.

A philosophy is not put to much of a test in ordinary times,
for in ordinary times philosophies are permitted to lie like sleeping
dogs. When it shows its inward metal is when the band begins
to play. The turmoils of the late lamentable war, it seems to me,
provided for such a trying out of fundamental ideas and attitudes
upon a colossal scale. The whole thinking of the world was thrown
into confusion; all the worst fears and prejudices of ignorant and
emotional men came to the front; it was a time, beyond all others
in modern history, when intellectual integrity was subjected to a
cruel strain. How did the *intelligentsia* of These States bear up
under that strain? What was the reaction of our learned men
to the challenge of organized hysteria, mob fear, incitement to
excess, downright insanity? How did they conduct themselves in
that universal whirlwind? They conducted themselves, I fear, in
a manner that must leave a brilliant question mark behind their
claim to independence and courage, to true knowledge and
dignity, to ordinary self-respect—in brief, to every quality that
belongs to the authentic aristocrat. They constituted themselves,
not a restraining influence upon the mob run wild, but the loudest
spokesmen of its worst imbecilities. They fed it with bogus history,
bogus philosophy, bogus idealism, bogus heroics. They manufactured blather for its entertainment. They showed themselves to
be as naïve as so many Liberty Loan orators, as emotional, almost,
as the spy hunters, and as disdainful of the ordinary intellectual

decencies as the editorial writers. I accumulated, in those great days, for the instruction and horror of posterity, a very large collection of academic arguments, expositions and pronunciamentos; it fills a trunk, and got me heavily into debt to three clipping bureaus. Its contents range from solemn hymns of hate in the learned (and even the theological) reviews and such official donkeyisms as the formal ratification of the so-called Sisson documents down to childish harangues to student-bodies, public demands that the study of the enemy language and literature be prohibited by law, violent denunciations of all enemy science as negligible and fraudulent, vitriolic attacks upon enemy magnificos, and elaborate proofs that the American Revolution was the result of a foul plot hatched in the Wilhelmstrasse of the time, to the wanton injury of two loving bands of brothers. I do not exaggerate in the slightest. The proceedings of Mr. Creel's amazing corps of "twenty-five hundred American historians" went further than anything I have described. And in every far-flung college town, in every one-building "university" on the prairie, even the worst efforts of those "historians" were vastly exceeded.

But I am forgetting the like phenomena on the other side of the bloody chasm? I am overlooking the darker crimes of the celebrated German professors? Not at all. Those crimes against all reason and dignity, had they been committed in fact, would not be evidence in favor of the Americans in the dock: the principle of law is too well accepted to need argument. But I venture to deny them, and out of a very special and singular knowledge, for I seem to be one of the few Americans who has ever actually read the proclamations of the German professors: all the most indignant critics of them appear to have accepted second-hand accounts of their contents. Having suffered the onerous labor of reading them, I now offer sworn witness to their relative mildness. Now and then one encounters in them a disconcerting bray. Now and then one weeps with sore heart. Now and then one is bogged in German made wholly unintelligible by emotion. But taking them as they stand, and putting them fairly beside the corresponding documents of American vintage, one is at once struck by their comparative suavity and decorum, their freedom from mere rhetoric and fustian—above all, by their effort to appeal to reason, such as it is, rather than to emotion. No German professor, from end to end of the war, put his hand to anything as transparently silly as the Sisson documents. No German professor essayed to prove that the Seven Years' War was caused by Downing Street. No German professor argued that the study of English would corrupt the soul. No German professor denounced Darwin as an ignoramus and Lister as a scoundrel. Nor was anything of the sort done, so far as I know, by any French professor. Nor even by any reputable English professor. All such honorable efforts on behalf of correct thought in wartime were monopolized by American professors. And if the fact is disputed, then I threaten upon some future day, when the stealthy yearning to forget has arisen, to print my proofs in parallel columns—the most esteemed extravagances of the German professors in one column and the corresponding masterpieces of the American professors in the other.

I do not overlook, of course, the self-respecting men who, in the midst of all the uproar, kept their counsel and their dignity. A small minority, hard beset and tested by the fire! Nor do I overlook the few sentimental fanatics who, in the face of devastating evidence to the contrary, proceeded upon the assumption that academic freedom was yet inviolable, and so got themselves cashiered, and began posturing in radical circles as martyrs, the most absurd of men. But I think I draw a fair picture of the general. I think I depict with reasonable accuracy the typical response of the only recognizable *intelligentsia* of the land to the first great challenge to their aristocratic aloofness—the first test in the grand manner of their freedom alike from the bellicose imbecility of the plutocracy and the intolerable fears and childish moral certainties of the mob. That test exposed them shamelessly. It revealed their fast allegiance to the one thing that is the antithesis of all free inquiry, of all honest hospitality to ideas, of all intellectual independence and integrity. They proved that they were correct—and in proving it they threw a brilliant light upon many mysteries of our national culture.

• I O •

The Intolerable Burden

Among others, upon the mystery of our literature—its faltering feebleness, its lack of genuine gusto, its dearth of salient personalities, its general air of poverty and imitation. What ails the beautiful letters of the Republic, I repeat, is what ails the general culture of the Republic—the lack of a body of sophisticated and civilized public opinion, independent of plutocratic control and superior to the infantile philosophies of the mob—a body of opinion showing the eager curiosity, the educated skepticism and the hospitality to ideas of a true aristocracy. This lack is felt by the American author, imagining him to have anything new to say, every day of his life. He can hope for no support, in ordinary cases, from the mob: it is too suspicious of all ideas. He can hope for no support from the spokesmen of the plutocracy: they are too diligently devoted to maintaining the intellectual *status quo*. He turns, then, to the *intelligentsia*—and what he finds is correctness! In his two prime functions, to represent the life about him accurately and to criticize it honestly, he sees that correctness arrayed against him. His representation is indecorous, unlovely, too harsh to be borne. His criticism is in contumacy to the ideals upon which the whole structure rests. So he is either attacked vigorously as an anti-patriot whose babblings ought to be put down by law, or enshrouded in a silence which commonly disposes of him even more effectively.

Soon or late, of course, a man of genuine force and originality is bound to prevail against that sort of stupidity. He will unearth an adherent here and another there; in the long run they may become numerous enough to force some recognition of him, even from the most immovable exponents of correctness. But the business is slow, uncertain, heart-breaking. It puts a burden upon the artist that ought not to be put upon him. It strains beyond reason his diligence and passion. A man who devotes his life to creating works of the imagination, a man who gives over all his strength and energy to struggling with problems that are essentially delicate and baffling and pregnant with doubt—such a man does not ask for recognition as a mere reward for his industry; he asks for it as a necessary *help* to his industry; he needs it as he needs decent subsistence and peace of mind. It is a grave damage to the artist and a grave loss to the literature when such a man as Poe has to seek consolation among his inferiors, and such a man as the Mark Twain of "What Is Man?" is forced to conceal his most profound beliefs, and such men as Dreiser and Cabell are exposed to incessant attacks by malignant stupidity. The notion that artists flourish upon adversity and misunderstanding, that they are able to function to the utmost in an atmosphere of indifference or hostility—this notion is nine-tenths nonsense. If it were true, then one would never hear of painters going to France or of musicians going to Germany. What the artist actually needs is comprehension of his aims and ideals by men he respects—not necessarily approval of his products, but simply an intelligent sympathy for him in the great agony of creation. And that sympathy must be more than the mere fellow-feeling of other craftsmen; it must come, in large part, out of a connoisseurship that is beyond the bald trade interest; it must have its roots in the intellectual curiosity of an aristocracy of taste. Billroth, I believe, was more valuable to Brahms than even Schumann. His eager interest gave music-making a solid dignity. His championship offered the musician a visible proof that his labors had got for him a secure place in a civilized and stable society, and that he would be judged by his peers, and safeguarded against the obtuse hostility of his inferiors.

No such security is thrown about an artist in America. It is not that the country lacks the standards that Dr. Brownell pleads for; it is that its standards are still those of a primitive and timorous society. The excesses of Comstockery are profoundly symbolical. What they show is the moral certainty of the mob in operation against something that is as incomprehensible to it as the theory of least squares, and what they show even more vividly is the distressing lack of any automatic corrective of that outrage—of any firm and secure body of educated opinion, eager to hear and test all intelligible ideas and sensitively jealous of the right to discuss them freely. When "The Genius" was attacked by the Comstocks, it fell to my lot to seek assistance for Dreiser among the *intel-*

ligentsia. I found them almost unanimously disinclined to lend a hand. A small number permitted themselves to be induced, but the majority held back, and not a few, as I have said, actually offered more or less furtive aid to the Comstocks. I pressed the matter and began to unearth reasons. It was, it appeared, dangerous for a member of the *intelligentsia,* and particularly for a member of the academic *intelligentsia,* to array himself against the mob inflamed —against the moral indignation of the sort of folk who devour vice reports and are converted by the Rev. Billy Sunday! If he came forward, he would have to come forward alone. There was no organized support behind him. No instinctive urge of class, no prompting of a great tradition, moved him to speak out for artistic freedom . . . England supplied the lack. Over there they have a mob too, and something akin to Comstockery, and a cult of hollow correctness—but they also have a caste that stands above all that sort of thing, and out of that caste came aid for Dreiser.

England is always supplying the lack—England, or France, or Germany, or some other country, but chiefly England. "My market and my reputation," said Prescott in 1838, "rest principally with England." To Poe, a few years later, the United States was "a literary colony of Great Britain." And there has been little change to this day. The English leisure class, says Prof. Dr. Veblen, is "for purposes of reputable usage the upper leisure class of this country." Despite all the current highfalutin about melting pots and national destinies the United States remains almost as much an English colonial possession, intellectually and spiritually, as it was on July 3, 1776. The American social pusher keeps his eye on Mayfair; the American literatus dreams of recognition by the London weeklies; the American don is lifted to bliss by the imprimatur of Oxford or Cambridge; even the American statesman knows how to cringe to Downing Street. Most of the essential policies of Dr. Wilson between 1914 and 1920—when the realistic English, finding him no longer useful, incontinently dismissed him —were, to all intents and purposes, those of a British colonial premier. He went into the Peace Conference willing to yield everything to English interests, and he came home with a treaty that was so extravagantly English that it fell an easy prey to the anti-English minority, ever alert for the makings of a bugaboo to scare the plain people. What lies under all this subservience is simple enough. The American, for all his braggadocio, is quite conscious of his intrinsic inferiority to the Englishman, on all cultural counts. He may put himself first as a man of business, as an adventurer in practical affairs or as a pioneer in the applied arts and sciences, but in all things removed from the mere pursuit of money and physical ease he well understands that he belongs at the second table. Even his recurrent attacks of Anglophobia are no more than Freudian evidences of his inferiority complex. He howls in order to still his inner sense of inequality, as he howls against imaginary enemies in order to convince himself that he is brave and against fabulous despotisms in order to prove that he is free. The English-man is never deceived by this hocus-pocus. He knows that it is always possible to fetch the rebel back into camp by playing upon his elemental fears and vanities. A few dark threats, a few patroniz-ing speeches, a few Oxford degrees, and the thing is done. More, the English scarcely regard it as hunting in the grand manner; it is a business of subalterns. When, during the early stages of the war, they had occasion to woo the American *intelligentsia,* what agents did they choose? Did they nominate Thomas Hardy, Joseph Conrad, George Moore and company? Nay, they nominated Conan Doyle, Coningsby Dawson, Alfred Noyes, Ian Hay, Chesterton, Kipling, Zangwill and company. In the choice there was high sagacity and no little oblique humor—as there was a bit later in the appointment of Lord Reading and Sir Auckland Geddes to Washington. The valuation they set upon the *aluminados* of the Republic was exactly the valuation they were in the habit of setting, at home, upon MM. of the Free Church Federation. They saw the eternal greengrocer beneath the master's gown and mortarboard. Let us look closely and we shall see him, too.

The essence of a self-reliant and autonomous culture is an unshakable egoism. It must not only regard itself as the peer of any other culture; it must regard itself as the superior of any other. You will find this indomitable pride in the culture of any truly first-rate nation: France, Germany or England. But you will not find it in the so-called culture of America. Here the decadent Anglo-Saxon majority still looks obediently and a bit wistfully toward the motherland. No good American ever seriously questions an English

judgment on an aesthetic question, or even on an ethical, philosophical or political question. There is, in fact, seldom any rational
reason why he should: it is almost always more mature, more
tolerant, more intelligent than any judgment hatched at home.
Behind it lies a settled scheme of things, a stable point of view,
the authority of a free intellectual aristocracy, the pride of tradition
and of power. The English are sure-footed, well-informed, persuasive. It is beyond their imagination that any one should seriously
challenge them. In this overgrown and oafish colony there is no
such sureness. The American always secretly envies the Englishman, even when he professes to flout him. The Englishman never
envies the American.

The extraordinary colonist, moved to give utterance to the
ideas bubbling within him, is thus vastly handicapped, for he must
submit them to the test of a culture that, in the last analysis, is
never quite his own culture, despite its dominance. Looking within
himself, he finds that he is different, that he diverges from the
English standard, that he is authentically American—and to be
authentically American is to be officially inferior. He thus faces
dismay at the very start: support is lacking when he needs it most.
In the motherland—in any motherland, in any wholly autonomous
nation—there is a class of men like himself, devoted to translating
the higher manifestations of the national spirit into ideas—men
differing enormously among themselves, but still united in common
cause against the lethargy and credulity of the mass. But in a
colony that class, if it exists at all, lacks coherence and certainty;
its authority is not only disputed by the inertia and suspiciousness
of the lower orders, but also by the superior authority overseas; it
is timorous and fearful of challenge. Thus it affords no protection
to an individual of assertive originality, and he is forced to go as a
suppliant to a quarter in which nothing is his by right, but everything must go by favor—in brief to a quarter where his very application must needs be regarded as an admission of his inferiority.
The burden of proof upon him is thus made double. Obviously, he
must be a man of very strong personality to surmount such obstacles triumphantly. Such strong men, of course, sometimes appear in a colony, but they always stand alone; their worst opposition is at home. For a colonial of less vigorous soul the battle is

almost hopeless. Either he submits to subordination and so wears docilely the inferior badge of a praiseworthy and tolerated colonist, or he deserts the minority for the far more hospitable and confident majority, and so becomes a mere mob-artist.

Examples readily suggest themselves. I give you Poe and Whitman as men strong enough to weather the adverse wind. The salient thing about each of these men was this: that his impulse to self-expression, the force of his "obscure, inner necessity," was so powerful that it carried him beyond all ordinary ambitions and prudences—in other words, that the ego functioned so heroically that it quite disregarded the temporal welfare of the individual. Neither Poe nor Whitman made the slightest concession to what was the predominant English taste, the prevailing English authority, of his time. And neither yielded in the slightest to the maudlin echoes of English notions that passed for ideas in the United States; in neither will you find any recognizable reflection of the things that Americans were saying and doing all about them. Even Whitman, preaching democracy, preached a democracy that not one actual democrat in a hundred thousand could so much as imagine. What happened? *Imprimis,* English authority, at the start, dismissed them loftily; they were, at best, simply rare freaks from the colonies. Secondly, American stupidity, falling into step, came near overlooking them altogether. The accident that maintained them was an accident of personality and environment. They happened to be men accustomed to social isolation and of the most meager wants, and it was thus difficult to deter them by neglect and punishment. So they stuck to their guns—and presently they were "discovered," as the phrase is, by men of a culture wholly foreign to them and perhaps incomprehensible to them, and thereafter, by slow stages, they began to win a slow and reluctant recognition in England (at first only from rebels and iconoclasts), and finally even in America. That either, without French prompting, would have come to his present estate I doubt very much. And in support of that doubt I cite again the fact that Poe's high talents as a critic, not having interested the French, have never got their deserts either in England or at home.

It is lesser men that we chiefly have to deal with in this world, and it is among lesser men that the lack of a confident intellectual viewpoint in America makes itself most evident. Examples are numerous and obvious. On the one hand, we have Fenimore Cooper first making a cringing bow for English favor, and then, on being kicked out, joining the mob against sense; he wrote books so bad that even the Americans of 1830 admired them. On the other hand, we have Henry James, a deserter made by despair; one so depressed by the tacky company at the American first table that he preferred to sit at the second table of the English. The impulse was, and is common; it was only the forthright act that distinguished him. And in the middle ground, showing both seductions plainly, there is Mark Twain—at one moment striving his hardest for the English *imprimatur*, and childishly delighted by every favorable gesture; at the next, returning to the native mob as its premier clown—monkey-shining at banquets, cavorting in the newspapers, shrinking poltroonishly from his own ideas, obscenely eager to give no offense. A much greater artist than either Poe or Whitman, so I devoutly believe, but a good deal lower as a man. The ultimate passion was not there; the decent householder always pulled the ear of the dreamer. His fate has irony in it. In England they patronize him: he is, for an American, not so bad. In America, appalled by his occasional ascents to honesty, his stray impulses to be wholly himself, the dunderheads return him to arm's length, his old place, and one of the most eminent of them, writing in the New York *Times*, argues piously that it is impossible to imagine him actually believing the commonplace heresies he put into "What Is Man?"

· I I ·

Epilogue

I have described the disease. Let me say at once that I have no remedy to offer. I simply set down a few ideas, throw out a few hints, attempt a few modest inquiries into causes. Perhaps my argument often turns upon itself: the field is weed-grown and paths are hard to follow. It may be that insurmountable natural obstacles stand in the way of the development of a distinctively

American culture, grounded upon a truly egoistic nationalism and supported by a native aristocracy. After all, there is no categorical imperative that ordains it. In such matters, when the conditions are right, nature often arranges a division of labor. A nation shut in by racial and linguistic isolation—a Sweden, a Holland or a France—is forced into autonomy by sheer necessity; if it is to have any intellectual life at all it must develop its own. But that is not our case. There is England to hold up the torch for us, as France holds it up for Belgium, and Spain for Latin America, and Germany for Switzerland. It is our function, as the younger and less confident partner, to do the simpler, rougher parts of the joint labor—to develop the virtues of the more elemental orders of men: industry, piety, docility, endurance, assiduity and ingenuity in practical affairs—the wood-hewing and water-drawing of the race. It seems to me that we do all this very well; in these things we are better than the English. But when it comes to those larger and more difficult activities which concern only the superior minority, and are, in essence, no more than products of its efforts to *demonstrate* its superiority—when it comes to the higher varieties of speculation and self-expression, to the fine arts and the game of ideas—then we fall into a bad second place. Where we stand, intellectually, is where the English non-conformists stand; like them, we are marked by a fear of ideas as disturbing and corrupting. Our art is imitative and timorous. Our political theory is hopelessly sophomoric and superficial; even English Toryism and Russian Bolshevism are infinitely more profound and pene-trating. And of the two philosophical systems that we have pro-duced, one is so banal that it is now imbedded in the New Thought, and the other is so shallow that there is nothing in it either to puzzle or to outrage a schoolmarm.

Nevertheless, hope will not down, and now and then it is supported by something rather more real than mere desire. One observes an undercurrent of revolt, small but vigorous, and some-times it exerts its force, not only against the superficial banality but also against the fundamental flabbiness, the intrinsic childish-ness of the Puritan *Anschauung*. The remedy for that childishness is skepticism, and already skepticism shows itself: in the icono-clastic political realism of Harold Stearns, Waldo Frank and company, in the groping questions of Dreiser, Cabell and Anderson, in the operatic rebellions of the Village. True imagination, I often think, is no more than a function of this skepticism. It is the dull man who is always sure, and the sure man who is always dull. The more a man dreams, the less he believes. A great literature is thus chiefly the product of doubting and inquiring minds in revolt against the immovable certainties of the nation. Shakespeare, at a time of rising democratic feeling in England, flung the whole force of his genius against democracy. Cervantes, at a time when all Spain was romantic, made a headlong attack upon romance. Goethe, with Germany groping toward nationalism, threw his influences on the side of internationalism. The central trouble with America is conformity, timorousness, lack of enterprise and audacity. A nation of third-rate men, a land offering hospitality only to fourth-rate artists. In Elizabethan England they would have bawled for democracy, in the Spain of Cervantes they would have yelled for chivalry, and in the Germany of Goethe they would have wept and beat their breasts for the Fatherland. Today, as in the day of Emerson, they set the tune. . . . But into the singing there occasionally enters a discordant note. On some dim tomorrow, perhaps, perchance, peradventure, they may be challenged.

Theodore Dreiser

‹‹‹‹‹‹‹‹‹‹‹‹‹‹‹‹‹‹‹‹‹‹‹‹‹‹‹‹‹‹‹‹›››››››››››››››››››››››››››››

· I ·

O UT of the desert of American fictioneering, so populous and yet so dreary, Dreiser stands up—a phenomenon inescapably visible, but disconcertingly hard to explain. What forces combined to produce him in the first place, and how has he managed to hold out so long against the prevailing blasts— of disheartening misunderstanding and misrepresentation, of Puritan suspicion and opposition, of artistic isolation, of commercial seduction? There is something downright heroic in the way the man has held his narrow and perilous ground, disdaining all compromise, unmoved by the cheap success that lies so inviting around the corner. He has faced, in his day, almost every form of attack that a serious artist can conceivably encounter, and yet all of them together have scarcely budged him an inch. He still plods along in the laborious, cheerless way he first marked out for himself; he is quite as undaunted by baited praise as by bludgeoning, malignant abuse; his later novels are, if anything, more unyieldingly dreiserian than his earliest. As one who has long sought to entice him in this direction or that, fatuously presuming to instruct him in what would improve him and profit him, I may well bear a reluctant and resigned sort of testimony to his gigantic steadfastness. It is almost as if any change in his manner, any concession to what is usual and esteemed, any amelioration of his blind, relentless exercises of *force majeure,* were a physical impossibility. One feels him at last to be authentically no more than a helpless instrument (or victim) of that inchoate flow of forces which he himself is so fond of depicting as at once the answer to the riddle of life, and a riddle ten times more vexing and accursed.

And his origins, as I say, are quite as mysterious as his motive power. To fit him into the unrolling chart of American, or even of English fiction, is extremely difficult. Save one thinks of H. B. Fuller (whose "With the Procession" and "The Cliff-Dwellers" are still remembered by Huneker, but by whom else?[1]), he seems to have had no forerunner among us, and for all the discussion of him that goes on, he has few avowed disciples, and none of them gets within miles of him. One catches echoes of him, perhaps, in Willa Sibert Cather, in Mary S. Watts, in David Graham Phillips, in Sherwood Anderson and in Joseph Medill Patterson, but, after all, they are no more than echoes. In Robert Herrick the thing descends to a feeble parody; in imitators further removed to sheer burlesque. All the latter-day American novelists of consideration are vastly more facile than Dreiser in their philosophy, as they are in their style. In the fact, perhaps, lies the measure of their difference. What they lack, great and small, is the gesture of pity, the note of awe, the profound sense of wonder —in a phrase, that "soberness of mind" which William Lyon Phelps sees as the hallmark of Conrad and Hardy, and which even the most stupid cannot escape in Dreiser. The normal American novel, even in its most serious forms, takes color from the national cocksureness and superficiality. It runs monotonously to ready explanations, a somewhat infantile smugness and hopefulness, a habit of reducing the unknowable to terms of the not worth knowing. What it cannot explain away with ready formulae, as in the later Winston Churchill, it snickers over as scarcely worth explaining at all, as in the later Howells. Such a brave and tragic book as "Ethan Frome" is so rare as to be almost singular, even with Mrs. Wharton. There is, I daresay, not much market for

---

[1] Fuller's comparative obscurity is one of the strangest phenomena of American letters. Despite his high achievement, he is seldom discussed, or even mentioned. Back in 1899 he was already so far forgotten that William Archer mistook his name, calling him Henry Y. Puller. *Vide* Archer's pamphlet, *The American Language* (New York, 1899).

that sort of thing. In the arts, as in the concerns of everyday, the American seeks escape from the insoluble by pretending that it is solved. A comfortable phrase is what he craves beyond all things —and comfortable phrases are surely not to be sought in Dreiser's stock.

I have heard argument that he is a follower of Frank Norris, and two or three facts lend it a specious probability. "McTeague" was printed in 1899; "Sister Carrie" a year later. Moreover, Norris was the first to see the merit of the latter book, and he fought a gallant fight, as literary advisor to Doubleday, Page & Co., against its suppression after it was in type. But this theory runs aground upon two circumstances, the first being that Dreiser did not actually read "McTeague," nor, indeed, grow aware of Norris, until after "Sister Carrie" was completed, and the other being that his development, once he began to write other books, was along paths far distant from those pursued by Norris himself. Dreiser, in truth, was a bigger man than Norris from the start; it is to the latter's unending honor that he recognized the fact instanter, and yet did all he could to help his rival. It is imaginable, of course, that Norris, living fifteen years longer, might have overtaken Dreiser, and even surpassed him; one finds an arrow pointing that way in "Vandover and the Brute" (not printed until 1914). But it swings sharply around in "The Epic of the Wheat." In the second volume of that incomplete trilogy, "The Pit," there is an obvious concession to the popular taste in romance; the thing is so frankly written down, indeed, that a play has been made of it, and Broadway has applauded it. And in "The Octopus," despite some excellent writing, there is a descent to a mysticism so fantastic and preposterous that it quickly passes beyond serious consideration. Norris, in his day, swung even lower—for example, in "A Man's Woman" and in some of his short stories. He was a pioneer, perhaps only half sure of the way he wanted to go, and the evil lures of popular success lay all about him. It is no wonder that he sometimes seemed to lose his direction.

Émile Zola is another literary father whose paternity grows dubious on examination. I once printed an article exposing what seemed to me to be a Zolaesque attitude of mind, and even some trace of the actual Zola manner, in "Jennie Gerhardt"; there came from Dreiser the news that he had never read a line of Zola, and knew nothing about his novels. Not a complete answer, of course; the influence might have been exerted at second hand. But through whom? I confess that I am unable to name a likely medium. The effects of Zola upon Anglo-Saxon fiction have been almost *nil;* his only avowed disciple, George Moore, has long since recanted and reformed; he has scarcely rippled the prevailing romanticism. . . . Thomas Hardy? Here, I daresay, we strike a better scent. There are many obvious likenesses between "Tess of the D'Urbervilles" and "Jennie Gerhardt" and again between "Jude the Obscure" and "Sister Carrie." All four stories deal penetratingly and poignantly with the essential tragedy of women; all disdain the petty, specious explanations of popular fiction; in each one finds a poetical and melancholy beauty. Moreover, Dreiser himself confesses to an enchanted discovery of Hardy in 1896, three years before "Sister Carrie" was begun. But it is easy to push such a fact too hard, and to search for likenesses and parallels that are really not there. The truth is that Dreiser's points of contact with Hardy might be easily matched by many striking points of difference, and that the fundamental ideas in their novels, despite a common sympathy, are anything but identical. Nor does one apprehend any ponderable result of Dreiser's youthful enthusiasm for Balzac, which antedated his discovery of Hardy by two years. He got from both men a sense of the scope and dignity of the novel; they taught him that a story might be a good one, and yet considerably more than a story; they showed him the essential drama of the commonplace. But that they had more influence in forming his point of view, or even in shaping his technique, than any one of half a dozen other gods of those young days—this I scarcely find. In the structure of his novels, and in their manner of approach to life no less, they call up the work of Dostoevsky and Turgenev far more than the work of either of these men—but of all the Russians save Tolstoi (as of Flaubert) Dreiser himself tells us that he was ignorant until ten years after "Sister Carrie." In his days of preparation, indeed, his reading was so copious and so disorderly that antagonistic influences must have well-nigh neutralized one another, and so left the curious youngster to work out his own method and his own philosophy.

Stevenson went down with Balzac, Poe with Hardy, Dumas *fils* with Tolstoi. There were even months of delight in Sienkiewicz, Lew Wallace and E. P. Roe! The whole repertory of the pedagogues had been fought through in school and college: Dickens, Thackeray, Hawthorne, Washington Irving, Kingsley, Scott. Only Irving and Hawthorne seem to have made deep impressions. "I used to lie under a tree," says Dreiser, "and read 'Twice Told Tales' by the hour. I thought 'The Alhambra' was a perfect creation, and I still have a lingering affection for it." Add Bret Harte, George Ebers, William Dean Howells, Oliver Wendell Holmes, and you have a literary stew indeed! . . . But for all its bubbling I see a far more potent influence in the chance discovery of Spencer and Huxley at twenty-three—the year of choosing! Who, indeed, will ever measure the effect of those two giants upon the young men of that era—Spencer with his inordinate meticulousness, his relentless pursuit of facts, his overpowering syllogisms, and Huxley with his devastating agnosticism, his insatiable questionings of the old axioms, above all, his brilliant style? Huxley, it would appear, has been condemned to the scientific hulks, along with bores innumerable and unspeakable; one looks in vain for any appreciation of him in treatises on beautiful letters.[2] And yet the man was a superb artist in works, a master-writer even more than a master-biologist, one of the few truly great stylists that England has produced since the time of Anne. One can easily imagine the effect of two such vigorous and intriguing minds upon a youth groping about for self-understanding and self-expression. They swept him clean, he tells us, of the lingering faith of his boyhood—a medieval, Rhenish Catholicism;—more, they filled him with a new and eager curiosity, an intense interest in the life that lay about him, a desire to seek out its hidden workings and underlying causes. A young man set afire by Huxley might perhaps make a very bad novelist, but it is a certainty that he could never make a sentimental and superficial one. There is

---

[2] For example, in "The Cambridge History of English Literature," which runs to fourteen large volumes and a total of nearly 10,000 pages, Huxley receives but a page and a quarter of notice, and his remarkable mastery of English is barely mentioned in passing. His two debates with Gladstone, in which he did some of the best writing of the century, are not noticed at all.

no need to go further than this single moving adventure to find the genesis of Dreiser's disdain of the current platitudes, his sense of life as a complex biological phenomenon, only dimly comprehended, and his tenacious way of thinking things out, and of holding to what he finds good. Ah, that he had learned from Huxley, not only how to inquire, but also how to report! That he had picked up a talent for that dazzling style, so sweet to the ear, so damnably persuasive, so crystal-clear!

But the more one examines Dreiser, either as writer or as theorist of man, the more his essential isolation becomes apparent. He got a habit of mind from Huxley, but he completely missed Huxley's habit of writing. He got a view of woman from Hardy, but he soon changed it out of all resemblance. He got a certain fine ambition and gusto out of Balzac, but all that was French and characteristic he left behind. So with Zola, Howells, Tolstoi and the rest. The tracing of likenesses quickly becomes rabbinism, almost cabalism. The differences are huge and sprout up in all directions. Nor do I see anything save a flaming up of colonial passion in the current efforts to fit him into a German frame, and make him an agent of Prussian frightfulness in letters. Such childish gabble one looks for in the New York *Times,* and there is where one actually finds it. Even the literary monthlies have stood clear of it; it is important only as material for that treatise upon the patrioteer and his bawling which remains to be written. The name of the man, true enough, is obviously Germanic, and he has told us himself, in "A Traveler at Forty," how he sought out and found the tombs of his ancestors in some little town of the Rhine country. There are more of these genealogical revelations in "A Hoosier Holiday," but they show a Rhenish strain that was already running thin in boyhood. No one, indeed, who reads a Dreiser novel can fail to see the gap separating the author from these half-forgotten forebears. He shows even less of German influence than of English influence.

There is, as a matter of fact, little in modern German fiction that is intelligibly comparable to "Jennie Gerhardt" and "The Titan," either as a study of man or as a work of art. The naturalistic movement of the eighties was launched by men whose eyes were upon the theatre, and it is in that field that nine-tenths of its force has been spent. "German naturalism," says George Madison Priest, quoting Gotthold Klee's "Grundzüge der deutschen Literaturgeschichte" "created a new type only in the drama."[3] True enough, it has also produced occasional novels, and some of them are respectable. Gustav Frenssen's "Jörn Uhl" is a specimen: it has been done into English. Another is Clara Viebig's "Das tägliche Brot," which Ludwig Lewisohn compares to George Moore's "Esther Waters." Yet another is Thomas Mann's "Buddenbrooks." But it would be absurd to cite these works as evidences of a national quality, and doubly absurd to think of them as inspiring such books as "Jennie Gerhardt" and "The Titan," which excel them in everything save workmanship. The case of Mann reveals a tendency that is visible in nearly all of his contemporaries. Starting out as an agnostic realist not unlike the Arnold Bennett of "The Old Wives' Tale," he has gradually taken on a hesitating sort of romanticism, and in one of his later books, "Königliche Hoheit" (in English, "Royal Highness"), he ends upon a note of sentimentalism borrowed from Wagner's "Ring." Fräulein Viebig has also succumbed to banal and extra-artistic purposes. Her "Die Wacht am Rhein," for all its merits in detail, is, at bottom, no more than an eloquent hymn to patriotism—a theme which almost always baffles novelists. As for Frenssen, he is a parson by trade, and carries over into the novel a good deal of the windy moralizing of the pulpit. All of these German naturalists—and they are the only German novelists worth considering —share the weakness of Zola, their *Stammvater*. They, too, fall into the morass that engulfed "Fécondité," and make sentimental propaganda.

I go into this matter in detail, not because it is intrinsically of any moment, but because the effort to depict Dreiser as a secret agent of the Wilhelmstrasse, told off to inject subtle doses of *Kultur* into a naïve and pious people, has taken on the proportions of an organized movement. The same critical imbecility which detects naught save a tomcat in Frank Cowperwood can find naught save an abhorrent foreigner in Cowperwood's creator.

---

[3] "A Brief History of German Literature" (New York: Chas. Scribner's Sons; 1909).

The truth is that the trembling patriots of letters, male and female, are simply at their old game of seeing a man under the bed. Dreiser, in fact, is densely ignorant of German literature, as he is of the better part of French literature, and of much of English literature. He did not even read Hauptmann until after "Jennie Gerhardt" had been written, and such typical German moderns as Ludwig Thoma, Otto Julius Bierbaum and Richard Dehmel remain as strange to him as Heliogabalus.

· 2 ·

In his manner, as opposed to his matter, he is more the Teuton, for he shows all of the racial patience and pertinacity and all of the racial lack of humor. Writing a novel is as solemn a business to him as trimming a beard is to a German barber. He blasts his way through his interminable stories by something not unlike main strength; his writing, one feels, often takes on the character of an actual siege operation, with tunnelings, drum fire, assaults in close order and hand-to-hand fighting. Once, seeking an analogy, I called him the Hindenburg of the novel. If it holds, then "The 'Genius'" is his Poland. The field of action bears the aspect, at the end, of a hostile province meticulously brought under the yoke, with every road and lane explored to its beginning, and every crossroads village laboriously taken, inventoried and policed. Here is the very negation of Gallic lightness and intuition, and of all other forms of impressionism as well. Here is no series of illuminating flashes, but a gradual bathing of the whole scene with white light, so that every detail stands out.

And many of those details, of course, are trivial; even irritating. They do not help the picture; they muddle and obscure it; one wonders impatiently what their meaning is, and what the purpose may be of revealing them with such a precise, portentous air. . . . Turn to page 703 of "The 'Genius.'" By the time one gets there, one has hewn and hacked one's way through 702 large pages of fine print—97 long chapters, more than 250,000 words. And yet, at this hurried and impatient point, with the *coda* already begun, Dreiser halts the whole narrative to explain the origin, nature and inner meaning of Christian Science, and to make us privy to a lot of chatty stuff about Mrs. Althea Jones, a professional healer, and to supply us with detailed plans and specifications of the apartment house in which she lives, works her tawdry miracles, and has her being. Here, in sober summary, are the particulars:

1. That the house is "of conventional design."
2. That there is "a spacious areaway" between its two wings.
3. That these wings are "of cream-coloured pressed brick."
4. That the entrance between them is "protected by a handsome wrought-iron door."
5. That to either side of this door is "an electric lamp support of handsome design."
6. That in each of these lamp supports there are "lovely cream-coloured globes, shedding a soft luster."
7. That inside is "the usual lobby."
8. That in the lobby is "the usual elevator."
9. That in the elevator is the usual "uniformed Negro elevator man."
10. That this Negro elevator man (name not given) is "indifferent and impertinent."
11. That a telephone switchboard is also in the lobby.
12. That the building is seven stories in height.

In "The Financier" there is the same exasperating rolling up of irrelevant facts. The court proceedings in the trial of Cowperwood are given with all the exactness of a parliamentary report in the London *Times*. The speeches of the opposing counsel are set down nearly in full, and with them the remarks of the judge, and after that the opinion of the Appellate Court on appeal, with the dissenting opinions as a sort of appendix. In "Sister Carrie" the thing is less savagely carried out, but that is not Dreiser's fault, for the manuscript was revised by some anonymous hand, and the printed version is but little more than half the length of the original. In "The Titan" and "Jennie Gerhardt" no such brake upon exuberance is visible; both books are crammed with details that serve no purpose, and are as flat as ditch-water. Even in the two volumes of personal record, "A Traveler at Forty" and "A Hoosier Holiday," there is the same furious accumulation of trivialities. Consider the former. It is without structure, without selection, without reticence. One arises from it as from a great babbling, half drunken. On the one hand the author fills a long and gloomy chapter with the story of the Borgias, apparently under the impression that it is news, and on the other hand he enters into intimate and inconsequential confidences about all the persons he meets en route, sparing neither the innocent nor the obscure. The children of his English host at Bridgely Level strike him as fantastic little creatures, even as a bit uncanny—and he duly sets it down. He meets an Englishman on a French train who pleases him much, and the two become good friends and see Rome together, but the fellow's wife is "obstreperous" and "haughty in her manner" and so "loud-spoken in her opinions" that she is "really offensive"—and down it goes. He makes an impression on a Mlle Marcelle in Paris, and she accompanies him from Monte Carlo to Ventimiglia, and there gives him a parting kiss and whispers, "*Avril-Fontainebleau*"—and lo, this sweet one is duly spread upon the minutes. He permits himself to be arrested by a fair privateer in Piccadilly, and goes with her to one of the dens of sin that suffragettes see in their nightmares, and cross-examines her at length regarding her ancestry, her professional ethics and ideals, and her earnings at her dismal craft—and into the book goes a full report of the proceedings. He is entertained by an eminent Dutch jurist in Amsterdam—and upon the pages of the chronicle it appears that the gentleman is "waxy" and "a little pedantic," and that he is probably the sort of "thin, delicate, well barbered" professor that Ibsen had in mind when he cast about for a husband for the daughter of General Gabler.

Such is the art of writing as Dreiser understands it and practices it—an endless piling up of minutiae, an almost ferocious tracking down of ions, electrons and molecules, an unshakable determination to tell it all. One is amazed by the mole-like diligence of the man, and no less by his exasperating disregard for the ease of his readers. A Dreiser novel, at least of the later canon, cannot be read as other novels are read—on a winter evening or summer afternoon, between meal and meal, traveling from New York to Boston. It demands the attention for almost a week, and uses up the faculties for a month. If, reading "The 'Genius,'" one were to become engrossed in the fabulous manner described in the publishers' advertisements, and so find oneself unable to put it down and go to bed before the end, one would get no sleep for three days and three nights.

Worse, there are no charms of style to mitigate the rigors of these vast steppes and pampas of narration. Joseph Joubert's saying that "words should stand out well from the paper" is quite incomprehensible to Dreiser; he never imitates Flaubert by writing for *"la respiration et l'oreille."* There is no painful groping for the inevitable word, or for what Walter Pater called "the gipsy phrase"; the common, even the commonplace, coin of speech is good enough. On the first page of "Jennie Gerhardt" one encounters "frank, open countenance," "diffident manner," "helpless poor," "untutored mind," "honest necessity," and half a dozen other stand-bys of the second-rate newspaper reporter. In "Sister Carrie" one finds "high noon," "hurrying throng," "unassuming restaurant," "dainty slippers," "high-strung nature," and "cool, calculating world"—all on a few pages. Carrie's sister, Minnie Hanson, "gets" the supper. Hanson himself is "wrapped up" in his child. Carrie decides to enter Storm and King's office, "no matter what." In "The Titan" the word "trig" is worked to death; it takes on, toward the end, the character of a banal and preposterous refrain. In the other books one encounters mates for it—words made to do duty in as many senses as the American verb "to fix" or the journalistic "to secure." . . .

I often wonder if Dreiser gets anything properly describable as pleasure out of this dogged accumulation of threadbare, undistinguished, uninspiring nouns, adjectives, verbs, adverbs, pronouns, participles and conjunctions. To the man with an ear for verbal delicacies—the man who searches painfully for the perfect word, and puts the way of saying a thing above the thing said—there is in writing the constant joy of sudden discovery, of happy accident. A phrase springs up full blown, sweet and caressing. But what joy can there be in rolling up sentences that have no more life and beauty in them, intrinsically, than so many election bulletins? Where is the thrill in the manufacture of such a paragraph as that in which Mrs. Althea Jones' sordid habitat is described with such inexorable particularity? Or in the laborious confection of such stuff as this, from Book I, Chapter IV, of "The 'Genius' "?:

The city of Chicago—who shall portray it! This vast ruck of life that had sprung suddenly into existence upon the dank marshes of a lake shore!

Or this from the epilogue to "The Financier":

There is a certain fish whose scientific name is *Mycteroperca Bonaci*, and whose common name is Black Grouper, which is of considerable value as an afterthought in this connection, and which deserves much to be better known. It is a healthy creature, growing quite regularly to a weight of two hundred and fifty pounds, and living a comfortable, lengthy existence because of its very remarkable ability to adapt itself to conditions. . . .

Or this from his pamphlet, "Life, Art and America":[4]

Alas, alas! for art in America. It has a hard stubby row to hoe.

But I offer no more examples. Every reader of the Dreiser novels must cherish astounding specimens—of awkward, platitudinous marginalia, of whole scenes spoiled by bad writing, of phrases as brackish as so many lumps of sodium hyposulphite. Here and there, as in parts of "The Titan" and again in parts of "A Hoosier Holiday," an evil conscience seems to haunt him and he gives hard striving to his manner, and more than once there emerges something that is almost graceful. But a backsliding always follows this phosphorescence of reform. "The 'Genius,'" coming after "The Titan," marks the high tide of his bad writing. There are passages in it so clumsy, so inept, so irritating that they seem almost unbelievable; nothing worse is to be found in the newspapers. Nor is there any compensatory deftness in structure, or solidity of design, to make up for this carelessness in detail. The well-made novel, of course, can be as hollow as the well-made play of Scribe—but let us at least have a beginning, a middle and an end! Such a story as "The 'Genius'" is as gross and shapeless as Brünnhilde. It billows and bulges out like a cloud of smoke, and its internal organization is almost as vague. There are episodes that, with a few chapters added, would make very respectable novels. There are chapters that need but a touch or two to be excellent short stories. The thing rambles, staggers, trips, heaves, pitches, struggles, totters, wavers, halts, turns aside, trembles on

---

[4] New York, 1917; reprinted from *The Seven Arts* for Feb., 1917.

the edge of collapse. More than once it seems to be foundering, both in the equine and in the maritime senses. The tale has been heard of a tree so tall that it took two men to see to the top of it. Here is a novel so brobdingnagian that a single reader can scarcely read his way through it. . . .

· 3 ·

Of the general ideas which lie at the bottom of all of Dreiser's work it is impossible to be in ignorance, for he has exposed them at length in "A Hoosier Holiday" and summarized them in "Life, Art and America." In their main outlines they are not unlike the fundamental assumptions of Joseph Conrad. Both novelists see human existence as a seeking without a finding; both reject the prevailing interpretations of its meaning and mechanism; both take refuge in "I do not know." Put "A Hoosier Holiday" beside Conrad's "A Personal Record," and you will come upon parallels from end to end. Or better still, put it beside Hugh Walpole's "Joseph Conrad," in which the Conradean metaphysic is condensed from the novels even better than Conrad has done it himself: at once you will see how the two novelists, each a worker in the elemental emotions, each a rebel against the current assurance and superficiality, each an alien to his place and time, touch each other in a hundred ways.

"Conrad," says Walpole, "is of the firm and resolute conviction that life is too strong, too clever and too remorseless for the sons of men." And then, in amplification: "It is as though, from some high window, looking down, he were able to watch some shore, from whose security men were forever launching little cockleshell boats upon a limitless and angry sea. . . . From his height he can follow their fortunes, their brave struggles, their fortitude to the very end. He admires their courage, the simplicity of their faith, but his irony springs from his knowledge of the inevitable end." . . .

Substitute the name of Dreiser for that of Conrad, and you will have to change scarcely a word. Perhaps one, to wit, "clever." I suspect that Dreiser, writing so of his own creed, would be tempted to make it "stupid," or, at all events, "unintelligible." The struggle of man, as he sees it, is more than impotent; it is gratuitous and purposeless. There is, to his eye, no grand ingenuity, no skillful adaptation of means to end, no moral (or even dramatic) plan in the order of the universe. He can get out of it only a sense of profound and inexplicable *dis*order. The waves which batter the cockleshells change their direction at every instant. Their navigation is a vast adventure, but intolerably fortuitous and inept—a voyage without chart, compass, sun or stars. . . .

So at bottom. But to look into the blackness steadily, of course, is almost beyond the endurance of man. In the very moment that its impenetrability is grasped the imagination begins attacking it with pale beams of false light. All religions, I daresay, are thus projected from the questioning soul of man, and not only all religions, but also all great agnosticisms. Nietzsche, shrinking from the horror of that abyss of negation, revived the Pythagorean concept of *der ewigen Wiederkunft*—a vain and blood-curdling sort of comfort. To it, after a while, he added explanations almost Christian—a whole repertoire of whys and wherefores, aims and goals, aspirations and significances. The late Mark Twain, in an unpublished work, toyed with an equally daring idea: that men are to some unimaginably vast and incomprehensible Being what the unicellular organisms of his body are to man, and so on *ad infinitum*. Dreiser occasionally inclines to much the same hypothesis; he likens the endless reactions going on in the world we know, the myriadal creation, collision and destruction of entities, to the slow accumulation and organization of cells *in utero*. He would make us specks in the insentient embryo of some gigantic Presence whose form is still unimaginable and whose birth must wait for Eons and Eons. Again, he turns to something not easily distinguishable from philosophical idealism, whether out of Berkeley or Fichte it is hard to make out—that is, he would interpret the whole phenomenon of life as no more than an appearance, a nightmare of some unseen sleeper or of men themselves, an "uncanny blur of nothingness"—in Euripides' phrase, "a song sung by an idiot, dancing down the wind." Yet again, he talks vaguely of the intricate polyphony of a cosmic orchestra, cacophonous to our dull ears. Finally, he puts the observed into the ordered, reading a purpose in the displayed event: "life was intended to sting and hurt" . . . But these are only gropings, and not to be read too critically. From speculations and explanations he always returns, Conrad-like, to the bald fact: to "the spectacle and stress of life." All he can make out clearly is "a vast compulsion which has nothing to do with the individual desires or tastes or impulses of individuals." That compulsion springs "from the settling processes of forces which we do not in the least understand, over which we have no control, and in whose grip we are as grains of dust or sand, blown hither and thither, for what purpose we cannot even suspect."[5] Man is not only doomed to defeat, but denied any glimpse or understanding of his antagonist. Here we come upon an agnosticism that has almost got beyond curiosity. What good would it do us, asks Dreiser, to know? In our ignorance and helplessness, we may at least get a slave's consolation out of cursing the unknown gods. Suppose we saw them striving blindly, too, and pitied them? . . .

But, as I say, this skepticism is often tempered by guesses at a possibly hidden truth, and the confession that this truth may exist reveals the practical unworkableness of the unconditioned system, at least for Dreiser. Conrad is far more resolute, and it is easy to see why. He is, by birth and training, an aristocrat. He has the gift of emotional detachment. The lures of facile doctrine do not move him. In his irony there is a disdain which plays about even the ironist himself. Dreiser is a product of far different forces and traditions, and is capable of no such escapement. Struggle as he may, and fume and protest as he may, he can no more shake off the chains of his intellectual and cultural heritage than he can change the shape of his nose. What that heritage is you may find out in detail by reading "A Hoosier Holiday," or in summary by glancing at the first few pages of "Life, Art and America." Briefly described, it is the burden of a believing mind, a moral attitude, a lingering superstition. One-half of the man's brain, so to speak, wars with the other half. He is intelligent, he is thoughtful, he is a sound artist—but there come moments when a dead hand falls

---

[5] "Life, Art and America," p. 5.

upon him, and he is once more the Indiana peasant, snuffing absurdly over imbecile sentimentalities, giving a grave ear to quackeries, snorting and eye-rolling with the best of them. One generation spans too short a time to free the soul of man. Nietzsche, to the end of his days, remained a Prussian pastor's son, and hence two-thirds a Puritan; he erected his war upon holiness, toward the end, into a sort of holy war. Kipling, the grandson of a Methodist preacher, reveals the tin-pot evangelist with increasing clarity as youth and its ribaldries pass away and he falls back upon his fundamentals. And that other English novelist who springs from the servants' hall—let us not be surprised or blame him if he sometimes writes like a bounder.

The truth about Dreiser is that he is still in the transition stage between Christian Endeavour and civilization, between Warsaw, Indiana and the Socratic grove, between being a good American and being a free man, and so he sometimes vacillates perilously between a moral sentimentalism and a somewhat extravagant revolt. "The 'Genius,'" on the one hand, is almost a tract for rectitude, a Warning to the Young; its motto might be *Scheut die Dirnen!* And on the other hand, it is full of a laborious truculence that can only be explained by imagining the author as heroically determined to prove that he is a plain-spoken fellow and his own man, let the chips fall where they may. So, in spots, in "The Financier" and "The Titan," both of them far better books. There is an almost moral frenzy to expose and riddle what passes for morality among the stupid. The isolation of irony is never reached; the man is still evangelical; his ideas are still novelties to him; he is as solemnly absurd in some of his floutings of the Code Américain as he is in his respect for Bouguereau, or in his flirtings with the New Thought, or in his naïve belief in the importance of novel-writing. Somewhere or other I have called all this the Greenwich Village complex. It is not genuine artists, serving beauty reverently and proudly, who herd in those cockroached cellars and bawl for art; it is a mob of half-educated yokels and cockneys to whom the very idea of art is still novel, and intoxicating—and more than a little bawdy.

Not that Dreiser actually belongs to this ragamuffin company. Far from it, indeed. There is in him, hidden deep down, a great instinctive artist, and hence the makings of an aristocrat. In his muddled way, held back by the manacles of his race and time, and his steps made uncertain by a guiding theory which too often eludes his own comprehension, he yet manages to produce works of art of unquestionable beauty and authority, and to interpret life in a manner that is poignant and illuminating. There is vastly more intuition in him than intellectualism; his talent is essentially feminine, as Conrad's is masculine; his ideas always seem to be deduced from his feelings. The view of life that got into "Sister Carrie," his first book, was not the product of a conscious thinking out of Carrie's problems. It simply got itself there by the force of the artistic passion behind it; its coherent statement had to wait for other and more reflective days. The thing began as a vision, not as a syllogism. Here the name of Franz Schubert inevitably comes up. Schubert was an ignoramus, even in music; he knew less about polyphony, which is the mother of harmony, which is the mother of music, than the average conservatory professor. But neverthe- less he had such a vast instinctive sensitiveness to musical values, such a profound and accurate feeling for beauty in tone, that he not only arrived at the truth in tonal relations, but even went beyond what, in his day, was known to be the truth, and so led an advance. Likewise, Giorgione da Castelfranco and Masaccio come to mind: painters of the first rank, but untutored, un- sophisticated, uncouth. Dreiser, within his limits, belongs to this sabot-shod company of the elect. One thinks of Conrad, not as artist first, but as savant. There is something of the icy aloofness of the laboratory in him, even when the images he conjures up pulsate with the very glow of life. He is almost as self-conscious as the Beethoven of the last quartets. In Dreiser the thing is more intimate, more disorderly, more a matter of pure feeling. He gets his effects, one might almost say, not by designing them, but by living them.

But whatever the process, the power of the image evoked is not to be gainsaid. It is not only brilliant on the surface, but mysterious and appealing in its depths. One swiftly forgets his intolerable writing, his mirthless, sedulous, repellent manner, in the face of the Athenian tragedy he instils into his seduced and soul-sick servant girls, his barbaric pirates of finances, his conquered and hamstrung supermen, his wives who sit and wait. He has, like Conrad, a sure talent for depicting the spirit in disintegration. Old Gerhardt, in "Jennie Gerhardt," is alone worth all the *dramatis personae* of popular American fiction since the days of "Rob o' the Bowl"; Howells could no more have created him, in his Rodinesque impudence of outline, than he could have created Tartuffe or Gargantua. Such a novel as "Sister Carrie" stands quite outside the brief traffic of the customary stage. It leaves behind it an unescapable impression of bigness, of epic sweep and dignity. It is not a mere story, not a novel in the customary American meaning of the word; it is at once a psalm of life and a criticism of life—and that criticism loses nothing by the fact that its burden is despair. Here, precisely, is the point of Dreiser's departure from his fellows. He puts into his novels a touch of the eternal *Weltschmerz*. They get below the drama that is of the moment and reveal the greater drama that is without end. They arouse those deep and lasting emotions which grow out of the recognition of elemental and universal tragedy. His aim is not merely to tell a tale; his aim is to show the vast ebb and flow of forces which sway and condition human destiny. One cannot imagine him consenting to Conan Doyle's statement of the purpose of fiction, quoted with characteristic approval by the New York *Times:* "to amuse mankind, to help the sick and the dull and the weary." Nor is his purpose to instruct; if he is a pedagogue it is only incidentally and as a weakness. The thing he seeks to do is to stir, to awaken, to move. One does not arise from such a book as "Sister Carrie" with a smirk of satisfaction; one leaves it infinitely touched.

· 4 ·

It is, indeed, a truly amazing first book, and one marvels to hear that it was begun lightly. Dreiser in those days (*circa* 1899), had seven or eight years of newspaper work behind him, in Chicago, St. Louis, Toledo, Cleveland, Buffalo, Pittsburgh and New York, and was beginning to feel that reaction of disgust which attacks all newspaper men when the enthusiasm of youth wears out. He had been successful, but he saw how hollow that success was, and how little surety it held out for the future. The theater was what chiefly lured him; he had written plays in his nonage, and he now proposed to do them on a large scale, and so get some of the easy dollars of Broadway. It was an old friend from Toledo, Arthur Henry, who turned him toward story-writing. The two had met while Henry was city editor of the *Blade*, and Dreiser a reporter looking for a job.[6] A firm friendship sprang up, and Henry conceived a high opinion of Dreiser's ability, and urged him to try a short story. Dreiser was distrustful of his own skill, but Henry kept at him, and finally, during a holiday the two spent together at Maumee, Ohio, he made the attempt. Henry had the manuscript typewritten and sent it to *Ainslee's Magazine*. A week or so later there came a check for $75.

This was in 1898. Dreiser wrote four more stories during the year following, and sold them all. Henry now urged him to attempt a novel, but again his distrust of himself held him back. Henry finally tried a rather unusual argument: he had a novel of his own on the stocks,[7] and he represented that he was in difficulties with it and in need of company. One day, in September, 1899, Dreiser took a sheet of yellow paper and wrote a title at random. That title was "Sister Carrie," and with no more definite plan than the mere name offered the book began. It went ahead steadily enough until the middle of October, and had come by then to the place where Carrie meets Hurstwood. At that point Dreiser left it in disgust. It seemed pitifully dull and inconsequential, and for two months he put the manuscript away. Then, under renewed urgings by Henry, he resumed the writing, and kept on to the place where Hurstwood steals the money. Here he went aground upon a comparatively simple problem; he couldn't devise a way to manage the robbery. Late in January he gave it up. But the faithful Henry kept urging him, and in March he resumed work, and soon had the story finished. The latter part, despite many distractions, went quickly. Once the manuscript was complete, Henry suggested various cuts, and in all about 40,000 words

---

[6] The episode is related in "A Hoosier Holiday."
[7] "A Princess of Arcady," published in 1900.

came out. The fair copy went to the Harpers. They refused it without ceremony and soon afterward Dreiser carried the manuscript to Doubleday, Page & Co. He left it with Frank Doubleday, and before long there came notice of its acceptance, and, what is more, a contract. But after the story was in type it fell into the hands of the wife of one of the members of the firm, and she conceived so strong a notion of its immorality that she soon convinced her husband and his associates. There followed a series of acrimonious negotiations, with Dreiser holding resolutely to the letter of his contract. It was at this point that Frank Norris entered the combat—bravely but in vain. The pious Barabbases, confronted by their signature, found it impossible to throw up the book entirely, but there was no nomination in the bond regarding either the style of binding or the number of copies to be issued, and so they evaded further dispute by bringing out the book in a very small edition and with modest unstamped covers. Copies of this edition are now eagerly sought by book collectors, and one in good condition fetches $25 or more in the auction rooms. Even the second edition (1907), bearing the imprint of B. W. Dodge & Co., carries an increasing premium.

The passing years work strange farces. The Harpers, who had refused "Sister Carrie" with a spirit bordering upon indignation in 1900, took over the rights of publication from B. W. Dodge & Co., in 1912, and reissued the book in a new (and extremely hideous) format, with a publisher's note containing smug quotations from the encomiums of the *Fortnightly Review,* the *Athenaeum,* the *Spectator,* the *Academy* and other London critical journals. More, they contrived humorously to push the date of their copyright back to 1900. But this new enthusiasm for artistic freedom did not last long. They had published "Jennie Gerhardt" in 1911 and they did "The Financier" in 1912, but when "The Titan" followed, in 1914, they were seized with qualms, and suppressed the book after it had got into type. In this emergency the English firm of John Lane came to the rescue, only to seek cover itself when the Comstocks attacked "The 'Genius,'" two years later. . . . For his high services to American letters, Walter H. Page, of Doubleday, Page & Co., was made ambassador to England, where "Sister Carrie" is regarded (according to the Harpers), as "the best story, on the whole, that has yet come out of America." A curious series of episodes. Another proof, perhaps, of that cosmic imbecility upon which Dreiser is so fond of discoursing. . . .

But of all this I shall say more later on, when I come to discuss the critical reception of the Dreiser novels, and the efforts made by the New York Society for the Suppression of Vice to stop their sale. The thing to notice here is that the author's difficulties with "Sister Carrie" came within an ace of turning him from novel-writing completely. Stray copies of the suppressed first edition, true enough, fell into the hands of critics who saw the story's value, and during the first year or two of the century it enjoyed a sort of esoteric vogue, and encouragement came from unexpected sources. Moreover, a somewhat bowdlerized English edition, published by William Heinemann in 1901, made a fair success, and even provoked a certain mild controversy. But the author's income from the book remained almost *nil*, and so he was forced to seek a livelihood in other directions. His history during the next ten years belongs to the tragi-comedy of letters. For five of them he was a Grub Street hack, turning his hand to any literary job that offered. He wrote short stories for the popular magazines, or special articles, or poems, according as their needs varied. He concocted fabulous tales for the illustrated supplements of the Sunday newspapers. He rewrote the bad stuff of other men. He returned to reporting. He did odd pieces of editing. He tried his hand at one-act plays. He even ventured upon advertisement writing. And all the while, the best that he could get out of his industry was a meager living.

In 1905, tiring of the uncertainties of this life, he accepted a post on the staff of Street & Smith, the millionaire publishers of cheap magazines, servant-girl romances and dime-novels, and here, in the very slums of letters, he labored with tongue in cheek until the next year. The tale of his duties will fill, I daresay, a volume or two in the autobiography on which he is said to be working; it is a chronicle full of achieved impossibilities. One of his jobs, for example, was to reduce a whole series of dime-novels, each 60,000 words in length, to 30,000 words apiece. He accomplished it by cutting each one into halves, and writing a new ending for the first half and a new beginning for the second, with new titles for both. This doubling of their property aroused the admiration of his employers; they promised him an assured and easy future in the dime-novel business. But he tired of it, despite this revelation of a gift for it, and in 1906 he became managing editor of the *Broadway Magazine,* then struggling into public notice. A year later he transferred his flag to the Butterick Building, and became chief editor of the *Delineator,* the *Designer* and other such gospels for the fair. Here, of course, he was as much out of water as in the dime-novel foundry of Street & Smith, but at all events the pay was good, and there was a certain leisure at the end of the day's work. In 1907, as part of his duties, he organized the National Child Rescue Campaign, which still rages as the *Delineator's* contribution to the Uplift. At about the same time he began "Jennie Gerhardt." It is curious to note that, during these same years, Arnold Bennett was slaving in London as the editor of *Woman.*

Dreiser left the *Delineator* in 1910, and for the next half year or so endeavored to pump vitality into the *Bohemian Magazine,* in which he had acquired a proprietary interest. But the *Bohemian* soon departed this life, carrying some of his savings with it, and he gave over his enforced leisure to "Jennie Gerhardt," completing the book in 1911. Its publication by the Harpers during the same year worked his final emancipation from the editorial desk. It was praised, and what is more, it sold, and royalties began to come in. A new edition of "Sister Carrie" followed in 1912, with "The Financier" hard upon its heels. Since then Dreiser has devoted himself wholly to serious work. "The Financier" was put forth as the first volume of "a trilogy of desire"; the second volume, "The Titan," was published in 1914; the third is yet to come. "The 'Genius'" appeared in 1915; "The Bulwark" is just announced. In 1912, accompanied by Grant Richards, the London publisher, Dreiser made his first trip abroad, visiting England, France, Italy and Germany. His impressions were recorded in "A Traveler at Forty," published in 1913. In the summer of 1915, accompanied by Franklin Booth, the illustrator, he made an automobile journey to his old haunts in Indiana, and the record is in "A Hoosier Holiday," published in 1916. His other writings include a volume of "Plays of the Natural and the Supernatural" (1916); "Life, Art and America," a pamphlet against Puritanism in letters (1917); a dozen or more short stories and novelettes, a few poems, and a three-act drama, "The Hand of the Potter."

Dreiser was born at Terre Haute, Indiana, on August 27, 1871, and, like most of us, is of mongrel blood, with the German, perhaps, predominating. He is a tall man, awkward in movement and nervous in habit; the boon of beauty has been denied him. The history of his youth is set forth in full in "A Hoosier Holiday." It is curious to note that he is a brother to the late Paul Dresser, author of "The Banks of the Wabash" and other popular songs, and that he himself, helping Paul over a hard place, wrote the affecting chorus:

> *Oh, the moon is fair tonight along the Wabash,*
> *From the fields there comes the breath of new-mown hay;*
> *Through the sycamores the candle lights are gleaming . . .*

But no doubt you know it.

· 5 ·

The work of Dreiser, considered as craftsmanship pure and simple, is extremely uneven, and the distance separating his best from his worst is almost infinite. It is difficult to believe that the novelist who wrote certain extraordinarily vivid chapters in "Jennie Gerhardt," and "A Hoosier Holiday," and, above all, in "The Titan," is the same who achieved the unescapable dullness of parts of "The Financier" and the general stupidity and stodginess of "The 'Genius.'" Moreover, the tide of his writing does not rise or fall with any regularity; he neither improves steadily nor grows worse steadily. Only half an eye is needed to see the superiority of "Jennie Gerhardt," as a sheer piece of writing, to "Sister Carrie," but on turning to "The Financier," which followed "Jennie Gerhardt" by an interval of but one year, one observes a falling off which, at its greatest, is almost indistinguishable from a collapse. "Jennie Gerhardt" is suave, persuasive, well-ordered, solid in structure, instinct with life. "The Financier," for all its merits in detail, is loose, tedious, vapid, exasperating. But had any critic, in the autumn of 1912, argued thereby that Dreiser was finished, that he had shot his bolt, his discomfiture would have come swiftly, for "The Titan," which followed in 1914, was almost as well done as "The Financier" had been ill done, and there are parts of it which remain, to this day, the very best writing that Dreiser has ever achieved. But "The 'Genius'"? Ay, in "The 'Genius'" the pendulum swings back again! It is flaccid, elephantine, doltish, coarse, dismal, flatulent, sophomoric, ignorant, unconvincing, wearisome. One pities the jurisconsult who is condemned, by Comstockian clamor, to plow through such a novel. In it there is a sort of humorless *reductio ad absurdum,* not only of the Dreiser manner, but even of certain salient tenets of the Dreiser philosophy. At its best it has a moral flavor. At its worst it is almost maudlin. . . .

The most successful of the Dreiser novels, judged by sales, is "Sister Carrie," and the causes thereof are not far to seek. On the one hand, its suppression in 1900 gave it a whispered fame that was converted into a public celebrity when it was republished in 1907, and on the other hand it shares with "Jennie Gerhardt" the capital advantage of having a young and appealing woman for its chief figure. The sentimentalists thus have a heroine to cry over, and to put into a familiar pigeon-hole; Carrie becomes a sort of Pollyanna. More, it is, at bottom, a tale of love—the one theme of permanent interest to the average American novel-reader, the chief stuffing of all our best-selling romances. True enough, it is vastly more than this—there is in it, for example, the astounding portrait of Hurstwood—but it seems to me plain that its relative popularity is by no means a test of its relative merit, and that the causes of that popularity must be sought in other directions. Its defect, as a work of art, is a defect of structure. Like Norris' "McTeague" it has a broken back. In the midst of the story of Carrie, Dreiser pauses to tell the story of Hurstwood—a memorably vivid and tragic story, to be sure, but still one that, considering artistic form and organization, does damage to the main business of the book. Its outstanding merit is its simplicity, its unaffected seriousness and fervor, the spirit of youth that is in it. One feels that it was written, not by a novelist conscious of his tricks, but by a novice carried away by his own flaming eagerness, his own high sense of the interest of what he was doing. In this aspect, it is perhaps more typically Dreiserian than any of its successors. And maybe we may seek here for a good deal of its popular appeal, for there is a contagion in naïveté as in enthusiasm, and the simple novel-reader may recognize the kinship of a simple mind in the novelist.

But it is in "Jennie Gerhardt" that Dreiser first shows his true mettle. . . . "The power to tell the same story in two forms," said George Moore, "is the sign of the true artist." Here Dreiser sets himself that difficult task, and here he carries it off with almost complete success. Reduce the story to a hundred words, and the same words would also describe "Sister Carrie." Jennie, like Carrie, is a rose grown from turnip-seed. Over each, at the start, hangs poverty, ignorance, the dumb helplessness of the Shudra, and yet in each there is that indescribable something, that element of essential gentleness, that innate inward beauty which levels all barriers of caste, and makes Esther a fit queen for Ahasuerus. Some Frenchman has put it into a phrase: *"Une âme grande dans un petit destin"*—a great soul in a small destiny. Jennie has some touch of that greatness; Dreiser is forever calling her "a big woman"; it is a refrain almost as irritating as the "trig" of "The Titan." Carrie, one feels, is of baser metal; her dignity never rises to anything approaching nobility. But the history of each is the history of the other. Jennie, like Carrie, escapes from the physical miseries of the struggle for existence only to taste the worse miseries of the struggle for happiness. Don't mistake me; we have here no maudlin tales of seduced maidens. Seduction, in truth, is far from tragedy for either Jennie or Carrie. The gain of each, until the actual event has been left behind and obliterated by experiences more salient and poignant, is greater than her loss, and that gain is to the soul as well as to the creature. With the rise from want to security, from fear to ease, comes an awakening of the finer perceptions, a widening of the sympathies, a gradual unfolding of the delicate flower called personality, an increased capacity for loving and living. But with all this, and as a part of it, there comes, too, an increased capacity for suffering—and so in the end, when love slips away and the empty years stretch before, it is the awakened and supersentient woman that pays for the folly of the groping, bewildered girl. The tragedy of Carrie and Jennie, in brief, is not that they are degraded, but that they are lifted up, not that they go to the gutter, but that they escape the gutter and glimpse the stars.

But if the two stories are thus variations upon the same somber theme, if each starts from the same place and arrives at the same dark goal, if each shows a woman heartened by the same hopes and tortured by the same agonies, there is still a vast difference between them, and that difference is the measure of the author's progress in his craft during the eleven years between 1900 and 1911. "Sister Carrie," at bottom, is no more than a first sketch, a rough piling up of observations and ideas, disordered and often incoherent. In the midst of the story, as I have said, the author forgets it, and starts off upon another. In "Jennie Gerhardt" there is no such flaccidity of structure, no such vacillation in aim, no such proliferation of episode. Considering that it is by Dreiser, it is extraordinarily adept and intelligent in design; only in "The Titan" has he ever done so well. From beginning to end the narrative flows logically, steadily, congruously. Episodes there are, of course, but they keep their proper place and bulk. It is always Jennie that stands at the center of the traffic; it is in Jennie's soul that every scene is ultimately played out. Her father and mother; Senator Brander, the god of her first worship; her daughter Vesta, and Lester Kane, the man who makes and mars her—all these are drawn with infinite painstaking, and in every one of them there is the blood of life. But it is Jennie that dominates the drama from curtain to curtain. Not an event is unrelated to her; not a climax fails to make clearer the struggles going on in her mind and heart.

It is in "Jennie Gerhardt" that Dreiser's view of life begins to take on coherence and to show a general tendency. In "Sister Carrie" the thing is still chiefly representation and no more; the image is undoubtedly vivid, but its significance, in the main, is left undisplayed. In "Jennie Gerhardt" this pictorial achievement is reinforced by interpretation; one carries away an impression that something has been said; it is not so much a visual image of Jennie that remains as a sense of the implacable tragedy that engulfs her. The book is full of artistic passion. It lives and glows. It awakens recognition and feeling. Its lucid ideational structure, even more than the artless gusto of "Sister Carrie," produces a penetrating and powerful effect. Jennie is no mere individual; she is a type of the national character, almost the archetype of the muddled, aspiring, tragic, fate-flogged mass. And the scene in which she is set is brilliantly national too. The Chicago of those great days of feverish money-grabbing and crazy aspiration may well stand as the epitome of America, and it is made clearer here than in any other American novel—clearer than in "The Pit" or "The Cliff-Dwellers"—clearer than in any book by an Easterner— almost as clear as the Paris of Balzac and Zola. Finally, the style of the story is indissolubly wedded to its matter. The narrative, in places, has an almost scriptural solemnity; in its very harshness and baldness there is something subtly meet and fitting. One cannot imagine such a history done in the strained phrases of Meredith or the fugal manner of Henry James. One cannot imagine that stark, stenographic dialogue adorned with the tinsel of pretty words. The thing, to reach the heights it touches, could have been done only in the way it has been done. As it stands, I would not take anything away from it, not even its journalistic banalities, its lack of humor, its incessant returns to C major. A primitive and touching poetry is in it. It is a novel, I am convinced, of the first consideration. . . .

In "The Financier" this poetry is almost absent, and that fact is largely to blame for the book's lack of charm. By the time we see him in "The Titan" Frank Cowperwood has taken on heroic proportions and the romance of great adventure is in him, but in "The Financier" he is still little more than an extra-pertinacious money-grubber, and not unrelated to the average stockbroker or corner grocer. True enough, Dreiser says specifically that he is more, that the thing he craves is not money but power—power to force lesser men to execute his commands, power to surround himself with beautiful and splendid things, power to amuse himself with women, power to defy and nullify the laws made for the timorous and unimaginative. But the intent of the author never really gets into his picture. His Cowperwood in this first stage is hard, commonplace, unimaginative. In "The Titan" he flowers out as a blend of revolutionist and voluptuary, a highly civilized Lorenzo the Magnificent, an immoralist who would not hesitate two minutes about seducing a saint, but would turn sick at the thought of harming a child. But in "The Financier" he is still in the larval state, and a repellent sordidness hangs about him.

Moreover, the story of his rise is burdened by two defects which still further corrupt its effect. One lies in the fact that Dreiser is quite unable to get the feel, so to speak, of Philadelphia, just as he is unable to get the feel of New York in "The 'Genius.'" The other is that the style of the writing in the book reduces the dreiserian manner to absurdity, and almost to impossibility. The incredibly lazy, involved and unintelligent description of the trial of Cowperwood I have already mentioned. We get, in this lumbering chronicle, not a cohesive and luminous picture, but a dull, photographic representation of the whole tedious process, beginning with an account of the political obligations of the judge and district attorney, proceeding to a consideration of the habits of mind of each of the twelve jurymen, and ending with a summary of the majority and minority opinions of the court of appeals, and a discussion of the motives, ideals, traditions, prejudices, sympathies and chicaneries behind them, each and severally. When Cowperwood goes into the market, his operations are set forth in their last detail; we are told how many shares he buys, how much he pays for them, what the commission is, what his profit comes to. When he comes into chance contact with a politician, we hear all about that politician, including his family affairs. When he builds and furnishes a house, the chief rooms in it are inventoried with such care that not a chair or a rug or a picture on the wall is overlooked. The endless piling up of such non-essentials cripples and incommodes the story; its drama is too copiously swathed in words to achieve a sting; the Dreiser manner devours and defeats itself.

But none the less the book has compensatory merits. Its character sketches, for all the cloud of words, are lucid and vigorous. Out of that enormous complex of crooked politics and crookeder finance, Cowperwood himself stands out in the round, comprehensible and alive. And all the others, in their lesser measures, are done almost as well—Cowperwood's pale wife, whimpering in her

empty house; Aileen Butler, his mistress; his doddering and eternally amazed old father; his old-fashioned, stupid, sentimental
mother; Stener, the City Treasurer, a dish-rag in the face of
danger; old Edward Malia Butler, that barbarian in a boiled
shirt, with his Homeric hatred and his broken heart. Particularly
old Butler. The years pass and he must be killed and put away, but
not many readers of the book, I take it, will soon forget him. Dreiser is at his best, indeed, when he deals with old men. In their
tragic helplessness they stand as symbols of that unfathomable
cosmic cruelty which he sees as the motive power of life itself.
More, even, than his women, he makes them poignant, vivid,
memorable. The picture of old Gerhardt is full of a subtle bright-
ness, though he is always in the background, as cautious and
penny-wise as an ancient crow, trotting to his Lutheran church,
pathetically ill-used by the world he never understands. Butler is
another such, different in externals, but at bottom the same dis-
mayed, questioning, pathetic old man. . . .

In "The Titan" there is a tightening of the screws, a clarifying
of the action, an infinite improvement in the manner. The book,
in truth, has the air of a new and clearer thinking out of "The
Financier," as "Jennie Gerhardt" is a new thinking out of "Sister
Carrie." With almost the same materials, the thing is given a new
harmony and unity, a new plausibility, a new passion and purpose.
In "The Financier" the artistic voluptuary is almost completely
overshadowed by the dollar-chaser; in "The Titan" we begin to
see clearly that grand battle between artist and man of money,
idealist and materialist, spirit and flesh, which is the informing
theme of the whole trilogy. The conflict that makes the drama,
once chiefly external, now becomes more and more internal; it is
played out within the soul of the man himself. The result is a
character sketch of the highest color and brilliance, a superb portrait of a complex and extremely fascinating man. Of all the personages in the Dreiser books, the Cowperwood of "The Titan"
is perhaps the most radiantly real. He is accounted for in every
detail, and yet, in the end, he is not accounted for at all; there
hangs about him, to the last, that baffling mysteriousness which
hangs about those we know most intimately. There is in him a
complete and indubitable masculinity, as the eternal feminine is

in Jennie. His struggle with the inexorable forces that urge him on as with whips, and lure him with false lights, and bring him to disillusion and dismay, is as typical as hers is, and as tragic. In his ultimate disaster, so plainly foreshadowed at the close, there is the clearest of all projections of the ideas that lie at the bottom of all Dreiser's work. Cowperwood, above any of them, is his protagonist.

The story, in its plan, is as transparent as in its burden. It has an austere simplicity in the telling that fits the directness of the thing told. Dreiser, as if to clear decks, throws over all the immemorial baggage of the novelist, making short shrift of "heart interest," conventional "sympathy," and even what ordinarily passes for romance. In "Sister Carrie," as I have pointed out, there is still a sweet dish for the sentimentalists; if they don't like the history of Carrie as a work of art they may still wallow in it as a sad, sad love story. Carrie is appealing, melting; she moves, like Marguerite Gautier, in an atmosphere of romantic depression. And Jennie Gerhardt, in this aspect, is merely Carrie done over— a Carrie more carefully and objectively drawn, perhaps, but still conceivably to be mistaken for a "sympathetic" heroine in a best-seller. A lady eating chocolates might jump from "Laddie" to "Jennie Gerhardt" without knowing that she was jumping ten thousand miles. The tear jugs are there to cry into. Even in "The Financier" there is still a hint of familiar things. The first Mrs. Cowperwood is sorely put upon; old Butler has the markings of an irate father; Cowperwood himself suffers the orthodox injustice and languishes in a cell. But no one, I venture, will ever fall into any such mistake in identity in approaching "The Titan." Not a single appeal to facile sentiment is in it. It proceeds from beginning to end in a forthright, uncompromising, confident manner. It is an almost purely objective account, as devoid of cheap heroics as a death certificate, of a strong man's contest with incontestable powers without and no less incontestable powers within. There is nothing of the conventional outlaw about him; he does not wear a red sash and bellow for liberty; fate wrings from him no melodramatic defiances. In the midst of the battle he views it with a sort of ironical detachment, as if lifted above himself by the sheer esthetic spectacle. Even in disaster he asks for no quarter, no generosity, no compassion. Up or down, he keeps his zest for the game that is being played, and is sufficient unto himself.

Such a man as this Cowperwood of the Chicago days, described romantically, would be indistinguishable from the wicked earls and seven-foot guardsmen of Ouida, Robert W. Chambers and The Duchess. But described realistically and cold-bloodedly, with all that wealth of minute and apparently inconsequential detail which Dreiser piles up so amazingly, he becomes a figure astonishingly vivid, lifelike and engrossing. He fits into no *a priori* theory of conduct or scheme of rewards and punishments; he proves nothing and teaches nothing; the forces which move him are never obvious and frequently unintelligible. But in the end he seems genuinely a man—a man of the sort we see about us in the real world—not a patent and automatic fellow, reacting docilely and according to a formula, but a bundle of complexities and contradictions, a creature oscillating between the light and the shadow—at bottom, for all his typical representation of a race and a civilization, a unique and inexplicable personality. More, he is a man of the first class, an Achilles of his world; and here the achievement of Dreiser is most striking, for he succeeds where all forerunners failed. It is easy enough to explain how John Smith courted his wife, and even how William Brown fought and died for his country, but it is inordinately difficult to give plausibility to the motives, feelings and processes of mind of a man whose salient character is that they transcend all ordinary experience. Too often, even when made by the highest creative and interpretative talent, the effort has resolved itself into a begging of the question. Shakespeare made Hamlet comprehensible to the groundlings by diluting that half of him which was Shakespeare with a half which was a college sophomore. In the same way he saved Lear by making him, in large part, a tedious and obscene old donkey—the blood brother of any average ancient of any average English taproom. Tackling Caesar, he was rescued by Brutus' knife. George Bernard Shaw, facing the same difficulty, resolved it by drawing a composite portrait of two or three London actor-managers and half a dozen English politicians. But Dreiser makes no such compromise. He bangs into the difficulties of his problem head on, and if he does not solve it absolutely, he at least makes an extraordinarily close approach to a solution. In "The Financier" a certain incredulity still hangs about Cowperwood; in "The Titan" he suddenly comes unquestionably real. If you want to get the true measure of this feat, put it beside the failure of Frank Norris with Curtis Jadwin in "The Pit." . . .

"The 'Genius,'" which interrupted the "trilogy of desire," marks the nadir of Dreiser's accomplishment, as "The Titan" marks its apogee. The plan of it, of course, is simple enough, and it is one that Dreiser, at his best, might have carried out with undoubted success. What he is trying to show, in brief, is the battle that goes on in the soul of every man of active mind between the desire for self-expression and the desire for safety, for public respect, for emotional equanimity. It is, in a sense, the story of Cowperwood told over again, but with an important difference, for Eugene Witla is a much less self-reliant and powerful fellow than Cowperwood, and so he is unable to muster up the vast resolution of spirits that he needs to attain happiness. "The Titan" is the history of a strong man. "The 'Genius'" is the history of a man essentially weak. Eugene Witla can never quite choose his route in life. He goes on sacrificing ease to aspiration and aspiration to ease to the end of the chapter. He vacillates abominably and forever between two irreconcilable desires. Even when, at the close, he sinks into a whining sort of resignation, the proud courage of Cowperwood is not in him; he is always a bit despicable in his pathos.

As I say, a story of simple outlines, and well adapted to the dreiserian pen. But it is spoiled and made a mock of by a donkeyish solemnity of attack which leaves it, on the one hand, diffuse, spineless and shapeless, and on the other hand, a compendium of platitudes. It is as if Dreiser, suddenly discovering himself a sage, put off the high passion of the artist and took to pounding a pulpit. It is almost as if he deliberately essayed upon a burlesque of himself. The book is an endless emission of the obvious, with touches of the scandalous to light up its killing monotony. It runs to 736 pages of small type; its reading is an unbearable weariness to the flesh; in the midst of it one has forgotten the beginning and is unconcerned about the end. Mingled with all the folderol, of course, there is stuff of nobler quality. Certain chapters stick in the memory; whole episodes lift themselves to the fervid luminosity of "Jennie Gerhardt"; there are character sketches that deserve all praise; one often pulls up with a reminder that the thing is the work of a proficient craftsman. But in the main it lumbers and jolts, wabbles and bores. A sort of ponderous imbecility gets into it. Both in its elaborate devices to shake up the pious and its imposing demonstrations of what every one knows, it somehow suggests the advanced thinking of Greenwich Village. I suspect, indeed, that the *vin rouge* was in Dreiser's arteries as he concocted it. He was at the intellectual menopause, and looking back somewhat wistfully and attitudinizingly toward the goatish days that were no more.

But let it go! A novelist capable of "Jennie Gerhardt" has rights, privileges, prerogatives. He may, if he will, go on a spiritual drunk now and then, and empty the stale bilges of his soul. Thackeray, having finished "Vanity Fair" and "Pendennis," bathed himself in the sheep's milk of "The Newcomes," and after "The Virginians" he did "The Adventures of Philip." Zola, with "Germinal," "La Débâcle" and "La Terre" behind him, recreated himself horribly with "Fécondité." Tolstoi, after "Anna Karenina," wrote "What Is Art?" Ibsen, after "Et Dukkehjem" and "Gengangere," wrote "Vildanden." The good God himself, after all the magnificence of Kings and Chronicles, turned Dr. Frank Crane and so botched his Writ with Proverbs. . . . A weakness that we must allow for. Whenever Dreiser, abandoning his fundamental skepticism, yields to the irrepressible human (and perhaps also divine) itch to label, to moralize, to teach, he becomes a bit absurd. Observe "The 'Genius,'" and parts of "A Hoosier Holiday" and of "A Traveler at Forty," and of "Plays of the Natural and the Supernatural." But in this very absurdity, it seems to me, there is a subtle proof that his fundamental skepticism is sound. . . .

I mention the "Plays of the Natural and the Supernatural." They are ingenious and sometimes extremely effective, but their significance is not great. The two that are "of the natural" are "The Girl in the Coffin" and "Old Ragpicker," the first a laborious evocation of the gruesome, too long by half, and the other an experiment in photographic realism, with a pair of policemen as its protagonists. All five plays "of the supernatural" follow a single plan. In the foreground, as it were, we see a sordid drama played out on the human plane, and in the background (or in the empyrean above, as you choose) we see the operation of the god-like imbecilities which sway and flay us all. The technical trick is well managed. It would be easy for such four-dimensional pieces to fall into burlesque, but in at least two cases, to wit, in "The Blue Sphere" and "In the Dark," they go off with an air. Superficially, these plays "of the supernatural" seem to show an abandonment to the wheezy, black bombazine mysticism which crops up toward the end of "The 'Genius.'" But that mysticism, at bottom, is no more than the dreiserian skepticism made visible. "For myself," says Dreiser somewhere, "I do not know what truth is, what beauty is, what love is, what hope is." And in another place: "I admit a vast compulsion which has nothing to do with the individual desires or tastes or impulses." The jokers behind the arras pull the strings. It is pretty, but what is it all about? . . . The criticism which deals only with externals sees "Sister Carrie" as no more than a deft adventure into realism. Dreiser is praised, when he is praised at all, for making Carrie so clear, for understanding her so well. But the truth is, of course, that his achievement consists precisely in making patent the impenetrable mystery of her, and of the tangled complex of striving and aspiration of which she is so helplessly a part. It is in this sense that "Sister Carrie" is a profound work. It is not a book of glib explanations, of ready formulae; it is, above all else, a book of wonder. . . .

Of "A Traveler at Forty" I have spoken briefly. It is heavy with the obvious; the most interesting thing in it is the fact that Dreiser had never seen St. Peter's or Picadilly Circus until he was too old for either reverence or romance. "A Hoosier Holiday" is far more illuminating, despite its platitudinizing. Slow in tempo, discursive, reflective, intimate, the book covers a vast territory, and lingers in pleasant fields. One finds in it an almost complete confession of faith, artistic, religious, even political. And not infrequently that confession takes the form of ingenuous confidences —about the fortunes of the house of Dreiser, the dispersed Dreiser clan, the old neighbors in Indiana, new friends made along the way. In "A Traveler at Forty" Dreiser is surely frank enough in his vivisections; he seldom forgets a vanity or a wart. In "A

Hoosier Holiday" he goes even further; he speculates heavily about all his *dramatis personae*, prodding into the motives behind their acts, wondering what they would do in this or that situation, forcing them painfully into laboratory jars. They become, in the end, not unlike characters in a novel; one misses only the neatness of a plot. Strangely enough, the one personage of the chronicle who remains dim throughout is the artist, Franklin Booth, Dreiser's host and companion on the long motor ride from New York to Indiana, and the maker of the book's excellent pictures. One gets a brilliant etching of Booth's father, and scarcely less vivid portraits of Speed, the chauffeur; of various persons encountered on the way; and of friends and relatives dredged up out of the abyss of the past. But of Booth one learns little save that he is a Christian Scientist and a fine figure of a man. There must have been much talk during those two weeks of careening along the highroad, and Booth must have borne some part in it, but what he said is very meagerly reported, and so he is still somewhat vague at the end—a personality sensed but scarcely apprehended.

However, it is Dreiser himself who is the chief character of the story, and who stands out from it most brilliantly. One sees in the man all the special marks of the novelist: his capacity for photographic and relentless observation, his insatiable curiosity, his keen zest in life as a spectacle, his comprehension of and sympathy for the poor striving of humble folks, his endless mulling of insoluble problems, his recurrent Philistinism, his impatience of restraints, his fascinated suspicion of messiahs, his passion for physical beauty, his relish for the gaudy drama of big cities; his incurable Americanism. The panorama that he enrolls runs the whole scale of the colors; it is a series of extraordinarily vivid pictures. The somber gloom of the Pennsylvania hills, with Wilkes-Barre lying among them like a gem; the procession of little country towns, sleepy and a bit hoggish; the flash of Buffalo, Cleveland, Indianapolis; the gargantuan coal-pockets and ore-docks along the Erie shore; the tinsel summer resorts; the lush Indiana farm lands, with their stodgy, bovine people—all of these things are sketched in simply, and yet almost magnificently. I know, indeed, of no book which better describes the American hinterland. Here we have no idle spying by a stranger, but a full-length representation by one who knows the thing he describes intimately, and is himself a part of it. Almost every mile of the road traveled has been Dreiser's own road in life. He knew those unkempt Indiana towns in boyhood; he wandered in the Indiana woods; he came to Toledo, Cleveland, Buffalo as a young man; all the roots of his existence are out there. And so he does his chronicle *con amore*, with many a sentimental dredging up of old memories, old hopes and old dreams.

Save for passages in "The Titan," "A Hoosier Holiday" marks the high tide of Dreiser's writing—that is, as sheer writing. His old faults are in it, and plentifully. There are empty, brackish phrases enough, God knows—"high noon" among them. But for all that, there is an undeniable glow in it; it shows, in more than one place, an approach to style; the mere wholesaler of words has become, in some sense, a connoisseur, even a voluptuary. The picture of Wilkes-Barre girt in by her hills is simply done, and yet there is imagination in it, and touches of brilliance. The somber beauty of the Pennsylvania mountains is vividly transferred to the page. The towns by the wayside are differentiated, swiftly drawn, made to live. There are excellent sketches of people—a courtly hotel-keeper in some God-forsaken hamlet, his self-respect triumphing over his wallow; a group of babbling Civil War veterans, endlessly mouthing incomprehensible jests; the half-grown beaux and belles of the summer resorts, enchanted and yet a bit staggered by the awakening of sex; Booth *père* and his sinister politics; broken and forgotten men in the Indiana towns; policemen, waitresses, farmers, country characters; Dreiser's own people—the boys and girls of his youth; his brother Paul, the Indiana Schneckenburger and Francis Scott Key; his sisters and brothers; his beaten, hopeless, pious father; his brave and noble mother. The book is dedicated to this mother, now long dead, and in a way it is a memorial to her, a monument to affection. Life bore upon her cruelly; she knew poverty at its lowest ebb and despair at its bitterest; and yet there was in her a touch of fineness that never yielded, a gallant spirit that faced and fought things through. One thinks, somehow, of the mother of Gounod. . . . Her son has not forgotten her. His book is her epitaph. He enters into her presence with love and with reverence and with something not far from awe. . . .

As for the rest of the Dreiser compositions, I leave them to your curiosity.

· 6 ·

Dr. William Lyon Phelps, the Lampson professor of English language and literature at Yale, opens his chapter on Mark Twain in his "Essays on Modern Novelists" with a humorous account of the critical imbecility which pursued Mark in his own country down to his last years. The favorite national critics of that era (and it extended to 1895, at the least) were wholly blind to the fact that he was a great artist. They admitted him, somewhat grudgingly, a certain low dexterity as a clown, but that he was an imaginative writer of the first rank, or even of the fifth rank, was something that, in their insanest moments, never so much as occurred to them. Phelps cites, in particular, an ass named Professor Richardson, whose "American Literature," it appears, "is still a standard work" and "a deservedly high authority"— apparently in colleges. In the 1892 edition of this *magnum opus,* Mark is dismissed with less than four lines, and ranked below Irving, Holmes and Lowell—nay, actually below Artemus Ward, Josh Billings and Petroleum V. Nasby! The thing is fabulous, fantastic, *unglaublich*—but nevertheless true. Lacking the "higher artistic or moral purpose of the greater humorists" (*exempli gratia,* Rabelais, Molière, Aristophanes!!), Mark is dismissed by this Professor Balderdash as a hollow buffoon. . . . But stay! Do not laugh yet! Phelps himself, indignant at the stupidity, now proceeds to credit Mark with a moral purpose! . . . Turn to "The Mysterious Stranger," or "What Is Man?" . . .

College professors, alas, never learn anything. The identical gentleman who achieved this discovery about old Mark in 1910, now seeks to dispose of Dreiser in the exact manner of Richardson. That is to say, he essays to finish him by putting him into Coventry, by loftily passing over him. "Do not speak of him," said Kingsley of Heine; "he was a wicked man!" Search the latest volume of the

Phelps revelation, "The Advance of the English Novel," and you will find that Dreiser is not once mentioned in it. The late O. Henry is hailed as a genius who will have "abiding fame"; Henry Sydnor Harrison is hymned as "more than a clever novelist," nay, "a valuable ally of the angels" (the right-thinker complex! art as a form of snuffling!), and an obscure Pagliaccio named Charles D. Stewart is brought forward as "the American novelist most worthy to fill the particular vacancy caused by the death of Mark Twain"—but Dreiser is not even listed in the index. And where Phelps leads with his baton of birch most of the other drovers of rah-rah boys follow. I turn, for example, to "An Introduction to American Literature," by Henry S. Pancoast, A.M., L.H.D., dated 1912. There are kind words for Richard Harding Davis, for Amélie Rives, and even for Will N. Harben, but not a syllable for Dreiser. Again, there is "A History of American Literature," by Reuben Post Halleck, A.M., LL.D., dated 1911. Lew Wallace, Marietta Holley, Owen Wister and Augusta Evans Wilson have their hearings, but not Dreiser. Yet again, there is "A History of American Literature Since 1870," by Prof. Fred Lewis Pattee,[8] instructor in "the English language and literature" somewhere in Pennsylvania. Pattee has praises for Marion Crawford, Margaret Deland and F. Hopkinson Smith, and polite bows for Richard Harding Davis and Robert W. Chambers, but from end to end of his fat tome I am unable to find the slightest mention of Dreiser.

So much for one group of heroes of the new Dunciad. That it includes most of the acknowledged heavyweights of the craft— the Babbitts, Mores, Brownells and so on—goes without saying; as Van Wyck Brooks has pointed out,[9] these magnificoes are austerely above any consideration of the literature that is in being. The other group, more courageous and more honest, proceeds by direct attack; Dreiser is to be disposed of by a moral *attentat*. Its leaders are two more professors, Stuart P. Sherman and H. W. Boynton, and in its ranks march the lady critics of the newspapers, with much shrill, falsetto clamor. Sherman is the only one of them who shows any intelligible reasoning. Boynton, as always, is a mere parroter of conventional phrases, and the objections of the

---

[8] New York: The Century Co.; 1916.   [9] In *The Seven Arts*, May, 1917.

ladies fade imperceptibly into a pious indignation which is in-distinguishable from that of the professional suppressors of vice.

What, then, is Sherman's complaint? In brief, that Dreiser is a liar when he calls himself a realist; that he is actually a natural-ist, and hence accursed. That "he has evaded the enterprise of representing human conduct, and confined himself to a representa-tion of animal behavior." That he "imposes his own naturalistic philosophy" upon his characters, making them do what they ought not to do, and think what they ought not to think. That "he has just two things to tell us about Frank Cowperwood: that he has a rapacious appetite for money, and a rapacious appetite for women." That this alleged "theory of animal behavior" is not only incorrect but downright immoral, and that "when one-half the world attempts to assert it, the other half rises in battle."[1]

Only a glance is needed to show the vacuity of all this *brutum fulmen*. Dreiser, in point of fact, is scarcely more the realist or the naturalist, in any true sense, than H. G. Wells or the later George Moore, nor has he ever announced himself in either the one character or the other—if there be, in fact, any difference between them that any one save a pigeon-holing pedagogue can discern. He is really something quite different, and, in his mo-ments, something far more stately. His aim is not merely to record, but to translate and understand; the thing he exposes is not the empty event and act, but the endless mystery out of which it springs; his pictures have a passionate compassion in them that it is hard to separate from poetry. If this sense of the universal and inexplicable tragedy, if this vision of life as a seeking without a finding, if this adept summoning up of moving images, is mis-taken by college professors for the empty, meticulous nastiness of Zola in "Pot-Bouille"—in Nietzsche's phrase, for "the delight to stink"—then surely the folly of college professors, as vast as it seems, has been underestimated. What is the fact? The fact is that Dreiser's attitude of mind, his manner of reaction to the phenomena he represents, the whole of his alleged "naturalistic philosophy," stems directly, not from Zola, Flaubert, Augier and the younger Dumas, but from the Greeks. In the midst of demo-

----

[1] The *Nation*, Dec. 2, 1915.

cratic cocksureness and Christian sentimentalism, of doctrinaire shallowness and professorial smugness, he stands for a point of view which at least has something honest and courageous about it; here, at all events, he is a realist. Let him put a motto to his books, and it might be:

Ἰὼ γενεαὶ βροτῶν,
Ὡς ὑμᾶς ἴσα καὶ τὸ μηδὲν
Ζώσας ἐναριθμῶ.

If you protest against that as too harsh for Christians and college professors, right-thinkers and forward-lookers, then you protest against "Oedipus Rex."[2]

As for the animal behavior prattle of the learned headmaster, it reveals, on the one hand, only the academic fondness for seizing upon high-sounding but empty phrases and using them to alarm the populace, and on the other hand, only the academic incapacity for observing facts correctly and reporting them honestly. The truth is, of course, that the behavior of such men as Cowperwood and Witla and of such women as Carrie and Jennie, as Dreiser describes it, is no more merely animal than the behavior of such acknowledged and undoubted human beings as Woodrow Wilson and Jane Addams. The whole point of the story of Witla, to take the example which seems to concern the horrified watchmen most, is this: that his life is a bitter conflict between the animal in him and the aspiring soul, between the flesh and the spirit, between what is weak in him and what is strong, between what is base and what is noble. Moreover, the good, in the end, gets its hooks into the bad: as we part from Witla he is actually bathed in the tears of remorse, and resolved to be a correct and godfearing man. And what have we in "The Financier" and "The Titan"? A conflict, in the ego of Cowperwood, between aspiration and ambition, between the passion for beauty and the passion for power. Is either passion animal? To ask the question is to answer it.

I single out Dr. Sherman, not because his pompous syllogisms have any plausibility in fact or logic, but simply because he may

---

[2] 1186–1189. So translated by Floyd Dell: "O ye deathward-going tribes of man, what do your lives mean except that they go to nothingness?"

well stand as archetype of the booming, indignant corrupter of criteria, the moralist turned critic. A glance at his paean to Arnold Bennett[3] at once reveals the true gravamen of his objection to Dreiser. What offends him is not actually Dreiser's shortcoming as an artist, but Dreiser's shortcoming as a Christian and an American. In Bennett's volumes of pseudo-philosophy—*e.g.*, "The Plain Man and His Wife" and "The Feast of St. Friend"—he finds the intellectual victuals that are to his taste. Here we have a sweet commingling of virtuous conformity and complacent optimism, of sonorous platitude and easy certainty—here, in brief, we have the philosophy of the English middle classes—and here, by the same token, we have the sort of guff that the half-educated of our own country can understand. It is the calm, superior numskullery that was Victorian; it is by Samuel Smiles out of Hannah More. The offence of Dreiser is that he has disdained this revelation and gone back to the Greeks. Lo, he reads poetry into "the appetite for women"—he rejects the Pauline doctrine that all love is below the diaphragm! He thinks of Ulysses, not as a mere heretic and criminal, but as a great artist. He sees the life of man, not as a simple theorem in Calvinism, but as a vast adventure, an enchantment, a mystery. It is no wonder that respectable schoolteachers are against him. . . .

The comstockian attack upon "The 'Genius'" seems to have sprung out of the same muddled sense of Dreiser's essential hostility to all that is safe and regular—of the danger in him to that mellowed Methodism which has become the national ethic. The book, in a way, was a direct challenge, for though it came to an end upon a note which even a Methodist might hear as sweet, there were undoubted provocations in detail. Dreiser, in fact, allowed his scorn to make off with his taste—and *es ist nichts fürchterlicher als Einbildungskraft ohne Geschmack.* The Comstocks arose to the bait a bit slowly, but none the less surely. Going through the volume with the terrible industry of a Sunday-school boy dredging up pearls of smut from the Old Testament, they achieved a list of no less than 89 alleged floutings of the code —75 described as lewd and 14 as profane. An inspection of these

---

[3] The New York *Evening Post*, Dec. 31, 1915.

specifications affords mirth of a rare and lofty variety; nothing could more cruelly expose the inner chambers of the moral mind. When young Witla, fastening his best girl's skate, is so overcome by the carnality of youth that he hugs her, it is set down as lewd. On page 51, having become an art student, he is fired by "a great, warm-tinted nude of Bouguereau"—lewd again. On page 70 he begins to draw from the figure, and his instructor cautions him that the female breast is round, not square—more lewdness. On page 151 he kisses a girl on mouth and neck and she cautions him: "Be careful! Mamma may come in"—still more. On page 161, having got rid of mamma, she yields "herself to him gladly, joyously" and he is greatly shocked when she argues that an artist (she is by way of being a singer) had better not marry—lewdness doubly damned. On page 245 he and his bride, being ignorant, neglect the principles laid down by Dr. Sylvanus Stall in his great works on sex hygiene—lewdness most horrible! But there is no need to proceed further. Every kiss, hug and tickle of the chin in the chronicle is laboriously snouted out, empanelled, exhibited. Every hint that Witla is no vestal, that he indulges his unchristian fleshliness, that he burns in the manner of I Corinthians, VII, 9, is uncovered to the moral inquisition.

On the side of profanity there is a less ardent pursuit of evidences, chiefly, I daresay, because their unearthing is less stimulating. (Beside, there is no law prohibiting profanity in books: the whole inquiry here is but so much *lagniappe*.) On page 408, in describing a character called Daniel C. Summerfield, Dreiser says that the fellow is "very much given to swearing, more as a matter of habit than of foul intention," and then goes on to explain somewhat lamely that "no picture of him would be complete without the interpolation of his various expressions." They turn out to be *God damn* and *Jesus Christ*—three of the latter and five or six of the former. All go down; the pure in heart must be shielded from the knowledge of them. (But what of the immoral French? They call the English *Goddams*.) Also, three plain *damns*, eight *hells*, one *my God*, five *by Gods*, one *go to the devil*, one *God Almighty* and one plain *God*. Altogether, 31 specimens are listed. "The 'Genius'" runs to 350,000 words. The profanity thus works out to somewhat less than one word in 10,000. . . . Alas, the comstockian proboscis, feeling for such offendings, is not as alert as when uncovering more savory delicacies. On page 191 I find an overlooked *by God*. On page 372 there are *Oh, God, God curse her*, and *God strike her dead*. On page 373 there are *Ah God, Oh God* and three other invocations of God. On page 617 there is *God help me*. On page 720 there is *as God is my judge*. On page 723 there is *I'm no damned good. . . .* But I begin to blush.

When the Comstock Society began proceedings against "The 'Genius,' " a group of English novelists, including Arnold Bennett, H. G. Wells, W. L. George and Hugh Walpole, cabled an indignant caveat. This bestirred the Author's League of America to activity, and its executive committee issued a minute denouncing the business. Later on a protest of American *literati* was circulated, and more than 400 signed, including such highly respectable authors as Winston Churchill, Percy MacKaye, Booth Tarkington and James Lane Allen, and such critics as Lawrence Gilman, Clayton Hamilton and James Huneker, and the editors of such journals as the *Century*, the *Atlantic Monthly* and the *New Republic*. Among my literary lumber is all the correspondence relating to this protest, not forgetting the letters of those who refused to sign, and some day I hope to publish it, that posterity may not lose the joy of an extremely diverting episode. The case attracted wide attention and was the theme of an extraordinarily violent discussion, but the resultant benefits to Dreiser were more than counterbalanced, I daresay, by the withdrawal of "The 'Genius' " itself.[4]

· 7 ·

Dreiser, like Mark Twain and Emerson before him, has been far more hospitably greeted in his first stage, now drawing to a close, in England than in his own country. The cause of this, I daresay, lies partly in the fact that "Sister Carrie" was in general circulation over there during the seven years that it remained suppressed on this side. It was during these years that such men as Arnold Bennett, Theodore Watts-Dunton, Frank Harris and

---

[4] [Footnote appears on following page.]

H. G. Wells, and such critical journals as the *Spectator*, the *Saturday Review* and the *Athenaeum* became aware of him, and so laid the foundations of a sound appreciation of his subsequent work. Since the beginning of the war, certain English newspapers have

---

[4] Despite the comstockian attack, Dreiser is still fairly well represented on the shelves of American public libraries. A canvass of the libraries of the 25 principal cities gives the following result, an × indicating that the corresponding book is catalogued, and a — that it is not:

	Sister Carrie	Jennie Gerhardt	The Financier	The Titan	A Traveler at Forty	The "Genius"	Plays of the Natural	A Hoosier Holiday
New York	×	—	—	×	×	×	×	×
Boston	—	—	—	—	×	—	×	—
Chicago	×	×	×	×	×	×	×	×
Philadelphia	×	×	×	×	×	×	×	×
Washington	—	—	—	—	×	—	×	—
Baltimore	—	—	—	—	×	—	—	—
Pittsburgh	—	—	×	×	×	×	—	×
New Orleans	—	—	—	—	—	—	—	—
Denver	×	×	×	×	×	×	×	×
San Francisco	×	×	×	×	×	—	—	×
St. Louis	×	×	×	×	×	—	×	—
Cleveland	×	×	×	×	—	×	×	—
Providence	—	—	—	—	—	—	—	—
Los Angeles	×	×	×	×	×	×	×	×
Indianapolis	×	×	×	—	×	—	×	×
Louisville	×	×	—	×	×	×	×	×
St. Paul	×	×	—	—	×	—	×	×
Minneapolis	×	×	×	—	×	—	×	—
Cincinnati	×	×	×	—	×	—	×	×
Kansas City	×	×	×	×	×	×	×	×
Milwaukee	—	—	—	—	×	—	×	×
Newark	×	×	×	×	×	×	×	×
Detroit	×	×	×	—	×	×	×	×
Seattle	×	×	—	—	×	—	×	×
Hartford	—	—	—	—	—	—	—	×

This table shows that but two libraries, those of Providence and New Orleans, bar Dreiser altogether. The effect of alarms from newspaper reviewers is indicated by the scant distribution of "The 'Genius,'" which is barred by 14 of the 25. It should be noted that some of these libraries issue certain of the books only under restrictions. This I know to be the case in Louisville, Los Angeles, Newark and Cleveland. The Newark librarian informs me that "Jennie Gerhardt" is to be removed altogether, presumably in response to some protest from local Comstocks. In Chicago "The 'Genius'" has been stolen, and on account of the withdrawal of the book the Public Library has been unable to get another copy.

echoed the alarmed American discovery that he is a literary agent of the Wilhelmstrasse, but it is to the honor of the English that this imbecility has got no countenance from reputable authority and has not injured his position.

At home, as I have shown, he is less fortunate. When criticism is not merely an absurd effort to chase him out of court because his ideas are not orthodox, as the Victorians tried to chase out Darwin and Swinburne, and their predecessors pursued Shelley and Byron, it is too often designed to identify him with some branch or other of "radical" poppycock, and so credit him with purposes he has never imagined. Thus Chautauqua pulls and Greenwich Village pushes. It the middle ground there proceeds the pedantic effort to dispose of him by labeling him. One faction maintains that he is a realist; another calls him a naturalist; a third argues that he is really a disguised romanticist. This debate is all sound and fury, signifying nothing, but out of it has come a valuation by Lawrence Gilman[5] which perhaps strikes very close to the truth. He is, says Mr. Gilman, "a sentimental mystic who employs the mimetic gestures of the realist." This judgment is apt in particular and sound in general. No such thing as a pure method is possible in the novel. Plain realism, as in Gorky's "Nachtasyl" and the war stories of Ambrose Bierce, simply wearies us by its vacuity; plain romance, if we ever get beyond our nonage, makes us laugh. It is their artistic combination, as in life itself, that fetches us—the subtle projection of the concrete muddle that is living against the ideal orderliness that we reach out for—the eternal war of experience and aspiration—the contrast between the world as it is and the world as it might be or ought to be. Dreiser describes the thing that he sees, laboriously and relentlessly, but he never forgets the dream that is behind it. "He gives you," continues Mr. Gilman, "a sense of actuality; but he gives you more than that: out of the vast welter and surge, the plethoric irrelevancies, . . . emerges a sense of the infinite sadness and mystery of human life." . . .[6]

"To see truly," said Renan, "is to see dimly." Dimness or

---

[5] The *North American Review*, Feb. 1916.

[6] Another competent valuation, by Randolph Bourne, is in *The Dial*, June 14, 1917.

mystery, call it what you will: it is in all these overgrown and formless, but profoundly moving books. Just what do they mean? Just what is Dreiser driving at? That such questions should be asked is only a proof of the straits to which pedagogy has brought criticism. The answer is simple: he is driving at nothing, he is merely trying to represent what he sees and feels. His moving impulse is no flabby yearning to teach, to expound, to make simple; it is that "obscure inner necessity" of which Conrad tells us, the irresistible creative passion of a genuine artist, standing spell-bound before the impenetrable enigma that is life, enamored by the strange beauty that plays over its sordidness, challenged to a wondering and half-terrified sort of representation of what passes understanding. And *jenseits von Gut und Böse.* "For myself," says Dreiser, "I do not know what truth is, what beauty is, what love is, what hope is. I do not believe any one absolutely and I do not doubt any one absolutely. I think people are both evil and well-intentioned." The hatching of the Dreiser bugaboo is here; it is the flat rejection of the rubber-stamp formulae that outrages petty minds; not being "good," he must be "evil"—as William Blake said of Milton, a true poet is always "of the devil's party." But in that very groping toward a light but dimly seen there is a measure, it seems to me, of Dreiser's rank and consideration as an artist. "Now comes the public," says Herman Bahr, "and de- mands that we explain what the poet is trying to say. The answer is this: If we knew exactly he would not be a poet. . . ."

The Sahara of the Bozart

‹‹‹‹‹‹‹‹‹‹‹‹‹‹‹‹‹‹‹‹‹‹‹‹‹‹‹‹‹‹‹‹‹‹‹›››››››››››››››››››››››››››››››

This produced a ferocious reaction in the South, and I was belabored for months, and even years afterward in a very extravagant manner. The essay in its final form, as it is here reproduced, dates sadly, but I have let it stand as a sort of historical document. On the heels of the violent denunciations of the elder Southerners there soon came a favorable response from the more civilized youngsters, and there is reason to believe that my attack had something to do with that revival of Southern letters which followed in the middle 1920's.

Alas, for the South! Her books have grown fewer—
She never was much given to literature.

IN the lamented J. Gordon Coogler, author of these elegiac lines, there was the insight of a true poet. He was the last bard of Dixie, at least in the legitimate line. Down there a poet is now almost as rare as an oboe-player, a dry-point etcher or a metaphysician. It is, indeed, amazing to contemplate so vast a vacuity. One thinks of the interstellar spaces, of the colossal reaches of the now mythical ether. Nearly the whole of Europe could be lost in that stupendous region of worn-out farms, shoddy cities and paralyzed cerebrums: one could throw in France, Germany and Italy, and still have room for the British Isles. And yet, for all its size and all its wealth and all the "progress" it babbles of, it is almost as sterile, artistically, intellectu-

From *A Mencken Chrestomathy*, 1949. Included in *Prejudices: Second Series*, 1920. Originally printed, in shorter form, in the New York *Evening Mail*, Nov. 13, 1917. Copyright 1920, 1949 by Alfred A. Knopf, Inc. Renewal copyright 1948 by H. L. Mencken.

ally, culturally, as the Sahara Desert. There are single acres in
Europe that house more first-rate men than all the states south
of the Potomac; there are probably single square miles in America. If the whole of the late Confederacy were to be engulfed by
a tidal wave tomorrow, the effect upon the civilized minority of
men in the world would be but little greater than that of a flood
on the Yang-tse-kiang. It would be impossible in all history to
match so complete a drying-up of a civilization.

I say a civilization because that is what, in the old days, the
South had, despite the Baptist and Methodist barbarism that
reigns down there now. More, it was a civilization of manifold
excellences—perhaps the best that the Western Hemisphere had
ever seen—undoubtedly the best that These States have ever seen.
Down to the middle of the last century, and even beyond, the
main hatchery of ideas on this side of the water was across the
Potomac bridges. The New England shopkeepers and theologians
never really developed a civilization; all they ever developed was a
government. They were, at their best, tawdry and tacky fellows,
oafish in manner and devoid of imagination; one searches the
books in vain for mention of a salient Yankee gentleman; as well
look for a Welsh gentleman. But in the South there were men of
delicate fancy, urbane instinct and aristocratic manner—in brief,
superior men—in brief, gentry. To politics, their chief diversion,
they brought active and original minds. It was there that nearly
all the political theories we still cherish and suffer under came to
birth. It was there that the crude dogmatism of New England was
refined and humanized. It was there, above all, that some attention was given to the art of living—that life got beyond and above
the state of a mere infliction and became an exhilarating experience. A certain notable spaciousness was in the ancient Southern
scheme of things. The *Ur*-Confederate had leisure. He liked to toy
with ideas. He was hospitable and tolerant. He had the vague
thing that we call culture.

But consider the condition of his late empire today. The picture gives one the creeps. It is as if the Civil War stamped out
every last bearer of the torch, and left only a mob of peasants
on the field. One thinks of Asia Minor, resigned to Armenians,
Greeks and wild swine, of Poland abandoned to the Poles. In all

that gargantuan paradise of the fourth-rate there is not a single picture gallery worth going into, or a single orchestra capable of playing the nine symphonies of Beethoven, or a single opera-house, or a single theater devoted to decent plays, or a single public monument that is worth looking at, or a single workshop devoted to the making of beautiful things. Once you have counted James Branch Cabell (a lingering survivor of the *ancien régime*: a scarlet dragon-fly imbedded in opaque amber) you will not find a single Southern prose writer who can actually write. And once you have—but when you come to critics, musical composers, painters, sculptors, architects and the like, you will have to give it up, for there is not even a bad one between the Potomac mudflats and the Gulf. Nor a historian. Nor a philosopher. Nor a theologian. Nor a scientist. In all these fields the South is an awe-inspiring blank—a brother to Portugal, Serbia and Albania.

Consider, for example, the present estate and dignity of Virginia—in the great days indubitably the premier American state, the mother of Presidents and statesmen, the home of the first American university worthy of the name, the *arbiter elegantiarum* of the Western World. Well, observe Virgina today. It is years since a first-rate man, save only Cabell, has come out of it; it is years since an idea has come out of it. The old aristocracy went down the red gullet of war; the poor white trash are now in the saddle. Politics in Virginia are cheap, ignorant, parochial, idiotic; there is scarcely a man in office above the rank of a professional job-seeker; the political doctrine that prevails is made up of hand-me-downs from the bumpkinry of the Middle West—Bryanism, Prohibition, all that sort of filthy claptrap; the administration of the law is turned over to professors of Puritanism and espionage; a Washington or a Jefferson, dumped there by some act of God, would be denounced as a scoundrel and jailed overnight.

Elegance, *esprit*, culture? Virginia has no art, no literature, no philosophy, no mind or aspiration of her own. Her education has sunk to the Baptist seminary level; not a single contribution to human knowledge has come out of her colleges in twenty-five years; she spends less than half upon her common schools, *per capita,* than any Northern state spends. In brief, an intellectual Gobi or Lapland. Urbanity, *politesse*, chivalry? Go to! It was in

Virginia that they invented the device of searching for contraband whiskey in women's underwear. . . . There remains, at the top, a ghost of the old aristocracy, a bit wistful and infinitely charming. But it has lost all its old leadership to fabulous monsters from the lower depths; it is submerged in an industrial plutocracy that is ignorant and ignominious. The mind of the state, as it is revealed to the nation, is pathetically naïve and inconsequential. It no longer reacts with energy and elasticity to great problems. It has fallen to the bombastic trivialities of the camp-meeting and the stump. One could no more imagine a Lee or a Washington in the Virginia of today than one could imagine a Huxley in Nicaragua.

I choose the Old Dominion, not because I disdain it, but precisely because I esteem it. It is, by long odds, the most civilized of the Southern states, now as always. It has sent a host of creditable sons northward; the stream kept running into our own time. Virginians, even the worst of them, show the effects of a great tradition. They hold themselves above other Southerners, and with sound pretension. If one turns to such a commonwealth as Georgia the picture becomes far darker. There the liberated lower orders of whites have borrowed the worst commercial bounderism of the Yankee and superimposed it upon a culture that, at bottom, is but little removed from savagery. Georgia is at once the home of the cotton-mill sweater, of the Methodist parson turned Savonarola and of the lynching bee. A self-respecting European, going there to live, would not only find intellectual stimulation utterly lacking; he would actually feel a certain insecurity, as if the scene were the Balkans or the China Coast. There is a state with more than half the area of Italy and more population than either Denmark or Norway, and yet in thirty years it has not produced a single idea. Once upon a time a Georgian printed a couple of books that attracted notice, but immediately it turned out that he was little more than an amanuensis for the local blacks—that his works were really the products, not of white Georgia, but of black Georgia. Writing afterward *as* a white man, he swiftly subsided into the fifth rank. And he is not only the glory of the literature of Georgia; he is, almost literally, the whole of the literature of Georgia —nay, of the entire art of Georgia.[1]

---

[1] The reference here, of course, was to Joel Chandler Harris.

Virginia is the best of the South today, and Georgia is perhaps the worst. The one is simply senile; the other is crass, gross, vulgar and obnoxious. Between lies a vast plain of mediocrity, stupidity, lethargy, almost of dead silence. In the North, of course, there is also grossness, crassness, vulgarity. The North, in its way, is also stupid and obnoxious. But nowhere in the North is there such complete sterility, so depressing a lack of all civilized gesture and aspiration. One would find it difficult to unearth a second-rate city between the Ohio and the Pacific that isn't struggling to establish an orchestra, or setting up a little theater, or going in for an art gallery, or making some other effort to get into touch with civilization. These efforts often fail, and sometimes they succeed rather absurdly, but under them there is at least an impulse that deserves respect, and that is the impulse to seek beauty and to experiment with ideas, and so to give the life of every day a certain dignity and purpose. You will find no such impulse in the South. There are no committees down there cadging subscriptions for orchestras; if a string quartet is ever heard there, the news of it has never come out; an opera troupe, when it roves the land, is a nine days' wonder. The little theater movement has swept the whole country, enormously augmenting the public interest in sound plays, giving new dramatists their chance, forcing reforms upon the commercial theater. Everywhere else the wave rolls high—but along the line of the Potomac it breaks upon a rock-bound shore. There is no little theater beyond. There is no gallery of pictures. No artist ever gives exhibitions. No one talks of such things. No one seems to be interested in such things.

As for the cause of this unanimous torpor and doltishness, this curious and almost pathological estrangement from everything that makes for a civilized culture, I have hinted at it already, and now state it again. The South has simply been drained of all its best blood. The vast hemorrhage of the Civil War half exterminated and wholly paralyzed the old aristocracy, and so left the land to the harsh mercies of the poor white trash, now its masters. The war, of course, was not a complete massacre. It spared a decent number of first-rate Southerners—perhaps even some of the very best. Moreover, other countries, notably France and Germany, have survived far more staggering butcheries, and even showed marked progress thereafter. But the war not only cost a great many valuable lives; it also brought bankruptcy, demoralization and despair in its train—and so the majority of the first-rate Southerners that were left, broken in spirit and unable to live under the new dispensation, cleared out. A few went to South America, to Egypt, to the Far East. Most came north. They were fecund; their progeny is widely dispersed, to the great benefit of the North. A Southerner of good blood almost always does well in the North. He finds, even in the big cities, surroundings fit for a man of condition. His peculiar qualities have a high social value, and are esteemed. He is welcomed by the codfish aristocracy as one palpably superior. But in the South he throws up his hands. It is impossible for him to stoop to the common level. He cannot brawl in politics with the grandsons of his grandfather's tenants. He is unable to share their fierce jealousy of the emerging black— the cornerstone of all their public thinking. He is anesthetic to their theological and political enthusiasms. He finds himself an alien at their feasts of soul. And so he withdraws into his tower, and is heard of no more. Cabell is almost a perfect example. His eyes, for years, were turned toward the past; he became a professor of the grotesque genealogizing that decaying aristocracies affect; it was only by a sort of accident that he discovered himself to be an artist. The South is unaware of the fact to this day; it regards Woodrow Wilson and John Temple Graves as much finer stylists, and Frank L. Stanton as an infinitely greater poet. If it has heard, which I doubt, that Cabell has been hoofed by the Comstocks, it unquestionably views that assault as a deserved rebuke to a fellow who indulges a lewd passion for fancy writing, and is a covert enemy to the Only True Christianity.

What is needed down there, before the vexatious public problems of the region may be intelligently approached, is a survey of the population by competent ethnologists and anthropologists. The immigrants of the North have been studied at great length, and anyone who is interested may now apply to the Bureau of Ethnology for elaborate data as to their racial strains, their stature and cranial indices, their relative capacity for education, and the changes that they undergo under American *Kultur*. But the older stocks of the South, and particularly the emancipated and dominant poor white trash, have never been investigated scientifically, and most of the current generalizations about them are probably wrong. For example, the generalization that they are purely Anglo-Saxon in blood. This I doubt very seriously. The chief strain down there, I believe, is Celtic rather than Saxon, particularly in the hill country. French blood, too, shows itself here and there, and so does Spanish, and so does German. The last-named entered from the northward, by way of the limestone belt just east of the Alleghenies. Again, it is very likely that in some parts of the South a good many of the plebeian whites have more than a trace of Negro blood. Interbreeding under concubinage produced some very light half-breeds at an early day, and no doubt appreciable numbers of them went over into the white race by the simple process of changing their abode. Not long ago I read a curious article by an intelligent Negro, in which he stated that it is easy for a very light Negro to pass as white in the South on account of the fact that large numbers of Southerners accepted as white have distinctly negroid features. Thus it becomes a delicate and dangerous matter for a train conductor or a hotelkeeper to challenge a suspect. But the Celtic strain is far more obvious than any of these others. It not only makes itself visible in physical stigmata —*e.g.*, leanness and dark coloring—but also in mental traits. For example, the religious thought of the South is almost precisely identical with the religious thought of Wales. There is the same naïve belief in an anthropomorphic Creator but little removed, in manner and desire, from an evangelical bishop; there is the same submission to an ignorant and impudent sacerdotal tyranny, and there is the same sharp contrast between doctrinal orthodoxy and private ethics. Read Caradoc Evans's ironical picture of the Welsh Wesleyans in his preface to "My Neighbors," and you will be instantly reminded of the Georgia and Carolina Methodists. The most booming sort of piety, in the South, is not incompatible with the theory that lynching is a benign institution. Two generations ago it was not incompatible with an ardent belief in slavery.

It is highly probable that some of the worst blood of western Europe flows in the veins of the Southern poor whites, now poor no longer. The original strains, according to every honest historian, were extremely corrupt. Philip Alexander Bruce (a Virginian of the old gentry) says in his "Industrial History of Virginia in the Seventeenth Century" that the first native-born generation was largely illegitimate. "One of the most common offenses against morality committed in the lower ranks of life in Virginia during the Seventeenth Century," he says, "was bastardy." The mothers of these bastards, he continues, were chiefly indentured servants, and "had belonged to the lowest class in their native country." Fanny Kemble Butler, writing of the Georgia poor whites of a century later, described them as "the most degraded race of human beings claiming an Anglo-Saxon origin that can be found on the face of the earth—filthy, lazy, ignorant, brutal, proud, penniless savages." The Sunday-school and the chautauqua, of course, have appreciably mellowed the descendants of these "savages," and their economic progress and rise to political power have done perhaps even more, but the marks of their origin are still unpleasantly plentiful. Every now and then they produce a political leader who puts their secret notions of the true, the good and the beautiful into plain words, to the amazement and scandal of the rest of the country. That amazement is turned into downright incredulity when news comes that his platform has got him high office, and that he is trying to execute it.

In the great days of the South the line between the gentry and the poor whites was very sharply drawn. There was absolutely no intermarriage. So far as I know there is not a single instance in history of a Southerner of the upper class marrying one of the bondwomen described by Mr. Bruce. In other societies characterized by class distinctions of that sort it is common for the lower class to be improved by extra-legal crosses. That is to say, the men of the upper class take women of the lower class as mistresses, and out of such unions spring the extraordinary plebeians who rise sharply from the common level, and so propagate the delusion that all other plebeians would do the same thing if they had the chance—in brief, the delusion that class distinctions are merely economic and conventional, and not congenital and genuine. But in the South the men of the upper classes sought their mistresses among the blacks, and after a few generations there was so much white blood in the black women that they were considerably more attractive than the unhealthy and bedraggled women of the poor whites. This preference continued into our own time. A Southerner of good family once told me in all seriousness that he had reached his majority before it ever occurred to him that a white woman might make quite as agreeable a mistress as the octaroons of his jejune fancy. If the thing has changed of late, it is not the fault of the Southern white man, but of the Southern mulatto women. The more sightly yellow girls of the region, with improving economic opportunities, have gained self-respect, and so they are no longer as willing to enter into concubinage as their grand-dams were.

As a result of this preference of the Southern gentry for mulatto mistresses there was created a series of mixed strains containing the best white blood of the South, and perhaps of the whole country. As another result the poor whites went unfertilized from above, and so missed the improvement that so constantly shows itself in the peasant stocks of other countries. It is a commonplace that nearly all Negroes who rise above the general are of mixed blood, usually with the white predominating. I know a great many Negroes, and it would be hard for me to think of an exception. What is too often forgotten is that this white blood is not the blood of the poor whites but that of the old gentry. The mulatto girls of the early days despised the poor whites as creatures distinctly inferior to Negroes, and it was thus almost unheard of for such a girl to enter into relations with a man of that submerged class. This aversion was based upon a sound instinct. The Southern mulatto of today is a proof of it. Like all other half-breeds he is an unhappy man, with disquieting tendencies toward anti-social habits of thought, but he is intrinsically a better animal than the pure-blooded descendant of the old poor whites, and he not infrequently demonstrates it. It is not by accident that the Negroes of the South are making faster progress, culturally, than the masses of the whites. It is not by accident that the only visible esthetic activity in the South is in their hands. No Southern composer has ever written music so good as that of half a dozen white-black composers who might be named. Even in politics, the Negro reveals a curious superiority. Despite the fact that the race question has been the main political concern of the Southern whites for two generations, to the practical exclusion of everything else, they have contributed nothing to its discussion that has impressed the rest of the world so deeply and so favorably as three or four books by Southern Negroes.

Entering upon such themes, of course, one must resign one's self to a vast misunderstanding and abuse. The South has not only lost its old capacity for producing ideas; it has also taken on the worst intolerance of ignorance and stupidity. Its prevailing mental attitude for several decades past has been that of its own hedge ecclesiastics. All who dissent from its orthodox doctrines are scoundrels. All who presume to discuss its ways realistically are damned. I have had, in my day, several experiences in point. Once, after I had published an article on some phase of the eternal race question,[2] a leading Southern newspaper replied by printing a column of denunciation of my father, then dead nearly twenty years—a philippic placarding him as an ignorant foreigner of dubious origin, inhabiting "the Baltimore ghetto" and speaking a dialect recalling that of Weber & Fields—two thousand words of incandescent nonsense, utterly false and beside the point, but exactly meeting the latter-day Southern notion of effective controversy. Another time, I published a short discourse on lynching, arguing that the sport was popular in the South because the backward culture of the region denied the populace more seemly recreations. Among such recreations I mentioned those afforded by brass bands, symphony orchestras, boxing matches, amateur athletic contests, horse races, and so on. In reply another great Southern journal denounced me as a man "of wineshop temperament, brass-jewelry tastes and pornographic predilections." In other words, brass bands, in the South, are classed with brass jewelry, and both are snares of the devil! To advocate setting up symphony orchestras is pornography! . . . Alas, when the touchy Southerner attempts a greater urbanity, the result is often even worse. Some time ago a colleague of mine printed an article deploring the arrested cultural development of Georgia. In reply he received a number of protests from patriotic Georgians, and all of them solemnly listed the glories of the state. I indulge in a few specimens:

---

[2] "Si Mutare Potest Aethiops Pellum Suam," *Smart Set*, Sept., 1917, pp. 138–42.

Who has not heard of Asa G. Candler, whose name is synonymous with Coca-Cola, a Georgia product?

The first Sunday school in the world was opened in Savannah.

Who does not recall with pleasure the writings of . . . Frank L. Stanton, Georgia's brilliant poet?

Georgia was the first state to organize a Boys' Corn Club in the South—Newton county, 1904.

The first to suggest a common United Daughters of the Confederacy badge was Mrs. Raynes, of Georgia.

The first to suggest a state historian of the United Daughters of the Confederacy was Mrs. C. Helen Plane (Macon convention, 1896).

The first to suggest putting to music Heber's "From Greenland's Icy Mountains" was Mrs. F. R. Goulding, of Savannah.

And so on, and so on. These proud boasts came, remember, not from obscure private persons, but from "leading Georgians" —in one case, the state historian. Curious sidelights upon the ex-Confederate mind! Another comes from a stray copy of a Negro paper. It describes an ordinance passed by the city council of Douglas, Ga., forbidding any trousers presser, on penalty of forfeiting a $500 bond, to engage in "pressing for both white and colored." This in a town, says the Negro paper, where practically all of the white inhabitants have "their food prepared by colored hands," "their babies cared for by colored hands," and "the clothes which they wear right next to their skins washed in houses where Negroes live"—houses in which the said clothes "remain for as long as a week at a time." But if you marvel at the absurdity, keep it dark! A casual word, and the united press of the South will be upon your trail, denouncing you bitterly as a scoundrelly damnyankee, a Bolshevik Jew.

Obviously, it is impossible for intelligence to flourish in such an atmosphere. Free inquiry is blocked by the idiotic certainties of ignorant men. The arts, save in the lower reaches of the gospel hymn, the phonograph and the political harangue, are all held in suspicion. The tone of public opinion is set by an upstart class but lately emerged from industrial slavery into commercial enterprise —the class of "bustling" business men, of "live wires," of commercial club luminaries, of "drive" managers, of forward-lookers and right-thinkers—in brief, of third-rate Southerners inoculated with all the worst traits of the Yankee sharper. One observes the curious effects of an old tradition of truculence upon a population now merely pushful and impudent, of an old tradition of chivalry upon a population now quite without imagination. The old repose is gone. The old romanticism is gone. The philistinism of the new type of town-boomer Southerner is not only indifferent to the ideals of the Old South; it is positively antagonistic to them. That philistinism regards human life, not as an agreeable adventure, but as a mere trial of rectitude and efficiency. It is overwhelmingly utilitarian and moral. It is inconceivably hollow and obnoxious. What remains of the ancient tradition is simply a certain charming civility in private intercourse—often broken down, alas, by the hot rages of Puritanism, but still generally visible. The Southerner, at his worst, is never quite the surly cad that the Yankee is. His sensitiveness may betray him into occasional bad manners, but in the main he is a pleasant fellow—hospitable, polite, good-humored, even jovial. . . . But a bit absurd. . . . A bit pathetic.

Criticism of Criticism

of Criticism

‹‹‹‹‹‹‹‹‹‹‹‹‹‹‹‹‹‹‹‹‹‹‹‹‹‹‹‹‹‹‹›››››››››››››››››››››››››››››››

VERY now and then, a sense of the futility of their daily endeavors falling suddenly upon them, the critics of Christendom turn to a somewhat sour and depressing consideration of the nature and objects of their own craft. That is to say, they turn to criticizing criticism. What is it in plain words? What is its aim, exactly stated in legal terms? How far can't it go? What good can it do? What is its normal effect upon the artist and the work of art?

Such a spell of self-searching has been in progress for several years past, and the critics of various countries have contributed theories of more or less lucidity and plausibility to the discussion. Their views of their own art, it appears, are quite as divergent as their views of the arts they more commonly deal with. One group argues, partly by direct statement and partly by attacking all other groups, that the one defensible purpose of the critic is to encourage the virtuous and oppose the sinful—in brief, to police the fine arts and so hold them in tune with the moral order of the world. Another group, repudiating this constabulary function, argues hotly that the arts have nothing to do with morality whatsoever—that their concern is solely with pure beauty. A third group holds that

(169)

the chief aspect of a work of art, particularly in the field of literature, is its aspect as psychological document—that if it doesn't help
men to know themselves it is nothing. A fourth group reduces the
thing to an exact science, and sets up standards that resemble algebraic formulae—this is the group of metrists, of contrapuntists and
of those who gabble of light-waves. And so, in order, follow groups
five, six, seven, eight, nine, ten, each with its theory and its proofs.

Against the whole corps, moral and aesthetic, psychological
and algebraic, stands Major J. E. Spingarn, U. S. A. Major Spingarn
lately served formal notice upon me that he had abandoned the
life of the academic grove for that of the armed array, and so
I give him his military title, but at the time he wrote his "Creative
Criticism" he was a professor in Columbia University, and I still
find myself thinking of him, not as a soldier extraordinarily literate,
but as a professor in rebellion. For his notions, whatever one may
say in opposition to them, are at least magnificently unprofessorial
—they fly violently in the face of the principles that distinguish the
largest and most influential group of campus critics. As witness:
"To say that poetry is moral or immoral is as meaningless as to say
that an equilateral triangle is moral and an isosceles triangle immoral." Or, worse: "It is only conceivable in a world in which
dinner-table conversation runs after this fashion: 'This cauliflower
would be good if it had only been prepared in accordance with
international law.'" One imagines, on hearing such atheism flying
about, the amazed indignation of Prof. Dr. William Lyon Phelps,
with his discovery that Joseph Conrad preaches "the axiom of
the moral law"; the "Hey, what's that!" of Prof. Dr. W. C. Brownell,
the Amherst Aristotle, with his eloquent plea for standards as iron-
clad as the Westminster Confession; the loud, patriotic alarm of
the gifted Prof. Dr. Stuart P. Sherman, of Iowa, with his maxim
that Puritanism is the official philosophy of America, and that all
who dispute it are enemy aliens and should be deported. Major
Spingarn, in truth, here performs a treason most horrible upon the
reverend order he once adorned, and having achieved it, he
straightway performs another and then another. That is to say, he
tackles all the antagonistic groups of orthodox critics seriatim, and
knocks them about unanimously—first the aforesaid agents of the
sweet and pious; then the advocates of unities, meters, all rigid

formulae; then the experts in imaginary psychology; then the historical comparers, pigeon-holers and makers of categories; finally, the professors of pure aesthetic. One and all, they take their places upon his operating table, and one and all they are stripped and anatomized.

But what is the anarchistic ex-professor's own theory?—for a professor must have a theory, as a dog must have fleas. In brief, what he offers is a doctrine borrowed from the Italian, Benedetto Croce, and by Croce filched from Goethe—a doctrine anything but new in the world, even in Goethe's time, but nevertheless long buried in forgetfulness—to wit, the doctrine that it is the critic's first and only duty, as Carlyle once put it, to find out "what the poet's aim really and truly was, how the task he had to do stood before his eye, and how far, with such materials as were afforded him, he has fulfilled it." For poet, read artist, or, if literature is in question, substitute the Germanic word *Dichter*—that is, the artist in words, the creator of beautiful letters, whether in verse or in prose. Ibsen always called himself a *Digter*, not a *Dramatiker* or *Skuespiller*. So, I daresay, did Shakespeare. . . . Well, what is this generalized poet trying to do? asks Major Spingarn, and how has he done it? That, and no more, is the critic's quest. The morality of the work does not concern him. It is not his business to determine whether it heeds Aristotle or flouts Aristotle. He passes no judgment on its rhyme scheme, its length and breadth, its iambics, its politics, its patriotism, its piety, its psychological exactness, its good taste. He may note these things, but he may not protest about them—he may not complain if the thing criticized fails to fit into a pigeon-hole. Every sonnet, every drama, every novel is *sui generis;* it must stand on its own bottom; it must be judged by its own inherent intentions. "Poets," says Major Spingarn, "do not really write epics, pastorals, lyrics, however much they may be deceived by these false abstractions; they express *themselves, and this expression is their only form.* There are not, therefore, only three or ten or a hundred literary kinds; there are as many kinds as there are individual poets." Nor is there any valid appeal *ad hominem.* The character and background of the poet are beside the mark; the poem itself is the thing. Oscar Wilde, weak and swine-like, yet wrote beautiful prose. To reject that prose on the ground that Wilde had filthy habits is as absurd as to reject "What Is Man?" on the ground that its theology is beyond the intelligence of the editor of the New York *Times*.

This Spingarn-Croce-Carlyle-Goethe theory, of course, throws a heavy burden upon the critic. It presupposes that he is a civilized and tolerant man, hospitable to all intelligible ideas and capable of reading them as he runs. This is a demand that at once rules out nine-tenths of the grown-up sophomores who carry on the business of criticism in America. Their trouble is simply that they lack the intellectual resilience necessary for taking in ideas, and particularly new ideas. The only way they can ingest one is by transforming it into the nearest related formula—usually a harsh and devastating operation. This fact accounts for their chronic inability to understand all that is most personal and original and hence most forceful and significant in the emerging literature of the country. They can get down what has been digested and redigested, and so brought into forms that they know, and carefully labeled by predecessors of their own sort—but they exhibit alarm immediately they come into the presence of the extraordinary. Here we have an explanation of Brownell's loud appeal for a tightening of standards—*i.e.*, a larger respect for precedents, patterns, rubber-stamps—and here we have an explanation of Phelps' inability to comprehend the colossal phenomenon of Dreiser, and of Boynton's childish nonsense about realism, and of Sherman's effort to apply the Espionage Act to the arts, and of More's querulous enmity to romanticism, and of all the fatuous pigeon-holing that passes for criticism in the more solemn literary periodicals.

As practiced by all such learned and diligent but essentially ignorant and unimaginative men, criticism is little more than a branch of homiletics. They judge a work of art, not by its clarity and sincerity, not by the force and charm of its ideas, not by the technical virtuosity of the artist, not by his originality and artistic courage, but simply and solely by his orthodoxy. If he is what is called a "right thinker," if he devotes himself to advocating the transient platitudes in a sonorous manner, then he is worthy of respect. But if he lets fall the slightest hint that he is in doubt about any of them, or, worse still, that he is indifferent, then he is a scoundrel, and hence, by their theory, a bad artist. Such pious piffle is horribly familiar among us. I do not exaggerate its terms. You will find it running through the critical writings of practically all the dull fellows who combine criticism with tutoring; in the words of many of them it is stated in the plainest way and defended with much heat, theological and pedagogical. In its baldest form it shows itself in the doctrine that it is scandalous for an artist —say a dramatist or a novelist—to depict vice as attractive. The fact that vice, more often than not, undoubtedly *is* attractive—else why should it ever gobble any of us?—is disposed of with a lofty gesture. What of it? say these birchmen. The artist is not a reporter, but a Great Teacher. It is not his business to depict the world as it is, but as it ought to be.

Against this notion American criticism makes but feeble headway. We are, in fact, a nation of evangelists; every third American devotes himself to improving and lifting up his fellow-citizens, usually by force; the messianic delusion is our national disease. Thus the moral *Privatdozenten* have the crowd on their side, and it is difficult to shake their authority; even the vicious are still in favor of crying vice down. "Here is a novel," says the artist. "Why didn't you write a tract?" roars the professor—and down the chute go novel and novelist. "This girl is pretty," says the painter. "But she has left off her undershirt," protests the headmaster—and off goes the poor dauber's head. At its mildest, this balderdash takes the form of the late Hamilton Wright Mabie's "White List of Books"; at its worst, it is comstockery, an idiotic and abominable thing. Genuine criticism is as impossible to such inordinately narrow and cocksure men as music is to a man who is tone-deaf. The critic, to interpret his artist, even to understand his artist, must be able to get into the mind of his artist; he must feel and comprehend the vast pressure of the creative passion; as Major Spingarn says, "aesthetic judgment and artistic creation are instinct with the same vital life." This is why all the best criticism of the world has been written by men who have had within them, not only the reflective and analytical faculty of critics, but also the gusto of artists—Goethe, Carlyle, Lessing, Schlegel, Saint-Beuve, and, to drop a story or two, Hazlitt, Hermann Bahr, Georg Brandes and James Huneker. Huneker, tackling "Also sprach Zarathustra," revealed its content in illuminating flashes. But tackled by Paul Elmer More, it became no more than a dull student's exercise, ill-naturedly corrected. . . .

So much for the theory of Major J. E. Spingarn, U. S. A., late professor of modern languages and literatures in Columbia University. Obviously, it is a far sounder and more stimulating theory than any of those cherished by the other professors. It demands that the critic be a man of intelligence, of toleration, of wide information, of genuine hospitality to ideas, whereas the others only demand that he have learning, and accept anything as learning that has been said before. But once he has stated his doctrine, the ingenious ex-professor, professor-like, immediately begins to corrupt it by claiming too much for it. Having laid and hatched, so to speak, his somewhat stale but still highly nourishing egg, he begins to argue fatuously that the resultant flamingo is the whole mustering of the critical *Aves*. But the fact is, of course, that criticism, as humanly practiced, must needs fall a good deal short of this intuitive re-creation of beauty, and what is more, it must go a good deal further. For one thing, it must be interpretation in terms that are not only exact but are also comprehensible to the reader, else it will leave the original mystery as dark as before— and once interpretation comes in, paraphrase and transliteration come in. What is recondite must be made plainer; the transcendental, to some extent at least, must be done into common modes of thinking. Well, what are morality, trochaics, hexameters, movements, historical principles, psychological maxims, the dramatic unities—what are all these save common modes of thinking, short cuts, rubber stamps, words of one syllable? Moreover, beauty as we know it in this world is by no means the apparition *in vacuo* that Dr. Spingarn seems to see. It has its social, its political, even its moral implications. The finale of Beethoven's C minor Symphony is not only colossal as music; it is also colossal as revolt; it says something against something. Yet more, the springs of beauty are not within itself alone, nor even in genius alone, but often in things without. Brahms wrote his Deutsches Requiem, not only because he was a great artist, but also because he was a good German. And in Nietzsche there are times when the divine afflatus takes a back seat, and the *spirochaetae* have the floor.

Major Spingarn himself seems to harbor some sense of this limitation on his doctrine. He gives warning that "the poet's intention must be judged at the moment of the creative act"— which opens the door enough for many an ancient to creep in. But limited or not, he at least clears off a lot of moldy rubbish, and gets further toward the truth than any of his former colleagues. They waste themselves upon theories that only conceal the poet's achievement the more, the more diligently they are applied; he, at all events, grounds himself upon the sound notion that there should be free speech in art, and no protective tariffs, and no *a priori* assumptions, and no testing of ideas by mere words. The safe ground probably lies between the contestants, but nearer Spingarn. The critic who really illuminates starts off much as he starts off, but with a due regard for the prejudices and imbecilities of the world. I think the best feasible practice is to be found in certain chapters of Huneker, a critic of vastly more solid influence and of infinitely more value to the arts than all the prating pedagogues since Rufus Griswold. Here, as in the case of Poe, a sensitive and intelligent artist re-creates the work of other artists, but there also comes to the ceremony a man of the world, and the things he has to say are apposite and instructive too. To denounce moralizing out of hand is to pronounce a moral judgment. To dispute the categories is to set up a new anti-categorical category. And to admire the work of Shakespeare is to be interested in his handling of blank verse, his social aspirations, his shot-gun marriage and his frequent concessions to the bombastic frenzy of his actors, and to have some curiosity about Mr. W. H. The really competent critic must be an empiricist. He must conduct his exploration with whatever means lie within the bounds of his personal limitation. He must produce his effects with whatever tools will work. If pills fail, he gets out his saw. If the saw won't cut, he seizes a club. . . .

Perhaps, after all, the chief burden that lies upon Major Spingarn's theory is to be found in its label. The word "creative" is a bit too flamboyant; it says what he wants to say, but it probably says a good deal more. In this emergency, I propose getting rid of the misleading label by pasting another over it. That is, I propose the substitution of "catalytic" for "creative," despite the fact that "catalytic" is an unfamiliar word, and suggests the dog-Latin of the seminaries. I borrow it from chemistry, and its meaning is really quite simple. A catalyzer, in chemistry, is a substance that helps two other substances to react. For example, consider the case of ordinary cane sugar and water. Dissolve the sugar in the water and nothing happens. But add a few drops of acid and the sugar changes into glucose and fructose. Meanwhile, the acid itself is absolutely unchanged. All it does is to stir up the reaction between the water and the sugar. The process is called catalysis. The acid is a catalyzer.

Well, this is almost exactly the function of a genuine critic of the arts. It is his business to provoke the reaction between the work of art and the spectator. The spectator, untutored, stands unmoved; he sees the work of art, but it fails to make any intelligible impression on him; if he were spontaneously sensitive to it, there would be no need for criticism. But now comes the critic with his catalysis. He makes the work of art live for the spectator; he makes the spectator live for the work of art. Out of the process comes understanding, appreciation, intelligent enjoyment—and that is precisely what the artist tried to produce.

Footnote on Criticism

<<<<<<<<<<<<<<<<<<<<<<<<<<<<<>>>>>>>>>>>>>>>>>>>>>>>>>>>

NEARLY all the discussions of criticism that I am ac
quainted with start off with a false assumption, to wit,
that the primary motive of the critic, the impulse which
makes a critic of him instead of, say, a politician, or a stockbroker,
is pedagogical—that he writes because he is possessed by a passion
to advance the enlightenment, to put down error and wrong, to
disseminate some specific doctrine: psychological, epistemological,
historical, or aesthetic. This is true, it seems to me, only of bad
critics, and its degree of truth increases in direct ratio to their
badness. The motive of the critic who is really worth reading—
the only critic of whom, indeed, it may be said truthfully that it is
at all possible to read him, save as an act of mental discipline—is
something quite different. That motive is not the motive of the
pedagogue, but the motive of the artist. It is no more and no less
than the simple desire to function freely and beautifully, to give
outward and objective form to ideas that bubble inwardly and
have a fascinating lure in them, to get rid of them dramatically and
make an articulate noise in the world. It was for this reason that
Plato wrote the "Republic," and for this reason that Beethoven
wrote the Ninth Symphony, and it is for this reason, to drop a
million miles, that I am writing the present essay. Everything else
is afterthought, mock-modesty, messianic delusion—in brief, affectation and folly. Is the contrary conception of criticism widely
cherished? Is it almost universally held that the thing is a brother

to jurisprudence, advertising, laparotomy, chautauqua lecturing and the art of the schoolmarm? Then certainly the fact that it is so held should be sufficient to set up an overwhelming probability of its lack of truth and sense. If I speak with some heat, it is as one who has suffered. When, years ago, I devoted myself diligently to critical pieces upon the writings of Theodore Dreiser, I found that practically every one who took any notice of my proceedings at all fell into either one of two assumptions about my underlying purpose: (*a*) that I had a fanatical devotion for Mr. Dreiser's ideas and desired to propagate them, or (*b*) that I was an ardent patriot, and yearned to lift up American literature. Both assumptions were false. I had then, and I have now, very little interest in many of Mr. Dreiser's main ideas; when we meet, in fact, we usually quarrel about them. And I am wholly devoid of public spirit, and haven't the least lust to improve American literature; if it ever came to what I regard as perfection my job would be gone. What, then, was my motive in writing about Mr. Dreiser so copiously? My motive, well known to Mr. Dreiser himself and to every one else who knew me as intimately as he did, was simply and solely to sort out and give coherence to the ideas of Mr. Mencken, and to put them into suave and ingratiating terms, and to discharge them with a flourish, and maybe with a phrase of pretty song, into the dense fog that blanketed the Republic.

The critic's choice of criticism rather than of what is called creative writing is chiefly a matter of temperament—perhaps, more accurately of hormones—with accidents of education and environment to help. The feelings that happen to be dominant in him at the moment the scribbling frenzy seizes him are feelings inspired, not directly by life itself, but by books, pictures, music, sculpture, architecture, religion, philosophy—in brief, by some other man's feelings about life. They are thus, in a sense, second-hand, and it is no wonder that creative artists so easily fall into the theory that they are also second-rate. Perhaps they usually are. If, indeed, the critic continues on this plane—if he lacks the intellectual agility and enterprise needed to make the leap from the work of art to the vast and mysterious complex of phenomena behind it—then they *always* are, and he remains no more than a fugleman or policeman to his betters. But if a genuine artist is concealed within him—if his feelings are in any sense profound and original, and his capacity for self-expression is above the average of educated men—then he moves inevitably from the work of art to life itself, and begins to take on a dignity that he formerly lacked. It is impossible to think of a man of any actual force and originality, universally recognized as having those qualities, who spent his whole life appraising and describing the work of other men. Did Goethe, or Carlyle, or Matthew Arnold, or Sainte-Beuve, or Macaulay, or even, to come down a few pegs, Lewes, or Lowell, or Hazlitt? Certainly not. The thing that becomes most obvious about the writings of all such men, once they are examined carefully, is that the critic is always being swallowed up by the creative artist—that what starts out as the review of a book, or a play, or other work of art, usually develops very quickly into an independent essay upon the theme of that work of art, or upon some theme that it suggests—in a word, that it becomes a fresh work of art, and only indirectly related to the one that suggested it. This fact, indeed, is so plain that it scarcely needs statement. What the pedagogues always object to in, for example, the *Quarterly* reviewers is that they forgot the books they were supposed to review, and wrote long papers—often, in fact, small books —expounding ideas suggested (or not suggested) by the books under review. Every critic who is worth reading falls inevitably into the same habit. He cannot stick to his task: what is before him is always infinitely less interesting to him than what is within him. If he is genuinely first-rate—if what is within him stands the test of type, and wins an audience, and produces the reactions that every artist craves—then he usually ends by abandoning the criticism of specific works of art altogether, and setting up shop as a general merchant in general ideas, *i.e.*, as an artist working in the materials of life itself.

Mere reviewing, however conscientiously and competently it is done, is plainly a much inferior business. Like writing poetry, it is chiefly a function of intellectual immaturity. The young literatus just out of the university, having as yet no capacity for grappling with the fundamental mysteries of existence, is put to writing reviews of books, or plays, or music, or painting. Very often he does it extremely well; it is, in fact, not hard to do well, for even decayed pedagogues often do it, as such graves of the intellect as the New York *Times* bear witness. But if he continues to do it, whether well or ill, it is a sign to all the world that his growth ceased when they made him *Artium Baccalaureus.* Gradually he becomes, whether in or out of the academic grove, a professor, which is to say, a man devoted to diluting and retailing the ideas of his superiors—not an artist, not even a bad artist, but almost the antithesis of an artist. He is learned, he is sober, he is painstaking and accurate—but he is as hollow as a jug. Nothing is in him save the ghostly echoes of other men's thoughts and feelings. If he were a genuine artist he would have thoughts and feelings of his own, and the impulse to give them objective form would be irresistible. An artist can no more withstand that impulse than a politician can withstand the temptations of a job. There are no mute, inglorious Miltons, save in the hallucinations of poets. The one sound test of a Milton is that he functions as a Milton. His difference from other men lies precisely in the superior vigor of his impulse to self-expression, not in the superior beauty and loftiness of his ideas. Other men, in point of fact, often have the same ideas, or perhaps even loftier ones, but they are able to suppress them, usually on grounds of decorum, and so they escape being artists, and are respected by right-thinking persons, and die with money in the bank, and are forgotten in two weeks.

Obviously, the critic whose performance we are commonly called upon to investigate is a man standing somewhere along the path leading from the beginning that I have described to the goal. He has got beyond being a mere cataloguer and valuer of other men's ideas, but he has not yet become an autonomous artist—he is not yet ready to challenge attention with his own ideas alone. But it is plain that his motion, in so far as he is moving at all, must be in the direction of that autonomy—that is, unless one imagines him sliding backward into senile infantilism: a spectacle not unknown to literary pathology, but too pathetic to be discussed here. Bear this motion in mind, and the true nature of his aims and purposes becomes clear; more, the incurable falsity of the aims and purposes usually credited to him becomes equally clear. He is not actually trying to perform an impossible act of arctic justice upon the artist whose work gives him a text. He is not trying with mathematical passion to find out exactly what was in that artist's mind at the moment of creation, and to display it precisely and in an ecstasy of appreciation. He is not trying to bring the work discussed into accord with some transient theory of aesthetics, or ethics, or truth, or to determine its degree of departure from that theory. He is not trying to lift up the fine arts, or to defend democracy against sense, or to promote happiness at the domestic hearth, or to convert sophomores into right-thinkers, or to serve God. He is not trying to fit a group of novel phenomena into the orderly process of history. He is not even trying to discharge the catalytic office that I myself, in a romantic moment, once sought to force upon him. He is, first and last, simply trying to express himself. He is trying to arrest and challenge a sufficient body of readers, to make them pay attention to him, to impress them with the charm and novelty of his ideas, to provoke them into an agreeable (or shocked) awareness of him, and he is trying to achieve thereby for his own inner ego the grateful feeling of a function performed, a tension relieved, a *katharsis* attained which Wagner achieved when he wrote "Die Walküre," and a hen achieves every time she lays an egg.

Joseph Conrad is moved by that necessity to write romances; Bach was moved to write music; poets are moved to write poetry; critics are moved to write criticism. The form is nothing; the only important thing is the motive power, and it is the same in all cases. It is the pressing yearning of every man who has ideas in him to empty them upon the world, to hammer them into plausible and ingratiating shapes, to compel the attention and respect of his equals, to lord it over his inferiors. So seen, the critic becomes a far more transparent and agreeable fellow than ever he was in the discourses of the psychologists who sought to make him a mere appraiser in an intellectual customs house, a gauger in a distillery of the spirit, a just and infallible judge upon the cosmic bench. Such offices, in point of fact, never fit him. He always bulges over their confines. So labeled and estimated, it inevitably turns out that the specific critic under examination is a very bad one, or no critic at all. But when he is thought of, not as pedagogue, but as artist, then he begins to take on reality, and, what is more, dignity. Carlyle was surely no just and infallible judge; on the contrary, he was full of prejudices, biles, naïvetés, humors. Yet he is read, consulted, attended to. Macaulay was unfair, inaccurate, fanciful, lyrical—yet his essays live. Arnold had his faults too, and so did Sainte-Beuve, and so did Goethe, and so did many another of that line—and yet they are remembered today, and all the learned and conscientious critics of their time, laboriously concerned with the precise intent of the artists under review, and passionately determined to set it forth with god-like care and to relate it exactly to this or that great stream of ideas—all these pedants are forgotten. What saved Carlyle, Macaulay and company is as plain as day. They were first-rate artists. They could make the thing charming, and that is always a million times more important than making it true.

Truth, indeed, is something that is believed in completely only by persons who have never tried personally to pursue it to its fastnesses and grab it by the tail. It is the adoration of second-rate men—men who always receive it at second-hand. Pedagogues believe in immutable truths and spend their lives trying to determine them and propagate them; the intellectual progress of man consists largely of a concerted effort to block and destroy their enterprise. Nine times out of ten, in the arts as in life, there is actually no truth to be discovered; there is only error to be exposed. In whole departments of human inquiry it seems to me quite unlikely that the truth ever *will* be discovered. Nevertheless, the rubber-stamp thinking of the world always makes the assumption that the exposure of an error is identical with the discovery of the truth—that error and truth are simple opposites. They are nothing of the sort. What the world turns to, when it has been cured of one error, is usually simply another error, and maybe one worse than the first one. This is the whole history of the intellect in brief. The average man of today does not believe in precisely the same imbecilities that the Greek of the fourth century before Christ believed in, but the things that he *does* believe in are often quite as idiotic. Perhaps this statement is a bit too sweeping. There is, year by year, a gradual accumulation of what may be called, provisionally, truths—there is a slow accretion of ideas that somehow manage to meet all practicable human tests, and so survive. But even so, it is risky to call them absolute truths. All that one may safely say of them is that no one, as yet, has demonstrated that they are errors. Soon or late, if experience teaches us anything, they are likely to succumb too. The profoundest truths of the Middle Ages are now laughed at by schoolboys. The profoundest truths of democracy will be laughed at, a few centuries hence, even by schoolteachers.

In the department of aesthetics, wherein critics mainly disport themselves, it is almost impossible to think of a so-called truth that shows any sign of being permanently true. The most profound of principles begins to fade and quiver almost as soon as it is stated. But the work of art, as opposed to the theory behind it, has a longer life, particularly if that theory be obscure and questionable, and so cannot be determined accurately. "Hamlet," the Mona Lisa, "Faust," "Dixie," "Parsifal," "Mother Goose," "Annabel Lee," "Huckleberry Finn"—these things, so baffling to pedagogy, so contumacious to the categories, so mysterious in purpose and utility—these things live. And why? Because there is in them the flavor of salient, novel and attractive personality, because the quality that shines from them is not that of correct demeanor but that of creative passion, because they pulse and breathe and speak, because they are genuine works of art. So with criticism. Let us forget all the heavy effort to make a science of it; it is a fine art, or nothing. If the critic, retiring to his cell to concoct his treatise upon a book or play or what-not, produces a piece of writing that shows sound structure, and brilliant color, and the flash of new and persuasive ideas, and civilized manners, and the charm of an uncommon personality in free function, then he has given something to the world that is worth having, and sufficiently justified his existence. Is Carlyle's "Frederick" true? Who cares? As well ask if the Parthenon is true, or the C minor Symphony, or "Wiener Blut." Let the critic who is an artist leave such necropsies to professors of aesthetics, who can no more determine the truth than he can, and will infallibly make it unpleasant and a bore.

It is, of course, not easy to practice this abstention. Two forces, one within and one without, tend to bring even a Hazlitt or a Huneker under the campus pump. One is the almost universal human susceptibility to messianic delusions—the irresistible

tendency of practically every man, once he finds a crowd in front
of him, to strut and roll his eyes. The other is the public demand,
born of such long familiarity with pedagogical criticism that no
other kind is readily conceivable, that the critic teach something
as well as say something—in the popular phrase, that he be constructive. Both operate powerfully against his free functioning,
and especially the former. He finds it hard to resist the flattery of
his customers, however little he may actually esteem it. If he knows
anything at all, he knows that his following, like that of every
other artist in ideas, is chiefly made up of the congenitally sub-
altern type of man and woman—natural converts, lodge joiners,
me-toos, stragglers after circus parades. It is precious seldom
that he ever gets a positive idea out of them; what he usually
gets is mere unintelligent ratification. But this troop, despite its
obvious failings, corrupts him in various ways. For one thing, it
enormously reenforces his belief in his own ideas, and so tends to
make him stiff and dogmatic—in brief, precisely everything that
he ought not to be. And for another thing, it tends to make him
(by a curious contradiction) a bit pliant and politic: he begins
to estimate new ideas, not in proportion as they are amusing or
beautiful, but in proportion as they are likely to please. So beset,
front and rear, he sometimes sinks supinely to the level of a professor, and his subsequent proceedings are interesting no more.
The true aim of a critic is certainly not to make converts. He must
know that very few of the persons who are susceptible to con-
version are worth converting. Their minds are intrinsically flabby
and parasitical, and it is certainly not sound sport to agitate minds
of that sort. Moreover, the critic must always harbor a grave doubt
about most of the ideas that they lap up so greedily—it must oc-
cur to him not infrequently, in the silent watches of the night,
that much that he writes is sheer buncombe. As I have said, I can't
imagine any idea—that is, in the domain of aesthetics—that is
palpably and incontrovertibly sound. All that I am familiar with,
and in particular all that I announce most vociferously, seem to
me to contain a core of quite obvious nonsense. I thus try to avoid
cherishing them too lovingly, and it always gives me a shiver to
see any one else gobble them at one gulp. Criticism, at bottom,
is indistinguishable from skepticism. Both launch themselves,

the one by aesthetic presentations and the other by logical presentations, at the common human tendency to accept whatever is approved, to take in ideas ready-made, to be responsive to mere rhetoric and gesticulation. A critic who believes in anything absolutely is bound to that something quite as helplessly as a Christian is bound to the Freudian garbage in the Book of Revelation. To that extent, at all events, he is unfree and unintelligent, and hence a bad critic.

The demand for "constructive" criticism is based upon the same false assumption that immutable truths exist in the arts, and that the artist will be improved by being made aware of them. This notion, whatever the form it takes, is always absurd—as much so, indeed, as its brother delusion that the critic, to be competent, must be a practitioner of the specific art he ventures to deal with, *i. e.,* that a doctor, to cure a belly-ache, must have a belly-ache. As practically encountered, it is disingenuous as well as absurd, for it comes chiefly from bad artists who tire of serving as performing monkeys, and crave the greater ease and safety of sophomores in class. They demand to be taught in order to avoid being knocked about. In their demand is the theory that instruction, if they could get it, would profit them—that they are capable of doing better work than they do. As a practical matter, I doubt that this is ever true. Bad poets never actually grow any better; they invariably grow worse and worse. In all history there has never been, to my knowledge, a single practitioner of any art who, as a result of "constructive" criticism, improved his work. The curse of all the arts, indeed, is the fact that they are constantly invaded by persons who are not artists at all—persons whose yearning to express their ideas and feelings is unaccompanied by the slightest capacity for charming expression—in brief, persons with absolutely nothing to say. This is particularly true of the art of letters, which interposes very few technical obstacles to the vanity and garrulity of such invaders. Any effort to teach them to write better is an effort wasted, as every editor discovers for himself; they are as incapable of it as they are of jumping over the moon. The only sort of criticism that can deal with them to any profit is the sort that employs them frankly as laboratory animals. It cannot cure them, but it can at least make an amusing and perhaps edifying show of them. It is idle to argue that the good in them is thus destroyed with the bad. The simple answer is that there *is* no good in them. Suppose Poe had wasted his time trying to dredge good work out of Rufus Dawes, author of "Geraldine." He would have failed miserably—and spoiled a capital essay, still diverting after three-quarters of a century. Suppose Beethoven, dealing with Gottfried Weber, had tried laboriously to make an intelligent music critic of him. How much more apt, useful and durable the simple note: "Arch-ass! Double-barreled ass!" Here was absolutely sound criticism. Here was a judgment wholly beyond challenge. Moreover, here was a small but perfect work of art.

Upon the low practical value of so-called constructive criticism I can offer testimony out of my own experience. My books are commonly reviewed at great length, and many critics devote themselves to pointing out what they conceive to be my errors, both of fact and of taste. Well, I cannot recall a case in which any suggestion offered by a constructive critic has helped me in the slightest, or even actively interested me. Every such wet-nurse of letters has sought fatuously to make me write in a way differing from that in which the Lord God Almighty, in His infinite wisdom, impels me to write—that is, to make me write stuff which, coming from me, would be as false as an appearance of decency in a Congressman. All the benefits I have ever got from the critics of my work have come from the destructive variety. A hearty slating always does me good, particularly if it be well written. It begins by enlisting my professional respect; it ends by making me examine my ideas coldly in the privacy of my chamber. Not, of course, that I usually revise them, but I at least examine them. If I decide to hold fast to them, they are all the dearer to me thereafter, and I expound them with a new passion and plausibility. If, on the contrary, I discern holes in them, I shelve them in a *pianissimo* manner, and set about hatching new ones to take their place. But constructive criticism irritates me. I do not object to being denounced, but I can't abide being schoolmastered, especially by men I regard as imbeciles.

I find, as a practicing critic, that very few men who write books are even as tolerant as I am—that most of them, soon or late, show signs of extreme discomfort under criticism, however polite its terms. Perhaps this is why enduring friendships between authors and critics are so rare. All artists, of course, dislike one another more or less, but that dislike seldom rises to implacable enmity, save between opera singer and opera singer, and creative author and critic. Even when the latter two keep up an outward show of good will, there is always bitter antagonism under the surface. Part of it, I daresay, arises out of the impossible demands of the critic, particularly if he be tinged with the constructive madness. Having favored an author with his good opinion, he expects the poor fellow to live up to that good opinion without the slightest compromise or faltering, and this is commonly beyond human power. He feels that any letdown compromises *him* —that his hero is stabbing him in the back, and making him ridiculous—and this feeling rasps his vanity. The most bitter of all literary quarrels are those between critics and creative artists, and most of them arise in just this way. As for the creative artist, he on his part naturally resents the critic's air of pedagogical superiority and he resents it especially when he has an uneasy feeling that he has fallen short of his best work, and that the discontent of the critic is thus justified. Injustice is relatively easy to bear; what stings is justice. Under it all, of course, lurks the fact that I began with: the fact that the critic is himself an artist, and that his creative impulse, soon or late, is bound to make him neglect the punctilio. When he sits down to compose his criticism, his artist ceases to be a friend, and becomes mere raw material for his work of art. It is my experience that artists invariably resent this cavalier use of them. They are pleased so long as the critic confines himself to the modest business of interpreting them— preferably in terms of their own estimate of themselves—but the moment he proceeds to adorn their theme with variations of his own, the moment he brings new ideas to the enterprise and begins contrasting them with their ideas, that moment they grow restive. It is precisely at this point, of course, that criticism becomes genuine criticism; before that it was mere reviewing. When a critic passes it he loses his friends. By becoming an artist, he becomes the foe of all other artists.

But the transformation, I believe, has good effects upon him:

it makes him a better critic. Too much *Gemütlichkeit* is as fatal to criticism as it would be to surgery or politics. When it rages un-impeded it leads inevitably either to a dull professorial sticking on of meaningless labels or to log-rolling, and often it leads to both. One of the most hopeful symptoms of the new *Aufklärung* in the Republic is the revival of acrimony in criticism—the renais-sance of the doctrine that aesthetic matters are important, and that it is worth the while of a healthy male to take them seriously, as he takes business, sport and amour. In the days when American literature was showing its first vigorous growth, the native criticism was extraordinarily violent and even vicious; in the days when American literature swooned upon the tomb of the Puritan *Kultur* it became flaccid and childish. The typical critic of the first era was Poe, as the typical critic of the second was Howells. Poe carried on his critical jehads with such ferocity that he often got into law suits, and sometimes ran no little risk of having his head cracked. He regarded literary questions as exigent and momentous. The lofty aloofness of the don was simply not in him. When he encountered a book that seemed to him to be bad, he attacked it almost as sharply as a Chamber of Commerce would attack a fanatic preaching free speech, or the corporation of Trinity Church would attack Christ. His opponents replied in the same berserker manner. Much of Poe's surviving ill-fame, as a drunkard and dead-beat, is due to their inordinate denunciations of him. They were not content to refute him; they constantly tried to dis-pose of him altogether. The very ferocity of that ancient row shows that the native literature, in those days, was in a healthy state. Books of genuine value were produced. Literature always thrives best, in fact, in an atmosphere of hearty strife. Poe, surrounded by admiring professors, never challenged, never aroused to the emotions of revolt, would probably have written poetry indis-tinguishable from the hollow stuff of, say, Prof. Dr. George E. Woodberry. It took the persistent (and often grossly unfair and dishonorable) opposition of Griswold *et al.* to stimulate him to his highest endeavors. He needed friends, true enough, but he also needed enemies.

Today, for the first time in years, there is strife in American criticism, and the Paul Elmer Mores and Hamilton Wright Mabies are no longer able to purr in peace. The instant they fall into stiff professorial attitudes they are challenged, and often with anything but urbanity. The *ex cathedra* manner thus passes out, and free discussion comes in. Heretics lay on boldly, and the professors are forced to make some defense. Often, going further, they attempt counter-attacks. Ears are bitten on. Noses are bloodied. There are wallops both above and below the belt. I am, I need not say, no believer in any magical merit in debate, no matter how free it may be. It certainly does not necessarily establish the truth; both sides, in fact, may be wrong, and they often are. But it at least accomplishes two important effects. On the one hand, it exposes all the cruder fallacies to hostile examination, and so disposes of many of them. And on the other hand, it melodramatizes the business of the critic, and so convinces thousands of bystanders, otherwise quite inert, that criticism is an amusing and instructive art, and that the problems it deals with are important. What men will fight for seems to be worth looking into.

The Poet and His Art

<<<<<<<<<<<<<<<<<<<<<<<<<<<<<<<>>>>>>>>>>>>>>>>>>>>>>>>>>>>>>>

POETRY is two quite distinct things, and may be either or both. One is a series of words that are intrinsically musical, in clang-tint and rhythm; as the single words *cellar-door* and *sarcoma* are musical. The other is a series of ideas, false in themselves, that offer a means of emotional and imaginative escape from the harsh realities of everyday. In brief, poetry is a comforting piece of fiction set to more or less lascivious music—a slap on the back in waltz time—a grand release of longings and repressions to the tune of flutes, harps, sackbuts, psalteries and the usual strings.

As I say, poetry may be either the one thing or the other— caressing music or caressing assurance. It need not necessarily be both. Consider a familiar example from "Othello":

> *Not poppy, nor mandragora,*
> *Nor all the drowsy syrups of the world*
> *Shall ever medicine thee to that sweet sleep*
> *Which thou owed'st yesterday.*

Here the sense, at best, is surely very vague. Probably not one auditor in a hundred, hearing an actor recite those glorious lines, attaches any intelligible meaning to the archaic word *owed'st*, the cornerstone of the whole sentence. Nevertheless, the effect is stupendous. The passage assaults and benumbs the faculties like the slow movement of Schumann's Rhenish Symphony; hearing it is a sensuous debauch; the man anesthetic to it could stand unmoved in Sainte-Chapelle. One easily recalls

From *A Mencken Chrestomathy*, 1949. Included in *Prejudices: Third Series*, 1922. First printed, in part, in the *Smart Set*, June 1920. Copyright 1922, 1949 by Alfred A. Knopf, Inc. Renewal copyright 1950 by H. L. Mencken.

many other such bursts of pure music, almost meaningless but infinitely delightful—in Poe, in Swinburne, in Marlowe. Two-thirds of the charm of reading Chaucer (setting aside the Rabelaisian comedy) comes out of the mere burble of the words; the meaning, to a modern, is often extremely obscure, and sometimes downright undecipherable. The whole fame of Poe, as a poet, is based upon five short poems. Of them, three are almost pure music. Their intellectual content is of the vaguest. No one would venture to reduce them to plain English. Even Poe himself always thought of them, not as statements of poetic ideas, but as simple utterances of poetic (*i.e.,* musical) sounds.

It was Sidney Lanier, himself a poet, who first showed the dependence of poetry upon music. He had little to say, unfortunately, about the clang-tint of words; what concerned him almost exclusively was rhythm. In "The Science of English Verse," he showed that the charm of this rhythm could be explained in the technical terms of music—that all the old gabble about dactyls and spondees was no more than a dog-Latin invented by men who were fundamentally ignorant of the thing they discussed. Lanier's book was the first (and last) intelligent work ever published upon the nature and structure of the sensuous content of English poetry. He struck out into such new and far paths that the professors of prosody still lag behind him, quite unable to understand a poet who was also a shrewd critic and a first-rate musician. But if, so deeply concerned with rhythm, he marred his treatise by forgetting clang-tint, he marred it still more by forgetting content. Poetry that is all music is obviously relatively rare, for only a poet who is also a natural musician can write it, and natural musicians are much rarer in the world than poets. Ordinary poetry, average poetry, thus depends in part upon its ideational material, and perhaps even chiefly. It is the *idea* expressed in a poem, and not the mellifluousness of the words used to express it, that arrests and enchants the average connoisseur. Often, indeed, he disdains this mellifluousness, and argues that the idea ought to be set forth without the customary pretty jingling, or, at most, with only the scant jingling that lies in rhythm —in brief, he wants his ideas in the altogether, and so advocates *vers libre.*

It was another American, this time F. C. Prescott, who first gave scientific attention to the intellectual content of poetry. His book is called "Poetry and Dreams." Its virtue lies in the fact that it rejects all the customary mystical and romantic definitions of poetry, and seeks to account for the thing in straightforward psychological terms. Poetry, says Prescott, is simply the verbal materialization of a daydream, an attempt to satisfy a longing by saying that it is satisfied. In brief, poetry represents imagination's bold effort to escape from the cold and clammy facts that hedge us in—to soothe the wrinkled and fevered brow with beautiful balderdash. On the precise nature of this beautiful balderdash you can get all the information you need by opening at random the nearest book of verse. The ideas you will find in it may be divided into two main divisions. The first consists of denials of objective fact; the second of denials of subjective fact. Specimen of the first sort:

> *God's in His heaven,*
> *All's right with the world.*

Specimen of the second:

> *I am the master of my fate;*
> *I am the captain of my soul.*

All poetry (forgetting, for the moment, its possible merit as mere sound) may be resolved into either the one or the other of these imbecilities—its essential character lies in its bold flouting of what every reflective adult knows to be the truth. The poet, imagining him to be sincere, is simply one who disposes of all the horrors of life on this earth, and of all the difficulties presented by his own inner weaknesses no less, by the elementary device of denying them. Is it a well-known fact that love is an emotion that is almost as perishable as eggs—that it is biologically impossible for a given male to yearn for a given female more than a few brief years? Then the poet disposes of it by assuring his girl that he will nevertheless love her forever—more, by pledging his word of honor that he believes that *she* will love *him* forever. Is it equally notorious that there is no such thing as justice in the world —that the good are tortured insanely and the evil go free and prosper? Then the poet composes a piece crediting God with a mysterious and unintelligible system of jurisprudence, whereby the torture of the good is a sort of favor conferred upon them for their goodness. Is it of almost equally widespread report that no healthy man likes to contemplate his own inevitable death—that even in time of war, with a vast pumping up of emotion to conceal the fact, every soldier hopes and believes that he, personally, will escape? Then the poet, first carefully introducing himself into a bomb-proof, achieves strophes declaring that he is free from all such weakness—that he will deliberately seek a rendezvous with death, and laugh ha-ha when the bullet finds him.

The precise nature of the imbecility thus solemnly set forth depends, very largely, of course, upon the private prejudices and yearnings of the poet, and the reception that is given it depends, by the same token, upon the private prejudices and yearnings of the reader. That is why it is often so difficult to get any agreement upon the merits of a definite poem, *i.e.*, to get any agreement upon its capacity to soothe. There is the man who craves only the animal delights of a sort of Moslem-Methodist paradise: to him "The Frost is on the Pumpkin" is a noble poem. There is the man who yearns to get out of the visible universe altogether and tread the fields of asphodel: for him there is delight only in the mystical stuff of Crashaw, Donne, Thompson and company. There is the man who revolts against the sordid Christian notion of immortality—an eternity to be spent flapping wings with pious greengrocers and Anglican bishops; he finds *his* escape in the gorgeous blasphemies of Swinburne. There is, to make an end, the man who, with an inferiority complex eating out of his heart, is moved by a great desire to stalk the world in heroic guise: he may go to the sonorous swanking of Kipling, or he may go to something more subtle, to some poem in which the boasting is more artfully concealed, say Christina Rossetti's "When I am Dead." Many men, many complexes, many secret yearnings! They collect, of course, in groups; if the group happens to be large enough the poet it is devoted to becomes famous. Kipling's fame is thus easily explained. He appealed to the commonest of all types of men, next to the sentimental type—which is to say, he appealed to the bully and braggart type, the chest-slapping type, the patriot type. Less harshly described, to the boy type. All of us have been Kiplingomaniacs at some time or other. I was myself a very ardent one at 17, and wrote many grandiloquent sets of verse in the manner of "Tommy Atkins" and "Fuzzy-Wuzzy." But if the gifts of observation and reflection have been given to us, we get over it. There comes a time when we no longer yearn to be heroes, but seek only ease— maybe even hope for quick extinction. Then we turn to Swinburne and "The Garden of Proserpine"—more false assurances, more mellifluous play-acting, another tinkling make-believe—but how sweet on blue days!

One of the things to remember here (too often it is forgotten, and Prescott deserves favorable mention for stressing it) is that a man's conscious desires are not always identical with his subconscious longings; in fact, the two are often directly antithetical. The real man lies in the depths of the subconscious, like a carp lurking in mud. His conscious personality is largely a product of his environment—the reaction of his subconscious to the prevailing notions of what is meet and seemly. Here, of course, I wander into platitude, for the news that all men are frauds was already stale in the days of Hammurabi. Freud simply translated the fact into pathological terms, added a bedroom scene, and so laid the foundations for his psychoanalysis. He made a curious mistake when he brought sex into the foreground of his new magic. He was, of course, quite right when he argued that, in civilized societies, sex impulses were more apt to be suppressed than any other natural impulses, and that the subconscious thus tends to be crowded with their ghosts. But in considering sex impulses, he forgot sex imaginings. Digging out, by painful cross-examination in a darkened room, some startling tale of carnality in his patient's past, he committed the incredible folly of assuming it to be literally true. More often than not, I believe, it was a mere piece of boasting, a materialization of desire—in brief, a poem. He should have psychoanalyzed a few poets instead of wasting all his time upon psychopathic women with sclerotic husbands. He would have dredged amazing things out of their subconsciouses, heroic as well as amorous. Imagine the billions of Boers, Germans, Irishmen and Hindus that Kipling would have confessed to killing!

A man's preferences in poetry constitute an excellent means of estimating his inner cravings and credulities. The music disarms his critical sense, and he confesses to cherishing ideas that he would repudiate with indignation if they were put into plain words. I say he cherishes those ideas. Maybe he simply tolerates them unwillingly; maybe they are no more than inescapable heritages from his barbarous ancestors, like his vermiform appendix. Think of the poems you like, and you will come upon many such intellectual fossils—ideas that you by no means subscribe to openly, but that nevertheless give you a strange joy. I put myself on the block as Exhibit A: there is my delight in Lizette Woodworth Reese's sonnet, "Tears." Nothing could do more violence to my conscious beliefs. Put into prose, the doctrine in the poem would make me laugh. There is no man in Christendom who is less a Christian than I am. But here the dead hand grabs me by the ear. My barbarian ancestors were converted to Christianity in the year 1535, and remained of that faith until near the middle of the eighteenth century. Observe, now, the load I carry; more than three hundred years of Christianity, and perhaps a thousand years (maybe even two, or three thousand) of worship of heathen gods before that—at the least, thirteen hundred years of uninterrupted belief in the immortality of the soul. Is it any wonder that, betrayed by the music of Miss Reese's Anglo-Saxon monosyllables, my conscious faith is lulled to sleep, thus giving my subconscious a chance to wallow in its immemorial superstition?

There are days when every one of us experiences this ontogenetic backfiring, and returns to an earlier stage of development. It is on such days that grown men play games, or cheer the flag, or fall in love. And it is then that they are in the mood for poetry, and get comfort out of its asseverations of the obviously not true. A truly civilized man, when he is wholly himself, derives no pleasure from hearing a poet state, as Browning stated, that all is well with the world. Such tosh not only does not please him; it definitely offends him, as he is offended by an idiotic article in a newspaper; it roils him to encounter so much stupidity in Christendom. But he may like it when he is drunk, or suffering from some low toxemia, or staggering beneath some great disaster. Then, as I say, the ontogenetic process reverses itself, and he slides back into infancy. Then he goes to poets, just as he goes to women and to theology. The very highest orders of men, perhaps, never suffer from such malaises of the spirit, or, if they suffer

(195)

from them, never succumb to them. Charles Darwin was such a man. There was never a moment in his life when he sought religious consolation, and there was never a moment when he turned to poetry; in fact, he regarded it as silly. Other first-rate men, more sensitive to the possible music in it, regard it with less positive aversion, but I have never heard of a truly first-rate man who got any permanent satisfaction out of its content. The Browning Societies of the latter part of the nineteenth century (and I choose the Browning Societies because Browning's poetry was often more or less logical in content, and thus above the ordinary intellectually) were not composed of such men as Huxley, Spencer, Lecky, Buckle and Trevelyan, but of third-rate schoolmasters, moony old maids, candidates for theosophy, literary vicars, and other such Philistines. The chief propagandist for Browning in the United States was not Henry Adams, or William Sumner, but an obscure professor of English who was also an ardent spook-chaser. And what is thus true ontogenetically is also true phylogenetically. That is to say, poetry is chiefly produced and esteemed by peoples that have not yet come to maturity. The Romans had a dozen poets of the first talent before they had a single prose writer of any skill whatsoever. So did the English.

In its character as a sort of music poetry is plainly a good deal more respectable, and makes an appeal to a far higher variety of reader, or, at all events, to a reader in a stage of greater mental clarity. A capacity for music—by which I mean melody, harmony and clang-tint—comes late in the history of every race. The savage can apprehend rhythm, but he is quite incapable of carrying a tune in any intelligible scale. The Negroes of our own South, who are commonly regarded as very musical, are actually only rhythmical; they never invent melodies, but only rhythms. And the whites to whom their barbarous dance-tunes chiefly appeal are in their own stage of culture. When one observes a room full of well-dressed men and women swaying and wriggling to the tune of some villainous mazurka from the Mississippi levees, one may assume very soundly that they are all the sort of folk who play golf and bridge. A great deal of superficial culture is compatible with that pathetic barbarism, and even a high degree of esthetic sophistication in other directions. The Greeks who built the Parthenon knew no more about music than a hog knows of predestination; they were almost as ignorant in that department as the modern Iowans or New Yorkers. It was not, indeed, until the Renaissance that music as we know it appeared in the world, and it was not until less than two centuries ago that it reached a high development. In Shakespeare's day music was just getting upon its legs in England; in Goethe's day it was just coming to full flower in Germany; in France and America it is still in the savage state. It is thus the youngest of the arts, and the most difficult, and hence the noblest. Any sane young man of twenty-two can write an acceptable sonnet, or draw a horse that will not be mistaken for an automobile, but before he may write even a bad string quartet he must go through a long and arduous training, just as he must strive for years before he may write prose that is instantly recognizable as prose, and not as a string of mere words.

The virtue of such great poets as Shakespeare does not lie in the content of their poetry, but in its music. The content of the Shakespearean plays, in fact, is often puerile, and sometimes quite incomprehensible. No scornful essays by George Bernard Shaw and Frank Harris were needed to demonstrate the fact; it lies plain in the text. One snickers sourly over the spectacle of generations of pedants debating the question of Hamlet's mental processes; the simple fact is that Shakespeare gave him no more mental processes than a Fifth Avenue rector has, but merely employed him as a convenient spout for some of the finest music ever got into words. As it is intoned on the stage by actors, it commonly loses content altogether. One cannot make out what the poor ham is saying; one can only observe that it is beautiful. There are whole speeches in the Shakespearean plays whose meaning is unknown even to scholars—and yet they remain favorites, and well deserve to. Who knows, again, what the sonnets are about? Is the bard talking about the innkeeper's wife at Oxford, or about a love affair of a pathological character? Some say one thing, and some another. But all who have ears must agree that the sonnets are extremely beautiful stuff—that the English language reaches in them the topmost heights of conceivable beauty. Shakespeare thus ought to be ranked among the musicians, along with Beethoven. As a philosopher he was a ninth-rater—but so was Ludwig. I wonder what he would have done with prose. I can't make up my mind about it. One day I believe that he would have written it as well as Dryden and the next day I begin to fear that he would have produced something as bad as Swinburne. He had the ear, but he lacked the logical sense. Poetry has done enough when it charms, but prose must also convince.

At the extremes there are indubitable poetry and incurable prose, and the difference is not hard to distinguish. Prose is simply a form of writing in which the author intends that his statements shall be accepted as conceivably true, even when they are about imaginary persons and events; its appeal is to the fully conscious and alertly reasoning man. Poetry is a form of writing in which the author attempts to disarm reason and evoke emotion, partly by presenting images that awaken a powerful response in the subconscious and partly by the mere sough and blubber of words. Poetry is not distinguished from prose, as John Livingston Lowes says in his "Convention and Revolt in Poetry," by an exclusive phraseology, but by a peculiar attitude of mind—an attitude of self-delusion, of fact-denying, of saying what isn't true. It is essentially an effort to elude facts, whereas prose is essentially a means of unearthing and exhibiting them. The gap is bridged by sentimental prose, which is half prose and half poetry. Immediately the thing acquires a literal meaning it ceases to be poetry; immediately it becomes capable of convincing an adult and perfectly sober man during the hours between breakfast and luncheon it is indisputably prose.

Once, after plowing through sixty or seventy volumes of bad verse, I described myself as a poetry-hater. The epithet was and is absurd. The truth is that I enjoy poetry as much as the next man—when the mood is on me. But what mood? The mood, in a few words, of intellectual and spiritual fatigue, the mood of revolt against the insoluble riddle of existence, the mood of disgust and despair. Poetry, then, is a capital medicine. First its sweet music lulls, and then its artful presentation of the beautifully improbable soothes and gives surcease. It is an escape from life, like religion, like alcohol, like a pretty girl. And to the mere sensuous joy in it, to the mere low delight in getting away from the world for a bit, there is added, if the poetry be good, something vastly better, something reaching out into the realm of the intelligent, to wit, appreciation of good workmanship. A sound sonnet is almost as pleasing an object as a well-written fugue. Well, who ever heard of a finer craftsman than William Shakespeare? His music was magnificent, he played superbly upon all the common emotions—and he did it magnificently, he did it with an air. No, I am no poetry-hater. But even Shakespeare I most enjoy, not on brisk mornings when I feel fit for any deviltry, but on dreary evenings when my old war wounds are troubling me, and bills are piled up on my desk, and I am too sad to work. Then I mix a stiff dram—and read poetry.

Professor Veblen

<<<<<<<<<<<<<<<<<<<<<<<<<<<<<<<<<<>>>>>>>>>>>>>>>>>>>>>>>>>>>>>>>>>>

An expansion of "Prof. Veblen and the Cow," which appeared in the *Smart Set* for May, 1919, and made a considerable pother. The events dealt with in this essay seem far away today, and perhaps a bit incredible, but they deserve to be recalled, for another and even more preposterous Veblen may be on us tomorrow. On the advent of the New Deal in 1933 some of the wizards at Washington tried to revive him, but this time he did not take and was soon forgotten again. I never met him, but years after 1919 I heard from some of his friends that my onslaught had greatly upset him, and, in fact, made him despair of the Republic. He died in 1929.

ACK in the year 1909, being engaged in a bombastic discussion with what was then known as an intellectual Socialist (like the rest of the *intelligentsia*, he succumbed to the first fife-corps of World War I, pulled down the red flag, damned Marx as a German spy, and began whooping for Woodrow Wilson and Otto Kahn), I was greatly belabored and incommoded by his long quotations from a certain Prof. Thorstein Veblen, then quite unknown to me. My antagonist manifestly attached a great deal of importance to these borrowed sagacities, for he often heaved them at me in lengths of a column or two, and urged me to read every word of them. I tried hard enough, but found it impossible going. The more I read them, in fact, the less I could make of them, and so in the end, growing impatient and impolite,

I denounced this Prof. Veblen as a geyser of pish-posh, refused to waste any more time upon his incomprehensible syllogisms, and applied myself to the other Socialist witnesses in the case, seeking to set fire to their shirts.

That old debate, which took place by mail (for the Socialist lived in levantine luxury on his country estate and I was a wage-slave attached to a city newspaper), was afterward embalmed in a dull book, and got the mild notice of a day. The book, by name, "Men vs. the Man,"[1] is now as completely forgotten as Baxter's "Saint's Rest" or the Constitution of the United States. I myself am perhaps the only man who remembers it at all, and the only thing I can recall of my opponent's argument (beyond the fact that it not only failed to convert me to Marxism, but left me a bitter and incurable scoffer at democracy in all its forms) is his curious respect for the aforesaid Veblen, and his delight in the learned gentleman's long, tortuous and (to me, at least) intolerably flapdoodlish phrases.

There was, indeed, a time when I forgot even this—when my mind was empty of the professor's very name. That was, say, from 1909 or thereabout to the middle of 1917. During those years, having lost all my former interest in Socialism, even as a species of insanity, I ceased to read its literature, and thus lost track of its Great Thinkers. The periodicals that I then gave an eye to, setting aside newspapers, were chiefly the familiar American imitations of the English weeklies of opinion, and in these the dominant Great Thinker was, first, the late Dr. William James, and, after his decease in 1910, Dr. John Dewey. The reign of James, as the illuminated will recall, was long and glorious. For three or four years running he was mentioned in every one of those American *Spectators* and *Saturday Reviews* at least once a week, and often a dozen times. Among the less somber gazettes of the Republic, to be sure, there were other heroes: Maeterlinck, Rabindranath Tagore, Judge Ben B. Lindsey, and so on, and still further down the literary and intellectual scale there were yet others: Hall Caine, Brieux and Jack Johnson among them, with paper-bag cookery and the twilight sleep to dispute their popularity. But on

---

[1] New York, 1910. The Socialist was Robert Rives La Monte.

the majestic level of the pre-Villard *Nation,* among the white and lavender peaks of professorial ratiocination, there was scarcely a serious rival to James. Now and then, perhaps, Jane Addams had a month of vogue, and during one winter there was a rage for Bergson, but taking one day with another, James held his own against the field.

His ideas, immediately they were stated, became the ideas of every pedagogue from Harvard to Leland Stanford, and the pedagogues rammed them into the skulls of the lesser *cerebelli.* When he died his ghost went marching on: it took three or four years to interpret and pigeon-hole his philosophical remains and to take down and redact his messages (via Sir Oliver Lodge, Little Bright-eyes, Wah-Wah the Indian Chief, and other gifted psychics) from the spirit world. But then, gradually, he achieved the ultimate, stupendous and irrevocable act of death, and there was a vacancy. To it Prof. Dr. Dewey was elected by the acclamation of all right-thinking and forward-looking men. He was an expert in pedagogics, metaphysics, psychology, ethics, logic, politics, pedagogical metaphysics, metaphysical psychology, psychological ethics, ethical logic, logical politics and political pedagogics. He was *artium magister, philosophiae doctor* and twice *legum doctor.* He had written a book called "How to Think." He sat in a professor's chair and caned sophomores for blowing spitballs. *Ergo,* he was the ideal candidate, and so he was nominated, elected and inaugurated, and for three years, more or less, he enjoyed a glorious reign in the groves of sapience, and the inferior *umbilicarii* venerated him as they had once venerated James.

I myself greatly enjoyed and profited by the discourses of this Prof. Dewey and was in hopes that he would last. Born of indestructible Vermont stock and a man of the highest bearable sobriety, he seemed likely to peg along almost *ad infinitum,* a gentle and charming volcano of correct thought. But it was not, alas, to be. Under cover of pragmatism, the serpent's metaphysic that James had left behind him, there was unrest beneath the surface. Young professors in remote and obscure universities, apparently as harmless as so many convicts in the death-house, were secretly flirting with new and red-hot ideas. Whole squads of them yielded in stealthy privacy to rebellious and often incomprehensible yearnings. Now and then, as if to reveal what was brewing, a hellmouth blazed and a Dr. Scott Nearing went sky-hooting through its smoke. One heard whispers of strange heresies —economic, sociological, even political. Gossip had it that pedagogy was hatching vipers, nay, was already brought to bed. But not much of this got into the home-made *Saturday Reviews* and *Athenaeums*—a hint or two maybe, but no more. In the main they kept to their old resolute demands for a pure civil-service, the budget system in Congress, the abolition of hazing at the Naval Academy, an honest primary, and justice to the Filipinos, with extermination of the Prussian monster added after August, 1914. And Dr. Dewey, on his remote Socratic Alp, pursued the calm reenforcement of the philosophical principles underlying these and all other lofty and indignant causes.

Then, of a sudden, Siss! Boom! Ah! Then, overnight, the up-springing of intellectual soviets, the headlong assault upon all the old axioms of pedagogical speculations, the nihilistic dethronement of Prof. Dewey—and rah, rah, rah for Prof. Dr. Thorstein Veblen! Veblen? Could it be—? Aye, it was! My old acquaintance! The *doctor obscurus* of my half-forgotten bout with the so-called intellectual Socialist! The Great Thinker redivivus! Here, indeed, he was again, and in a few months—almost it seemed a few days —he was all over the *Nation*, the *Dial*, the *New Republic* and the rest of them, his books and pamphlets began to pour from the the presses, the newspapers reported his every wink and whisper, and everybody who was anybody began gabbling about him. The spectacle, I do not hesitate to say, somewhat disconcerted me and even distressed me. On the one hand, I was sorry to see so learned and interesting a man as Dr. Dewey sent back to the insufferable dungeons of Columbia, there to lecture in imperfect Yiddish to classes of Grand Street Platos. And on the other hand, I shrunk supinely from the appalling job, newly rearing itself before me, of re-reading the whole canon of the singularly laborious and muggy, the incomparably tangled and unintelligible works of Prof. Veblen.

But if a sense of duty tortures a man, it also enables him to achieve prodigies, and so I managed to get through the whole infernal job. I read "The Theory of the Leisure Class" (1899), I read "The Theory of Business Enterprise" (1904), and then I read "The Instinct of Workmanship" (1914). A hiatus followed; I was racked by a severe neuralgia, with delusions of persecution. On recovering I tackled "Imperial Germany and the Industrial Revolution" (1915). Marasmus for a month, and then "The Nature of Peace and the Terms of its Perpetuation" (1917). What ensued was never diagnosed; probably it was some low infection of the mesentery or spleen. When it passed off, leaving only an asthmatic cough, I read "The Higher Learning in America" (1918), and then went to Mt. Clemens to drink the Glauber's salts. Eureka! the business was done! It had strained me, but now it was over. Alas, a good part of the agony had been needless. What I found myself aware of, coming to the end, was that practically the whole system of Prof. Veblen was in his first book and his last—that is, in "The Theory of the Leisure Class," and "The Higher Learning in America."[2] I pass on the news to literary archeologists. Read these two, and you won't have to read the others. And if even two daunt you, then read the first. Once through it, though you will have missed many a pearl and many a pain, you will have an excellent grasp of the gifted metaphysician's ideas.

For those ideas, in the main, were quite simple, and often anything but revolutionary in essence. What was genuinely remarkable about them was not their novelty, or their complexity, nor even the fact that a professor should harbor them; it was the astoundingly grandiose and rococo manner of their statement, the almost unbelievable tediousness and flatulence of the gifted headmaster's prose, his unprecedented talent for saying nothing in an august and heroic manner. There are tales of an actress of the last generation, probably Sarah Bernhardt, who could put pathos and even terror into a recitation of the multiplication table. Something of the same talent, raised to a high power, was in this Prof. Veblen. If one tunneled under his great moraines and stalagmites of words, dug down into his vast kitchen-midden of discordant and raucous polysyllables, blew up the hard, thick shell of his almost theological manner, what one found in his discourse was chiefly a mass of platitudes—the self-evident made horrifying, the obvious in terms of the staggering.

---

[2] He wrote four books between *The Higher Learning* and his death in 1929, but they were only reboilings of old bones, and attracted no notice.

Marx, I daresay, had said a good deal of it long before him, and what Marx overlooked had been said over and over again by his heirs and assigns. But Marx, at this business, labored under a technical handicap; he wrote in German, a language he actually understood. Prof. Veblen submitted himself to no such disadvantage. Though born, I believe, in These States, and resident here all his life, he achieved the effect, perhaps without employing the means, of thinking in some unearthly foreign language—say Swahili, Sumerian or Old Bulgarian—and then painfully clawing his thoughts into a copious but uncertain and book-learned English. The result was a style that affected the higher cerebral centers like a constant roll of subway expresses. The second result was a sort of bewildered numbness of the senses, as before some fabulous and unearthly marvel. And the third result, if I make no mistake, was the celebrity of the professor as a Great Thinker. In brief, he stated his hollow nothings in such high, astounding terms that inevitably arrested and blistered the right-thinking mind. He made them mysterious. He made them shocking. He made them portentous. And so, flinging them at naïve and believing souls, he made them stick and burn.

Consider this specimen—the first paragraph of Chapter XIII of "The Theory of the Leisure Class":

> In an increasing proportion as time goes on, the anthropomorphic cult, with its code of devout observances, suffers a progressive disintegration through the stress of economic exigencies and the decay of the system of status. As this disintegration proceeds, there come to be associated and blended with the devout attitude certain other motives and impulses that are not always of an anthropomorphic origin, nor traceable to the habit of personal subservience. Not all of these subsidiary impulses that blend with the bait of devoutness in the later devotional life are altogether congruous with the devout attitude or with the anthropomorphic apprehension of sequence of phenomena. Their origin being not the same, their action upon the scheme of devout life is also not in the same direction. In many ways they traverse the underlying norm of subservience or vicarious life to which the code of devout observances and the ecclesiastical and sacerdotal institutions are to be traced as their substantial basis. Through the presence of these alien motives the social and industrial regime of status gradually disintegrates, and the canon of personal sub-

servience loses the support derived from an unbroken tradition. Extraneous habits and proclivities encroach upon the field of action occupied by this canon, and it presently comes about that the ecclesiastical and sacerdotal structures are partially converted to other uses, in some measure alien to the purpose of the scheme of devout life as it stood in the days of the most vigorous and characteristic development of the priesthood.

Well, what have we here? What does this appalling salvo of rhetorical artillery signify? What was the sweating professor trying to say? Simply that in the course of time the worship of God is commonly corrupted by other enterprises, and that the church, ceasing to be a mere temple of adoration, becomes the head-quarters of these other enterprises. More simply still, that men sometimes vary serving God by serving other men, which means, of course, serving themselves. This bald platitude, which must be obvious to any child who has ever been to a church bazaar, was here tortured, worried and run through rollers until it spread out to 241 words, of which fully 200 were unnecessary. The next paragraph was even worse. In it the master undertook to explain in his peculiar dialect the meaning of "that non-reverent sense of esthetic congruity with the environment which is left as a residue of the latter-day act of worship after elimination of its anthropomorphic content." Just what did he mean by this "non-reverent sense of esthetic congruity"? I studied the whole paragraph for three days, halting only for prayer and sleep, and I came to certain conclusions. What I concluded was this: he was trying to say that many people go to church, not because they are afraid of the devil but because they enjoy the music, and like to look at the stained glass, the potted lilies and the rev. pastor. To get this profound and highly original observation upon paper, he wasted, not merely 241, but more than 300 words. To say what might have been said on a postage stamp he took more than a page in his book.

And so it went, alas, alas, in all his other volumes—a cent's worth of information wrapped in a bale of polysyllables. In "The Higher Learning in America" the thing perhaps reached its damndest and worst. It was as if the practice of that incredibly obscure and malodorous style were a relentless disease, a sort of progressive intellectual diabetes, a leprosy of the horse sense. Words were flung upon words until all recollection that there must be a meaning in them, a ground and excuse for them, were lost. One wandered in a labyrinth of nouns, adjectives, verbs, pronouns, adverbs, prepositions, conjunctions and participles, most of them swollen and nearly all of them unable to walk. It was, and is, impossible to imagine worse English, within the limits of intelligible grammar. It was clumsy, affected, opaque, bombastic, windy, empty. It was without grace or distinction and it was often without the most elementary order. The professor got himself enmeshed in his gnarled sentences like a bull trapped by barbed wire, and his efforts to extricate himself were quite as furious and quite as spectacular. He heaved, he leaped, he writhed; at times he seemed to be at the point of yelling for the police. It was a picture to bemuse the vulgar and to give the judicious grief.

Worse, there was nothing at the bottom of all this strident wind-music—the ideas it was designed to set forth were, in the overwhelming main, poor ideas, and often they were ideas that were almost idiotic. The concepts underlying, say, "The Theory of the Leisure Class" were simply Socialism and well water; the concepts underlying "The Higher Learning in America" were so childishly obvious that even the poor drudges who wrote editorials for newspapers often voiced them, and when, now and then, the professor tired of this emission of stale bosh and attempted flights of a more original character, he straightway came tumbling down into absurdity. What the reader then had to struggle with was not only intolerably bad writing, but also loose, flabby, cocksure and preposterous thinking. . . . Again I take refuge in an example. It is from Chapter IV of "The Theory of the Leisure Class." The problem before the author here had to do with the social convention which, in pre-Prohibition 1899, frowned upon the consumption of alcohol by women—at least to the extent to which men might consume it decorously. Well, then, what was his explanation of this convention? Here, in brief, was his process of reasoning:

> 1. The leisure class, which is the predatory class of feudal times, reserves all luxuries for itself, and disapproves their use by members of the lower classes, for this use takes away their charm by taking away their exclusive possession.

2. Women are chattels in the possession of the leisure class, and hence subject to the rules made for inferiors. "The patriarchal tradition . . . says that the woman, being a chattel, should consume only what is necessary to her sustenance, except so far as her further consumption contributes to the comfort or the good repute of her master."

3. The consumption of alcohol contributes nothing to the comfort or good repute of the woman's master, but "detracts sensibly from the comfort or pleasure" of her master. *Ergo*, she is forbidden to drink.

This, I believe, was a fair specimen of the Veblenian ratiocination. Observe it well, for it was typical. That is to say, it started off with a gratuitous and highly dubious assumption, proceeded to an equally dubious deduction, and then ended with a platitude which begged the whole question. What sound reason was there for believing that exclusive possession was the hallmark of luxury? There was none that I could see. It might be true of a few luxuries, but it was certainly not true of the most familiar ones. Did I enjoy a decent bath because I knew that John Smith could not afford one—or because I delighted in being clean? Did I admire Beethoven's Fifth Symphony because it was incomprehensible to Congressmen and Methodists—or because I genuinely loved music? Did I prefer kissing a pretty girl to kissing a charwoman because even a janitor may kiss a charwoman—or because the pretty girl looked better, smelled better and kissed better?

Confronted by such considerations, it seemed to me that there was little truth left in Prof. Veblen's theory of conspicuous consumption and conspicuous waste—that what remained of it, after it was practically applied a few times, was no more than a wraith of balderdash. What could have been plainer than his failure in the case of the human female? Starting off with a platitude, he ended in absurdity. No one could deny, I was willing to grant, that in a clearly limited sense, women occupied a place in the world—or, more accurately, aspired to a place in the world—that had some resemblance to that of a chattel. Marriage, the goal of their only honest and permanent hopes, invaded their individuality; a married woman (I was thinking, remember, of 1899) became the function of another individuality. Thus the appearance she presented to the world was often the mirror of her husband's egoism. A rich man hung his wife with expensive clothes and jewels for the same reason, among others, that he drove an expensive car: to notify everybody that he could afford it—in brief, to excite the envy of Marxians. But he also did it, let us hope, for another and far more powerful reason, to wit, that he delighted in her, that he loved her—and so wanted to make her gaudy and happy. This reason, to be sure, was rejected by the Marxians of the time, as it is rejected by those of ours, but nevertheless, it continued to appeal very forcibly, and so continues in our own day, to the majority of normal husbands in the nations of the West. The American husband, in particular, dresses his wife like a circus horse, not primarily because he wants to display his wealth upon her person, but because he is a soft and moony fellow and ever ready to yield to her desires, however preposterous. If any conception of her as a chattel were actively in him, even unconsciously, he would be a good deal less her slave. As it is, her vicarious practice of conspicuous waste commonly reaches such a development that her master himself is forced into renunciations—which brought Prof. Dr. Veblen's theory to self-destruction.

His final conclusion was as unsound as his premises. All it came to was a plain begging of the question. Why does a man forbid his wife to drink all the alcohol she can hold? Because, he said, it "detracts sensibly from his comfort or pleasure." In other words, it detracts from his comfort and pleasure because it detracts from his comfort and pleasure. Meanwhile, the real answer is so plain that even a professor should know it. A man forbids his wife to drink too much because, deep in his secret archives, he has records of the behavior of other women who drank too much, and is eager to safeguard his wife's connubial rectitude and his own dignity against what he knows to be certain invasion. In brief, it is a commonplace of observation, familiar to all males beyond the age of twenty-one, that once a woman is drunk the rest is a mere matter of time and place: the girl is already there. A husband, viewing this prospect, perhaps shrinks from having his chattel damaged. But let us be soft enough to think that he may also shrink from seeing humiliation and bitter regret inflicted upon one who is under his protection, and one whose dignity and happiness are precious to him, and one whom he regards with deep and (I surely hope) lasting affection. A man's grandfather is surely not his chattel, even by the terms of the Veblen theory, yet I am sure that no sane man would let the old gentleman go beyond a discreet cocktail or two if a bout of genuine bibbing were certain to be followed by the complete destruction of his dignity, his chastity and (if a Presbyterian) his immortal soul.

One more example of the Veblenian logic and I must pass on. On page 135 of "The Theory of the Leisure Class" he turned his garish and buzzing searchlight upon another problem of the domestic hearth, this time a double one. First, why do we have lawns around our country houses? Secondly, why don't we use cows to keep them clipped, instead of employing Italians, Croatians and blackamoors? The first question was answered by an appeal to ethnology: we delight in lawns because we are the descendants of "a pastoral people inhabiting a region with a humid climate"—because our dolicho-blond ancestors had flocks, and thus took a keen professional interest in grass. (The Marx *motif!* The economic interpretation of history in E flat.) But why don't *we* keep flocks? Why do we renounce cows and hire Jugo-Slavs? Because "to the average popular apprehension a herd of cattle so pointedly suggests thrift and usefulness that their presence . . . would be intolerably cheap." Plowing through a bad book from end to end, I could find nothing sillier than this. Here, indeed, the whole "theory of conspicuous waste" was exposed for precisely what it was: one per cent platitude and ninety-nine per cent nonsense. Had the genial professor, pondering his great problems, ever taken a walk in the country? And had he, in the course of that walk, ever crossed a pasture inhabited by a cow (*Bos taurus*)? And had he, making that crossing, ever passed astern of the cow herself? And had he, thus passing astern, ever stepped carelessly, and—

III

Politics

＊ · ＊ · ＊ · ＊ · ＊

From his earliest newspaper days Mencken was a commentator on politics, local, national, and international. As a journalist he wrote more in this field than in any other, and his writing was exceptionally well informed. It had much hard work behind it, including attendance at the political conventions and contact with politicians of all ranks and persuasions. Not infrequently Mencken's advice was sought by these men on matters of tactics and strategy, and sometimes even members of the judiciary would ask his views in cases with political overtones. In the last newspaper article he was to write for the Baltimore Sun he offered unsolicited advice to the Supreme Bench of Baltimore in a case being held sub judice. Negroes had been barred from playing tennis in the public parks, an order Mencken thought was silly, and the matter was on appeal. He was fully aware of the court's attitude (when cases were under advisement) toward newspaper discussions of the kind he was writing, and on the whole he approved of it, but the piece was composed with such ingenuity that the court would have made itself absurd if it had taken official notice of it.

Mencken enjoyed the company of politicians, and he had a high regard for the attractiveness and ability of many of them. But he was constantly disturbed by the gulf between their public and private views. He would know at first hand that a candidate was aware that his programs were incapable of fulfillment, and he could never accustom himself to the candidate's wholesale commitment to them. Once, when he was closeted with a Presidential candidate in the latter's drawing room on a campaign train, the matter of such promises came up. The candidate conceded that the promises he was making at every whistle stop could never be carried out, except through a miracle. "You forget," the candidate added, "that our agreement in the premises must remain

(213)

purely personal. You are not a candidate for President of the United States. I am."

Mencken's treatment of candidates for office was civil, and his weapon against those to whom he was opposed usually went no further than raillery. But when he felt the candidate or politician deserved it, his pieces could be as cruel as any written in modern times. The article on Bryan, published in its first form in the Baltimore Evening Sun *the day after Bryan's death at Dayton, Tennessee, is included here as a specimen. He also followed the curious, self-imposed rule that he would not write a completely favorable piece on any occupant of the Presidency.*

In common with all political journalists, he was free in his predictions of events to come. His most famous venture in this realm was the statement that if Roosevelt could be beaten at all, it could be "with a Chinaman, or even a Republican." This was immediately twisted by the press to "a Chinaman could beat Roosevelt." He replied after the election, when he was reminded of the prophecy, that "they didn't run a Chinaman, they ran Landon."

The Politician

<<<<<<<<<<<<<<<<<<<<<<<<<<<<<<<<<>>>>>>>>>>>>>>>>>>>>>>>>>>>>>>

HALF the sorrows of the world, I suppose, are caused by making false assumptions. If the truth were only easier to ascertain the remedy for them would consist simply of ascertaining it and accepting it. This business, alas, is usually impossible, but fortunately not always: now and then, by some occult process, half rational and half instinctive, the truth gets itself found out and an ancient false assumption goes overboard. I point, in the field of the social relations, to one which afflicted the human race for millenniums: that one, to wit, which credited the rev. clergy with a mysterious wisdom and awful powers. Obviously, it has ceased to trouble all the superior varieties of men. It may survive in those remote marches where human beings go to bed with the cows, but certainly it has vanished from the cities. Asphalt and the apostolic succession, indeed, seem to be irreconcilable enemies. I can think of no clergyman in any great American city today whose public dignity and influence are much above those of an ordinary Class I Babbitt. It is hard for even the most diligent and passionate of the ancient order to get upon the first pages of the newspapers; he must make a clown-show, discreditable to his fraying cloth, or he must blush unseen. When bishops begin launching thunderbolts against heretics, the towns do not tremble; they laugh. When elders denounce sin, sin only grows more popular. Imagine a city man getting a notice from the ordinary of his diocese that he had been excommunicated. It would trouble him far less, I venture, than his morning *Katzenjammer*.

The reason for all this is not hard to find. All the superior varieties of men—and even the lowest varieties of city workmen are at least superior to peasants—have simply rid themselves of their old belief in devils. Hell no longer affrights and palsies them, and so the magic of those who profess to save them from it no longer impresses them. That profession, I believe, was bogus, and its acceptance was therefore a false assumption. Being so, it made men unhappy; getting rid of it has delivered them. They are no longer susceptible to ecclesiastical alarms and extortions; *ergo*, they sleep and eat better. Think of what life must have been under such princes of damnation as Cotton Mather and Jonathan Edwards, with even bartenders and metaphysicians believing in them! And then compare it to life under Bishop Manning and the Rev. Dr. John Roach Straton, with only a few half-wits believing in them! Or turn to the backwoods of the Republic, where the devil is still feared, and with him his professional exterminators. In the country towns the clergy are still almost as influential as they were in Mather's day, and there, as everyone knows, they remain public nuisances, and civilized life is almost impossible. In such Neolithic regions nothing can go on without their consent, on penalty of anathema and hell-fire; as a result, nothing goes on that is worth recording. It is this survival of sacerdotal authority, I begin to believe, and not hookworm, malaria or the event of April 9, 1865, that is chiefly responsible for the cultural paralysis of the late Confederate States. The South lacks big cities; it is run by its country towns—and in every country town there is some Baptist *mullah* who rules by scaring the peasantry. The false assumption that his pretensions are sound, that he can actually bind and loose, that contumacy to him is a variety of cursing God—this false assumption is what makes the yokels so uneasy, so nervous, and hence so unhappy. If they could throw it off they would burn fewer Aframericans and sing more songs. If they could be purged of it they would be purged of Ku Kluxry too.

The cities got rid of that false assumption half a century ago, and have been making cultural progress ever since. Somewhat later they got rid of its brother, to wit, respect for government, and, in particular, respect for its visible agents, the police. That respect—traditional, and hence irrational—had been, for years, in increasingly unpleasant collision with a great body of obvious facts. The police, by assumption austere and almost sacrosanct, were gradually discovered to be, in reality, a pack of rogues and but little removed, save by superior impudence and enterprise, from the cut-throats and purse-snatchers they were set to catch. When, a few decades ago, the American people, at least in the big cities, began to accept them frankly for what they were—when the old false assumption of their integrity and public usefulness was quietly abandoned and a new and more accurate assumption of their roguery was adopted in its place—when this change was effected there was a measurable increase, I believe, in the public happiness. It no longer astonished anyone when policemen were taken in evildoing; indignation therefore abated, and with it its pains. If, before that time, the corps of Prohibition enforcement officers—*i.e.*, a corps of undisguised scoundrels with badges— had been launched upon the populace, there would have been a great roar of wrath, and much anguished gnashing of teeth. People would have felt themselves put upon, injured, insulted. But with the old false assumption about policemen removed from their minds, they met the new onslaught calmly and even smilingly. Today no one is indignant over the fact that the extortions of these new *Polizei* increase the cost of potable alcohol. The false assumption that the police are altruistic agents of a benevolent state has been replaced by the sound assumption that they are gentlemen engaged assiduously, like the rest of us, in finding meat and raiment for their families and in laying up funds to buy Liberty Bonds in the next war to end war. This is human progress, for it increases human happiness.

So much for the evidence. The deduction I propose to make from it is simply this: that a like increase would follow if the American people could only rid themselves of another and worse false assumption that still rides them—one that corrupts all their thinking about the great business of politics, and vastly augments their discontent and unhappiness—the assumption, that is, that politicians are divided into two classes, and that one of those classes is made up of good ones. I need not argue, I hope, that this assumption is almost universally held among us. Our whole politics, indeed, is based upon it, and has been based upon it since the earliest days. What is any political campaign save a concerted effort to turn out a set of politicians who are admittedly bad and put in a set who are thought to be better? The former assumption, I believe, is always sound; the latter is just as certainly false. For if experience teaches us anything at all it teaches us this: that a good politician, under democracy, is quite as unthinkable as an honest burglar. His very existence, indeed, is a standing subversion of the public good in every rational sense. He is not one who serves the common weal; he is simply one who preys upon the commonwealth. It is to the interest of all the rest of us to hold down his powers to an irreducible minimum, and to reduce his compensation to nothing; it is to his interest to augment his powers at all hazards, and to make his compensation all the traffic will bear. To argue that these aims are identical is to argue palpable nonsense. The politician, at his ideal best, never even remotely approximated in practice, is a necessary evil; at his worst he is an almost intolerable nuisance.

What I contend is simply that he would be measurably less a nuisance if we got rid of our old false assumption about him, and regarded him in the cold light of fact. At once, I believe, two-thirds of his obnoxiousness would vanish. He would remain a nuisance, but he would cease to be a swindler; the injury of having to pay freight on him would cease to be complicated by the insult of being rooked. It is the insult and not the injury that makes the deeper wounds, and causes the greater permanent damage to the national psyche. All of us have been trained, since infancy, in putting up with necessary evils, plainly recognized *as* evils. We know, for example, that the young of the human species commonly smell badly; that garbage men, bootblacks and messenger boys commonly smell worse. These facts are not agreeable, but they remain tolerable because they are universally assumed—because there is no sense of having been tricked and cozened in their perennial discovery. But try to imagine how distressing fatherhood would become if prospective fathers were all taught that the human infant radiates an aroma like the rose—if the truth came constantly as a surprise! Each fresh victim of the deception would feel that he had been basely swindled—that his own child was somehow bogus. Not infrequently, I suppose, he would be tempted to make away with it in some quiet manner, and have another—only to be shocked again. That procedure would be idiotic, admittedly, yet it is exactly the one we follow in politics. At each election we vote in a new set of politicians, insanely assuming that they are better than the set turned out. And at each election we are, as they say in the Motherland, done in.

Of late the fraud has become so gross that the plain people begin to show a great restlessness under it. Like animals in a cage, they trot from one corner to another, endlessly seeking a way out. If the Democrats win one year, it is a pretty sure sign that they will lose the next year. State after state becomes doubtful, pivotal, skittish; even the solid South begins to break. In the cities it is still worse. An evil circle is formed. First the poor taxpayers, robbed by the politicians of one great party and then by those of the other, turn to a group of free-lance rogues in the middle ground—non-partisan candidates, Liberals, reformers or whatnot: the name is unimportant. Then, flayed and pillaged by these gentry as they never were by the old-time professionals, they go back in despair to the latter, and are flayed and pillaged again. Back to Bach! Back to Tammany! Tammany reigns in New York because the Mitchel outfit was found to be intolerable—in other words, because the reformers were found to be even worse than the professionals. Is the fact surprising? Why should it be? Reformers and professionals are alike politicians in search of jobs; both are trying to bilk the taxpayers. Neither ever has any other motive. If any genuinely honest and altruistic politician had come to the surface in America in my time I'd have heard of him, for I have always frequented newspaper offices, and in a newspaper office the news of such a marvel would cause a dreadful tumult. I can recall no such tumult. The unanimous opinion of all the journalists that I know, excluding a few Liberals who are obviously somewhat balmy—they all believed, for example, that the late war would end war—is that, since the days of the national Thors and Wotans, no politician who was not out for himself, and for himself alone, has ever drawn the breath of life in the United States.

The gradual disintegration of Liberalism among us, in fact, offers an excellent proof of the truth of my thesis. The Liberals have come to grief by fooling their customers, not merely once too often, but a hundred times too often. Over and over again they have trotted out some new hero, usually from the great open spaces, only to see him taken in the immemorial malpractices within ten days. Their graveyard, indeed, is filled with cracked and upset headstones, many covered with ribald pencilings. Every time there is a scandal in the grand manner the Liberals lose almost as many general officers as either the Democrats or Republicans. Of late, racked beyond endurance by such catastrophes at home, they have gone abroad for their principal heroes; losing humor as well as hope, they now ask us to venerate such astounding paladins as the Hon. Béla Kun, a gentleman who, in any American state, would not only be in the calaboose, but actually in the death-house. But this absurdity is only an offshoot of a deeper one. Their primary error lies in making the false assumption that some politicians are better than others. This error they share with the whole American people.

I propose that it be renounced, and contend that its renunciation would greatly rationalize and improve our politics. I do not argue that there would be any improvement in our politicians; on the contrary, I believe that they would remain substantially as they are today, and perhaps grow even worse. But what I do argue is that recognizing them frankly for what they are would instantly and automatically dissipate the indignation caused by their present abominations, and that the disappearance of this indignation would promote the public contentment and happiness. Under my scheme there would be no more false assumptions and no more false hopes, and hence no more painful surprises, no more bitter resentment of fraud, no more despair. Politicians, in so far as they remained necessary, would be kept at work—but not with any insane notion that they were archangels. Their rascality would be assumed and discounted, as the rascality of the police is now assumed and discounted. Machinery would be gradually developed to limit it and counteract it. In the end, it might be utilized in some publicly profitable manner, as the insensitiveness to filth of garbage men is now utilized, as the reverence of the clergy for capitalism is now utilized. The result, perhaps, would be a world no better than the present one, but it would at least be a world more intelligent.

In all this I sincerely hope that no one will mistake me for one who shares the indignation I have spoken of—that is, for one who believes that politicians can be made good, and cherishes a fond scheme for making them so. I believe nothing of the sort. On the contrary, I am convinced that the art and mystery they practice is essentially and incurably anti-social—that they must remain irreconcilable enemies of the common weal until the end of time. But I maintain that this fact, in itself, is not a bar to their employment. There are, under Christian civilization, many necessary offices that demand the possession of anti-social talents. A professional soldier, regarded realistically, is much worse than a professional politician, for he is a professional murderer and kidnaper, whereas the politician is only a professional sharper and sneak-thief. A clergyman, too, begins to shrink and shrivel on analysis; the work he does in the world is basically almost indistinguishable from that of an astrologer, a witch-doctor or a fortuneteller. He pretends falsely that he can get sinners out of hell, and collects money from them on that promise, tacit or express. If he had to go before a jury with that pretension it would probably go hard with him. But we do not send him before a jury; we grant him his hocus-pocus on the ground that it is necessary to his office, and that his office is necessary to civilization, so-called. I pass over the journalist delicately; the time has not come to turn state's evidence. Suffice it to say that he, too, would probably wither under a stiff cross-examination. If he is no murderer, like the soldier, then he is at least a sharper and swindler, like the politician.

What I plead for, if I may borrow a term in disrepute, is simply *Realpolitik, i. e.*, realism in politics. I can imagine a political campaign purged of all the current false assumptions and false pretenses—a campaign in which, on election day, the voters went to the polls clearly informed that the choice before them was not between an angel and a devil, a good man and a bad man, an altruist and a go-getter, but between two frank go-getters, the one, perhaps, excelling at beautiful and nonsensical words and the other at silent and prehensile deeds—the one a chautauqua orator and the other a porch-climber. There would be, in that choice, something candid, free and exhilarating. Buncombe would be adjourned. The voter would make his selection in the full knowledge of all the facts, as he makes his selection between two heads of cabbage, or two evening papers, or two brands of chewing tobacco. Today he chooses his rulers as he buys bootleg whiskey, never knowing precisely what he is getting, only certain that it is not what it pretends to be. The Scotch may turn out to be wood alcohol or it may turn out to be gasoline; in either case it is not Scotch. How much better if it were plainly labeled, for wood alcohol and gasoline both have their uses—higher uses, indeed, than Scotch. The danger is that the swindled and poisoned consumer, despairing of ever avoiding them when he doesn't want them, may prohibit them even when he does want them, and actually enforce his own prohibition. The danger is that the hopeless voter, forever victimized by his false assumption about politicians, may in the end gather such ferocious indignation that he will abolish them teetotally and at one insane swoop, and so cause government by the people, for the people and with the people to perish from this earth.

Imperial Purple

<<<<<<<<<<<<<<<<<<<<<<<<<<<<<<<<<>>>>>>>>>>>>>>>>>>>>>>>>>>>>>>>>>

Most of the rewards of the Presidency, in these days, have come to be very trashy. The President continues, of course, to be an eminent man, but only in the sense that Jack Dempsey, Lindbergh, Babe Ruth and Henry Ford have been eminent men. He sees little of the really intelligent and amusing people of the country: most of them, in fact, make it a sort of point of honor to avoid him. His time is put in mainly with shabby politicians and other such designing fellows—in brief, with rogues and ignoramuses. When he takes a little holiday his customary companions are vermin that no fastidious man would consort with. Dr. Harding, forced to entertain them, resorted to poteen as an analgesic; Dr. Coolidge loaded them aboard the *Mayflower*, and then fled to his cabin, took off his vest and shirt, and went to sleep; Dr. Hoover hauled them to the Rapidan at 60 miles an hour, and back at 80 or 90.

The honors that are heaped upon a President are seldom of a kind to impress and content a civilized man. People send him turkeys, opossums, pieces of wood from the *Constitution*, goldfish, carved peach kernels, models of the state capitols of Wyoming and Arkansas, and pressed flowers from the Holy Land. Once a year some hunter in Montana or Idaho sends him 20 pounds of bear-steak, usually collect. It arrives in a high state, and has to be fed to the White House dog. He receives 20 or 30 chain-prayer letters every day, and fair copies of 40 or 50 sets of verse. Colored clergy-

From *A Mencken Chrestomathy*, 1949. Originally printed in the Baltimore *Evening Sun*, Aug. 17, 1931.

men send him illustrated Bibles, madstones and boxes of lucky powders, usually accompanied by applications for appointment as collector of customs at New Orleans, Mobile or Wilmington, N. C., or as Register of the Treasury. His public rewards come in the form of LL.D.'s from colleges eager for the publicity—and on the same day others precisely like it are given to a champion lawn-tennis player, a banker known to be without heirs of his body, and a general in the army. No one ever thinks to give him any other academic honor; he is never made a Litt.D., a D.D., an S.T.D., a D.D.S., or a J.U.D., but always an LL.D. Dr. Hoover, to date, has 30 or 40 such degrees. He apparently knows as little about law as a court catchpoll, but he is more solidly *legum doctor* than Blackstone or Pufendorf.

The health of a President is watched very carefully, not only by the Vice-President but also by medical men detailed for the purpose by the army or navy. These medical men have high-sounding titles, and perform the duties of their office in full uniform, with swords on one side and stethoscopes on the other. The diet of their imperial patient is rigidly scrutinized. If he eats a few peanuts they make a pother; if he goes in for some steamed hard crabs at night, washed down by what passes in Washington for malt liquor, they complain to the newspapers. Every morning they look at his tongue, take his pulse and temperature, determine his blood pressure, and examine his eye-grounds and his knee-jerks. The instant he shows the slightest sign of being upset they clap him into bed, post Marines to guard him, put him on a regimen fit for a Trappist, and issue bulletins to the newspapers.

When a President goes traveling he never goes alone, but always with a huge staff of secretaries, Secret Service agents, doctors, nurses, and newspaper reporters. Even so stingy a fellow as Dr. Coolidge had to hire two whole Pullman cars to carry his entourage. The cost, to be sure, is borne by the taxpayers, but the President has to put up with the company. As he rolls along thousands of boys rush out to put pennies on the track, and now and then one of them loses a finger or a toe, and the train has to be backed up to comfort his mother, who, it usually turns out, cannot speak English. When the train arrives anywhere all the town bores and scoundrels gather to greet the Chief Magistrate, and that night he has to eat a bad dinner, and to listen to three hours of bad speeches.

The President has less privacy than any other American. Thousands of persons have the right of access to him, beginning with the British Ambassador and running down to the secretary of the Republican county committee of Ziebach county, South Dakota. Among them are the 96 members of the United States Senate, perhaps the windiest and most tedious group of men in Christendom. If a Senator were denied admission to the White House the whole Senate would rise in indignation. And if the minister from Albania were kicked out even the French and British Ambassadors would join in protesting. Many of these gentlemen drop in, not because they have anything to say, but simply to prove to their employers or customers that they can do it. How long they stay is only partly determined by the President himself. Dr. Coolidge used to get rid of them by falling asleep in their faces, but that device is impossible to Presidents with a more active interest in the visible world. It would not do to have them heaved out by the Secret Service men or by the White House police, or to insult and affront them otherwise, for many of them have wicked tongues. On two occasions within historic times Presidents who were irritable with such bores were reported in Washington to be patronizing the jug, and it took a lot of fine work to put down the scandal.

All day long the right hon. lord of us all sits listening solemnly to bores and quacks. Anon a secretary rushes in with the news that some eminent movie actor or football coach has died, and the President must seize a pen and write a telegram of condolence to the widow. Once a year he is repaid by receiving a cable on his birthday from King George. Such things are cherished by Presidents, and they leave them, *post mortem*, to the Library of Congress. Anon there comes a day of public ceremonial, and a chance to make a speech. Alas, it must be made at the annual banquet of some organization that is discovered, at the last minute, to be made up mainly of gentlemen under indictment, or at the tomb of some statesman who escaped impeachment by a hair. Twenty million voters with IQ's below 60 have their ears glued to the radio; it takes four days' hard work to concoct a speech without a sensible word in it. Next day a dam must be opened somewhere. Four Senators get drunk and try to neck a lady politician built like an overloaded tramp steamer. The Presidential automobile runs over a dog. It rains.

In Memoriam: W. J. B.

In its first form this was printed in the Baltimore *Evening Sun*, July 27, 1925, the day after Bryan's death at Dayton, Tenn. I reworked it for the *American Mercury*, Oct., 1925. My adventures as a newspaper correspondent at the Scopes trial are told in my *Newspaper Days* (New York, 1943).

Has it been duly marked by historians that William Jennings Bryan's last secular act on this globe of sin was to catch flies? A curious detail, and not without its sardonic overtones. He was the most sedulous fly-catcher in American history, and in many ways the most successful. His quarry, of course, was not *Musca domestica* but *Homo neandertalensis*. For forty years he tracked it with coo and bellow, up and down the rustic backways of the Republic. Wherever the flambeaux of chautauqua smoked and guttered, and the bilge of idealism ran in the veins, and Baptist pastors dammed the brooks with the sanctified, and men gathered who were weary and heavy laden, and their wives who were full of Peruna and as fecund as the shad (*Alosa sapidissima*), there the indefatigable Jennings set up his traps and spread his bait. He knew every country town in the South and West, and he could crowd the most remote of them to suffocation by simply winding his horn. The city proletariat, transiently flustered by him in 1896, quickly penetrated his buncombe and would have no more of him; the cockney gallery jeered

(227)

him at every Democratic national convention for twenty-five years. But out where the grass grows high, and the horned cattle dream away the lazy afternoons, and men still fear the powers and principalities of the air—out there between the corn-rows he held his old puissance to the end. There was no need of beaters to drive in his game. The news that he was coming was enough. For miles the flivver dust would choke the roads. And when he rose at the end of the day to discharge his Message there would be such breathless attention, such a rapt and enchanted ecstasy, such a sweet rustle of amens as the world had not known since Johann fell to Herod's ax.

There was something peculiarly fitting in the fact that his last days were spent in a one-horse Tennessee village, beating off the flies and gnats, and that death found him there. The man felt at home in such simple and Christian scenes. He liked people who sweated freely, and were not debauched by the refinements of the toilet. Making his progress up and down the Main Street of little Dayton, surrounded by gaping primates from the upland valleys of the Cumberland Range, his coat laid aside, his bare arms and hairy chest shining damply, his bald head sprinkled with dust—so accoutred and on display, he was obviously happy. He liked getting up early in the morning, to the tune of cocks crowing on the dunghill. He liked the heavy, greasy victuals of the farmhouse kitchen. He liked country lawyers, country pastors, all country people. He liked country sounds and country smells.

I believe that this liking was sincere—perhaps the only sincere thing in the man. His nose showed no uneasiness when a hillman in faded overalls and hickory shirt accosted him on the street, and besought him for light upon some mystery of Holy Writ. The simian gabble of the crossroads was not gabble to him, but wisdom of an occult and superior sort. In the presence of city folks he was palpably uneasy. Their clothes, I suspect, annoyed him, and he was suspicious of their too delicate manners. He knew all the while that they were laughing at him—if not at his baroque theology, then at least at his alpaca pantaloons. But the yokels never laughed at him. To them he was not the huntsman but the prophet, and toward the end, as he gradually forsook mundane politics for more ghostly concerns, they began to elevate him in their hierarchy. When he died he was the peer of Abraham. His old enemy, Wilson, aspiring to the same white and shining robe, came down with a thump. But Bryan made the grade. His place in Tennessee hagiography is secure. If the village barber saved any of his hair, then it is curing gallstones down there today.

But what label will he bear in more urbane regions? One, I fear, of a far less flattering kind. Bryan lived too long, and descended too deeply into the mud, to be taken seriously hereafter by fully literate men, even of the kind who write schoolbooks. There was a scattering of sweet words in his funeral notices, but it was no more than a response to conventional sentimentality. The best verdict the most romantic editorial writer could dredge up, save in the humorless South, was to the general effect that his imbecilities were excused by his earnestness—that under his clowning, as under that of the juggler of Notre Dame, there was the zeal of a steadfast soul. But this was apology, not praise; precisely the same thing might be said of Mary Baker G. Eddy. The truth is that even Bryan's sincerity will probably yield to what is called, in other fields, definitive criticism. Was he sincere when he opposed imperialism in the Philippines, or when he fed it with deserving Democrats in Santo Domingo? Was he sincere when he tried to shove the Prohibitionists under the table, or when he seized their banner and began to lead them with loud whoops? Was he sincere when he bellowed against war, or when he dreamed of himself as a tin soldier in uniform, with a grave reserved at Arlington among the generals? Was he sincere when he fawned over Champ Clark, or when he betrayed Clark? Was he sincere when he pleaded for tolerance in New York, or when he bawled for the faggot and the stake in Tennessee?

This talk of sincerity, I confess, fatigues me. If the fellow was sincere, then so was P. T. Barnum. The word is disgraced and degraded by such uses. He was, in fact, a charlatan, a mountebank, a zany without sense or dignity. His career brought him into contact with the first men of his time; he preferred the company of rustic ignoramuses. It was hard to believe, watching him at Dayton, that he had traveled, that he had been received in civilized societies, that he had been a high officer of state. He seemed only a poor clod like those around him, deluded by a childish theology, full of an almost pathological hatred of all learning, all human dignity, all beauty, all fine and noble things. He was a peasant come home to the barnyard. Imagine a gentleman, and you have imagined everything that he was not. What animated him from end to end of his grotesque career was simply ambition—the ambition of a common man to get his hand upon the collar of his superiors, or, failing that, to get his thumb into their eyes. He was born with a roaring voice, and it had the trick of inflaming half-wits. His whole career was devoted to raising those half-wits against their betters, that he himself might shine.

His last battle will be grossly misunderstood if it is thought of as a mere exercise in fanaticism—that is, if Bryan the Fundamentalist Pope is mistaken for one of the bucolic Fundamentalists. There was much more in it than that, as everyone knows who saw him on the field. What moved him, at bottom, was simply hatred of the city men who had laughed at him so long, and brought him at last to so tatterdemalion an estate. He lusted for revenge upon them. He yearned to lead the anthropoid rabble against them, to punish them for their execution upon him by attacking the very vitals of their civilization. He went far beyond the bounds of any merely religious frenzy, however inordinate. When he began denouncing the notion that man is a mammal even some of the hinds at Dayton were agape. And when, brought upon Clarence Darrow's cruel hook, he writhed and tossed in a very fury of malignancy, bawling against the veriest elements of sense and decency like a man frantic—when he came to that tragic climax of his striving there were snickers among the hinds as well as hosannas.

Upon that hook, in truth, Bryan committed suicide, as a legend as well as in the body. He staggered from the rustic court ready to die, and he staggered from it ready to be forgotten, save as a character in a third-rate farce, witless and in poor taste. It was plain to everyone who knew him, when he came to Dayton, that his great days were behind him—that, for all the fury of his hatred, he was now definitely an old man, and headed at last for silence. There was a vague, unpleasant manginess about his appearance; he somehow seemed dirty, though a close glance showed him as carefully shaven as an actor, and clad in immaculate linen. All the hair was gone from the dome of his head, and it had begun to fall out, too, behind his ears, in the obscene manner of Samuel Gompers. The resonance had departed from his voice; what was once a bugle blast had become reedy and quavering. Who knows that, like Demosthenes, he had a lisp? In the old days, under the magic of his eloquence, no one noticed it. But when he spoke at Dayton it was always audible.

When I first encountered him, on the sidewalk in front of the office of the rustic lawyers who were his associates in the Scopes case, the trial was yet to begin, and so he was still expansive and amiable. I had printed in the *Nation,* a week or so before, an article arguing that the Tennessee anti-evolution law, whatever its wisdom, was at least constitutional—that the yahoos of the state had a clear right to have their progeny taught whatever they chose, and kept secure from whatever knowledge violated their superstitions. The old boy professed to be delighted with the argument, and gave the gaping bystanders to understand that I was a publicist of parts. Not to be outdone, I admired the preposterous country shirt that he wore—sleeveless and with the neck cut very low. We parted in the manner of two ambassadors.

But that was the last touch of amiability that I was destined to see in Bryan. The next day the battle joined and his face became hard. By the end of the week he was simply a walking fever. Hour by hour he grew more bitter. What the Christian Scientists call malicious animal magnetism seemed to radiate from him like heat from a stove. From my place in the courtroom, standing upon a table, I looked directly down upon him, sweating horribly and pumping his palm-leaf fan. His eyes fascinated me; I watched them all day long. They were blazing points of hatred. They glittered like occult and sinister gems. Now and then they wandered to me, and I got my share, for my reports of the trial had come back to Dayton, and he had read them. It was like coming under fire.

Thus he fought his last fight, thirsting savagely for blood. All sense departed from him. He bit right and left, like a dog with rabies. He descended to demagogy so dreadful that his very associates at the trial table blushed. His one yearning was to keep his yokels heated up—to lead his forlorn mob of imbeciles against the foe. That foe, alas, refused to be alarmed. It insisted upon seeing the whole battle as a comedy. Even Darrow, who knew better, occasionally yielded to the prevailing spirit. One day he lured poor Bryan into the folly I have mentioned: his astounding argument against the notion that man is a mammal. I am glad I heard it, for otherwise I'd never believe it. There stood the man who had been thrice a candidate for the Presidency of the Republic—there he stood in the glare of the world, uttering stuff that a boy of eight would laugh at. The artful Darrow led him on: he repeated it, ranted for it, bellowed it in his cracked voice. So he was prepared for the final slaughter. He came into life a hero, a Galahad, in bright and shining armor. He was passing out a poor mountebank.

Last Words

❮❮❮❮❮❮❮❮❮❮❮❮❮❮❮❮❮❮❮❮❮❮❮❮❮❮❯❯❯❯❯❯❯❯❯❯❯❯❯❯❯❯❯❯❯❯❯❯❯❯❯❯❯

ONE of the merits of democracy is quite obvious: it is perhaps the most charming form of government ever devised by man. The reason is not far to seek. It is based
upon propositions that are palpably not true—and what is not true,
as everyone knows, is always immensely more fascinating and
satisfying to the vast majority of men than what is true. Truth has a
harshness that alarms them, and an air of finality that collides with
their incurable romanticism. They turn, in all the great emergencies
of life, to the ancient promises, transparently false but immensely
comforting, and of all those ancient promises there is none more
comforting than the one to the effect that the lowly shall inherit
the earth. It is at the bottom of the dominant religious system of
the modern world, and it is at the bottom of the dominant political
system. Democracy gives it a certain appearance of objective and
demonstrable truth. The mob man, functioning as citizen, gets a
feeling that he is really important to the world—that he is
genuinely running things. Out of his maudlin herding after rogues
and mountebanks there comes to him a sense of vast and mysterious power—which is what makes archbishops, police sergeants and
other such magnificoes happy. And out of it there comes, too, a
conviction that he is somehow wise, that his views are taken
seriously by his betters—which is what makes United States
Senators, fortune-tellers and Young Intellectuals happy. Finally,
there comes out of it a glowing consciousness of a high duty

triumphantly done—which is what makes hangmen and husbands happy.

All these forms of happiness, of course, are illusory. They don't last. The democrat, leaping into the air to flap his wings and praise God, is forever coming down with a thump. The seeds of his disaster lie in his own stupidity: he can never get rid of the naïve delusion—so beautifully Christian!—that happiness is something to be got by taking it away from the other fellow. But there are seeds, too, in the very nature of things: a promise, after all, is only a promise, even when it is supported by divine revelation, and the chances against its fulfillment may be put into a depressing mathematical formula. Here the irony that lies under all human aspiration shows itself: the quest for happiness, as usual, brings only *un*happiness in the end. But saying that is merely saying that the true charm of democracy is not for the democrat but for the spectator. That spectator, it seems to me, is favored with a show of the first cut and caliber. Try to imagine anything more heroically absurd! What grotesque false pretenses! What a parade of obvious imbecilities! What a welter of fraud! But is fraud unamusing? Then I retire forthwith as a psychologist. The fraud of democracy, I contend, is more amusing than any other—more amusing even, and by miles, than the fraud of religion. Go into your praying-chamber and give sober thought to any of the more characteristic democratic inventions. Or to any of the typical democratic prophets. If you don't come out paled and palsied by mirth then you will not laugh on the Last Day itself, when Presbyterians step out of the grave like chicks from the egg, and wings blossom from their scapulae, and they leap into interstellar space with roars of joy.

I have spoken hitherto of the possibility that democracy may be a self-limiting disease, like measles. It is, perhaps, something more: it is self-devouring. One cannot observe it objectively without being impressed by its curious distrust of itself—its apparently ineradicable tendency to abandon its whole philosophy at the first sign of strain. I need not point to what happens invariably in democratic states when the national safety is menaced. All the great tribunes of democracy, on such occasions, convert themselves, by a process as simple as taking a deep breath, into despots of an almost fabulous ferocity. Nor is this process confined to times of alarm and terror: it is going on day in and day out. Democracy always seems bent upon killing the thing it theoretically loves. All its axioms resolve themselves into thundering paradoxes, many amounting to downright contradictions in terms. The mob is competent to rule the rest of us—but it must be rigorously policed itself. There is a government, not of men, but of laws—but men are set upon benches to decide finally what the law is and may be. The highest function of the citizen is to serve the state—but the first assumption that meets him, when he essays to discharge it, is an assumption of his disingenuousness and dishonor. Is that assumption commonly sound? Then the farce only grows the more glorious.

I confess, for my part, that it greatly delights me. I enjoy democracy immensely. It is incomparably idiotic, and hence incomparably amusing. Does it exalt dunderheads, cowards, trimmers, frauds, cads? Then the pain of seeing them go up is balanced and obliterated by the joy of seeing them come down. Is it inordinately wasteful, extravagant, dishonest? Then so is every other form of government: all alike are enemies to decent men. Is rascality at the very heart of it? Well, we have borne that rascality since 1776, and continue to survive. In the long run, it may turn out that rascality is an ineradicable necessity to human government, and even to civilization itself—that civilization, at bottom, is nothing but a colossal swindle. I do not know. I report only that when the suckers are running well the spectacle is infinitely exhilarating. But I am, it may be, a somewhat malicious man: my sympathies, when it comes to suckers, tend to be coy. What I can't make out is how any man can believe in democracy who feels for and with them, and is pained when they are debauched and made a show of. How can any man be a democrat who is sincerely a democrat?

I V

<<<<<<<<<<<<<<<>>>>>>>>>>>>

American Journalism

＊ · ＊ · ＊ · ＊ · ＊

Mencken applied for a job on a Baltimore paper the day after his father's funeral. He was eighteen years old, and he remained a working newspaperman the rest of his active life. He possessed exceptional skill for almost any stint that came his way in the practice of the craft, from police-court reporter to managing editor. In addition, he had two qualities that lifted him to the top level: he was prodigal of his talents, and he had a settled point of view that enabled him to see things in a pattern.

His first task in the day's work was to turn out good newspaper copy. Whatever articles or books he might write were the product of the hours that were left over. In the course of his life he wrote many millions of words for the newspapers. Much of it was hackwork, but it was hackwork of a superior order, and some of it he was able to salvage for his books. He never cut corners or held back choice bits for his publications elsewhere. He had a prodigality rarely witnessed in a writer of his abilities. A Coleridge could regret the waste of the prime and manhood of his intellect in his press work, but Mencken was too free of self-consciousness and vanity, too dedicated to his lifework, ever to entertain these thoughts.

The perspective from which he saw events as a journalist is illustrated by an incident that occurred as World War II approached. The chief of one of America's intelligence services returned from a tour of duty abroad to head the division in Washington. Intelligence estimates from his agents at home and in foreign countries passed over his desk daily. Among them, from time to time, were included clippings of Mencken's newspaper appraisals of the world situation. The intelligence chief discovered that not infrequently Mencken's determinations were more revelatory than those of his own agents. Under the impression

(239)

that Mencken had exceptional sources of information, the chief went to Baltimore to learn what they were. He was assured by Mencken that the articles were the product of a diligent reading of the nation's press and Mencken's fitting the pieces into a coherent whole.

In 1934 Mencken was chosen by the Washington correspondents to speak at their Gridiron Dinner. President Roosevelt was to be the second speaker. Mencken prepared his text and, as was customary, submitted it to the White House. Its tone was pleasant and marked by the usual flashes of humor. But Mencken was mousetrapped by the New Dealers he had begun to snipe at in his articles. The President's response was a scathing summary of the deficiencies of the newspaper world, from reporter to publisher. The effect was electric: the President was reading from Mencken's "Journalism in America," reprinted here.

Mencken not only did more than his share of a newspaperman's work, but he made a habit of participating in the fringe activities of his papers, from singing carols on Christmas Eve in the pressroom for the benefit of the employees' children to attending the meetings of professional associations of journalists. A year before his stroke he was present at the annual meeting of the National Conference of Editorial Writers. He was under the impression that the meeting would consist of a round-table discussion in which he would participate. He was surprised when he was called on for a speech, but he summed up in not many words the experience of a lifetime. His final advice to his editorial colleagues was practical: when there is nothing to comment on intelligently, that day omit the editorial page altogether.

Journalism in America

‹‹‹‹‹‹‹‹‹‹‹‹‹‹‹‹‹‹‹‹‹‹‹‹‹‹‹‹‹‹‹‹‹‹‹‹‹›››››››››››››››››››››››››››››››››››

• I •

ONE of the agreeable spiritual phenomena of the great age in which we live is the soul-searching now going on among American journalists. Fifteen years ago, or even ten years ago, there was scarcely a sign of it. The working newspaper men of the Republic, of whom I have had the honor to be one since the last century, were then almost as complacent as so many Federal judges, movie magnates, or major-generals in the army. When they discussed their puissant craft at all, it was only to smack their chests proudly, boasting of their vast power in public matters, of their adamantine resistance to all the less tempting varieties of bribes, and of the fact that a politician of enlightened self-interest, giving them important but inaccurate news confidently, could rely upon them to mangle it beyond recognition before publishing it. I describe a sort of Golden Age, and confess frankly that I can't do so without a certain yielding to emotion. Salaries had been going up since the dawn of the new century, and the journalist, however humble, was beginning to feel his oats. For the first time in history he was paid as well as the human cranes and steam shovels slinging rolls of paper in the cellar. He began to own two hats, two suits of clothes, two pairs of shoes, two walking-sticks, even two belts. He ceased to feed horribly in one-arm lunchrooms and began to dine in places with fumigated waitresses, some of a considerable pulchritude and amiability, and red-shaded table lamps. He was, as such things are reckoned, happy. But at the heart of his happiness, alas, there yet gnawed a cankerworm. One enemy remained in his world, unscotched and apparently unscotchable, to wit, the business manager. The business manager, at will, could send up a blue slip and order him fired. In the face of that menace from below-stairs his literary superiors were helpless, up to and including the editor-in-chief. All of them were under the hoof of the business manager, and all the business manager ever thought of was advertising. Let an advertiser complain that his honor had been impugned or his *clavi* abraded, and off went a head.

It was the great war for human freedom, I suspect and allege, that brought the journalist deliverance from that last and most abominable hazard: he was, perhaps, one of the few real beneficiaries of all the carnage. As the struggle grew more savage on Flanders fields and business grew better and better at home, reporters of any capacity whatever got to be far too scarce to fire loosely. Moreover, the business manager, with copy pouring over his desk almost unsolicited, began to lose his old dread of advertisers, and then even some of his natural respect for them. It was a sellers' market, in journalism as in the pants business. Customers were no longer kissed; the lesser among them actually began to stand in line. The new spirit, so strange and so exhilarating, spread like a benign pestilence, and presently it began to invade even the editorial rooms. In almost every American city, large or small, some flabbergasted advertiser, his money in his hand, sweat pouring from him as if he had seen a ghost, was kicked out with spectacular ceremonies. All the principal papers, suddenly grown rich, began also to grow independent, virtuous, touchy, sniffish. No —————— could dictate to them, God damn! So the old free reading notices of the Bon Marché and the Palais Royal disappeared, salaries continued to climb, and the liberated journalist, taking huge breaths of thrilling air, began to think of himself as a professional man.

Upon that cogitation he is still engaged, and all the weeklies that print the news of the craft are full of its fruits. He elects representatives and they meet in lugubrious conclave to draw up codes of ethics. He begins to read books dealing with professional questions of other sorts—even books not dealing with professional questions. He changes his old cynical view of schools of journalism, and is lured, now and then, into lecturing in them himself. He no longer thinks of his calling as a business, like the haberdasher's or tallow chandler's, or as a game, like the stockbroker's or faro-dealer's, but as a profession, like the jurisconsult's or gynecologist's. His purpose is to set it on its legs as such—to inject plausible theories into its practice, and rid it of its old casualness and opportunism. He no longer sees it as a craft to be mastered in four days, and abandoned at the first sign of a better job. He begins to talk darkly of the long apprenticeship necessary to master its technic, of the wide information and sagacity needed to adorn it, of the high rewards that it offers—or may offer later on—to the man of true talent and devotion. Once he thought of himself, whenever he thought at all, as what Beethoven called a free artist —a gay adventurer careening down the charming highways of the world, the gutter ahead of him but ecstasy in his heart. Now he thinks of himself as a fellow of weight and responsibility, a beginning publicist and public man, sworn to the service of the born and unborn, heavy with duties to the Republic and to his profession.

In all this, I fear, there is some illusion, as there always is in human thinking. The journalist can no more see himself realistically than a bishop can see himself realistically. He gilds and engauds the picture, unconsciously and irresistibly. For one thing, and a most important one, he is probably somewhat in error about his professional status. He remains, for all his dreams, a hired man —the owner downstairs, or even the business manager, though he doesn't do it very often now, is still free to demand his head— and a hired man is not a professional man. The essence of a professional man is that he is answerable for his professional conduct only to his professional peers. A physician cannot be fired by any one, save when he has voluntarily converted himself into a jobholder; he is secure in his livelihood so long as he keeps his health, and can render service, or what they regard as service, to his patients. A lawyer is in the same boat. So is a dentist. So, even, is a horse-doctor. But a journalist still lingers in the twilight zone, along

(243)

with the trained nurse, the embalmer, the rev. clergy and the great majority of engineers. He cannot sell his services directly to the consumer, but only to entrepreneurs, and so those entrepreneurs have the power of veto over all his soaring fancies. His codes of ethics are all right so long as they do not menace newspaper profits; the moment they do so the business manager, now quiescent, will begin to growl again. Nor has he the same freedom that the lawyers and the physicians have when it comes to fixing his own compensation; what he faces is not a client but a boss. Above all, he is unable, as yet, to control admission to his craft. It is constantly recruited, on its lowest levels, from men who have little professional training or none at all, and some of these men master its chief mysteries very quickly. Thus even the most competent journalist faces at all times a severe competition, easily expanded at need, and cannot afford to be too saucy. When a managing editor is fired there is always another one waiting to take his place, but there is seldom another place waiting for the managing editor.

All these things plainly diminish the autonomy of the journalist, and hamper his effort to lift his trade to professional rank and dignity. When he talks of codes of ethics, indeed, he only too often falls into mere tall talk, for he cannot enforce the rules he so solemnly draws up—that is, in the face of dissent from above. Nevertheless, his discussion of the subject is still not wholly absurd, for there remain plenty of rules that he *can* enforce, and I incline to think that there are more of them than of the other kind. Most of the evils that continue to beset American journalism today, in truth, are not due to the rascality of owners nor even to the Kiwanian bombast of business managers, but simply and solely to the stupidity, cowardice and Philistinism of working newspaper men. The majority of them, in almost every American city, are still ignoramuses, and proud of it. All the knowledge that they pack into their brains is, in every reasonable cultural sense, useless; it is the sort of knowledge that belongs, not to a professional man, but to a police captain, a railway mail-clerk, or a board-boy in a brokerage house. It is a mass of trivialities and puerilities; to recite it would be to make even a barber beg for mercy. What is missing from it, in brief, is everything worth knowing—everything that enters into the common knowledge of educated men. There are managing editors in the United States, and scores of them, who have never heard of Kant or Johannes Müller and never read the Constitution of the United States; there are city editors who do not know what a symphony is, or a streptococcus, or the Statute of Frauds; there are reporters by the thousand who could not pass the entrance examination for Harvard or Tuskegee, or even Yale. It is this vast and militant ignorance, this widespread and fathomless prejudice against intelligence, that makes American journalism so pathetically feeble and vulgar, and so generally disreputable. A man with so little intellectual enterprise that, dealing with news daily, he can go through life without taking in any news that is worth knowing—such a man, you may be sure, is lacking in professional dignity quite as much as he is lacking in curiosity. The delicate thing called honor can never be a function of stupidity. If it belongs to those men who are genuinely professional men, it belongs to them because they have lifted themselves to the plane of a true aristocracy, in learning as well as in liberty—because they have deliberately and successfully separated themselves from the great masses of men, to whom learning is an insult and liberty an agony. The journalists, in seeking to acquire that status, put the cart before the horse.

• 2 •

The facts that I here set forth are well known to every American newspaper man who rises above the ice-wagon driver level, and in those sad conferences which mark every gathering of the craft they do not go undiscussed. Even the American Society of Newspaper Editors, *i.e.*, of those journalists who have got into golf clubs and become minor Babbitts, has dealt with them at some of its annual pow-wows, albeit very gingerly and with many uneasy glances behind the door. But in general journalism suffers from a lack of alert and competent professional criticism; its slaves, afflicted by a natural inferiority complex, discountenance free speaking as a sort of treason; I have myself been damned as a public enemy for calling attention, ever and anon, to the intolerable incompetence and quackery of all save a small minority of the

Washington correspondents. This struthion fear of the light is surely not to be noted in any of the actual professions. The medical men, in their trade journals, criticize one another frankly and sharply, and so do the lawyers in theirs: the latter, indeed, are not above taking occasional hacks at the very judges, their lawful fathers and patterns of grace. As for the clergy, every one knows that they devote a large part of their professional energy to refuting and damning their brethren, and that not a few of them do it on public stumps, with the laity invited. So, also, in the fine arts. It is impossible for an architect to affront humanity with a blotch without hearing from other architects, and it is impossible for a poet to print anything at all without tasting the clubs of other poets. Even dramatists, movie actors, chiropractors and politicians criticize one another, and so keep themselves on tiptoe. But not journalists. If a Heywood Broun is exasperated into telling the truth about the manhandling of a Snyder trial, or a Walter Lippmann exposes the imbecility of the Russian "news" in a New York *Times,* or an Oswald Garrison Villard turns his searchlight on a Boston *Herald* or a Washington *Star,* it is a rarity and an indecorum. The organs of the craft—and there are journals for journalists, just as there are doctors for doctors—are all filled with bilge borrowed from Rotary and Kiwanis. Reading them, one gathers the impression that every newspaper proprietor in the United States is a distinguished public figure, and every circulation manager a wizard. The editorial boys, it appears, never fall down on their jobs; they are not only geniuses, but also heroes. Some time ago, having read all such journals assiduously for years, I stopped my subscriptions to them. I found that I preferred the clip-sheet of the Methodist Board of Temperance, Prohibition and Public Morals.

But if there is thus little or no frank and open discussion of the evils that beset journalism in the Republic, there is a great deal of private discontent and soul-searching, and it shows itself in all the fantastic codes of ethics that issue from embattled professors of journalism in the great rolling-mills of learning, and from editorial associations in the cow states. In such codes, I am sorry to have to repeat, I take no stock. Most of them are the handiwork of journalists of no professional importance whatever, and, what is worse, of no apparent sense. They run the scale from metaphysical principia worthy of Rotary to sets of rules fit only for the government of a Y. M. C. A. lamasery or a state's prison. They concern themselves furiously with abuses which are not peculiar to journalism but run through the whole of American life, and they are delicately silent about abuses that are wholly journalistic, and could be remedied quickly and without the slightest difficulty. Their purpose, I believe, is largely rhetorical. They give a certain ease and comfort to the laboring patient without letting any of his blood. Nevertheless, I am glad to see them multiply, for though most of them may be hollow today, there is always a chance that some solid substance may get into them tomorrow. If they accomplish nothing else at the moment, they at least accustom the journalist to the notion that his craft needs an overhauling. His old romantic optimism oozes out of him. He is no longer quite happy. Out of his rising discomforts, I believe, there will issue eventually a more realistic attitude toward the problems that confront him, and on some bright day in the future he may address himself rationally to the hard business of solving them. Most of them, I believe, are clearly soluble. More, most of them can be solved by working newspaper men, without any help from experts in ethics. What they call for is not any transcendental gift for righteousness, but simply ordinary professional competence and common sense.

For example, the problem of false news. How does so much of it get into the American newspapers, even the good ones? Is it because journalists, as a class, are habitual liars, and prefer what is not true to what is true? I don't think it is. Rather, it is because journalists are, in the main, extremely stupid, sentimental and credulous fellows—because nothing is easier than to fool them—because the majority of them lack the sharp intelligence that the proper discharge of their duties demands. The New York *Times* did not print all its famous blather and balderdash about Russia because the Hon. Mr. Ochs desired to deceive his customers, or because his slaves were in the pay of Russian reactionaries, but simply and solely because his slaves, facing the elemental professional problem of distinguishing between true news and false, turned out to be incompetent. All around the borders of Russia sat propagandists hired to fool them. In many cases, I have no doubt, they detected that purpose, and foiled it; we only know what they printed, not what they threw into their wastebaskets. But in many other cases they succumbed easily, and even ridiculously, and the result was the vast mass of puerile rubbish that Mr. Lippmann later made a show of. In other words, the editors of the American newspaper most brilliantly distinguished above its fellows for its news-gathering enterprise turned out to be unequal to a job of news-gathering presenting special but surely not insuperable difficulties. It was not an ethical failure, but a purely technical failure. And so was the same eminent newspaper's idiotic misreporting of the news from China in the early part of 1927, and the grotesque paralysis of the whole American press in the face of the Miami hurricane in 1926.

Obviously, the way to diminish such failures in future is not to adopt sonorous platitudes borrowed from the realtors, the morticians, the sanitary plumbers and Kiwanis, but to undertake an overhauling of the faulty technic, and of the incompetent personnel responsible for it. This overhauling, of course, will take some intelligence, but I don't think it will make demands that are impossible. The bootlegging, legal or delicatessen professions, confronted by like demands, would quickly furnish the talent necessary to meet them; I see no reason why the profession of journalism should not measure up as well. What lies in the way of it is simply the profound, maudlin sentimentality of the average American journalist—his ingenuous and almost automatic belief in everything that comes to him in writing. One would think that his daily experience with the written word would make him suspicious of it; he himself, in fact, believes fondly that he is proof against it. But the truth is that he swallows it far more often than he rejects it, and that his most eager swallowing is done in the face of the plainest evidence of its falsity. Let it come in by telegraph, and his mouth flies open. Let it come in by telegraph *from a press association* and down it goes at once. I do not say, of course, that *all* press association news is thus swallowed by news editors. When the means are readily at hand, he often attempts to check it, and sometimes even rejects it. But when such checking presents difficulties—in other words, when deceit is especially easy, and should be guarded against most vigilantly—he succumbs nine times out of ten, and without a struggle. It was precisely by this process that the editors of the *Times,* otherwise men of extraordinary professional alertness, were victimized by the Russian "news" that made that paper ridiculous. In the face of great improbabilities, they interpreted their inability to dispose of them as a license to accept them as truth. Journalism will be a sounder and more dignified profession when a directly contrary interpretation of the journalist's duty prevails. There will then be less news in the papers, but it will at least have the merit of being true.

Nor is the typical American journalist's credulity confined to such canards and roorbacks from far places. He is often victimized just as easily at home, despite his lofty belief that he is superior to the wiles of press agents. The plain fact is that most of the stuff he prints now emanates from press agents, and that his machinery for scrutinizing it is lamentably defective. True enough, the bold, gay liars employed by theatrical managers and opera singers no longer fool him as they used to; he has grown so suspicious of them that he often turns them out when they have real news. But what of the press agents of such organizations as the Red Cross, the Prohibition Unit, the Near-East Relief, the Chamber of Commerce of the United States, the Department of Justice, the Y. M. C. A., and the various bands of professional patriots? I do not say that the press agents of such bodies are always or necessarily liars; all I say is that, nine times out of ten, their statements are accepted as true by the newspapers without any attempt to determine accurately whether they are true or not. They may be simple statements of plain fact; they may, on the contrary, conceal highly dubious purposes, of organizations and individuals. In both cases they are set forth in the same way—solemnly and without comment. Who, ordinarily, would believe a Prohibition agent? Perhaps a Federal judge in his robes of office and full of seized evidence; I can think of no one else. Yet the American newspapers are filled every day with the dreadful boasts and threats of such frauds: it is set before the people, not as lies, but as news. What is the purpose of such rubbish? Its purpose, obviously, is to make it appear that the authors are actually enforcing Prohibition—in other words, to make them secure in their jobs. Every newspaper man in America knows that Prohibition is not being enforced—and yet it is rarely that an American newspaper comes out in these days without a gaudy story on its first page, rehearsing all the old lies under new and blacker headlines.

I do not argue here, of course, that only demonstrable facts are news. There are times and occasions when rumor is almost as important as the truth—when a newspaper's duty to its readers requires it to tell them not only what has happened, but also what is reported, what is threatened, what is merely said. What I contend is simply that such quasi-news, such half-baked and still dubious news, should be printed for exactly what it is—that it ought to be clearly differentiated from news that, by an overwhelming probability, is true. That differentiation is made easily and as a matter of course by most European newspapers of any dignity. When they print a dispatch from the Russian border they indicate its source, and not infrequently follow it with a cynical comment. If they had Prohibition agents on their hands, they would print the fulminations of those gentlemen in the same way— with plain warnings to stop, look and listen. In brief, they make every reasonable effort to make up for their own technical limitations as news-gatherers—they do the best they can, and say so frankly when it is not very good. I believe that American newspapers might imitate them profitably. If it were done, then the public's justifiable distrust of all newspapers, now rising, would tend to ebb. They would have to throw off their present affectation of omniscience, but they would gain a new repute for honesty and candor; they would begin to seem more reliable when they failed than they now seem when they succeed. The scheme I propose would cost nothing; on the contrary, it would probably save expense. It would throw no unbearable burden upon the journalistic mind; it would simply make it more cautious and alert. Best of it, it would increase the dignity of journalism without resort to flapdoodlish and unenforceable codes of ethics, by Mush out of Tosh.

· 3 ·

In their private communions, though seldom in public, the more conscientious and unhappy variety of journalists commonly blame the woes of the craft upon the entrance into newspaper ownership of such opulent vacuums as Cyrus H. K. Curtis and the late Frank A. Munsey. As a result of the application of chain-store methods to journalism by these amiable Vandals there are fewer papers than there used to be, and the individual journalist is less important. All the multitudinous Hearst papers are substantially identical, and so are all the Scripps-Howard papers, and all the Curtis papers, and so were the Munsey papers in the great days of that pathetic man. There is little room, on the papers of such chains, for the young man who aspires to shine. Two thirds of their contents are produced in great factories, and what remains is chiefly a highly standardized bilge. In the early days of Hearst, when he had only a few widely scattered papers, his staffs were manned by men of great professional enterprise and cunning, and some of them became celebrated in the craft, and even generally. But now a Hearst paper, however inflammatory, is no more than a single unit in a long row of filling-stations, and so it tends to attract only the duller and less picturesque sort of men. There is scarcely a Hearst managing editor today who amounts to anything professionally, or is heard of outside his own dung-hill. The platitudes of Brisbane and Dr. Frank Crane serve as pabulum for all of them. What they think is what the machines at the central factory think; what they do is determined by men they have never seen. So with the Scripps-Howard slaves, and the slaves of Cox, and those of Curtis, and all the rest. Their predecessors of a generation ago were gaudy adventurers, experimenters, artists; they themselves are golf-players, which is to say, blanks. They are well paid, but effectively knee-haltered. The rewards of their trade used to come in freedom, opportunity, the incomparable delights of self-expression; now they come in money.

But the sweet goes with the bitter. The newspapers of today, though they may be as rigidly standardized as Uneeda biscuits, are at least solvent: they are no longer the paltry freebooters that they used to be. A Munsey, perhaps, is a jackass, but he is at least honest; no one seriously alleges that his papers are for sale; even the sinister Wall Street powers that Liberals see in the background must get what they want out of him by being polite to him, not by simply sending him orders. The old-timers, contemplating the ghastly spectacle of a New York *Sun* submerged in the Munsey swamp and an *Evening Post* descending from a Villard to a Curtis, forget conveniently how bad most of the papers they once worked for really were. In the town where I began there were five papers, and four of them were cheap, trashy, stupid and corrupt. They all played politics for what there was in it, and leaped obscenely every time an advertiser blew his nose. Every other American city of that era was full of such papers—dreadful little rags, venal, vulnerable and vile. Not a few of them made great pretensions, and were accepted by a naïve public as organs of the enlightenment. Today, I believe, such journalistic street-walkers are very rare. The consolidations that every old-timer deplores have accomplished at least one good thing: they have got the newspapers, in the main, out of the hands of needy men. When orders come from a Curtis or a Munsey today the man who gets them, though he may regard them as ill-advised and even as idiotic, is seldom in any doubt as to their good faith. He may execute them without feeling that he has been made an unwilling party to an ignominious barter. He is not condemned daily to acts whose true purpose he would not dare to put into words, even to himself. His predecessor, I believe, often suffered that dismaying necessity: he seldom had any illusions about the *bona fides* of his boss. It took the whole force of his characteristic sentimentality to make him believe in his paper, and not infrequently even that sentimentality was impotent without the aid of ethyl alcohol.

Thus there is something to be said for the new newspaper Babbitts, as reluctant as every self-respecting journalist must be to say it. And in what is commonly said against them there is not infrequently a certain palpable exaggeration and injustice. Are they responsible for the imbecile editorial policies of their papers, for the grotesque lathering of such mountebanks as Coolidge and Mellon, for the general smugness and lack of intellectual enterprise that pervades American journalism? Perhaps they are. But do they issue orders that their papers shall be printed in blowsy, clumsy English? That they shall stand against every decent thing, and in favor of everything that is meretricious and ignoble? That they shall wallow in trivialities, and manhandle important news? That their view of learning shall be that of a bartender? Has any newspaper proprietor ever issued orders that the funeral orgies of a Harding should be described in the language of a Tennessee revival? Or that helpless men, with the mob against them, should be pursued without fairness, decency or sense? I doubt it. I doubt, even, that the Babbitts turned Greeleys are responsible, in the last analysis, for the political rubbish that fills their papers—the preposterous anointing of Coolidge, the craven yielding to such sinister forces as the Ku Klux Klan and the Anti-Saloon League, the incessant, humorless, degrading hymning of all sorts of rogues and charlatans. The average newspaper proprietor, I suspect, gets nine-tenths of his political ideas from his own men. In other words, he is such an ass that he believes political reporters, and especially his own political reporters. They have, he fancies, wide and confidential sources of information: their wisdom is a function of their prestige as his agents. What they tell him is, in the long run, what he believes, with certain inconsiderable corrections by professionals trying to work him. If only because they have confidential access to him day in and day out, they are able to introduce their own notions into his head. He may have their jobs in his hands, but they have his ears and eyes, so to speak, in theirs.

Even the political garbage that emanates from Washington, and especially from the typewriters of the more eminent and puissant correspondents there resident, is seldom inspired, I am convinced, by orders from the Curtis or Munsey at home: its sources are rather to be sought in the professional deficiencies of the correspondents themselves—a class of men of almost incredible credulity. In other words, they are to be sought, not in the corruption and enslavement of the press, but in the incompetence of the press. The average Washington correspondent, I believe, is honest enough, as honesty goes in the United States, though his willingness to do press work for the National Committees in campaign time and for other highly dubious agencies at other times is not to be forgotten. What ails him mainly is that he is a man without sufficient force of character to resist the blandishments that surround him from the moment he sets foot in Washington. A few men, true enough, resist, and their papers, getting the benefit of it, become notable for their independence and intelligence, but the great majority succumb almost at once.

A few months of associating with the gaudy magnificoes of the town, and they pick up its meretricious values, and are unable to distinguish men of sense and dignity from mountebanks. A few clumsy overtures from the White House, and they are rattled and undone. They come in as newspaper men, trained to get the news and eager to get it; they end as tin-horn statesmen, full of dark secrets and unable to write the truth if they tried. Here I spread no scandal and violate no confidence. The facts are familiar to every newspaper man in the United States. A few of the more intelligent managing editors, cynical of ever counteracting the effects of the Washington miasma, seek to evade them by frequently changing their men. But the average managing editor is too stupid to deal with such difficulties. He prints balderdash because he doesn't know how to get anything better—perhaps, in many cases, because he doesn't know that anything better exists. Drenched with propaganda at home, he is quite content to take more propaganda from Washington. It is not that he is dishonest, but that he is stupid—and, being stupid, a coward. The resourcefulness, enterprise and bellicosity that his job demands are simply not in him. He doesn't wear himself out trying to get the news, as romance has it; he slides supinely into the estate and dignity of a golf-player. American journalism suffers from too many golf-players. They swarm in the Washington Press Gallery. They, and not their bosses, are responsible for most of the imbecilities that now afflict their trade.

· 4 ·

The journalists of the United States will never get rid of those afflictions by putting the blame on Dives, and never by making speeches at one another in annual conventions, and never by drawing up codes of ethics that most of their brethren will infallibly laugh at, as a Congressman laughs at a gentleman. The job before them—that is, before the civilized minority of them—is to purge their trade before they seek to dignify it—to clean house before they paint the roof and raise a flag. Can the thing be done? It not only can be done: it *has* been done. There are at least a

dozen newspapers in the United States that already show a determined effort to get out of the old slough. Any managing editor in
the land, if he has the will, can carry his own paper with them.
He is under no compulsion, save rarely, to employ this or that
hand; it is not often that owners, or even business managers, take
any interest in that business, save to watch the payroll. Is his paper
trifling, ill-informed, petty and unfair? Is its news full of transparent absurdities? Are its editorials ignorant and without sense?
Is it written in English full of *clichés* and vulgarities—English that
would disgrace a manager of prize-fighters or a county superintendent of schools? Then the fault belongs plainly, not to some
remote man, but to the proximate man—to the man who lets such
drivel go by. He could get better if he wanted it, you may be
sure. There is in all history no record of a newspaper owner who
complained because his paper was well-edited. And I know of no
business manager who objected when the complaints pouring in
upon him, of misrepresentations, invasions of privacy, gross inac-
curacies and other such nuisances, began to lighten.

Not a few managing editors, as I say, are moving in the right
direction. There has been an appreciable improvement, during the
past dozen years, in the general tone of American newspapers.
They are still full of preposterous blather, but they are measurably
more accurate, I believe, than they used to be, and some of them
are better written. A number of them are less absurdly partisan,
particularly in the smaller cities. Save in the South and in the
remoter fastnesses of New England the old-time party organ has
gone out of fashion. In the big cities the faithful hacks of the New
York *Tribune* type have begun to vanish. With them has gone the
old-time drunken reporter, and in his place is appearing a young
fellow of better education, and generally finer metal. The up-
lifters of the craft try to make him increase, and to that end
encourage schools of journalism. But these seminaries, so far,
show two palpable defects. On the one hand, they are seldom
manned by men of any genuine professional standing, or of any
firm notion of what journalism is about. On the other hand, they
are nearly all too easy in their requirements for admission. Probably half of them, indeed, are simply refuges for students too stupid
to tackle the other professions. They offer snap courses, and they

promise quick jobs. The result is that the graduates coming out of them are mainly second-raters—that young men and women issuing from the general arts courses make better journalistic material.

What ails these schools of journalism is that they are not yet professional schools, but simply trade schools. Their like is to be found, not in the schools of medicine and law, but in the institutions that teach barbering, bookkeeping and scenario-writing. Obviously, the remedy for their general failure is to borrow a leaf from the book of the medical men, and weed out the incompetents, not after they have finished, but before they have begun. Twenty-five years ago any yokel who had got through the three R's was free to study medicine in the United States. In three years, and sometimes in two years, he was turned out to practice upon his fellow hinds, and once he had his license it was a practical impossibility to challenge him. But now there is scarcely a medical school in the United States that does not demand a bachelor's degree or its equivalent as a prerequisite to entrance, and the term of study in all of them is four years, and it must be followed by at least one year of hospital service. This reform was not achieved by passing laws against the old hedge schools: it was achieved simply by setting up the competition of good schools. The latter gradually elbowed the former out. Their graduates had immense advantages. They had professional prestige from the moment of their entrance into practice. The public quickly detected the difference between them and their competitors from the surviving hedge schools. Soon the latter began to disintegrate, and now all save a few of them have disappeared. The medical men improved their profession by making it more difficult to become a medical man. Today the thing is a practical impossibility to any young man who is not of genuine intelligence.

But at least two-thirds of the so-called schools of journalism still admit any aspirant who can make shift to read and write. The pedagogues who run them cannot be expected to devote much thought or money to improving them; they are in the position of the quacks who used to run the hedge medical schools. The impulse toward improvement, if it ever comes at all, must come from the profession they presume to serve. Here is a chance for the editorial committees and societies of journalists that now spring up on all sides. Let them abandon their vain effort to frame codes of ethics and devote themselves to the nursery. If they can get together a committee on schools of journalism as wise and as bold as the Council on Medical Education of the American Medical Association they will accomplish more in a few years than they can hope to accomplish with academic codes of ethics in half a century.

All the rest will follow. The old fond theory, still surviving in many a newspaper office, that it is somehow discreditable for a reporter to show any sign of education and culture, that he is most competent and laudable when his intellectual baggage most closely approaches that of a bootlegger—this theory will fall before the competition of novices who have been adequately trained, and have more in their heads than their mere training. Journalism, compared to the other trades of literate men, is surely not unattractive, even today. It is more amusing than the army or the cloth, and it offers a better living at the start than either medicine or the law. There is a career in it for the young man of original mind and forceful personality—a career leading to power and even to a sort of wealth. In point of fact, it has always attracted such young men, else it would be in an even lower state than it is now. It would attract a great many more of them if its public opinion were more favorable to them—if they were less harassed by the commands of professional superiors of no dignity, and the dislike of fellows of no sense. Every time two of them are drawn in they draw another. The problem is to keep them. That is the central problem of journalism in the United States today.

I seem to be in a mood for constructive criticism. Let me add one more pearl of wisdom before I withdraw. I put it in the form of a question. Suppose the shyster lawyers of every town organized a third-rate club, called it the Bar Association, took in any Prohibition agent or precinct politician who could raise the dues, and then announced publicly, from the courthouse steps, that it represented the whole bar, and that membership in it was an excellent form of insurance—that any member who paid his dues would get very friendly consideration, if he ever got into trouble, from the town's judges and district attorney. And suppose the decent lawyers of the town permitted this preposterous pretension to go unchallenged—and some of them even gave countenance to it by joining the club. How long would the legal profession in that town retain its professional honor and dignity? How many laymen, after two or three years, would have any respect left for *any* lawyer, even a judge?

Yet the journalists of the United States permit that precise thing to go on under their noses. In almost every city of the country there is a so-called Press Club, and at least three-fourths of them are exactly like the hypothetical Bar Association that I have described. They are run by newspaper men of the worst type—many of them so incompetent and disreputable that they cannot even get jobs on newspapers. They take the money of all the town grafters and rascals on the pretense that newspaper favors go with its receipt. They are the resorts of idlers and blackmailers. They are nuisances and disgraces. Yet in how many towns have they been put down? In how many towns do the decent newspaper men take any overt action against them? My proposal is very simple. I propose that they be shut up, East, West, North and South, before anything more is said about codes of newspaper ethics.

The Hills of Zion

<<<<<<<<<<<<<<<<<<<<<<<<<<<<<<<>>>>>>>>>>>>>>>>>>>>>>>>>>>>>>>>

In its first form this was a dispatch to the Baltimore *Evening Sun.* I wrote it on a roaring hot Sunday afternoon in a Chattanooga hotel room, naked above the waist and with only a pair of BVD's below.

IT was hot weather when they tried the infidel Scopes at Dayton, Tenn., but I went down there very willingly, for I was eager to see something of evangelical Christianity as a going concern. In the big cities of the Republic, despite the endless efforts of consecrated men, it is laid up with a wasting disease. The very Sunday-school superintendents, taking jazz from the stealthy radio, shake their fire-proof legs; their pupils, moving into adolescence, no longer respond to the proliferating hormones by enlisting for missionary service in Africa, but resort to necking instead. Even in Dayton, I found, though the mob was up to do execution upon Scopes, there was a strong smell of antinomianism. The nine churches of the village were all half empty on Sunday, and weeds choked their yards. Only two or three of the resident pastors managed to sustain themselves by their ghostly science; the rest had to take orders for mail-order pantaloons or work in the adjacent strawberry fields; one, I heard, was a barber. On the courthouse green a score of sweating theologians debated the darker passages of Holy Writ day and night, but I soon found that they were all volunteers, and that the local faithful, while interested in their exegesis as an intellectual exercise, did not permit it to impede the

From *A Mencken Chrestomathy*, 1949. Included in *Prejudices: Fifth Series*, 1926. First printed in the Baltimore *Evening Sun.* Copyright 1926 by Alfred A. Knopf, Inc. Renewal copyright 1954 by H. L. Mencken.

indigenous debaucheries. Exactly twelve minutes after I reached the village I was taken in tow by a Christian man and introduced to the favorite tipple of the Cumberland Range: half corn liquor and half Coca-Cola. It seemed a dreadful dose to me, but I found that the Dayton illuminati got it down with gusto, rubbing their tummies and rolling their eyes. I include among them the chief local proponents of the Mosaic cosmogony. They were all hot for Genesis, but their faces were far too florid to belong to teetotalers, and when a pretty girl came tripping down the main street, which was very often, they reached for the places where their neckties should have been with all the amorous enterprise of movie actors. It seemed somehow strange.

An amiable newspaper woman of Chattanooga, familiar with those uplands, presently enlightened me. Dayton, she explained, was simply a great capital like any other. That is to say, it was to Rhea county what Atlanta was to Georgia or Paris to France. That is to say, it was predominantly epicurean and sinful. A country girl from some remote valley of the county, coming into town for her semi-annual bottle of Lydia Pinkham's Vegetable Compound, shivered on approaching Robinson's drug-store quite as a country girl from upstate New York might shiver on approaching the Metropolitan Opera House. In every village lout she saw a potential white-slaver. The hard sidewalks hurt her feet. Temptations of the flesh bristled to all sides of her, luring her to Hell. This newspaper woman told me of a session with just such a visitor, holden a few days before. The latter waited outside one of the town hot-dog and Coca-Cola shops while her husband negotiated with a hardware merchant across the street. The newspaper woman, idling along and observing that the stranger was badly used by the heat, invited her to step into the shop for a glass of Coca-Cola. The invitation brought forth only a gurgle of terror. Coca-Cola, it quickly appeared, was prohibited by the country lady's pastor, as a levantine and Hell-sent narcotic. He also prohibited coffee and tea—and pies! He had his doubts about white bread and boughten meat. The newspaper woman, interested, inquired about ice-cream. It was, she found, not specifically prohibited, but going into a Coca-Cola shop to get it would be clearly sinful. So she offered to get a saucer of it, and bring it out to the sidewalk. The visitor vacillated—and came near being lost. But God saved her in the nick of time. When the newspaper woman emerged from the place she was in full flight up the street. Later on her husband, mounted on a mule, overtook her four miles out the mountain pike.

This newspaper woman, whose kindness covered city infidels as well as Alpine Christians, offered to take me back in the hills to a place where the old-time religion was genuinely on tap. The Scopes jury, she explained, was composed mainly of its customers, with a few Dayton sophisticates added to leaven the mass. It would thus be instructive to climb the heights and observe the former at their ceremonies. The trip, fortunately, might be made by automobile. There was a road running out of Dayton to Morgantown, in the mountains to the westward, and thence beyond. But foreigners, it appeared, would have to approach the sacred grove cautiously, for the upland worshipers were very shy, and at the first sight of a strange face they would adjourn their orgy and slink into the forest. They were not to be feared, for God had long since forbidden them to practice assassination, or even assault, but if they were alarmed a rough trip would go for naught. So, after dreadful bumpings up a long and narrow road, we parked our car in a little woodpath a mile or two beyond the tiny village of Morgantown, and made the rest of the approach on foot, deployed like skirmishers. Far off in a dark, romantic glade a flickering light was visible, and out of the silence came the rumble of exhortation. We could distinguish the figure of the preacher only as a moving mote in the light: it was like looking down the tube of a dark-field microscope. Slowly and cautiously we crossed what seemed to be a pasture, and then we stealthily edged further and further. The light now grew larger and we could begin to make out what was going on. We went ahead on all fours, like snakes in the grass.

From the great limb of a mighty oak hung a couple of crude torches of the sort that car inspectors thrust under Pullman cars when a train pulls in at night. In the guttering glare was the preacher, and for a while we could see no one else. He was an immensely tall and thin mountaineer in blue-jeans, his collarless shirt open at the neck and his hair a tousled mop. As he preached he paced up and down under the smoking flambeaux, and at each turn he thrust his arms into the air and yelled "Glory to God!" We crept nearer in the shadow of the cornfield, and began to hear more of his discourse. He was preaching on the Day of Judgment. The high kings of the earth, he roared, would all fall down and die; only the sanctified would stand up to receive the Lord God of Hosts. One of these kings he mentioned by name, the king of what he called Greece-y.[1] The king of Greece-y, he said, was doomed to Hell. We crawled forward a few more yards and began to see the audience. It was seated on benches ranged round the preacher in a circle. Behind him sat a row of elders, men and women. In front were the younger folk. We crept on cautiously, and individuals rose out of the ghostly gloom. A young mother sat suckling her baby, rocking as the preacher paced up and down. Two scared little girls hugged each other, their pigtails down their backs. An immensely huge mountain woman, in a gingham dress, cut in one piece, rolled on her heels at every "Glory to God!" To one side, and but half visible, was what appeared to be a bed. We found afterward that half a dozen babies were asleep upon it.

The preacher stopped at last, and there arose out of the darkness a woman with her hair pulled back into a little tight knot. She began so quietly that we couldn't hear what she said, but soon her voice rose resonantly and we could follow her. She was denouncing the reading of books. Some wandering book agent, it appeared, had come to her cabin and tried to sell her a specimen of his wares. She refused to touch it. Why, indeed, read a book? If what was in it was true, then everything in it was already in the Bible. If it was false, then reading it would imperil the soul. This syllogism from the Caliph Omar complete, she sat down. There followed a hymn, led by a somewhat fat brother wearing silver-rimmed country spectacles. It droned on for half a dozen stanzas, and then the first speaker resumed the floor. He argued that the gift of tongues was real and that education was a snare. Once his children could read the Bible, he said, they had enough. Beyond lay only infidelity and damnation. Sin stalked the cities. Dayton

---

[1] Grecia? *Cf.* Daniel VIII, 21.

itself was a Sodom. Even Morgantown had begun to forget God. He sat down, and a female aurochs in gingham got up. She began quietly, but was soon leaping and roaring, and it was hard to follow her. Under cover of the turmoil we sneaked a bit closer.

A couple of other discourses followed, and there were two or three hymns. Suddenly a change of mood began to make itself felt. The last hymn ran longer than the others, and dropped gradually into a monotonous, unintelligible chant. The leader beat time with his book. The faithful broke out with exultations. When the singing ended there was a brief palaver that we could not hear, and two of the men moved a bench into the circle of light directly under the flambeaux. Then a half-grown girl emerged from the darkness and threw herself upon it. We noticed with astonishment that she had bobbed hair. "This sister," said the leader, "has asked for prayers." We moved a bit closer. We could now see faces plainly, and hear every word. At a signal all the faithful crowded up to the bench and began to pray—not in unison, but each for himself. At another they all fell on their knees, their arms over the penitent. The leader kneeled facing us, his head alternately thrown back dramatically or buried in his hands. Words spouted from his lips like bullets from a machine-gun—appeals to God to pull the penitent back out of Hell, defiances of the demons of the air, a vast impassioned jargon of apocalyptic texts. Suddenly he rose to his feet, threw back his head and began to speak in the tongues[2] —blub-blub-blub, gurgle-gurgle-gurgle. His voice rose to a higher register. The climax was a shrill, inarticulate squawk, like that of a man throttled. He fell headlong across the pyramid of supplicants.

From the squirming and jabbering mass a young woman gradually detached herself—a woman not uncomely, with a pathetic homemade cap on her head. Her head jerked back, the veins of her neck swelled, and her fists went to her throat as if she were fighting for breath. She bent backward until she was like half a hoop. Then she suddenly snapped forward. We caught a flash of the whites of her eyes. Presently her whole body began to be convulsed—great throes that began at the shoulders and ended at

---

[2] Mark xvi, 17.

the hips. She would leap to her feet, thrust her arms in air, and then hurl herself upon the heap. Her praying flattened out into a mere delirious caterwauling. I describe the thing discreetly, and as a strict behaviorist. The lady's subjective sensations I leave to infidel pathologists, privy to the works of Ellis, Freud and Moll. Whatever they were, they were obviously not painful, for they were accompanied by vast heavings and gurglings of a joyful and even ecstatic nature. And they seemed to be contagious, too, for soon a second penitent, also female, joined the first, and then came a third, and a fourth, and a fifth. The last one had an extraordinary violent attack. She began with mild enough jerks of the head, but in a moment she was bounding all over the place, like a chicken with its head cut off. Every time her head came up a stream of hosannas would issue out of it. Once she collided with a dark, undersized brother, hitherto silent and stolid. Contact with her set him off as if he had been kicked by a mule. He leaped into the air, threw back his head, and began to gargle as if with a mouthful of BB shot. Then he loosed one tremendous, stentorian sentence in the tongues, and collapsed.

By this time the performers were quite oblivious to the profane universe and so it was safe to go still closer. We left our hiding and came up to the little circle of light. We slipped into the vacant seats on one of the rickety benches. The heap of mourners was directly before us. They bounced into us as they cavorted. The smell that they radiated, sweating there in that obscene heap, half suffocated us. Not all of them, of course, did the thing in the grand manner. Some merely moaned and rolled their eyes. The female ox in gingham flung her great bulk on the ground and jabbered an unintelligible prayer. One of the men, in the intervals between fits, put on his spectacles and read his Bible. Beside me on the bench sat the young mother and her baby. She suckled it through the whole orgy, obviously fascinated by what was going on, but never venturing to take any hand in it. On the bed just outside the light the half a dozen other babies slept peacefully. In the shadows, suddenly appearing and as suddenly going away, were vague figures, whether of believers or of scoffers I do not know. They seemed to come and go in couples. Now and then a couple at the ringside would step out and vanish into the black night.

After a while some came back, the males looking somewhat sheepish. There was whispering outside the circle of vision. A couple of Model T Fords lurched up the road, cutting holes in the darkness with their lights. Once someone out of sight loosed a bray of laughter.

All this went on for an hour or so. The original penitent, by this time, was buried three deep beneath the heap. One caught a glimpse, now and then, of her yellow bobbed hair, but then she would vanish again. How she breathed down there I don't know; it was hard enough six feet away, with a strong five-cent cigar to help. When the praying brothers would rise up for a bout with the tongues their faces were streaming with perspiration. The fat harridan in gingham sweated like a longshoreman. Her hair got loose and fell down over her face. She fanned herself with her skirt. A powerful old gal she was, plainly equal in her day to a bout with obstetrics and a week's washing on the same morning, but this was worse than a week's washing. Finally, she fell into a heap, breathing in great, convulsive gasps.

Finally, we got tired of the show and returned to Dayton. It was nearly eleven o'clock—an immensely late hour for those latitudes—but the whole town was still gathered in the courthouse yard, listening to the disputes of theologians. The Scopes trial had brought them in from all directions. There was a friar wearing a sandwich sign announcing that he was the Bible champion of the world. There was a Seventh-Day Adventist arguing that Clarence Darrow was the beast with seven heads and ten horns described in Revelation xiii, and that the end of the world was at hand. There was an evangelist made up like Andy Gump, with the news that atheists in Cincinnati were preparing to descend upon Dayton, hang the eminent Judge Raulston, and burn the town. There was an ancient who maintained that no Catholic could be a Christian. There was the eloquent Dr. T. T. Martin, of Blue Mountain, Miss., come to town with a truck-load of torches and hymn-books to put Darwin in his place. There was a singing brother bellowing apocalyptic hymns. There was William Jennings Bryan, followed everywhere by a gaping crowd. Dayton was having a roaring time. It was better than the circus. But the note of devotion was simply not there; the Daytonians, after listening a while, would slip away to

Robinson's drug-store to regale themselves with Coca-Cola, or to the lobby of the Aqua Hotel, where the learned Raulston sat in state, judicially picking his teeth. The real religion was not present. It began at the bridge over the town creek, where the road makes off for the hills.

The Spell of Journalism

‹‹‹‹‹‹‹‹‹‹‹‹‹‹‹‹‹‹‹‹‹‹‹‹‹‹‹‹‹‹‹‹‹‹‹‹›››››››››››››››››››››››››››››››››

THE recollections here embalmed, I should say at once, have nothing in common with the high, astounding tales of journalistic derring-do that had a considerable run several years ago, after the devourers of best-sellers had begun to tire of medical memoirs. In the second half of the period here covered I became a city editor, which is to say, a fellow of high mightiness in a newspaper office, and at the very end I was lifted by one of fate's ironies into even higher dignities, but the narrative has principally to do with my days as a reporter, when I was young, goatish and full of an innocent delight in the world. My adventures in that character, save maybe in one or two details, were hardly extraordinary; on the contrary they seem to me now, looking back upon them nostalgically, to have been marked by an excess of normalcy. Nevertheless, they had their moments—in fact, they were made up, subjectively, of one continuous, unrelenting, almost delirious moment—and when I revive them now it is mainly to remind myself and inform historians that a newspaper reporter, in those remote days, had a grand and gaudy time of it, and no call to envy any man.

In the long, busy years following I had experiences of a more profound and even alarming nature, and if the mood were on me I could fill a book with inside stuff almost fit to match the high, astounding tales aforesaid. I roamed, in the practice of my trade, from the river Jordan in the East to Hollywood in the West, and

---

from the Orkney Islands in the North to Morocco and the Spanish Main in the South, and, like every other journalist, I met, listened to and smelled all sorts of magnificoes, including Presidents and Vice-Presidents, generals and admirals, bishops and archbishops, murderers and murderesses, geniuses both scientific and literary, movie and stage stars, heavyweight champions of the world, Class A and Class B royalties, judges and hangmen, millionaires and labor goons, and vast hordes of other notables, including most of the recognized Caesars and Shakespeares of journalism. I edited both newspapers and magazines, some of them successes and some of them not, and got a close, confidential view of the manner in which opinion is formulated and merchanted on this earth. My own contributions to the mess ran to millions of words, and I came to know intimately many of its most revered confectioners. More than once I have staggered out of editorial conferences dripping cold sweat, and wondering dizzily how God got along for so many years without the *New Republic* and the Manchester *Guardian*. And at other times I have marveled that the human race did not revolt against the imposture, dig up the carcass of Johann Gutenberg, and heave it to the buzzards and hyenas in some convenient zoo.

A newspaper man in active practice finds it hard to remain a mere newspaper man: he is constantly beset by temptations to try other activities, and if he manages to resist them it takes a kind of fortitude that less protean men, badgered only by their hormones and their creditors, never have need of. I was born, happily, with no more public spirit than a cat, and have thus found it relatively easy to throw off all the commoner lures, but there have been times when the sirens fetched me clearly below the belt, and I did some wobbling. In 1912, though no one will ever believe it, I was groomed surreptitiously as a dark horse for the Democratic Vice-Presidential nomination, and if one eminent American statesman, X, had not got tight at the last minute, and another, Y, kept unaccountably sober, I might have become immortal. Two years later I was offered $30,000 cash, deposited in a bank to my order, to write anti-Prohibition speeches for the illiterates in the two Houses of Congress. A little further on an Episcopal bishop asked me to tackle and try to throw a nascent convert, female and rich, who had thrice slipped out of his hands at the very brink of the font. Another time the prophet of a new religion, then very prosperous in the Middle West, offered to consecrate me as a bishop myself, with power to bind and loose; and almost simultaneously I was arrested on Boston Common on a charge of vending obscene literature to the young gentlemen of Harvard. I have seen something of the horrors of war, and much too much of the worse horrors of peace. On five several occasions I have been offered the learned degree of *legum doctor,* though few men are less learned in the law than I am, or have less respect for it; and at other times I have been invited to come in and be lynched by the citizens of three of the great Christian states of the Union.

Such prodigies and monstrosities I could pile up for hours, along with a lot of instructive blabbing about what this or that immortal once told me off the record, for I have had the honor of encountering three Presidents of the United States in their cups, not to mention sitting Governors of all the states save six. But I bear in mind Sir Thomas Overbury's sneer at the fellow who "chooseth rather to be counted a spy than not a politician, and maintains his reputation by naming great men familiarly," and so hold my peace: let some larval Ph.D. dig the dirt out of my papers marked "Strictly Private: Destroy Unread" after I shove off for bliss eternal. In the present book my only purpose is to try to re-create for myself, and for any one who may care to follow me, the gaudy life that young newspapers reporters led in the major American cities at the turn of the century. I believed then, and still believe today, that it was the maddest, gladdest, damndest existence ever enjoyed by mortal youth. At a time when the respectable bourgeois youngsters of my generation were college freshmen, oppressed by simian sophomores and affronted with balderdash daily and hourly by chalky pedagogues, I was at large in a wicked seaport of half a million people, with a front seat at every public show, as free of the night as of the day, and getting earfuls and eyefuls of instruction in a hundred giddy arcana, none of them taught in schools. On my twenty-first birthday, by all orthodox cultural standards, I probably reached my all-time low, for the heavy reading of my teens had been abandoned in favor of life itself, and I did not return seriously to the lamp until a time near the end of this record. But it would be an exaggeration to say that I was ignorant, for if I neglected the humanities I was meanwhile laying in all the worldly wisdom of a police lieutenant, a bartender, a shyster lawyer, or a midwife. And it would certainly be idiotic to say that I was not happy. The illusion that swathes and bedizens journalism, bringing in its endless squads of recruits, was still full upon me, and I had yet to taste the sharp teeth of responsibility. Life was arduous, but it was gay and carefree. The days chased one another like kittens chasing their tails.

Whether or not the young journalists of today live so spaciously is a question that I am not competent to answer, for my contacts with them, of late years, have been rather scanty. They undoubtedly get a great deal more money than we did in 1900, but their freedom is much less than ours was, and they somehow give me the impression, seen at a distance, of complacency rather than intrepidity. In my day a reporter who took an assignment was wholly on his own until he got back to the office, and even then he was little molested until his copy was turned in at the desk; today he tends to become only a homunculus at the end of a telephone wire, and the reduction of his observations to prose is commonly farmed out to literary castrati who never leave the office, and hence never feel the wind of the world in their faces or see anything with their own eyes. I well recall my horror when I heard, for the first time, of a journalist who had laid in a pair of what were then called bicycle pants and taken to golf: it was as if I had encountered a stud-horse with his hair done up in frizzes, and pink bowknots peeking out of them. It seemed, in some vague way, ignominious, and even a bit indelicate. I was shocked almost as much when I first heard of reporters joining labor unions, and describing themselves as wage slaves. The underlying ideology here, of course, was anything but new, for I doubt that there has ever been a competent reporter in history who did not regard the proprietors of his paper as sordid rascals, all dollars and no sense. But it is one thing (a) to curl the lip over such wretches, and quite another thing (b) to bellow and beat the breast under their atrocities, just as it is one thing (a^2) to sass a cruel city editor with, so to speak, the naked hands, and another thing (b^2) to confront him from behind a phalanx of government agents and labor bravoes. The *a* operations are easy to reconcile with the old-time journalist's concept of himself as a free spirit and darling of the gods, licensed by his high merits to ride and deride the visible universe; the *b*'s must suggest inevitably a certain unhappy self-distrust, perhaps not without ground.

Like its companion volume, "Happy Days" (1940), this book is mainly true, but with occasional stretchers. I have checked my recollections whenever possible, and found them reasonably accurate. For the rest, I must throw myself upon the bosom of that "friendly and judicious reader" to whom Charles Lamb dedicated the Essays of Elia—that understanding fellow, male or female, who refuses to take "everything perversely in the absolute and literal sense," but gives it "a fair construction, as to an after-dinner conversation."

V

American English

Mencken's interest in American English first developed at the turn of the century when, as a police-court reporter in Baltimore, he was attracted by the peculiarities of speech he heard from both sides of the court rail. By 1910 he had accumulated enough material to begin publication of newspaper articles on the subject in the Baltimore Evening Sun, *and in August 1913, he printed his first magazine piece, "The American: His Language" in the* Smart Set, *the opening of which became the opening of the first edition of* The American Language, *published in 1919. The book was probably written in 1915 or 1916, and was put in final form in 1918. It was the product of leisure provided by the atmosphere of World War I, which had compelled him to suspend his role as a critic of public affairs. A second edition followed in 1921, a third in 1923, and a fourth in 1936, all completely revised and enlarged. Thereafter he published two huge supplements to the fourth edition, the first in 1945, and the second in 1948. Again, the fourth edition resulted from the restrictions imposed by World War II on his normal mode of writing. In 1963 an excellent one-volume abridged edition of the fourth edition and its two supplements appeared under the editorship of Professor Raven I. McDavid, Jr.*

The first edition of The American Language *was an immediate popular and critical success. Mencken thought the work inferior to* A Book of Prefaces, *published in 1917, which had been given only three favorable reviews, but he was nevertheless pleased by the book's reception. He received a large amount of material from professional philologists and the public for use in future editions, and he subscribed to a clipping service to keep track of articles and other material in the field. His labors eventually stimulated the founding in 1925 of* American Speech, *a journal devoted to the subject. This circumstance somewhat surprised him, for, as he remarked, he was not normally given to good works. What pleased him most was the cordial reception given all editions by the learned world generally. There were exceptions, but the only one which stung him was a lack of acknowledgment from the* Dictionary of American English on Historical Principles, *which began to appear in 1936, notwithstanding the fact, as he remarked, that his book had been mined by the editors. However, due acknowledgment was given in the next printing.*

In the first three editions of The American Language, *Mencken had argued that American speech was clearly becoming distinct from its parent stem, and that the differences between English and American would continue to increase. On the analogy of the Irish dialect of English, a dialect he regarded as much less important than American, he thought this a gain, and cited the extraordinary contributions of Douglas Hyde, J. M. Synge, and Lady Gregory. In America, he said on the final page of the third edition:*

> *given the poet, there may suddenly come a day when our* theirns *and* would'a hads *will take on the barbaric stateliness of the peasant locutions of old Maurya in "Riders to the Sea." They seem grotesque and absurd today because the folks who use them seem grotesque and absurd. But that is a too facile logic and under it is a false assumption. In all human beings, if only understanding be brought to the business, dignity will be found, and that dignity cannot fail to reveal itself, soon or late, in the words and phrases with which they make known their hopes and aspirations and cry out against the meaninglessness of life.*

In the fourth edition he reversed his main argument. He thought that since 1923 English had been so greatly influenced by American that the Englishman, on an early tomorrow, would speak a kind of American dialect.

In the Preface to Supplement Two he closed his last accounting with the subject by observing that his labors over the years had not been those of an "expert in linguistics," but of "a journalist interested in languages" whose principal virtue was the "homely virtue of diligence." Professor McDavid takes the position that this estimate is the product of "excessive modesty." However, in conversation, Mencken admitted he possessed one of the rarest of all accomplishments: he was absolutely bilingual. He could speak English, as in this phrase, and American, as in this here one.

The American Language

❮❮❮❮❮❮❮❮❮❮❮❮❮❮❮❮❮❮❮❮❮❮❮❮❮❮❮❮❮❮❯❯❯❯❯❯❯❯❯❯❯❯❯❯❯❯❯❯❯❯❯❯❯❯❯❯❯❯❯❯

• I •

The Earliest Alarms

THE first American colonists had perforce to invent Americanisms, if only to describe the unfamiliar landscape and weather, flora and fauna confronting them. Half a dozen that are still in use are to be found in Captain John Smith's "Map of Virginia," published in 1612, and there are many more in the works of the New England annalists. As early as 1621 Alexander Gill was noting in his "Logonomia Anglica" that *maize* and *canoe* were making their way into English.[1] But it was reserved for one Francis Moore, who came out to Georgia with Oglethorpe in 1735, to raise the earliest alarm against this enrichment of English from the New World, and so set the tone that English criticism has maintained ever since. Thus he described Savannah, then a village only two years old:

> It stands upon the flat of a Hill; the Bank of the River (which they in barbarous English call a *bluff*) is steep, and about forty-five foot perpendicular.[2]

[1] "British Recognition of American Speech in the Eighteenth Century," by Allen Walker Read, *Dialect Notes*, Vol. VI, Pt. VI, 1933, p. 313.

[2] "A Voyage to Georgia, Begun in the Year 1735" (London, 1744), p. 24. Moore was something of an adventurer. He went to West Africa for the Royal Africa Company in 1730, and got into obscure difficulties on the river Gambia. But when he came to Georgia in 1735 it was in the prosaic character of storekeeper to the colony. He arrived late in the year and remained until July, 1736. In 1738 he was back, staying this time until 1743. His subsequent career is unknown.

John Wesley arrived in Georgia the same year, and from his diary for December 2, 1737, comes the Oxford Dictionary's earliest example of the use of the word. But Moore was the first to notice it, and what is better to the point, the first to denounce it, and for that pioneering he must hold his honorable place in this history. In colonial times, of course, there was comparatively little incitement to hostility to Americanisms, for the stream of Englishmen coming to America to write books about their sufferings had barely begun to flow, and the number of American books reaching London was very small. But by 1754 literary London was already sufficiently conscious of the new words arriving from the New World for Richard Owen Cambridge, author of "The Scribleriad," to be suggesting[3] that a glossary of them would soon be in order, and two years later the finicky and always anti-American Samuel Johnson was saying, in a notice of Lewis Evans's "Geographical, Historical, Political, Philosophical, and Mechanical Essays,"[4] substantially what many English reviewers still say with dogged piety:

> This treatise is written with such elegance as the subject admits, tho' not without some mixture of the American dialect, a tract [*i.e.*, trace] of corruption to which every language widely diffused must always be exposed.

As the Revolution drew on, the English discovered varieties of offensiveness on this side of the ocean that greatly transcended the philological, and I can find no record of any denunciation of Americanisms during the heat of the struggle itself. When, on July 20, 1778, a committee appointed by the Continental Congress to arrange for the "publick reception of the sieur Gerard, minister plenipotentiary of his most christian majesty," brought in a report recommending that "all replies or answers" to him should be "in the language of the United States,"[5] no notice of the contumacy

---

[3] In the *World,* No. 102, Dec. 12, 1754. Quoted by Read.

[4] The *Literary Magazine,* Sept.–Oct., 1756. Evans's book was published in Philadelphia in 1755 by Benjamin Franklin and D. Hall. It was accompanied by the author's "General Map of the Middle British Colonies in America."

[5] "Secret Journals of the Continental Congress," Vol. II, p. 95. In the earlier editions of the present book I said that these instructions were issued to Franklin on his appointment as Minister to France. Where I picked up the error I don't recall. It was corrected by the late Fred Newton Scott in the *Saturday Review of Literature,* Oct. 11, 1924. The instructions to Franklin, dated Oct. 12, 1778, contained no mention of language.

seems to have been taken in the Motherland. But a few months
before Cornwallis was finally brought to heel at Yorktown the
subject was resumed, and this time the attack came from a Briton
living in America, and otherwise ardently pro-American. He was
John Witherspoon (1723–94), a Scottish clergyman who had come
out in 1769 to be president of Princeton *in partibus infidelium.*

Witherspoon took to politics when the war closed his college,
and was elected a member of the New Jersey constitutional con-
vention. In a little while he was promoted to the Continental
Congress, and in it he sat for six years as its only member in holy
orders. He signed both the Declaration of Independence and the
Articles of Confederation, and was a member of the Board of
War throughout the Revolution. But though his devotion to the
American cause was thus beyond question, he was pained by the
American language, and when, in 1781, he was invited to contribute a series of papers to the *Pennsylvania Journal and Weekly
Advertiser* of Philadelphia, he seized the opportunity to denounce
it, albeit in the politic terms proper to the time. Beginning with
the disarming admission that "the vulgar in America speak much
better than the vulgar in England, for a very obvious reason, *viz.,*
that being much more unsettled, and moving frequently from
place, they are not so liable to local peculiarities either in accent
or phraseology," he proceeded to argue that Americans of education showed a lamentable looseness in their "public and solemn
discourses."

> I have heard in this country, in the senate, at the bar, and
> from the pulpit, and see daily in dissertations from the press, errors
> in grammar, improprieties and vulgarisms which hardly any person
> of the same class in point of rank and literature would have fallen
> into in Great Britain.

Witherspoon's mention of "the senate" was significant, for he
must have referred to the Continental Congress, and it is fair to
assume that at least some of the examples he cited to support his
charge came from the sacred lips of the Fathers. He divided these
"errors in grammar, improprieties and vulgarisms" into eight
classes, as follows:

1. Americanisms, or ways of speaking peculiar to this country.
2. Vulgarisms in England and America.

3. Vulgarisms in America only.
4. Local phrases or terms.
5. Common blunders arising from ignorance.
6. Cant phrases.
7. Personal blunders.
8. Technical terms introduced into the language.[6]

By Americanisms, said Witherspoon,

> I understand an use of phrases or terms, or a construction of sentences, even among people of rank and education, different from the use of the same terms or phrases, or the construction of similar sentences in Great Britain. It does not follow, from a man's using these, that he is ignorant, or his discourse upon the whole inelegant; nay, it does not follow in every case that the terms or phrases used are worse in themselves, but merely that they are of American and not of English growth. The word *Americanism*, which I have coined for the purpose, is exactly similar in its formation and significance to the word *Scotticism*.

Witherspoon listed twelve examples of Americanisms falling within his definition, and despite the polite assurance I have just quoted, he managed to deplore all of them. His first was the use of *either* to indicate more than two, as in "The United States, or *either* of them." This usage seems to have had some countenance in the England of the early seventeenth century, but it had gone out there by Witherspoon's day, and it has since been outlawed by the schoolmarm in the United States. His second caveat was laid against the American use of *to notify*, as in "The police *notified* the coroner." "In English," he said somewhat prissily, "we do not *notify* the person of the thing, but *notify* the thing to the person." But *to notify*, in the American sense, was simply an example of archaic English, preserved like so many other archaisms in America, and there was, and is, no plausible logical or grammatical objection to it.[7] Witherspoon's third Americanism

---

[6] Witherspoon's papers appeared under the heading of "The Druid." This list and the foregoing quotation are from No. V, printed on May 9, 1781. The subject was continued in No. VI on May 16, and in No. VII (in two parts) on May 23 and 30. All the papers are reprinted in "The Beginnings of American English," edited by M. M. Mathews (Chicago, 1931). They are also to be found in Witherspoon's "Collected Works," edited by Ashbel Green, Vol. IV (New York, 1800–01).

[7] The Oxford Dictionary's first example is dated 1440. After 1652 all the examples cited are American, until 1843, when the usage reappears in England.

was *fellow countrymen,* which he denounced as "an evident tau-
tology," and his fourth was the omission of *to be* before the second
verb in such constructions as "These things were ordered delivered
to the army." His next three were similar omissions, and his remaining five were the use of *or* instead of *nor* following *neither,*
the use of *certain* in "A *certain* Thomas Benson" (he argued that
"A *certain person called* Thomas Benson" was correct), the use
of *incident* in "Such bodies are *incident* to these evils," and the use
of *clever* in the sense of worthy, and of *mad* in the sense of angry.

It is rather surprising that Witherspoon found so few Americanisms for his list. Certainly there were many others, current in
his day, that deserved a purist's reprobation quite as much as
those he singled out, and he must have been familiar with them.
Among the verbs a large number of novelties had come into American usage since the middle of the century, some of them revivals
of archaic English verbs and others native inventions—*to belittle,
to advocate, to progress, to notice, to table, to raise* (for *to grow*),
*to deed, to locate, to ambition, to deputize, to compromit, to
appreciate* (in the sense of increase in value), *to eventuate,* and
so on. Benjamin Franklin, on his return to the United States in
1785, after nine years in France, was impressed so unpleasantly
by *to advocate, to notice, to progress* and *to oppose* that on December 26, 1789 he wrote to Noah Webster to ask for help in
putting them down, but they seem to have escaped Witherspoon.
He also failed to note the changes of meaning in the American
use of *creek, shoe, lumber, corn, barn, team, store, rock, cracker*
and *partridge.* Nor did he have anything to say about American
pronunciation, which had already begun to differ materially from
that of Standard English.

Witherspoon's strictures, such as they were, fell upon deaf
ears, at least in the new Republic. He was to get heavy support,
in a little while, from the English reviews, which began to belabor everything American in the closing years of the century, but
on this side of the ocean the tide was running the other way, and
as the Revolution drew to its victorious close there was a widespread tendency to reject English precedent and authority altogether, in language no less than in government. In the case of the
language, several logical considerations supported that dispo-

sition, though the chief force at the bottom of it, of course, was probably only national conceit. For one thing, it was apparent to the more astute politicians of the time that getting rid of English authority in speech, far from making for chaos, would encourage the emergence of home authority, and so help to establish national solidarity, then the great desideratum of desiderata. And for another thing, some of them were farsighted enough to see that the United States, in the course of the years, would inevitably surpass the British Isles in population and wealth, and to realize that its cultural independence would grow at the same pace.

Something of the sort was plainly in the mind of John Adams when he wrote to the president of Congress from Amsterdam on September 5, 1780, suggesting that Congress set up an academy for "correcting, improving and ascertaining the English language." There were such academies, he said, in France, Spain, and Italy, but the English had neglected to establish one, and the way was open for the United States. He went on:

> It will have a happy effect upon the union of States to have a public standard for all persons in every part of the continent to appeal to, both for the signification and pronunciation of the language. . . . English is destined to be in the next and succeeding centuries more generally the language of the world than Latin was in the last or French is in the present age. The reason of this is obvious, because the increasing population in America, and their universal connection and correspondence with all nations will, aided by the influence of England in the world, whether great or small, force their language into general use, in spite of all the obstacles that may be thrown in their way, if any such there should be.[8]

Six years before this, in January, 1774, some anonymous writer, perhaps also Adams, had printed a similar proposal in the *Royal American Magazine*. That it got some attention is indicated by the fact that Sir John Wentworth, the Loyalist Governor of New Hampshire, thought it of sufficient importance to enclose a reprint of it in a dispatch to the Earl of Dartmouth, Secretary of State for the Colonies, dated April 24. I quote from it briefly:

---

[8] The letter is reprinted in full in "The Beginnings of American English," before cited, pp. 41–43.

The English language has been greatly improved in Britain within a century, but its highest perfection, with every other branch of human knowledge, is perhaps reserved for this land of light and freedom. As the people through this extensive country will speak English, their advantages for polishing their language will be great, and vastly superior to what the people of England ever enjoyed. I beg leave to propose a plan for perfecting the English language in America, thro' every future period of its existence; *viz.:* That a society for this purpose should be formed, consisting of members in each university and seminary, who shall be stiled *Fellows of the American Society of Language;* That the society . . . annually publish some observations upon the language, and from year to year correct, enrich and refine it, until perfection stops their progress and ends their labor.[9]

Whether this article was Adams's or not, he kept on returning to the charge, and in a second letter to the president of Congress, dated September 30, 1780, he expressed the hope that, after an American Academy had been set up, England would follow suit.

This I should admire. England will never more have any honor, excepting now and then that of imitating the Americans. I assure you, Sir, I am not altogether in jest. I see a general inclination after English in France, Spain and Holland, and it may extend throughout Europe. The population and commerce of America will force their language into general use.[1]

In his first letter to the president of Congress Adams deplored the fact that "it is only very lately that a tolerable dictionary [of English] has been published, even by a private person,[2] and there is not yet a passable grammar enterprised by any individual." He did not know it, but at that very moment a young schoolmaster in the backwoods of New York was preparing to meet both lacks. He was Noah Webster. Three years later he returned to Hartford, his birthplace, and brought out his "Grammatical Institute of the English Language," and soon afterward he began the labors which finally bore fruit in his "*American* Dictionary of the English

---

[9] The full text is in "The Beginnings of American English," just cited.
[1] For this letter I am indebted to George Philip Krapp: "The English Language in America," Vol. I, p. 7.
[2] His reference, of course, was to Johnson's Dictionary, first published in 1755.

Language" in 1828.[3] Webster was a pedantic and rather choleric fellow—someone once called him "the critic and cockcomb-general of the United States"—and his later years were filled with ill-natured debates over his proposals for reforming English spelling, and over the more fanciful etymologies in his dictionary. But though, in this enlightened age, he would scarcely pass as a philologian, he was extremely well read for his time, and if he fell into the blunder of deriving all languages from the Hebrew of the Ark, he was at least shrewd enough to notice the relationship between Greek, Latin and the Teutonic languages before it was generally recognized. He was always at great pains to ascertain actual usages, and in the course of his journeys from state to state to perfect his copyright on his first spelling-book[4] he accumulated a large amount of interesting and valuable material, especially in the field of pronunciation. Much of it he utilized in his "Dissertations on the English Language," published at Boston in 1789.

In the opening essay of this work he put himself squarely behind Adams. He foresaw that the new Republic would quickly outstrip England in population, and that virtually all its people would speak English. He proposed therefore that an American standard be set up, independent of the English standard, and that it be inculcated in the schools throughout the country. He argued that it should be determined, not by "the practise of any particular class of people," but by "the general practise of the nation," with due regard, in cases where there was no general practise, to "the principle of analogy." He went on:

> As an independent nation, our honor requires us to have a system of our own, in language as well as government. Great Britain, whose children we are, and whose language we speak, should no longer be *our* standard; for the taste of her writers is already corrupted,[5] and her language on the decline. But if it were

---

[3] His "Compendious Dictionary of the English Language," a sort of trial balloon, was published in 1806. There is a brief but good account of his dictionary-making in "A Survey of English Dictionaries," by M. M. Mathews; London, 1933, pp. 37–45.

[4] Published in 1783. There was no national copyright until 1790.

[5] Later on in the same essay Webster sought to support this doctrine by undertaking an examination of Johnson, Gibbon, Hume, Robertson, Home, Kaims and Blair. Of Johnson he said: "His style is a mixture of Latin and English; an intoler-

not so, she is at too great a distance to be our model, and to instruct us in the principles of our own tongue. . . . Several circumstances render a future separation of the American tongue from the English necessary and unavoidable. . . . Numerous local causes, such as a new country, new associations of people, new combinations of ideas in arts and sciences, and some intercourse with tribes wholly unknown in Europe, will introduce new words into the American tongue. These causes will produce, in a course of time, a language in North America as different from the future language of England as the modern Dutch, Danish and Swedish are from the German, or from one another: like remote branches of a tree springing from the same stock, or rays of light shot from the same center, and diverging from each other in proportion to their distance from the point of separation. . . . We have therefore the fairest opportunity of establishing a national language and of giving it uniformity and perspicuity, in North America, that ever presented itself to mankind. Now is the time to begin the plan.[6]

What Witherspoon thought of all this is not recorded. Maybe he never saw Webster's book, for he was going blind in 1789, and lived only five years longer. Webster seems to have got little support for what he called his Federal English from the recognized illuminati of the time;[7] indeed, his proposals for a reform of American spelling, set forth in an appendix to his "Dissertations," were denounced roundly by some of them, and the rest were only lukewarm. He dedicated the "Dissertations" to Franklin, but

---

able composition of Latinity, affected smoothness, scholastic accuracy, and roundness of periods." And of Gibbon: "It is difficult to comprehend his meaning and the chain of his ideas, as fast as we naturally read. . . . The mind of the reader is constantly dazzled by a glare of ornament, or charmed from the subject by the music of the language."

[6] The successive parts of the quotation are from pp. 20, 22, 22–3, and 36.

[7] The members of the Philological Society of New York, organized in 1788, were for him, but they were young men of little influence, and their society lasted only a year or so. Webster became a member on March 17, 1788, but on Dec. 20 he left New York. The president was Josiah O. Hoffman and among the members were William Dunlap, the painter and dramatist, and Samuel L. Mitchell. On Aug. 27 Ebenezer Hazard, then Postmaster-General of the Confederation, wrote to a friend in Boston that Webster was "the monarch" of the society. In April, 1788 Webster printed in his *American Magazine* a notice saying that its purpose was that of "ascertaining and improving the American tongue." On July 4, 1788 the society passed a resolution approving the first part of his Grammatical Institute. See "The Philological Society of New York," by Allen Walker Read, *American Speech*, April, 1934.

Franklin delayed acknowledging the dedication until the last days of 1789, and then ventured upon no approbation of Webster's linguistic Declaration of Independence. On the contrary, he urged him to make war upon various Americanisms of recent growth, and perhaps with deliberate irony applauded his "zeal for preserving the purity of our language." A year before the "Dissertations" appeared, Dr. Benjamin Rush anticipated at least some of Webster's ideas in "A Plan of a Federal University,"[8] and they seem to have made some impression on Thomas Jefferson, who was to ratify them formally in 1813;[9] but the rest of the contemporaneous sages held aloof, and in July, 1800, the *Monthly Magazine and American Review* of New York printed an anonymous denunciation, headed "On the Scheme of an American Language," of the notion that "grammars and dictionaries should be compiled by natives of the country, not of the British or English, but of the *American* tongue." The author of this tirade, who signed himself C, displayed a violent Anglomania. "The most suitable name for our country," he said, "would be that which is now appropriated only to a part of it: I mean New England." While admitting that a few Americanisms were logical and necessary—for example, *Congress, president* and *capitol*—he dismissed all the rest as "manifest corruptions." A year later, a savant using the *nom de plume* of Aristarcus delivered a similar attack on Webster in a series of articles contributed to the *New England Palladium* and reprinted in the *Port Folio* of Philadelphia, the latter "a notoriously Federalistic and pro-British organ." "If the Connecticut lexicographer," he said, "considers the retaining of the English

---

[8] Contributed to the *American Museum* for 1788. Under the heading of Philology he said: "Instruction in this branch of literature will become the more necessary in America as our intercourse must soon cease with the bar, the stage and the pulpit of Great Britain, from whence [sic] we received our knowledge of the pronunciation of the English language. Even modern English books should cease to be the models of style in the United States. The present is the age of simplicity of writing in America. The turgid style of Johnson, the purple glare of Gibbon, and even the studied and thick-set metaphors of Junius are all equally unnatural and should not be admitted into our country."

[9] In a letter from Monticello, August 16, to John Waldo, author of "Rudiments of English Grammar."—On August 12, 1801 Jefferson wrote to James Madison: "I view Webster as a mere pedagogue, of very limited understanding and very strong prejudices and party passion," but this was with reference to a political matter. In his letter to Waldo, Jefferson adopted Webster's ideas categorically, and professed to believe that "an American dialect will be formed."

language as a badge of slavery, let him not give us a Babylonish dialect in its stead, but adopt, at once, the language of the aborigines."[1]

But if the illuminati were thus chilly, the plain people supported Webster's scheme for the emancipation of American English heartily enough, though very few of them could have heard of it. The period from the gathering of the Revolution to the turn of the century was one of immense activity in the concoction and launching of new Americanisms, and more of them came into the language than at any time between the earliest colonial days and the rush to the West. Webster himself lists some of these novelties in his "Dissertations," and a great many more are to be found in Richard H. Thornton's "American Glossary"[2]—for example, *black-eye* (in the sense of defeat), *block* (of houses), *bobolink, bookstore, bootee* (now obsolete), *breadstuffs, buckeye, buckwheat-cake, bull-snake, bundling* and *buttonwood,* to go no further than the *b's.* It was during this period, too, that the American meanings of such words as *shoe, corn, bug, bureau, mad, sick, creek, barn* and *lumber* were finally differentiated from the English meanings, and that American peculiarities in pronunciation began to make themselves felt. Despite the economic difficulties which followed the Revolution, the general feeling was that the new Republic was a success, and that it was destined to rise in the world as England declined. There was a widespread contempt for everything English, and that contempt extended to the canons of the mother-tongue.

· 2 ·

The English Attack

But the Jay Treaty of 1794 gave notice that there was still some life left in the British lion, and during the following years

---

[1] See "Towards a Historical Aspect of American Speech Consciousness," by Leon Howard, *American Speech,* April, 1930.
[2] Published in two volumes (Philadelphia and London, 1912). Thornton, who died in 1925, left a large amount of additional material, and its publication was begun in *Dialect Notes,* Vol. VI, Pt. III, 1931.

the troubles of the Americans, both at home and abroad, mounted at so appalling a rate that their confidence and elation gradually oozed out of them. Simultaneously, their pretensions began to be attacked with pious vigor by patriotic Britishers, and in no field was the fervor of these brethren more marked than in those of literature and language. To be sure, there were Englishmen, then as now, who had a friendly and understanding interest in all things American, including even American books, and some of them took the trouble to show it, but they were not many. The general tone of English criticism, from the end of the eighteenth century to the present day, has been one of suspicion, and not infrequently it has been extremely hostile. The periods of remission, as often as not, have been no more than evidences of adroit politicking, as when Oxford, in 1907, helped along the graceful liquidation of the Venezuelan unpleasantness of 1895 by giving Mark Twain an honorary D.C.L. In England all branches of human endeavor are alike bent to the service of the state, and there is an alliance between society and politics, science and literature, that is unmatched anywhere else on earth. But though this alliance, on occasion, may find it profitable to be polite to the Yankee, and even to conciliate him, there remains an active aversion under the surface, born of the incurable rivalry between the two countries, and accentuated perhaps by their common tradition and their similar speech. Americanisms are forcing their way into English all the time, and of late they have been entering at a truly dizzy pace, but they seldom get anything properly describable as a welcome, save from small sects of iconoclasts, and every now and then the general protest against them rises to a roar. As for American literature, it is still regarded in England as somewhat barbaric and below the salt, and the famous sneer of Sydney Smith, though time has made it absurd in all other respects, is yet echoed complacently in many an English review of American books.[3]

---

[3] "In the four quarters of the globe, who reads an American book? or goes to an American play? or looks at an American picture or statue? What does the world yet owe to American physicians or surgeons? What new substances have their chemists discovered? or what old ones have they analyzed? What new constellations have been discovered by the telescopes of Americans? What have they done in mathematics? Who drinks out of American glasses? or eats from American plates? or wears American coats or gowns? or sleeps in American blankets? Finally, under which of the old tyrannical governments of Europe is every sixth man a slave, whom

There is an amusing compilation of some of the earlier dia-
tribes in William B. Cairns's "British Criticisms of American
Writings, 1783–1815."[4] Cairns is not so much concerned with
linguistic matters as with literary criticism, but he reprints a number of extracts from the pioneer denunciations of Americanisms,
and they surely show a sufficient indignation. The attack began
in 1787, when the *European Magazine and London Review* fell
upon the English of Thomas Jefferson's "Notes on the State of
Virginia," and especially upon his use of *to belittle,* which, according to Thornton, was his own coinage. "*Belittle!*" it roared.
"What an expression! It may be an elegant one in Virginia, and
even perfectly intelligible; but for our part, all we can do is to
guess at its meaning. For shame, Mr. Jefferson! Why, after tram-
pling upon the honour of our country, and representing it as little
better than a land of barbarism—why, we say, perpetually tram-
ple also upon the very grammar of our language, and make that
appear as Gothic as, from your description, our manners are rude?
—Freely, good sir, will we forgive all your attacks, impotent as
they are illiberal, upon our *national character;* but for the future
spare—O spare, we beseech you, our mother-tongue!" The *Gentleman's Magazine* joined the charge in May, 1798, with sneers for
the "uncouth . . . localities" [*sic*] in the "Yankey dialect" of Noah
Webster's "Sentimental and Humorous Essays," and the *Edinburgh* followed in October, 1804, with a patronizing article upon
John Quincy Adams's "Letters on Silesia." "The style of Mr.
Adams," it said, "is in general very tolerable English; which, for
an American composition, is no moderate praise." The usual American book of the time, it went on, was full of "affectations and
corruptions of phrase," and they were even to be found in "the
enlightened state papers of the two great Presidents." The *Edinburgh* predicted that a "spurious dialect" would prevail, "even at
the Court and in the Senate of the United States," and that the
Americans would thus "lose the only badge that is still worn of

---

his fellow-creatures may buy, and sell and torture." All this was a part of a
review of Adam Seybert's "Statistical Annals of the United States," *Edinburgh
Review,* Jan.–May, 1820.

    [4] *University of Wisconsin Studies in Language and Literature,* No. 1 (Madison,
Wis., 1918).

our consanguinity." The appearance of the five volumes of Chief Justice Marshall's "Life of George Washington," from 1804 to 1807, brought forth corrective articles from the *British Critic,* the *Critical Review,* the *Annual,* the *Monthly,* and the *Eclectic.* The *Edinburgh,* in 1808, declared that the Americans made "it a point of conscience to have no aristocratical distinctions—even in their vocabulary." They thought, it went on, "one word as good as another, provided its meaning be as clear." The *Monthly Mirror,* in March of the same year, denounced "the corruptions and barbarities which are hourly obtaining in the speech of our transatlantic colonies [*sic*]," and reprinted with approbation a parody by some anonymous Englishman of the American style of the day. Here is an extract from it, with the words that the author regarded as Americanisms in italics:

> In America authors are to be found who make use of new or obsolete words which no good writer in this country would employ; and were it not for my *destitution* of leisure, which obliges me to hasten the *occlusion* of these pages, as I *progress* I should *bottom* my assertation on instances from authors of the first *grade;* but were I to render my sketch *lengthy* I should *illy* answer the purpose which I have in view.

The *British Critic,* in April, 1808, admitted somewhat despairingly that the damage was already done—that "the common speech of the United States has departed very considerably from the standard adopted in England." The others, however, sought to stay the flood by invective against Marshall, and, later, against his rival biographer, the Rev. Aaron Bancroft. The *Annual,* in 1808, pronounced its anathema upon "that torrent of barbarous phraseology" which was pouring across the Atlantic, and which threatened "to destroy the purity of the English language." In Bancroft's "Life of George Washington" (1808), according to the *British Critic,* there were "new words, or old words in a new sense," all of them inordinately offensive to Englishmen, "at almost every page," and in Joel Barlow's "The Columbiad" (1807; reprinted in England in 1809) the *Edinburgh* found "a great multitude of words which are radically and entirely new, and as utterly foreign as if they had been adopted from the Hebrew or Chinese," and "the perversion of a still greater number of English words from their proper use or signification, by employing nouns substantive for verbs, adjectives for substantives, &c." The *Edinburgh* continued:

> We have often heard it reported that our transatlantic brethren were beginning to take it amiss that their language should still be called English; and truly we must say that Mr. Barlow has gone far to take away that ground of reproach. The groundwork of his speech, perhaps may be English, as that of the Italian is Latin; but the variations amount already to more than a change of dialect; and really make a glossary necessary for most untravelled readers.

Some of Barlow's novelties, it must be granted, were fantastic enough—for example, *to vagrate* and *to ameed* among the verbs, *imkeeled* and *homicidious* among the adjectives, and *coloniarch* among the nouns. But many of the rest were either obsolete words whose use was perfectly proper in heroic poetry, or nonce-words of obvious meaning and utility. Some of the terms complained of by the *Edinburgh* are in good usage at this moment—for example, *to utilize, to hill, to breeze, to spade* (the soil), *millenial, crass,* and *scow.*[5] But to the English reviewers of the time words so unfamiliar were not only deplorable on their own account; they were also proofs that the Americans were a sordid and ignoble people with no capacity for prose, or for any of the other elegances of life.[6] "When the vulgar and illiterate lose the force of their animal spirits," observed the *Quarterly* in 1814, reviewing J. K. Paulding's "Lay of the Scottish Fiddle" (1813), "they become mere clods. . . . The founders of American society brought to the composition of their nation few seeds of good taste, and no rudiments of liberal science." To which may be added Southey's judgment in a letter to Landor in 1812: "See what it is to have a nation to take its place among civilized states before it has either gentlemen or scholars! They have in the course of twenty years acquired a distinct national character for low and lying knavery;

---

[5] See "A Historical Note on American English," by Leon Howard, *American Speech*, Sept., 1927.

[6] Cairns says that the *Edinburgh*, the *Anti-Jacobin*, the *Quarterly*, and the *European Magazine and London Review* were especially virulent. He says that the *Monthly*, despite my quotations, was always "kindly toward America" and that the *Eclectic* was, "on the whole, fair." The *Literary Magazine and British Review* he describes as enthusiastically pro-American, but it lived only a short time.

and so well do they deserve it that no man ever had any dealings with them without having proofs of its truth." Landor, it should be said, entered a protest against this, and on a somewhat surprising ground, considering the general view. "Americans," he said, "speak our language; they read 'Paradise Lost.'" But he hastened to add, "I detest the American character as much as you do."

The War of 1812 naturally exacerbated this animosity, though when the works of Irving and Cooper began to be known in England some of the English reviewers moderated their tone. Irving's "Knickerbocker" was not much read there until 1815, and not much talked about until "The Sketch-Book" followed it in 1819, but Scott had received a copy of it from Henry Brevoort in 1813, and liked it and said so. Byron mentioned it in a letter to his publisher, Murray, on August 7, 1821. We are told by Thomas Love Peacock that Shelley was "especially fond of the novels of Charles Brockden Brown, the American," but Cairns says there is no mention of the fact, if it be a fact, in any of Shelley's own writings, or in those of his other friends. "Knickerbocker" was published in 1809, the *North American Review* began in May, 1815, Bryant's "Thanatopsis" was printed in its pages in 1817, and Paulding's "The Backwoodsman," with an American theme and an American title, came out a year later, but Cooper's "Precaution" was still two years ahead, and American letters were yet in a somewhat feeble state. John Pickering, so late as 1816, said that "in this country we can hardly be said to have any authors by profession," and Justice Story, three years later, repeated the saying and sought to account for the fact. "So great," said Story, "is the call for talents of all sorts in the active use of professional and other business in America that few of our ablest men have leisure to devote exclusively to literature or the fine arts. . . . This obvious reason will explain why we have so few professional authors, and those not among our ablest men." In 1813 Jefferson, anticipating both Pickering and Story, had written to John Waldo:

> We have no distinct class of literati in our country. Every man is engaged in some industrious pursuit, and science is but a secondary occupation, always subordinate to the main business of life. Few, therefore, of those who are qualified have leisure to write.

Difficulties of communication hampered the circulation of such native books as were written. "It is much to be regretted," wrote Dr. David Ramsay, of Charleston, S. C., to Noah Webster in 1806, "that there is so little intercourse in a literary way between the States. As soon as a book of general utility comes out in any State it should be for sale in all of them." Ramsay asked for little; the most he could imagine was a sale of 2,000 copies for an American work in America. But even that was apparently beyond the possibilities of the time. It would be a mistake, however, to assume that the Americans eschewed reading altogether; on the contrary, there is some evidence that they read many English books. In 1802 the *Scot's Magazine* reported that at a book-fair held shortly before in New York the sales ran to 520,000 volumes, and that a similar fair was projected for Philadelphia. Six years before this the London book-seller, Henry Lemoine, made a survey of the American book trade for the *Gentleman's Magazine*.[7] He found that very few books were being printed in the country, and ascribed the fact to the high cost of labor, but he encountered well-stocked bookstores in New York, Philadelphia and Baltimore, and plenty of customers for their importations. He went on:

> Their sales are very great, for it is scarcely possible to conceive the number of readers with which every little town abounds. The common people are on a footing, in point of literature, with the middle ranks in Europe; they all read and write, and understand arithmetic. Almost every little town now furnishes a small circulating-library. . . . Whatever is useful sells, but publications on subjects merely speculative, and rather curious than important, controversial divinity, and voluminous polemical pieces, as well as heavy works on the arts and sciences, lie upon the importer's hands. They have no ready money to spare for anything but what they find useful.

But other visitors were much less impressed by the literary gusto of the young Republic. Henry Wansey, who came out in 1794, reported in his "Excursion to the United States of North America"[8] that the American libraries were "scanty," that their

---

[7] November, 1796. I take what follows from Cairns.
[8] Salisbury, 1796. Wansey stayed but two months, and his journey was confined to the region between Boston and Philadelphia.

collections were "almost entirely of modern books," and that they were deficient in "the means of tracing the history of questions, . . . a want which literary people felt very much, and which it will take some years to remedy." And Captain Thomas Hamilton, in his "Men and Manners in America,"[9] said flatly that "there is . . . nothing in the United States worthy of the name of library. Not only is there an entire absence of learning, in the higher sense of the term, but an absolute want of the material from which alone learning can be extracted. At present an American might study every book within the limits of the Union, and still be regarded in many parts of Europe—especially in Germany—as a man comparatively ignorant. Why does a great nation thus voluntarily continue in a state of intellectual destitution so anomalous and humiliating?" According to Hamilton, all the books imported from Europe for public institutions during the fiscal year 1829–30 reached a value of but $10,829.

But whatever the fact here, there can be no doubt that the Americans were quickly aware of every British aspersion upon their culture, whether it appeared in a book or in one of the reviews. If nothing else was read, such things were certainly read, and they came with sufficient frequency, and were couched in terms of sufficient offensiveness, to keep the country in a state of indignation for years. The flood of books by English visitors began before the end of the eighteenth century, and though many of them were intended to be friendly, there was in even the friendliest of them enough of what Cairns calls "the British knack for saying gracious things in an ungracious way" to keep the pot of fury boiling. At the other extreme the thing went to fantastic lengths. The *Quarterly Review,* summing up in 1814, accused the Americans of a multitude of strange and hair-raising offenses— for example, employing naked colored women to wait upon them at table, kidnapping Scotsmen, Welshmen and Hollanders and

---

[9]Published in Edinburgh in 1833, and reprinted in Philadelphia the same year. The book did not bear Hamilton's name, but was ascribed on the title page to "the author of 'Cyril Thornton.'" Hamilton was a younger brother to Sir William Hamilton, the metaphysician, and a friend to Sir Walter Scott. He was himself a frequent contributor to *Blackwood's.* "Cyril Thornton," published in 1827, was a successful novel, and remained in favor for many years. Hamilton died in 1842. "Men and Manners in America" was translated into French and twice into German.

selling them into slavery, and fighting one another incessantly under rules which made it "allowable to peel the skull, tear out the eyes, and smooth away the nose." In this holy war upon the primeval damyankee William Gifford, editor of the *Anti-Jacobin* in 1797–98, and after 1809 the first editor of the *Quarterly,* played an extravagant part,[1] but he was diligently seconded by Sydney Smith, Southey, Thomas Moore and many lesser lights. "If the [English] reviewers get hold of an American publication," said J. K. Paulding in "Letters From the South" in 1817, "it is made use of merely as a pretext to calumniate us in some way or other." There is an instructive account of the whole uproar in the fifth volume of John Bach McMaster's "History of the People of the United States From the Revolution to the Civil War." McMaster says that it was generally believed that the worst calumniators of the United States were subsidized by the British government, apparently in an effort to discourage emigration. He goes on:

> The petty annoyances, the little inconveniences and unpleasant incidents met with in all journeys, were grossly exaggerated and cited as characteristic of daily life in the States. Men and women met with at the inns and taverns, in the stage-coaches and far-away country towns, were described not as so many types, but as the typical Americans. The abuse heaped on public men by partisan newspapers, the charges of corruption made by one faction against the other, the scandals of the day, were all cited as solemn truth.

Even the relatively mild and friendly Captain Hamilton condescended to such tactics. This is what he had to say of Thomas Jefferson:

> The moral character of Jefferson was repulsive. Continually puling about liberty, equality, and the degrading curse of slavery,

---

[1] Gifford was a killer in general practice, and his onslaughts on Wordsworth, Shelley and Keats are still remembered. He retired from the *Quarterly* in 1824 with a fortune of £25,000—the first magazine editor in history to make it pay. On his death in 1826 he was solemnly buried in Westminster Abbey. The *Quarterly,* despite its anti-American ferocity, was regularly reprinted in Boston. But when its issue for July, 1823 appeared with an extraordinarily malignant review of William Faux's "Memorable Days in America" (London, 1823) the American publishers were warned that it contained a libel on "a distinguished individual at Washington," and accordingly withheld it.

he brought his own children to the hammer, and made money of his debaucheries.[2]

Such violent assaults, in the long run, were bound to breed defiance, but while they were at their worst they produced a contrary effect. "The nervous interest of Americans in the impressions formed of them by visiting Europeans," says Allan Nevins,[3] "and their sensitiveness to British criticism in especial, were long regarded as constituting a salient national trait." The native authors became extremely self-conscious and diffident, and the educated classes, in general, were daunted by the torrent of abuse: they could not help finding in it an occasional reasonableness, an accidental true hit. The result was uncertainty and skepticism in native criticism. "The first step of an American entering upon a literary career," said Henry Cabot Lodge, writing of the first quarter of the century,[4] "was to pretend to be an Englishman in order that he might win the approval, not of Englishmen, but of his own countrymen." Cooper, in his first novel, "Precaution" (1820), chose an English scene, imitated English models, and obviously hoped to placate the English critics thereby. Irving, too, in his earliest work, showed a considerable discretion, and his "Knickerbocker" was first published anonymously. But this puerile spirit did not last long. The English libels were altogether too vicious to be received lying down; their very fury demanded that they be met with a united and courageous front. Cooper, in his second novel, "The Spy" (1821), boldly chose an American setting and American characters, and though the influence of his wife, who came of a Loyalist family, caused him to avoid any direct at-

[2] See also "The Cambridge History of American Literature," Vol. I (New York, 1917), pp. 205–8; "As Others See Us," by John Graham Brooks (New York, 1909), Ch. VII; "James Kirke Paulding," by Amos L. Herold (New York, 1926), Ch. IV; "American Social History as Recorded by British Travellers," by Allan Nevins (New York, 1923), pp. 3–26 and pp. 111–138; "One Hundred Years of Peace," by Henry Cabot Lodge (New York, 1913), pp. 41–55; and "The English Traveller in America," 1785–1835, by Jane Louise Mesick (New York, 1922), pp. 241–45. There is a brief but comprehensive view of the earlier period in "British Recognition of American Speech in the Eighteenth Century," by Allen Walker Read, *Dialect Notes*, Vol. VI, Pt. VI, 1933. A bibliography of British books of American travel is in "The Cambridge History of American Literature," Vol. I, pp. 468–90, and another, annotated, in Nevins, pp. 555–68.

[3] "American Social History as Recorded by British Travelers" (New York, 1923), p. 3.

[4] In his essay, Colonialism in America, in "Studies in History" (Boston, 1884).

tack upon the English, he attacked them indirectly, and with great effect, by opposing an immediate and honorable success to their derisions. "The Spy" ran through three editions in four months, and was followed by a long line of thoroughly American novels. In 1828 Cooper undertook a detailed reply to the more common English charges in "Notions of the Americans," but he was still too cautious to sign his name to it: it appeared as "by a Travelling Bachelor." By 1834, however, he was ready to apologize formally to his countrymen for his early truancy in "Precaution." Irving, who was even more politic, and suffered moreover from Anglomania in a severe form, nevertheless edged himself gradually into the patriot band, and by 1828 he was brave enough to refuse the *Quarterly's* offer of a hundred guineas for an article on the ground that it was "so persistently hostile to our country" that he could not "draw a pen in its service."

The real counter-attack was carried on by lesser men—the elder Timothy Dwight, John Neal, Edward Everett, Charles Jared Ingersoll, J. K. Paulding, and Robert Walsh, Jr., among them. Neal went to England, became secretary to Jeremy Bentham, forced his way into the reviews, and so fought the English on their own ground. Walsh set up the *American Review of History and Politics,* the first American critical quarterly, in 1811, and eight years later published "An Appeal From the Judgments of Great Britain Respecting the United States of America." Everett performed chiefly in the *North American Review* (founded in 1815), to which he contributed many articles and of which he was editor from 1820 to 1824. Wirt published his "Letters of a British Spy" in 1803, and Ingersoll followed with "Inchiquin the Jesuit's Letters on American Literature and Politics" in 1811. In January, 1814 the *Quarterly* reviewed "Inchiquin" in a particularly violent manner, and a year later Dwight replied to the onslaught in "Remarks on the Review of Inchiquin's Letters Published in the *Quarterly Review,* Addressed to the Right Honorable George Canning, Esq." Dwight ascribed the *Quarterly* diatribe to Southey. He went on:

> Both the travelers and the literary journalists of [England] have, for reasons which it would be idle to inquire after and useless to allege, thought it proper to caricature the Americans. Their

pens have been dipped in gall; and their representations have been, almost merely, a mixture of malevolence and falsehood.

Dwight rehearsed some of the counts in the *Quarterly's* indictment—that "the president of Yale College tells of a *conflagrative* brand," that Jefferson used *to belittle,* that *to guess* was on the tongues of all Americans, and so on. "You charge us," he said, "with making some words, and using others in a peculiar sense. . . . You accuse us of forming projects to get rid of the English language; 'not,' you say, 'merely by barbarizing it, but by abolishing it altogether, and substituting a new language of our own.'" His reply was to list, on the authority of Pegge's "Anecdotes of the English Language," 105 vulgarisms common in London—for example, *potecary* for apothecary, *chimly* for chimney, *saace* for sauce, *kiver* for cover, *nowheres* for nowhere, *scholard* for scholar, and *hisn* for his—to accuse "members of Parliament" of using *diddled* and *gullibility*[5] and to deride the English provincial dialects as "unintelligible gabble."

But in this battle across the ocean it was Paulding who got in the most licks, and the heaviest ones. In all he wrote five books dealing with the subject. The first, "The Diverting History of John Bull and Brother Jonathan" (1812), was satirical in tone, and made a considerable popular success. Three years later he followed it with a more serious work, "The United States and England," another reply to the *Quarterly* review of "Inchiquin." The before-mentioned "Letters From the South" came out in 1817, and in 1822 Paulding resumed the attack with "A Sketch of Old England," a sort of *reductio ad absurdum* of the current English books of American travels. He had never been to England, and the inference was that many of the English travelers had never been to America. Finally, in 1825, he resorted to broad burlesque in "John Bull in America, or The New Munchausen."[6] Now and

---

[5] At that time both words were neologisms. The Oxford Dictionary's first example of *gullibility* is dated 1793. So late as 1818 it was denounced by the Rev. H. J. Todd, one of the improvers of Johnson's Dictionary, as "a low expression, sometimes used for *cullibility.*" The Oxford's first example of *to diddle* is dated 1806.

[6] This book, like John Bull and Brother Jonathan, seems to have had readers for a generation or more. So late as 1867 the Scribners brought out a new edition of the two in a single volume, under the title of "The Bulls and Jonathans," with a preface by William I. Paulding. It still makes amusing reading.

then some friendly aid came from the camp of the enemy. Cairns shows that, while the *Quarterly,* the *European Magazine* and the *Anti-Jacobin* were "strongly anti-American" and "deliberately and dirtily bitter," three or four of the lesser reviews displayed a fairer spirit, and even more or less American bias. After 1824, when the *North American Review* gave warning that if the campaign of abuse went on it would "turn into bitterness the last drops of good-will toward England that exist in the United States," even *Blackwood's* became somewhat conciliatory.

· 3 ·

American "Barbarisms"

But this occasional tolerance for things American was never extended to the American language. Most of the English books of travel mentioned Americanisms only to revile them, and even when they were not reviled they were certainly not welcomed. The typical attitude was well set forth by Captain Hamilton in "Men and Manners in America," already referred to as denying that the United States of 1833 had any libraries. "The amount of bad grammar in circulation," he said, "is very great; that of barbarisms [*i.e.,* Americanisms] enormous." Worse, these "barbarisms" were not confined to the ignorant, but came almost as copiously from the lips of the learned.

> I do not now speak of the operative class, whose massacre of their mother-tongue, however inhuman, could excite no astonishment; but I allude to the great body of lawyers and traders; the men who crowd the exchange and the hotels; who are to be heard speaking in the courts, and are selected by their follow-citizens to fill high and responsible offices. Even by this educated and respectable class, the commonest words are often so transmogrified as to be placed beyond recognition of an Englishman.

Hamilton then went on to describe some of the prevalent "barbarisms":

> The word *does* is split into two syllables, and pronounced *do-es. Where,* for some incomprehensible reason, is converted into

whare, there into *thare;* and I remember, on mentioning to an
acquaintance that I had called on a gentleman of taste in the arts,
he asked "whether he *shew* (showed) me his pictures." Such words
as *oratory* and *dilatory* are pronounced with the penult syllable
long and accented: *missionary* becomes *missionairy, angel, ángel,
danger, dánger,* etc.

But this is not all. The Americans have chosen arbitrarily to
change the meaning of certain old and established English words,
for reasons they cannot explain, and which I doubt much whether
any European philologist could understand. The word *clever*
affords a case in point. It has here no connexion with talent, and
simply means pleasant or amiable. Thus a good-natured blockhead
in the American vernacular is a *clever* man, and having had this
drilled into me, I foolishly imagined that all trouble with regard
to this word, at least, was at an end. It was not long, however,
before I heard of a gentleman having moved into a *clever* house,
of another succeeding to a *clever* sum of money, of a third embark-
ing in a *clever* ship, and making a *clever* voyage, with a *clever*
cargo; and of the sense attached to the word in these various combinations, I could gain nothing like a satisfactory explanation. . . .

The privilege of barbarizing the King's English is assumed by
all ranks and conditions of men. Such words as *slick, kedge* and
boss, it is true, are rarely used by the better orders; but they assume
unlimited liberty in the use of *expect, reckon, guess* and *calculate,*
and perpetrate other conversational anomalies with remorseless
impunity.

This Briton, as usual, was as full of moral horror as of grammatical disgust, and put his denunciation upon the loftiest of
grounds. He concluded:

I will not go on with this unpleasant subject, nor should I have
alluded to it, but I feel it something of a duty to express the
natural feeling of an Englishman at finding the language of
Shakespeare and Milton thus gratuitously degraded. Unless the
present progress of change be arrested by an increase of taste and
judgment in the more educated classes, there can be no doubt that,
in another century, the dialect of the Americans will become utterly
unintelligible to an Englishman, and that the nation will be cut off
from the advantages arising from their participation in British
literature. If they contemplate such an event with complacency, let
them go on and prosper; they have only to *progress* in their
present course, and their grandchildren bid fair to speak a jargon

as novel and peculiar as the most patriotic American linguist can desire.[7]

All the other English writers of travel books took the same line, and so did the stay-at-homes who hunted and abhorred Americanisms from afar. Mrs. Frances Trollope reported in her "Domestic Manners of the Americans" (1832) that during her whole stay in the Republic she had seldom "heard a sentence elegantly turned and correctly pronounced from the lips of an American": there was "always something either in the expression or the accent" that jarred her feelings and shocked her taste. She concluded that "the want of refinement" was the great American curse. Captain Frederick Marryat, in "A Diary in America" (1839), observed that "it is remarkable how very debased the language has become in a short period in America," and then proceeded to specifications—for example, the use of *right away* for immediately, of *mean* for ashamed, of *clever* in the senses which stumped Captain Hamilton, of *bad* as a deprecant of general utility, of *admire* for like, of *how?* instead of *what?* as an interrogative, of *considerable* as an adverb, and of such immoral verbs as *to suspicion* and *to opinion.* Marryat was here during Van Buren's administration, when the riot of Americanisms was at its wildest, and he reported some really fantastic specimens. Once, he said, he heard "one of the first men in America" say, "Sir, if I had done so, I should not only have doubled and trebled, but I should have *fourbled* and *fivebled* my money." Unfortunately, it is hard to believe that an American who was so plainly alive to the difference between *shall* and *will*, *should* and *would*, would have been unaware of *quadrupled* and *quintupled.* No doubt there was humor in the country, then as now, and visiting Englishmen were sometimes taken for rides.

Captain Basil Hall, who was here in 1827 and 1828, and published his "Travels in North America" in 1829, was so upset by some of the novelties he encountered that he went to see Noah Webster, then seventy years old, to remonstrate. Webster upset him still further by arguing stoutly that "his countrymen had not only a right to adopt new words, but were obliged to modify the

---

[7] The quotations are from pp. 127–9.

language to suit the novelty of the circumstances, geographical and political, in which they were placed." The lexicographer went on to observe judicially that "it is quite impossible to stop the progress of language—it is like the course of the Mississippi, the motion of which, at times, is scarcely perceptible; yet even then it possesses a momentum quite irresistible. Words and expressions will be forced into use, in spite of all the exertions of all the writers in the world."

"But surely," persisted Hall, "such innovations are to be deprecated?"

"I don't know that," replied Webster. "If a word becomes universally current in America, where English is spoken, why should it not take its station in the language?"

To this Hall made an honest British reply. "Because," he said, "there are words enough already."

Webster tried to mollify him by saying that "there were not fifty words in all which were used in America and not in England" —an underestimate of large proportions—but Hall went away muttering.

Marryat, who toured the United States ten years after Hall, was chiefly impressed by the American verb *to fix*, which he described as "universal" and as meaning "to do anything." It also got attention from other English travelers, including Godfrey Thomas Vigne, whose "Six Months in America" was printed in 1832, and Charles Dickens, who came in 1842. Vigne said that it had "perhaps as many significations as any word in the Chinese language," and proceeded to list some of them—"to be done, made, mixed, mended, bespoken, hired, ordered, arranged, procured, finished, lent or given." Dickens thus dealt with it in one of his letters home to his family:

> I asked Mr. Q. on board a steamboat if breakfast be nearly ready, and he tells me yes, he should think so, for when he was last below the steward was *fixing* the tables—in other words, laying the cloth. When we have been writing and I beg him . . . to collect our papers, he answers that he'll *fix* 'em presently. So when a man's dressing he's *fixing* himself, and when you put yourself under a doctor he *fixes* you in no time. T'other night, before we came on board here, when I had ordered a bottle of mulled claret, and waited some time for it, it was put on the table with an apology

from the landlord (a lieutenant-colonel) that he fear'd it wasn't properly *fixed*. And here, on Saturday morning, a Western man, handing his potatoes to Mr. Q. at breakfast, inquired if he wouldn't take some of "these *fixings*" with his meat.[8]

In another letter, written on an Ohio river steamboat on April 15, 1842, Dickens reported that "out of Boston and New York" a nasal drawl was universal, that the prevailing grammar was "more than doubtful," that the "oddest vulgarisms" were "received idioms," and that "all the women who have been bred in slave States speak more or less like Negroes." His observations on American speech habits in his "American Notes" (1842) were so derisory that they drew the following from Emerson:

> No such conversations ever occur in this country in real life, as he relates. He has picked up and noted with eagerness each odd local phrase that he met with, and when he had a story to relate, has joined them together, so that the result is the broadest caricature.[9]

Almost every English traveler of the years between the War of 1812 and the Civil War was puzzled by the strange signs on American shops. Hall couldn't make out the meaning of *Leather and Finding Store*, though he found *Flour and Feed Store* and *Clothing Store* self-explanatory, albeit unfamiliar. Hamilton, who followed in 1833, failed to gather "the precise import" of *Dry-Goods Store*, and was baffled and somewhat shocked by *Coffin Warehouse* (it would now be *Casketeria!*) and *Hollow Ware*, *Spiders*, and *Fire-Dogs*. But all this was relatively mild stuff, and after 1850 the chief licks at the American dialect were delivered, not by English travelers, most of whom had begun by then to find it more amusing than indecent, but by English pedants who did not stir from their cloisters. The climax came in 1863, when the Very Rev. Henry Alford, D.D., dean of Canterbury, printed his "Plea for the Queen's English."[1] He said:

---

[8] The letter appears in John Forster's "Life of Charles Dickens" (London, 1872–74), Book III, Chapter V. It is reprinted in Allan Nevins's "American Social History as Recorded by British Travelers" (New York, 1923), p. 268. It was written on a canal-boat nearing Pittsburgh, and dated March 28, 1842.

[9] "Journal," Nov. 25, 1842.

[1] A second edition followed in 1864, and an eighth was reached by 1880. There was also an American edition. In October, 1864, an American resident in England, G. Washington Moon by name, brought out a counterblast, "The Dean's English."

Look at the process of deterioration which our Queen's English has undergone at the hands of the Americans. Look at those phrases which so amuse us in their speech and books; at their reckless exaggeration and contempt for congruity; and then compare the character and history of the nation—its blunted sense of moral obligation and duty to man; its open disregard of conventional right when aggrandisement is to be obtained; and I may now say, its reckless and fruitless maintenance of the most cruel and unprincipled war in the history of the world.

It will be noted that Alford here abandoned one of the chief counts in Sydney Smith's famous indictment, and substituted its exact opposite. Smith had denounced slavery, whereas Alford, by a tremendous feat of moral virtuosity, was now denouncing the war to put it down! But Samuel Taylor Coleridge had done almost as well in 1822. The usual English accusation at that time, as we have seen, was that the Americans had abandoned English altogether and set up a barbarous jargon in its place. Coleridge, speaking to his friend Thomas Allsop, took the directly contrary tack. "An American," he said, "by his boasting of the superiority of the Americans generally, but especially in their language, once provoked me to tell him that 'on that head the least said the better, as the Americans presented the extraordinary anomaly of a *people without a language.* [Allsop's italics] That they had mistaken the English language for baggage (which is called *plunder* in America), and had stolen it.'" And then the inevitable moral reflection: "Speaking of America, it is believed a fact verified beyond doubt that some years ago it was impossible to obtain a copy of the Newgate Calendar, as they had all been bought up by the Americans, whether to suppress the blazon of their forefathers, or to assist in their genealogical researches, I could never learn satisfactorily."[2]

This reached a seventh edition by 1884. Moon employed the ingenious device of turning Alford's pedantries upon him. He showed that the dean was a very loose and careless writer, and often violated his own rules. Another American, Edward S. Gould, bombarded him from the same ground in "Good English, or Popular Errors in Language" (New York, 1867). Alford was a favorite scholar of the time. He wrote Latin odes and a history of the Jews before he was ten years old, and in later life was the first editor of the *Contemporary Review* and brought out a monumental edition of the New Testament in Greek. He was born in 1810, served as dean of Canterbury from 1857 to 1871, and died in the latter year.

[2] "Letters, Conversations and Recollections of S. T. Coleridge," edited by Thomas Allsop (London, 1836).

· 4 ·

The English Attitude Today

Smith, Alford and Coleridge have plenty of heirs and assigns
in the England of today. There is in the United States, as everyone knows, a formidable sect of Anglomaniacs, and its influence
is often felt, not only in what passes here for society, but also in
the domains of politics, finance, pedagogy and journalism, but the
corresponding sect of British Americophils is small and feeble,
though it shows a few respectable names. It is seldom that anything specifically American is praised in the English press, save,
of course, some new manifestation of American Anglomania. The
realm of Uncle Shylock remains, at bottom, the "brigand confederation" of the *Foreign Quarterly,* and on occasion it becomes
again the "loathsome creature, . . . maimed and lame, full of sores
and ulcers," of Dickens. In the field of language an Americanism
is generally regarded as obnoxious *ipso facto,* and when a new
one of any pungency begins to force its way into English usage
the guardians of the national linguistic chastity belabor it with
great vehemence, and predict calamitous consequences if it is
not put down. If, despite these alarms, it makes progress, they
often switch to the doctrine that it is really old English, and
search the Oxford Dictionary for examples of its use in Chaucer's
time, or even in the Venerable Bede's;[3] but while it is coming in
they give it no quarter. Here the unparalleled English talent for
discovering moral obliquity comes into play, and what begins as
an uproar over a word sometimes ends as a holy war to keep the
knavish Yankee from undermining and ruining the English *Kultur*
and overthrowing the British Empire. The crusade has abundant
humors. Not infrequently a phrase denounced as an abominable
Americanism really originated in the London music-halls, and is
unknown in the United States. And almost as often the denuncia-

---

[3] "This dichotomy," says Allen Walker Read in "British Recognition of American Speech in the Eighteenth Century," *Dialect Notes,* Vol. VI, Pt. VI, 1933, p. 331,
"runs through most British writing on American speech . . . : on the one hand the
Americans are denounced for introducing corruptions into the language, and on the
other hand those very expressions are eagerly claimed as of British origin to show
that the British deserve the credit for them."

tion of it is sprinkled with genuine Americanisms, unconsciously picked up.

The English seldom differentiate between American slang and Americanisms of legitimate origin and in respectable use: both belong to what they often call the American slanguage.[4] It is most unusual for an American book to be reviewed in England without some reference to its strange (so one gathers) generally unpleasant diction. The Literary Supplement of the London *Times* is especially alert in this matter. It discovers Americanisms in the writings of even the most decorous American authors, and when none can be found it notes the fact, half in patronizing approbation and half in incredulous surprise. Of the 240 lines it gave to the first two volumes of the Dictionary of American Biography, 31 were devoted to animadversions upon the language of the learned authors.[5] The Manchester *Guardian* and the weeklies of opinion follow dutifully. The *Guardian,* in a review of Dr. Harry Emerson Fosdick's "As I See Religion," began by praising his "telling speech," but ended by deploring sadly his use of the "full-blooded Americanisms which sometimes make even those who do not for a moment ques-

---

[4] According to *American Speech* (Feb. 1930, p. 250) this term was invented in 1925 or thereabout. At that time the English war debt to the United States was under acrimonious discussion, and Uncle Sam became Uncle Shylock.

[5] Aug. 29, 1929. The passage is perhaps worth quoting in full: "The literary style of the articles is, in most instances, suitable to their purpose. Some of them afford obvious indications of their country of origin, as when we read that Bishop Asbury was at no time a *well man,* or that Chester A. Arthur's chief did not uphold the power of the Conkling *crowd,* or that Robert Bacon announced his *candidacy* for the Senate, or that Governor Altgeld *protested* the action of President Cleveland, or that Dr. W. Beaumont, when a doctor's apprentice, learned to *fill* prescriptions, or that J. G. Blaine *raised* a family of seven children, or that Prof. B. P. Bowne tested the progress of his pupils by a written *quiz.* The article on Blaine contains a curious illustration of the peculiar American use of the word *politician.* We read that 'however much Blaine was a politician, it seems to be the fact that from 1876 he was the choice of the majority, or of the largest faction, of Republicans.' One naturally wonders why it should be thought surprising for a politician to win popular support within his own party. The explanation is that *politician* is here very nearly a synonym for *wire-puller* or *intriguer,* and the point the writer wishes to make is that Blaine's influence was not wholly due to his adroit manipulation of the political machine." The following is from the *Times'* review of Hervey Allen's "Toward the Flame" (*Literary Supplement,* June 7, 1934): "Mr. Allen may or not feel complimented by the statement that apart from military terms which appear strange to us, there is not an Americanism in his strong and supple prose; but the fact adds to an English reader's pleasure. Yet one would like to know what were the functions of the individual called the colonel's *striker.*" The English term for *striker,* as the reviewer might have discovered by consulting the Oxford Dictionary, is *batman.* Both signify a military servant.

tion America's right and power to contribute to the speech which we use in common wince as they read."[6] One learns from J. L. Hammond that the late C. P. Scott, for long the editor of the *Guardian*, had a keen nose for Americanisms, and was very alert to keep them out of his paper. Says Hammond:

> He would go bustling into a room, waving a cutting or a proof, in which was an obscure phrase, a preciosity, or an Americanism. "What does he mean by this? He talks about a *final showdown?* An Americanism, I suppose. What does it mean? Generally known? I don't know it. Taken from cards? I never heard of it."[7]

This war upon Americanisms is in progress all the time, but it naturally has its pitched battles and its rest-periods between. For months there may be relative quiet on the linguistic Western front, and then some alarmed picket fires a gun and there is what the German war *communiqués* used to call a sharpening of activity. As a general thing the English content themselves with artillery practice from their own lines, but now and then one of them boldly invades the enemy's country. This happened, for example, in 1908, when Charles Whibley contributed an extremely acidulous article on "The American Language" to the *Bookman* (New York) for January. "To the English traveler in America," he said, "the language which he hears spoken about him is at once a puzzle and a surprise. It is his own, yet not his own. It seems to him a caricature of English, a phantom speech, ghostly yet familiar, such as he might hear in a land of dreams." Mr. Whibley objected violently to many characteristic American terms, among them, *to locate, to operate, to antagonize, transportation, commutation* and *proposition*. "These words," he said, "if words they may be called, are hideous to the eye, offensive to the ear, meaningless to the brain." The onslaught provoked even so mild a man as Dr. Henry W. Boynton to action, and in the *Bookman* for March of the same year he published a spirited rejoinder. "It offends them [the English]," he said, "that we are not thoroughly ashamed of ourselves for not being like them." Mr. Whibley's article was reprinted with this counterblast, so that readers of the magazine might judge

---

[6] Weekly edition, Aug. 26, 1932, p. 175.
[7] C. P. Scott of the Manchester *Guardian* (London, 1934), p. 314.

the issues fairly. The controversy quickly got into the newspapers, and was carried on for months, with American patriots on one side and Englishmen and Anglomaniacs on the other.

I myself once helped to loose such an uproar, though quite unintentionally. Happening to be in London in the winter of 1929–30, I was asked by Mr. Ralph D. Blumenfeld, the American-born editor of the *Daily Express,* to do an article for his paper on the progress of Americanisms in England since my last visit in 1922. In that article I ventured to say:

> The Englishman, whether he knows it or not, is talking and writing more and more American. He becomes so accustomed to it that he grows unconscious of it. Things that would have set his teeth on edge ten years ago, or even five years ago, are now integral parts of his daily speech. . . . In a few years it will probably be impossible for an Englishman to speak, or even to write, without using Americanisms, whether consciously or unconsciously. The influence of 125,000,000 people, practically all headed in one direction, is simply too great to be resisted by any minority, however resolute.

The question whether or not this was sound will be examined in Chapters VI and XII. For the present it is sufficient to note that my article was violently arraigned by various volunteer correspondents of the *Express* and by contributors to many other journals. One weekly opened its protest with "That silly little fellow, H. L. Mencken, is at it again" and headed it "The American Moron," and in various other quarters I was accused of a sinister conspiracy against the mother-tongue, probably political or commercial in origin, or maybe both. At this time the American talkie was making its first appearance in England, and so there was extraordinary interest in the subject, for it was obvious that the talkie would bring in far more Americanisms than the silent movie; moreover, it would also introduce the hated American accent. On February 4, 1930 Sir Alfred Knox, a Conservative M.P., demanded in the House of Commons that the Right Hon. William Graham, P.C., then president of the Board of Trade, take steps to "protect the English language by limiting the import of American talkie films." In a press interview he said:

I don't go to the cinema often, but I had to be present at one a few days ago, when an American talkie film was shown. The words and accent were perfectly disgusting, and there can be no doubt that such films are an evil influence on our language. It is said that 30,000,000 [British] people visit the cinemas every week. What is the use of spending millions on education if our young people listen to falsified English spoken every night?[8]

There had been another such uproar in 1927, when an International Conference on English was held in London, under the presidency of the Earl of Balfour. This conference hardly got beyond polite futilities, but the fact that the call for it came from the American side[9] made it suspect from the start, and its deliberations met with unconcealed hostility. On June 25, 1927, the *New Statesman* let go with a heavy blast, rehearsing all the familiar English objections to Americanisms. It said:

> It is extremely desirable, to say the least, that every necessary effort should be made to preserve some standard of pure idiomatic English. But from what quarter is the preservation of such a standard in any way threatened? The answer is "Solely from America." Yet we are asked to collaborate with the Americans on the problem; we are to make bargains about our own tongue; there is to be a system of give and take. . . . Why should we offer to discuss the subject at all with America? We do not want to interfere with their language; why should they seek to interfere with ours? That their huge hybrid population of which only a small minority are even racially Anglo-Saxons should use English as their chief medium of intercommunication is our misfortune, not our fault. They certainly threaten our language, but the only way in which we can effectively meet that threat is by assuming—in the words of

---

[8] According to the Associated Press, Mr. Graham pointed to the Cinematographic Act as designed to encourage British films, but added: "I'm not prepared to place direct restrictions on the importations of American talking films into this country."

[9] It was issued in March, 1922, and was signed by the late James W. Bright, then professor of English at the Johns Hopkins; Charles H. Grandgent of Harvard; Robert Underwood Johnson, secretary of the American Academy of Arts and Letters; John Livingston Lowes of Harvard; John M. Manly of the University of Chicago; Charles G. Osgood of Princeton, and the late Fred Newton Scott of the University of Michigan. A reply was received in October, 1922, from an English committee consisting of the Earl of Balfour, Dr. Robert Bridges and Sir Henry Newbolt, but it was not until five years later that the conference was actually held. It will be referred to again a bit later on.

the authors of "The King's English"[1] that "Americanisms are foreign words and should be so treated."

The proposal that a permanent Council of English be formed, with 50 American members and 50 from the British Empire, brought the *New Statesman* to the verge of hysterics. It admitted that such a council "might be very useful indeed," but argued that it "ought not to include more than one Scotsman and one Irishman, and should certainly not include even a single American." Thus it reasoned:

> The American language is the American language, and the English language is the English language. In some respects the Americans may fairly claim superiority. *Sidewalk*, for example, is a better word than *pavement*, and *fall* an infinitely better word than *autumn*. If we do not adopt these better words it is simply because of their "American flavor"; and the instinct which makes us reject them, though unfortunate in certain cases, is profoundly right. The only way to preserve the purity of the English language is to present a steadily hostile resistance to every American innovation. From time to time we may adopt this word or that, or sometimes a whole vivid phrase. But for all serious lovers of the English tongue it is America that is the only dangerous enemy. She must develop her own language and allow us to develop ours.

The other English journals were rather less fierce in their denunciation of the council and its programme, but very few of them greeted either with anything approaching cordiality.[2] The *Times*, obviously trying to be polite, observed that "without offense it may be said that no greater assaults are made on the common

---

[1] By H. W. and F. G. Fowler (Oxford, 1908).

[2] There is an account of their attitude, with quotations, by Dr. Kemp Malone of the Johns Hopkins, who was an American delegate to the conference, in *American Speech*, April, 1928, p. 261. The conference held two sessions, both at the quarters of the Royal Society of Literature. On the first day Lord Balfour presided, and on the second day Dr. Johnson. The speakers on the first day were Lord Balfour, Dr. Canby, George Bernard Shaw, Prof. Lloyd Jones of the British Broadcasting Corporation, Sir Israel Gollancz, Dr. Lowes, and Dr. Johnson. Those on the second day were Dr. Canby, Dr. Louise Pound of the University of Nebraska, Professor F. S. Boas, Dr. Lowes, Sir Henry Newbolt, and J. C. Squire. In addition to the speakers, those in attendance were Dr. Scott, Dr. George Philip Krapp, Prof. W. H. Wagstaff, Prof. J. Dover Wilson, Prof. A. Lloyd James, Dr. W. A. Craigie, and John Bailey. The conference was financed by the Commonwealth Fund, with some aid from Thomas W. Lamont. Later on the support of the Commonwealth Fund was withdrawn, and so the project to form a permanent Council of English fell through.

language than in America," and the *Spectator* ventured the view
that in the United States English was departing definitely from
the home standard, and was greatly "imposed upon and influenced
by a host of immigrants from all the nations of Europe." This in-
sistence that Americans are not, in any cultural sense, nor even in
any plausible statistical sense, Anglo-Saxons is to be found in many
English fulminations upon the subject. During the world war,
especially after 1917, they were hailed as blood-brothers, but that
lasted only until the first mention of war-debts. Ever since 1920
they have been mongrels again, as they were before 1917, and
most discussions of Americanisms include the objection that yielding to them means yielding to a miscellaneous rabble of inferior
tribes, some of them, by English standards, almost savage. There
was a time when the American in the English menagerie of comic
foreigners was Hiram Q. Simpkins or Ulysses X. Snodgrass, a
Yankee of Puritan, and hence of vaguely English stock, but on
some near tomorrow he will probably be Patrick Kraus, Rastus
O'Brien, Ole Ginzberg, or some other such fantastic compound of
races.

The complaint that Americanisms are inherently unintelligible
to civilized Christians is often heard in England, though not as
often as in the past. It is a fact that they frequently deal with
objects and ideas that are not familiar to the English, and that
sometimes they make use of metaphors rather too bold for the
English imagination. In consequence, there has been a steady
emission of glossaries since the earliest days, some of them on a
large scale. The first seems to have been that of the Rev. Jonathan
Boucher, which was probably drawn up before 1800, but was not
published until 1832, when it appeared in the second edition of
his "Glossary of Archaic and Provincial Words."[3] It was followed

---

[3] Boucher, who was born in England in 1737, came out to Virginia in 1759
as a private tutor. In 1762 he returned home to take holy orders, but was soon
back in Virginia as rector of Hanover parish. He also conducted a school, and
one of his pupils was young John Parke Custis, Washington's stepson. Boucher
made the most of this connection. In 1770 he became rector at Annapolis, and
soon afterward he married an heiress and bought a plantation on the Maryland
side of the Potomac. His Loyalist sentiments got him into difficulties as the Revolution approached, and in 1775 he returned to England, where he died in 1804.
In 1797 he published "A View of the Causes and Consequences of the American
Revolution," a series of thirteen sermons. After his death his friends began the
publication of his "Glossary of Archaic and Provincial Words," on which he had

by that of David Humphreys, one of the Hartford Wits, which was printed as an appendix to his play, "The Yankey in England," in 1815.[4] A year later came John Pickering's "Vocabulary or Collection of Words and Phrases Which Have Been Supposed to be Peculiar to the United States of America." Pickering got many of his words from the current English reviews of American books, and his purpose was the double, and rather contradictory, one of proving to the English reviewers that they were good English, and of dissuading Americans from using them.[5] Roblcy Dunglison's glossary followed in 1829–30, John Mason Peck's in 1834,[6] J. O. Halliwell-Phillips's "Dictionary of Archaisms and Provincialisms, Containing Words Now Obsolete in England, All of Which Are Familiar and in Common Use in America" in 1850, John Russell Bartlett's "Glossary of Words and Phrases Usually Regarded as Peculiar to the United States" (about 3,725 terms) in 1848, A. L.

---

been engaged for thirty years. The first part, covering part of the letter A, came out in 1807. In 1832 the Rev. Joseph Hunter and Joseph Stevenson undertook to continue the work, but it got no further than Bl. Boucher's brief glossary of Americanisms appeared in the introduction to this second edition. It listed but 38 words. With it was printed Absence: a Pastoral; "drawn from the life, from the manners, customs and phraseology of planters (or, to speak more pastorally, of the rural swains) inhabiting the Banks of the Potomac, in Maryland." Boucher accused the Americans of "making all the haste they conveniently can to rid themselves of" the English language. "It is easy to foresee," he said, "that, in no very distant period, their language will become as independent of England as they themselves are, and altogether as unlike English as the Dutch or Flemish is unlike German, or the Norwegian unlike the Danish, or the Portuguese unlike Spanish." Absence is reprinted in *Dialect Notes,* Vol. VI, Pt. VII, 1933, with a commentary by Allen Walker Read.

[4] It is reprinted in "The Beginnings of American English," by M. M. Mathews; (Chicago, 1931), pp. 56–63. About 280 terms are listed. They are mainly New England dialect forms, but one finds a few Americanisms that were in general use, and have survived, *e.g., breadstuffs, spook, nip* (a measure of drink), *to boost, to stump,* and *tarnation.*

[5] Pickering's long introductory essay, but not his vocabulary, is reprinted in Mathews, pp. 65–76. On March 18, 1829, Dr. T. Romeyn Beck, a New York physician and antiquary, read a paper on the Pickering book before the Albany Institute. It was published in the *Transactions* of the Institute for 1830, and is reprinted by Mathews, pp. 78–85.

[6] Dunglison's glossary, dealing with about 190 terms, was published in three instalments in the *Virginia Literary Museum.* It was reprinted in *Dialect Notes,* Vol. V, Pt. X, 1927, with a commentary by Allen Walker Read. Peck's appeared in his Emigrant's Guide and Gazetteer of the State of Illinois, first published in 1834, and reissued with revisions in 1836 and 1837. See John Mason Peck and the American Language, by Elrick B. Davis, *American Speech,* Oct., 1926. "An examination of the vocabulary of the 1837 edition," says Davis, "shows that out of 648 specific words used in strategic positions only 313 show a history in the Oxford Dictionary complete in Peck's use of them before 1789, the year of his birth."

Elwin's "Glossary of Supposed Americanisms" (about 465 terms) in 1859, Maximilien Schele de Vere's "Americanisms" (about 4,000 terms) in 1872, John S. Farmer's "Americanisms Old and New" (about 5,000 terms) in 1889, Sylva Clapin's "New Dictionary of Americanisms" (about 5,250 terms) in 1902, and Richard H. Thornton's "American Glossary" (about 3,700 terms) in 1912. These were mainly the work of philological amateurs, and only Thornton's two volumes had any scientific value.

So long ago as 1913 Sir Sidney Low, who had lived in America and had a sound acquaintance with Americanisms, suggested ironically in an article in the *Westminster Gazette* that American be taught in the English schools. This was before the movie invasion, and he reported that the English business man was "puzzled by his ignorance of colloquial American" and "painfully hampered" thereby in his handling of American trade. He went on:

> In the United States the study of the English tongue forms part of the educational scheme. . . . I think we should return the compliment. We ought to learn the American language in our schools and colleges. At present it is strangely neglected by the educational authorities. They pay attention to linguistic attainments of many other kinds, but not to this. How many thousands of youths are at this moment engaged in puzzling their brains over Latin and Greek grammar only Whitehall knows. Every well-conducted seminary has some instructor who is under the delusion that he is teaching English boys and girls to speak French with a good Parisian accent. We teach German, Italian, even Spanish, Russian, modern Greek, Arabic, Hindustani. For a moderate fee you can acquire a passing acquaintance with any of these tongues at the Berlitz Institute and the Gouin Schools. But even in these polyglot establishments there is nobody to teach you American. I have never seen a grammar of it or a dictionary. I have searched in vain at the book-sellers for "How to Learn American in Three Weeks" or some similar compendium. Nothing of the sort exists. The native speech of one hundred millions of civilized people is as grossly neglected by the publishers as it is by the schoolmasters. You can find means to learn Hausa or Swahili or Cape Dutch in London more easily than the expressive, if difficult, tongue which is spoken in the office, the barroom, the tramcar, from the snows of Alaska to the mouths of the Mississippi, and is enshrined in a literature that is growing in volume and favor every day.

Low quoted an extract from an American novel then appearing serially in an English magazine—an extract including such Americanisms as *side-stepper, saltwater-taffy, Prince-Albert* (coat), *boob, bartender* and *kidding*, and many characteristically American extravagances of metaphor. It might be well argued, he said, that this strange dialect was as near to "the tongue that Shakespeare spoke" as "the dialect of Bayswater or Brixton," but that philological fact did not help to its understanding. "You might almost as well expect him [the British business man] to converse freely with a Portuguese railway porter because he tried to stumble through Caesar when he was in the Upper Fourth at school."

At the time Low published his article the invasion of England by Americanisms was just beginning in earnest, and many words and phrases that have since become commonplaces there were still strange and disquieting. Writing in the London *Daily Mail* a year or so later W. G. Faulkner thought it necessary to explain the meanings of *hobo, hoodlum, bunco-steerer, dead-beat, flume, dub, rubberneck, drummer, sucker, dive* (in the sense of a thieves' resort), *clean up, graft* and *to feature*, and another interpreter, closely following him, added definitions of *hold-up, quitter, rube, shack, bandwagon, road-agent, cinch, live-wire* and *scab*.[7] This was in the early days of the American-made movie, and Faulkner denounced its terminology as "generating and encouraging mental indiscipline." As Hollywood gradually conquered the English cinema palaces,[8] such warnings became more frequent and more

---

[7] In Thornton's "American Glossary" *hobo* is traced to 1891, *hold-up* and *bunco* to 1887, *dive* to 1882, *dead-beat* to 1877, *hoodlum* to 1872, *road-agent* to 1866, *drummer* to 1836, and *flume* to 1792.

[8] The first American films reached England in 1907, but until 1915 they came in such small numbers that they were not separated, in the customs returns, from "optical supplies and equipment." In 1915 their total value was fixed at £47,486. But the next year it leaped to £349,919, and thereafter it mounted, with occasional recessions, to the peak of £880,240 in 1927. These values represented, of course, only the cost of the actual films, not that of the productions. In 1927 the Cinematograph Films Act was passed. It provided that all English exhibitors would have to show at least 5% of English-made films after Sept. 30, 1928, 7½% after the same date in 1930, 10% after 1931, 12½% after 1932, 15% after 1933, and 20% from Sept. 30, 1935 onward. The English duty is 1d. a foot on positives and 5d. on negatives. I am indebted for these figures and for those following to Mr. Lynn W. Meekins, American commercial attaché in London, and Mr. Henry E. Stebbins, assistant trade commissioner.

angry, and in 1920 the London *Daily News* began a formal agitation of the subject, with the usual pious editiorials and irate letters from old subscribers. I quote a characteristic passage from one of the latter:

> I visited two picture theaters today for the express purpose of collecting slang phrases and of noticing the effect of the new language on the child as well as on the adult. What the villain said to the hero when the latter started to argue with him was, "*Cut out* that *dope*," and a hundred piping voices repeated the injunction. The comic man announced his marriage to the Belle of Lumbertown by saying, "I'm *hitched*."

On January 22, 1920 the London bureau of the Associated Press made this report:

> England is apprehensive lest the vocabularies of her youth become corrupted through incursions of American slang. Trans-Atlantic tourists in England note with interest the frequency with which resort is made to "Yankee talk" by British song and play writers seeking to enliven their productions. Bands and orchestras throughout the country when playing popular music play American selections almost exclusively. American songs monopolize the English music hall and musical comedy stage. But it is the subtitle of the American moving picture film which, it is feared, constitutes the most menacing threat to the vaunted English purity of speech.

When the American talkie began to reinforce the movie, in 1929,[9] there was a fresh outburst of indignation, but this time it had a despairist undertone. Reinforced by the spoken word, Americanisms were now coming in much faster than they could be challenged and disposed of. "Within the past few years," said Thomas Anderson in the Manchester *Sunday Chronicle* for January 12, 1930, "we have gradually been adopting American habits

---

[9] After the introduction of the talkie the imports of American films showed a great decline in value. They dropped from £861,592 in 1929, to £506,477 in 1930, and to £130,847 in 1932. In part this was due to the operation of the Cinematograph Films Act, but in larger part it was produced by a change in trade practice. In the silent days many positives were sent to England, but since the talkie came in the film companies have been sending negatives and duplicating them in England. Thus the total annual footage is probably but little less than it was in 1929. Of the 476 imported films shown in England, Scotland and Wales in 1933, 330 were American, and according to Henry J. Gibbs, writing in the *Black-shirt*, "their value was 90 to 95% of the total."

of speech, American business methods, and the American outlook." To which Jameson Thomas added in the London *Daily
Express* for January 21:

> One must admit that we write and speak Americanisms. So
> long as Yankeeisms came to us insidiously we absorbed them
> carelessly. They have been a valuable addition to the language,
> as nimble coppers are a valuable addition to purer currency. But
> the talkies have presented the American language in one giant
> meal, and we are revolted.

But this revolt, in so far as it was real at all, was apparently
confined to the aged: the young of the British species continued
to gobble down the neologisms of Hollywood and to imitate the
Hollywood intonation. "Seldom do I hear a child speak," wrote a
correspondent of the London *News Chronicle* on June 15, 1931,
"who has not attached several Americanisms to his vocabulary,
which are brought out with deliberation at every opportunity."
During the next few years the English papers printed countless
protests against this corruption of the speech of British youth, but
apparently to no avail. Nor was there any halt when Col. F. W. D.
Bendall, C.M.G., M.A., an inspector of the Board of Education,
began stumping the country in an effort to further the dying
cause of linguistic purity.[1] Nor when the chief constable—*i.e.*,
chief of police—of Wallasey, a suburb of Liverpool, issued this
solemn warning in his annual report:

> I cannot refrain from commenting adversely on the pernicious
> and growing habit of . . . youths to use Americanisms, with nasal
> accompaniment, in order to appear, in their own vernacular, *tough
> guys*. On one of my officers going to search him, a young house-

---

[1] The following is from the Denby *Herald's* report of an address by Col.
Bendall before the Dudley Literary Society on January 31, 1931: "He suggested
that though it was true that American had a remarkable capacity for growth, there
was no need to suppose that it would eventually settle the form which English
must take. Such a state of affairs would necessarily result either in a wider divergence between literary and spoken English or in literary English becoming affected.
The former position would lead to a loss of subtlety in spoken English and to
literature's becoming unintelligible to the masses, while to illustrate how deplorable
the latter would be, the speaker read a part of Mr. Mencken's translation of the
Declaration of Independence into modern American." The colonel's apparently
grave acceptance of my burlesque as a serious specimen of "modern American"
was matched by a sage calling himself John O'London in "Is It Good English?";
London, 1924, p. 92. After quoting the opening paragraph of my version, he said
solemnly, "I hope 'these States' will suppress all such translations."

breaker told him to "*Lay off, cop.*" *Oh-yeahs* are frequent in answer to charges, and we are promised *shoots up in the burg* [*sic*] and threatened to be *bumped off.*[2]

Parallel with this alarmed hostility to the jargon of the movies and the talkies, much of it borrowed from the American underworld, there has gone on in England a steady opposition to the more decorous varieties of American. I have already mentioned the *Times'* sneering review of the first two volumes of the "Dictionary of American Biography." Back in 1919 H. N. Brailsford, the well-known English publicist, who has been in the United States many times and often contributes to American magazines, actually objected to the vocabulary of the extremely precious and Anglomaniacal Woodrow Wilson, then in action in Versailles. "The irruption of Mr. Wilson upon our scene," he wrote in the London *Daily Herald* on August 20, "threatens to modify our terminology. If one knew the American language (as I do not)," and so on.[3] A little while before this a leading English medical journal had been protesting against the Americanisms in an important surgical monograph.[4] Translations done in the United States are so often denounced that denouncing them has become a sort of convention. There was a storm of unusual violence, in 1925, over the plays of Luigi Pirandello. Their merit had been recognized in America earlier than in England—indeed, some of them had been forbidden, at least in English, by the English censor—and in consequence the first translations were published in this country. What followed when they reached England was thus described by the London correspondent of the *Bookman* (New York) in its issue for September, 1925:

> A strange situation has arisen over the Pirandello translations. These were made in America, and they contain phraseology which

---

[2] Chief Constable's Report for the Year Ended 31st December, 1932 (Wallasey, 1933), p. 13.

[3] In the London *Times* for June 15, 1927, George Bernard Shaw was reported as saying: "When President Wilson came to this country he gave us a shock by using the world *obligate* instead of *oblige*. It showed that a man could become President in spite of that, and we asked ourselves if a man could become King of England if he used the world *obligate*. We said at once that it could not be done."

[4] Review in the *Medical Press*, Sept. 17, 1919, of an article by MacCarty and Connor in *Surgery, Gynecology and Obstetrics*. "In the study of the terminology of diseases of the breast," said the reviewer, "[the authors] suggest a scheme which seems simple, but unfortunately for British understanding, it is written in American."

is peculiarly American. As a consequence they have been generally condemned in the English press as being translations from one foreign tongue into another. . . . It will be understood that when an English reader is used to calling comfits *sweets* and finds them called *candies* he feels he is not getting an English equivalent of the Italian author's word.

This correspondence was signed Simon Pure; its actual author, I am informed, was Rebecca West. She expressed the opinion that English translations of foreign books were frequently offensive to Americans, and for like reasons. "It seems to me to be a pity," she continued, "that the habit should have grown up among Continental authors of selling 'world rights in the English language.' If the English translation does not satisfy the Americans, and the American translation does not please the English, it would surely be far better that there should be two translations." In a long reply to this, published in the *Saturday Review of Literature* (New York) for December 26, 1925, Ernest Boyd—himself a translator of wide experience, born in Ireland, educated there and in England, for seven years a member of the British consular service, and resident in New York since 1920—denied that there was any hostility to English translations in this country. "English translators," he said, "are accepted at their own—or their publishers'— valuation in America," but American translators "are received with prejudice and criticized with severity" in England. The American edition of Pirandello's plays consisted of two volumes, one translated by Dr. Arthur Livingston of Columbia University, and the other by Edward Storer, an Englishman. Said Mr. Boyd:

> Dr. Livingston, the American, is taken to task though his Italian scholarship is well authenticated and beyond dispute. Mr. Storer, on the contrary, is an Englishman, and his translations are so defective in places as to show a complete misunderstanding of the text, but no complaints have been raised on that score. . . . One might have thought that the proper claim would be that a competent person, and only a competent person, irrespective of nationality, should translate. But British nationality is more important than American scholarship, apparently.

The ensuing debate ran on for several years; in fact, it is still resumed from time to time, with the English champions holding stoutly to the doctrine that there can be but one form of English pure and undefiled, and that it must, shall and will be the Southern English variety. Thus Raymond Mortimer in the *Nation and Athenaeum* for July 28, 1928:

> It is most unfortunate that American publishers should be able to buy the English as well as the American rights of foreign books. For the result usually is that these books remain permanently closed to the English reader.[5]

The English objection is not alone to the American vocabulary; it is also to the characteristic American style, which begins to differ appreciably from the normal English style. In every recent discussion of the matter the despairist note that I was mentioning a few paragraphs back is audible. There was a time when the English guardians of the mother-tongue tried to haul American into conformity by a kind of *force majeure*, but of late they seem to be resigned to its differentiation, and are concerned mainly about the possibility that Standard English may be considerably modified by its influence. As I have noted, H. W. and F. G. Fowler, in "The King's English," were deciding so long ago as 1906 that "Americanisms are foreign words, and should be so treated." They admitted that American had its points of superiority —"*Fall* is better on the merits than *autumn,* in every way; it is short, Saxon (like the other three season names), picturesque;

---

[5] Many more examples might be added, some of them not without their humors. Back in 1921 J. C. Squire (now Sir John) was protesting bitterly because an American translator of the Journal of the Goncourts "spoke of a *pavement* as a *sidewalk.*" See the *Literary Review* of the New York *Evening Post,* July 23, 1921. In Dostoevsky: "Letters and Reminiscences," translated from the Russian by S. S. Koteliansky and J. Middleton Murry (New York, 1923; American binding of English sheets) there is this note, p. 282: "Saltykov, Mihail Efgrafovich (who used the pseudonym N. Schedrin), author of the Golovlevs, one of the greatest of Russian novels, which has been translated into French and American, but not yet into English." Such sneers are now answered by defiance as often as with humility. When Dr. Edgar J. Goodspeed, professor of Biblical and patristic Greek at the University of Chicago, published his new version of the New Testament (Chicago, 1923) he boldly called it "an American translation," and in it he as boldly employed Americanisms in place of the English forms of the Authorized Version. Thus *corn,* meaning wheat in England but maize in America, was changed to *wheat* in Mark II, 23, Mark IV, 28, and Matthew XII, 1. Similarly, when Ezra Pound published "Ta Hio: the Great Learning" (*University of Washington Chapbooks,* No. 14; Seattle, 1928) he described it on the title-page as "newly rendered into the American language." See American and English translations of "The Oppermanns," by Edmund E. Miller, *American Speech,* Oct., 1935.

it reveals its derivation to everyone who uses it, not to the scholar only, like *autumn*"—but they protested against taking even the most impeccable Americanisms into English. "The English and the American language and literature," they argued, "are both good things, but they are better apart than mixed." In 1910 the Encyclopedia Britannica (Eleventh Edition) admitted that this falling apart had already gone so far that it was "not uncommon to meet with American newspaper articles of which an untravelled Englishman would hardly be able to understand a sentence." "The fact is," said the London *Times Literary Supplement* for January 21, 1926, in a review of G. P. Krapp's "The English Language in America," "that in spite of the greater frequency of intercourse the two idioms *have* drifted apart; farther apart than is, perhaps, generally recognized. . . . A British visitor in America, if he has any taste for the niceties of language, experiences something of the thrills of contact with a foreign idiom, for he hears and reads many things which are new to him and not a few which are unintelligible." "If the American temperament, despite its general docility, persists in its present attitude towards a standardized language," said Ernest Weekley in "Adjectives—and Other Words" (1930), "spoken American must eventually become as distinct from English as Yiddish is from classical Hebrew." Or, added Professor J. Y. T. Greig of Newcastle in "Breaking Priscian's Head" (1929), as "Spanish is from Portuguese."

This echo of Noah Webster is itself echoed frequently by other English publicists and philologians. There is, indeed, a school of English thought which holds that the United States is not only drifting away from the mother country linguistically, but is fundamentally differentiated from it on wider cultural grounds. "Those who have had to do with Americans," said Geoffrey Grigson in the London *Morning Post* for February 13, 1934, "will not mistake them for our intimate cousins, our near psychic relations." He continued:

> They are linked to us by many strands of sympathy, but they are a different people, or a number of different peoples. Their language, their real literature—witness Poe, Hawthorne, Melville, James, Ransom, Macleish, Hemingway—are different; and one might say even that the more they are English the more they are

alien. The New Englander, for example, feels and thinks differently; his communal, political, and person "mythology"—to use a convenient word for those bodies of fiction and "belief" which unite each social entity—differentiates him completely from an Englishman. I am not sure, in fact, that we cannot more easily get to understand the soul of Frenchman, Italian, German, Spaniard even. After all, we belong geographically and spiritually to the European cultural *bloc*.

The late Cecil Chesterton was saying something to the same general effect in the London *New Witness* so long ago as 1915. "I do not believe," he wrote, "that nations ever quarrel merely because they feel that they do not understand each other. That attitude of mind of itself tends to produce a salutary humility on the one side and a pleasantly adventurous curiosity on the other. What really produces trouble between peoples is when one is quite certain that it understands the other—and in fact doesn't. And I am perfectly certain that that has been from the first one of the primary causes of trouble between England and America."[6] To which may be added the following from an article by Herbert Agar in the *New Statesman* for August 8, 1931:

> The English should try to cope with their philological ignorance. They should train themselves to realize that it is neither absurd nor vulgar that a language which was once the same should in the course of centuries develop differently in different parts of the world. If such were not the case, we should all still be speaking a sort of Ur-Sanskrit. Just as French and Italian may be described as divergent forms of modern Latin, so it would be helpful to think of the language of Oxford and the language of Harvard as divergent forms of modern English. It is perhaps a pity, from the point of view of international good feeling, that the two forms have not diverged a little further. At any rate, when the Englishman can learn to think of American as a language, and not merely as a ludicrously unsuccessful attempt to speak as he himself speaks, when he can learn to have for American only the normal intolerance of the provincial mind for all foreign tongues, then there will come a great improvement in Anglo-American relations. For even though Americans realize the absurdity of the English attitude toward their language, nevertheless they remain

[6] The article is summarized, with long extracts, in the *Literary Digest* for June 19, 1915, p. 1468.

deeply annoyed by it. This is natural, for a man's language is his very soul. It is his thoughts and almost all his consciousness. Laugh at a man's language, and you have laughed at the man himself in the most inclusive sense.

But not all Englishmen, of course, indulge themselves in the derision that Mr. Agar denounces. The prevailing tone of English opinion remains loftily anti-American, in linguistic as in other matters, but there have arisen in late years two factions which take a more moderate position, the one contending that American speech is really not the barbaric jargon it is commonly thought to be, and the other arguing boldly that its peculiarities, though maybe somewhat uncouth, nevertheless have a merit of their own. A representative spokesman of the first faction is Sir Charles Strachey, M.C.M.G., a former official of the Foreign and Colonial Offices. On May 2, 1931, he wrote to the London *Times* to protest against the assumption that the argot of Chicago gunmen is the official language of the United States. "American diplomatic correspondence," he said, "is always a model of correct English, and it would be a gross error to suppose that the United States Ambassador calls revenue the *dough* or the *berries*, and refers to his Italian colleagues as a *wop*." But this Strachey faction is not large, and as a general thing even the language of American diplomacy grates on English nerves, as I was lately noting in the case of H. N. Brailsford's objection to the style of Woodrow Wilson.

The revolutionary theory that the American language actually has some merit seems to have been launched by William Archer, a Scotsman, in an article entitled "American Today," printed somewhat prudently, not in England, but in *Scribner's Magazine* for February, 1899. "New words," he said, "are begotten by new conditions of life; and as American life is far more fertile of new conditions than ours, the tendency toward neologism cannot but be stronger in America than in England. American has enormously enriched the language, not only with new words, but (since the American mind is, on the whole, quicker and wittier than the English) with apt and luminous colloquial metaphors." Twenty years later Archer returned to the matter, this time on English soil, in an article written for the *Westminster Gazette*.[7] In it he

---

[7] Reprinted in the *Literary Review* of the New York *Evening Post*, July 23, 1921.

protested vigorously against the English habit of "pulling a wry face over American expressions, not because they are inherently bad, but simply because they are American. The vague and unformulated idea behind all such petty cavillings," he continued, "is that the English language is in danger of being corrupted by the importation of Americanisms, and that it behooves us to establish a sort of quarantine in order to keep out the detrimental germs. This notion is simply one of the milder phases of the Greater Stupidity."

Two years before this, Frank Dilnot, an English journalist with American experience, had come out for American in a large way. "Show me the alert Englishman," he wrote,[8] "who will not find a stimulation in those nuggety word-groupings which are the commonplaces in good American conversation. They are like flashes of crystal. They come from all kinds of people—who are brilliantly innocent of enriching the language. . . . The American tongue, written or spoken with its alteration from the English of England, is a potent and penetrating instrument, rich in new vibrations, full of joy as well as shocks for the unsuspecting visitor." In May, 1920, Richard Aldington joined the American party in an article contributed to *Poetry* (Chicago). In it he made an eloquent plea for American linguistic independence, and praised the development of a characteristically American idiom by the American poets and novelists of the day. "Are Americans," he demanded,

> to write the language which they speak, which is slowly but inevitably separating itself from the language of England, or are they to write a devitalized idiom learned painfully from books or from a discreet frequentation of London literary cliques? . . . Englishmen of letters and literary journalists may publish these exhortations and practise their refinements: in vain—a vast and increasingly articulate part of the English-speaking and English-writing world will ignore them. Another century may see English broken into a number of dialects or even different languages, spoken in Canada, Australia, South Africa, the United States and England. The result may eventually be similar to the break-up of Latin.

This pro-American party is still small, but it can show some well-known names. The late Robert Bridges, Poet Laureate and

---

[8] "The New America" (New York, 1919), Ch. III.

founder of the Society for Pure English, was in sympathy with
it,[9] and it has got support from Wyndham Lewis, Edward Shanks,
Virgina Woolf and Sir John Foster Fraser. "The Americans," said
Mrs. Woolf in the *Saturday Review of Literature* on August 1,
1925, "are doing what the Elizabethans did—they are coining new
words. They are instinctively making the language adapt itself to
their needs." She continued:

> In England, save for the impetus given by the war, the word-
> coining power has lapsed; our writers vary the metres of their
> poetry, remodel the rhythms of prose, but one may search English
> fiction in vain for a single new word. It is significant that when
> we want to freshen our speech, we borrow from American—
> *poppycock, rambunctious, flip-flop, booster, good mixer.* All the
> expressive, ugly, vigorous slang which creeps into use among us,
> first in talk, later in writing, comes from across the Atlantic.

In February, 1925, H. E. Moore printed an elaborate defense
of Americanisms in the *English Review*, then edited by Austin
Harrison. He contrasted the tendency to academic tightness in
Standard English with the greater naturalness of American, and
give high praise to some of the salient characters of the latter—

---

[9] The Society was organized in 1913, but the intervention of the war suspended
its proceedings until 1918. The first of its Tracts was issued in October, 1919.
The original committee consisted of Dr. Bridges, Henry Bradley, Sir Walter
Raleigh and L. Pearsall Smith, the last-named an American living in England. In
Tract No. 1 one of its purposes was stated to be the encouragement of "those
who possess the word-making faculty," and another was the enrichment of Standard
English with dialectic and "democratic" forms and usages. In Tract No. XXIV,
1926, Dr. Bridges protested against an allegation that the Society was "working
for uniformity and standardization against idiom and freedom. Our readers," he
went on, "know that this is not what we intend or desire; indeed teachers, who as
a class advocate standardization of speech as the necessary basis for general tuition,
sometimes complain of us as mischief-makers because we do not support them
more thoroughly." In 1922 Dr. Bridges wrote to Dr. H. S. Canby: "We desire as
many American subscribers as possible, *in order to make our Society seem as much
American as it is English.* [His italics.] There is a great and natural prejudice in
America against English dictation in the matter of our language, and that followed,
I think, as a protest against the insular contempt which the English felt a couple
of generations ago for American forms of speech. We now in England feel very
differently and the S.P.E. would certainly treat American usages and preferences
with full respect" (*Literary Review*, May 20, 1922). "The S.P.E.," says J. Y. T.
Greig in "Breaking Priscian's Head" (London, 1929), "despite its inauspicious
name, has done a great deal of splendid work, but only because it happened to be
founded by, and to have remained under, the control of men like Dr. Bridges,
Mr. L. P. Smith, and Mr. H. W. Fowler. This was a fortunate and very rare accident. In wrong hands it would have long ago become a dreadful curse, a veritable
Inquisition and Congregation of the Propaganda rolled into one."

its hospitality to neologisms, its fertility in effective metaphor, its "fluid" spelling. "As this divergence of English and American," he said, "has proceeded through strata of English derision and American defiance it has tended to become deliberate and constructive. England and academic America generally have asserted the old criteria. But they have been swept aside by America's egalitarian millions, and established changes have now made any acceptance of literary Southern English impossible." "I have never found it possible," said Mr. Shanks in the London *Evening Standard* in 1931,

> to understand why with so many people there should be an automatic objection to anything that can be called an Americanism. An Americanism is an expression adopted by those who speak our common language but who live in the United States. There are more of them than there are of us, and so one would suppose, on democratic principles, that their choice was entitled at least to our serious consideration. There are, in fact, more of them than of all the other English-speaking peoples put together, and a majority vote on the question to whom the language really belongs would certainly give a verdict against us. Yet, for many of us "Americanism" is simply a term of abuse. . . . The facts that we ought to realise and that we ignore when we talk loftily about "Americanisms" are that America is making a formidable contribution to the development of our language and that all our attempts to reject that contribution will in the long run be vain—quite apart from the other fact that we ought to rejoice in this proof that the language is still alive and capable of learning from experience.

Writing a year later, Sir John Fraser[1] made a vigorous attack upon the dominant anti-American party, and accused it of trying absurdly to halt a process of inevitable change. He said:

> Quite respectable people, very refined, even literary gents and prelates, would faint were they not so angry at the Americanization of our ways, and particularly the degradation of our speech. Why? If we take up the position that because we are British we must be right there is no argument. But if the Anglicization of the world is good, why is the Americanization of England bad? . . . Is our language to remain staid and dignified like a piece of furniture made when good Victoria was Queen, or, as we live in

---

[1] London *Sunday Graphic*, Jan. 3, 1932.

swiftly shifting times, aeroplanes and record-smashing cars, is there something to be said for adapting our ways of speech to the newer generations? . . . Then there is the other school, which is called the Oxford manner, though mostly adopted by people who know nothing about Oxford. With their stuffy, roof-of-the-mouth inflections [*sic*] they have developed a speech of their own. . . . I prefer slangy American.

In *Life and Letters* for April, 1934, Wyndham Lewis argued at length that, even if it were rational, it was too late for the English to stem the advance of American. He said:

> While England was a uniquely powerful empire-state, ruled by an aristocratic caste, its influence upon the speech as upon the psychology of the American ex-colonies was overwhelming. But today that ascendancy has almost entirely vanished. The aristocratic caste is nothing but a shadow of itself, the cinema has brought the American scene and the American dialect nightly into the heart of England, and the Americanizing process is far advanced. . . . There has been no reciprocal movement of England into the United States; indeed, with the New American nationalism, England is deliberately kept out. . . . So the situation is this, as far as our common language is concerned: the destiny of England and the United States is more than ever one, but it is now the American influence that is paramount. The tables have effectively been turned in this respect.

Finally, I extract a few sentences of sage advice from a radio speech to his fellow-countrymen by Alistair Cooke, of the British Broadcasting Corporation:

> When you hear an expression that seems a little odd to you, don't assume it was invented by a music-hall comedian trying to be smart. It was probably spoken by Lincoln or Paul Jones. . . . And when you hear a strange pronunciation remember you are not hearing a chaotic speech that anyone has deliberately changed. . . . It is the cultivated speech of a New England gentleman of 1934, and it happens in essentials also to be the cultivated speech you would have heard in London over two hundred years ago.[2]

---

[2] Printed as "That Dreadful American," *Listener,* Jan. 30, 1935.

Hell and Its Outskirts

‹‹‹‹‹‹‹‹‹‹‹‹‹‹‹‹‹‹‹‹‹‹‹‹‹‹‹‹‹‹‹‹‹› ›››››››››››››››››››››››››››››››

> *It doesn't matter what they preach,*
> *Of high or low degree:*
> *The old Hell of the Bible*
> *Is Hell enough for me.*
>
> *'Twas preached by Paul and Peter;*
> *They spread it wide and free;*
> *'Twas Hell for old John Bunyan*
> *And it's Hell enough for me.*

THE author of these elegiac strophes, Frank Lebby Stanton, has been moldering in the red clay of Georgia for a long, long while, but what he wrote went straight to the hearts of the American people, and there it still glows warmly. Hell remains the very essence not only of their dogmatic theology but also of their everyday invective. They employ it casually more than any other *Kulturvolk*, and perhaps more than all others put together. They have enriched it with a vast store of combinations, variations, licks, breaks, and riffs. They have made it roar and howl, and they have made it coo and twitter. It helps to lift them when supersonic waves of ecstasy rush through their lymphatic systems, and it soothes them when they roll in the barbed wire of despair. To find its match, you must go to the Buddhist *Om mani padma Hum*, meaning anything you please, or the Moslem *al-hamdu lil'lah*, meaning the same, or the ancient Mesopotamian

Word from the Abyss, *Muazaga-gu-abzu*. Even so, *hell* is far ahead, for, compared to it, all these ejaculations have a pale and pansy cast, as does *hell* itself in nearly every other language; e.g., *enfer* in French, *infierno* in Spanish, *helvede* in Danish, *jigoku* in Japanese, and *Hölle* in German. So long ago as 1880, in the appendix on "The Awful German Language" to "A Tramp Abroad," Mark Twain derided *Hölle* as "chipper, frivolous and unimpressive" and marveled that anyone invited to go there could "rise to the dignity of feeling insulted." He had never heard, apparently, of the even more flaccid Finnish *manala*, which in These States would be the name of an infant food or perhaps of a female infant among the Bible-searchers of the Dust Bowl.

Hell is one of the most ancient and honorable terms in English, and etymologists in their dusty cells have traced it to the first half of the ninth century. It is thus appreciably older than either *home* or *mother* and nearly five centuries older than its great rival, *damn*. But it was not until Shakespeare's time that it began to appear in the numerous blistering phrases that now glorify it—e.g., *go to hell, to hell with, hell to pay, hell is loose, hellcat*, and so on—and even then it rose only to be knocked down, for Shakespeare's time also saw the beginnings of the Puritan murrain, and once the bluenoses were in power they put down all strong language with a brutal hand. At the Restoration, of course, it was reliberated, but only in a spavined state. The Cavaliers, male and female, were great swearers, but their oaths were nearly all cautious and cushioned. Such examples as *gadzooks, zounds, 'sdeath, 'sblood, by'r Lady, a plague on't, rat me, split my windpipe, marry*, and *burn me* are heard in America today, when they are heard at all, only among candidates in theology and Boy Scouts. The English, indeed, have never recovered from the blight of Puritanism, and their swearing strikes all other civilized peoples as puny. They are constantly working up a pother over such forms as *bloody*, which to the rest of the world are quite innocuous. *Good gracious*, which appeared in Oliver Goldsmith's "Good Natur'd Man" in 1768, seems to have been regarded in that day as pretty pungent, and *mercy*, which preceded it by some years, was frowned upon as blasphemous. "Our armies," says Uncle Toby in "Tristram Shandy," "swore terribly in Flanders," but at home such virtuosity was rare, even among the military. In the wars of our own time, the swearing of the English has provoked the contempt of both their allies and their enemies. In both World War I and World War II, they depended mainly upon a couple of four-letter words that are obscene but not profane, and what they made of them showed little ingenuity or imagination. The American military borrowed these terms in a spirit probably more derisory than admiring, and dropped them the instant they were restored to Mom.

But as the brethren of the Motherland lost their Elizabethan talent for wicked words it was transferred to these shores. Even the Puritans of New England, once they settled down, took to cussing out one another in a violent manner, and thousands of them were sent to the stocks or whipping post for it by their baffled magistrates. The heroes of the Revolution not only swore in all the orthodox forms but also invented a new expletive, *tarnation*, which survived until the Mexican War. As Dr. Louise Pound has demonstrated with great learning, both *tarnation* and *darn* were derived from *eternal* and the former preceded the latter in refined use. George Washington himself cut loose with *hell* and *damn* whenever the imbecilities of his brass went too far. But it was the great movement into the West following the War of 1812 that really laid the foundations of American profanity and got *hell* firmly on its legs. Such striking forms as *to raise hell, to hell around, hell-bent for election, to be hell on, to play hell with, what the hell, heller, merry hell, hellish, hellcat, hell on wheels, hell and high water, from hell to breakfast, a hoot in hell, the hell of it, hell's a-poppin', the hell you say, hell with the lid off,* and *the hinges of hell* were then invented by the gallant fellows, many of them fugitives from Eastern sheriffs, who legged it across the great plains to die for humanity at the hands of Indians, buffalo, catamounts, rattlesnakes, bucking broncos, and vigilance committees. For nearly two generations nine-tenths of the new terms in America, whether profane or not, came from the region beyond Wheeling, West Virginia, and were commonly called Westernisms. It was not until after the Civil War that the newspaper wits of the East began to contribute to the store, and not until after World War I that concocting such things became the monopoly of Hollywood press agents, radio mountebanks, and Broadway columnists.

The great upsurge of *hell* that rose to a climax in the Mexican War era naturally upset the contemporary wowsers, and they busied themselves launching euphemistic surrogates. Some of these seem to have been imported from the British Isles, along with Dundreary whiskers, soda water, and bathing; for example, *by heck*, which originated there as a substitute for *by Hector*, itself a substitute for *by God*, but was already obsolete at home by the time it appeared in America. Here it not only flourished among the prissy in its prototypical form but also moved over into the domain of *hell* and gave birth to *a heck of a, to raise heck, to run like heck, colder than heck, to play heck with, to beat heck, what the heck,* and *go to heck*. Other deputies for *hell* were invented on American soil, notably *thunder* and *blazes*. *Go to thunder* in the sense of *go to hell* is traced by the "Dictionary of American English" to 1848 and marked an Americanism, and at about the same time *thunderation* began to be used for *damnation*. But soon *thunderation* was used in place of *hell*, as in *what the thunderation*. It is possible that German immigration helped to spread it in its various forms, for a favorite German expletive in those days was *Donnerwetter*; i.e., thundery weather. But this is only a guess, and, like all other learned men, I am suspicious of guessing.

After the Civil War there was another great upsurge of wowserism, culminating in the organization of the Comstock Society in 1873[1] and of the Woman's Christian Temperance Union the year following. Neither organization devoted itself specifically to profanity, but the moral indignation that radiated from both of them soon began to afflict it, and by 1880 it was being denounced violently in thousands of far-flung evangelical pulpits. In this work, the leader was the Reverend Sam Jones, who had been converted and ordained a Methodist clergyman in 1872. Sam roared against cussing as he roared against boozing, but the Devil fetched him by seducing him into using stronger and stronger language himself, and toward the end of his life I more than once heard

---

[1] Its legal name was The New York Society for the Suppression of Vice. In 1947 that name was changed to the Society to Maintain Public Decency. Old Anthony Comstock was snatched up to Heaven in 1915 and succeeded by John S. Sumner.

him let go with objurgations that would have cheered a bouncer clearing out a Sailor's Bethel. Even the Catholics, who ordinarily never mistake the word for the deed, joined the crusade, and in 1882 they were reviving the Holy Name Society, which had been organized back in 1274 and then forgotten. This combined assault had some effect; indeed, it probably had much more effect than it has been given credit for. At all events, the lush profanity of the Civil War era began to shrink and pale, and such unearthly oaths as *Jesus Christ and John Jacob Astor, by the high heels of St. Patrick,* and *by the double-barreled jumping Jiminetty* began to vanish from the American repertory. *God damn* kept going downhill throughout my youth in the eighties and nineties, and by the time I came of age I seldom used it. Many new euphemisms took the places of the forthright oaths of an earlier day, and one of them, *hully gee,* quickly became so innocuous that when Edward W. Townsend introduced it into "Chimmie Fadden," in 1895, it fell almost as flat as the four-letter words with which the lady novelists now pepper their pages.

But *hell* and *damn* somehow survived this massacre—maybe because the new euphemisms left a man choking and gasping when the steam really rose in his gauges, or maybe because some amateur canon lawyer discovered that in their naked state, uncoupled to sacred names, they are not officially blasphemous. Whatever the reason, American profanity was saved, and to this day it revolves around them and recruits itself from their substance. *Damn* is plainly the feebler of the two, despite its crashing effect when used by a master. *Hell* is enormously more effective, if only because it is more protean. For one phrase embodying the former there are at least forty embodying the latter, and many of them are susceptible to elegant and ingenious permutations. It is impossible for *damn* to bust loose, or to freeze over; it is impossible to knock it out of anyone, or to give it to anyone, or to beat it, or to raise it, or to think of a snowball or a bat in it, or to link it to high water, or to be *damn*-bent for election, or to plunge from *damn*-to-breakfast, or to *damn* around, or to get the *damn* out of any place, or to pull its lid off, or to think of it as having hubs or hinges. There is no such thing as a *damn*-hound, a *damn*cat, a *damn*hole, or a *damn*ion. Nothing is as black as *damn,* as busy as *damn,* as hot (or cold) as *damn,* or as deep, crazy, dumb, clever, cockeyed, crooked, touchy, dead, drunk, nervous, dull, expensive, scared, funny, hungry, lonely, mad, mean, poor, real, rotten, rough, serious, sick, smart, or sore as *damn. Damn* is a simple verb and its only child is a simple adjective, but *hell* ranges over all the keys of the grammatical scale and enters into combinations as avidly as oxygen.

There was a time when men learned in the tongues turned trembling backs upon such terms, but in recent years they have shown a libido for studying them, and the result is a rising literature. One of the earliest of the new monographs upon the subject —and still one of the best—was published in *American Speech* in August, 1931, by Dr. L. W. Merryweather. Probing scientifically, he discovered a great deal about *hell* that no one had ever noticed before. It can be slung about, he found, through nearly all the parts of speech. It can be used to represent almost every shade of meaning from yes to no, so that *hell of a time* may mean both the seraphic felicity of a police sergeant in a brewery and the extreme discomfort of a felon in the electric chair. A thing may be either *hotter than hell* or *colder than hell.* A *hellcat* may be either a woman so violent that her husband jumps overboard or nothing worse than a college cheerleader. *What in hell* is a mere expression of friendly interest, but *who the hell says so* is a challenge to fight. Merryweather threw out the suggestion that the upsurge and proliferation of *hell* in the Old West may have been due to Mormon influence. The Saints, he said, were very pious fellows and avoided the vain use of sacred names, but they were also logicians and hence concluded that the use of terms of precisely opposite connotation might be allowable, and even praiseworthy. At all events, they began to swear *by hell* and to call ordinary Christians *hellions* and *sons of hell,* and these terms were quickly borrowed by the miners, trappers, highwaymen, and others who invaded their Zion, and out of them flowed some of the most esteemed terms in *hell* of today. Whether Merryweather was right here I do not presume to say, but in another of his conclusions he undoubtedly slipped, as even savants sometimes do. "Today," he said, "*hell* fills so large a place in the American vulgate that it will probably be worn out in a few years more, and will become obsolescent." We all know now that nothing of the sort has happened. *Hell*, in fact, is flourishing as never before. I have many hundreds of examples of its use in my archives, and new ones are being added almost every day.

A large number of swell ones were assembled into a monograph by another scholar, Dr. Bartlett Jere Whiting, published in *Harvard Studies and Notes in Philology and Literature*, Vol. XX, 1938. Whiting, a sequestered philologian interested chiefly in Old and Middle England, sought his material not in the market place but in books—mostly novels of the 1920–37 period. But even within this narrow and somewhat dephlogisticated field he found enough phrases based on *hell* to fill twenty-four pages of the austere journal in which he wrote. I have space for only a few examples: *holy hell, fifteen kinds of hell, to batter hell into, assorted hell, the seven hinges of hell, thicker than fiddlers in hell, four naked bats out of hell, like a shot out of hell, the chance of a celluloid collar in hell, three hurrahs in hell, hell's own luck, hell up Sixth Street, hell on toast, from hell to Harvard, hell gone from nowhere, like a hangman from hell, hell's half acre, hell-for-leather,* and *what the red* (or *bloody*) *hell.* Whiting duly noted *hell of a business, hurry, jam, job, life, mess, place, note, row, time,* and *way* but overlooked George Ade's *hell of a Baptist.* He added some euphemisms for *hell*—for example, *billy-be-damned, billy-ho,* and *blazes*—but he had to admit that these "makeshifts and conscience-easers," as he called them, were all pretty feeble.

Robert Southey, more than a century ago, investigated the names of the principal devils of Hell, and not only printed a list of them in one of his books but also suggested that some might be useful as cuss words; e.g., *Lacahabarrutu, Buzache, Knockadawe, Baa,* and *Ju.* There were, however, no takers for his suggestion and he got no further with the subject. In Harlem, according to Zora Neale Hurston, the dark geographers have discovered that there is a hotter Hell lying somewhat south of the familiar Christian resort, and have given it the name of *Beluthahatchie.* So far, not much has been learned about its amperage, sociology, or public improvements, but its temperature has been fixed tentatively somewhere between that of a blast furnace and that of the sun. These Afro-American explorers also believe that their spectroscopes have found three suburbs of Hell proper, by name *Diddy-wah-diddy*, *Ginny Gall*, and *West Hell*. Unhappily, not much is known about them, though several ghosts returned to earth report that *Diddy-wah-diddy* is a sort of Long Island, given over mainly to eating houses and night clubs, and that *West Hell* lies beyond the railroad tracks and is somewhat tacky.

The Vocabulary of the Drinking Chamber

‹‹‹‹‹‹‹‹‹‹‹‹‹‹‹‹‹‹‹‹‹‹‹‹‹‹‹‹‹‹‹‹›››››››››››››››››››››››››››››››

ARTENDERS, as a class, are probably the most adept practical psychologists on earth, but they have never given much attention to purely humanistic studies, as, for example, semantics. One result is that their professional argot is pretty meager; indeed, it might reasonably be described as infirm. At least ninety-five per cent of them, in speaking of the tools and *materia* of their craft, use the threadbare words of every day. A glass, to them, is simply a *glass*, a bung starter is a *bung starter*, a bouncer is a *bouncer*, rye whiskey is *rye*, a cocktail is a *cocktail*, gin is *gin*, and so on *ad finem*. There are, to be sure, occasional Winchells among them, but no such Winchell has ever concocted anything to raise the hackles of a linguistic pathologist. When they call a garrulous client an *auctioneer*, or a *souse* a *trance*, he barely flutters an eyelid, nor does he find much to lift him in *squirt gun* for a Seltzer siphon, *sham* for a glass with a false bottom, *stick* for the handle of a beer spigot, or *comb* for the instrument that slices off the supererogatory suds from a stoup of beer. Even *cop's bottle* for the worst whiskey in the house seems to him to be close to the obvious; what else, indeed, could it be called? College boys, in their opprobrious names for their books, their professors, and

From *The New Yorker*, Nov. 6, 1948. Copyright 1948 by *The New Yorker* Magazine, Inc.

(335)

the females who prey upon them, have developed a great many niftier and hotter words, and railroad men, to cite only one group of workingmen, have invented so rich and bizarre a vocabulary that it transcends the poor jargon of the booze slingers as the spiral nebula in Andromeda transcends the flash of a match.

A good way to discover the paucity of bartenders' neologistic powers is to ask yourself what they call themselves. Have they ever invented a fancy name comparable to the *mortician* of the undertakers, the *realtor* of the real-estate jobbers, the *ecdysiast* of the strip teasers, or the *cosmetologist* of the beauté-shoppé gals? Alas, they have not, and it seems very unlikely that they ever will. Even so silly a term as *mixologist* was devised not by a practicing bartender but by some forgotten journalist writing in the *Knicker-bocker Magazine* in 1856. He intended it sportively and it has remained on that level ever since, along with *colonel* for a whiskey drummer and *professor* for a kneader of pugilists. In 1901, the *Police Gazette,* then at the apex of its educational influence, attempted to revive and glorify *mixologist,* but the effort failed miserably, and *bar clerk* was soon substituted, and likewise failed. *Barman,* borrowed from the English, has been put forward from time to time, and there used to be an International *Barmen* Association in New York, but I can no longer find it in the Manhattan telephone book, and its former spot is now held by the International *Bartenders* School, on Forty-sixth Street, which has a Yale for its Harvard in the *Bartenders* School, Inc., on Forty-ninth Street. Both have excellent reputations in scholastic circles. All the existing unions in the profession, so far as I have been able to track them down, use plain *bartender* in their titles, and so do the various social clubs, choral societies, and leagues against prohibition and Communism. Some time ago, Oscar Haimo, of the Hotel Pierre, described himself as *maître de bar* in the advertising of his latest book, "Cocktails and Wine Digest," but I have yet to hear a second for it. Nor is there any visible support for *server,* which made its début in New Jersey late in 1910 and seems to have died the death by January 1, 1911. Forgetting the vulgar *barkeeper* and *barkeep,* only *bartender* survives, a lowly word but a sound one. It arose from unknown sources during the Gothic Age of American boozing, *c.* 1855, and is of purely American genesis, though the English now toy with it. So is *barroom*, which was used by John Adams in 1807. And so is *bar* (the room, not the service counter), which was first heard of in 1788. The English *barmaid* has never caught on in this country; perhaps it suggests too strongly the poetic but smelly *milkmaid*. There are many females behind our more democratic bars, and I know one in Baltimore who is a first-rate artist, but if you called her a *barmaid*, she would crown you with the cop's bottle.

The failure of the bartenders to enrich the vocabulary of their art and mystery is matched by the reluctance of professional philologians to investigate the terms already existing. This reluctance, of course, may be due to the fact that booze studies are frowned upon on most college campuses, and hence bring no promotion to the ambitious pedagogue; also, there may be something in the fact that men learned in the tongues commonly carry their liquor badly, and sometimes have to be sent home from their annual powwows in charge of trained nurses. Whatever the truth about this, it remains a matter of record that they have done next to nothing to clear up the etymologies of boozology and that the origins of many of our salient drinking terms—for example, *cocktail*, *Mickey Finn*, and *highball*—are quite as dark as the origins of the things themselves. In this emergency, as might be expected, a great many amateurs have thrown themselves into the breach, and the result is a mass of surmise and speculation that gives the scientific student a lot of pain. I have in my archives perhaps forty of fifty such etymologies for *cocktail*, but can only report sadly that nearly all of them are no more than baloney. The most plausible that I have encountered was launched upon humanity by Stanley Clisby Arthur, author of "Famous New Orleans Drinks and How to Mix Them," a classical work. It is to the effect that the *cocktail* was invented, along about 1800, by Antoine Amédée Peychaud, a refugee from Santo Domingo who operated a New Orleans pharmacy in the Rue Royale. This Peychaud was a Freemason, and his brethren in the craft took to dropping in at his drugstore after their lodge meetings. A hospitable fellow, he regaled them with a toddy made of French brandy, sugar, water, and a bitters of a secret formula, brought from Santo Domingo. Apparently running short of toddy glasses, he served this mixture in double-ended eggcups, called, in French *"coquetiers."* The true pronunciation of the word was something on the order of *"ko-kayt-yay,"* but his American friends soon mangled it to *"cock-tay"* and then to *"cocktail."* The composition of the bitters he used remained secret, and they are known as Peychaud's to this day. His brandy came from the Sazerac du Forge et Fils distillery at Limoges, and its name survives in the Sazerac cocktail, though this powerful drug is now usually made of rye whiskey, with the addition of Peychaud's bitters, absinthe, lemon peel, and sugar.

As I have said, this etymology has more plausibility than most, and I'd like to believe it, if only to ease my mind, but some obvious question marks follow it. First, why didn't Arthur give his authorities? It is hard to believe that he remembered back to 1800 himself, and if there were intervening chroniclers, then why didn't he name them? And if he got his facts from original documents—say, in the old Cabildo—then why didn't he supply titles, dates, and pages? A greater difficulty lies in the fact that the searchers for the "Dictionary of American English" unearthed a plain mention of the *cocktail* in the Hudson (N.Y.) *Balance* for May 13, 1806, in which it was defined as "a stimulating liquor composed of spirits of any kind, sugar, water and bitters." How did Peychaud's invention, if it *was* his invention, make its way from New Orleans to so remote a place as Hudson, New York, in so short a time, and how did it become generalized on the way? At the start of its journey it was a concoction of very precise composition—as much so as the Martini or Manhattan of today—but in a very few years it was popping up more than a thousand miles away, with an algebraic formula, $x + C_{12} H_{22} O_{11} + H_2O + y$, that can be developed, by substitution, into almost countless other formulas, all of them making authentic cocktails. Given *any* hard liquor, *any* diluent, and *any* addition of aromatic flavoring, and you have one instantly. What puzzles me is how this massive fact, so revolutionary in human history and so conducive to human happiness, jumped so quickly from New Orleans to the Hudson Valley. It seems much more likely that the *cocktail* was actually known and esteemed in the Albany region some time before Peychaud shook up his first Sazerac on the lower Mississippi. But, lacking precise proof to this effect, I am glad to give that Mousterian soda jerker full faith and credit, and to greet him with huzzas for his service to humanity.

Cocktails are now so numerous that no bartender, however talented, can remember how to make all of them, or even the half of them. In the "Savoy Cocktail Book," published in 1930, the number listed is nearly seven hundred, and in the "Bartender's Guide," by Trader Vic, published in 1947, it goes beyond sixteen hundred. No man short of a giant could try them all, and nine-tenths of them, I believe, would hardly be worth trying. The same sound instinct that prompts the more enlightened minority of mankind to come in out of a thunderstorm has also taught it to confine its day-in-and-day-out boozing to about a dozen standard varieties —the *Martini*, the *Manhattan*, the *Daiquiri*, the *Side Car*, the *Orange Blossom*, the *Alexander*, the *Bronx*, and a few others. The lexicographer John Russell Bartlett, in the fourth edition of his "Dictionary of Americanisms," 1877, also listed the *Jersey* and the *Japanese*, but neither survives except in the bartenders' guides, which no bartender ever reads. The "Dictionary of American English" traces the *Manhattan* only to 1894, but that is absurd, for I saw a justice of the Supreme Court of the United States drink one in a Washington barroom in 1886. The others that I have mentioned, save the *Martini* and the *Bronx*, are not listed in any dictionary at hand, though millions of them go down the esophagi of one-hundred-per-cent Americans every week, and maybe every day. A correspondent tells me that the *Daiquiri* was invented by American engineers marooned at Daiquiri, near Santiago de Cuba, in 1898; they ran out of whiskey and gin but found a large supply of pale Cuban rum, and got it down by mixing it with lime juice. The origin of the *Martini* is quite unknown to science, though I have heard the suggestion that its name comes from that of Martin Luther. The origin of *Bronx* ditto; all that is known is that it preceded the *Bronx Cheer*. The origin of the *Alexander* ditto, despite some fancy theories. The *Old-fashioned* is supposed to be the grandfather of them all, and it really may be, for its formula greatly resembles that of the Hudson *Balance* cocktail of 1806, but the fact remains that Bartlett did not mention it in 1877 and that it is not to be found in any earlier reference works, not even the *Congressional Globe*, predecessor of the *Congressional Record*.

Some time ago, the St. Louis *Post-Dispatch*, a high-toned paper, dug up a local historian who testified that the *highball* was named by Lilburn McNair, a grandson of the first governor of Missouri and a shining light of St. Louis bar society in the nineties. It seems to be true that the name was first heard about that time, for *highball* was never applied before to a mixture of rye or bourbon and soda or tap water, and Scotch whiskey did not come upon the American market until the early nineties. (My father, trying his first shot of it in 1894, carried on in a violent manner, and died, four years later, believing that it was made by quack saloonkeepers in their cellars, of creosote and sweet spirits of nitre.) But there are old-timers in Boston who say that the first *highball* was shoved across the bar at the Parker House there, and the late Patrick Gavin Duffy, an eminent bartender of New York, claimed in his "The Official Mixer's Manual" that he borned it at the old Ashland House in 1895. Why the name? Most of the authorities say that it arose from the fact that the bartenders of the nineties called a glass a *ball* and that *highball* flowed naturally from the fact that what was formerly a whiskey-and-soda needed a taller glass than a straight whiskey. But all the bartenders above eighty that I am acquainted with say that *ball* was never used for a glass. Other authorities report that *highball* was lifted from the railroad men, who use the term for go ahead. But this sounds pretty thin, for if the railroad men of that era had ever detected a bartender putting water (and especially soda water) into whiskey, they would have butchered him on the spot. Thus the matter stands. I pant for light, but there is no light.

The history of *Mickey Finn* is equally murky. Herbert Asbury says, in his "Gem of the Prairie," a history of the rise of culture in Chicago, that the name was borrowed from that of a Chicago saloonkeeper who had been a lush-roller in his early days and operated a college for pickpockets in connection with his saloon. The patrons of the place were a somewhat mischievous lot, and not infrequently Finn had to go to the aid of his bouncer. They used the side arms in vogue at the time—to wit, bung starters, shillelaghs, joints of gas pipe, and lengths of garden hose filled with BB shot—but the work was laborious, and Finn longed for something sneakier and slicker. One day, a colored swami named

Hall offered to mix him a dose that would knock out the friskiest patient in a few minutes. The formula turned out to be half an ounce of chloral hydrate in a double slug of pseudo-whiskey. It worked so well that many of those to whom it was given landed in the morgue, and Finn was so pleased with it that he gave it his name. I have a very high opinion of Asbury's lexicographical and sociological parts, but I am still waiting to hear him explain how *Mickey Finn* became transferred from a dose comparable to an atomic bomb to a drink of bathtub gin with a drop or two of croton oil in it—a mixture that certainly got rid of the customer but did him no more permanent harm than a draught of Glauber's salts. Also, I am waiting to hear from him why a Chicago saloon-keeper had to wait for a colored necromancer to tell him about *knockout drops,* which had been familiar in American criminal circles since the first Grant administration. My own great-uncle, Julius by name, got a massive shot of them in Wheeling, West Virginia, in 1870, and was never the same man afterward.

These few examples reveal the pitfalls, booby traps, and other difficulties that strew the path of anyone seriously interested in the origin and history of booze terms. The dictionaries, always prissy, avoid most of them as they avoid the immemorial four-letter words. You will not find *Mickey Finn* in the great Webster of 1934, or in the "Dictionary of American English," or in the "Supplement to the New English Dictionary." It appears, to be sure, in some of the newer and smaller dictionaries, but almost always with the equivocal definition of "a drugged drink." So far as I have been able to discover, only "Words: The New Dictionary," brought out in 1947, says that its essential medicament is a cathartic, not a narcotic. Even Berrey and Van den Bark, in their invaluable "American Thesaurus of Slang," 1942, are content to list it under the rubric of *strong liquor,* along with *forty-rod, pop-skull,* and *third rail,* though I should add that they note that tramps and criminals now use it to designate any laxative victual. *Highball* is listed in nearly all the dictionaries published since 1930, but not one of them attempts its etymology. Nor does any of them try to unravel the mystery of *cocktail.*

V I

<<<<<<<<<<<<<<>>>>>>>>>>>>>>

Religion and Morals

＊ · ＊ · ＊ · ＊ · ＊

When Mencken began his studies in American English, he was venturing into a scholarly field in which there was little competition. It was otherwise with his works on religion and morals. Here he was pitting himself against the best scholarly and philosophical minds the West had known over a period of twenty-five hundred years. He could not hope, and in the end it would have been futile, to master the enormous literature on these subjects; but he had the sure instinct of the scholar, and during the years he was preparing himself for this task, he came upon the books and thought essential to his view of the subjects.

He once described himself as a "materialist of the materialists," and it was from this position that he approached the subject of religion. From his early newspaper days he had skirmished with various Protestant ministers, yet throughout his life clergymen were among his friends. When he started his daily column "The Free Lance" in 1911 for the Baltimore Evening Sun, he was told that he could write on any subject, provided the column was irresponsible and readable. Later a caveat was added that he must not attack the Christian Church. Mencken kept to the conditions, but the Methodist ministers, aroused by his onslaughts on Baltimore's uplifters, denounced him in unison at a public meeting. The editor, a fair man, released him from his pledge, and said he could reply. As Mencken was later to remark, the reply went on for the remaining years of the life of the column; in fact, it continued until he stopped writing altogether. The Treatise on the Gods was an attempt to get at the roots of the subject and to state his ideas in a systematic manner.

Mencken saw religion in all its forms throughout history as a contrivance of man to obtain the good will of the powers that appear

(345)

to operate the universe. In conversation he once discussed Havelock Ellis's notion that at bottom religion was the art of achieving an emotional relationship with the world conceived as a whole. Mencken thought this plain nonsense. The idea of a man having a relationship with the world "as a whole" was an impossible one. Man's relationships were always immediate, with his wife, his employer, the tax collector, the books he read, and the music he heard. Wordsworth's conception of a serene mood in which

We see into the life of things

he also thought untenable. He did not deny that mystics reported such experiences, but since they could also be induced by drugs, lack of sleep, starvation, and other factors, he believed the safer course was to await an explanation by medicine or biology.

He thought of his book as a twentieth-century modernization of nineteenth-century materialism. The data that had accumulated in anthropology, psychology, and allied fields since the days of Huxley was of large proportions, and Mencken attempted to organize it and to state in readable form the main conclusions to be drawn from it. He kept rigorously to his subject with uncompromising skepticism, and he ignored the various efforts, ranging from the fifth century B.C. to the present day, to refute skepticism by the substitution of a philosophical view of the world for the religious one. In all this he was following in the footsteps of his youthful idol, Huxley. His claim for the book, as he told his brother August, was that it was "the first work of art on the anti-religious side after Huxley."

His volume on morals was published four years after his study of religion, and follows the same form even to chapter headings and the colophon. Its premise is the ancient one that the subject matter of ethics is susceptible to treatment by rational methods, exactly as are physics and biology. Admittedly the task is one of great difficulty in the ethical field, but no more satisfactory view of the problem has been suggested.

The Treatise on the Gods *was a popular success, with two printings before publication and a sale of 13,000 copies in its first year. The* Treatise on Right and Wrong, *which appeared during the Depression, did not fare as well.*

The Nature and Origin

of Religion

≪≪≪≪≪≪≪≪≪≪≪≪≪≪≪≪≪≪≪≪≪≪≪≪≪≪≫≫≫≫≫≫≫≫≫≫≫≫≫≫≫≫≫≫≫≫≫≫≫≫≫≫

· I ·

THE ancient and curious thing called religion, as it shows itself in the modern world, is often so overladen with excrescences and irrelevancies that its fundamental nature tends to be obscured. When we hear of it in everyday life, it is usually in connection with some grandiose pretension by its priests or practitioners or some unseemly row or scandal among them, religious only by courtesy. It is employed by such pretenders as a sanction for moral theories, for political and economic dogmas, for reforms (or for opposition to them) in laws and manners, for social protests and revolutions, and even for purely private enterprises, including the commercial and the amorous. In Christian Europe, as everyone knows, it is the plaything of political charlatans, clerical and lay; in America it is used as a club and a cloak by both politicians and moralists, all of them lusting for power and most of them palpable frauds. Some of the most bitter religious controversies of this age of hatreds—for example, the war over Prohibition in the United States, the long struggle over the Pope's temporal power in Italy, and that between church and state in Germany, Russia and Mexico—have had little to do with religion, properly so called. But it serves so conveniently to give a high dignity and authority to this or that faction, otherwise plainly in want of a respectable case, that it is constantly lugged in by the heels, to its own grave damage and discredit and the complete destruction of common sense and common decency. The fact, no doubt, accounts at least partly for the slowness with which some of the capital problems of mankind approach solution, especially in the fields of morals and government: their discussion is often so contaminated by pseudo-religious considerations that a rational and realistic dealing with them becomes impossible. It accounts unquestionably for the general feeling that religion itself is a highly complicated and enigmatical thing, with functions so diverse and sinister that plain men had better avoid thinking of them, as they avoid thinking of the Queen's legs and the King's death.

Nevertheless, it is quite simple at bottom. There is nothing really secret or complex about it, no matter what its professors may allege to the contrary. Whether it happens to show itself in the artless mumbo-jumbo of a Winnebago Indian or in the elaborately refined and metaphysical rites of a Christian archbishop, its single function is to give man access to the powers which seem to control his destiny, and its single purpose is to induce those powers to be friendly to him. That function and that purpose are common to all religions, ancient or modern, savage or civilized, and they are the only common characters that all of them show. Nothing else is essential. Religion may repudiate every sort of moral aim or idea, and still be authentically religion. It may confine itself to the welfare of the votary in this world, rejecting immortality and even the concept of the soul, and yet hold its character and its name. It may reduce its practices to hollow formulae, without immediate logical content. It may imagine its gods as beings of unknown and unknowable nature and faculties, or it may imagine them as creatures but slightly different from men. It may identify them with animals, natural forces, or inanimate objects, on the earth or in the vague skies. It may credit them with virtues which, in man, would be inconceivable, or lay to them vices and weaknesses which, in man, would be unendurable. It may think of them as numerous or as solitary, as mortal or as immortal. It may elect them and depose them, choose between them, rotate them in office, arrange them in hierarchies, punish them, kill them. But so long as it believes them to be able at their will to condition the fate of man, whether on this earth or elsewhere, and so long as it professes to be capable of influencing that will to his benefit, that long it is religion, and as truly deserving of the name as the most highly wrought theological system ever heard of.

• 2 •

In its pure and simple form religion is not often encountered today. It is almost as rare, indeed, as pure democracy or pure reason. It tends inevitably to gather the accretions that I have mentioned, some of them suitable to it and some not. The first man who sought to propitiate the inimical and impenetrable powers of the air must have done it with certain outcries and certain gestures of abasement, and thereby he laid the foundations of liturgy and ceremonial. His first apparent success, observed by his marveling and perhaps envious fellows, made a priest of him, and straightway theology was born. There are, in truth, psychological impediments to pure religion, deeply implanted in the common nature of man. He is not, ordinarily, capable of the profound and overmastering feeling that its practice demands. His discontents, in the main, are transient, and his yearnings come and go with easy fluency, changing day by day. Nor has he the intellectual resolution and audacity, the hard drive of character, needed for a direct onslaught upon the gods. The thought of facing them in their rainbow crowns and robes of lightning appalls him; his inferiority complex gets in the way; he has all he can do to face the policeman on the beat and his own wife. Thus the business of wrestling with Omnipotence tends to fall into the hands of specialists, which is to say, into the hands of men who by habit and training are subnormally god-shy and have a natural talent for remonstrance and persuasion. These specialists, by the method of trial and error, develop a professional technique, and presently it is so complicated and so highly formalized that the layman can scarcely comprehend it. He may retain a lively sense of its purpose, and even lend a hand in some of its procedures, but he is quite content to leave the general management of the business to priests.

The Catholic Mass offers a case in point. Every adult Catholic has been instructed in the nature and meaning of that ceremonial, and is supposed to participate in every important step of it. At a certain place he is admitted by a sacerdotal miracle into the actual presence of the Son of God, and there, in theory, performs an act of personal worship, directly and without any further priestly intervention. But it would surely be too much to assume that the average Catholic, at this place, really does anything of the sort. The hortatory literature of the church, in fact, is largely devoted to upbraiding him for failing to do so. The Mass, with its strange language and esoteric ceremonials, is simply too much for him: he comes to regard it less as a means of worship than as a symbol and witness of his willingness to be worshiped for. He resorts to it on Sunday morning as a public notice that he is of a generally religious cast of mind, and of specifically Catholic views. When he thinks of it seriously at all, he thinks of it as principally the priest's affair, not his own. His bare presence, with due regard to certain matters of etiquette, is enough in his mind to establish his piety, and so get him his fair share of grace, *i.e.*, his fair share of the Almighty's special favor, reserved for the faithful.

Within all the great religions there arise, from time to time, cults which seek to rid worship of this formalization and artificiality. One of the most familiar of them is called mysticism. It has appeared not only in all three of the principal branches of Christianity, but also in Moslemism, Buddhism, Brahmanism, and Taoism, and even in the barbaric shamanism of Central Asia and the crude animism of the North American Indians. There were mystics among the ancient Jews, and their ideas give pungency and glamour to the Book of Revelation. St. Augustine inclined toward mystical practices, and the cult was prosperous so early as the fourth century, especially in the Eastern church. It came into the Western church with monasticism, which was originally grounded upon it, and found adherents in such magnificoes as Eckhart of St. Gall, Bernard of Clairvaux, Francis of Assisi, Ignatius Loyola, Thomas Aquinas, St. Catherine of Siena and St. Theresa. Luther, in his early days, was a mystic, and later on there were many more among the Protestants. There are survivors in our own day, despite the general decay of religion. The Holy

(350)

Rollers, when they are possessed by the Holy Ghost and address God directly in the tongues, practice what may be called a form of mysticism, and so do the Trappists when they engage in their silent and interminable grovelings. The Calvinistic process of redemption that dour Presbyterians visualize is essentially private and mystical, and so is the process of spiritual purification imagined by the Christian Scientists.

The essence of mysticism is that it breaks down all barriers between the devotee and his god, and thereby makes the act of worship a direct and personal matter. In theory, no ceremony is required, nor any priest, nor even any teacher. The mystic brings himself into contact with Omnipotence by any device which pleases his fancy, and can be demonstrated to work in his case. He may resort to magical formulae, to narcotics, to violent physical activity, or to painful ascetic practices, or he may accomplish his purpose very simply by introspection and prayer. The main thing is that, without the aid of any human agent, he comes face to face with his god, and can make his wants known directly. The intervention of a liturgy, as of a priest, would be absurd; not even articulate speech is necessary. Here we have religion in a nearly pure form, with god and suppliant in the easy posture of physician and patient or parent and child.

The priests of all faiths naturally view such practices with suspicion, for they tend to discount the value of dogma and to make the devotee self-reliant and intractable. Open any treatise upon pastoral theology and you will find the author warning his sacerdotal readers against old women who pray too much and are otherwise too intimate with God. If all of the faithful inclined to mysticism, and had a talent for it, there would be empty pews in the churches and the whole ecclesiastical structure would begin to rock. But the taste for it, while very far from common, is still too powerful when it is encountered to be put down altogether, so the gentlemen of the cloth have usually tried to keep it within bounds by countenancing it and regulating it. The rules of the various Catholic orders are ingeniously drawn to that end. Piety is encouraged and protected, but the devotee is kept under the eye of judicious superiors, and thus restrained from any indecorous familiarity with the Most High. Further than this discreet policing it would be unsafe to go, for a downright prohibition of mysticism would be only too plainly a prohibition of religion.

But there is really no need for the gentlemen of the cloth to be alarmed, for not many human beings, as we have seen, are fit for private encounters with the gods. The rest prefer to transact their business at a distance and through intermediaries. Thus mysticism (and every other form of pure religion with it) tends to yield constantly to liturgy, dogma and priestcraft. In the end, the way the thing is done begins to count for more than the aim in doing it, and that aim itself is converted, by the magnificent rationalizations of theology, into something that it is not. The process is familiar in everyday life; it is encountered at every step in the history of religion, and especially of Christianity. Protestantism itself, in its earliest phases, was plainly a movement toward mysticism: its purpose, at least in theory, was to remove the priestly veil separating man from the revealed Word of God. But that veil was restored almost instantly, and by the year 1522, five years after Wittenberg, Luther was damning the Anabaptists with all the ferocious certainty of a medieval Pope, and his followers were docilely accepting his teaching. The Lutherans have been horribly priest-ridden ever since. They are even more subservient to sacerdotal authority, indeed, than the Catholics, for most of them take theology more seriously.

Their fellow abhorrers of the Roman Harlot have gone down the common road almost as far. I point to the Baptists. The theology of the Baptists, theoretically, is simple to the point of austerity. Their sole repository of the truth is the King James Bible, and once he has assented to a few simple principles of faith, every Baptist is free to interpret the revelations therein as he pleases. The church has no hierarchy, nor indeed any ecclesiastical organization. Every congregation hires its own pastor, and may ordain anyone to the office. The highest denominational body is a mere steering committee and has no authority in canon law over even the meanest crossroads church. Nevertheless, it must be plain that the Baptists, at least in the United States, submit to an ecclesiastical tyranny of extraordinary pretensions. Their pastors not only expound Holy Writ to them with great assurance and indignation, but also presume to lay down regulations governing their private conduct in many far-flung fields, including the moral, the political, the connubial and the convivial. These regulations, speaking generally, are respected and obeyed; there are Baptists, to be sure, who protest against them as *ultra vires,* but there are not many who openly flout them. The reason is not far to seek. The majority of Baptists, like the majority of non-Baptists, have very little private talent for religion. They have neither the intrepidity necessary for gaining access to God and making their wants known to Him, nor the erudition needed to interpret His dark wishes and commands. Thus they are forced to resort to professionals. In other words, they are thrown into the arms of priests, as the pious have been thrown since the memory of man runneth not to the contrary, at all times and everywhere.

· 3 ·

It is highly probable, indeed, that the first priest appeared in the world simultaneously with the first religion; nay, that he actually invented it. We know nothing positive, of course, about what happened in that remote and creepy time, but we do know something—though maybe not as much as we ought to know— about the nature of man, and that knowledge teaches us that great inventions are always made, not by men in the mass or even by small groups, but by extraordinary individuals. The Greek mythographers sensed the fact, and so transferred the invention of books from the vague Phoenicians to the concrete Cadmus. In all other mythologies there is the same astute recognition of leaders and innovators. The invention of fire-making apparatus is never ascribed to a whole tribe, nor even to a group within it, but always to a single Fire-Bringer, and usually he is felt to be so unusual that he is credited with a divine character. In later ages the acquired imbecility of the learned made war upon this primeval good sense, and there was much weighty gabble about folk-art, and, what is worse, about folk *works* of art. But now even pedants are aware that nothing of the sort has ever been seen in the world. The very myths themselves are the compositions, not of the folk, but of professional artists—humble, perhaps, but gifted more than most. So with folk-songs. So with theological dogmas. So with theories of government. So, indeed, with college yells.

Certainly religion must be granted to be one of the greatest inventions ever made on earth. It not only probably antedated all the rest, including even fire-making; it was also more valuable to the Dawn Man than any or all of them. For it had the peculiar virtue of making his existence endurable. For many generations, perhaps for many thousands of years, he had been finding life increasingly unpleasant, for the cells of his cortex had been gradually proliferating, and the more they proliferated the more he was afflicted by a new curse: the power to think. Having escaped his enemies and eaten his fill, he could no longer take his brutal ease under a kindly tree. The dog-like beasts who were his play-mates and the apes who were his sardonic cousins were far happier. Their minds were empty; they could not generalize experience; they were innocent. But man suffered under the stealthy, insidious assaults of his awakening brain, now bulging and busy like a bulb in spring. It not only caused him to remember the tree that came near falling upon him last week; it also enabled him to picture the tree that might actually fetch him tomorrow. He began to live in a world of multiplied hazards and accidents, some of them objec-tively real and some residing in the spooky shades of his burgeon-ing consciousness. Once he had been content, like his faunal inferiors, to rejoice over the danger escaped; now he was harried by a concept of danger in general, and tortured by speculations about its how and why.

Three devices for dealing with this accumulating unpleasant-ness lay before him. There was, first, the device of seeking out the causes of things, and endeavoring either to modify them or to anticipate their consequences, so that the tree would not fall, or, if it fell, its fall could be foreseen and evaded. This was the device of knowledge, and with it came in the beginnings of the scientific spirit, the dawn of invention and discovery. There was, second, the device of getting rid of unpleasantness by denying that it was unpleasant—the adoption of the theory that the tree, falling on a man, really did not break his head, or that a broken head, for some reason imagined and stated, was better than a sound one. This was the device of poetry. There was, third and finally, the device of trying to halt the falling of trees by appealing or protest-ing to the unseen but palpable powers which resided in their branches, or somewhere else aloft, and caused them to fall. This was the device of magic or religion.

I incline to believe that the third device was adopted before either of the other two. It made very little demand upon the imagination and almost none upon the nascent faculty of reason. The sequence of cause and effect that it presented was completely natural and self-evident. Who has not seen a baby, bumped by toddling into a chair, strike at it angrily and jabber anathemas upon it? Who has not seen a puppy, pricked by a thorn, snap at it and get pricked again? All mammals, in truth, seem to have an inborn tendency to identify causation with volition. They are naturally pugnacious, and life to them consists largely of a search for something or someone to blame it on. Every dog, as a sage once observed, has found its god, and worships him with its tail; it might be added that the same god, if young, male and of high spirits, has a dreadful facility for changing suddenly into a demon. The creatures of other classes and phyla attack the unfriendliness of the world with different weapons. The birds and the insects, to name but two, are highly scientific. There is no evidence that they practice any form of religion, but in inventiveness they are far superior to all mammals save man. The comon sparrow builds a nest which surpasses anything ever shaped by an elephant or a lion, and the ant and the bee engage in engineering operations which make the ingenuities of even the higher apes seem puerile. If ants and bees have any conception of religion at all, they are probably atheists. They never cry over spilt milk; they proceed diligently to lick it up. But in the veins of primitive man ran none of their cold, acrid, persevering blood; he was a mammal, and as a mammal he naturally made his first attempt to better his lot, not by adding labor to his other pains, but by seeking to placate or destroy his enemies and by courting his friends. Of these enemies and friends the most potent were those who lay beyond his mortal eye.

· 4 ·

The earliest religion, I daresay, arose out of some extraordinary series of calamities, unprecedented and intolerable. As the cells of his cortex multiplied, primitive man found even the ordinary discomforts of life increasingly disagreeable, but it is probable that he was still too close to his infra-human forebears to do anything about them. When it rained, and there was no cave or thicket handy, he simply got wet, as the other mammals got wet. When food was scarce he chewed on twigs. When it was cold he shivered. When a rival stole his wife he went without the domestic consolations until the rival tired of her, or he could make and wive a widow. All such misfortunes were unpleasant, and the new trick of thinking made them more so, but they tended to be transient, and they were not often fatal, nor even disabling. Beyond them lurked others of a greater fearsomeness: drowning, dropping sunstruck, getting killed by lightning, by wild beasts or by falling rocks and trees, dying in general. An inimical volition seemed to lurk in all of them. It was not hard to imagine some evil will throwing down the avalanche, or sending the lightning, or drawing the drowning man down to death. In fact, it was easier to imagine it than not to imagine it.

But I find myself doubting that any of these disasters was sufficiently poignant and shocking to arouse the Dawn Man to anything resembling general measures against them. They came as a normal thing, too infrequently for that, and they had the peculiarity that those who suffered them commonly died in the process, and were thus unable to think of remedies and preventives. If the survivors gave earnest thought to them at all, it was probably to the effect that they themselves had escaped once and would likely escape the next time. That attitude is common to this day. When it is encountered in soldiers it is called bravery and when it is encountered in philosophers it is called optimism. Under it there lies a certain rationalization, conscious or unconscious, of the probabilities, but its main constituent is simply a lethargic habit of mind, a disinclination to think. To primitive man thinking was even more unpalatable than it is to modern Christians. He did it badly, as they do, and his brief experience of it had taught him that it brought him only woe.

What was needed, to arouse him to the immense feat of ratiocination which gave birth to religion, was a calamity so vast that he could not put it out of mind, and yet so merciful that it left him alive and thinking. No one, of course, will ever know what it was, nor when or whence it came, nor whether it took the form of a single shocking blow or of a long series of smaller but accumulating disasters. In the folk-art of most races there are what seem to be echoes of it—greatly distorted, perhaps, but still seeming to point to some actual experience. The Flood story is a common example. It is encountered, not only in the Old Testament, but also in the mythologies of peoples as far apart as the Persians, the ancient Greeks, the Hindus, the primitive Peruvians and Mexicans, and the Polynesians. Only the tribes of Africa seem to lack it, and no doubt it will be found there as ethnological research advances. As we have it from the Jews, who got it from the Babylonians, who got it from the Sumerians, it is placed in a relatively advanced stage of human progress, and so the effect of the deluge is represented as being, not the invention of religion, but the mere reform of a religion already existing. But that detail is unimportant, for it is always the habit of man to reincarnate his heroes and divinities, so that Barbarossa and Odin tend to become indistinguishable, and Moses is forever reappearing—in our time as Joseph Smith, Mary Baker G. Eddy and a long series of lesser prophets. No doubt Noah, as a small boy, heard in his *Chedar* school of an *Ur*-Noah, and played with a toy ark. And the *Ur*-Noah that he heard of probably had predecessors of his own.

The persistence of this Flood myth suggests a hypothetical reconstruction of the invention of religion. It remains, to be sure, only hypothetical, and if any facts are in it then the chances are that they only repeat parallel facts at other times and places, but it will serve the present purpose well enough. I pitch on a stretch of grassland for the scene—a stretch of grassland in a wide valley, with a small river bisecting it. On one bank of the river there was a bit of higher land, broken by rock masses and covered with trees. The people of the valley found this higher land very attractive. There were caves on it for shelter, there were nuts and berries to eat, and there were birds and small game. They came to regard it as their refuge and citadel, as the center of their common life, as what we would call their home. When dangerous beasts roved in the grassland, or there were heavy rains, or it was cold and windy, or the lightnings flashed, or the sun was intolerably hot, they took shelter in its caves. Therein they devoured their food, housed their sick, had their babies, rested from their labors, and dreamed their murky dreams.

One spring there came great rains in the valley, and on their heels a flood of melting snow. The little river turned into a big one, and was presently over its banks. Foot by foot it spread across the grassland, until there was water everywhere, as far as the eye could see. But still the rains kept falling. Soon the flood lapped at the base of the higher ground, and by and by it began creeping near the top. One night it rolled into the lowermost cave, cut off the occupants, and drowned a mother and her child. The next morning it was making for other caves, higher up the slope, and before dark the people deserted all of them, and gathered on the summit, huddled, wet and half dead with terror. One can scarcely think of them as silent. They took counsel, they gave voice to their distress, they cried out. The rising water seemed to them like a living thing. It moved upon them like one, it menaced them like one, it would devour them like one. Already a mother and her child had gone into its maw, wiped out as if gobbled by a tiger. Who would go next? Would all go, one by one? In terror they wailed and protested, seeking to dissuade the water, to placate it, to scare it off. But always it came nearer, and soon famine was added to the greater horror, for all their food was gone.

It is not hard to imagine the hideous scene—the paralyzing fright, the despair, the false hopes, the bitter desperation. Nor is it hard to imagine one man more desperate than the rest—more desperate, and hence braver. Maybe he was the mate of the woman devoured, the father of the lost child. One pictures him resolved upon a last, violent, fantastic attempt to dissuade the monster. The rest, pressed together on the summit, are silent and hopeless by now, but he steps boldly forth. He stands out and hurls his objurgations across the flood. He goes close to the edge and bombards the enemy with stones. Growing bolder, he stalks into the water and belabors it with his club. His fellows, appalled, shrink back: at every instant they expect to see him drawn in, following the mother and her child. But he comes back safely. He comes back proudly, shaking himself. He has at least done something. The terror of the others begins to be tempered with the sneaking envy called admiration. Rough men, facing all their lives a world of hazards and enemies, they know courage when they see it. . . . And next morning the flood begins to recede.

· 5 ·

I like to think of religion as beginning thus, not with propitiation but with remonstrance, not with groveling but with defiance. The hypothesis is certainly as good as another. It accounts for all the necessary facts, and leaves out of account all irrelevant refinements and sophistications, by theology out of poetry. It does not reason backward from the complicated wants and aspirations of civilized man, like so many of the theories advanced by the learned; it assumes that the Dawn Man actually stood at the dawn, and was but one remove from his indelicate uncle, the ape. It depicts him as keeping within the bounds of his probable observation and experience, as making no dizzy and unlikely leap into a world of transcendental shapes. The concept of the supernatural, indeed, must have come much later. To primitive man all things were natural. He did not think of waters and lightnings, winds and avalanches as differing in essence from tigers and wolves; he thought of them as substantially identical to tigers and wolves. Not until ages later, in all probability, did his children formulate the concept of a category of beings quite unlike ordinary beings, and qualitatively superior to them. Thus the earliest imaginable religion, in the strict sense, had no gods; it simply had powers of an extraordinary potency, to be dealt with as ordinary powers were dealt with, but with a certain exaggeration of effort. If, as I have assumed, remonstrance and intimidation were the first weapons used against them, then it is also reasonable to assume that something akin to propitiation, or at all events of thanksgiving, soon followed. For it is hard to think of early man upbraiding the waters which made his world a desolation and then neglecting to laud the sun which warmed him back to life.

But if these waters did not constitute a god, the brave fellow who bawled and flogged them down was still unquestionably a priest. He had discovered what seemed to be a way to inflict his will upon powers that were otherwise immovable, and had thus rendered a vast service to the whole tribe. You may be sure that this service got its reward in adulation, and that he did not shrink therefrom. The power to think was still a novelty in the world, but vanity was already ancient, and so was the yearning for power. This first priest was the owner of a valuable arcanum. He could accomplish something that other men were incapable of. One may fancy him slowly developing his technique, no doubt by the method of trial and error. One may fancy him, too, slowly widening the field of its efficacy. If he could stop floods, then it was easy to believe that he could also ward off the lightnings. Here there was a chance for his public repute to increase more quickly, for of every thousand, or two, or ten thousand persons menaced and alarmed by lightning flashes only one was hit. Thus he made devotees, and was presently in receipt of gratifying revenues. People came to him with all sorts of troubles, as they go to priests today. He took on the aloof, philosophical air of a dermatologist contemplating an eczema: he learned how to avoid making promises and yet hold the confidence of his customers. He gave some thought to the form and content of his incantations, and thereby invented the first ritual. He devised, perhaps, a distinctive costume for himself, to mark him off from the common run of men. He made friends with the women especially, for women are always the chief custodians of woe. He did no work.

But it was not all easy sailing. The gift of blarney went with the sacerdotal office, in the earliest days as now, but there must have been failures occasionally which even the richest blarney could not explain away. One can imagine the rage of a hunter who, on going on *safari*, paid a stiff fee for the protection of his wife and children, and then returned from the hills to find them all drowned, or struck by lightning, or devoured by a saber-toothed tiger, or crushed by a falling tree, or done to death by snakes or ants. It was a delicate situation for the primeval priest, and he was lucky if he got out of it with nothing worse than a cracked head. To this day, in the remoter parts of Italy and Polynesia, the simple folk, when one of their gods fails them, take it out by smashing his image. Even on higher levels there is the same unpleasant resort to the axiom that it is unfair to exact something for nothing, and one hears that soldiers wounded in the wars are commonly very suspicious of their regimental chaplains. No doubt the first priest made some narrow escapes. If he survived to die naturally, as natural death was understood in that gory era, it was probably only by the aid of casuistry, which is thus as old as theology, and remains its chief staff in our own enlightened day.

But there was something that gave the pioneer pastor even more concern than the murmuring of dissatisfied clients, and that was the appearance of rivals. They must have come upon the scene at a very early stage, for the new trade of priestcraft had attractions that were plainly visible to any bright and ambitious young man. It carried an air of pleasing novelty; there was daring in it, and thrills therewith; it made for popularity and a spacious and lazy life; dignity belonged to it; above all, it seemed easy. To be sure, we may assume that the first practitioner hastened to spread the word that there was vastly more to it than appeared on the surface—that under his facile whoops and gyrations glowed a peculiar inward illumination, highly refined in its nature and hard to achieve. Hints of the same sort still come from the holy men: it is not, they let it be understood, their overt acts which count, nor even the arcanum to which they are privy, but their own singular state of interior grace, partly engendered by the apostolic laying on of hands, and partly the fruit of an inborn gift for holiness.

But the first priest probably found it much harder to support such pretensions than it is today, for the science of theology was still in its infancy. One can easily imagine rivals essaying to talk him down, and even laughing at him. Was the tribe as a whole with him or against him? The chances are that it was more or less divided, for in the domain of religion the human mind is naturally somewhat flighty, and what one man believes another is sure to doubt. If the first priest was prudent, as he probably was, he soon grasped the fact that his monopoly could not last, and sought to save what he could of it by compromise. That is to say, he sought to dispose of his most formidable rival by admitting him as an apprentice and so gaining his help. Thus two priests bloomed where only one had bloomed before, and presently there was a whole guild of them, and they began to act in cooperation, pooling their professional secrets and equipment, accumulating a tradition, and acquiring a definite place in society.

This organization of their business no doubt saved their necks

(361)

on more than one occasion, for it enabled them to defend themselves to some effect when their ghostly technique failed and they faced an indignant clientele. They could not only make a better physical resistance; they could also make a better forensic resistance, for the ideas that occurred to them in the course of their professional deliberations *in camera*, and were therein labored to a high state of finish, would operate against the plain people with extraordinary force. Thus theology got on its legs, both as a science and as an art, and with it its faithful handmaiden, homiletics. The sacerdotal office began to be associated with eloquence, with learning, with a smooth and ready plausibility, with the trick of getting out of tight corners neatly.

But though the first priests, by resorting to cooperation, thus escaped disaster, they made it impossible, by the same stroke, for any of their number to become king. The eldest among them, at the start, had been plainly headed for that office, and without rivals at his heels he would have got it. Anyone could see that he was superior, in more ways than one, to the Old Man who then held it, or what passed for it. Was the Old Man a mighty hunter? Then so was the priest, and a far mightier than any who hunted wolves, tigers or other men, for his quarry was the dreadful shape that rode the lightnings and the baleful presence that caused the waters to rise, and caves to be flooded, and people to be drowned. He had a kind of wisdom that was palpably rarer and more delicate than any Old Man's. He had, too, the charm of strangeness; his feats were new in the world; he was, in a sense, like a being from another planet; he shared some of the dark, exquisite mystery of the powers he professed to rule. Moreover, he probably had youth, or, at all events, less hoariness of age than the Old Man, and that fact would not pass unnoticed among the women.

· 6 ·

But the moment one priest turned into two all these qualifications for kingship went for naught, for one was destroyed that was greater than all of them, and that was the character of a single and indivisible man. The simple savages of those days had not yet formulated the concept of government by committee; they wanted to be led, when there was leading to be done, by a leader who could come to decisions instantly, and whose familiar frame, heaving into battle, was his sufficient ensign and guidon. They were yet close cousins to the brutes who hunted in packs, always with one leader, not two, or three, or a dozen. They had no communal policy save that of forthright attack upon whatever seemed to menace them; they had not yet invented congresses, plebiscites or even councils of war: their minds were still too primitive to be equal to the colossal intellectual feat—perhaps the most revolutionary, when it was achieved at last, in the whole history of man—of lifting reflection from its natural place after action, or, at best, alongside, and putting it in front.

So the priests, powwowing and quarreling among themselves, failed to wrest kingship from the Old Man. The theology which saved them also ruined them. The Old Man knew less than even the least of them, but what he knew had a higher practical value, and was instantly applicable, and needed no argument to support it. As human society developed he was challenged by other and less purely biological leaders, but always they came one by one, bringing the same homely goods that he had to offer and speaking his own simple language. The earliest history that we know of tells us of single kings; never of boards and commissions. Not infrequently they succumbed to rivals, but always the rivals who beat them reigned alone. But the first priests to leave definite records were already organized in droves, with complicated gradations of rank. Among the early Egyptians and the peoples of Mesopotamia they had elaborate hierarchies, and constituted a separate caste, clearly superior to the rest of the population but still subject to the king. In India they constitute such a separate caste to this day —the Brahmans. The ancient Jews had a whole tribe of them—the Levites, who were later shouldered out by the Aaronites. These Aaronites became so powerful that even kings could not take away their high privileges and prerogatives; but though they were immensely lordly they never became actually royal. Now and then, in history, we hear of kings who were also priests, or even gods, but almost always it turns out on investigation that they were kings first and became priests only afterward. The case of

David is familiar, and that of the Egyptian pharaohs will be recalled. The former Czar of Russia was a sort of high priest, but only *ex officio*. The King of England is another.

The common people have always rejoiced over a show of piety in their rulers: it flatters them to have a sign that the inferiority they must suffer on this earth has its compensation in equality before God. There are many examples in history of rulers who were ardent devotees. The late Queen Victoria was of that company, and so was Kaiser Wilhelm II when he was on the throne: in the role of head of the state church of Prussia he not infrequently delivered sermons, and some of them revealed a pretty gift for theology. It seems to be generally felt that the President of the United States ought to be a member of some church or other—safely Protestant, of course—and that he should attend its public ceremonials more or less regularly. Roosevelt II began praying fervently as soon as he got to the White House, though before that his devotions had been inconspicuous. Hoover, after years of backsliding, became a passionate Quaker the moment he was nominated. And so on back to George Washington, a vestryman. Thomas Jefferson and Abraham Lincoln seem to have been the only Presidents of a definitely irreligious cut, and they were discreetly silent upon the subject while in office. When a ruler thus submits gracefully to the religious ideas prevailing among his people he greatly augments his prestige and popularity. Believers are consoled and even skeptics are reassured, for skepticism commonly distrusts iconoclasm quite as much as it distrusts orthodoxy. It is felt to be dangerous, in modern states, to make religious speculation a public matter.

The clergy repay this friendly recognition of their place in society by an almost unfailing devotion to the constituted authorities. When they take part in rebellions, it is almost always against subversive usurpers, not legitimate rulers. At all times and everywhere they have been the bulwark of orthodoxy in politics—in England during the long constitutional struggle that culminated in the Reform Bill of 1832, in Russia during the three-cornered war between autocracy, democracy and Communism, in Italy during the Risorgimento, in Germany in 1848, and in Spain yesterday. Their prayers always go up for kings, not for rebels and reformers. During the American Revolution the priests of the established church were almost unanimously loyal to King George, and during the Civil War the clergy of the South remained faithful to the Southern economic system, and to slavery as a part of it. The great religious reformers have never preached the liberation of the masses. Luther, Calvin and John Wesley were all on the side of authority. The Catholic church is for it everywhere today, and the more intransigent it is the better the church likes it. Thus the patriotism of a priest is hard to distinguish from the patriotism of a stockbroker. When he is found questioning the established order it usually develops, upon inquiry, that he is also questioning the tenets of his church, and is on his way to heresy.

· 7 ·

Among the learned there is a frenzy to differentiate between religion and magic, and whole shelves of books have been written upon the theme. The magician, it is explained, is one who professes to control the powers he deals with; the priest attempts only to propitiate them. The magician pretends to be able to work evil as well as good; the priest works only good. The magician deals with all sorts of shapes, some supernatural and others not; the priest deals only with gods and their attendant angels. The magician claims a control over material substances; the priest confines himself to spiritual matters.

Such distinctions have been set up in great number, but, as it seems to me, to no useful purpose. It may be that there are magicians who are not also priests, but it would be hard to find a priest who is not, in some sense, a magician. Let us turn, for illustration, to the rev. clergy of Holy Church. When the celebrant of Mass comes to the Consecration, and, in the words of the Fourth Lateran Council, "the whole substance of the bread is changed into the body of Christ, and the whole substance of the wine into His blood, the species alone remaining"—when this daily miracle is performed, it must be plain that there is an indubitably magical quality in it. The simple carbohydrate of the bread, a purely material substance, is changed into a complicated congeries of other material substances, and so with the alcohol of the wine. Only the "species," or "accidents," *i.e.*, the outward appearances, of the bread and wine remain; otherwise they are completely transformed into flesh and blood. Here we have all the characteristics of a magical act, as experts set them forth: the suspension of natural laws, the transmutation of a material substance, the use of a puissant verbal formula, and the presence of an adept. If it be argued that the essential miracle is performed, not by the priest but by God, then it may be answered that, as a matter of historical fact, God has never performed it since the Last Supper save at a priest's behest and with his aid, and that if the priest should neglect any important part of the prescribed formula the whole transaction would fail.

But the point needs no laboring, for it doesn't make much difference what a thing is called, so long as its intrinsic character is clearly apprehended. Magic or religion: it is all one. Theologians themselves dispose of the matter by calling everything they do an act of religion, including even such operations as bedizening themselves with high-sounding titles and dignities, superior to any ever claimed by Christ, and laying taxes upon the faithful for their own aggrandizement; if that is how they feel about it, let them have their way. Their earliest forerunners, we may be sure, wasted no time upon any such bandying with words. They were aware of no difference between magic and religion, but practiced both with easy consciences. The first priest, indeed, by any modern definition, was far more the magician than the priest. If he saw the flood that he put down as a living thing, then he saw it as a living thing differing in no essential from himself. It plainly had free will, as he had, and, having free will, it must have had consciousness, but that will and that consciousness were not transcendental; they responded to ordinary terrestrial stimuli, and could be controlled by human means. I suppose the first priest, if he thought about it at all, thought that he had overcome the flood by scaring it. Its subsidence followed his volley of objurgations: the logic in that fact was strong enough to convince any theologian ever heard of. There was no intervention by a higher power, summoned to the business by the priest's words, for no higher power had yet been imagined. Purpose and malignancy could be detected in floods and tempests, as they could be detected in tigers and hyenas, but there was no evidence that they differed in any manner from the purpose and malignancy of man.

This naïve view of the matter, however, could not last. As the new art of thinking developed and primitive man began to feel somewhat at ease in its exercise, it must have occurred to more than one speculative mind that the power exercised by the priest was really of an extraordinary character. He could do things that no other man could hope to do; he could force his will upon other wills that were notably sturdy and recalcitrant. The best hunter thought he had performed a not inconsiderable feat when he had brought a tiger down, but here was a man who could bring down the dreadful forces residing in the waters and the lightnings. Was he, in fact, an ordinary man? If the vast powers he professed to possess were real, then how did he come to possess them? And why were they not found in other men?

I suspect that the early priests, facing this dawn of the critical spirit, soon found themselves in the situation in front of Pope Pius IX in 1870. Confronted by a revival and epidemic of Gallicanism which menaced not only his temporal power but also his spiritual authority, he was forced to seek a ground for his pretensions that would be beyond the reach of challenge and denial. He found it in the doctrine of papal infallibility. In other words, he found it in the doctrine that he was not, in fact, an ordinary man. No doubt the early priests went much the same route. It had become increasingly difficult for them to convince skeptics that the gifts they exercised were like the gifts of other men, but only greater and grander; it was necessary for them to pretend to gifts which differentiated them from other men in kind as well as in degree. That step, it is probable, took them further than they had any intention of going, and maybe to their embarrassment. Its effect was to make them, for all practical purposes, gods.

If I suggest that they were embarrassed thereby, it is for a plain reason. So long as they were ordinary men their occasional— or even frequent—failures were not fatal to their pretensions, for other men also failed at times. Everyone knew of a hunter who had gone out to kill a tiger, and got killed himself. Everyone knew of failures in other enterprises, some of them easy. It was thus not unnatural that priests, facing the potent shapes that they habitually dealt with, should also come to grief now and then. But the minute they began to pretend that there was something in them that was superior to anything in those shapes, and differed in kind from anything in ordinary men, that minute it became unreasonable for them to fail. Failure now took on the appearance, not of an ordinary human calamity, but of proof of false pretenses. They found themselves in the unpleasant situation of the popes after 1870, with the riddle of organic evolution confronting their newly won infallibility, and no doubt they tried, for a time, to get out of the difficulty as the popes have sought to dispose of the riddle: by delicate evasion. But the subtleties suitable to modern theologians did not fit their realistic time: the reasoning that went on among their clients, in so far as any went on at all, was of the harsh, literal variety observed among children. Either they were superior beings or they were not superior beings. Either they had within them wills which could best the wills of flood and storm, and hence stood clearly above the wills of ordinary men, or they were frauds. I daresay that while this question was being debated, perhaps over a stretch of thousands of years, there was a high mortality among priests, and every great public catastrophe was followed by a massacre. And if not by a massacre, then at least by an unpleasant disgorging of spoils and a painful running of the gauntlet.

· 8 ·

The way out was plain enough. What the priest couldn't prove himself, he could prove very easily of the powers he dealt with. Their extraordinary puissance was admitted by the very skeptics who were his enemies; it was, indeed, the foundation of the case of the skeptics. What was easier than to grant it—and then add something to it? That addition produced the first gods, in the true sense. The priest himself had been transiently a god, and some trace of his early divinity has clung to his heirs and assigns ever since, but it is only too obvious that he was also a mere man, and, as men ran in the world, of none too savory a kind. The concept of a being both god and man was still beyond the nascent imagination of *Homo sapiens:* millenniums would have to come and go before even specialists in theology would pretend to be able to grasp it. But it was easy for the simplest of men to imagine a category of beings who were superior to any beings in human form, even including priests, and it was a logical step to acknowledge that dealing with them was a complex and difficult matter, and that an occasional failure was thus no disgrace. They could be intimidated at times, given the proper technique, and they could be wooed and bamboozled at other times, but there were yet times when they refused to yield for any reason that pleased them or for no reason at all.

This view of them, as it gained acceptance, vastly increased the security and influence of the priests. On the one hand, it saved them from accountability when they failed, and on the other hand it gave a new dignity and authority to their technique when they succeeded. One may be sure that they did not neglect to refine that technique in the light of experience. What worked once—whether genuflection, or outcry, or *passacaglia*—was cherished to be tried again, and when it failed on that second trial, steps were taken to remedy the deficiencies that it revealed. Priestcraft thus became a more and more complicated discipline, with characters suggesting both an art and a science. A native talent was no longer sufficient for its practice; the practitioner also had to be trained. To this day, whether upon the low level of savage superstition or upon the shining heights of Christian culture, his training remains a tedious and laborious process. Even a Baptist pastor, though he may preach without knowing anything else, cannot preach until he knows the Bible.

The primitive priest, as we have followed him, had now come to the point where, when luck ran his way, he could fight and conquer beings of a supernatural potency—in fact, nascent gods. But as yet he had to fight them alone, or, at all events, with no aid save that of his fellows, and so the business, though it was safer than it used to be, continued to be full of unpleasant hazards. If there were times when he prevailed brilliantly, there were still times when he failed dismally. What he needed, obviously, was reinforcement from the high realm of his awful antagonists, that the chances of battle might be more equitable. In other words, what he needed was the aid of other gods. I suspect that he got it, when it came at last, quite fortuitously, and perhaps to his considerable surprise. There was, let us say, a great forest fire or a grass fire, and he went into action against it as in duty bound. The people, trembling, were helpless; if he could not stay the monster disaster was upon them. He stood out bravely, trying his most trusted gesticulations one by one, and hurling his blackest imprecations at the flames. But his magic simply would not work. The fire came on and he retreated before it, along with the Old Man, the hunters and the rest. Then, to the joy and amazement of all, something happened. Clouds rolled up; the skies darkened; there was a splutter of rain. Anon there was a downpour—and the fire god was routed.

What more natural than to give thanks? What more logical than to hail and praise the good god who had overcome the bad one? True religion, in the most modern and delicate sense, was born at that moment. If the worker of marvels, in the past, had been no more than a magician, he was now genuinely a priest, with gods working for him. That is the hallmark of a priest to this day; he has a god working for him. He is a public expert in all that pertains to that god. He knows what is pleasing to it and what offends it. He interprets and expounds its occult desires, and executes its dark and arbitrary mandates. He has avenues of approach to it that are closed to ordinary men. He can, by appropriate representations, induce it to change inconvenient decrees, and he can summon its aid when his own decrees are flouted.

One may be sure that the first priest to manacle a god was not slow to see the advantages in his new situation. He became, at one stroke, infinitely more powerful than he had ever been before. Hitherto, despite the steady advances in his art, there had remained something equivocal and uncomfortable about his position: he had been, when he succeeded, almost a god himself, and when he failed, no more than a poor charlatan, laughed at by the very children. But now, with a god in his service, and then another, and then a whole hierarchy, he was securely somebody and what he had to say was attended to. When he let it be known that there were certain things, done by the people, that would gratify the gods and insure their aid, these things began to be regarded as virtuous, upright, moral. When he announced that other things were frowned upon, they straightway became sins. The two categories were carefully marked off by the priest. The acts in the first he commanded, and those in the second he forbade. Religion ceased to be a mere trembling before unsearchable enmities, and became a way of life. The priest found himself a law-giver.

True enough, there were still failures, but they were no longer dangerous to him. His day of taking the blame had passed; he could now throw it upon the people. Did fires rage and the sky remain dry? Then it was because the faithful had forgotten their plain duties. They had done something that they ought not to have done, or left undone something that they ought to have done. They had neglected some act of obligation, bungled some formula of devotion, yielded to some sin. Above all, they had failed in their obedience to the priest. At great pains he had taught them what would please the gods, but in their days of ease they had gone gadding after false lures. Now, with calamity upon them, they were paying for it. It was not the priest's fault. He was not only innocent; he was actually injured, for they had rewarded all his trouble with ingratitude. This ingratitude itself soon became a sin. It was just as bad, it appeared, to flout the priest as it was to flout the gods. It remains so to this day, and in the fact lies the chief dignity of the sacerdotal office. The priest, as such, cannot err, for his mandates are the mandates of the gods, and, being unable to err, he cannot really fail. When the gods blast the faithful it is not a sign that the priest's ministrations have gone for naught; it is a sign that the people have not been worthy of them. The ire of the gods is the penalty of human weakness. If there were no sin there would be no sorrow.

There is every reason for believing that this emergence of the priest as infallible law-giver goes back to the earliest days of religion. At the very dawn of recorded history he was already secure in the role. There were other law-givers, to be sure, but within the field of his peculiar interests and capacities he was not often challenged. His rivals, however powerful, could not hope to unhorse him, for behind him stood the omnipotent gods. If, put to the test of defiance, he could not induce those gods to send down their punitive lightnings instanter, he could always rely upon them doing it soon or late. The first ensuing calamity justified him, and got him back whatever authority he had lost—and calamities were plentiful in those remote days, as they are now. They remain the most potent weapons in the armamentarium of the priest. He may rest assured that, soon or late, they will come, and he may rest assured that when they do come their victims will turn to him for aid and consolation. Whenever there is blood upon the moon, and multitudes of human beings are heavy laden and sore beset, religion revives and flourishes. It was so when the Roman Empire began to disintegrate and the whole Western world was plunged into chaos; it was so when the wars of nationalism began, at the close of the Middle Ages; it was so when the Industrial Revolution made slaves of half the people of England. Always, in time of bloodshed, pestilence and poverty, of misery and despair, there is what theologians call a spiritual awakening. But when peace and plenty caress the land the priest has a hard time keeping his flock at prayer, and great numbers desert him altogether, as they desert his colleagues in cheer and comfort, the poet and the political reformer.

· 9 ·

So far I have said nothing whatever about the soul, nor about the theological theory, so familiar to modern man, that it never dies, but goes on serenely after the death of its owner, maybe in Heaven, maybe in Hell, and maybe lingering somewhere between. The omission has not been accidental but deliberate, for I can find no reason to believe that early man had any conception of such an entity, though he plainly had a more or less clear notion of the psyche, or, perhaps more accurately, of the will. The will he could easily sense and savor, as even dogs sense and savor it. He felt within him the stirrings of his own, and he observed the operation of wills of the same kind in other men, in the lower animals, and even in inanimate things. When a stone on a hillside, hitherto motionless, began suddenly to roll downhill, it was natural and inevitable for him to conclude that it had will to do so. In the same way he saw the workings of will in thunder and lightning, in rain and fire, in snow and hail, in the rising and setting of the sun, and in the seasonal leafing and decline of trees. To this day children reason in the same way, as Jean Piaget sets forth instructively in "The Child's Conception of the World." They begin their conscious lives by assuming that all things are likewise conscious, and then revise that assumption to include only things that move, and then, coming to the border of critical thinking, cut it down to things that move of themselves.

Primitive man was surely not critical. His mental habits, in so far as we can determine them across the void of millenniums, were those of a child just barely able to think at all. It was thus easier for him to imagine will in things than not to imagine it, and so a concept of conscious purpose probably went into the first law of causation that he formulated. But this will that he imagined (or psyche, or consciousness, or spirit, or personality, or Ka, or whatever you choose to call it) was certainly not the thing that modern theologians think of as the soul. It moved the body in which it lived, but it was still bound by that body. When the body was destroyed, it also was destroyed. There is no reason to believe that primitive man, in the first days of his muddled grappling with the unknown, ever thought of it as existing independently. All the evidence before him ran in the other direction. A dead man could no longer fight; a fire put out could burn no more; when the sun went down for the night its will to warm and comfort went with it. Was the will of the first god in a different category? It is not likely. That will, too, had its corporeal embodiment: its operations could be apprehended only physically. To have imagined it as existing outside and apart from that corporeal embodiment would have strained the nascent imagination of early man beyond its reasonable and probable capacity. And what he could not imagine of the gods he could scarcely imagine of himself. The soul was to be invented in due course, but not yet.

Virtuosi of theology, who, as we shall often see in this work, are sometimes far from critical in their ways of thought, ground their theory that a belief in the soul goes back to the first days of religion upon two very dubious pieces of evidence. The first is the fact that something somehow resembling it is believed in almost universally by the savages of today, even the lowest. The second is the fact that in some of the caves once inhabited by early man there are indications that he carefully buried his dead brothers, or otherwise put them away, and as carefully surrounded them with objects which suggest that he expected them to rise again. But there is nothing in either of these facts of a genuinely persuasive nature. To begin with the first, what savages believe today is by no means a safe indicator of what primitive man believed, for their ancestry is just as long as our own, and they have been exposed to the same processes of change that we have been exposed to, though perhaps in lesser degree. Some of them, perhaps, have been living, ever since the dawn of human history, on a plane but little above that of the apes, but others show abundant evidence that they have been up in the world and then come down again. The superstitions of the latter represent, not only ideas that they have evolved themselves, but also ideas inherited from forebears of a superior and now half-forgotten culture. Even the former always show signs of outside influence, for there is no tribe in the world that is completely isolated. Thus what savages believe about the soul tells us next to nothing about what our earliest progenitors believed. The lowest African tribesman of today is far above the first priest, for he is the heir and assign of long generations of highly subtle and ingenious theologians. It is, indeed, reported by missionaries that he sometimes criticizes the salient Christian dogmas with such skill that it is difficult to argue him down. Not infrequently, precipitating his criticism into overt acts, he has to be dealt with by the secular arm.

The evidence from the cave burials is even more shaky. In the first place, they do not appear until a relatively late date— perhaps tens of thousands of years after primitive man had begun to support priests. In the second place, it is plainly not necessary to assume, from what they reveal about his disposition of the dead, that he had any conception of an immortal soul. All they show is that he did not abandon his fallen comrades to the hyenas. But do atheists today? Do even animals? Surely not always. All of us have seen a dog watching by the carcass of its dead mate, and the books of big game hunters are full of stories to the same effect.

Köhler (or is it Yerkes?) tells of a mother baboon who, when her baby died, clutched it to her breast for days and weeks—until, in fact, its poor body was reduced to leather and bones. Primitive man, I suspect, did little more. He had still to be convinced of the irrevocability, in all cases, of somatic death. He saw an occasional fellow, struck by clubs or stones, fall unconscious, and yet revive and survive. He knew that he himself went to sleep at night, and yet awoke again in the morning. It must have been hard for him to decide, in any given case, that a dead man was actually dead forever. So he prudently cherished the body in his cave, and when the process of decay convinced him at last that there would be no awakening he got rid of it by sinking it into the floor. Perhaps he continued to hope even when decay was far gone, for his graves were shallow, and a sleeper come to life in one of them might have got out very easily.

The things that he deposited with the dead offer no evidence that he believed in an immortal soul, separate from and independent of the body. Their significance has been exaggerated by thinking of them in terms of the funerary objects in vogue among far later and more sophisticated peoples. What more natural than to put a fallen hunter's weapons by his side? Suppose he should awake when no one was by—wouldn't he need them? So with food. So with clothing. There remains the red ochre that certain peoples of the Stone Age smeared over corpses: in some graves large amounts of it have been found. Long treatises have been written to prove that it had some profound and transcendental significance, but it seems to me to be far easier to believe that primitive man saw it as no more than a surrogate for lost blood.

The dead man, more often than not, had met his death by violence, and to the accompaniment of hemorrhage. The causal connection between that hemorrhage and his loss of consciousness must have been plain to even the most unreflective, as it would be plain today to a child. What more reasonable, then, than to try to replace it with something that, to primitive eyes, closely resembled it, even to the extent of substantial identity? Blood and ochre were both red, and redness was a character that was considerably more salient and arresting than any other that primitive eyes could detect in either substance. It took mankind tens of thousands of years to get past such superficialities to the more important realities beneath; the process is not yet complete. The whole history of religion, indeed, and of magic with it, is a history of objects looked upon as essentially alike because they shared, to use the theological terminology, the same "species" or "accidents." To this day the wine used at the Eucharist is almost invariably red, not white. I have heard of Mississippi Baptists who, in fear that even unfermented grape-juice might deliver them to the Rum Demon, used Coca-Cola, but I have never heard of them using soda-pop.

· I O ·

The learned, in their speculations regarding the genesis of religious ideas in primitive man, would get farther and fare better if they disregarded the dubious analogies presented by the thinking of relatively advanced savages, prehistoric or of today, and addressed themselves to an examination of the thinking of very young children. Much remains to be ascertained and charted in that field but not a little is already known. The behaviorists, for example, have made great progress in the study of infantile emotions. They find that the only recognizable one in the newborn child is fear. The world it inhabits, like the world of the lowest savages, is filled with inscrutable and forbidding shapes. It can see things only dimly, and what it sees is seldom reassuring. Further than that it is simply an automaton, with a few primitive instincts to get it through the day.

Its first muddled attempts at observation, as we have seen by Piaget's studies, lead it into a naïve animism. Everything that it is cognizant of seems to be animated by a conscious purpose, usually inimical but sometimes friendly—its rattle as well as its nurse, the bottle that satisfies its hunger as well as the fly that disturbs its sleep. As it becomes aware of more and more objects, the number of wills is simply increased. Its toys begin to take on definite personalities; it divides them into good and evil as it divides its elders or other children. So with natural phenomena. The clouds, hiding the moon, have killed it. The thunder is a voice. The sun is alive "because it keeps coming back." Even when, with the dawn of the critical spirit, some of these concepts are abandoned, it is usually only to make way for others that are but one degree removed from the animistic. The sun, ceasing to be alive, now moves "because someone pushes it."

The principal someone in this world of unfathomable presences is the mother, and after her comes the father. To the child gradually tightening its grasp upon reality they inevitably take on the character of gods. They are, as Pierre Bovet says in "Le Sentiment Religieux," both omniscient and omnipotent. Nothing seems to be beyond their powers. They are not only gods; they are also priests, which, as a practical matter, is often something higher. They can control all the evil purposes that lurk in things; they are masters of the unknown and unknowable. Children have no other gods. When, later on, domestic pedagogy introduces them to an unseen Presence who lurks in the skies there ensues a simple transference of faith and credit. This Presence, at first, is comprehended only dimly, and sometimes He is confused transiently with the sun or the moon, but in His final shape He is always a grandiose Father, watching over little boys and girls. He accumulates reality and authority in two stages. The first is marked by the discovery that the actual mother and father are not really omniscient and omnipotent—that they may be deceived and their will resisted: this discovery had its parallel in primitive man's dawning doubts about the might of the priest as a prime mover. The second stage is marked by the observation that God demands a *quid pro quo* for His favors—that, like mother and father, He functions only according to certain patterns, often uncomfortable to the votary; the parallel is to be found in the primitive priest's invention of moral duty and pious obligation.

The likeness might be pushed further: I point to it only to suggest that in it may be found a clue to the origin of the soul. Piaget supplies some significant facts. The child, at one stage, is unable to take in the concept of death as final. It is simply a departure into that murky realm whence babies issue, and in the face of it certain questions inevitably suggest themselves: "Do people turn back into babies when they get quite old? . . . When you die, do you grow up again?" There may be an echo here of the speculations of primitive man, once he had begun to think at all: it seems, indeed, more likely than not. To him, as to the child, the mysteries of birth and death must have seemed almost identical. A child that, in its mother's body, had had no visible will issued into the world and developed one, and a man who plainly had one lost it by dying. It was probably a philosophical impossibility, as we have seen, for the earliest man to imagine it existing independently—that is, without some bodily investiture. Naturally, then, he thought of it as transferring itself from one body to another. It left an old man as he was dying and entered into a baby as it was born.

This belief, in one form or another, survives into our own day. Among the Papupo-Melanesian savages described by Bronislaw Malinowski in "The Father in Primitive Psychology" (as among many savages in other parts of the world) there is no understanding of the physiological role of the father. He is the mother's husband, her lover and provider, but is not thought to share with her in bringing forth the child. She becomes pregnant by the act of ancestral spirits, who insert a spirit into her womb: it is not a new creation, but simply the spirit of one who, being dead, tires of life on Tuma, the island of the departed, and craves another whirl on earth. Nor are such beliefs confined to savages. They have been entertained by civilized man for many centuries, and lie at the bottom of some of the most subtle and elegant of modern religions—for example, Brahmanism. Christianity, for reasons that we shall see in a moment, has never toyed with them, but there are traces of them in the more occult and extravagant parts of the Jewish Cabala and in the doctrines of the Shiite sect of Moslems. The theosophists, as everyone knows, ground their whole system upon such a concept of transferable psyches. But a transferable psyche, though it has begun to show some of the characters of a soul, is not yet a true one. The essential qualities of a soul, as the most authoritative Christian theology views the matter, are, first, that it is personal to one individual, and, second, that when he dies it goes on existing indefinitely. If it were imagined as common to two or more individuals, then the Last Judgment would present judicial difficulties beyond the ingenuity even of God. And if it could die, then it might escape Him altogether, and so make His jurisprudence ridiculous. So Christianity has no traffic with metempsychosis.

The Nature and Origin of Religion

The soul, I believe, has been a thing of slow growth. It has probably had a phylogenetic history almost as long as that of man himself. Our remote ancestors, when they began to speculate about the great mysteries of birth and death, and gradually formulated the notion that the will which went out of a man dying entered into a child newborn, must have presently asked themselves just how the transfer was effected, and where the will lingered while awaiting it. Children, obviously, were not born every day. There might be a death, and no woman near her term. No doubt it was long held, as I have said, that the psyche of a dead man lingered in his carcass, or at all events in the vicinity. In case he should revive he would need it again; in case he was doomed to revive no more it would be in waiting for the next birth. Maybe the care of the dead, in the course of time, was inspired by the second notion quite as much as by the first. The stock of psyches had to be kept sweet, and treated with respect. In all this, dreams would reinforce speculation. Everyone, sleeping, had conversed with the dead. They could be seen plainly, always in a shape substantially identical with their earthly form; they talked freely and showed all of the desires and habits of mind of the living; they could be consoling, chatty, instructive, bellicose, threatening, vengeful, lustful, heroic; moreover, they could move about. Thus the ghost was born, a sort of anthropoid ancestor of the soul. It began almost at once to be dreaded, for though it was in many respects like a living man, it yet had ways of its own, and some of them were unpleasantly mysterious and menacing. People took to blaming ghosts, and especially the ghosts of unpopular men, for a variety of minor calamities, too trivial to be laid to the gods. Quite naturally, the business of dealing with them was handed over to the priests, who were already experts in whatever was disagreeable.

But the ghost was still far from the thing that modern theologians call a soul, for it was bound to an earthly investiture and could be restored to that investiture or to another, and it was anything but immortal. The ghosts that men saw in dreams—and pretty soon, by an easy step of the fancy, when awake, especially at night—were all relatively recent, for the memory of man was yet somewhat infantile and hazy, and there was no history to re-

(379)

inforce it. A mother might dream of a baby dead a dozen years, and a man traversing a dark wood might encounter his slain father, but that was as far as it went. He seldom encountered his father's father, and never the grandfather of his grandfather. The ghost thus had a limited span of life, and it continues to show that defective durability to this day. Among savages there is a practically universal belief that, by appropriate devices, it may be killed, or, at all events, reduced to inertia and impotence. Even on higher levels ghost lore is largely a lore of exorcism and extermination. So long as a given ghost behaves with reasonable decency it is viewed with more or less equanimity, for experience teaches that it can't last indefinitely, but if it shows any active unpleasantness steps are taken to put it down. Its life is thus precarious, as man's is. And when it dies, either by natural senility or as a result of operations by the priest, it is dead in bitter reality, for so far as I know there is no concept anywhere of a ghost of the second degree, or ghost's ghost.

· I I ·

There must have been active speculation at a very early day about the precise duration of a ghost's life, for it was a matter of practical concern to primitive man. How long could spirits be preserved in or near the bodies of the dead, that there might be a ready supply when children were born? How long was it necessary to put up with a ghost who made a nuisance of himself, and resisted the efforts of the priests to make away with him? The priests, appealed to for authoritative information on these points, probably showed the usual theological division of opinion. There was a party which held that all ghosts die very soon; there was an opposition party which gave them longer life. As the memory of man improved this second party naturally tended to prevail, for he could now remember men long dead, and so dream about them and see their ghosts. History, getting on its legs, helped too; there began to be traditions of heroes in the remote past, and uneasy sleepers occasionally saw them and had talk with them. Thus the life-span of the ghost was gradually stretched out, and there arose a new speculation as to how it was spent, and where.

Did ghosts continue to hang about their earthly clay, sometimes making themselves visible to man and sometimes withdrawing into invisibility, or did they have quarters of their own, remote from those of man, from which they issued intermittently, as the impulse moved them? It was a pretty question, and it fevered theologians for thousands of years. Even in the great days of Egypt, when the cult of the dead reached its apogee, they were far from agreeing. So far apart, indeed, did the Right and Left parties stand that for practical purposes they were forced into a sort of compromise, whereby the soul was divided into two halves, one of which remained by the body and the other of which departed to some vague bourne in the Nile Delta, of indefinite situation and extent. This habit of thinking of the soul as multiple is common among savages today, so common that the professors of comparative religion have invented a special name for it: polypsychism. Some of the American Indian tribes, in the days before they became realtors and Rotarians, recognized two souls, and some of the African tribes three. The Malays, to this day, think they can distinguish no less than seven. There is the psyche proper, which dies when a man dies; there is the ghost which issues from its corpse; there is a shadow-soul corresponding to the shadow that followed him while he was alive; there is the reflection-soul which he saw in woodland pools, and so on.

But primitive man, it is probable, was far less inventive. The thing he thought of, when he speculated about the dead, was simply the psyche turned ghost. Wherever that ghost lurked, whether by the corpse or far away, it was plainly more or less uncomfortable, else it would not be so often on the prowl. It certainly must have known, having been a man itself, that its grisly appearances in the night were far from pleasant to those it accosted; thus it must have been impelled to make them by discontents sufficiently sharp to overcome its natural decency. It is likely that we have here the beginnings of Heaven and Hell. The two, at the start, were probably indistinguishable, as they still were in the time of the Egyptians. Certain ghosts, inhabiting the vague region of the dead, were unhappy and walked the night, to the terror of the living; others, more comfortable, were never seen or heard from. This vague place of their abiding, under the name of Sheol, survived into the day of the Jewish prophets. It survives into our own day, somewhat embellished by the advances of theological science, as the Catholic Purgatory.

The Swiss-American, James H. Leuba, after a lifetime spent in investigating the psychology of religion, held that the belief of primitive man in the more or less limited survival of ghosts, still almost universal among savages, had very little relation to the belief of the so-called civilized races in the immortality of the soul. The former was based upon what, to our remotest ancestors, must have seemed sound objective evidence—the evidence of shadows, of reflections, of shapes seen at night. The latter, in the jargon of psychology, is only a sort of wish neurosis: it is grounded, not upon objective evidence, but upon a despairing, colicky feeling that this world we live in is hopeless, and that there must be another beyond to correct its intolerable injustices. It is, said Leuba, "a child of the craving for rationality." Thus it could not have come into acceptance until a relatively late period in the history of man, after he had begun to speculate elaborately and painfully about the nature and aims of his existence. I incline to think that its authors were not theologians at all, but metaphysicians, which is to say, men professionally devoted to concocting recondite and gratuitous theories about man and the universe.

Theologians, as a class, avoid such puerile exercises; they are practical men, dealing daily with harsh and pressing realities. Immortality, as they preach it in the modern world, is but little more than a handy device for giving force and effect to their system of transcendental jurisprudence: what it amounts to is simply a threat that the contumacious will not be able to escape them by dying. Not many of them, I am sure, can actually imagine the life eternal, and most of them, in all probability, waste no effort trying to do so. They leave that feat to the aforesaid metaphysicians, to the class of scientists who try to reconcile science and revelation, and to spiritualists, all of whom have greatly damaged the dignity and authority of theology by trying to enrich its ideology. I am myself a theologian of considerable gifts, and yet I can no more imagine immortality than I can imagine the Void which existed before matter took form. Neither, I suspect, can the Pope.

The Nature and Origin

of Morality

❮❮❮❮❮❮❮❮❮❮❮❮❮❮❮❮❮❮❮❮❮❮❮❮❮❮❮❮❮❯❯❯❯❯❯❯❯❯❯❯❯❯❯❯❯❯❯❯❯❯❯❯❯❯❯❯❯❯❯

• I •

CHILDREN come into the world without any visible understanding of the difference between good and bad, right
and wrong, but some sense of it is forced upon them
almost as soon as they learn the difference between light and dark,
hot and cold, sweet and sour. It is a kind of knowledge that seems
to be natural and essential to all creatures living in societies, and
it shows itself in many of the lower animals quite as well as in
human beings. To be sure, they do not appear to formulate a
concept of evil *per se,* and certainly they know nothing about the
highly metaphysical abstraction that mankind calls sin, but many
species are well acquainted with concrete acts of wickedness, and
punish them severely. Theft and adultery are familiar examples.
A dog will pursue and, if it can, castigate another dog which steals
its bone, and an ape will try to kill any bachelor intruder which
makes too free with its wives. This sharp and often bloody dis-
crimination between *meum* and *tuum* is to be observed not only
in mammals, but also in animals of lower orders, including birds,
insects and even fishes. Much of the uproar that goes on among
sparrows and starlings is caused by conflicts over property rights,
and everyone has seen two goldfishes in a globe fighting over a

speck of food, with one claiming it and trying to gobble it and the other seeking to make off with it.

A German popular naturalist, Dr. Theodor Zell, has gone to the length of writing a treatise called "Moral in der Tierwelt" (Morality in the Animal World), in which he argues that many species, especially among the social insects, entertain not only the somewhat negative idea of vice but also the positive idea of virtue. The ants, he says, are better citizens than the members of any known human society, for they never go on strike. If the workers of a given colony should quit work their queen would starve, and each of them would enjoy thereby the democratic privilege of aspiring to her power and circumstance, but they never cease to feed her so long as any food is obtainable. Thus they are true patriots, and show a luxuriant development of that loyalty to the established order which is put so high among the virtues by human beings. It appears also, sometimes in curious forms, among rather more complex but still untutored and infidel creatures. Thus we are told by travelers that certain monkeys have a great aversion to a brother who, on being taken by men, lives contentedly in captivity, and that they try to kill him when they can get at him. They seem to feel, however dimly, that he has repudiated a solemn obligation to the tribe, and they punish the crime as men might.

Here it may be argued that such acts and attitudes in the lower animals are purely instinctive, and that it would be irrational to dignify them by calling them moral. But to that it may be answered that the motives and impulses lying behind many of the moral concepts of human beings seem to be instinctive in exactly the same sense, and almost to the same extent. No teaching is required to induce a baby to recognize a given rattle as its own; all the power of pedagogy must be devoted to inducing it to surrender its property on demand. Nor is there any reason to believe that the various manifestations of sexual rivalry among men are any nobler in origin than those observed among apes or dogs; the whole tendency of an advancing culture is to obliterate them, not to nourish them. In the days when anthropology was a pseudoscience chiefly cultivated by missionaries there was a belief that the lower races of men had no morals at all—that they yielded to their impulses in a naïve and irrational manner, and had no conception whatever of property rights, whether in goods or in women, or of duties, whether to their gods or to their fellow men. But it is now known that savages are really rather more moral, if anything, than civilized men. Their ethical systems, in some ways, differ from ours, just as their grammatical systems differ, and their theological and governmental systems, but even the most primitive of them submit unquestioningly to complicated and onerous duties and taboos, and not only suffer punishment willingly when the Old Adam lures them into false steps, but also appear to be tortured by what, on higher levels, is called conscience—to the extent, at times, of falling into such vapors of remorse that they languish and die.

Primitive man, in this respect as in others, seems to have been much like the savages of today. At the time when we get our first vague glimpse of him, lurking in the dark of his spooky caves, he was already a family man, and hence had certain duties, rights and responsibilities. We know, of course, very little about him, but we are at least reasonably sure that he did not habitually share his wife with all comers, or kill and eat his children, or fail in what he conceived to be his duty to the gods. To that extent, at least, he was a moral agent, and as completely so as any Christian. Later on in human history, when men discovered the art of writing and began to record their thoughts and doings for posterity, they devoted almost as much time and energy to setting down their notions of right and wrong as they gave to recording their prodigies and glories. In the very first chapter of the collection of hoary documents which we call the Bible there are confident moral mandates, and similar ones are to be found in the ancient books of every other people. The earliest conquerors and despots of whom we have any news seem to have regarded themselves, precisely like their colleagues of today, as the heralds of an ethical enlightenment, and every one of them was apparently just as eager as the celebrated Hammurabi to be known as "the king of righteousness."

In the world that we now live in the moral sense seems to be universally dispersed, at all events among normal persons beyond infancy. No traveler has ever discovered a tribe which failed to show it. There are peoples so primitive that their religion is hard to distinguish from a mere fear of the dark, but there is none so low that it lacks a moral system, elaborate and unyielding. Nor is that system often challenged, at least on the lower cultural levels, by those who lie under it. The rebellious individual may evade it on occasion, but he seldom denies its general validity. To find any such denial on a serious scale one must return to Christendom, where a bold and impatient reexamination of the traditional ethical dogma has followed the collapse of the old belief in revelation. But even in Christendom the most formidable critics of the orthodox system are still, as a rule, profoundly moral men, and the reform they propose is not at all an abandonment of moral imperatives, but simply a substitution of what they believe to be good ones for what they believe to be bad ones. This has been true of every important iconoclast from Hobbes to Lenin, and it was preeminently true of the arch-iconoclast Nietzsche. His furious attack upon the Christian ideal of humility and abnegation has caused Christian critics to denounce him as an advocate of the most brutal egoism, but in point of fact, he proposed only the introduction of a new and more heroic form of renunciation, based upon abounding strength rather than upon hopeless weakness; and in his maxim "Be hard!" there was just as much sacrifice of immediate gratification to ultimate good as you will find in any of the *principia* of Jesus.

The difference between moral systems is thus very slight, and if it were not for the constant pressure from proponents of virtues that have no roots in ordinary human needs, and hence appeal only to narrow and abnormal classes of men, it would be slighter still. All of the really basic varieties of moral good have been esteemed as such since the memory of mankind runneth not to the contrary, and all of the basic wickednesses have been reprehended. The Second Commandment preached by Jesus (Mark XII, 31) was preached by the Gautama Buddha six centuries before Him, and it must have been hoary with age when the Gautama Buddha made it the center of his system. Similarly, the Ten Commandments of Exodus and Deuteronomy were probably thousands of years old when the Jewish scribes first reduced them to writing. Finally, and in the same way, the Greeks lifted their concept of wisdom as the supreme good out of the stream of time, and if we think of them today as its inventors, it is only because we are more familiar with their ethical speculations than we are with those of more ancient peoples.

The five fundamental prohibitions of the Decalogue—those leveled at murder, theft, trespass, adultery and false witness—are to be found in every moral system ever heard of, and seem to be almost universally supported by human opinion. This support, of course, does not mean that they are observed with anything properly describable as pedantic strictness; on the contrary, they are evaded on occasion, both by savages and by civilized men, and some of them are evaded very often. In the United States, for example, the situations in which killing a fellow human being is held to be innocent are considerably more numerous than those in which it is held to be criminal, and even in England, the most moral of great nations, there are probably almost as many. So with adultery. So, again, with theft, trespass and false witness. Theft and trespass shade by imperceptible gradations into transactions that could not be incommoded without imperiling the whole fabric of society, and bearing false witness is so easy to condone that bishops are sometimes among its most zealous practitioners. But despite this vagueness of moral outline and this tolerance of the erring the fact remains that all normal and well-disposed men, whether civilized or uncivilized, hold it to be axiomatic that murder, theft, trespass, adultery and false witness, in their cruder and plainer forms, are anti-social and immoral enterprises, and no one argues seriously, save maybe in time of war, when all the customary moral sanctions are abandoned, that they should be countenanced. When they are perpetrated in a naked manner, without any concession to the ancient and ineradicable feeling against them, they are viewed with abhorrence, and the guilty are severely punished.

· 2 ·

But if the fundamental moral ideas of all peoples are thus pretty much the same—and they tend toward that identity on the side of the virtues almost as often as on the side of the vices—the nature of the authority which men put behind them differs considerably from time to time and place to place. No one glancing through the Nicomachean Ethics can fail to see at once that the sanctions which seemed apposite and persuasive to Aristotle were not the sanctions which appeared nearly four centuries later in the Beatitudes. To Aristotle "the moral activities" were "purely human," and the business of defining and estimating them was a matter for philosophers, not for priests. He scoffed at the idea that the gods could be either moral or immoral in the human sense, and believed that the only thing men and women could learn from them was their serenity. To him, as to Socrates, virtue was mainly a function of wisdom, and the chief means of attaining it, and happiness with it, was "some form of contemplative activity."

But to Jesus it was simply obedience to the will of Yahweh, and the way to it ran through an humble and a contrite heart. There was, to Him, no merit in wisdom, not even in moral wisdom, but only in submission. The thing to do was to follow faithfully the precept of Yahweh, the tribal protector of the Jews and the pattern of all goodness, and to carry out in the trusting manner of a little child such of his special mandates as could be intercepted and interpreted. Thus the ethical doctrine of Jesus was based almost wholly upon supernatural commands, many of them arbitrary and unintelligible, and the surmises and experiments of human reason had little if anything to do with it. To this day the system that He founded, despite the adept use of casuistry by its defenders, remains fundamentally contemptuous of reason, and some of its characteristic principles—for example, its exaltation of poverty, chastity and obedience—have yet to be squared with a sound social philosophy. But to Aristotle reason was everything and the will of the gods nothing. If he could not justify a given article of conduct on purely logical grounds he was inclined to reject it.

There is yet a third way to account for ethical ideas, and that is by the device of laying them to the inherent nature of man. From this point of view neither revelation nor reason has any validity: the moving force is a body of impulses and habits that stretches back to the infancy of the race, and is at least in some part an inheritance from pre-human ancestors. Perhaps Aristotle alluded to it darkly when he spoke of "moral qualities that are thought to be the outcome of the physical constitution"; it did not get much attention, however, until the Earl of Shaftesbury stated it clearly in his "Inquiry Concerning Virtue or Merit" (1699), and it was not studied seriously until the time of Darwin.

In Darwin's first great work, "The Origin of Species," he depicted life on earth as a merciless struggle for survival, and left scarcely any room in the picture for moral restraints. This neglect seriously incommoded some of his disciples, for it was plain that such restraints existed, and not only on the human level; thus they were compelled to look for them outside what Huxley called "the cosmic process," which is to say, in some extra-natural realm. Any such necessity, to men of their generally skeptical cast of mind, was bound to be embarrassing, for the only extra-natural realm conveniently at hand was that of the Judaeo-Christian Yahweh, which they were certainly not eager to enter. After they had sweated and panted over this dilemma for twelve long years Darwin came to their rescue with the celebrated fourth and fifth chapters of "The Descent of Man." It was these chapters, even more than anything in "The Origin of Species," which gave him the evil name among Christians that he still enjoys in Arkansas. For in them he laid the whole moral passion of man, even in its loftiest forms, to what he called, perhaps somewhat loosely, instinct, and brought forward evidence tending to show, as he thought, that the same moving force was present in many of the lower animals.

Its genesis he sought in the structure and evolution of the family. Below a certain level, as everyone knows, nothing resembling the family exists. The adult creatures lay their eggs and then go about their business; the young come forth fully able to fend for themselves. But as one comes up the scale the young appear at earlier and earlier stages of their development, until finally they are born quite helpless. Their helplessness naturally requires that they be helped, and this help commonly comes from their mothers, with their fathers sometimes lending a hand. Thus the family appears in the world, and within its fold, according to Darwin, the social instincts develop. The parent animal, having learned to perform services for its young, to take pleasure in their company, and to feel sympathy for them, cannot well remain completely indifferent to the young of other adults, or to those adults themselves. And the young, having learned to trust to their parents for aid, and to sport and play with their brethren, grow up with an amiable attitude toward other individuals.

Darwin added cautiously that "these feelings and services are by no means extended to all the individuals of the same species, but only to those of the same association"; nevertheless, once they exist there is no psychological impediment to a gradual extension of their range. He believed that, in man, three things have contributed to that extension, and so created the great body of moral sentiments, *i.e.*, of impulses to positive benevolence and negative restraint. The first is the development of human intelligence, which enables man to weigh his conflicting instincts, and urges him to yield oftenest to those which give him the most durable satisfaction. The second is the appearance of language, which causes a common opinion to form, and a sense of the common good. The third is habit. Darwin argued that these factors were sufficient to account for all the essential phenomena of morality, even the highest. We shall look into his ideas at greater length in Chapter II.

· 3 ·

The lines between the three fundamental moral theories, of course, are not sharply drawn, and it is quite possible for a given moralist to found his system upon two of them, and even upon all three. Thus Aristotle, though he believed firmly that all ethical problems could be worked out by a purely intellectual process, almost like problems in algebra, could yet admit that "some moral qualities" might be "the outcome of the physical constitution" and that others might have "a close affinity in many respects with the passions," which are plainly irrational; moreover, like most other Greek philosophers of his time, he had not quite divested himself of a sneaking belief in the gods, and in consequence he occasionally discussed ethics in terms of their probable desires. In the same way Darwin, besides making intelligence almost as important in his system as instinct, confessed that "the reverence or fear of the gods or spirits" must also be considered by every professor of morals—if not because such beings actually exist, then at least because multitudes of men believe that they do, and act upon that belief in daily life.

Contrariwise, not many moral theologians of any dignity halt their exposition with a bald statement of what the gods command. Always they make some effort to prove that it is in accord both with human reason and with what they conceive to be the eternal nature of man. Or nearly always. In the Christian moral system, as we now know it, a few elements remain that cannot be rationalized, but have to be accounted for on the ground that Yahweh's mind is so much superior to the human mind that certain of its mandates must be forever inscrutable to man ("How unsearchable are his judgments, and his ways past finding out!"), but such wholly unfathomable mysteries are not numerous. In the main, theologians profess to know precisely why this or that ordinance was issued by the gods, and precisely what it is intended to achieve. Knowing such things, in fact, is their principal business in the world. They are specialists in penetrating the impenetrable, or they are nothing.

As a practical matter, all moral systems of any complexity gather in virtues and wickednesses based upon each of the three sanctions—the theological, the logical and the biological. In the Christian system, for example, one act may be forbidden on the ground that it is repugnant to God, another on the ground that it is in contempt of sound reason, and a third on the ground that it does violence to the nature of man. Acts belonging to the first category decrease in number and importance as belief in revelation decays, but enough of them survive to condition, to some extent, our everyday thinking on moral matters, and even to color our secular jurisprudence.

A familiar example is blasphemy. There is obviously nothing in the nature of man to interdict it (even theologians, in fact, recognize that the impulse to it is a natural "weakness"), nor is there any impediment to it in reason, save maybe on grounds of taste and decorum, for if it is logical for a believer to call upon his gods for help, then it is equally logical for him to abuse them roundly (as is the habit of Italian peasants and African cannibals) when they mock his faith by failing him. What gives blasphemy a bad name in Christendom is simply the Third Commandment, supported by such glosses as Leviticus xxiv, 16 and Mark iii, 29. There is never any complaint about it from non-believers; on the contrary, they commonly esteem it, at least in its more seemly forms, as an effective weapon against both the general piety and their own inherited qualms. When one hears of a concerted effort to put it down—as by the organization of Holy Name Societies among Catholics—it always appears that the chief appeal is to revelation unadorned: the thing is evil simply because Yahweh frowns upon it. And when there is a civil prosecution, as still sometimes happens, notably in the English-speaking countries, it is always evident that the animus behind it is theological rather than legal. In other words, the prohibition of blasphemy is what the anthropologists call a taboo. It is a survival from the day when our savage forebears feared not only to irritate their gods, but even to name them.

In the index to my copy of the Nicomachean Ethics I can find no reference to the offense; if Aristotle mentions it in his text I have forgotten the passage and can't find it. It had, indeed, little terror for the speculative and realistic Greeks, and when they accused anyone of it, as in the case of Socrates, it was only to give a pious flourish to the bill of charges against an unpopular man, condemned before he was heard. The Romans, though their moral sanctions were less purely metaphysical than those of the Greeks, had no specific law against blasphemers, and no apparent abhorrence of them. If they were proceeded against at all, it was simply as disturbers of the public order. Nor is there anything against them in the sanctions of the post-Darwinian moralists, save in so far as their acts break the peace, and thus outrage the social instinct. "It is to the Jewish and Christian Law," says Dr. W. F. Geikie-Cobb, a learned English patrologist, "that we have to look for the creation of the offense of blasphemy." And Law, of course, is here used in the sense that Jesus understood it, as a synonym for a divine mandate, or, as an anthropologist would say, for taboo.

But not many true analogues of the prohibition of blasphemy survive in the civil codes of civilized countries. Even among professing Christians there is a tendency to neglect and reject whatever has no other authority behind it than the command of Yahweh, published by his amanuenses of the Old and New Testaments. Thus Protestants in general are very careless about resorting to the sacraments, though failure to do so is still a mortal sin to Catholics. Nor do they pay any noticeable heed to what Catholic moral theologians call the "supernatural precepts"—faith, hope and charity—or to the Catholic ordinances for fasts. Both Catholics and Protestants long ago put the Tenth Commandment on the shelf, and both, relying upon various passages in Paul's epistles (and conveniently forgetting Matthew v, 17–18 and Luke xvi, 17), ignore the whole of Leviticus.

Even the Jews, including the most orthodox among them, have discreetly edited the Law. They still observe the sacrament of circumcision and they still respect the taboos on eating pork, oysters, eels, shrimp, crabs, lobsters and clams, and butter or milk with meat, but they no longer feast on locusts, beetles and grasshoppers (Leviticus xi, 22), just as they no longer execute witches (Exodus xxii, 18), or stone an ox that gores a man (*ibid.* xxi, 28), or bar him "that is wounded in the stones, or hath his privy member cut off," from the synagogue (Deuteronomy xxiii, 1). According to the Catholic moral theologians, McHugh and Callan, the Mosaic Law was handed down "when experience had proved that knowledge is not sufficient to make men virtuous," and was abrogated when further experience showed that "external observance is not sufficient for holiness." The Jews accept the first half of this, but not the second: they still think of themselves as bound by the Law. But it grows more and more vague to them as year follows year, and many of them, exposed to the growing skepticism of Christendom, scarcely know what it is. More than once I have greatly astonished a Jewish friend by assuring him that he was perfectly free, under Yahweh, to dine upon June bugs.

VII

Persons

＊ · ＊ · ＊ · ＊ · ＊

In his long writing career Mencken published many studies of poli-
ticians, writers, musicians, newspapermen, and other persons of more
or less prominence. Some he knew personally, and some he knew only
through their books or other activities. The accounts extended from
vignettes to analyses running to many thousands of words. Of those
that appear here, the Cooper piece gives Mencken's view of his first
important predecessor as a critic of American life. Mencken wrote a
fair amount about Mark Twain in his Smart Set *days, but much of it*
is buried in articles addressed purportedly to other subjects. Long
before the academic world sensed Mark Twain's importance, Mencken
had proclaimed it with vigor. He wrote three full-dress studies of
Huneker; one, the longest, was a critical appraisal for A Book of
Prefaces; *another, nostalgic recollections prompted by Huneker's death,*
was turned out in three days for the Century Magazine; *and the last,*
the one included here, was an extension and rewriting of the Century
piece. He maintained polite contacts with Ambrose Bierce, who ad-
mired his prose, and the two of them attended Percival Pollard's cre-
mation in Baltimore, where Bierce entertained Mencken with macabre
accounts of other funerals. Bierce predicted hopefully that the grief-
stricken widow would immolate herself in the flames (she remarried
several months later), and recommended that Pollard's ashes be made
into bullets to be discharged at stupid publishers. Mencken had a deep
admiration for Beethoven, and thought the first movement of the
"Eroica" unparalleled. But he rated Wagner as the best musician who
ever lived, and "Die Meistersinger" as "the greatest single work of art
ever produced by man." It might be noted that, although Mencken's
writings may give the opposite impression, his use of the superlative in
praise of specific books or other works of art is rare. Saintsbury was
more free with them than any other critic of his rank, but Mencken,
as he himself observed, made it a rule to employ them with chariness.

James Fenimore Cooper

<<<<<<<<<<<<<<<<<<<<<<<<<<<<<<<<>>>>>>>>>>>>>>>>>>>>>>>>>>>>>>>>

IN 1838, the year of "The American Democrat," Cooper was forty-nine, but there was no sign in him of the dying fires which usually come with middle age. Before the year was out he was to publish five separate books, running to seven volumes in all, and by the end of 1841 he was to write and print the eight volumes of four more, including "The Pathfinder," "The Deerslayer" and his excellent history of the United States Navy. The energy of the man was really almost beyond belief. Since his return from Europe, late in 1835, he had been engaged continuously in brawls of every imaginable sort, whether political, social, monetary or legal, and yet he had somehow found the time to keep up his dogged and furious writing. One lawsuit is usually sufficient to paralyze an artist, as the example of Beethoven so sadly attests, but Cooper, with a dozen on his hands, managed to pour out novel after novel, to project vast and complicated histories, to reduce his observations in Europe to a row of fat volumes, and to belabor his fellow Americans with pamphlets and pronunciamentoes, philippics and pasquinades. His litigations still await a historian of his own industry, learned in both the annals of the law and the dark secrets of the heart. Meanwhile, his prohibition of a biography, though it has been disregarded in the letter, has been observed in the spirit, for Lounsbury's life leaves him vaguer than any other bigwig of his time, and the rest of the writing upon him, forgetting Carl Van Doren's brief but admirable essay, is mainly trash.

Originally printed as Introduction to *The American Democrat,* by James Fenimore Cooper, 1931. Copyright 1931 by Alfred A. Knopf, Inc. Renewal copyright 1959 by Alfred A. Knopf, Inc.

Cooper was probably the first American to write about Americans in a really frank spirit. The fact has been pretty well forgotten by the college tutors who now boil sophomores in the "Leatherstocking Tales," but during his last ten or twelve years on earth it was what his countrymen chiefly remembered when they thought of him. He began, ironically enough, as an apologist for them, and while he was abroad as tourist and consul he wrote a great deal of soothing stuff on the subject, including a formal treatise and three bad novels, now happily expunged from the record. But when he returned home after seven years' absence he was led to reexamine the evidence, and the fruits of that re-examination, being bitter in taste, got him magnificently disliked. What he discovered, searching the national scene, was that the democratic panacea, after all, was a fraud like any other. The young Republic had rid itself of one gang of political streptococci, only to take on another. There were no more kings and nobles, but the country swarmed with demagogues, and the more Cooper studied them the less he admired them. His conclusions he precipitated into the pamphlets and pronunciamentoes aforesaid, and of the lot "The American Democrat" was at once the shrewdest and the most offensive. It was not, of course, a complete repudiation of democracy, as the alarmed reviewers of the time alleged. But it went into the defects and dangers of democracy with acrid realism, and so poor Cooper got the name of a sniffish and unpatriotic fellow, and was accused of all sorts of aristocratic pretensions, immensely obnoxious to the free citizens of a free and glorious state.

The fact that one may read it today without more than an occasional cough behind the hand is the best of testimonies to its sagacity. How many other treatises on politics have held up for a century? How many of even fifty years ago are worth reading now? Cooper, to be sure, made some bad guesses: for example, he figured that Congress would beat the President, and reduce him to a gaudy nonentity, like the King of England and the President of France. But we may forgive him here for a natural error, for that is the way the stream was running in his time, and he could not foresee the change of course that would come with the Civil War. In general, his prophecies were as sound as his observations were accurate. He saw clearly how democracy warred upon the free functioning of genuinely superior men—how it kept them out of public life, and so forced them into silence and sterility, and robbed the commonwealth of their sense and decency. And he saw as clearly how the rule of the majority must tend toward a witless and malignant tyranny, anti-social in its motives and evil almost beyond endurance in its effects. These, as we now know, are the chief burdens of the democratic form of government, and under them it is beginning to break down. Cooper discerned them in its springtime, and sought valiantly to throw them off before it was too late.

He failed, but his book remains—a simple, sound and sensible tract, moderate in tone and extraordinarily astute in its conclusions. It is the work of a man who had large confidence in the fundamental democratic scheme of things, despite all his qualms. He knew that democracy, even if it failed, would have some useful by-products—that its dogma of equality, even though false, had certain uses for human dignity. I think the event has justified that assurance. The Americano, whatever his faults, is at least a less abject and groveling fellow than the Englishman. He may venerate such fifth-rate men as Harding and Coolidge, but he still falls a good deal short of venerating such complete vacuums as King George V. So on lower levels. In his view of the secular magnificoes who come and go—Morgan, the Rockefellers, Andy Carnegie, Andy Mellon, Henry Ford, and so on—there is surely none of the base and menial adulation which in England bathes a lord. To him, more often than not, they are largely comic characters, and in his envy of them there is a sufficient admixture of irony to keep it from becoming quite ignoble. Thus he retains a modicum of dignity, imbecile though he may be. I incline to think that that modicum of dignity is the chief and perhaps the only gift of democracy to mankind. At all events, I don't seem to recall any other.

With it, of course, go severe penalties. Dignity slides into vanity. The inferior man, looking upward, concludes that he is as good as his betters, and then, by an easy stage, that he is better. The result is a vast setting up of new values, all of them repugnant to civilization. The virtues of the cow-yard become the official virtues of the nation. Laws are drawn to coerce every citizen into such habits and ways of thought that he will be acceptable to country pastors. The thing becomes a furious game, begun by ignoramuses and carried on by rogues. In the end a candid world contemplates a government whose chief executive fashions his policy to please Methodist bishops, and whose legislators leap as those bishops crack their whips, and whose highest judicial officers owe office to them, and are not permitted to forget it. And behind roars a system of law which seems to have the chief aim of finding out what civilized men prefer to do, and prohibiting it under barbarous penalties. Here is democracy carried out to the last desperate place of decimals, but it is surely not the democracy that Cooper put his trust in.

His text defines the thing quite differently. Of what use is freedom, he demands, if "every one is not master of his own innocent acts and associations?" And what right has any man to call himself a democrat if he "will submit to be dictated to in those habits over which neither law nor morality [he means, of course, civilized law and rational morality] assumes a right of control?" The true democrat, "recognizing the right of all to participate in power, . . . will proudly maintain his own independence of vulgar domination," and "the same principle and manliness that would induce him to depose a royal despot will induce him to resist a vulgar tyrant." The doctrine could not be put more succinctly, or more eloquently. It was launched into an America that was in the throes of the Jackson *jacquerie,* and so it got no hearing, but of late it has come to life again, and a great deal will be heard of it hereafter. Or so, at all events, one may hope.

The chief criticism that Cooper had to meet in his day was to the effect that he was a purse-conscious, overbearing and snooty fellow, proud of his fame, proud of his money and proud of his birth—in brief, a sort of backwoods *Junker,* ever eager to elbow lesser folk off the sidewalk. The charge perhaps had some psychological justification, for modesty is seldom encountered in the literati, and never in those who have made a splash. Nevertheless, Cooper kept his vanity, if he really had as much as was said, in admirable check, and his discussion of "the duties of station" shows that he saw clearly how little genuine aristocracy is a matter of privilege and how much a matter of responsibility. If he urges his "superior" Americans to oppose the encroachments of the mob, it is not because it will work them any private benefit but because it will work a benefit to the nation. The power that is naturally in their hands, democracy or no democracy, must be used to further the freedom of all—and not merely freedom to take a hand in the government, but also and more especially freedom to resist the government. Here Cooper's doctrine is curiously like that of Jefferson. He sees liberty, not primarily as the right to govern, but as the right to rebel. "It is a public duty to guard against all excesses of public power, whether inflicted by mere opinion *or under the forms of law*." The citizen owes no duty of compliance when what is sought to be done to him ought not to be done. It is his duty, as it is his right, to guard against the tyranny of law by remembering the crude and vulgar process by which the laws of a democratic country are made, and the generally sorry character of those who make them.

Cooper, by the standards of his time, was a gentleman, and he was well aware that as such he belonged to a small and far from popular minority. In large part his book is devoted to an argument that the gentleman, after all, has a plausible place in a democratic society, if only as a standing protest against the leveling that everywhere goes on. That leveling, by the democratic theory, is upward, but in actuality it is downward, for the mob suspects and resents superiorities, whereas inferiorities give it a pleasant glow. It would be dangerous for an aspirant to the Presidency to be a man of learning, or to excel at any of the fine arts, or to be of noble lineage. If he professes some science or art, say history, as Woodrow Wilson did, then he must at least profess it badly, like Wilson again. If he is a lawyer, like McKinley, Coolidge or Taft, then he must be an incompetent one. And if, like Roosevelt, he pretends to gentle birth, then it must be mainly only pretense. Cooper, himself a shining example of what he called the man of "liberal attainments," had a vast disdain for such quacks, and saw in their success only a proof of their quackery. The qualities he esteemed were the sound ones of genuine learning, honest and useful achievement, and unruffled independence of spirit—especially the last. "All greatness of character," he said, "is dependent on individuality." The important man is the odd man, the unfettered man, the man who plows his own furrow. He is the sole repository of honor, national as well as personal. Cooper grieved to see him gradually disappearing from American public life, his place taken by the servile and scurvy fellow who now dominates the whole political scene. "They who do not see and feel the importance of possessing a class of such men in a community, to give it tone, a high and farsighted policy, and lofty views in general, can know little of history, and have not reflected on the inevitable consequences of admitted causes."

Cooper believed passionately in the Bill of Rights, but he was well aware of its limitations. At most, he observed shrewdly, it simply drew a line under the reserved powers of the states, any one of which could nullify the principles it set forth. He saw that a better safeguard to liberty lay in the independence of the law-makers, for the more that independence was stressed the easier it would be to get able and self-respecting men into Congress. So he launched himself violently against the theory, first rising in his time, that a Congressman was no more than an office boy for his constituents, bound to carry out their whims. The event has proved that his reasoning was perfectly sound. Today we confront a Congress made up of men who play the limber jenkins, not indeed to their constituents, but to the rogues and charlatans who inflame and prey upon their constituents, and everyone knows how little the Bill of Rights stays them. They have driven such tunnels through it that it is now only a shell. Worse, the habit of subservience has extended also to the executive department and the judiciary, and *Marbury vs. Madison* is in as sad a state of debility as the Bill of Rights itself. All the checks and balances, in fact, have ceased to function, and there is no effective obstacle to any imaginable sort of governmental excess. Cooper saw the shadow of that tyranny closing over Congress, but he was too early to envision the bureaucracy that was to come in with the Civil War, or the collapse of the judiciary afterward. When he wrote, John Marshall was but three years dead, and the Anti-Saloon League's pens for fattening candidates for the Federal bench were still undreamed of.

It must be confessed that a certain priggishness shows itself in some of his pages. Not only is there a Johnsonian roll in his prose; there is also a touch of the brittle old lexicographer's pedantry in some of his attitudes. His chapter on the American language, then first differentiating itself from orthodox English, might have been written by a schoolma'am. He even goes to the length of arguing gravely that either ought to be pronounced *eyether* and neither *neyther*—a sheer absurdity, with no support whatever in either etymology or common sense. Here, as in other philological cases, the instinct of the folk has triumphed over the imbecility of pedagogues, and democracy, perhaps, has earned some praise. Cooper's castigation of American hyperbole is equally prudish and preposterous. He had been in Europe so long that it shocked him, precisely as it shocks the English mountebanks who rove the country today, exposing themselves condescendingly at tea parties and snuffling for dollars. It apparently never occurred to him that what set his teeth on edge was the best of all evidences that a new and vigorous national life was in the making in America, and that putting down its natural and inevitable manifestations was as hopeless a task as putting down the tides. Fortunately, his chapter on language is plainly irrelevant and *ultra vires,* and so the reader with humor may conveniently skip it.

He makes up for it by his two brief paragraphs on eating and drinking. They are marred, to be sure, by a dash of what Nietzsche called moralic acid, but there is still proof in them that they were penned by a man who had had his legs, in his day, under many a gorgeous board, and his nose into more than well water. "The Americans," he roared, "are the grossest feeders of any civilized nation known." Is it true today? I incline to believe that it is not. The English, with their monotonous roasts, their ghastly boiled fish and their unspeakable vegetables, are now the undisputed champions in that department: to quote Nietzsche again, their cookery is but one remove from cannibalism. Our own cookery is still in a backward state, and the cooking-school ma'ms are trying hard to make it worse, but its materials grow so rich and varied that spoiling them altogether becomes increasingly difficult. We eat, indeed, far better than our fathers, at least if we live in cities. In Cooper's time an American dinner must have been horrible beyond words. Let it be remembered to his credit that he protested indignantly, and even bitterly. Here and there—who knows?—he may have agitated a conscience and translated a frying-pan to the ash-barrel. If so, he served his country well.

The rest of his diatribe seems to have won no customers. Its sole effect was to make him unpopular. He lived long enough to see the kind of democracy that he admired go into final eclipse under Jackson, and the kind he loathed triumphant. His warnings were gloomy, but the event was always gloomier still. He was dead ten years when the Civil War finally blew the old Republic to pieces, and brought in that hegemony of the ignorant and ignoble which yet afflicts us.

Mark Twain

I BELIEVE that "Huckleberry Finn" is one of the great master-pieces of the world, that it is the full equal of "Don Quixote" and "Robinson Crusoe," that it is vastly better than "Gil Blas," "Tristram Shandy," "Nicholas Nickleby" or "Tom Jones." I believe that it will be read by human beings of all ages, not as a solemn duty but for the honest love of it, and over and over again, long after every book written in America between the years 1800 and 1860, with perhaps three exceptions, has disappeared entirely save as a classroom fossil. I believe that Mark Twain had a clearer vision of life, that he came nearer to its elementals and was less deceived by its false appearances, than any other American who has ever presumed to manufacture generalizations, not excepting Emerson. I believe that, admitting all his defects, he wrote better English, in the sense of cleaner, straighter, vivider, saner English, than either Irving or Hawthorne. I believe that four of his books—"Huck," "Life on the Mississippi," "Captain Stormfield's Visit to Heaven," and "A Connecticut Yankee"—are alone worth more, as works of art and as criticisms of life, than the whole output of Cooper, Irving, Holmes, Mitchell, Stedman, Whittier and Bryant. I believe that he ranks well above Whitman and certainly not below Poe. I believe that he was the true father of our national literature, the first genuinely American artist of the blood royal. . . .

He was one of the great artists of all time. He was the full equal of Cervantes and Molière, Swift and Defoe. He was and is the one authentic giant of our national literature.

From the *Smart Set*, Feb. 1913.

James Gibbons Huneker

⋘⋘⋘⋘⋘⋘⋘⋘⋘⋘⋘⋘⋘⋘⋙⋙⋙⋙⋙⋙⋙⋙⋙⋙⋙⋙⋙⋙⋙

· I ·

THE world that James Gibbons Huneker knew, celebrated and adorned has gone down the dreadful chutes of time, and already begins to seem as fabulous as the world of John Paleologus. In Europe the great crusade for democracy finished it, and in the United States it was blasted by the *jacquerie* whose horrible symbol is Prohibition. He lived long enough to see it disintegrate and vanish from sight, with all its easy well-being, its calm and amiable curiosities, its pleasant cockiness—himself, by that time, become a mere show for pathologists, with one leg thrust through the crematory door. I have never known a man whose falling years were more melancholy. The work of his life was behind him and he knew it: what he did of an evening for *The World* was only a laborious boiling of the pot. On all sides loomed wrack and wreck, rust and ruin. The old battles were over and half forgotten; the old delights were under the Methodist interdict; of the old friends, more were dead than alive; all the ancient and charming haunts were dark.

I saw him only infrequently in those sad days, for, save to do his evening newspaper stint, he seldom ventured out of his remote and somewhat mysterious Brooklyn lair. There was, indeed, nothing to bring him, for there was no place to go. New York was still on its lugubrious Prohibition honeymoon, and the art of the bootician was yet as primitive as painting in the time of Giovanni Cimabue. Lüchow's, with the Pilsner taps running Coca-Cola, was an inferno of protesting ghosts; Scheffel Hall was dark and creepy; old Sieg had closed the Kaiser-Keller and departed for parts unknown; Jack's and Rogers' were ready to give up; even the spaghetti joints were going dry. During the summer of 1920 Huneker had gone to London for *The World,* and there, grinding out 25,000 words of correspondence in five weeks, he put in his afternoons at the resurrected Gambrinius, flushing his clogged pipes with the elixir of happier days. "It is," he wrote to me, with an autumnal glare of the old rapture, "genuine Pilsner from Bohemia! It has expelled the sugar from my blood!" But when he got back to Brooklyn there was only tea to drink, and so the sugar returned, and soon the news began to go about that the old boy was done for. My last word from him came on January 22, 1921. " 'Painted Veils,' " he wrote, "has aroused the anger of the barnyard school of fictionists and its critics, much to my joy. Anything to make imbeciles realize their imbecility!" But that joy was not to be for long. Two weeks later, on February 9, he died. Prohibition was one year and twenty-one days old.

So passed one of the most charming fellows ever heard of, and the best critic of the American first line. The young professors who write literary history for sophomores seldom mention him today, but there was vastly more in him than in all their N. P. Willises and Charles Dudley Warners—nay, than in all their Lowells and Howellses. Alone among the men of his generation he knew precisely which way the literary current was running, and alone among them he kept his bark in the middle of the stream to the end. It is not enough to say that he was the chief man in the movement of the 90's on this side of the ocean; he was, indeed, the only man who mattered at all, for he was the only one who never wavered. The rest went this way and that way —into popularity, into preciosity, into futility and banality. Some even fetched up in the movies! But Huneker stuck. The tune that he piped in 1891—and with what lovely shakes, appoggiaturas and grimaces!—he was still piping in 1920. To clear out the tripe-sellers in all of the seven arts—that was his first purpose. To bring in better men—odd men, men of free fancy, sometimes even wild men—that was his second. No American, not even Poe, ever

dragged in more of them, or made the dragging in a more exhilarating show.

For years, indeed, he was our official introducer of esthetic
and philosophical ambassadors, and if now and then he gave
an incautious whoop for a newcomer whose fraudulence became obvious a moment later, then let us not forget that he always
made amends for it by giving extra measure next day. He was the
first American to write about Ibsen with anything approaching
rational understanding of the artist behind the whiskers; he was
the first to sense the true stature of Nietzsche, both as dithyram-
bist and as metaphysician; he was in the forefront of the army
corps that discovered George Bernard Shaw. At a time when
Turgenev and Dostoevsky were still setting Howells to a guilty
trembling, he was thumping the tom-tom boldly for Huysmans,
Rimbaud and Villiers de l'Isle Adam. Did he praise Sudermann
too much? Then remember that it was the Sudermann of "Frau
Sorge" and "Sodoms Ende"—and consider how much worse some
of his contemporaries were let in: for example, Percival Pollard by
Robert W. Chambers and La Atherton. "My temperament," he
once said, "has always inclined to the excessive, the full-blown, the
flamboyant." It made him succumb a shade too easily, no doubt, to
the mountebankish Maeterlinck, but it was not too excessive and
full-blown to let him discern instantly the difference between the
reigning godkins of 1895 and Gerhart Hauptmann. It was exactly
his *héliogabalisme,* indeed, that led him to some of his most solid
pioneering: for Strindberg among dramatists, for Stirner among
philosophers, and for Richard Strauss among composers.

"To spill his own soul: that should be the critic's aim." The
soul that Huneker spilled so lavishly in his heyday—how many
millions of words he must have written, first and last!—was
perhaps the most colorful, as it was assuredly the most charming,
ever turned loose in these sorry states. The man was essentially and
inescapably civilized. He believed completely in the importance
of ideas, the high value of beauty. Emerging by some inadvertence
of the gods from the spiritual slums of Philadelphia, soberly bred
and badly fed, he showed from the start all the fine gustos of a
born connoisseur. Life to him was never a trial to be endured or
a lesson to be learned, but always a magnificent adventure. I knew
him best in his later years, when the marks of illness were already

upon him and the world that he was most at home in was already on the way to collapse, but never do I recall any relaxation of his immense curiosity or any lessening in his hospitality to novelty. What he brought back from Paris as a young man was what chiefly characterized him to the end of his days: his capacity for enthusiasm. It seems to me that he had that capacity to a degree unmatched in any other American, before or since; he was an Emerson purged of the last drop of moralic acid, a Howells liberated completely from the New England malaria. When his soul went adventuring among masterpieces (real and so-to-speak) it did not go in Sunday broadcloth; it went with vine-leaves in its gaseous and flaming hair. The one aim of the arts, by his philosophy, was to make the spirit glad—to set it to dancing, in Nietzsche's phrase, with arms and legs. He had absolutely no feeling for extra-esthetic values, whether sound or false. If the work that stood before him was honest, if it was original, if it was beautifully and thoroughly alive, then he was for it to his last corpuscle. What if it violated all the accepted canons of decorum? Then let the canons of decorum go hang! What if it lacked all purpose to improve and lift up? Then so much the better! What if it outraged all men of right feeling, and made them blush, tremble and cough behind their hands? Then damn all men of right feeling forevermore!

Along with this critical antinomianism, so strange in the America that he came back to in the early 8o's and so revolting to most Americans, there went something that was also, in all probability, part of the loot of Paris: an insatiable curiosity about the artist as man. To a Frenchman, as every one knows, a painter is never a mere painter, nor a composer a mere composer; he is also a husband and a lover, a consumer of victuals, a drinker of good or bad wine, a politician, a public spectacle, a citizen and patriot, a Christian or a heathen, the host of microbes, the partisan of a metaphysical theory. So in the eye of Huneker. His curiosity in such secret directions sometimes went to extravagant lengths. He mingled criticism and gossip in a way unheard of by the audience that followed Hamilton Wright Mabie. He liked to prod into marriages, liaisons, feuds literary and carnal, lawsuits, vices, scandals of all sorts. The guzzling and drabbing of Liszt interested him profoundly, and he found in them a clue to the Hungarian rhapsodies. He always thought of Wagner, not in terms of howling sopranos and grunting basses, but in terms of the Triebschen idyl and the Bayreuth court. Tschaikovsky's love affairs, to him, explained the "Romeo et Juliette" atrocity, and Dvořák's herculean capacity for cocktails the gorgeous last movement of "From the New World." He was far more interested in Walt Whitman as man, I think, than in Walt Whitman as poet. A man of wide travels, endless contacts and enormous reading, he picked up such details everywhere, and filed them away in his archives, well-indexed and instantly available. So far as I can recall, he never wrote a piece of criticism without adding to it a piece of biography. Even his most casual newspaper stuff was packed with gossip.

• 2 •

And what gossip it was! It made his conversation the most delightful imaginable. There was not only stupendous information in it; there was also a gaudy sort of malice—as there is, indeed, in all conversation worth hearing. I recall sessions at Lüchow's, with old August himself hovering in the background, that were veritable debauches of sly and stimulating scandal. Down went a *Seidel* of Pilsner—and out came the authentic last words of Whitman, gasped into poor Horace Traubel's solicitous ear, and too horrible, almost, to be remembered in a Christian land. Down went another—and out came a precise and meticulous description of Liszt's vast flotilla of warts and wens: the purple ones and the pale ones, the big ones and the little ones. Down went a third— and the theme was the virtuous love affairs of Gounod, or Wagner's encounter with the lascivious Swedish baroness, or the true story of Zola's asphyxiation, or the details of the affair between Duse and D'Annunzio, or Shaw's heroic but vain efforts to throw off the Thirty-nine Articles, or the secret causes of Tschaikovsky's suicide, or the early lives of the de Reszke brothers in their Polish home, or the varying talents and idiosyncrasies of Lillian Russell's first four husbands. Down went a fourth—and there was coruscating, confidential discourse upon the defects in the Boehm system, the

merits of German bathrooms, the difficulties of Brahms' Capriccio
in B minor, the proper tuning of the viol da gamba, the metaphysical errors of the Gnostics, the neckties of Richard Harding Davis,
the bad red wines at Wiesbaden, the worse red wines at Capri, the
Pilsner at Carlsbad, the Pilsner at Vienna, the Pilsner at Prague,
the Pilsner at Pilsen.

What should one drink with a *Rebhuhn* in *Weinkraut?* What
is best for Moselle *Katzenjammer?* Who really invented the
saxophone, and now roasts in Hell for it? What would be the effect
of Hoboken steam beer upon a Bavarian? Where is the authentic
home of *bouillabaisse?* Does the study of Latin and Greek spoil
women for love? Are the great German brewers, the Pschorrs,
honestly proud that Richard Strauss is their cousin? Did the
tubercle bacillus improve or injure Chopin's music? What assassin
invented the New York scheme of frying soft crabs in batter? Why
were boiled potatoes always served with *Rinderbrust mit Meer-
rettig?* Did the invention of macaroni precede or follow the invention of the pipe-organ? Was St. Thomas Aquinas really an atheist
in disguise? Why were all the German dictionaries silent about the
etymology of *Risi-Bisi?* I have heard him discuss all these grave
and gloomy problems, the while Otto and Emil hauled in the
Pilsner and his tonsils comfortably steamed. He was full of strange
and fantastic information, much of it plainly apocryphal, but all
of it immensely amusing. His musical anecdotes went back to the
days of Johann Georg Albrechtsberger and embraced the latest
conductor in Broadway. Raphael Joseffy was his authority in all
things pianistic—with Pachmann as a sort of court of appeals.
Joseffy told him this; Pachmann assured him of that. He knew how
much Rubinstein could drink, and why d'Albert left his second,
third and fourth wives. You will find a lot to the same effect in
"Old Fogy" and "Steeplejack," but the best was reserved for the
Biertisch. He was its greatest adornment in the western world.
His feet under its blackened oak, with Otto hovering to one side
and Emil to the other, he was truly magnificent. I have heard
them all, but he was the best. His conversation, indeed, made his
books seem almost funereal.

Just what arts he included among the seven I don't know, but
certainly cooking must have been one of them. Imagine such a
man spending his last days on a diet, with only gluten-bread to eat

and only unsweetened tea to drink! It was torture that would have made Prometheus yell. "The stomach of Vienna," he said in one of his books, "first interested me; not its soul." Even above the Strauss waltzes he put the *Apfelstrudel* and the *Kaiserschmarrn*. But the ear crowded the palate pretty closely: he was a musician before he was anything else. Turn to "Steeplejack," where he tells of his youth and its dreams: "I would fain be a pianist, a composer of music." The pianist he remained to the end of his days, ever concerned about *tempi*, traditions, shades of interpretation, but if he ever wrote any music he took good care to burn it. My guess is that it would have been Chopinesque, for a sentimentalist was concealed in him—more, it stuck out. Chopin was his first love and his last love, and of all his books he was proudest of the one on the Polish tuberose. In his last month of life he wrote to me about the new German translation—how well it was done, how beautifully it was bound, how punctilious the publisher had been about sending him a check while the mark still had some value. His volume on Liszt had blood in it too, but from the head rather than from the heart. The emperor of warts and wens he venerated as the greatest pianist of them all, but for Chopin he had a genuine devotion, almost a vocation: Chopin was his god.

For orchestral music, though what he wrote about Brahms and Strauss was brilliant with insight, he had less feeling: he was essentially a pianist. Nor was he a partisan of the opera: the singers interested him far more than the thick, heavy music and the preposterous staging, and not much that he wrote about Wagner was better than "Isolde's Mother" in "Mezzotints." In his declining years, somewhat upset in judgment, he devoted nearly a whole book to Mary Garden, a favorite warbler of the time. There was a touch of precision in his make-up that craved the pearly clarity of the black keys and white; he could see through a piano piece, but a symphony in the grand manner, I half suspect, often left him uneasy. Once he told me that he believed most of the classical symphonies, and especially Mozart's, sounded better in four-hand piano arrangement than in the concert-hall. In that form he knew all of them backward and forward, from Haydn's Surprise to César Franck's in D minor. And he had a wide and profound knowledge, too, of chamber music, and especially of that kind which found room for the piano. For vocal music he cared

a great deal less, for, like most sound musicians, he found unpleasant tones in the human voice. His rage for Mary Garden was
surely not grounded upon any solid admiration for the singer;
what interested him was the charm of the woman.

It is common news that in the other arts he sometimes slipped
sadly. For many years painters were his everyday associates, but
what he wrote of painting never showed him at its best. When he
had gone with the Post-Impressionists he had gone about as far as
he could go: the ensuing chromomaniacs puzzled him a good
deal more than they delighted him. In the theater he was so much
the eclectic that it was often difficult to tell which way he was
headed: Maeterlinck, Hervieu, Brieux, and Wedekind apparently
looked much the same to him. This eclecticism, more than once,
led him into dubious waters, and only the endless resources of
his immense cleverness got him back to dry land. But when the
dramatist was also a philosopher he could write about him with
great persuasiveness. The early Shaw, in his hands, took on a
coherence that was probably only an afterthought to Shaw himself.
And he wrote superbly about Hauptmann. Here the dramatic
critic merged with the critic of letters. He was on the lookout in
that direction to the end, though while the music season raged he
had little time for reading. If he was not the first to hail William
McFee, then he was not far from the second. And he did some
valiant whooping for Joseph Conrad long before the general roar.

· 3 ·

Huneker's excess of eclecticism, his chief defect, was probably
largely grounded upon simple amiability. There was little of the
berserker in him. He detested what he called the tripe-sellers of
the market-place as much as most, but he seldom attacked them
head-on. His method was the indirect one of crying up the sellers
of honest red herring. He disliked combat, and was no hand at
sanitary tearing down. Thus he made no splash as a critic of critics:
to him they were all able and honest fellows, doing their level
damnedest to nourish the enlightenment—even J. Ranken Towse
of *The Evening Post,* even the half-fabulous Henry J. Finck of the

same eminent paper. In "Steeplejack," to be sure, there are some tart things about William Winter, the greatest bad critic who ever lived, but he puts the worst of them off on Charlie McLellan, the librettist of "The Belle of New York." The New York of his time swarmed with critical mountebanks, and some of them attained to dangerous influence, but Huneker never addressed himself to clearing them out: he was content to offer better stuff, and let it go at that. The fine bellicosity of a Shaw was simply not in him. He had his share of malice, but it never rose to indignation. He enjoyed making "imbeciles realize their imbecility," but he harbored no longing to crack their heads.

Here politeness often verged upon timorousness, and that timorousness, I believe, had its roots in the curious modesty of the man. I have never known an artist who was more sincerely humble. Thrown all his life long among actors, opera singers, piano and fiddle players, novelists, star newspaper reporters, painters, critics and other such shameless exhibitionists, he yet managed to remain self-effacing himself. It always seemed a bit incredible to him when some one praised his work, and he was visibly uncomfortable whenever it was compared, to his credit, with that of others. I recall arguing with him for hours that most of his fellow music critics in New York were palpable charlatans, with nothing even remotely approaching a sound knowledge of music, and no apparent talent for writing. He refused flatly to grant me any case at all. He said I exaggerated. I set up impossible standards. I forgot the harsh rigors of their nightly labor. I blamed poor slaves for the sins of their papers. And so on and so on, endlessly to the same effect. The best I could dredge out of him was a categorical admission that it was an idiocy to praise Massenet and denounce Richard Strauss. The same had been done by one of his colleagues, but he refused to apply the principle to the man. In his private psychiatry idiocy was divided, like sin, into two kinds: the venial and the mortal. The idiocies of his friends were all venial.

This modesty, by a strange twist, made him grasp somewhat absurdly at certain kinds of recognition. When, running out of bad novelists, the National Institute of Arts and Letters offered him its ribbon, he accepted at once. It was, in essence, a comic episode: election to the colored Elks would have been far less inappropriate. But it was a long while before he could see it that way; at the start it seemed to him to be a high and undeserved honor, even a condescension! Toward the end of his life he came to a more rational view of it, and he died protesting that he had never worn the badge of the society. Instead—but let him tell it himself: "Last Summer (1920), in London, I wore a button sent to me by the *Bürgermeister* of Vienna, conferring upon me the freedom of that unhappy city. I did this for the sake of sheer paradox; beside, it was a touchstone for Austrian and German waiters working as Swiss in the Gambrinus and other beer-halls. I wish you could have seen the look of mingled awe and astonishment when they saw the button! *Ach, Herr Jessus, sint Sie Oestreicher?* . . . I don't blame you for wanting to shoot me if I had worn the other button."

But it had tickled him quietly in its day, for it seemed a help up the fragile beanstalk he was always talking of. "I tried to climb," he says in "Steeplejack," summing up his life at sixty, "but my muscles were undeveloped and wings I had none to speak of; the consequences may be well imagined. Many a tumble, broken bones, and what sentimentalists would describe as shattered illusions. . . . Life has been the Barmecide's feast to me—you remember the Arabian Nights—no sooner did I covet a rare dish than fate whisked it out of my reach. I love painting and sculpture: I may only look, but never own either pictures or marbles. I would fain be a pianist, a composer of music: I am neither. Nor a poet. Nor a novelist, actor, playwright. I have written of many things from architecture to zoölogy without grasping their inner substance. I am Jack of the Seven Arts, master of none. . . . My story is the story of an unquiet soul who voyaged from city to city, country to country, in search of something, he knew not what. The golden grapes of desire were never plucked, the marvellous mirage of the Seven Arts never overtaken, the antique and beautiful porches of philosophy, the solemn temples of religion never penetrated."

And a great deal more to the same melancholy effect. The Pilsner taps had been running Coca-Cola for a year when these words were set down, else I should have my suspicions. It was the worst critical judgment in a lifetime of critical judgments. Huneker surely did not live in vain. True, he left no school, save maybe transiently, and all the young critics of today turn away from his innocent delight in all lovely and amusing things to seek inspiration in the moral sitz-baths of More, Babbitt and company. But even the young critics owe him an immense debt—a vaster debt, indeed, than they will ever owe to their current masters. For it was Huneker, more than any other, who cleared the grove of the far worse masters next preceding—the Mabies and William Winters, the Fincks and Brander Matthewses, the Tartuffes and Pecksniffs, the literary Sunday-school superintendents and vice-crusaders, the concocters of White Lists of books, the shrill fuglemen of bad painting, maudlin music, valentine poetry, tin-pot drama and bogus criticism. Huneker was ever so polite to them, but when he had had his say they were done. He brought in a clearer, cleaner air. He knew vastly more than they did, and he said it infinitely better. The art of criticism, as they practiced it, was a branch of Christian endeavor; its aim was to make more and better Presbyterians; it ranged in tone from the solemn grunting of a bishop denouncing birth control to the kittenish whimsicality of a suburban curate trying to shock the Ladies' Aid Society. Huneker related it to living ideas, to all the great movements of human forces, to life itself. The world to him was a single entity, and each of the seven arts was a brother to all the others. To him a new play in Copenhagen, if only truth was in it, had inevitable repercussions in New York. Himself a divine mongrel, half Irish and the rest God knows what, he knew no nationalities and no schools. Whatever was genuinely original, whatever said something really new, whatever brought some bit of the unknown down into the known—that was unfailingly interesting to him, and he knew how to make it interesting to others—interesting and important.

So he plowed his ground and planted his seed. At a time when the Winters and Matthewses were still snuffling over the cup-and-saucer plays of Robertson, the puerile artificialities of Scribe and Sardou, and "The Man in the Iron Mask," he was preaching the new and revolutionary dramaturgy of Ibsen and Strindberg. In the golden age of Rosa Bonheur's "Horse Fair," and the saccharine covers of the *Ladies' Home Journal* he was expounding the ideas of the Post-Impressionists. In the midst of "Hearts and Flowers,"

Tosti's "Goodbye" and the Sousa marches, he was busy with spade work for Brahms and Richard Strauss. And before even the youngest professors had got over Schopenhauer, he was hauling ashore the devil-fish, Nietzsche. No stranger poisons ever came through the customs than those he brought in his baggage. No man among us ever urged more ardently, or with sounder knowledge or greater persuasiveness, that civilized catholicity of taste which downs and damns the snarling narrowness of Little Bethel. He was, in his amiable way, the sworn and relentless foe to all "the traps that snare the attention from poor or mediocre workmanship—the traps of sentimentalism, of false feeling, of cheap pathos, of the cheap moral." He was the complete antithesis to all the brummagem "Philistines of culture" who "clutter the market-place with their booths, mischievous half-art and tubs of tripe and soft soap." On the surface, as I have said, it may seem that the work of his lifetime went for little or nothing. There is a swing back to the pious, pseudo-intellectual flummery that he abhorred. Bad critics, failing at the trade, turn professors, moralists, tub-thumpers. But Huneker, dead, is still alive enough to pull powerfully the other way. His influence, surviving him, is a formidable obstacle to complete surrender. In the midst of the prayer-meeting one hears anon his ribald laugh and his reassuring *"Grüss Gott!"*

His criticism had the florid and baroque charm of the man himself: it was the product of an exuberant, a lavish and a happy soul. It had the shimmering surface of an ornate and intricate fabric, and beneath there was a great richness. Despite its enormous allusiveness, it was never a mere *pastiche;* the selection of authorities, Christian and heathen, virtuous and wicked, far and near, was made delicately, discreetly, with unerring taste and judgment. And in the summing up there was always the clearest possible statement of the whole matter, with a gaudy jest to drive it home. What finally emerged was a body of doctrine that came, I believe, very close to the truth. It seldom shows any sign of wearing out; it remains, in all essentials, as sound today as when it was set down. Thus Huneker left his mark upon his time. No man could have been less a reformer by inclination, and yet he became a reformer beyond compare. He emancipated criticism in America from its old bondage to sentimentality and stupidity, and with it he emancipated all the arts themselves.

(418)

Ambrose Bierce

‹‹‹‹‹‹‹‹‹‹‹‹‹‹‹‹‹‹‹‹‹‹‹‹‹‹‹‹‹‹‹›››››››››››››››››››››››››››››››

Bierce disappeared in Mexico in 1914
and is supposed to have been killed there.

THE reputation of Bierce has always radiated an occult, artificial, drug-store scent. He has been hymned in a passionate, voluptuous, inordinate way by a small band of disciples, and he has been passed over altogether by the great majority of American critics, and no less by the great majority of American readers. Certainly it would be absurd to say that he is generally read, even by the *intelligentsia*. Most of his books, in fact, are out of print and almost unobtainable, and there is little evidence that his massive "Collected Works," printed in twelve volumes between 1909 and 1912, have gone into anything even remotely approaching a wide circulation.

I have a suspicion, indeed, that Bierce did a serious disservice to himself when he put those twelve volumes together. Already an old man at the time, he permitted his nostalgia for his lost youth to get the better of his critical faculty, never very powerful at best, and the result was a depressing assemblage of worn-out and fly-blown stuff, much of it quite unreadable. If he had boiled the collection down to four volumes, or even to six, it might have got him somewhere, but as it is, his good work is lost in a morass of bad and indifferent work. I doubt that anyone save the Bierce fanatics aforesaid has ever plowed through the whole twelve

From *A Mencken Chrestomathy*, 1949. Included in *Prejudices: Sixth Series*, 1927. With additions from the *American Mercury*, Sept. 1929. Copyright 1927 by Alfred A. Knopf, Inc. Renewal copyright 1955 by H. L. Mencken.

volumes. They are filled with epigrams against frauds long dead and forgotten, and echoes of old and puerile newspaper controversies, and experiments in fiction that belong to a dark and expired age. But in the midst of all this blather there are some pearls —more accurately, there are two of them. One consists of the series of epigrams called "The Devil's Dictionary"; the other consists of the war stories, commonly called "Tales of Soldiers and Civilians." Among the latter are some of the best war stories ever written—things fully worthy to be ranged beside Zola's "L'Attaque du Moulin," Kipling's "The Taking of Lungtungpen," or Ludwig Thoma's "Ein Bayrischer Soldat." And among the former are some of the most gorgeous witticisms in the English language.

Bierce, I believe, was the first writer of fiction ever to treat war realistically. He antedated even Zola. It is common to say that he came out of the Civil War with a deep and abiding loathing of slaughter—that he wrote his war stories in disillusion, and as a sort of pacifist. But this is certainly not believed by anyone who knew him, as I did in his last years. What he got out of his services in the field was not a sentimental horror of it, but a cynical delight in it. It appeared to him as a sort of magnificent *reductio ad absurdum* of all romance. The world viewed war as something heroic, glorious, idealistic. Very well, he would show how sordid and filthy it was—how stupid, savage and degrading. But to say this is not to say that he disapproved it. On the contrary, he vastly enjoyed the chance its discussion gave him to set forth dramatically what he was always talking about and gloating over: the infinite imbecility of man. There was nothing of the milk of human kindness in old Ambrose; he did not get the nickname of Bitter Bierce for nothing. What delighted him most in this life was the spectacle of human cowardice and folly. He put man, intellectually, somewhere between the sheep and the horned cattle, and as a hero somewhere below the rats. His war stories, even when they deal with the heroic, do not depict soldiers as heroes; they depict them as bewildered fools, doing things without sense, submitting to torture and outrage without resistance, dying at last like hogs in Chicago. So far in this life, indeed, I have encountered no more thorough-going cynic than Bierce was. His disbelief in man went even further than Mark Twain's; he was quite unable to imagine the heroic, in any ordinary sense. Nor, for that matter, the wise. Man to him, was the most stupid and ignoble of animals. But at the same time the most amusing. Out of the spectacle of life about him he got an unflagging and Gargantuan joy. The obscene farce of politics delighted him. He was an almost amorous connoisseur of theology and theologians. He howled with mirth whenever he thought of a professor, a doctor or a husband.

Another character that marked him, perhaps flowing out of this same cynicism, was his curious taste for the macabre. All of his stories show it. He delighted in hangings, autopsies, dissecting-rooms. Death to him was not something repulsive, but a sort of low comedy—the last act of a squalid and rib-rocking buffoonery. When, grown old and weary, he departed for Mexico, and there—if legend is to be believed—marched into the revolution then going on, and had himself shot, there was certainly nothing in the transaction to surprise his acquaintances. The whole thing was typically Biercian. He died happy, one may be sure, if his executioners made a botch of dispatching him—if there was a flash of the grotesque at the end. Once I enjoyed the curious experience of going to a funeral with him. His conversation to and from the crematory was superb—a long series of gruesome but highly amusing witticisms. He had tales to tell of crematories that had caught fire and singed the mourners, of dead bibuli whose mortal remains had exploded, of widows guarding the fires all night to make sure that their dead husbands did not escape. The gentleman whose carcass we were burning had been a literary critic. Bierce suggested that his ashes be molded into bullets and shot at publishers, that they be presented to the library of the New York Lodge of Elks, that they be mailed anonymously to Ella Wheeler Wilcox, then still alive. Later on, when he heard that they had been buried in Iowa, he exploded in colossal mirth. The last time I saw him he predicted that the Christians out there would dig them up and throw them over the state line. On his own writing desk, he once told me, he kept the ashes of his son. I suggested idly that the ceremental urn must be a formidable ornament. "Urn hell!" he answered. "I keep them in a cigar-box!"

Bierce followed Poe in most of his short stories, but it is only a platitude to say that he wrote better than Poe. He had a far firmer grasp upon character; he was less literary and more observant. Unluckily, his stories seemed destined to go the way of Poe's. Their influence upon the modern American short story, at least upon its higher levels, is almost nil. When they are imitated at all, it is by the lowly hacks who manufacture thrillers for the pulp magazines. Meanwhile, it remains astonishing that his wit is so little remembered. In "The Devil's Dictionary" are some of the most devastating epigrams ever written. "Ah, that we could fall into women's arms without falling into their hands": it is hard to find a match for that in Oscar himself. I recall another: "Opportunity: a favorable occasion for grasping a disappointment." Another: "Once: enough." A third: "Husband: one who, having dined, is charged with the care of the plate." A fourth: "Our vocabulary is defective: we give the same name to woman's lack of temptation and man's lack of opportunity." A fifth: "Slang is the speech of him who robs the literary garbage cans on their way to the dump."

Bierce's critical judgments were often silly, as when he put Longfellow above Whitman, and not infrequently they were strongly colored by personal considerations, as when he overpraised George Sterling's poem, "The Wine of Wizardry." He was too little read to be a sound critic of letters, and he lacked the capacity to separate the artist from the man. Even his treatise on the art of writing, "Write it Right," is full of puerilities, for it never seems to have occurred to him that language, like literature, is a living thing, and not a mere set of rules. Writing of the trade he practiced all his life, he wrote like a somewhat saucy schoolma'am, and when another schoolma'am lifted his stuff the theft went almost undetected. His own style was extraordinarily tight and unresilient, and his fear of rhetoric often took all the life out of his ideas. His stories, despite their melodramatic effectiveness, begin to seem old-fashioned; they belong to the era before the short story ceased to be a formal intellectual exercise and became a transcript of life. The people in them simply do not live and breathe; Ring Lardner, whose manner Bierce would have detested, did a hundred times better in that direction. They are probably read today, not as literature, but as shockers. Their appalling gruesomeness is what keeps in them such life as they have. Some of them deserve a better kind of immortality.

Bierce's social criticism, like his literary criticism, was often amusing but seldom profound. It had, however, the virtue of being novel in its day, and so it made its mark. He was the first American to lay about him with complete gusto, charging and battering the frauds who ranged the country. The timorousness of Mark Twain was not in him; no head was lofty enough to escape his furious thwack. Such berserk men have been rare in our history; the normal Americano, even when he runs amok, shows a considerable discretion. But there was no more discretion in Bierce than you will find in a runaway locomotive. Had he been a more cautious man, the professors of literature would be politer to him today.

Beethoven

BEETHOVEN was one of those lucky men whose stature, viewed in retrospect, grows steadily. How many movements have there been to put him on the shelf? At least a dozen in the hundred years since his death. There was one in New York in 1917, launched by idiot critics and supported by the war fever: his place, it appeared, was to be taken by such prophets of the new enlightenment as Stravinsky. The net result of that movement was simply that the best orchestra in America went to pot—and Beethoven survived unscathed. Surely the nineteenth century was not deficient in master musicians. It produced Schubert, Schumann, Chopin, Wagner and Brahms, to say nothing of a whole horde of Dvořáks, Tschaikovskys, Debussys, Verdis and Puccinis. Yet it gave us nothing better than the first movement of the Eroica. That movement, the first challenge of the new music, remains its last word. It is the noblest piece of absolute music ever written in the sonata form, and it is the noblest piece of program music. In Beethoven, indeed, the distinction between the two became purely imaginary. Everything he wrote was, in a way, program music, including even the first two symphonies, and everything was absolute music.

It was a bizarre jest of the gods to pit Beethoven, in his first days in Vienna, against Papa Haydn. Haydn was undeniably a genius of the first water, and, after Mozart's death, had no ap-

From A Mencken Chrestomathy, 1949. Included in Prejudices: Fifth Series, 1926. First printed in part in the Baltimore Evening Sun, April 24, 1922, and in part in the American Mercury, April 1926. Copyright 1926 by Alfred A. Knopf, Inc. Renewal copyright 1954 by H. L. Mencken.

parent reason to fear a rival. If he did not actually create the symphony as we know it today, then he at least enriched the form with its first genuine masterpieces—and not with a scant few, but literally with dozens. Tunes of the utmost loveliness gushed from him like oil from a well. More, he knew how to manage them; he was a master of musical architectonics. But when Beethoven stepped in, poor old Papa had to step down. It was like pitting a gazelle against a bull. One colossal bellow, and the combat was over. Musicians are apt to look at it as a mere contest of technicians. They point to the vastly greater skill and ingenuity of Beethoven—his firmer grip upon his materials, his greater daring and resourcefulness, his far better understanding of dynamics, rhythms and clang-tints—in brief, his tremendously superior musicianship. But that was not what made him so much greater than Haydn—for Haydn, too, had his superiorities; for example, his far readier inventiveness, his capacity for making better tunes. What lifted Beethoven above the old master was simply his greater dignity as a man. The feelings that Haydn put into tone were the feelings of a country pastor, a rather civilized stockbroker, a viola player gently mellowed by Kulmbacher. When he wept it was with the tears of a woman who has discovered another wrinkle; when he rejoiced it was with the joy of a child on Christmas morning. But the feelings that Beethoven put into his music were the feelings of a god. There was something olympian in his snarls and rages, and there was a touch of hell-fire in his mirth.

It is almost a literal fact that there is not a trace of cheapness in the whole body of his music. He is never sweet and romantic; he never sheds conventional tears; he never strikes orthodox attitudes. In his lightest moods there is the immense and inescapable dignity of the ancient prophets. He concerns himself, not with the transient agonies of romantic love, but with the eternal tragedy of man. He is a great tragic poet, and like all great tragic poets, he is obsessed by a sense of the inscrutable meaninglessness of life. From the Eroica onward he seldom departs from that theme. It roars through the first movement of the C minor, and it comes to a stupendous final statement in the Ninth. All this, in his day, was new in music, and so it caused murmurs of surprise and even indignation. The step from Mozart's Jupiter to the first movement of the Eroica was uncomfortable; the Viennese began to wriggle in their stalls. But there was one among them who didn't wriggle, and that was Franz Schubert. Turn to the first movement of his Unfinished or to the slow movement of his Tragic, and you will see how quickly the example of Beethoven was followed—and with what genius. There was a long hiatus after that, but eventually the day of November 6, 1876, dawned in Karlsruhe, and with it came the first performance of Brahms' C minor. Once more the gods walked in the concert hall. They will walk again when another Brahms is born, and not before. For nothing can come out of an artist that is not in the man. What ails the music of all the Tschaikovskys, Mendelssohns—and Chopins? What ails it is that it is the music of shallow men. It is often, in its way, lovely. It bristles with charming musical ideas. It is infinitely ingenious and workmanlike. But it is as hollow, at bottom, as a bull by an archbishop. It is the music of second-rate men.

Beethoven disdained all their artifices: he didn't need them. It would be hard to think of a composer, even of the fourth rate, who worked with thematic material of less intrinsic merit. He borrowed tunes wherever he found them; he made them up out of snatches of country jigs; when he lacked one altogether he contented himself with a simple phrase, a few banal notes. All such things he viewed simply as raw materials; his interest was concentrated upon their use. To that use of them he brought the appalling powers of his unrivaled genius. His ingenuity began where that of other men left off. His most complicated structures retained the overwhelming clarity of the Parthenon. And into them he got a kind of feeling that even the Greeks could not match; he was preeminently a modern man, with all trace of the barbarian vanished. Into his gorgeous music there went all of the high skepticism that was of the essence of the eighteenth century, but into it there also went the new enthusiasm, the new determination to challenge and beat the gods, that dawned with the nineteenth.

The older I grow, the more I am convinced that the most portentous phenomenon in the whole history of music was the first public performance of the Eroica on April 7, 1805. The manufacturers of program notes have swathed that gigantic work in so many layers of banal legend and speculation that its intrinsic merits have been almost forgotten. Was it dedicated to Napoleon I? If so, was the dedication sincere or ironical? Who cares—that is, who with ears? It might have been dedicated, just as well, to Louis XIV, Paracelsus or Pontius Pilate. What makes it worth discussing, today and forever, is the fact that on its very first page Beethoven threw his hat into the ring and laid his claim to immortality. Bang!—and he is off. No compromise! No easy bridge from the past! The Second Symphony is already miles behind. A new order of music has been born. The very manner of it is full of challenge. There is no sneaking into the foul business by way of a mellifluous and disarming introduction; no preparatory hemming and hawing to cajole the audience and enable the conductor to find his place in the score. Nay! Out of silence comes the angry crash of the tonic triad, and then at once, with no pause, the first statement of the first subject—grim, domineering, harsh, raucous, and yet curiously lovely—with its astounding collision with that electrical C sharp. The carnage has begun early; we are only in the seventh measure. In the thirteenth and fourteenth comes the incomparable roll down the simple scale of E flat—and what follows is all that has ever been said, perhaps all that ever *will* be said, about music-making in the grand manner. What was afterward done, even by Beethoven, was done in the light of that perfect example. Every line of modern music that is honestly music bears some sort of relation to that epoch-making first movement.

The rest of the Eroica is Beethovenish, but not quintessence. There is a legend that the funeral march was put in simply because it was a time of wholesale butchery, and funeral marches were in fashion. No doubt the first-night audience in Vienna, shocked and addled by the piled-up defiances of the first movement, found the lugubrious strains grateful. But the *scherzo?* Another felonious assault upon poor Papa Haydn! Two giants boxing clumsily, to a crazy piping by an orchestra of dwarfs. No wonder some honest Viennese in the gallery yelled: "I'd give another kreutzer if the thing would stop!" Well, it stopped finally, and then came something reassuring—a theme with variations. Everyone in Vienna knew and esteemed Beethoven's themes with variations. He was, in fact, the rising master of themes with variations in the town. But a joker remained in the pack. The variations grew more and more complex and surprising. Strange novelties got into them. The polite exercises became tempestuous, moody, cacophonous, tragic. At the end a harsh, hammering, exigent row of chords—the C minor Symphony casting its sinister shadow before.

It must have been a great night in Vienna. But perhaps not for the actual Viennese. They went to hear "a new grand symphony in D sharp" (*sic!*). What they found in the Theater-an-der-Wien was a revolution.[1]

---

[1] The reader with any curiosity about Beethoven's method of planning and writing the stupendous first movement will find plenty to his taste in "The Unconscious Beethoven," by Ernest Newman (New York, 1927). It is a story packed with almost incredible marvels.

VIII

<<<<<<<<<<<<<<>>>>>>>>>>>>>>

Memories

＊ · ＊ · ＊ · ＊ · ＊

As some writers are their own favorite authors, one of Mencken's favorite subjects was himself. For decades Baltimoreans were enlivened in the Sunpapers with his accounts of recurrent bouts with asthma, his discovery of a sound razor blade, what he preferred to drink and the type of glass to serve it in, the kind of pavement he liked to walk on, and endless other such trivia. It was all set forth with verve and it was never dull.

With the age of sixty almost around the corner, and with some leisure at his disposal, he turned his hand to sketches of his boyhood. The first was published in 1936 in The New Yorker, a magazine he admired. The piece was so successful that he thereafter contributed ten more to the magazine, then added nine others to the collection and incorporated them all in the volume Happy Days. The book closed with an experience in his tenth year. Blanche Knopf was pleased with the volume itself and with its reception, and she pressed Mencken to write an account of each decade of his life. Mencken replied that the years of his teens were too serious to be treated lightly and declined. But he had opened up a vein which engaged him and delighted a new public; he therefore published two more volumes, one an account of his early newspaper days, and the other a potpourri of unconnected reminiscences extending from his tenth to his fifty-sixth year.

He thought of the volumes solely as entertainment, and in that aspect they more than fulfill their aim. No more delightful recollections exist in English. But between the lines, reciting the amusing experiences, is always the essential Mencken, gay, unintimidatable, Spartan-like in his perseverance, gazing with wondering blue eyes at the world's absurdities.

Recollections

of Notable Cops

<<<<<<<<<<<<<<<<<<<<<<<<<<<<<<<<<<>>>>>>>>>>>>>>>>>>>>>>>>>>>>>>>>>>

SOME time ago I read in a New York paper that fifty or sixty
college graduates had been appointed to the metropolitan
police force, and were being well spoken of by their superiors. The news astonished me, for in my reportorial days there was
simply no such thing in America as a book-learned cop, though
I knew a good many who were very smart. The force was then
recruited, not from the groves of Academe, but from the ranks of
workingmen. The best police captain I ever knew in Baltimore
was a meat-cutter by trade, and had lost one of his thumbs by a
slip of his cleaver, and the next best was a former bartender. All
the mounted cops were ex-hostlers passing as ex-cavalrymen, and
all the harbor police had come up through the tugboat and gar-
bage-scow branches of the merchant marine. It took a young reporter a little while to learn how to read and interpret the reports
that cops turned in, for they were couched in a special kind of
English, with a spelling peculiar to itself. If a member of what
was then called "the finest" had spelled *larceny* in any way save
larsensy, or *arson* in any way save *arsony*, or *fracture* in any way
save *fraxr*, there would have been a considerable lifting of eye-
brows. I well recall the horror of the Baltimore cops when the
first board to examine applicants for places on the force was set

From *Newspaper Days*, 1941. First printed in *The New Yorker*, Sept. 20, 1941.
Copyright 1941 by Alfred A. Knopf, Inc.

up. It was a harmless body headed by a political dentist, and the hardest question in its first examination paper was "What is the plural of *ox?*," but all the cops in town predicted that it would quickly contaminate their craft with a great horde of what they called "professors," and reduce it to the level of letter-carrying or school-teaching.

But, as I have noted, their innocence of *literae humaniores* was not necessarily a sign of stupidity, and from some of them, in fact, I learned the valuable lesson that sharp wits can lurk in unpolished skulls. I knew cops who were matches for the most learned and unscrupulous lawyers at the Baltimore bar, and others who had made monkeys of the oldest and crabbedest judges on the bench, and were generally respected for it. Moreover, I knew cops who were really first-rate policemen, and loved their trade as tenderly as so many art artists or movie actors. They were badly paid, but they carried on their dismal work with unflagging diligence, and loved a long, hard chase almost as much as they loved a quick, brisk clubbing. Their one salient failing, taking them as a class, was their belief that any person who had been arrested, even on mere suspicion, was unquestionably and *ipso facto* guilty. But that theory, though it occasionally colored their testimony in a garish manner, was grounded, after all, on nothing worse than professional pride and *esprit de corps*, and I am certainly not one to hoot at it, for my own belief in the mission of journalism has no better support than the same partiality, and all the logic I am aware of stands against it.

In those days that pestilence of Service which torments the American people today was just getting under way, and many of the multifarious duties now carried out by social workers, statisticians, truant officers, visiting nurses, psychologists, and the vast rabble of inspectors, smellers, spies and bogus experts of a hundred different faculties either fell to the police or were not discharged at all. An ordinary flatfoot in a quiet residential section had his hands full. In a single day he might have to put out a couple of kitchen fires, arrange for the removal of a dead mule, guard a poor epileptic having a fit on the sidewalk, catch a runaway horse, settle a combat with table knives between husband and wife, shoot a cat for killing pigeons, rescue a dog or a baby from a sewer, bawl out a white-wings for spilling garbage, keep order on the sidewalk at two or three funerals, and flog half a dozen bad boys for throwing horse-apples at a blind man. The cops downtown, especially along the wharves and in the red-light districts, had even more curious and complicated jobs, and some of them attained to a high degree of virtuosity.

As my memory gropes backward I think, for example, of a strange office that an old-time roundsman named Charlie had to undertake every spring. It was to pick up enough skilled workmen to effect the annual redecoration and refurbishing of the Baltimore City Jail. Along about May 1 the warden would telephone to police headquarters that he needed say, ten head of painters, five plumbers, two blacksmiths, a tile-setter, a roofer, a bricklayer, a carpenter and a locksmith, and it was Charlie's duty to go out and find them. So far as I can recall, he never failed, and usually he produced two or three times as many craftsmen of each category as were needed, so that the warden had some chance to pick out good ones. His plan was simply to make a tour of the saloons and stews in the Marsh Market section of Baltimore, and look over the drunks in congress assembled. He had a trained eye, and could detect a plumber or a painter through two weeks' accumulation of beard and dirt. As he gathered in his candidates, he searched them on the spot, rejecting those who had no union cards, for he was a firm believer in organized labor. Those who passed were put into storage at a police station, and there kept (less the unfortunates who developed delirium tremens and had to be handed over to the resurrection men) until the whole convoy was ready. The next morning Gene Grannan, the police magistrate, gave them two weeks each for vagrancy, loitering, trespass, committing a nuisance, or some other plausible misdemeanor, the warden had his staff of master-workmen, and the jail presently bloomed out in all its vernal finery.

Some of these toilers returned year after year, and in the end Charlie recognized so many that he could accumulate the better part of his convoy in half an hour. Once, I remember, he was stumped by a call for two electricians. In those remote days there were fewer men of that craft in practice than today, and only one could be found. When the warden put on the heat Charlie sent

him a trolleycar motorman who had run away from his wife and
was trying to be shanghaied for the Chesapeake oyster fleet. This
poor man, being grateful for his security in jail, made such eager
use of his meager electrical knowledge that the warden decided
to keep him, and even requested that his sentence be extended.
Unhappily, Gene Grannan was a pretty good amateur lawyer,
and knew that such an extension would be illegal. When the
warden of the House of Correction, which was on a farm twenty
miles from Baltimore, heard how well this system was working,
he put in a requisition for six experienced milkers and a choir
leader, for he had a herd of cows and his colored prisoners loved
to sing spirituals. Charlie found the choir leader in no time, but
he bucked at hunting for milkers, and got rid of the nuisance by
sending the warden a squad of sailors who almost pulled the
poor cows to pieces.

Gene had been made a magistrate as one of the first fruits of
the rising reform movement in Baltimore, and was a man of the
chastest integrity, but he knew too much about reformers to
admire them, and lost no chance to afflict them. When, in 1900,
or thereabout, a gang of snoopers began to tour the red-light districts, seeking to harass and alarm the poor working women there
denizened, he instructed the gals to empty slops on them, and
acquitted all who were brought in for doing it, usually on the
ground that the complaining witnesses were disreputable persons,
and could not be believed on oath. One day, sitting in his frowsy
courtroom, I saw him gloat in a positively indecent manner when
a Methodist clergyman was led out from the cells by Mike Hogan,
the turnkey. This holy man, believing that the Jews, unless they
consented to be baptized, would all go to Hell, had opened a
mission in what was then still called the Ghetto, and sought to
save them. The adults, of course, refused to have anything to do
with him, but he managed, after a while, to lure a number of
kosher small boys into his den, chiefly by showing them magic-
lantern pictures of the Buffalo Bill country and the Holy Land.
When their fathers heard of this there was naturally an uproar, for
it was a mortal sin in those days for an orthodox Jew to enter a
Goy Schul. The ritual for delousing offenders was an arduous one,
and cost both time and money. So the Jews came clamoring to

(435)

Grannan, and he spent a couple of hours trying to figure out some charge to lay against the evangelist. Finally, he ordered him brought in, and entered him on the books for "annoying persons passing by and along a public highway, disorderly conduct, making loud and unseemly noises, and disturbing religious worship." He had to be acquitted, of course, but Gene scared him so badly with talk of the penitentiary that he shut down his mission forthwith, and left the Jews to their post-mortem sufferings.

As I have noted in Chapter II, Gene was a high favorite among us young reporters, for he was always good for copy, and did not hesitate to modify the course of justice in order to feed and edify us. One day an ancient German, obviously a highly respectable man, was brought in on the incredible charge of beating his wife. The testimony showed that they had been placidly married for more than 45 years, and seldom exchanged so much as a bitter word. But the night before, when the old man came home from the saloon where he played *Skat* every evening, the old woman accused him of having drunk more than his usual ration of eight beers, and in the course of the ensuing debate he gave her a gentle slap. Astounded, she let off an hysterical squawk, an officious neighbor rushed in, the cops came on his heels, and so the old man stood before the bar of justice, weeping copiously and with his wife weeping even more copiously beside him. Gene pondered the evidence with a frown on his face, and then announced his judgment. "The crime you are accused of committing," he said, "is a foul and desperate one, and the laws of all civilized countries prohibit it under heavy penalties. I could send you to prison for life, I could order you to the whipping-post [it still exists in Maryland, and for wife-beaters only], or I could sentence you to be hanged. [Here both parties screamed.] But inasmuch as this is your first offense I will be lenient. You will be taken hence to the House of Correction, and there confined for twenty years. In addition, you are fined $10,000." The old couple missed the fine, for at mention of the House of Correction both fainted. When the cops revived them, Gene told the prisoner that, on reflection, he had decided to strike out the sentence, and bade him go and sin no more. Husband and wife rushed out of the courtroom hand in hand, followed by a cop with the umbrella and market basket that the old woman had forgotten. A week or two later news came in that she was ordering the old man about in a highly cavalier manner, and had cut down his evenings of *Skat* to four a week.

The cops liked and admired Gene, and when he was in good form he commonly had a gallery of them in his courtroom, guffawing at his whimsies. But despite his popularity among them he did not pal with them, for he was basically a very dignified, and even somewhat stiff fellow, and knew how to call them down sharply when their testimony before him went too far beyond the bounds of the probable. In those days, as in these, policemen led a social life almost as inbred as that of the justices of the Supreme Court of the United States, and outsiders were seldom admitted to their parties. But reporters were exceptions, and I attended a number of cop soirees of great elegance, with the tables piled mountain-high with all the delicacies of the season, and a keg of beer every few feet. The graft of these worthy men, at least in my time, was a great deal less than reformers alleged and the envious common people believed. Most of them, in my judgment, were very honest fellows, at least within the bounds of reason. Those who patrolled the fish markets naturally had plenty of fish to eat, and those who manned the police boats in the harbor took a certain toll from the pungy captains who brought up Baltimore's supplies of watermelons, cantaloupes, vegetables, crabs and oysters from the Eastern Shore of Maryland: indeed, this last impost amounted to a kind of *octroi,* and at one time the harbor force accumulated so much provender that they had to seize an empty warehouse on the waterfront to store it. But the pungy captains gave up uncomplainingly, for the pelagic cops protected them against the thieves and highjackers who swarmed in the harbor, and also against the land police. I never heard of cops getting anything that the donor was not quite willing and even eager to give. Every Italian who ran a peanut stand knew that making them free of it was good institutional promotion and the girls in the red-light districts liked to crochet neckties, socks and pulse-warmers for them. It was not unheard of for a cop to get mashed on such a girl, rescue her from her life of shame, and set her up as a more or less honest woman. I knew of several cases in which holy matrimony followed. But the more ambitious girls, of course, looked higher, and some of them, in my time, made very good marriages. One actually married a banker, and another died only a few years ago as the faithful and much respected wife of a prominent physician. The cops always laughed when reformers alleged that the wages of sin were death—specifically, that women who sold their persons always ended in the gutter, full of dope and despair. They knew that the overwhelming majority ended at the altar of God, and that nearly all of them married better men than they could have had any chance of meeting and roping if they had kept their virtue.

One dismal New Year's day I saw a sergeant lose an excellent chance to pocket $138.66 in cash money: I remember it brilliantly because I lost the same chance at the same moment. There had been the usual epidemic of suicides in the waterfront flophouses, for the dawn of a new year turns the thoughts of homeless men to peace beyond the dissecting-room, and I accompanied the sergeant and a coroner on a tour of the fatal scenes. One of the dead men was lying on the fifth floor of a decaying warehouse that had been turned into ten-cent sleeping quarters, and we climbed up the long stairs to inspect him. All the other bums had cleared out, and the hophead clerk did not offer to go with us. We found the deceased stretched out in a peaceful attitude, with the rope with which he had hanged himself still around his neck. He had been cut down, but then abandoned.

The sergeant loosed the rope, and began a search of the dead man's pockets, looking for means to identify him. He found nothing whatever of that sort, but from a pants pocket he drew out a fat wad of bills, and a hasty count showed that it contained $416. A situation worthy of Scribe, or even Victor Hugo! Evidently the poor fellow was one of the Russell Sages that are occasionally found among bums. His money, I suppose, had been diminishing, and he had bumped himself off in fear that it would soon be all gone. The sergeant looked at the coroner, the coroner looked at me, and I looked at the sergeant. Then the sergeant wrapped up the money in a piece of newspaper lying nearby, and handed it to the coroner. "It goes," he said sadly, "to the state of Maryland. The son-of-a-bitch died intestate, and with no heirs."

The next day I met the coroner, and found him in a low frame of mind. "It was a sin and a shame," he said, "to turn that money over to the State Treasury. What I could have done with $138.67! (I noticed he made a fair split, but collared one of the two odd cents.) Well, it's gone now—damn the luck! I never *did* trust that flatfoot."

A Girl from Red Lion, P.A.

◀◀◀◀◀◀◀◀◀◀◀◀◀◀◀◀◀◀◀◀◀◀◀◀◀◀◀◀◀◀◀◀▶▶▶▶▶▶▶▶▶▶▶▶▶▶▶▶▶▶▶▶▶▶▶▶▶▶▶▶▶▶▶

SOMEWHERE in his lush, magenta prose Oscar Wilde speaks of the tendency of nature to imitate art—a phenomenon often observed by persons who keep their eyes open. I first became aware of it, not through the pages of Wilde, but at the hands of an old-time hack-driver named Peebles, who flourished in Baltimore in the days of this history. Peebles was a Scotsman of a generally unfriendly and retiring character, but nevertheless he was something of a public figure in the town. Perhaps that was partly due to the fact that he had served twelve years in the Maryland Penitentiary for killing his wife, but I think he owed much more of his eminence to his adamantine rectitude in money matters, so rare in his profession. The very cops, indeed, regarded him as an honest man, and said so freely. They knew about his blanket refusal to take more than three or four times the legal fare from drunks, they knew how many lost watches, wallets, stick-pins and walking-sticks he turned in every year, and they admired as Christians, though deploring as cops, his absolute refusal to work for them in the capacity of stool-pigeon.

Moreover, he was industrious as well as honest, and it was the common belief that he had money in five banks. He appeared on the hack-stand in front of the old Eutaw House every evening at nine o'clock, and put in the next five or six hours shuttling merrymakers and sociologists to and from the red-light districts. When this trade began to languish he drove to Union Station, and there kept watch until his two old horses fell asleep. Most of the

From *Newspaper Days*, 1941. First printed in *The New Yorker*, Feb. 15, 1941. Copyright 1941 by Alfred A. Knopf, Inc.

strangers who got off the early morning trains wanted to go to the nearest hotel, which was only two blocks away, so there was not a great deal of money in their patronage, but unlike the other hackers Peebles never resorted to the device of driving them swiftly in the wrong direction and then working back by a circuitous route.

A little after dawn one morning in the early autumn of 1903, just as his off horse began to snore gently, a milk-train got in from lower Pennsylvania, and out of it issued a rosy-cheeked young woman carrying a pasteboard suitcase and a pink parasol. Squired up from the train level by a car greaser with an eye for country beauty, she emerged into the sunlight shyly and ran her eye down the line of hacks. The other drivers seemed to scare her, and no wonder, for they were all grasping men whose evil propensities glowed from them like heat from a stove. But when she saw Peebles her feminine intuition must have told her that he could be trusted, for she shook off the car greaser without further ado, and came up to the Peebles hack with a pretty show of confidence.

"Say, mister," she said, "how much will you charge to take me to a house of ill fame?"

In telling of it afterward Peebles probably exaggerated his astonishment a bit, but certainly he must have suffered something rationally describable as a shock. He laid great stress upon her air of blooming innocence, almost like that of a cavorting lamb. He said her two cheeks glowed like apples, and that she smelled like a load of hay. By his own account he stared at her for a full minute without answering her question, with a wild stream of confused surmises racing through his mind. What imaginable business could a creature so obviously guileless have in the sort of establishment she had mentioned? Could it be that her tongue had slipped—that she actually meant an employment office, the Y.W.C.A., or what not? Peebles, as he later elaborated the story, insisted that he had cross-examined her at length, and that she had not only reiterated her question in precise terms, but explained that she was fully determined to abandon herself to sin and looked forward confidently to dying in the gutter. But in his first version he reported simply that he had stared at her dumbly until his amazement began to wear off, and then motioned to her to climb into his hack. After all, he was a common carrier, and obliged by law to haul all comers, regardless of their private projects and intentions. If he yielded anything to his Caledonian moral sense it took the form of choosing her destination with some prudence. He might have dumped her into one of the third-rate bagnios that crowded a street not three blocks from Union Station, and then gone on about his business. Instead, he drove half way across town to the high-toned studio of Miss Nellie d'Alembert, at that time one of the leaders of her profession in Baltimore, and a woman who, though she lacked the polish of Vassar, had sound sense, a pawky humor, and progressive ideas.

I had become, only a little while before, city editor of the *Herald,* and in that capacity received frequent confidential communications from her. She was, in fact, the source of a great many useful news tips. She knew everything about everyone that no one was supposed to know, and had accurate advance information, in particular, about Page 1 divorces, for nearly all the big law firms of the town used her facilities for the manufacture of evidence. There were no Walter Winchells in that era, and the city editors of the land had to depend on volunteers for inside stuff. Such volunteers were moved (*a*) by a sense of public duty gracefully performed, and (*b*) by an enlightened desire to keep on the good side of newspapers. Not infrequently they cashed in on this last. I well remember the night when two visiting Congressmen from Washington got into a debate in Miss Nellie's music-room, and one of them dented the skull of the other with a spittoon. At my suggestion the other city editors of Baltimore joined me in straining journalistic ethics far enough to remove the accident to Mt. Vernon place, the most respectable neighborhood in town, and to lay the fracture to a fall on the ice.

My chance leadership in this public work made Miss Nellie my partisan, and now and then she gave me a nice tip and forgot to include the other city editors. Thus I was alert when she called up during the early afternoon of Peebles' strange adventure, and told me that something swell was on ice. She explained that it was not really what you could call important news, but simply a sort of human-interest story, so I asked Percy Heath to go to see her, for though he was now my successor as Sunday editor, he still did an occasional news story, and I knew what kind he enjoyed especially. He called up in half an hour, and asked me to join him. "If you don't hear it yourself," he said, "you will say I am pulling a fake."

When I got to Miss Nellie's house I found her sitting with Percy in a basement room that she used as a sort of office, and at once she plunged into the story.

"I'll tell you first," she began, "before you see the poor thing herself. When Peebles yanked the bell this morning I was sound asleep, and so was all the girls, and Sadie the coon had gone home. I stuck my head out of the window, and there was Peebles on the front steps. I said: 'Get the hell away from here! What do you mean by bringing in a drunk at this time of the morning? Don't you know us poor working people gotta get some rest?' But he hollered back that he didn't have no drunk in his hack, but something he didn't know what to make of, and needed my help on, so I slipped on my kimono and went down to the door, and by that time he had the girl out of the hack, and before I could say 'scat' he had shoved her in the parlor, and she was unloading what she had to say.

"Well, to make a long story short, she said she come from somewheres near a burg they call Red Lion, P.A., and lived on a farm. She said her father was one of them old rubes with whiskers they call Dunkards, and very strict. She said she had a beau in York, P.A., of the name of Elmer, and whenever he could get away he would come out to the farm and set in the parlor with her, and they would do a little hugging and kissing. She said Elmer was educated and a great reader, and he would bring her books that he got from his brother, who was a train butcher on the Northern Central, and him and her would read them. She said the books was all about love, and that most of them was sad. Her and Elmer would talk about them while they set in the parlor, and the more they talked about them the sadder they would get, and sometimes she would have to cry.

"Well, to make a long story short, this went on once a week or so, and night before last Elmer come down from York with some more books, and they set in the parlor, and talked about love. Her old man usually stuck his nose in the door now and then, to see that there wasn't no foolishness, but night before last he had a bilious attack and went to bed early, so her and Elmer had it all to theirself in the parlor. So they quit talking about the books, and Elmer began to love her up, and in a little while they was hugging and kissing to beat the band. Well, to make a long story short, Elmer went too far, and when she come to herself and kicked him out she realized she had lost her honest name.

"She laid awake all night thinking about it, and the more she thought about it the more scared she got. In every one of the books her and Elmer read there was something on the subject, and all of the books said the same thing. When a girl lost her honest name there was nothing for her to do excepting to run away from home and lead a life of shame. No girl that she ever read about ever done anything else. They all rushed off to the nearest city, started this life of shame, and then took to booze and dope and died in the gutter. Their family never knew what had became of them. Maybe they landed finally in a medical college, or maybe the Salvation Army buried them, but their people never heard no more of them, and their name was rubbed out of the family Bible. Sometimes their beau tried to find them, but he never could do it, and in the end he usually married the judge's homely daughter, and moved into the big house when the judge died.

"Well, to make a long story short, this poor girl lay awake all night thinking of such sad things, and when she got up at four thirty a.m. and went out to milk the cows her eyes was so full of tears that she could hardly find their spigots. Her father, who was still bilious, give her hell, and told her she was getting her just punishment for setting up until ten and eleven o'clock at night, when all decent people ought to be in bed. So she began to suspect that he may have snuck down during the evening, and caught her, and was getting ready to turn her out of the house and wash his hands of her, and maybe even curse her. So she decided to have it over and done with as soon as possible, and last night, the minute he hit the hay again, she hoofed in to York, P.A., and caught the milk-train for Baltimore, and that is how Peebles found her at Union Station and brought her here. When I asked her what in hell she wanted all she had to say was 'Ain't this a house of ill fame?', and it took me an hour or two to pump her story out of her. So now I have got her upstairs under lock and key, and as soon as I can get word to Peebles I'll tell him to take her back to Union Station, and start her back for Red Lion, P.A. Can you beat it?"

Percy and I, of course, demanded to see the girl, and presently Miss Nellie fetched her in. She was by no means the bucolic Lillian Russell that Peebles' tall tales afterward made her out, but she was certainly far from unappetizing. Despite her loss of sleep, the dreadful gnawings of her conscience and the menace of an appalling retribution, her cheeks were still rosy, and there remained a considerable sparkle in her troubled blue eyes. I never heard her name, but it was plain that she was of four-square Pennsylvania Dutch stock, and as sturdy as the cows she serviced. She had on her Sunday clothes, and appeared to be somewhat uncomfortable in them, but Miss Nellie set her at ease, and soon she was retelling her story to two strange and, in her sight, probably highly dubious men. We listened without interrupting her, and when she finished Percy was the first to speak.

"My dear young lady," he said, "you have been grossly misinformed. I don't know what these works of fiction are that you and Elmer read, but they are as far out of date as Joe Miller's Jest-Book. The stuff that seems to be in them would make even a newspaper editorial writer cough and scratch himself. It may be true that, in the remote era when they appear to have been written, the penalty of a slight and venial slip was as drastic as you say, but I assure you that it is no longer the case. The world is much more humane than it used to be, and much more rational. Just as it no longer burns men for heresy or women for witchcraft, so it has ceased to condemn girls to lives of shame and death in the gutter for the trivial dereliction you acknowledge. If there were time I'd get you some of the more recent books, and point out passages showing how moral principles have changed. The only thing that is frowned on now seems to be getting caught. Otherwise, justice is virtually silent on the subject.

"Inasmuch as your story indicates that no one knows of your crime save your beau, who, if he has learned of your disappearance, is probably scared half to death, I advise you to go home, make some plausible excuse to your pa for lighting out, and resume your care of his cows. At the proper opportunity take your beau to the pastor, and join him in indissoluble love. It is the safe, respectable and hygienic course. Everyone agrees that it is moral, even moralists. Meanwhile, don't forget to thank Miss Nellie. She might have helped you down the primrose way; instead, she has restored you to virtue and happiness, no worse for an interesting experience."

The girl, of course, took in only a small part of this, for Percy's voluptuous style and vocabulary were beyond the grasp of a simple milkmaid. But Miss Nellie, who understood English much better than she spoke it, translated freely, and in a little while the troubled look departed from those blue eyes, and large tears of joy welled from them. Miss Nellie shed a couple herself, and so did all the ladies of the resident faculty, for they had drifted downstairs during the interview, sleepy but curious. The practical Miss Nellie inevitably thought of money, and it turned out that the trip down by milk-train and Peebles' lawful freight of $1 had about exhausted the poor girl's savings, and she had only some odd change left. Percy threw in a dollar and I threw in a dollar, and Miss Nellie not only threw in a third, but ordered one of the ladies to go to the kitchen and prepare a box-lunch for the return to Red Lion.

Sadie the coon had not yet come to work, but Peebles presently bobbed up without being sent for, and toward the end of the afternoon he started off for Union Station with his most amazing passenger, now as full of innocent jubilation as a martyr saved at the stake. As I have said, he embellished the story considerably during the days following, especially in the direction of touching up the girl's pulchritude. The cops, because of their general confidence in him, swallowed his exaggerations, and I heard more than one of them lament that they had missed the chance to handle the case professionally. Percy, in his later years, made two or three attempts to put it into a movie scenario, but the Hays office always vetoed it.

How the girl managed to account to her father for her mysterious flight and quick return I don't know, for she was never heard from afterward. She promised to send Miss Nellie a picture postcard of Red Lion, showing the new hall of the Knights of Pythias, but if it was ever actually mailed it must have been misaddressed, for it never arrived.

Beaters of Breasts

O N September 1, in the presidential campaign year of 1936, I received an office chit from Paul Patterson, publisher of the Baltimore *Sunpapers,* proposing that I go to Boston to cover the Harvard tercentenary orgies, then just getting under way. On September 3, after a day given over, at least in theory, to prayer and soul-searching, I replied as follows:

> The more I think over the Harvard project, the less it lifts me. I'd much prefer to join Alf Landon. I like politicoes much better than I like professors. They sweat more freely and are more amusing.

My prayer and soul-searching, of course, were purely bogus, as such exercises only too often are. I had actually made up my mind in favor of the politicians a great many years before, to wit, in 1900 or thereabout, when I was still an infant at the breast in journalism. They shocked me a little at my first intimate contact with them, for I had never suspected, up to then, that frauds so bold and shameless could flourish in a society presumably Christian, and under the eye of a putatively watchful God. But as I came to know them better and better I began to develop a growing admiration, if not for their virtue, then at least for their professional virtuosity, and at the same time I discovered that many of them, in their private character, were delightful fellows, whatever their infamies *ex officio.* This appreciation of them, in the years following, gradually extended itself into a friendly interest in quacks of all sorts, whether theological, economic, military, philanthropic, judicial, literary, musical or sexual, and including even the professorial, and in the end that interest made me a sort of expert on the science of rooking the confiding, with a large acquaintance among practitioners of every species. But though I thus threw a wide net I never hauled in any fish who seemed to me to be the peers of the quacks political—not, indeed, by many a glittering inch. Even the Freudians when they dawned, and the chiropractors, and the penologists, and the social engineers, and the pedagogical wizards of Teachers College, Columbia, fell a good deal short of many Congressmen and Senators that I knew, not to mention Governors of sovereign American states. The Governors, in fact, were for long my favorites, for they constituted a class of extraordinarily protean rascals, and I remember a year when, of the forty-eight then in office, four were under indictment by grand juries, and one was actually in jail. Of the rest, seven were active Ku Kluxers, three were unreformed labor leaders, two were dipsomaniacs, five were bogus war heroes, and another was an astrologer.

My high opinion of political mountebanks remains unchanged to this day, and I suspect that when the history of our era is written at last it may turn out that they have been one of America's richest gifts to humanity. On only one point do I discover any doubt, and that is on the point whether those who really believe in their hocus-pocus—for example, Woodrow Wilson—are to be put higher or lower, in entertainment value, to those who are too smart —for example, Huey Long. Perhaps the question answers itself, for very few of the second class, in the long run, are able to resist their own buncombe, and I daresay that Huey, if the Japs had not cut him down prematurely, would have ended by believing more or less in his share-the-wealth apocalypse, though not, of course, to the extent of sharing his share. After the death of William Jennings Bryan, in 1926, I printed an estimate of his life and public services which dismissed him as a quack pure and unadulterated, but in the years since I have come to wonder if that was really just. When, under the prodding of Clarence Darrow, he made his immortal declaration that man is not a mammal, it seemed to me to be a mere bravura piece by a quack sure that his customers would take anything. But I am now more than half

convinced that Jennings really believed it, just as he believed that
Jonah swallowed the whale. The same phenomenon is often visible
in other fields of quackery, especially the theological. More than
once I have seen a Baptist evangelist scare himself by his own
alarming of sinners, and quite as often I have met social workers
who actually swallowed at least a third of their sure-cures for all
the sorrows of the world. Let us not forget that Lydia Pinkham,
on her deathbed, chased out her doctors and sent for a carboy of
her Vegetable Compound, and that Karl Marx (though not En-
gels) converted himself to Socialism in his declining years.

It amazes me that no one has ever undertaken a full-length
psychological study of Bryan, in the manner of Gamaliel Bradford
and Lytton Strachey, for his life was long and full of wonders. My
own contacts with him, unhappily, were rather scanty, though I
reported his performances, off and on, from 1904 to 1926, a period
of nearly a quarter of a century. The first time I saw him show in
the grand manner was at the Democratic national convention of
1904, in St. Louis. He had been the party candidate for the presidency in 1896 and 1900, and was to be the candidate again in
1908, but in 1904 the gold Democrats were on top and he was
rejected in favor of Alton B. Parker, a neat and clean but bewildered judge from somewhere up the Hudson, now forgotten by all
save political antiquarians. Jennings made a stupendous fight
against Parker, and was beaten in the end only by a resort to
gouging *a posteriori* and kneeing below the belt. On a hot, humid
night, with the hall packed, he elbowed his way to the platform
to deliver what he and everyone else thought would be his vale-
dictory. He had prepared for it by announcing that he had come
down with laryngitis and could scarcely speak, and as he began
his speech it was in a ghostly whisper. That was long before the
day of loud-speakers, so the gallery could not hear him, and in a
minute it was howling to him to speak louder, and he was going
through the motion of trying to do so. In his frayed alpaca coat
and baggy pants he was a pathetic figure, and that, precisely, is
what he wanted to appear.

But galleries are always brutal, and this one was worse than
most. It kept on howling, and in a little while the proceedings had
to be suspended while the sergeants-at-arms tried to restore order.

(449)

How long the hiatus continued I forget, but I well remember how it ended. One of the dignitaries in attendance was the late J. Ham Lewis, then in the full splendor of his famous pink whiskers. He sat at a corner of the platform where everyone in the house could see him, and so sitting, with the fetid miasma from 15,000 Democrats rising about him, he presently became thirsty. Calling a page, he sent out for a couple of bottles of beer, and when they came in, sweating with cold, he removed the caps with a gold opener, parted his vibrissae with a lordly gesture, and proceeded to empty the beer down his esophagus. The galleries, forgetting poor Jennings, rose on their hind legs and gave Ham three loud cheers, and when they were over it was as if an electric spark had been discharged, for suddenly there was quiet, and Jennings could go on.

The uproar had nettled him, for he was a vain fellow, and when he uttered his first words it was plain that either his indignation had cured his laryngitis or he had forgotten it. His magnificent baritone voice rolled out clearly and sonorously, and in two minutes he had stilled the hostility of the crowd and was launched upon a piece of oratory of the very first chop. There were hundreds of politicians present who had heard his Cross of Gold speech in Chicago in 1896, and they were still more or less under its enchantment, but nine-tenths of them were saying the next day that this St. Louis speech was even more eloquent, even more gaudy, even more overpowering. Certainly I listened to it myself with my ears wide open, my eyes apop and my reportorial pencil palsied. It swept up on wave after wave of sound like the *finale* of the first movement of Beethoven's Eroica, and finally burst into such coruscations that the crowd first gasped and then screamed. "You *may* say," roared Jennings, "that I have not fought a good fight. [*A pause.*] You *may* say that I have not run a good race. [*A longer pause, with dead silence in the galleries.*] But *no* man [*crescendo*] shall say [*a catch in the baritone voice*] that I have not kept the faith!!!!"

That was long, long ago, in a hot and boozy town, in the decadent days of an American era that is now as far off as the Würm Glaciation, but I remember it as clearly as if it were last night. What a speech, my masters! What a speech! Like all really great art, it was fundamentally simple. The argument in it, so far as I can recall it at all, was feeble, and the paraphrase of II Timothy IV, 7 was obvious. But how apt, how fit and meet, how tremendously effective! If the galleries had been free to vote, Bryan would have been nominated on the spot, and to the tune of ear-splitting hallelujahs. Even as it was, there was an ominous stirring among the delegates, boughten though most of them were, and the leaders, for ten minutes, were in a state of mind not far from the panicky. I well recall how they darted through the hall, slapping down heresy here and encouraging the true faith there. Bryan, always the perfect stage manager, did not wait for this painful afterglow. He knew that he was done for, and he was too smart to be on hand for the formal immolation. Instead, he climbed down from the platform and made his slow way out of the hall, his huge catfish mouth set in a hard line, his great eyes glittering, his black hair clumped in sweaty locks over his epicycloid dome. He looked poor and shabby and battered, but he was pathetic no more. The Money Power had downed him, but his soul was marching on. Some one in the galleries started to sing "John Brown's Body" in a voice of brass, but the band leader shut it off hastily by breaking into "The Washington *Post* March." Under cover of the banal strains the leaders managed to restore law and order in the ranks. The next morning Parker was nominated, and on the Tuesday following the first Monday of the ensuing November he was laid away forever by Roosevelt I.

I missed Bryan's comeback in 1908, but I saw him often after that, and was present, as I have recorded, at his Gethsemane among the Bible searchers at Dayton, Tenn., though I had left town before he actually ascended into Heaven. He was largely responsible for the nomination of Woodrow Wilson at Baltimore in 1912, and was rewarded for his services by being made Secretary of State. In New York, in 1924, after howling against Wall Street for nearly three weeks, he accepted the nomination of its agent and attorney, John W. Davis, of Piping Rock, W. Va., and took in payment the nomination of his low comedy brother, Charlie, to second place on the ticket. During the great war upon the Rum Demon he hung back until the triumph of Prohibition began to seem inevitable, and then leaped aboard the band wagon with loud, exultant gloats. In brief, a fraud. But I find myself convinced, nevertheless, that his support of the Good Book against Darwin and company was quite sincere—that is, as sincerity runs among politicoes. When age began to fetch him the fear of Hell burgeoned out of his unconscious, and he died a true Christian of the Hookworm Belt, full of a malignant rage against the infidel.

Bryan was essentially and incurably a yap, and never had much of a following in the big cities. At the New York convention of 1924 the Tammany galleries razzed him from end to end of his battle against the Interests, and then razzed him again, and even more cruelly, when he sold out for the honor of the family. He made speeches nearly every day, but they were heard only in part, for the moment he appeared on the platform the Al Smith firemen in the galleries began setting off their sirens and the cops on the floor began shouting orders and pushing people about. Thus the setting was not favorable for his oratory, and he made a sorry showing. But when he had a friendly audience he was magnificent. I heard all the famous rhetoricians of his generation, from Chauncey M. Depew to W. Bourke Cockran, and it is my sober judgment, standing on the brink of eternity, that he was the greatest of them all. His voice had something of the caressing richness of Julia Marlowe's, and he could think upon his feet much better than at a desk. The average impromptu speech, taken down by a stenographer, is found to be a bedlam of puerile clichés, thumping non sequiturs and limping, unfinished sentences. But Jennings emitted English that was clear, flowing and sometimes not a little elegant, in the best sense of the word. Every sentence had a beginning, a middle and an end. The argument, three times out of four, was idiotic, but it at least hung together.

I never traveled with him on his tours of the cow country, but it was my good fortune to accompany various other would-be heirs to Washington and Lincoln on theirs, and I always enjoyed the experience, though it meant heavy work for a reporter, and a certain amount of hardship. No politician can ever resist a chance to make a speech, and sometimes, in the regions where oratory is still esteemed, that chance offers twenty or thirty times a day. What he has to say is seldom worth hearing, but he roars it as if it were gospel, and in the process of wearing out his vocal chords he also wears out the reporters. More than once, accompanying such a geyser, I have been hard at it for eighteen hours out of the twenty-four, and have got nothing properly describable as a meal until 11:30 p.m. Meanwhile, unless there is an occasional lay-over in some hotel, it is hard to keep clean, and in consequence after a couple of weeks of campaigning the entourage of a candidate for the highest secular office under God begins to smell like a strike meeting of longshoremen.

Of all the hopefuls I have thus accompanied on their missionary journeys—it is perhaps only a coincidence that each and every one of them was licked—the most amusing was Al Smith. By the time he made his campaign in 1928 he was very well known to the country, and so he attracted large crowds everywhere. Sometimes, of course, those crowds were a good deal more curious than cordial, for Al passed, in the pellagra and chigger latitudes, as no more than a secret agent of the Pope, and it was generally believed that he had machineguns aboard his campaign train, and was ready to turn them loose at a word from Rome. But the only time he met with actual hostility was not in the tall grass but in the metropolis of Louisville, and the persons who tried to fetch him there were not credulous yokels but city slickers. His meeting was held in a large hall, and every inch of it was jammed. When Al and his party got to the place they found it uncomfortably warm, but that was hardly surprising, for big crowds always engender calories. But by the time the candidate rose to speak the heat was really extraordinary, and before he was half way through his speech he was sweating so copiously that he seemed half drowned. The dignitaries on the platform sweated too, and so did the vulgar on the floor and in the galleries. Minute by minute the temperature seemed to increase, until finally it became almost unbearable. When Al shut down at last, with his collar a rag and his shirt and pants sticking to his hide, the thermometer must have stood at 100 degrees at least, and there were plenty who guessed that it stood at 110. Not until the campaign party got back to its train did the truth reach it. There then appeared an apologetic committee with the news that the city administration of Louisville, which was currently Republican, had had its goons fire up the boilers under the hall, deliberately and with malice prepense.

The plan had been to wreck the meeting by frying it, but the plotters had underestimated the endurance of a politico with an audience in front of him, and also the endurance of an American crowd feasting its eyes upon a celebrated character. It took Al twenty-four hours to cool off, but I had noted no falling off in his oratorical amperage. He had, in fact, hollered even louder than usual, and his steaming customers had howled with delight. What his speech was about I can't tell you, and neither, I daresay, could anyone else who was present.

The truth is that some of his most effective harangues in that campaign were probably more or less unintelligible to himself. The common report was that he knew nothing about national issues, and that he had never, in fact, been across the North River before he was nominated, or even so much as looked across, so he carried a Brain Trust with him to help him prove that this report was all a lie, and its members prepared the first draft of every one of his set speeches. Its chief wizard was the famous Mrs. Belle Israels Moskowitz, but she did not travel with the candidate; instead, she remained at his G.H.Q. in New York, bossing a huge staff of experts in all the known departments of human knowledge, and leaving the field work to two trusties—the Hon. Joseph M. Proskauer, a justice of the Supreme Court of New York, and the Hon. Bernard L. Shientag, then a justice of the New York City court. The two learned judges and their secretaries sweated almost as hard every day as Al sweated in that hall in Louisville. They had a car to themselves, and it was filled with files, card indexes and miscellaneous memoranda supplied from time to time by Mrs. Moskowitz. Every morning they would turn out bright and early to concoct Al's evening speech—usually on some such unhappy and unfathomable subject (at least to the candidate himself) as the tariff, the League of Nations, Farm Relief, the Alaskan fisheries, or the crimes of the Chicago Board of Trade. They would work away at this discourse until noon, then stop for lunch, and then proceed to finish it. By three or four o'clock it was ready, and after a fair copy had been sent to Al it would be mimeographed for the use of the press.

Al's struggles with it were carried on *in camera*, so I can't report upon them in any detail, but there is reason to believe that he often made heavy weather of mastering his evening's argument. By the time he appeared on the platform he had reduced it to a series of notes on cards, and from these he spoke—often thunderously and always to the great delight of the assembled Democrats. But not infrequently his actual speech resembled the draft of the two judges only to the extent that the ritual of the Benevolent and Protective Order of Elks resembles the Book of Mormon and the poetry of John Donne. The general drift was there, but that was about all—and sometimes even the drift took a new course. The rest was a gallimaufry of Al's recollections of the issues and arguments in a dozen New York campaigns, with improvisations suggested by the time, the place and the crowd. It was commonly swell stuff, but I'd certainly be exaggerating if I said it showed any profound grasp of national issues. Al, always shrewd, knew that a Chicago crowd, or a rural Missouri crowd, or a crowd in Tennessee, Michigan or Pennsylvania did not differ by more than four per cent from a New York crowd, so he gave them all the old stuff that he had tried with such success in his state campaigns, and it went down again with a roar. Never in my life have I heard louder yells than those that greeted him at Sedalia, Mo., in the very heart of the no-more-scrub-bulls country. His meeting was held in the vast cattle-shed of a county fair, and among the 20,000 persons present there were some who had come in by flivver from places as far away as Nebraska, Oklahoma, and even New Mexico. The subject of his remarks that night, as set by the two judges, was the tariff, but he had forgotten it in five minutes, and so had his audience. There were stenographers present to take down what he said, and transcripts of it were supplied to the press-stand sheet by sheet, but only a few correspondents actually sent it out. The rest coasted on the judges' draft, disseminated by the press associations during the late afternoon and released at 8 p.m., as he arose to speak. Thus all the Americans who still depended on the newspapers for their news—and there were plenty of them left in 1928—were duped into accepting what the two laborious jurisconsults had written for what Al had actually said. I do not know, but the thought has often crossed my mind, that Hoover's overwhelming victory in November may have been due, at least in part, to that fact.

Al bore up pretty well under the rigors of the campaign, but now and then he needed a rest, and it was provided by parking his train on a side-track for a quiet night, usually in some sparsely settled region where crowds could not congregate. After his harrying of Tennessee, and just before he bore down upon Louisville to be fried, there was such a hiatus in rural Kentucky. When I turned out in the morning I found that the train was laid up in a lovely little valley of the Blue Grass country, with nothing in sight save a few farmhouses and a water-tank, the latter about a mile down the track. My colleague, Henry M. Hyde, suggested that we go ashore to stretch our legs, and in a little while we were hanging over a fence some distance to the rear of the train, admiring a white-painted house set in a grove of trees. Presently two handsome young girls issued from the house, and asked us prettily to have breakfast with their mother, who was a widow, and themselves. We accepted at once, and were very charmingly entertained. In the course of the conversation it appeared that another daughter, not present, aspired to be the postmistress of the village behind the tank down the track, and Hyde, always gallant, promised at once that he would see Al, and get her a promise of the appointment come March 4, 1929.

When we got back to the train Hyde duly saw Al, and the promise was made instantly. Unhappily, Hoover won in November, and it seemed hopeless to ask his Postmaster-General to make good on Al's pledge. Four years of horror came and went, but the daughter down in the Blue Grass kept on hugging her ambition. When Roosevelt II was elected in 1932 her mother got into communication with Hyde, suggesting that the new administration should be proud and eager to make good on the promise of the Democratic standard-bearer four years before, even though that standard-bearer had since taken his famous walk. Hyde put the question up to Jim Farley, and Farley, a man very sensitive to points of honor, decided that Roosevelt was bound to carry out the official promises of his predecessor, however revolting they might be. An order was thereupon issued that the daughter be made postmistress at the water-tank at once, and Hyde went to bed that night feeling that few other Boy Scouts had done better during the day. But alas and alas,

(456)

it turned out that the tank was a fourth-class post office, that appointments to such offices were under the Civil Service, and that candidates had to be examined. Farley so advised the widow's daughter and she took the examination, but some other candidate got a higher mark, and the scrupulous Jim decided that he could not appoint her. Hyde and I often recall the lamentable episode, and especially the agreeable first canto of it. Never in all my wanderings have I seen a more idyllic spot than that secluded little valley in the Blue Grass, or had the pleasure of being entertained by pleasanter people than the widow and her daughters. The place was really Arcadian, and Hyde and I wallowed in its bucolic enchantments while Al caught up with lost sleep on his funeral train.

He was, in his day, the most attractive of all American politicoes, but it would be going too far to say that he was any great shakes as an orator. Compared to Bryan he was a BB shot to a twelve-inch shell, and as he was passing out of public life there was arising a rhetorician who was even greater than Bryan, to wit, Gerald L. K. Smith. As I have said, I have heard all the really first-chop American breast-beaters since 1900, and included among them have been not only the statesmen but also the divines, for example, Sam Jones, Gipsy Smith, Father Coughlin and Billy Sunday, but among them all I have encountered none worthy of being put in the same species, or even in the same genus, as Gerald. His own early training was gained at the sacred desk but in maturity he switched to the hustings, so that he now has a double grip upon the diaphragms and short hairs of the *Anthropoidea.* Add to these advantages of nurture the natural gifts of an imposing person, a flashing eye, a hairy chest, a rubescent complexion, large fists, a voice both loud and mellow, terrifying and reassuring, *sforzando* and *pizzicato,* and finally, an unearthly capacity for distending the superficial blood-vessels of his temples and neck, as if they were biceps—and you have the makings of a boob-bumper worth going miles to see and hear, and then worth writing home about. When I first heard Gerald, at the convention of the Townsend old-age pension fans at Cleveland in 1936, I duly wrote home about him to the *Sun-paper,* and in the following fervent terms:

His speech was a magnificent amalgam of each and every American species of rabble-rousing, with embellishments borrowed from the Algonquin Indians and the Cossacks of the Don. It ran the keyboard from the softest sobs and gurgles to the most ear-splitting whoops and howls, and when it was over the 9000 delegates simply lay back in their pews and yelled.

Never in my life, in truth, have I ever heard a more effective speech. In logical content, to be sure, it was somewhat vague and even murky, but Dr. Townsend's old folks were not looking for logical content: what they had come to Cleveland for was cheer, consolation, the sweet music of harps and psalteries. Gerald had the harps and psalteries, and also a battery of trumpets, trombones and bass-drums. When he limned the delights of a civilization offering old-age pensions to all, with $200 cash a month for every gaffer and another $200 for the old woman, he lifted them up to the highest heaven, and when he excoriated the Wall Street bankers, millionaire steel magnates, Chicago wheat speculators and New Deal social engineers who sneered at the vision, he showed them the depths of the lowest hell. Nor was it only the believing and in fact already half-dotty old folks who panted under his eloquence: he also fetched the minority of sophisticates in the hall, some of them porch-climbers in Dr. Townsend's entourage and the rest reporters in the press-stand. It is an ancient convention of American journalism, not yet quite outlawed by the Newspaper Guild, that the press-stand has no opinion—that its members, consecrated to fair reports, must keep their private feelings to themselves, and neither cheer nor hiss. But that convention went out of the window before Gerald had been hollering five minutes. One and all, the boys and gals of the press abandoned their jobs, leaped upon their rickety desks, and gave themselves up to the voluptuous enjoyment of his whooping. When the old folks yelled, so did the reporters yell, and just as loudly. And when Gerald, sweating like Al at Louisville, sat down at last, and the press resumed its business of reporting his remarks, no one could remember what he had said.

A few weeks later I saw him give an even more impressive exhibition of his powers. At the Townsend convention just described one of the guest speakers had been the Rev. Charles E. Coughlin, the radio priest, who, in return for Dr. Townsend's politeness in inviting him, invited the doctor and Gerald to speak at his own convention, scheduled to be held in Cleveland a few weeks later. But Gerald's immense success apparently sicklied him o'er with a green cast of envy, and when the time came he showed a considerable reluctance to make good. Finally, he hit upon the device of putting Gerald and the doctor off until the very end of his convention, by which time his assembled customers would be so worn out by his own rabble-rousing that nothing short of an earthquake could move them. On the last day, in fact, they were so worn out, for Coughlin kept banging away at them from 10 a.m. to 8 p.m., with no breaks for meals. The device was thus a smart one, but his reverence, for all his smartness, was not smart enough to realize that Gerald was actually an earthquake. First, old Townsend was put up, and the general somnolence was only increased, for he is one of the dullest speakers on earth. But then, with the poor morons hardly able to keep their eyes open, Gerald followed—and within five minutes the Coughlin faithful had forgotten all about their fatigues, and also all about Coughlin, and were leaping and howling like the Townsend old folks. It was a shorter speech than the other, for Coughlin, frowning, showed his itch to cut it off as soon as possible and Gerald was more or less uneasy, but it was even more remarkable. Once more the boys and gals in the press-stand forgot their Hippocratic oath and yielded themselves to pure enjoyment, and once more no one could recall, when it was over, what its drift had been, but that it was a masterpiece was agreed by all. When Gerald came to Cleveland it was in the humble role of a follower of the late Huey Long, jobless since Huey's murder on September 10, 1935. But when he cleared out after his two speeches it was in the lofty character of the greatest rabble-rouser since Peter the Hermit.

Coughlin, it seems to me, is a much inferior performer. He has a velvet voice, and is thus very effective on the radio, but like his great rival on the air, Roosevelt II, he is much less effective face to face. For one thing, he is almost totally lacking in dramatic gesture, for his long training at the mike taught him to stick firmly to one spot, lest the fans lose him in the midst of his howling. It is, of course, impossible for an orator with passion in him to remain really immovable, so Coughlin has developed a habit of enforcing his points by revolving his backside. This saves him from going off the air, but it is somewhat disconcerting, not to say indecent, in the presence of an audience. After the convention of his half-wits in Cleveland in 1936 a report was circulated that he was experimenting with a mike fixed to his shoulders by a stout framework, so that he could gesture normally without any risk of roaring futilely into space, but if he actually ever used it I was not present, and so cannot tell you about it.

I X

‹‹‹‹‹‹‹‹‹‹‹‹‹‹››››››››››››››

Letters

⌘ · ⌘ · ⌘ · ⌘ · ⌘

August Mencken, by careful calculations, has concluded that his brother wrote a minimum of seventy-five thousand letters. Mr. Guy Forgue, the editor of the Mencken correspondence, estimates that about fifteen thousand of them are in public or private collections. Mencken was a polite man; his practice was to answer all letters on the day of their arrival. As a rule he kept no copies, but his secretary preserved many of her notebooks, and after his stroke his enforced leisure was partially occupied with their transcription under his supervision. Mencken was not a correspondent for correspondence's sake. He was an exceptionally busy man, and his letters were written for a particular purpose. Many of these were no more than notes of acknowledgment and have no intrinsic value; but at all periods of his life there are others which shed light on his motives or amplify his ideas. Altogether they constitute the most complete correspondence record of a major American writer yet made public.

He was a stylist of ability, he was also a conversationalist of the first rank. These two qualities combine in his letters to give them their vivid interest. When the mood was upon him, Mencken could be as engaging a monologist as we are told Huneker was; but he was also a master at the joint exploration of a subject with a companion. As a man talking he was at once gay and serious, humorous and witty, spontaneous, and above all, gratifying. All these characteristics appear in his letters, which are seldom dull. For some unaccountable reason the letters of some of the world's most effective writers are tedious. Pepys's letters, for example, are almost unreadable. Mencken's are as absorbing as his books.

As a critic and editor Mencken had a special interest in encouraging younger writers. He tried to read all the periodicals, both estab-

(463)

lished and transient, where talent might be uncovered. The young writer who caught his eye, or who had hopefully mailed him some work, would, if the piece justified it, receive a warm response. The notes were short, and said, in substance: "You are well on the way to learning your business, stick to it." Mr. Forgue has exhumed from Sherwood Anderson's writings an account of the gratitude felt by the young men and women of the time:

> *We got the letters and the letters made us proud. "Well, I had a letter from Henry Mencken today."*
> *You said it offhand, but in your heart you felt that it was like being knighted by a king.*
> *You knew damn well the others felt the same.*

Mencken's letters have his unmistakable stamp. He would begin a note to a stranger: "I have your note of April 6th, addressed to Mr. S. Mencken. The only S. Mencken I know of is my uncle Siegmund. He is in the lime and cement business, and knows nothing of book reviewing." He would close a good-natured response to a critical letter from Ezra Pound with the remark: "Meanwhile, please don't try to alarm a poor old man by yelling at him and making faces. It has been tried before." And sometimes he would be lavish in sending thanks for a favorable notice of his writings: "As George Cohan says, I thank you; my family thanks you; my valet, Rudolph, thanks you; my Bierbruder, George Nathan, thanks you; my pastor thanks you; my brother, Wolfgang, thanks you; my chauffeur, Étienne, thanks you; my secretary, Miss Goldberg, thanks you; my accompanist, Signor Sforzando, thanks you." There is no indication in Mencken's letters that they were written for posterity.

George Jean Nathan said he had never known a man who had so much fun out of life as Mencken had in the Smart Set *years. His exuberance of spirit overflowed in many directions, not the least of which was the harmless hoaxes he perpetrated on his friends in his letters. His friends would be the recipients of tracts against alcohol and immodest dress, or of a stone fragment certified by "H. L. Mencken, Inspector" to be a genuine madstone guaranteed to cure all ailments save impotence. Students working on the Mencken letters and on other Mencken material today are sometimes apt to mistake fiction for fact; some of the hoaxes are seemingly so realistic that his brother August's present-day efforts to correct misapprehensions, although based on knowledge of the facts, are not infrequently resisted.*

Letters

❮❮❮❮❮❮❮❮❮❮❮❮❮❮❮❮❮❮❮❮❮❮❮❮❮❮❮❮❮❮❯❯❯❯❯❯❯❯❯❯❯❯❯❯❯❯❯❯❯❯❯❯❯❯❯❯❯❯❯❯

To THEODORE DREISER

H. L. Mencken
1524 Hollins St.
Baltimore
April 23rd [*1911*]

DEAR DREISER:—

When "Jennie Gerhardt" is printed it is probable that more than one reviewer will object to its length, its microscopic detail, its enormous painstaking—but rest assured that Heinrich Ludwig von Mencken will not be in that gang. I have just finished reading the ms.—every word of it, from first to last—and I put it down with a clear notion that it should remain as it stands. The story comes upon me with great force; it touches my own experience of life in a hundred places; it preaches (or perhaps I had better say exhibits) a philosophy of life that seems to me to be sound; altogether I get a powerful effect of reality, stark and unashamed. It is drab and gloomy, but so is the struggle for existence. It is without humor, but so are the jests of that great comedian who shoots at our heels and makes us do our grotesque dancing.

I needn't say that it seems to me an advance above "Sister Carrie." Its obvious superiority lies in its better form. You strained (or perhaps even broke) the back of "Sister Carrie" when you let Hurstwood lead you away from Carrie. In "Jennie Gerhardt" there is no such running amuck. The two currents of interest, of spiritual unfolding, are very deftly managed. Even when they do not actually coalesce, they are parallel and close together. Jennie is never out of Kane's life, and after their first meeting, she is never

---

Throughout the letters section, the footnotes are Guy Forgue's. *Ed.*

out of his. The reaction of will upon will, of character upon character, is splendidly worked out and indicated. In brief, the story hangs together; it is a complete whole; consciously or unconsciously, you have avoided the chief defect of "Sister Carrie."

It is difficult, just rising from the book, to describe the impression I bring away. That impression is of a living whole, not of a fabric that may be unraveled and examined in detail. In brief, you have painted so smoothly and yet so vigorously that I have no memory of brush strokes. But for one thing, the great naturalness of the dialogue sticks in mind. In particular, you have been extremely successful with Gerhardt. His speeches are perfect: nothing could be nearer to truth. I am well aware that certain persons are impatient of this photographic accuracy. Well, let them choose their poison. As for me, I prefer the fact to the fancy. You have tried to depict a German of a given type—a type with which I, by chance, happen to be very familiar. You have made him as thoroughly alive as Huck Finn.

These are random, disordered notes. When the time comes, I'll reduce my thoughts to order and write a formal, intelligible review. At the moment I am too near the book. I rather distrust my own enthusiasm for it. Perhaps I read my own prejudices and ideas into it. My interest is always in the subjective event, seldom or never in the objective event. That is why I like "Lord Jim." Here you have got very close to the very well-springs of action. The march of episodes is nothing: the slow unfolding of character is everything.

If anyone urges you to cut down the book bid that one be damned. And if anyone argues that is is over-gloomy call the police. Let it stand as it is. Its bald, forthright style; its scientific, unemotional piling up of detail; the incisive truthfulness of its dialogue; the stark straightforwardness of it all—these are merits that need no praise. It is at once an accurate picture of life and a searching criticism of life. And that is my definition of a good novel.

Here and there I noted minor weaknesses. For one thing, it is doubtful that Jennie would have been able to conceal from so sophisticated a man as Kane the fact that she had had a child. Child-bearing leaves physical marks, and those marks commonly persist for five or six years. But there are, of course, exceptions to this rule. Not many readers, I suppose, will raise the point. Again, if I remember correctly, you speak of L. S. & M. S. "shares" as being worth $1,000 par. Don't you mean bonds? If bonds, the income would be fixed and could not fluctuate. Again you give Kane $5,000 income from $75,000 at 6 per cent. A small thing—but everywhere else you are so utterly careful that small errors stick out.

A final word: the least satisfactory personage in the book is Jennie herself. Not that you do not account for her, from head to heels—but I would have preferred, had I the choice, a more typical kept woman. She is, in brief, uncompromisingly exceptional, almost unique, in several important details. Her connection with her mother and father and with the facts of her life grows, at times, very fragile. But I can well understand how her essential plausibility must have reacted upon you—how your own creation must have dragged you on. There is always Letty Pace to show Jennie's limitations. In her class she is a miracle, and yet she never quite steps out of that class.

But I go back to the effect of the book as a whole. That effect, believe me, is very powerful. I must go to Hardy and Conrad to find its like. David Phillips, I believe, might have done such a story had he lived, but the best that he actually wrote, to wit, "The Hungry Heart," goes to pieces beside "Jennie." I mean this in all seriousness. You have written a novel that no other American of the time could have written, and even in England there are not six men who, with your material, could have reached so high a level of reality. My earnest congratulations. By all means let me see that third book. "Jennie" shows immense progress in craftsmanship. As a work of art it is decidedly superior to "Sister Carrie."

I'll return the ms. by express tomorrow morning. Maybe chance will throw us together soon and we'll have a session over "Jennie." At the moment I am rather too full of the story as a human document to sit down in cold blood and discourse upon its merits and defects as a work of art. I know that it is immensely good, but I have still to get my reasons reduced to fluent words.

God keep you. As for me, I lately enjoyed the first of the

season's rashers of crab à la creole. With genuine Muenchener to
flush the esophagus afterward.

Yours,

H. L. M.

Reading this over it seems damned cold. [What] I really
want to say is just—"Hurrah!" You have put over a truly *big*
thing.

◇◇◇◇◇◇◇◇◇◇◇◇

To WILLARD HUNTINGTON WRIGHT

H. L. Mencken
1524 Hollins St.
Baltimore
December 20th [*1911*]

DEAR WRIGHT:—

My sincere congratulations on the Christmas Book Section.[1]
You have got guts into it: the stuff is sound and has an air. In
particular, I like the notice of "The Indian Lily."[2] For why? Because I sent the S. S. last week a notice that follows yours almost
idea for idea! You'll see it in the February number—a plain
psychic steal from you. The book disposes of the notion that
Sudermann is a dead one. Who else could have done "The Purpose," or "The Song of Death," or "Autumn," or that Christmas
story? Once more I bang my seidel on the table and bawl "Die
Wacht Am Rhein." We Dutch may be vulgar eaters, but we have
a few good men left.

Poor Pollard passed in painlessly, but very pathetically.[3] A
month or so ago headaches seized him and pretty soon he began
to show signs of mental disturbance. On December 5, the bone-
head horse-doctors at Milford having diagnosed grip, his wife
brought him to Baltimore for treatment. Unfortunately she landed
him, before I knew anything about it, in an E flat homeopathic
hospital. There nothing seems to have been done for him. The
homeopaths said he was getting on "nicely"—and Mrs. Pollard

---

[1] [Of the Los Angeles *Times*. G.F.]

[2] ["The Indian Lily," by Hermann Sudermann (New York: B. W. Huebsch;
1912), was reviewed by Mencken in the *Smart Set* for February 1912. G.F.]

[3] [Percival Pollard (1869–1911) was a Baltimore critic and the former literary
reviewer of *Town Topics*. G.F.]

went back to Milford to lock up the house and get some clothes. While she was away Pollard was suddenly paralyzed and became unconscious.

That was last Sunday a week. I was out at dinner and couldn't be found, but an old fellow named Burrows, who knew Pollard, happened to drop into the hospital and found out what was going on. He set up a loud and righteous bellow and demanded a consultation with Harvey Cushing, of the Johns Hopkins, the greatest brain surgeon in America. Cushing diagnosed a brain abscess and decided to operate at once. But Mrs. Pollard was somewhere on the road and couldn't be reached. Poor Burrows, until he found me, after midnight, was in a hell of a sweat, being afraid that Pollard would die on the table and that he (Burrows) would be blamed. But I joined with him in authorizing the operation (there was nothing else to do, for Pollard was dying) and Cushing operated at 1:30 in the morning. He found one whole lobe of the brain involved. The thing was utterly hopeless. So Pollard was put to bed and there was nothing to do but wait for the end. Fortunately enough, when Mrs. Pollard returned next morning, she approved the whole proceeding.

Pollard lasted until the past Sunday. He never regained consciousness a moment. Yesterday, according to his wish, we cremated him at the local crematory. Present: Mrs. Pollard, Mrs. Burrows and another woman; Ambrose Bierce, Neale the publisher and myself. A pathetically small party for so clever a fellow, so decent a friend. I had an Episcopal preacher I know (he also knew Pollard slightly) read a few words at the undertaker's. Then we went to the crematory, the women returning at once, but Bierce, Neale and I waiting to the end. The business there was over in five minutes. I am holding the ashes here. Later on they will probably be sent to Iowa, where Pollard's parents are buried. Mrs. Pollard went back to Milford this afternoon. She has an invalid mother and a sister, but no child. I think Pollard left property enough to keep her.

Pollard's last book, "Vagabond Journeys," came out on the day of his funeral. Neale came down from New York with the first three copies. He landed at the undertaker's with them. They actually went to the poor fellow's funeral.

I'm glad you get a chuckle, now and then, out of the Free

Lance stuff.[4] Most of it, of course, is purely local. Privately, I am thinking of reducing my newspaper work a good deal to make time for other business. Thayer of the Smart Set pursues me with propositions and I am inclined to take some of them. This under your hat. I want to stay in Baltimore, on account of my family and the property that will have to keep me when I am old. This, I believe, can be managed. Thayer, by the way, is willing to start that knock-em-down quarterly I mentioned to you, though it may be a year or two before he gets the Smart Set going and can come to it. You are elected and inaugurated in advance. He will pay cash for stuff. Of all this, of course, say nothing.

If you can possibly manage it, you must make that Munich trip with old McDannald and me.[5] Mac is a noble beer-drinker: a Virginian with a figure like Taft's and German brains. We sail April 16 and return by June 3 or 4. Total cost: not over $450.

Yours,
Mencken

◇◇◇◇◇◇◇◇◇◇◇◇

(SENT TO BURTON RASCOE WITH AN
    UNIDENTIFIED LETTER)

[*Summer 1920?*]

ADDENDUM ON AIMS:

If I have any definite purpose at the moment it is to get an audience wider than the home audience. This seems likely of accomplishment. Vincent O'Sullivan's brief references to me in the Mercure de France have opened the way for the possible French translation of "On Democracy," and he has now printed a long article on me in the London New Witness (G. K. Chesterton's paper) for November 28.[6] The London Athenaeum has reviewed

---

[4] [The Free Lance was a column that Mencken wrote for the Baltimore *Evening Sun* from May 8, 1911, until October 23, 1915, and in which he commented freely and somewhat tartly on local or general matters. It was discontinued because Mencken's position had become untenable after the war broke out in Europe. G.F.]

[5] [A. H. McDannald was a Baltimore *Sun* reporter, who later became editor of the *Encyclopedia Americana*. G.F.]

[6] ["Notes on Democracy" was not translated into French, unlike "In Defense of Women" and "Selected Prejudices." Mencken was never too well-known in France. Vincent O'Sullivan's article: "La littérature Americaine," in the *Mercure de France* for January 16, 1919. G.F.]

"Prejudices" favorably, and the London Times has noticed it. In Germany I have had a four column article in the Continental Times, and I am now in contact with various Germans who will introduce my ensuing books. In Denmark, Georg Brandes has read some of my books, and professed interest in them. E. A. Boyd told me that when he visited Brandes a year ago, B. told him that the three Americans who interested him most were Dreiser, E. W. Howe and me. (This is confidential.) I also have a good booster in South America, and he will do my "On Democracy" into Spanish.[7]

I believe, and have often argued, that the battle of ideas should be international—that is idiotic to expect any one country to offer hospitality to every imaginable sort of man. I do not fit into the United States very well. My skepticism is intolerably offensive to the normal American man; only the man under strong foreign influences sees anything in it save a gross immorality. The Sherman reaction is typical and quite honest.[8] If the notions of the right-thinkers are correct, then such stuff as mine (and particularly such stuff as I shall write hereafter) ought to be put down by law. I believe that, in the long run, it *will* be put down by law—that free speech is too dangerous to a democracy to be permitted. But I do not complain about this fact. If Knopf cannot print my books following "On Democracy" I shall print them in Zürich or Leipzig. The Puritans have a right to determine the laws of their own country. And I reject the sentimentality that the minority also has rights.

Note on my relations to Nathan:

We are constantly accused of imitating each other. This is absurd. No two men could possibly be more unlike, in style and thought. Nathan detests philosophical questions, and particularly political questions; he sees life purely as idiotic spectacle. I delight in such questions, though I reject all solutions. Nathan aims at a very complex style; I aim at the greatest possible lucidity. Our point of contact is our common revulsion from American senti-

---

[7] [A good booster: Isaac Goldberg (1887–1938), specialist of South American literature, and author of a book on Mencken.   G.F.]
[8] [Sherman: Stuart P. Sherman.   G.F.]

mentality. We are both essentially foreigners. But he is more French than anything else, and I am more German than anything else. We work together amicably because we are both lonely, and need some support. He dislikes the American Language book because it is full of facts, and has never read it. I dislike his interest in the theater, which seems to me to be an intellectual hogpen. But we come together on several essentials, e.g. our common disinclination to know authors or to belong to literary coteries, our lack of national feeling, and (perhaps most important) our similar attitudes toward money, religion, women, etc. We seldom disagree on literary judgments; it is very rare for either to exercise his veto in buying stuff for the Smart Set. Both of us think the same, for example, about Cabell, Dreiser, Cather, Dunsany, Conrad, Anatole France, etc. Both have the same (almost pathological) aversion to worldly failure; we dislike having anything to do with men who are so bad at their jobs that they can't live decently by them. Neither regards writing books as a job: it is the *reward* of a job. Both of us detest martyrs of all sorts.

My relations to Dreiser:

The common notion that I discovered Dreiser is bosh. He had written "Sister Carrie" before I ever met him. I probably helped him appreciably after "Jennie Gerhardt," but it is not inconceivable that he would have been better off if I had never written a line about him. We remained on good terms so long as I was palpably his inferior—a mere beater of drums for him. But when I began to work out notions of my own it quickly appeared that we were much unlike. Dreiser is a great artist, but a very ignorant and credulous man. He believes, for example, in the Ouija board. My skepticism, and, above all, my contempt for the peasant, eventually offended him. We are still, of course, very friendly, but his heavy sentimentality and his naïve yearning to be a martyr make it impossible for me to take him seriously— that is, as man. As artist, I believe that he has gone backward— but he is still a great man. Think of "Twelve Men."

I know no other first-rate artist. I know Hergesheimer, but only slightly, and his rather gaudy vanity repels me. I have never met Cabell. I have met La Cather but once. Dunsany but once—

he is an ass. I have never met Vincent O'Sullivan, who has written about me. I have never even seen such men as Howells, Herrick, Garland, etc. I know Ed Howe, and like him. He is the very best type of American—simple, shrewd and lively in mind. I mean the real American—not the Judaized New Yorker.

On Influences:

I have never consciously imitated any man save the anonymous editorial writer of the New York Sun. The man who made a critic of me was Robert I. Carter, an old New York Herald man, then managing editor of the Baltimore Herald, and my boss (circa 1912).[9] He taught me a lot, but particularly one thing—that the first desideratum in criticism is to be *interesting*. What has become of him I don't know. I haven't heard from him in years. Next to Carter, I learned most from Percival Pollard—particularly the value, to a critic, of concentrating on a few men. Pollard used Ambrose Bierce; I used Dreiser. I seldom read criticism. The work of such men as Brownell, More, Sherman, etc. seems to me to be simply silly—a dull emission of the obviously untrue.

I believe that the public likes criticism only in so far as it is a good show, which means only in so far as it is bellicose. The crowd is always with the prosecution. Hence, when I have to praise a writer, I usually do it by attacking his enemies. And when I say the crowd I mean all men. My own crowd is very small and probably somewhat superior, but it likes rough-house just as much as a crowd around a bulletin-board. All the favorable notices of "Prejudices" show an obvious delight in my onslaughts on Cobb, Veblen, Howells, Hamlin Garland, Sydnor Harrison, Shaw, etc. Such doings, of course, involve reprisals. I am myself attacked with great vigor. Not infrequently I am attacked unfairly, e.g., by the fellows who accused me, during the war, of German propaganda, which was just as unfair as accusing a man, in Catholic Ireland, of being an Orangeman. But such attacks do not annoy me. I am skeptic enough to believe that some other fellow's notions of honor may be quite as sound as my own. Moreover, there is always a certain amount of truth in every attack, however dishonest.

---

[9] [The date should be 1900. G.F.]

Ethical note:

I have no superstitions about critical honor. I lean toward men I like and away from men I dislike. The calm, Judicial judgment makes me laugh. It is a symptom of a delusion of infallibility. I am often wrong. My prejudices are innumerable, and often idiotic. My aim is not to determine facts, but to function freely and pleasantly—as Nietzsche used to say, to dance with arms and legs.

Critical:

All of my work hangs together, once the main ideas under it are discerned. Those ideas are chiefly of a skeptical character. I believe that nothing is unconditionally true, and hence I am opposed to every statement of positive truth and to every man who states it. Such men seem to me to be either idiots or scoundrels. To one category or the other belong all theologians, professors, editorial writers, right-thinkers, etc. I am against patriotism because it demands the acceptance of propositions that are obviously imbecile, e.g., that an American Presbyterian is the equal of Ludendorff. I am against democracy for the same reason: it rests upon lunacy. To me democracy seems to be founded upon the inferior man's envy of his superior—of the man who is having a better time. This is also the origin of Puritanism. I detest all such things. I acknowledge that many men are my superiors, and always defer to them. In such a country as the United States, of course, few such men are to be encountered. Hence my foreignness: most of the men I respect are foreigners. But this is not my fault. I'd be glad to respect Americans if they were respectable. George Washington was. I admire him greatly. It seems to me that, within our own time, Germany has produced more such men than any other country. Next to Germany, England. Italy has not produced a single first-rate man in years, and France has produced very few since the fall of the Empire.

I detest men who meanly admire mean things, e.g., fellows who think that Rockefeller is a great man. I also detest poltroons —that is, men who seek unfair advantages in combat. In my gladiatorial days on the Baltimore Sun I never attacked a single man who was without means of hitting back. Often I insisted upon the paper giving him the means—I controlled space that was dedicated to anyone who wanted to attack me. No man was ever refused this space. My objection to Americans is that they like to fight with the enemy strapped to a board. Hence the persecution of Germans, lynching, the American Legion, the American Protective Association, the attack on Spain, the wars with Nicaragua, Santo Domingo, etc. This poltroonery is not essentially American; it is simply democratic; the inferior man always shows it. I never complain about an attack, however unfair.

As I say, all my work hangs together. Whether it appears to be burlesque, or serious criticism, or mere casual controversy, it is always directed against one thing: unwarranted pretension. It always seeks to expose a false pretense, to blow up a wobbly axiom, to uncover a sham virtue. My experience of the world teaches me that the best people are those who make no profession of being good—that all who do, absolutely without exception, are frauds. I regard Wilson as the archetype of the hypocrite—an incurable damned liar, utterly without honor.

My weapon is adapted to the enemy and the fight. Sometimes I try to spoof them, and sometimes I use a club. But the end is always the same. I have no general aim save this—that is, I do not aspire to set up any doctrine of my own. Few doctrines seem to me to be worth fighting for. I can't understand the martyr. Far from going to the stake for a Great Truth, I wouldn't even miss a meal for it. My notion is that all the larger human problems are insoluble, and that life is quite meaningless—a spectacle without purpose or moral. I detest all efforts to read a moral into it. I do not write because I want to make converts. In point of fact, I seldom make one—and then it is embarrassing. I write because the business amuses me. It is the best of sports. But all the fun is over by the time a book is printed. The reviews are seldom interesting. In particular, the favorable ones often depress me, for they credit me with purposes that I revolt against; they seek to make a Great Teacher out of me.

I am, tested by the prevailing definitions, a bad American. I do not believe the country has the glorious future that patrioteers talk of. It will probably remain second-rate for centuries—a mere milch cow for England. All of the American ideals, so-called, that I know of seem to me to be idiotic. If they were sound, I'd probably jump into the nearest river. The sort of country they conjure up would be simply a paradise of bounders—forward-lookers, right-thinkers, all sorts of stupid cowards. I do not believe that civilized life is possible under a democracy. Unless the Germans shoot all of their present democratic statesmen, Germany will sink to the level of the United States. But I do not care. No matter what happens, here or elsewhere, I shall be dead by 1950.

I am an extreme libertarian, and believe in absolute free speech, especially for anarchists, Socialists and other such fools. Once all those fellows were free to gabble ad lib., democracy would be reduced to an absurdity: the mob would go stark crazy. I am against jailing men for their opinions, or, for that matter, for anything else. I am opposed to all religions, because all of them seek to throttle opinion. I do not believe in education, and am glad I never went to a university. Beyond the rudiments, it is impossible to teach anything. All the rest the student acquires himself. His teacher merely makes it difficult for him. I never learned anything in school. As I look back, I remember but one teacher with pleasure. He saved me a whole year by insisting upon promoting me when all of the other asses were trying to teach me what I already knew.

It is my belief that democracy is inimical to literature, as to all other fruits of civilization, but this seems to me to be a fact of no importance. All it amounts to is this: that the artist in America can never have a large audience and must expect to encounter positive hostility—Comstockery, college-professorism, etc. But such handicaps are not fatal. They should merely spur on a genuinely good man. I believe every civilized American should help such men—not as a duty, but as a pleasure. Make it a duty, and it at once becomes dishonest.

My style of writing is chiefly grounded upon an early enthusiasm for Huxley, the greatest of all masters of orderly exposition. He taught me the importance of giving to every argument a simple structure. As for the fancy work on the surface, it comes chiefly from an anonymous editorial writer in the New York Sun, circa 1900. He taught me the value of apt phrases. My vocabulary is pretty large; it probably runs to 25,000 words. It represents much labor. I am constantly expanding it. I believe that a good phrase is better than a Great Truth—which is usually buncombe. I delight in argument, not because I want to convince, but because argument itself is an end.

Finally, I have no ambition to be praised by eminent professors. The reviews of my "American Language" actually made me sick. I don't want to get into the school literature books when I die. All I want is time to write half a dozen books that I have in mind. They will not deal with other books. In fact, I'll write very little about books hereafter. All my criticism is, at bottom, a criticism of ideas, not of mere books. But ideas—i.e., the follies and imbecilities of men—interest me. Blowing them up is the noblest of human occupations.

[*Unsigned*]

◇◇◇◇◇◇◇◇◇◇◇◇

To THE EDITOR OF *The Nation*
(*Communicated by Carl Van Doren*)[1]

September 6th [*1920*]

DEAR SIR:–

With the highest respect, my duty to my grandchildren impels me to protest against being shoved out of your ivory tower, as happens in your issue of September 4, page 263. I am no more a radical in letters than I am in politics, and I surely do not propose that the universities, such as they are, should cease teaching "Euripides and Lucretius, Montaigne and Voltaire, Kant and Goethe, Hazlitt (Hatzfeldt?) and Shelley (Scholle?)," and begin teaching Vachel Lindsay and Dreiser, Amy Lowell and George Sterling (a most immoral fellow: he refused the gilt-edged purple of the National Institute of Arts and Letters with scorn), Gerald Stanley Lee and Harry Kemp. All I ask is that they put a soft pedal upon Fenimore Cooper and James Russell Lowell, Edmund

---

[1] [Carl Van Doren (1885–1950) was then literary editor of the *Nation*. On September 4, 1920, the *Nation* had printed an anonymous article (written by Ludwig Lewisohn) entitled "The Ivory Tower," denouncing Mencken on the grounds that he despised the classics and showed no awareness of "the continuity of human culture." G.F.]

Clarence Stedman and Fanny Fern, Paul Elmer More and Hamilton Wright Mabie. If this is too much to ask, then God help us all!

In other words, the combat is not between the new men of
today and the indubitable classics, but between the new men of
today and the bogus classics. In this combat I favor the new men,
not because they are to be mentioned in the same breath with the
indubitable classics, but simply and solely because, compared to
the bogus classics, they are vastly more honest, interesting, ingenious, enterprising and alive. To go to music, the choice is not
between Richard Strauss and Beethoven, but between Richard
Strauss and Prof. Ludwig Blatz, instructor in harp, piano, violin,
ukelele and theory in the Hannah More Academy for Baptist
Young Ladies. I advocate all honest and diligent men, especially
when they are against me. I am against all tripe-sellers and false-
faces, let the chips fall where they may.

This letter is NOT for publication. I am decidedly opposed
to vain discussions of what John Doe thinks and what is in
Richard Roe's secret heart. But I read the Nation so diligently and
admire it so enormously that you must permit me this private
effort to avoid getting into its aviary of evil birds. If necessary,
I'll kiss the First Folio Shakespeare, or give three cheers for
Joseph Addison. But please don't try me with no bunk about
George E. Woodberry being a greater poet than Lizette Reese, or
Mrs. Humphrey Ward having it all over Dreiser.

Sincerely yours,

H. L. Mencken

❖❖❖❖❖❖❖❖❖❖❖❖❖

To UPTON SINCLAIR

H. L. Mencken
1524 Hollins St.
Baltimore
August 24th [1923]

DEAR SINCLAIR:—

"The Goslings," unluckily, finds me in an unexpected situation. I am leaving the Smart Set next month to start a new serious
review, and hence cannot buy a serial for the former. And the new
review probably will not begin before January, and so it could not

use any substantial part of "The Goslings" before the publication of the complete book. The Los Angeles section, as it stands, would make, of course, far more than one installment, and in view of the plan upon which you have written it I see no way to cut it materially without grave damage to it. So the whole scheme seems to blow up. The enclosed stuff is excellent. I have read every word of it, and with constant interest.

Now to the new review. Knopf is to be the publisher, and it is to be a genuinely first-rate monthly, well printed on good paper. I shall try to cut a rather wide swathe in it, covering politics, economics, the exact sciences, etc., as well as belles lettres and the other fine arts. I have some promises of stuff from men who have something to say and know how to write, and I hope to stir up the animals. In politics it will be, in the main, Tory, but *civilized* Tory. You know me well enough to know that there will be no quarter for the degraded cads who now run the country. I am against you and against the Liberals because I believe you chase butterflies, but I am even more against your enemies.

Nothing would delight me more [than] to have a roaring article from you in the first number. I go further, and suggest a subject. Why not a sort of reminiscent and autobiographical chapter, "aus meinem Leben," rehearsing realistically your adventures as a reformer—not the objective facts and struggles, but the psychological adventures and observations. Isn't it a fact that the majority of people, even those who are most obviously oppressed, are quite devoid of any comprehension of liberty—that they are contented in their wallow? Haven't you, as a matter of actual experience, found them apathetic and even hostile? It is my own observation that liberty seems dangerous to all ordinary men— that respect for it and love of it are confined to small classes. Think of the doings of the American Legion!

But maybe this notion doesn't appeal to you. If not, what other ideas have you? I needn't point out that this new review would get you before an entirely new audience—a cynical one, perhaps, and impatient of exhortation, but nevertheless one with a keen relish for wit and a decent attitude toward opponents. Give the matter your prayers.

Yours,
Mencken

◇◇◇◇◇◇◇◇◇◇◇◇◇

To GEORGE JEAN NATHAN[2]

The American Mercury
October 19th [*1924*]

DEAR GEORGE:–

What I am thinking of is the future—two, five or ten years hence. In particular, I am thinking of my own future. As things stand, I see nothing ahead save a round of dull drudgery, with no chance to lift the magazine out of casualness and triviality and to make it of solid dignity and influence. Its present apparent success, I believe, is largely illusory. It is appealing mainly to a superficial and unstable class of readers. Their support is not to be depended on. They buy it at the newsstands, and gabble about it intermittently, but they are not permanently interested in ideas. What the magazine needs is a sounder underpinning. It must develop a more coherent body of doctrine, and maintain it with more vigor. It must seek to lead, not a miscellaneous and frivolous rabble, but the class that is serious at bottom, however much it may mock conventional seriousness. There is great significance, I believe, in the fact that the most successful thing we have ever printed, and by long odds, was the Kent article on Coolidge. It proved that the civilized minority, after all, *does* take politics seriously.[3]

You mention the Smart Set, and say that I was wrong about it. I believe, on the contrary, that I was right every time. The Smart Set went to pot because it was too trivial—because it interested intelligent readers only intermittently, and then only when they were in trifling moods—when they were, so to speak, a bit stewed intellectually. Eventually, many of them tired of it—because it got nowhere. Their reading of the magazine be-

---

[2] [It was not long before Mencken and Nathan disagreed on the editorial policy of the *Mercury;* George Jean Nathan cared nothing for politics, and Mencken cared less and less for art. On February 19, 1925, Nathan ceased being co-editor and became contributing editor; but it was not until 1930 that he left the magazine entirely. The following letter throws some light on what the public long considered a mystery. G.F.]

[3] [The Kent article: "Mr. Coolidge," by Frank R. Kent, in the August 1924 *Mercury.* G.F.]

came irregular, and so its circulation declined. As you will recall, I proposed at least a dozen times that we put more solid stuff into it. We could never agree as to the character of this solid stuff, and I thus lost interest in it. During its last three or four years I certainly put no hard work and thought into it. I simply slopped along. I don't want to do this with the American Mercury. Too much is at stake in it. On the Smart Set we could hide behind the obvious handicaps—the absurd name, the wretched printing, the imbecility of Warner, and so on. But now we are out in the open, with the harsh sunlight on us.

I believe that either of us, convinced of all this and with a simple and vigorous policy, could make the American Mercury something very much better than it is, and give it eventually the solid position of the Atlantic, or even a better position. Its chances are not unlike those which confronted the Atlantic in the years directly after the Civil War: it has an opportunity to seize leadership of the genuinely civilized minority of Americans. But I doubt that the job thus presented is one for two men: divided councils make for too much irresolution and compromise. In particular, I doubt that you and I could carry it off together. Our interests are too far apart. We see the world in wholly different colors. When we agree, it is mainly on trivialities. This fundamental difference was of relatively small consequence on the Smart Set, for neither of us took the magazine very seriously: the presence of Warner made it impossible. But it is different with the American Mercury. I see no chance of coming close together. On the contrary, I believe that we are drifting further and further apart. I cite an obvious proof of it: we no longer play together. Another: when we sit down to discuss the magazine itself we are off it in ten minutes.

What is to be done I don't know. But I believe the matter ought to be talked out. I can see clearly only what is ahead for myself. My current job tends to irritate me. I am tied to routine, and much of it is routine that shouldn't be thrown on me—for example, watching the printer, and especially the make-up man. Page 374 in the November issue is in point. If I get out of contact with the office for three days my desk is in chaos. All this makes it a practical impossibility for me to do what I ought to do, and what Sedgwick does—that is, track down ideas, manuscripts and authors. I have duties that are antagonistic, and that kill each other. If I go on, I'll slide inevitably, in self-protection, into the easier of them. In other words, I'll do precisely what I did on the Smart Set. I could work with a competent slave, but I can't work when I must be that slave myself.

But I don't want to make this a roster of grievances. You have your own troubles, and some of them are worse than mine. All I suggest is that we sit down and look at the situation realistically, and try to remedy it if it can be remedied. It goes without saying that I am willing to go on as now until a remedy can be found. But nothing is to be gained by evasions. It ought to be clearly understood by all hands that I am dissatisfied with the present scheme, and that its continuance is bound to make me less and less useful to the magazine. Look at my December book article: it is dreadful stuff. I therefore propose a palaver. Why should we quarrel? Either I am right or I am wrong. If I am right, I assume that everyone will agree. If I am wrong, I engage to shut up.

[*M.*]

◇◇◇◇◇◇◇◇◇◇◇

To SARA P. HAARDT[4]

H. L. Mencken
1524 Hollins St.
Baltimore.
January 22, 1925

DEAR SARA:—

You tell me too little about yourself. How do you feel? I don't preach patience to you so much as cynicism: it is the most comforting of philosophies. You will get over your present difficulties only to run into something worse, and so on until the last sad scene. Make up your mind to it—and then make the best of it. If you can't write a book a year, then write one every two years.

---

[4] [Sara Haardt's health was never very good; at the time of this letter, she was under treatment in a Maryland sanitarium for tuberculosis of the lungs. G.F.]

I believe that life is a constant oscillation between the sharp horns of dilemmas. I work like a dog, and accomplish nothing that really interests me. Once I gave up all routine work and devoted myself to a book: I was sick of it in six months, and went back to answering letters and reading MSS.

Nevertheless, life remains livable. Biological necessities keep us going. It is the feeling of exerting effort that exhilarates us, as a grasshopper is exhilarated by jumping. A hard job, full of impediments, is thus more satisfying than an easy job. When I get letters from Germ. *Gelehrten*, complaining that they are having a hell of a time, I always congratulate them. They will do good work, and enjoy it. The men at the Rockefeller Institute, with money to pay for everything they want, are unhappy, and the place is full of intrigue.

But I run on *à la* Polonius. Please excuse poor pen.

Yours,

M.

◇◇◇◇◇◇◇◇◇◇◇◇

To UPTON SINCLAIR

H. L. Mencken
1524 Hollins St.
Baltimore
September 9th [1926]

DEAR SINCLAIR:—

Your questions are easy. The government brings my magazine to you only unwillingly. It tried to ruin my business, and failed only by an inch. It charges too much for postal orders, and loses too many of them. A corporation of idiot Chinamen could do the thing better. Its machine for putting out fires is intolerably expensive and inefficient. It seldom, in fact, actually puts out a fire: they burn out. In 1904 two square miles of Baltimore burnt down. I lost a suit of clothes, the works of Richard Harding Davis, and a gross of condoms. The Army had nothing to do with the discovery of the cause of yellow fever. Its bureaucrats persecuted the men who did the work. They could have done it much more quickly if they been outside the army. It took years of effort to in-

(483)

duce the government to fight mosquitoes, and it does the work very badly today. There is malaria everywhere in the South. It is mainly responsible for the prevalence of religion down there.

You shock me with your government worship. It is unmanly. Today I got word from a friend who lately had a session with a Department of Justice moron. The moron told him that I was on the official list of Bolshevik agents, and that the American Mercury was backed by Russian money. What do you make of that! I am tempted to confess.

Yours,
Mencken

◇◇◇◇◇◇◇◇◇◇◇◇◇

To UPTON SINCLAIR

H. L. Mencken
1524 Hollins St.
Baltimore
May 2, 1936

DEAR SINCLAIR:

I can see nothing unfair or insulting in that somewhat jocose but still quite reasonable speculation. When you proposed to become the savior and boss of California, and then of the United States, you invited the opinion of every citizen as to your qualifications, and with them, of your probable course of action in office. If my own views in that direction differ from your own it may be only because I am a better psychologist than you are. It seems to me that you are a professional messiah like any other, and would perform precisely like the rest if you got the chance. Once in power, you would certainly not be too polite to the money-mad widows and orphans whose stocks and bonds now haunt your dreams.

I admit that you have done more or less hollering for free speech, but how much of it did you do during the war, when free speech was most in danger? My recollection is that you actually supported Wilson. If I am right, then you also gave aid and comfort to A. Mitchell Palmer. Well, so did every other Socialist in this great Republic—every one, that is, save a handful.

The handful went to jail—for example, Rose Pastor Stokes and Gene Debs.

Your frank disapproval of my controversial technic induces me to say with equal frankness that I think your own is much worse. You have spent your life making reckless charges against all sorts of people—some of them, as when you alleged categorically that the American Mercury was financed by unnamed "men of wealth," completely false—and yet you set up a horrible clatter every time you are put on the block yourself. It seems to me that a world-saver ought to be more philosophical, not to say more sportsmanlike.

I am against the violation of civil rights by Hitler and Mussolini as much as you are, and well you know it. But I am also against the wholesale murders, confiscations and other outrages that have gone on in Russia. I think it is fair to say that you pseudo-Communists are far from consistent here. You protest, and with justice, every time Hitler jails an opponent, but you forget that Stalin and company have jailed and murdered a thousand times as many. It seems to me, and indeed the evidence is plain, that compared to the Moscow brigands and assassins, Hitler is hardly more than a common Ku Kluxer and Mussolini almost a philanthropist.

If you will denounce the orgy of sadistic fury that has gone on in Russia in terms at least as violent as those you have applied to your political opponents for years past, then I'll be glad to print your denunciation, and to hail you with joy as a convert to fair play. And if you will acknowledge publicly that your quack friend, Dr. Albert Abrams, was a fraud, and that your support of his spondylotherapy was idiotic, then I'll engage to cease mentioning it. But you can't ask me to stop discussing you freely, and speculating about your political and other hallucinations so long as you keep on trying to get on the public payroll, trafficking with (and being gulled by) such obvious demagogues as Roosevelt, making whoopee out of the pathetic hopes and illusions of poor and miserable people, and reviling everyone who shows better taste and better sense than you do.

In political controversy there is such a thing as give-and-take. If you want to speak your mind freely, you must let your opponents speak their minds freely, even when what they have to say collides with your vanity and violates your peculiar notions of the true, the good and the beautiful, whether in politics, theology or pathology. It seems to me that you fail here. You are far, far better on the give than on the take. No man in American history has denounced more different people than you have, or in more violent terms, and yet no man that I can recall complains more bitterly when he happens to be hit. Why not stop your caterwauling for a while, and try to play the game according to the rules?

Yours,
Mencken

◇◇◇◇◇◇◇◇◇◇◇◇

To UPTON SINCLAIR

H. L. Mencken
1524 Hollins St.
Baltimore
May 12, 1936

MY DEAR SINCLAIR:

You duck artfully, but not enough to get out of range. *Exemplia gratia:*

1. You protested when the late A. Mitchell Palmer jailed Reds, but all the while you supported his boss, Wilson. In other words, you objected to the St. Valentinc's Day massacre, but certified to the virtue of Al Capone.

2. The American Mercury was *not* backed by "gentlemen of wealth." Every cent of the small sum it took to launch it was supplied by its publisher, Alfred Knopf. In a few months the magazine was paying its own way. When I showed your nonsense to Knopf, he laughed, and in the American Mercury for February, 1928 I laughed too, as all sensible men laugh at palpable imbecilities.

3. The difference between Abrams's spondylotherapy and his electronic vibrations was the difference between tweedledum and tweedledee. Both were bald and shameless frauds. If you will produce evidence that Lord Horder, or any other reputable

medical man, ever said that either would cure syphilis and cancer, which is what Abrams claimed for both, I'll stop mentioning your childish belief in his *bona fides*.

You evade the question of your political sword-swallowing. What is to be thought of a great lover of the down-trodden who ran for Congress as a Socialist in 1920, for the United States Senate as a Socialist in 1922, for Governor of California as a Socialist in 1926, and then popped up in 1934 as a life-long Democrat, and entered upon negotiations with such professional politicians as Franklin D. Roosevelt and Jim Farley, and incidentally, was taken for a ride? What is to be thought of him save that he has learned, like any other chronic job-seeker, to rise above principle? What is to be thought of him save that the itch for office has got him down, and is burning him up?

According to news items reaching the East, you were lately running for something or other again. The people of California, it appears, turned you down, along with your brother messiah, Dr. Townsend. With the utmost friendliness, I can only say that I think they showed sound judgment. They have had plenty of chance to estimate both you and Townsend, and they prefer anybody else, including even Hoover. They refused to follow you as a Socialist, they refused to follow you as a Prohibitionist, they refused to follow you as an electronic vibrator, they refused to follow you as a thought transferer, they refused to follow you as a Democrat, and now they refuse to follow you as anything whatsoever. The rule is that three strikes are out. To the bench, Comrad; to the bench!

Yours,
Mencken

X

<<<<<<<<<<<<>>>>>>>>>>>>>

Miscellany

❀ · ❀ · ❀ · ❀ · ❀

Mencken's miscellaneous writing constitutes the bulk of his work. In 1949 he published a selection of miscellany in a volume entitled A Mencken Chrestomathy. *It is a large book, but it represents only a fraction of this material. In many ways it is the most satisfying of all Mencken's books, and in the whole range of American letters it has no parallel. It is a work that can be read simply as recreation, for, although it is full of serious judgments in a variety of fields, they are overlaid with the Mencken exuberancy, which overshadows everything else. As a writer he was many things, and not least of all a comic genius. Some of the subjects to which he gave his most earnest efforts— American English, the nature of religion and morals—are of such a nature that, with the passage of time, his writing on them may survive only historically. In fields of rapidly accumulating data, studies like Mencken's are seldom the last word. But his miscellaneous writings have qualities of a different order. They are the product of an acute observer of the human scene who was attracted by both its droll and its tragic aspects.*

Mencken experimented with literary forms, particularly the brief comment and the aphorism. In fact, the last volume to which he put his hand, which was published after his death, was a notebook. The comment and the aphorism are, of course, well-known forms to the European man of letters, but they have never been extensively culti-vated by his American counterpart. Mencken's control of both forms was evident early in his career. He also experimented with sketches of human types in the tradition of Theophrastus and La Bruyère, and published twenty-two of them, for the most part in the Smart Set. *For example:*

THE ROMANTIC

There is a variety of man whose eye inevitably exaggerates, whose ear inevitably hears more than the band plays, whose imagination inevitably doubles and triples the news brought in by his five senses. He is the enthusiast, the believer, the romantic. He is the sort of fellow who, if he were a bacteriologist, would report the streptococcus pyogenes to be as large as a St. Bernard dog, as intelligent as Socrates, as beautiful as Beauvais Cathedral and as respectable as a Yale professor.

All twenty-two sketches are collected in the Mencken Chrestomathy.

Christmas Story

❮❮❮❮❮❮❮❮❮❮❮❮❮❮❮❮❮❮❮❮❮❮❮❮❮❮❮❮❮❮❮❯❯❯❯❯❯❯❯❯❯❯❯❯❯❯❯❯❯❯❯❯❯❯❯❯❯❯❯❯❯

ᴅᴇsᴘɪᴛᴇ all the snorting against them in works of divinity, it has always been my experience that infidels—or free-thinkers, as they usually prefer to call themselves—are a generally estimable class of men, with strong overtones of the benevolent and even of the sentimental. This was certainly true, for example, of Leopold Bortsch, *Totsäufer*[1] for the Scharnhorst Brewery, in Baltimore, forty-five years ago, whose story I have told, alas only piecemeal, in various previous communications to the press. If you want a bird's-eye view of his character, you can do no better than turn to the famous specifications for an ideal bishop in I Timothy ɪɪɪ, 2–6. So far as I know, no bishop now in practice on earth meets those specifications precisely, and more than one whom I could mention falls short of them by miles, but Leopold qualified under at least eleven of the sixteen counts, and under some of them he really shone.

He was extremely liberal (at least with the brewery's money), he had only one wife (a natural blonde weighing a hundred and eighty-five pounds) and treated her with great humanity, he was (I quote the text) "no striker . . . not a brawler," and he was preeminently "vigilant, sober, of good behavior, given to hospitality, apt to teach." Not once in the days I knew and

---

First printed as "Stare Decisis" in *The New Yorker*, Dec. 30, 1944. Copyright 1944, 1946 by H. L. Mencken. The story was published by Alfred A. Knopf, Inc., in 1946 as a small volume with illustrations by Bill Crawford. It carried an acknowledgment by H.L.M. that "in writing it I had valuable suggestions from my brother, August Mencken."

[1] A *Totsäufer* (literally, dead-drinker) is a brewery's customers' man. One of his most important duties is to carry on in a wild and inconsolable manner at the funerals of saloonkeepers.

admired him, *c.* 1900, did he ever show anything remotely resembling a bellicose and rowdy spirit, not even against the primeval Prohibitionists of the age, the Lutheran pastors who so often plastered him from the pulpit, or the saloonkeepers who refused to lay in Scharnhorst beer. He was a sincere friend to the orphans, the aged, all blind and one-legged men, ruined girls, opium fiends, Chinamen, oyster dredgers, ex-convicts, the more respectable sort of colored people, and all the other oppressed and unfortunate classes of the time, and he slipped them, first and last, many a substantial piece of money.

Nor was he the only Baltimore infidel of those days who thus shamed the churchly. Indeed, the name of one of his buddies, Fred Ammermeyer, jumps into my memory at once. Fred and Leopold, I gathered, had serious dogmatic differences, for there are as many variations in doctrine between infidels as between Christians, but the essential benignity of both men kept them on amicable terms, and they often cooperated in good works. The only noticeable difference between them was that Fred usually tried to sneak a little propaganda into his operations—a dodge that the more scrupulous Leopold was careful to avoid. Thus, when a call went out for Bibles for the paupers lodged in Bayview, the Baltimore almshouse, Fred responded under an assumed name with a gross that had to be scrapped at once, for he had marked all the more antinomian passages with a red, indelible pencil—for example, Proverbs VII, 18–19; Luke XII, 19; I Timothy v, 23; and the account of David's dealing with Uriah in II Samuel XI. Again, he once hired Charlie Metcalfe, a small-time candy manufacturer, to prepare a special pack of chocolate drops for orphans and ruined girls with a deceptive portrait of Admiral Dewey on the cover and a print of Bob Ingersoll's harangue over his brother's remains at the bottom of each box. Fred had this subversive exequium reprinted many times, and distributed at least two hundred and fifty thousand copies in Baltimore between 1895 and 1900. There were some Sunday-school scholars who received, by one device or another, at least a dozen. As for the clergy of the town, he sent each and every one of them a copy of Paine's "Age of Reason" three or four times a year—always disguised as a special-delivery or registered letter marked "Urgent." Finally, he employed seedy rabble-rousers to mount soapboxes at downtown street corners on Saturday nights and there bombard the assembled loafers, peddlers, and cops with speeches which began seductively as excoriations of the Interests and then proceeded inch by inch to horrifying proofs that there was no hell.

But in the masterpiece of Fred Ammermeyer's benevolent career there was no such attempt at direct missionarying; indeed, his main idea when he conceived it was to hold up to scorn and contumely, by the force of mere contrast, the crude missionarying of his theological opponents. This idea seized him one evening when he dropped into the Central Police Station to pass the time of day with an old friend, a police lieutenant who was then the only known freethinker on the Baltimore force. Christmas was approaching and the lieutenant was in an unhappy and rebellious frame of mind—not because he objected to its orgies as such, or because he sought to deny Christians its beautiful consolations, but simply and solely because he always had the job of keeping order at the annual free dinner by the massed missions of the town to the derelicts of the waterfront, and that duty compelled him to listen politely to a long string of pious exhortations, many of them from persons he knew to be whited sepulchres.

"Why in hell," he observed impatiently, "do all them goddam hypocrites keep the poor bums waiting for two, three hours while they get off their goddam whimwham? Here is a hall full of men who ain't had nothing to speak of to eat for maybe three, four days, and yet they have to set there smelling the turkey and the coffee while ten, fifteen Sunday-school superintendents and W.C.T.U. sisters sing hymns to them and holler against booze. I tell you, Mr. Ammermeyer, it ain't human. More than once I have saw a whole row of them poor bums pass out in faints, and had to send them away in the wagon. And then, when the chow is circulated at last, and they begin fighting for the turkey bones, they ain't hardly got the stuff down before the superintendents and the sisters begin calling on them to stand up and confess whatever skulduggery they have done in the past, whether they really done it or not, *with us cops standing all around*. And every man Jack of them knows that if they don't lay it on plenty thick there won't be no encore of the giblets and stuffing, and two times out of three there ain't no encore anyhow, for them psalm singers are the stingiest outfit outside hell and never give a starving bum enough solid feed to last him until Christmas Monday. And not a damned drop to drink! Nothing but coffee—and without no milk! I tell you, Mr. Ammermeyer, it makes a man's blood boil."

Fred's duly boiled, and to immediate effect. By noon the next day he had rented the largest hall on the waterfront and sent word to the newspapers that arrangements for a Christmas party for bums to end all Christmas parties for bums were under way. His plan for it was extremely simple. The first obligation of hospitality, he announced somewhat prissily, was to find out precisely what one's guests wanted, and the second was to give it to them with a free and even reckless hand. As for what his proposed guests wanted, he had no shade of doubt, for he was a man of worldly experience and he had also, of course, the advice of his friend the lieutenant, a recognized expert in the psychology of the abandoned.

First and foremost, they wanted as much malt liquor as they would buy themselves if they had the means to buy it. Second, they wanted a dinner that went on in rhythmic waves, all day and all night, until the hungriest and hollowest bum was reduced to breathing with not more than one cylinder of one lung. Third, they wanted not a mere sufficiency but a riotous superfluity of the best five-cent cigars on sale on the Baltimore wharves. Fourth, they wanted continuous entertainment, both theatrical and musical, of a sort in consonance with their natural tastes and their station in life. Fifth and last, they wanted complete freedom from evangelical harassment of whatever sort, before, during, and after the secular ceremonies.

On this last point, Fred laid special stress, and every city editor in Baltimore had to hear him expound it in person. I was one of those city editors, and I well recall his great earnestness, amounting almost to moral indignation. It was an unendurable outrage, he argued, to invite a poor man to a free meal and then make him wait for it while he was battered with criticism of his ways, however well intended. And it was an even greater outrage to call upon him to stand up in public and confess to all the false steps of what may have been a long and much troubled life. Fred was determined, he said, to give a party that would be devoid of all the blemishes of the similar parties staged by the Salvation Army, the mission helpers, and other such nefarious outfits. If it cost him his last cent, he would give the bums of Baltimore massive and unforgettable proof that philanthropy was by no means a monopoly of gospel sharks—that its highest development, in truth, was to be found among freethinkers.

It might have cost him his last cent if he had gone it alone, for he was by no means a man of wealth, but his announcement had hardly got out before he was swamped with offers of help. Leopold Bortsch pledged twenty-five barrels of Scharnhorst beer and every other *Totsäufer* in Baltimore rushed up to match him. The Baltimore agents of the Pennsylvania two-fer factories fought for the privilege of contributing the cigars. The poultry dealers of Lexington, Fells Point, and Cross Street markets threw in barrel after barrel of dressed turkeys, some of them in very fair condition. The members of the boss bakers' association, not a few of them freethinkers themselves, promised all the bread, none more than two days old, that all the bums of the Chesapeake littoral could eat, and the public-relations counsel of the Celery Trust, the Cranberry Trust, the Sauerkraut Trust, and a dozen other such cartels and combinations leaped at the chance to serve.

If Fred had to fork up cash for any part of the chow, it must have been for the pepper and salt alone. Even the ketchup was contributed by social-minded members of the Maryland canners' association, and with it they threw in a dozen cases of dill pickles, chowchow, mustard, and mincemeat. But the rent of the hall had to be paid, and not only paid but paid in advance, for the owner thereof was a Methodist deacon, and there were many other expenses of considerable size—for example, for the entertainment, the music, the waiters and bartenders, and the mistletoe and immortelles which decorated the hall. Fred, if he had desired, might have got the free services of whole herds of amateur musicians and elocutionists, but he swept them aside disdainfully, for he was determined to give his guests a strictly professional show. The fact that a burlesque company starved out in the Deep South was currently stranded in Baltimore helped him here, for its members were glad to take an engagement at an inside rate, but the musicians' union, as usual, refused to let art or philanthropy shake its principles, and Fred had to pay six of its members the then prevailing scale of four dollars for their first eight hours of work and fifty cents an hour for overtime. He got, of course, some contributions in cash from rich freethinkers, but when the smoke cleared away at last and he totted up his books, he found that the party had set him back more than a hundred and seventy-five dollars.

Admission to it was by invitation only, and the guests were selected with a critical and bilious eye by the police lieutenant. No bum who had ever been known to do any honest work—even such light work as sweeping out a saloon—was on the list. By Fred's express and oft-repeated command it was made up wholly of men completely lost to human decency, in whose favor nothing whatsoever could be said. The doors opened at 11 a.m. of Christmas Day, and the first canto of the dinner began instantly. There were none of the usual preliminaries—no opening prayer, no singing of a hymn, no remarks by Fred himself, not even a fanfare by the band. The bums simply shuffled and shoved their way to the tables and simultaneously the waiters and sommeliers poured in with the chow and the malt. For half an hour no sound was heard save the rattle of crockery, the chomp-chomp of mastication, and the grateful grunts and "Oh, boy!"s of the assembled underprivileged.

Then the cigars were passed round (not one but half a dozen to every man), the band cut loose with the tonic chord of G major, and the burlesque company plunged into Act I, Sc. 1 of "Krausmeyer's Alley." There were in those days, as old-timers will recall, no less than five standard versions of this classic, ranging in refinement all the way from one so tony that it might have been put on at the Union Theological Seminary down to one so rowdy that it was fit only for audiences of policemen, bums, newspaper reporters, and medical students. This last was called the Cincinnati version, because Cincinnati was then the only great American city whose mores tolerated it. Fred gave instructions that it was to be played *à outrance* and *con fuoco*, with no salvo of slapsticks, however brutal, omitted, and no *double-entendre*, however daring. Let the boys have it, he instructed the chief comedian, Larry Snodgrass, straight in the eye and direct from the wood. They were poor men and full of sorrow, and he wanted to give them, on at least one red-letter day, a horse doctor's dose of the kind of humor they really liked.

In that remote era the girls of the company could add but little to the exhilarating grossness of the performance, for the strip tease was not yet invented and even the shimmy was still only nascent, but they did the best they could with the muscle dancing launched by Little Egypt at the Chicago World's Fair, and that best was not to be sneezed at, for they were all in hearty sympathy with Fred's agenda, and furthermore, they cherished the usual hope of stage folk that Charles Frohman or Abe Erlanger might be in the audience. Fred had demanded that they all appear in red tights, but there were not enough red tights in hand to outfit more than half of them, so Larry Snodgrass conceived the bold idea of sending on the rest with bare legs. It was a revolutionary indelicacy, and for a startled moment or two the police lieutenant wondered whether he was not bound by his Hippocratic oath to raid the show, but when he saw the whole audience leap up and break into cheers, his dubieties vanished, and five minutes later he was roaring himself when Larry and the other comedians began paddling the girls' cabooses with slapsticks.

I have seen many a magnificent performance of "Krausmeyer's Alley" in my time, including a Byzantine version called "Krausmeyer's Dispensary," staged by the students at the Johns Hopkins Medical School, but never have I seen a better one. Larry and his colleagues simply gave their all. Wherever, on ordinary occasions, there would have been a laugh, they evoked a roar, and where there would have been roars they produced something akin to asphyxia and apoplexy. Even the members of the musicians' union were forced more than once to lay down their fiddles and cornets and bust into laughter. In fact, they enjoyed the show so vastly that when the comedians retired for breath and the girls came out to sing "Sweet Rosie O'Grady" or "I've Been Workin' on the Railroad," the accompaniment was full of all the outlaw *glissandi* and *sforzandi* that we now associate with jazz.

(499)

The show continued at high tempo until 2 p.m., when Fred shut it down to give his guests a chance to eat the second canto of their dinner. It was a duplicate of the first in every detail, with second and third helpings of turkey, sauerkraut, mashed potatoes, and celery for everyone who called for them, and a pitcher of beer in front of each guest. The boys ground away at it for an hour, and then lit fresh cigars and leaned back comfortably for the second part of the show. It was still basically "Krausmeyer's Alley," but it was a "Krausmeyer's Alley" adorned and bedizened with reminiscences of every other burlesque-show curtain raiser and afterpiece in the repertory. It went on and on for four solid hours, with Larry and his pals bending themselves to their utmost exertions, and the girls shaking their legs in almost frantic abandon. At the end of an hour the members of the musicians' union demanded a cut-in on the beer and got it, and immediately afterward the sommeliers began passing pitchers to the performers on the stage. Meanwhile, the pitchers on the tables of the guests were kept replenished, cigars were passed round at short intervals, and the waiters came in with pretzels, potato chips, celery, radishes, and chipped beef to stay the stomachs of those accustomed to the free-lunch way of life.

At 7 p.m. precisely, Fred gave the signal for a hiatus in the entertainment, and the waiters rushed in with the third canto of the dinner. The supply of roast turkey, though it had been enormous, was beginning to show signs of wear by this time, but Fred had in reserve twenty hams and forty pork shoulders, the contribution of George Wienefeldter, president of the Weinefeldter Bros. & Schmidt Sanitary Packing Co., Inc. Also, he had a mine of reserve sauerkraut hidden down under the stage, and soon it was in free and copious circulation and the guests were taking heroic hacks at it. This time they finished in three-quarters of an hour, but Fred filled the time until 8 p.m. by ordering a seventh-inning stretch and by having the police lieutenant go to the stage and assure all hands that any bona-fide participant found on the streets, at the conclusion of the exercises, with his transmission jammed would not be clubbed and jugged, as was the Baltimore custom at the time, but returned to the hall to sleep it off on the floor. This announcement made a favorable impression, and the brethren settled down for the resumption of the show in a very pleasant mood. Larry and his associates were pretty well fagged out by now, for the sort of acting demanded by the burlesque profession is very fatiguing, but you'd never have guessed it by watching them work.

At ten the show stopped again, and there began what Fred described as a *Bierabend,* that is, a beer evening. Extra pitchers were put on every table, more cigars were handed about, and the waiters spread a substantial lunch of rye bread, rat-trap cheese, ham, bologna, potato salad, liver pudding, and *Blutwurst.* Fred announced from the stage that the performers needed a rest and would not be called upon again until twelve o'clock, when a midnight show would begin, but that in the interval any guest or guests with a tendency to song might step up and show his or their stuff. No less than a dozen volunteers at once went forward, but Fred had the happy thought of beginning with a quartet, and so all save the first four were asked to wait. The four laid their heads together, the band played the vamp of "Sweet Adeline," and they were off. It was not such singing as one hears from the Harvard Glee Club or the Bach Choir at Bethlehem, Pennsylvania, but it was at least as good as the barbershop stuff that hillbillies now emit over the radio. The other guests applauded politely, and the quartet, operating briskly under malt and hop power, proceeded to "Don't You Hear Dem Bells?" and "Aunt Dinah's Quilting Party." Then the four singers had a nose-to-nose palaver and the first tenor proceeded somewhat shakily to a conference with Otto Strauss, the leader of the orchestra.

From where I sat, at the back of the hall, beside Fred, I could see Otto shake his head, but the tenor persisted in whatever he was saying, and after a moment Otto shrugged resignedly and the members of the quartet again took their stances. Fred leaned forward eagerly, curious to hear what their next selection would be. He found out at once. It was "Are You Ready for the Judgment Day?," the prime favorite of the period in all the sailors' bethels, helping-up missions, Salvation Army bum traps, and other such joints along the waterfront. Fred's horror and amazement and sense of insult were so vast that he was completely speechless, and all I heard out of him while the singing went on was a series of sepulchral groans. The man was plainly suffering cruelly, but what could I do? What, indeed, could anyone do? For the quartet had barely got half way through the first stanza of the composition before the whole audience joined in. And it joined in with even heartier enthusiasm when the boys on the stage proceeded to "Showers of Blessings," the No. 2 favorite of all seasoned mission stiffs, and then to "Throw Out the Lifeline," and then to "Where Shall We Spend Eternity?," and then to "Wash Me, and I Shall Be Whiter Than Snow."

Half way along in this orgy of hymnody, the police lieutenant took Fred by the arm and led him out into the cold, stinging, corpse-reviving air of a Baltimore winter night. The bums, at this stage, were beating time on the tables with their beer glasses and tears were trickling down their noses. Otto and his band knew none of the hymns, so their accompaniment became sketchier and sketchier, and presently they shut down altogether. By this time the members of the quartet began to be winded, and soon there was a halt. In the ensuing silence there arose a quavering, boozy, sclerotic voice from the floor. "Friends," it began, "I just want to tell you what these good people have done for me—how their prayers have saved a sinner who seemed past all redemption. Friends, I had a good mother, and I was brought up under the influence of the Word. But in my young manhood my sainted mother was called to heaven, my poor father took to rum and opium, and I was led by the devil into the hands of wicked men—yes, and wicked women, too. Oh, what a shameful story I have to tell! It would shock you to hear it, even if I told you only half of it. I let myself be . . ."

I waited for no more, but slunk into the night. Fred and the police lieutenant had both vanished, and I didn't see Fred again for a week. But the next day I encountered the lieutenant on the street, and he hailed me sadly. "Well," he said, "what could you expect from them bums? It was the force of habit, that's what it was. They have been eating mission handouts so long they can't help it. Whenever they smell coffee, they begin to confess. Think of all that good food wasted! And all that beer! And all them cigars!"

The Divine Afflatus

<<<<<<<<<<<<<<<<<<<<<<<<<<<<<<<<<>>>>>>>>>>>>>>>>>>>>>>>>>>>>>>>>>

THE suave and edematous Chesterton, in a late effort to earn the honorarium of a Chicago newspaper, composed a thousand words of labored counterblast to what is called inspiration in the arts. The thing itself, he argued, has little if any actual existence; we hear so much about it because its alleged coyness and fortuitousness offer a convenient apology for third-rate work. The man taken in such third-rate work excuses himself on the ground that he is a helpless slave of some power that stands outside him, and is quite beyond his control. On days when it favors him he teems with ideas and creates masterpieces, but on days when it neglects him he is crippled and impotent—a fiddle without a bow, an engine without steam, a tire without air. All this, according to Chesterton, is nonsense. A man who can really write at all, or paint at all, or compose at all should be able to do it at almost any time, provided only "he is not drunk or asleep."

So far Chesterton. The formula of the argument is simple and familiar: to dispose of a problem all that is necessary is to deny that it exists. But there are plenty of men, I believe, who find themselves unable to resolve the difficulty in any such cavalier manner—men whose chief burden and distinction, in fact, is that they do not employ formulae in their thinking, but are thrown constantly upon industry, ingenuity and the favor of God. Among such men there remains a good deal more belief in what is vaguely called inspiration. They know by hard experience that there are days when their ideas flow freely and clearly, and days when they are dammed up damnably. Say a man of that sort has a good day. For some reason quite incomprehensible to him all his mental processes take on an amazing ease and slickness. Almost without conscious effort he solves technical problems that have badgered him for weeks. He is full of novel expedients, extraordinary efficiencies, strange cunnings. He has a feeling that he has suddenly and unaccountably broken through a wall, dispersed a fog, got himself out of the dark. So he does a double or triple stint of the best work that he is capable of—maybe of far better work than he has ever been capable of before—and goes to bed impatient for the morrow. And on the morrow he discovers to his consternation that he has become almost idiotic, and quite incapable of any work at all.

I challenge any man who trades in ideas to deny that he has this experience. The truth is that he has it constantly. It overtakes poets and contrapuntists, critics and dramatists, philosophers and journalists; it may even be shared, so far as I know, by advertisement writers, chautauqua orators and the rev. clergy. The characters that all anatomists of melancholy mark in it are the irregular ebb and flow of the tides, and the impossibility of getting them under any sort of rational control. The brain, as it were, stands to one side and watches itself pitching and tossing, full of agony but esentially helpless. Here the man of creative imagination pays a ghastly price for all his superiorities and immunities; nature takes revenge upon him for dreaming of improvements in the scheme of things. Sitting there in his lonely room, gnawing the handle of his pen, racked by his infernal quest, horribly bedeviled by incessant flashes of itching, toothache, eyestrain and evil conscience—thus tortured, he makes atonement for his crime of being intelligent. The normal man, the healthy and honest man, the good citizen and householder—this man, I daresay, knows nothing of all that travail. It is reserved especially for artists and metaphysicians. It is the particular penalty of those who pursue strange butterflies into dark forests, and go fishing in enchanted and forbidden streams.

Let us, then, assume that the fact is proved: the nearest poet is a witness to it. But what of the underlying mystery? How are we to account for that puckish and inexplicable rise and fall of inspiration? My questions, of course, are purely rhetorical. Explanations exist; they have existed for all time; there is always a well-known solution to every human problem—neat, plausible, and wrong. The ancients, in the case at bar, laid the blame upon the gods: sometimes they were remote and surly, and sometimes they were kind. In the Middle Ages lesser powers took a hand in the matter, and so one reads of works of art inspired by Our Lady, by the Blessed Saints, by the souls of the departed, and even by the devil. In our own day there are explanations less supernatural but no less fanciful—to wit, the explanation that the whole thing is a matter of pure chance, and not to be resolved into any orderly process—to wit, the explanation that the controlling factor is external circumstance, that the artist happily married to a dutiful wife is thereby inspired—finally, to make an end, the explanation that it is all a question of Freudian complexes, themselves lurking in impenetrable shadows. But all of these explanations fail to satisfy the mind that is not to be put off with mere words. Some of them are palpably absurd; others beg the question. The problem of the how remains, even when the problem of the why is disposed of. What is the precise machinery whereby the cerebrum is bestirred to such abnormal activity on one day that it sparkles and splutters like an arc light, and reduced to such feebleness on another day that it smokes and gutters like a tallow dip?

In this emergency, having regard for the ages-long and unrelieved sufferings of artists great and small, I offer a new, simple, and at all events not ghostly solution. It is supported by the observed facts, by logical analogies and by the soundest known principles of psychology, and so I present it without apologies. It may be couched, for convenience, in the following brief terms: that inspiration, so-called, is a function of metabolism, and that it is chiefly conditioned by the state of the intestinal flora—in larger words, that a man's flow of ideas is controlled and determined, both quantitatively and qualitatively, not by the whims of the gods, nor by the terms of his armistice with his wife, nor by the combinations of some transcendental set of dice, but by the chemical content of the blood that lifts itself from his liver to his brain, and that this chemical content is established in his digestive tract, particularly south of the pylorus. A man may write great poetry when he is drunk, when he is cold and miserable, when he is bankrupt, when he has a black eye, when his wife glowers at him across the table, when his children lie dying of smallpox; he may even write it during an earthquake, or while crossing the English channel, or in the midst of a Methodist revival, or in New York. But I am so far gone in materialism that I am disposed to deny flatly and finally, and herewith do deny flatly and finally, that there has lived a poet in the whole history of the world, ancient or modern, near or far, who ever managed to write great poetry, or even passably fair and decent poetry, at a time when he was suffering from stenosis at any point along the thirty-foot *via dolorosa* running from the pylorus to the sigmoid flexure. In other words, when he was—

But perhaps I had better leave your medical adviser to explain. After all, it is not necessary to go any further in this direction; the whole thing may be argued in terms of the blood stream —and the blood stream is respectable, as the duodenum is an outcast. It is the blood and the blood only, in fact, that the cerebrum is aware of; of what goes on elsewhere it can learn only by hearsay. If all is well below, then the blood that enters the brain through the internal carotid is full of the elements necessary to bestir the brain-cells to their highest activity; if, on the contrary, anabolism and katabolism are going on ineptly, if the blood is not getting the supplies that it needs and not getting rid of the wastes that burden it, then the brain-cells will be both starved and poisoned, and not all the king's horses and all the king's men can make them do their work with any show of ease and efficiency. In the first case the man whose psyche dwells in the cells will have a moment of inspiration—that is, he will find it a strangely simple and facile matter to write his poem, or iron out his syllogism, or make his bold modulation from F sharp minor to C major, or get his flesh-tone, or maybe only perfect his swindle. But in the second case he will be stumped and helpless. The more he tries, the more vividly he will be conscious of his impotence. Sweat will stand out in beads upon his brow, he will fish patiently for the elusive thought, he will try coaxing and subterfuge, he will retire to his ivory tower, he will tempt the invisible powers with black coffee, tea, alcohol and the alkaloids, he may even curse God and invite death—but he will not write his poem, or iron out his syllogism, or find his way into C major, or get his flesh-tone, or perfect his swindle.

Fix your eye upon this hypothesis of metabolic inspiration, and at once you will find the key to many a correlative mystery. For one thing, it quickly explains the observed hopelessness of trying to pump up inspiration by mere hard industry—the essential imbecility of the 1,000 words a day formula. Let there be stenosis below, and not all the industry of a Hercules will suffice to awaken the lethargic brain. Here, indeed, the harder the striving, the worse the stagnation—as every artist knows only too well. And why not? Striving in the face of such an interior obstacle is the most cruel of enterprises—a business more nerve-racking and exhausting than reading a newspaper or watching a bad play. The pain thus produced, the emotions thus engendered, react upon the liver in a manner scientifically displayed by Dr. George W. Crile in his "Man: An Adaptive Mechanism," and the result is a steady increase in the intestinal demoralization, and a like increase in the pollution of the blood. In the end the poor victim comes to a familiar pass; beset on the one hand by impotence and on the other hand by an impatience grown pathological, he gets into a state indistinguishable from the frantic. It is at such times that creative artists suffer most atrociously. It is then that they writhe upon the sharp spears and red-hot hooks of a jealous and unjust Creator for their invasion of His monopoly. It is then that they pay a grisly super-tax upon their superiority to the great herd of law-abiding and undistinguished men. The men of this herd never undergo any comparable torture; the agony of the artist is quite beyond their experience and even beyond their imagination. No catastrophe that could conceivably overtake a lime and cement dealer, a curb-broker, a lawyer, a plumber or a Presbyterian is to be mentioned in the same breath with the torments that, to the most minor of poets, are familiar incidents of his professional life, and, to such a man as Poe, or Beethoven, or Brahms, are the commonplaces of every day. Beethoven suffered more during the composition of the Fifth Symphony than all the judges on the supreme benches of the world have suffered jointly since the time of the Gerousia.

Again, my hypothesis explains the fact that inspiration, save under extraordinary circumstances, is never continuous for more than a relatively short period. A banker, a barber or a manufacturer of patent medicines does his work day after day without any noticeable rise or fall of efficiency; save when he is drunk, jailed or ill in bed the curve of his achievement is flattened out until it becomes almost a straight line. But the curve of an artist, even of the greatest of artists, is frightfully zigzagged. There are moments when it sinks below the bottom of the chart, and immediately following there may be moments when it threatens to run off the top. Some of the noblest passages written by Shakespeare are in his worst plays, cheek by jowl with padding and banality; some of the worst music of Wagner is in his finest music dramas. There is, indeed, no such thing as a flawless masterpiece. Long labored, it may be gradually enriched with purple passages—the high inspirations of widely separated times crowded together— but even so it will remain spotty, for those purple passages will be clumsily joined, and their joints will remain as apparent as so many false teeth. Only the most elementary knowledge of psychology is needed to show the cause of the zigzagging that I have mentioned. It lies in the elemental fact that the chemical constitution of the blood changes ever hour, almost every minute. What it is at the beginning of digestion is not what it is at the end of digestion, and in both cases it is enormously affected by the nature of the substances digested. No man, within twenty-four hours after eating a meal in a Pennsylvania Railroad dining-car, could conceivably write anything worth reading. A tough beefsteak, I daresay, has ditched many a promising sonnet, and bad beer, as every one knows, has spoiled hundreds of sonatas. Thus inspiration rises and falls, and even when it rises twice to the same height it usually shows some qualitative difference—there is the inspiration, say, of spring vegetables and there is the inspiration of autumn fruits. In a long work the products of greatly differing inspirations, of greatly differing streams of blood, are hideously intermingled, and the result is the inevitable spottiness that I have mentioned. No one but a maniac argues that "Die Meistersinger" is *all* good. One detects in it days when Wagner felt, as the saying goes, like a fighting cock, but one also detects days when he arose in the morning full of acidosis and despair— days when he turned heavily from the Pierian spring to castor oil.

Moreover, it must be obvious that the very conditions under which works of art are produced tend to cause great aberrations in metabolism. The artist is forced by his calling to be a sedentary man. Even a poet, perhaps the freest of artists, must spend a good deal of time bending over a desk. He may conceive his poems in the open air, as Beethoven conceived his music, but the work of reducing them to actual words requires diligent effort in camera. Here it is a sheer impossibility for him to enjoy the ideal hygienic conditions which surround the farmhand, the curb-broker and the sailor. His viscera are congested; his eyes are astrain; his muscles are without necessary exercise. Furthermore, he probably breathes bad air and goes without needed sleep. The result is inevitably some disturbance of metabolism, with a vitiated blood supply and a starved cerebrum. One is always surprised to encounter a poet who is ruddy and stout; the standard model is a pale and flabby stenotic, kept alive by patent medicines. So with the painter, the musical composer, the sculptor, the artist in prose. There is no more confining work known to man than instrumentation. The composer who has spent a day at it is invariably nervous and ill. For hours his body is bent over his music-paper, the while his pen engrosses little dots upon thin lines. I have known composers, after a week or so of such labor, to come down with auto-intoxication in its most virulent forms. Perhaps the notorious ill health of Beethoven, and the mental breakdowns of Schumann, Tschaikovsky and Hugo Wolf had their origin in this direction. It is difficult, going through the history of music, to find a single composer in the grand manner who was physically and mentally up to par.

I do not advance it as a formal corollary, but no doubt this stenosis hypothesis also throws some light upon two other immemorial mysteries, the first being the relative aesthetic sterility of women, and the other being the low aesthetic development of certain whole classes, and even races of men, *e.g.*, the Puritans, the Welsh and the Confederate Americans. That women suffer from stenosis far more than men is a commonplace of internal medicine; the weakness is chiefly to blame, rather than the functional peculiarities that they accuse, for their liability to headache. A good many of them, in fact, are habitually in the state of health which, in the artist, is accompanied by an utter inability to work. This state of health, as I have said, does not inhibit *all* mental activity. It leaves the powers of observation but little impaired; it does not currupt common sense; it is not incompatible with an intelligent discharge of the ordinary duties of life. Thus a lime and cement dealer, in the midst of it, may function almost as well as when his metabolic processes are perfectly normal, and by the same token a woman chronically a victim to it may yet show all the sharp mental competence which characterizes her sex. But here the thing stops. To go beyond—to enter the realm of constructive thinking, to abandon the mere application of old ideas and essay to invent new ideas, to precipitate novel and intellectual concepts out of the chaos of memory and perception—this is quite impossible to the stenotic. *Ergo,* it is unheard of among classes and races of men who feed grossly and neglect personal hygiene; the pill-swallower is the only artist in such groups. One may thus argue that the elder Beecham saved poetry in England, as the younger Beecham saved music. . . . But, as I say, I do not stand behind the hypothesis in this department, save, perhaps, in the matter of women. I could amass enormous evidences in favor of it, but against them there would always loom the disconcerting contrary evidence of the Bulgarians. Among them, I suppose, stenosis must be unknown—but so are all the fine arts.

"*La force et la faiblesse de l'esprit,*" said Rochefoucauld, "*sont mal nommées; elles ne sont, en effect, que la bonne ou la mauvaise des organes du corps.*" Science wastes itself hunting in the other direction. We are flooded with evidences of the effects of the mind on the body, and so our attention is diverted from the enormously greater effects of the body on the mind. It is rather astonishing that the Wassermann reaction has not caused the latter to be investigated more thoroughly. The first result of the general employment of that great diagnostic device was the discovery that thousands of cases of so-called mental disease were really purely physical in origin—that thousands of patients long supposed to have been crazed by seeing ghosts, by love, by grief, or by reverses in the stock-market were actually victims of the small but extremely enterprising *spirochaete pallida*. The news heaved a bomb into psychiatry, but it has so far failed to provoke a study of the effects of other such physical agents. Even the effects of this one agent remain to be inquired into at length. One now knows that it may cause insanity, but what of the lesser mental aberrations that it produces? Some of these aberrations may be actually beneficial. That is to say, the mild toxemia accompanying the less virulent forms of infection may stimulate the brain to its highest functioning, and so give birth to what is called genius—a state of mind long recognized, by popular empiricism, as a sort of half-way station on the road to insanity. Beethoven, Nietzsche and Schopenhauer suffered from such mild toxemias, and there is not the slightest doubt that their extraordinary mental activity was at least partly due to the fact. That tuberculosis, in its early stages, is capable of the same stimulation is a commonplace of observation. The consumptive may be weak physically, but he is usually very alert mentally. The history of the arts, in fact, shows the names of hundreds of inspired consumptives.

Here a physical infirmity produces a result that is beneficial, just as another physical infirmity, the stenosis aforesaid, produces a result that is baleful. The artist often oscillates horribly between the two effects; he is normally anything but a healthy animal. Perfect health, indeed, is a boon that very few men above the rank of clodhoppers ever enjoy. What health means is a degree of adaptation to the organism's environment so nearly complete that there is no irritation. Such a state, it must be obvious, is not often to be observed in organisms of the highest complexity. It is common, perhaps, in the earthworm. This elemental beast makes few demands upon its environment, and is thus subject to few diseases. It seldom gets out of order until the sands of its life are run, and then it suffers one grand illness and dies forthwith. But man is forever getting out of order, for he is enormously complicated—and the higher he rises in complexity, the more numerous and the more serious are his derangements. There are whole categories of diseases, *e.g.*, neurasthenia and hay fever, that afflict chiefly the more civilized and delicate ranks of men, leaving the inferior orders unscathed. Good health in man, indeed, is almost invariably a function of inferiority. A professionally healthy man, *e.g.*, an acrobat, an osteopath or an ice-wagon driver, is always stupid. In the Greece of the great days the athletes we hear so much about were mainly slaves. Not one of the eminent philosophers, poets or statesmen of Greece was a good high-jumper. Nearly all of them, in fact, suffered from the same malaises which afflict their successors of today, as you will quickly discern by examining their compositions. The aesthetic impulse, like the thirst for truth, might almost be called a disease. It seldom if ever appears in a perfectly healthy man.

But we must take the aloes with the honey. The artist suffers damnably, but there is compensation in his dreams. Some of his characteristic diseases cripple him and make his whole life a misery, but there are others that seem to help him. Of the latter, the two that I have mentioned carry with them concepts of extreme obnoxiousness. Both are infections, and one is associated in the popular mind with notions of gross immorality. But these concepts of obnoxiousness should not blind us to the benefits that apparently go with the maladies. There are, in fact, maladies much more obnoxious, and they carry no compensating benefits. Cancer is an example. Perhaps the time will come when the precise effects of these diseases will be worked out accurately, and it will be possible to gauge in advance their probable influence upon this or that individual. If that time ever comes the manufacture of artists will become a feasible procedure, like the present manufacture of soldiers, capons, right-thinkers and doctors of philosophy. In those days the promising young men of the race, instead of being protected from such diseases at all hazards, will be deliberately infected with them, as soils are now inoculated with nitrogen-liberating bacteria. . . . At the same time, let us hope, some progress will be made against stenosis. It is, after all, simply a question of technique, like the artificial propagation of the race by the device of Dr. Jacques Loeb. The poet of the future, come upon a period of doldrums, will not tear his hair in futile agony. Instead, he will go to the nearest clinic, and there get his rasher of Bulgarian bacilli, or an injection of some complex organic compound out of a ductless gland, or an order on a masseur, or a diet list, or perchance a barrel of Russian oil.

(512)

Star-Spangled Men

<<<<<<<<<<<<<<<<<<<<<<<<<<<<<<<<<<>>>>>>>>>>>>>>>>>>>>>>>>>>>>>>>>>>

This piece belongs to my private archeology. It is dated beyond repair, but I print it because it is full of my view of the issues
and leaders of World War I. In World War II, I took a similar line,
but by that time I had ceased to write on public matters and so not
much indication of it got on paper. In World War I, as I indicate,
there were no gauds for civilians, but that lack was remedied in a
wholesale manner in World War II.

I OPEN the memoirs of General Grant, Volume II, at the place
where he is describing the surrender of General Lee, and
find the following:

I was without a sword, as I usually was when on horseback
on the field, and wore a soldier's blouse for a coat, with the
shoulder straps of my rank to indicate to the army who I was.

Anno 1865. I look out of my window and observe an officer
of the United States Army passing down the street. Anno 1922.
Like General Grant, he is without a sword. Like General Grant,
he wears a sort of soldier's blouse for a coat. Like General Grant,
he employs shoulder straps to indicate to the army who he is.
But there is something more. On the left breast of this officer, apparently a major, there blazes so brilliant a mass of color that, as
the sun strikes it and the flash bangs my eyes, I wink, catch my
breath and sneeze. There are two long strips, each starting at the
sternum and disappearing into the shadows of the axilla—every
hue in the rainbow, the spectroscope, the kaleidoscope—imperial
purples, *sforzando* reds, wild Irish greens, romantic blues, loud

From *A Mencken Chrestomathy*, 1949. Included in *Prejudices: Third Series*, 1922.
First printed in the *New Republic*, Sept. 29, 1920. Copyright 1922 by Alfred A.
Knopf, Inc. Renewal copyright 1950 by H. L. Mencken.

yellows and oranges, rich maroons, sentimental pinks, all the half-tones from ultra-violet to infra-red, all the vibrations from the impalpable to the unendurable. A gallant *Soldat* indeed! How he would shame a circus ticket-wagon if he wore all the medals and badges, the stars and crosses, the pendants and lavallières, that go with those ribbons! . . . I glance at his sleeves. A simple golden stripe on the one—six months beyond the raging main. None on the other—the Kaiser's cannon missed him.

Just what all these ribbons signify I am sure I don't know; probably they belong to campaign medals and tell the tale of butcheries in foreign and domestic parts—mountains of dead Filipinos, Mexicans, Haitians, Dominicans, West Virginia miners, perhaps even Prussians. But in addition to campaign medals and the Distinguished Service Medal there are now certainly enough foreign orders in the United States to give a distinct brilliance to the national scene, viewed, say, from Mars. The Frederician tradition, borrowed by the ragged Continentals and embodied in Article I, Section 9, of the Constitution, lasted until 1918, and then suddenly blew up; to mention it today is a sort of indecorum, and tomorrow, no doubt, will be a species of treason. Down with Frederick; up with John Philip Sousa! Imagine what Sir John Pershing would look like at a state banquet of his favorite American order, the Benevolent and Protective one of Elks, in all the Byzantine splendor of his casket of ribbons, badges, stars, garters, sunbursts and cockades—the lordly Bath of the grateful motherland, with its somewhat disconcerting "Ich dien"; the gorgeous tricolor baldrics, sashes and festoons of the Légion d'Honneur; the grand cross of SS. Maurizio e Lazzaro of Italy; the Danilo of Montenegro, with its cabalistic monogram of Danilo I and its sinister hieroglyphics; the breastplate of the Paulownia of Japan, with its rising sun of thirty-two white rays, its blood-red heart, its background of green leaves and its white ribbon edged with red; the mystical St. Saviour of Greece, with its Greek motto and its brilliantly enameled figure of Christ; above all, the Croix de Guerre of Czecho-Slovakia, a new one and hence not listed in the books, but surely no shrinking violet.

Alas, Pershing was on the wrong side—that is, for one with a fancy for gauds of that sort. The most blinding of all known

orders is the Medijie of Turkey, which not only entitles the holder
to four wives, but also requires him to wear a red fez and a frozen
star covering his whole façade. I was offered this order by Turk-
ish spies during the war, and it wobbled me a good deal. The
Alexander of Bulgaria is almost as seductive. The badge consists
of an eight-pointed white cross, with crossed swords between the
arms and a red Bulgarian lion over the swords. The motto is *"Za
Chrabrost!"* Then there are the Prussian orders—the Red and
Black Eagles, the Pour le Mérite, the Prussian Crown, the Hohen-
zollern and the rest. And the Golden Fleece of Austria—the
noblest of them all. Think of the Golden Fleece on a man born
in Linn County, Missouri. . . . I begin to doubt that the General
would have got it, even supposing him to have taken the other
side. The Japs, I note, gave him only the grand cordon of the
Paulownia, and the Belgians and Montenegrins were similarly
cautious. There are higher classes. The highest of the Paulownia
is only for princes, which is to say, only for non-Missourians.

Pershing is the champion, with General March a bad second.
March is a K.C.M.G., and entitled to wear a large cross of white
enamel bearing a lithograph of the Archangel Michael and the
motto, *"Auspicium Melioris Aevi,"* but he is not a K.C.B.[1] Admirals
Benson and Sims are also grand crosses of Michael and George,
and like most other respectable Americans, members of the
Legion of Honor, but they seem to have been forgotten by the
Greeks and Montenegrins.[2] British-born and extremely Anglomaniacal Sims[3] refused the Distinguished Service Medal of his
adopted country, but is careful to mention in "Who's Who in
America" that his grand cross of Michael and George was con-

---

[1] March went to the Philippines as commander of the forgotten Astor Battery
and saw long and hard service here. He was a commander of the artillery in the
A.E.F. and later its chief of staff. He retired from the army in 1921. He had many
decorations besides the grand cross of the order of St. Michael and St. George, including the grand cordon of the Chia Ho of China and that of Polonia Restituta.

[2] Benson was chief of naval operations in World War I. He had the order of
the Rising Sun of Japan, the order of St. Gregory the Great, conferred by the
Pope, and a gold medal struck in his honor by New Mexico. He died in 1932.

[3] Sims was born in Canada. He was commander of the naval forces in European
waters throughout World War I. He had Japanese, Belgian and Italian orders, and
was an LL.D. of Yale, Harvard, Tufts, Pennsylvania, Columbia, Williams, Juniata,
Stevens, McGill, Queen's, California, Union, Wesleyan, and Cambridge (England).
He died in 1936.

ferred upon him, not by some servile gold-stick, but by "King George of England";[4] Benson omits mention of His Majesty, as do Pershing and March. It would be hard to think of any other American officers, real or bogus, who would refuse the D.S.M., or, failing it, the grand decoration of chivalry of the Independent Order of Odd Fellows. I once saw the latter hung, with ceremonies of the utmost magnificence, upon a bald-headed tinner who had served the fraternity long and faithfully; as he marched down the hall toward the throne of the Supreme Exalted Pishposh a score of scared little girls, the issue of other tinners, strewed his pathway with roses, and around the stem of each rose was a piece of glittering tinfoil. The band meanwhile played "The Rosary," and, at the conclusion of the spectacle, as fried oysters were served, "Wien bleibt Wien."

It was, I suspect, by way of the Odd Fellows and other such gaudy heirs to the Deutsche Ritter and the Rosicrucians that the lust to gleam and jingle got into the arteries of the American people. For years the austere tradition of Washington's day served to keep the military bosom bare of spangles, but all the while a weakness for them was growing in the civil population. Rank by rank, they became Knights of Pythias, Odd Fellows, Red Men, Nobles of the Mystic Shrine, Knights Templar, Patriarchs Militant, Elks, Moose, Woodmen of the World, Foresters, Hoo-Hoos, Ku Kluxers —and in every new order there were thirty-two degrees, and for every degree there was a badge, and for every badge there was a yard of ribbon. The Nobles of the Mystic Shrine, chiefly paunchy wholesalers of the Rotary Club species, are not content with swords, baldrics, stars, garters, jewels; they also wear red fezzes. The Elks run to rubies. The Red Men array themselves like Sitting Bull. The patriotic ice-wagon drivers and Methodist deacons of the Ku Klux Klan carry crosses set with incandescent lights. An American who is forced by his profession to belong to many such orders—say a life insurance solicitor, an undertaker or a dealer in oil stock—accumulates a trunk full of decorations, many of them weighing a pound. There is a mortician in Hagerstown, Md., who has been initiated eighteen times. When he robes

---

[4] From 1922 onward he struck this out.

himself to plant a fellow joiner he weighs three hundred pounds and sparkles and flashes like the mouth of Hell itself. He is entitled to bear seven swords, all jeweled, and to hang his watch chain with the golden busts of nine wild animals, all with precious stones for eyes. Put beside this lowly washer of the dead, Pershing newly polished would seem almost like a Trappist.

But even so the civil arm is robbed of its just dues in the department of gauds and radioactivity, no doubt by the direct operation of military vanity and jealousy. Despite a million proofs (and perhaps a billion eloquent arguments) to the contrary, it is still the theory at the official ribbon counter that the only man who serves in a war is the man who serves in uniform. This is soft for the Bevo officer,[5] who at least has his service stripes and the spurs that gnawed into his desk, but it is hard upon his brother Elmer, the dollar-a-year man, who worked twenty hours a day for fourteen months buying soap-powder, canned asparagus and raincoats for the army of God. Elmer not only labored with inconceivable diligence; he also faced hazards of no mean order, for on the one hand was his natural prejudice in favor of a very liberal rewarding of commercial enterprise, and on the other hand were his patriotism and his fear of Atlanta Penitentiary. I daresay that many and many a time, after working his twenty hours, he found it difficult to sleep the remaining four hours. I know, in fact, survivors of that obscure service who are far worse wrecks today than Pershing is. Their reward is—what? Winks, sniffs, innuendoes. If they would indulge themselves in the now almost universal American yearning to go adorned, they must join the Knights of Pythias. Even the American Legion fails them, for though it certainly does not bar non-combatants, it insists that they shall have done their non-combating in uniform.

What I propose is a variety of the Distinguished Service Medal for civilians—perhaps, better still, a distinct order for civilians, closed to the military and with badges of different colors and areas, to mark off varying services to democracy. Let it run, like the Japanese Paulownia, from high to low—the lowest class

---

[5] A Bevo officer was one who fought the wicked Hun from a desk in Washington. The name derived from that of a near-beer of the time.

for the patriot who sacrificed only time, money and a few nights'
sleep; the highest for the great martyr who hung his country's
altar with his dignity, his decency and his sacred honor. For
Elmer and his nervous insomnia, a simple rosette, with an iron
badge bearing the national motto, "Safety First"; for the university president who prohibited the teaching of the enemy language in his learned grove, heaved the works of Goethe out of the
university library, cashiered every professor unwilling to support
Woodrow for the first vacancy in the Trinity, took to the stump
for the National Security League,[6] and made two hundred
speeches in moving picture theaters—for this giant of loyal endeavor let no 100 per cent American speak of anything less than
the grand cross of the order, with a gold badge in stained glass, a
baldric of the national colors, a violet plug hat with a sunburst on
the side, the privilege of the floor of Congress, and a pension of
$10,000 a year. After all, the cost would not be excessive; there
are not many of them. Such prodigies of patriotism are possible
only to rare and gifted men. For the grand cordons of the order,
e.g., college professors who spied upon and reported the seditions
of their associates, state presidents of the American Protective
League,[7] alien property custodians, judges whose sentences of
conscientious objectors mounted to more than 50,000 years, members of George Creel's herd of 2,000 American historians, the authors of the Sisson documents,[8] etc.—pensions of $10 a day would
be enough, with silver badges and no plug hats. For the lower

---

[6] A band of patriots which made a deafening uproar in the 1914–1918 era.
Its fronts were Elihu Root and Alton B. Parker.

[7] An organization of amateur detectives working under the aegis of the Department of Justice. In 1917 its operatives reported that I was an intimate associate
and agent of "the German monster, Nietzsky," and I was solemnly investigated.
But I was a cunning fellow in those days and full of a malicious humor, so I not
only managed to throw off the charge but even to write the report upon myself.
I need not say that it gave me a clean bill of health—and I still have a carbon to
prove it. As a general rule the American Protective League confined itself to easier
victims. Its specialty was harassing German waiters.

[8] Creel served as chairman of what was called the Committee on Public Information from 1917 to 1919. Its chief business was to propagate the official doctrine as to the causes and issues of the war. To that end Creel recruited his horde
of college historians and they solemnly certified to the truth of everything that
emanated from Washington and London. The Sisson documents were supposed to
show a sinister conspiracy of the Russian Communists, but what the specifications
were I forget. Creel's committee was also in charge of newspaper censorship during
the war.

ranks, bronze badges and the legal right to the title of "The Hon.,"
already every true American's by courtesy.

Not, of course, that I am insensitive to the services of the
gentlemen of those lower ranks, but in such matters one must
go by rarity rather than by intrinsic value. If the grand cordon or
even the nickel-plated eagle of the third class were given to
every patriot who bored a hole through the floor of his flat to get
evidence against his neighbors, the Krausmeyers, and to every
one who visited the Hofbräuhaus nightly, denounced the Kaiser
in searing terms, and demanded assent from Emil and Otto, the
waiters, and to every one who notified the catchpolls of the Department of Justice when the wireless plant was open in the garret
of the Arion Liedertafel, and to all who took a brave and forward
part in slacker raids, and to all who lent their stenographers funds
at 6 per cent to buy Liberty bonds at 4¼ per cent, and to all who
sold out at 99 and then bought in again at 83.56, and to all who
served as jurors or perjurers in cases against members and ex-
members of the I.W.W., and to the German-American members
of the League for German Democracy, and to all the Irish who
snitched upon the Irish—if decorations were thrown about with
any such lavishness, then there would be no nickel left for our
bathrooms. On the civilian side as on the military side the great
rewards of war go, not to mere dogged industry and fidelity, but
to originality—to the unprecedented, the arresting, the bizarre.
The New York *Tribune* liar who invented the story about the
German plant for converting the corpses of the slain into soap did
more for democracy and the Wilsonian idealism, and hence deserves a more brilliant recognition, than a thousand uninspired
hawkers of atrocity stories supplied by Viscount Bryce and his
associates. For that great servant of righteousness the grand
cordon, with two silver badges and the chair of history at Columbia, would be scarcely enough; for the ordinary hawkers any precious metal would be too much.

Whether or not the Y.M.C.A. has decorated its chocolate
peddlers and soul-snatchers I do not know; since the chief
Y.M.C.A. lamasery in my town of Baltimore became the scene
of a homosexual scandal I have ceased to frequent evangelical
society. If not, then there should be some governmental recog-

nition of these highly characteristic heroes of the war for democracy. The veterans of the line, true enough, dislike them excessively, and have a habit of denouncing them obscenely when the corn-juice flows. They charged too much for cigarettes; they tried to discourage the amiability of the ladies of France; they had a habit of being absent when the shells burst in air. Well, some say this and some say that. A few, at least, of the pale and oleaginous brethren must have gone into the Master's work because they thirsted to save souls, and not simply because they desired to escape the trenches. And a few, I am told, were anything but unpleasantly righteous, as a round of Wassermanns would show. If, as may be plausibly argued, these Soldiers of the Double Cross deserve to live at all, then they surely deserve to be hung with white enameled stars of the third class, with gilt dollar marks superimposed. Motto: "Glory, glory, hallelujah!"

But what of the vaudeville actors, the cheer leaders, the doughnut fryers, the camp librarians, the press agents? I am not forgetting them. Let them be distributed among all the classes from the seventh to the eighth, according to their sufferings for the holy cause. And the agitators against Beethoven, Bach, Brahms, Wagner, Richard Strauss, all the rest of the cacophonous Huns? And the specialists in the crimes of the German professors? And the collectors for the Belgians, with their generous renunciation of all commissions above 80 per cent? And the pathologists who denounced Johannes Müller as a fraud, Karl Ludwig as an imbecile, and Paul Ehrlich as a thief? And the patriotic chemists who discovered arsenic in dill pickles, ground glass in pumpernickel, bichloride tablets in Bismarck herring, pathogenic organisms in aniline dyes? And the inspired editorial writers of the New York *Times* and *Tribune*, the Boston *Transcript*, the Philadelphia *Ledger*, the Mobile *Register*, the Jones Corners *Eagle*? And the headline writers? And the Columbia, Yale and Princeton professors? And the authors of books describing how the Kaiser told them the whole plot in 1913, while they were pulling his teeth or shining his shoes? And the ex-ambassadors? And the *Nietzschefresser*? And the chautauqua orators? And the four-minute men?[9]

---

[9] These were bores who visited the movie parlors of the time and broke in upon "The Perils of Pauline" with brief but rousing speeches. How many were in

And the Methodist pulpit pornographers who switched so facilely from vice-crusading to German atrocities? And Dr. Newell Dwight Hills? And Dr. Henry van Dyke?[1] And the Vigilantes?[2] Let no grateful heart forget them!

Palmer and Burleson I leave for special legislation.[3] If mere university presidents, such as Nicholas Murray Butler, are to have the grand cross, then Palmer deserves to be rolled in malleable gold from head to foot, and polished until he blinds the cosmos —then Burleson must be hung with diamonds like Mrs. Warren and bathed in spotlights like Gaby Deslys. . . . Finally, I reserve a special decoration, to be conferred *in camera* and worn only in secret chapter, for husbands who took chances and refused to read anonymous letters from Paris: the somber badge of the Ordre de la Cuculus Canorus, first and only class.

---

practice first and last I do not know, but there must have been hundreds of thousands. They were chiefly recruited from the ranks of Rotarians, Kiwanians, chautauquans, evangelical clergymen, and minor politicial aspirants.

[1] Hillis was a Presbyterian clergyman, but went over to the Congregationalists and spent most of his life in the old pulpit of Henry Ward Beecher in Brooklyn. He brought out a book called "German Atrocities" in 1918, in which all of the most fantastic inventions of the English propaganda bureau were treated gravely. Such horrors apparently fascinated him, and he wallowed in them in a really obscene manner. He died in 1929. Van Dyke, another Presbyterian, took the same line, though less violently. He had been pastor of the Brick Presbyterian Church in New York, but in the war era was professor of English literature at Princeton. He was taken gravely as a poet and essayist in his day, and rose to be president of the National Institute of Arts and Letters, but his writings were hollow and he is now pretty well forgotten. He died in 1933.

[2] An organization of professional patriots analogous to the American Protective League, but even worse. Its heroic members specialized in daubing yellow paint on the houses of persons suspected of having doubts about the Wilson idealism. In some regions they also resorted to assault, always at odds of at least 10 to 1.

[3] A. Mitchell Palmer, a Quaker, was Attorney General under Wilson. He was the superintendent of many ferocious spy-hunts. He died in 1936. Albert Sidney Burleson was Wilson's Postmaster General. He specialized in the censorship of the mails. He died in 1937.

Death:

A Philosophical Discussion

‹‹‹‹‹‹‹‹‹‹‹‹‹‹‹‹‹‹‹‹‹‹‹‹‹‹‹‹‹‹‹‹‹›››››››››››››››››››››››››››››››

The back parlor of an American home. A dim suggestion of festivity: strange chairs, the table pushed back, a decanter and glasses. A heavy, suffocating, discordant scent of flowers—roses, carnations, lilies, gardenias. A general stuffiness and mugginess, as if it were raining outside, which it isn't.

A door leads into the front parlor. It is open, and through it the flowers may be seen. They are banked about a long black box with huge nickel handles, resting upon two folding horses. Now and then a man comes into the front room from the street door, his shoes squeaking hideously. Each visitor approaches the long black box, looks into it with ill-concealed repugnance, snuffles softly, and then backs off toward the door. A clock on the mantelpiece ticks loudly.

In the back parlor six pallbearers sit upon chairs, all of them bolt upright, with their hands on their knees. They are in their Sunday clothes, and their hats are on the floor beside their chairs. Each wears upon his lapel the gilt badge of a fraternal order, with a crepe rosette. In the gloom they are indistinguishable; all of them talk in the same strained, throaty whisper. Between their remarks they pause, clear their throats, blow their noses, and shuffle in their chairs. They are intensely uncomfortable.

From A Mencken Chrestomathy, 1949. Included in A Book of Burlesques, 1916. First printed in the Smart Set, Dec. 1914. Copyright 1916 by Alfred A. Knopf, Inc. Renewal copyright 1944 by H. L. Mencken.

Death: A Philosophical Discussion

Tempo: Adagio lamentoso, with occasionally a rise to andante maesto. So:

FIRST PALLBEARER Who woulda thought that *he* woulda been the next?

SECOND PALLBEARER Yes; you never can tell.

THIRD PALLBEARER (*An oldish voice, oracularly.*) We're here today and gone tomorrow.

FOURTH PALLBEARER I seen him no longer ago than Chewsday. He never looked no better. Nobody would have—

FIFTH PALLBEARER I seen him Wednesday. We had a glass of beer together in the Huffbrow Kaif. He was laughing and cutting up like he always done.

SIXTH PALLBEARER You never know who it's gonna hit next. Him and me was pallbearers together for Hen Jackson no more than a month ago, or say five weeks.

FIRST PALLBEARER Well, a man is lucky if he goes off quick. If I had *my* way I wouldn't want no better way.

SECOND PALLBEARER My brother John went thataway. He dropped like a stone, settin' there at the supper table. They had to take his knife outen his hand.

THIRD PALLBEARER I had an uncle to do the same thing, but without the knife. He had what they call appleplexy. It runs in my family.

FOURTH PALLBEARER They say it's in *his'n*, too.

FIFTH PALLBEARER But he never looked it.

SIXTH PALLBEARER No. Nobody woulda thought *he* woulda been the next.

FIRST PALLBEARER   Them are the things you never can tell anything about.

SECOND PALLBEARER   Ain't it true!

THIRD PALLBEARER   We're here today and gone tomorrow.
   (*A pause. Feet are shuffled. Somewhere a door bangs.*)

FOURTH PALLBEARER (*Brightly.*)   He looks elegant. I hear he never suffered none.

FIFTH PALLBEARER   No; he went too quick. One minute he was alive and the next minute he was dead.

SIXTH PALLBEARER   Think of it: dead so quick!

FIRST PALLBEARER   Gone!

SECOND PALLBEARER   Passed away!

THIRD PALLBEARER   Well, we all have to go *some* time.

FOURTH PALLBEARER   Yes; a man never knows but what his turn'll come next.

FIFTH PALLBEARER   You can't tell nothing by looks. Them sickly fellows generally lives to be old.

SIXTH PALLBEARER   Yes; the doctors say it's the big stout person that goes off the soonest. They say pneumoney never kills none but the healthy.

FIRST PALLBEARER   So I have heered it said. My wife's youngest brother weighed 240 pounds. He was as strong as a mule. He could lift a whiskey-barrel, and then some. Once I seen him drink damn near a whole keg of beer. Yet it finished him in less'n a week—and *he* had it mild.

SECOND PALLBEARER   It seems that there's a lot of it this winter.

(524)

THIRD PALLBEARER Yes; I hear of people taken with it every day. My brother Sam's oldest is down with it.

FOURTH PALLBEARER I had it myself once. I was out of my head for four weeks.

FIFTH PALLBEARER That's a good sign.

SIXTH PALLBEARER Yes; you don't die as long as you're out of your head.

FIRST PALLBEARER It seems to me that there is a lot of sickness around this year.

SECOND PALLBEARER I been to five funerals in six weeks.

THIRD PALLBEARER I beat you. I been to six in five weeks, not counting this one.

FOURTH PALLBEARER A body don't hardly know what to think of it scarcely.

FIFTH PALLBEARER That's what *I* always say: you can't tell who'll be next.

SIXTH PALLBEARER Ain't it true! Just think of *him*.

FIRST PALLBEARER Yes; nobody woulda picked *him* out.

SECOND PALLBEARER Nor my brother John, neither.

THIRD PALLBEARER Well, what *must* be *must* be.

FOURTH PALLBEARER Yes; it don't do no good to kick. When a man's time comes he's got to go.

FIFTH PALLBEARER We're lucky if it ain't us.

SIXTH PALLBEARER So I always say. We ought to be thankful.

FIRST PALLBEARER   That's the way *I* always feel about it.

SECOND PALLBEARER   It wouldn't do *him* no good, no matter *what* we done.

THIRD PALLBEARER   We're here today and gone tomorrow.

FOURTH PALLBEARER   But it's hard all the same.

FIFTH PALLBEARER   It's hard on *her*.

SIXTH PALLBEARER   Yes, it is. Why should *he* go?

FIRST PALLBEARER   It's a question nobody ain't ever answered.

SECOND PALLBEARER   Nor never won't.

THIRD PALLBEARER   You're right there. I talked to a preacher about it once, and even *he* couldn't give no answer to it.

FOURTH PALLBEARER   The more you think about it the less you can make it out.

FIFTH PALLBEARER   When I seen him last Wednesday he had no more ideer of it than what you had.

SIXTH PALLBEARER   Well, if I had *my* choice, that's the way I would always want to die.

FIRST PALLBEARER   Yes; that's what *I* say. I am with you there.

SECOND PALLBEARER   Yes; you're right, bothen you. It don't do no good to lay sick for months, with doctors' bills eatin' you up, and then have to go anyhow.

THIRD PALLBEARER   No; when a thing has to be done, the best thing to do is to get it done and over with.

FOURTH PALLBEARER   That's just what I said to my wife when I heerd.

FIFTH PALLBEARER   But nobody hardly thought that *he* woulda been the next.

SIXTH PALLBEARER   No; but that's one of them things you can't tell.

FIRST PALLBEARER   You never know *who'll* be the next.

SECOND PALLBEARER   It's lucky you don't.

THIRD PALLBEARER   I guess you're right.

FOURTH PALLBEARER   That's what my grandfather used to say: you never know what is coming.

FIFTH PALLBEARER   Yes; that's the way it goes.

SIXTH PALLBEARER   First one, and then somebody else.

FIRST PALLBEARER   Who it'll be you can't say.

SECOND PALLBEARER   *I* always say the same: we're here today—

THIRD PALLBEARER (*Cutting in jealously and humorously*).   And tomorrow we ain't here.

(*A subdued and sinister snicker. It is followed by sudden silence. There is a shuffling of feet in the front room, and whispers. Necks are craned. The pallbearers straighten their backs, and hitch their coat collars. The clergyman has arrived. From above comes the sound of weeping.*)

The Libertine

<<<<<<<<<<<<<<<<<<<<<<<<<<<<<<<<<>>>>>>>>>>>>>>>>>>>>>>>>>>>

THE average man of our time and race is quite incapable of all these incandescent and intriguing divertisements. He is far more virtuous than they make him out, far less schooled in sin, far less enterprising and ruthless. I do not say, of course, that he is pure in heart, for the chances are that he isn't; what I do say is that, in the overwhelming majority of cases, he is pure in act, even in the face of temptation. And why? For several main reasons, not to go into minor ones. One is that he lacks the courage. Another is that he lacks the money. Another is that he is fundamentally moral, and has a conscience. It takes more sinful initiative than he has in him to plunge into any affair save the most casual and sordid; it takes more ingenuity and intrepidity than he has in him to carry it off; it takes more money than he can conceal from his consort to finance it. A man may force his actual wife to share the direst poverty, but even the least vampirish woman of the third part demands to be courted in what, considering his station in life, is the grand manner, and the expenses of that grand manner scare off all save a small minority of specialists in deception. So long, indeed, as a wife knows her husband's income accurately, she has a sure means of holding him to his oaths.

Even more effective than the fiscal barrier is the barrier of poltroonery. The one character that distinguishes man from the other higher vertebrata, indeed, is his excessive timorousness, his

---

easy yielding to alarms, his incapacity for adventure without a crowd behind him. In his normal incarnation he is no more capable of initiating an extra-legal affair—at all events, above the mawkish harmlessness of a flirting match with a cigar girl in a café—than he is of scaling the battlements of hell. He likes to think of himself doing it, just as he likes to think of himself leading a cavalry charge or climbing the Matterhorn. Often, indeed, his vanity leads him to imagine the thing done, and he admits by winks and blushes that he is a bad one. But at the bottom of all that tawdry pretence there is usually nothing more material than an oafish smirk at some disgusted shop-girl, or a scraping of shins under the table. Let any woman who is disquieted by reports of her husband's derelictions figure to herself how long it would have taken him to propose to her if left to his own enterprise, and then let her ask herself if so pusillanimous a creature could be imaged in the role of Don Giovanni.

Finally, there is his conscience—the accumulated sediment of ancestral faint-heartedness in countless generations, with vague religious fears and superstitions to leaven and mellow it. What! a conscience? Yes, dear friends, a conscience. That conscience may be imperfect, inept, unintelligent, brummagem. It may be indistinguishable, at times, from the mere fear that some one may be looking. It may be shot through with hypocrisy, stupidity, play-acting. But nevertheless, as consciences go in Christendom, it is genuinely entitled to the name—and it is always in action. A man, remember, is not a being *in vacuo*; he is the fruit and slave of the environment that bathes him. One cannot enter the House of Commons, the United States Senate, or a prison for felons without becoming, in some measure, a rascal. One cannot fall over-board without shipping water. One cannot pass through a modern university without carrying away scars. And by the same token one cannot live and have one's being in a modern democratic state, year in and year out, without falling, to some extent at least, under that moral obsession which is the hallmark of the mob-man set free. A citizen of such a state, his nose buried in Nietzsche, "Man and Superman," and other such advanced literature, may caress himself with the notion that he is an immoralist, that his soul is full of soothing sin, that he has cut himself loose from the revelation of God. But all the while there is a part of him that remains a sound Christian, a moralist, a right-thinking and forward-looking man. And that part, in times of stress, asserts itself. It may not worry him on ordinary occasions. It may not stop him when he swears, or takes a nip of whiskey behind the door, or goes motoring on Sunday; it may even let him alone when he goes to a leg-show. But the moment a concrete Temptress rises before him, her nose snow-white, her lips rouged, her eyelashes drooping provokingly—the moment such an abandoned wench has at him, and his lack of ready funds begins to conspire with his lack of courage to assault and wobble him—at that precise moment his conscience flares into function, and so finishes his business. First he sees difficulty, then he sees danger, then he sees wrong. The result? The result is that he slinks off in trepidation, and another vampire is baffled of her prey.

It is, indeed, the secret scandal of Christendom, at least in the Protestant regions, that most men are faithful to their wives. You will travel a long way before you find a married man who will admit that *he* is, but the facts are the facts, and I am surely not one to flout them.

Random Notes

<<<<<<<<<<<<<<<<<<<<<<<<<<<<<<<<>>>>>>>>>>>>>>>>>>>>>>>>>>>>>>

W E MUST respect the other fellow's religion, but only in the sense and to the extent that we respect his theory that his wife is beautiful and his children smart.

In a country of pushers and yearners, what a joy it is to meet a man who envies no one and wants to be nothing that he is not!

All the great enterprises of the world are run by a few smart men: their aids and associates run down by rapid stages to the level of sheer morons. Everyone knows that this is true of government, but we often forget that it is equally true of private undertakings. In the average great bank, or railroad, or other corporation the burden of management lies upon a small group. The rest are ciphers.

The unreliability of history is one of the crying scandals of civilization. To this day no really convincing account of the origins of the Civil War has been written. Worse, there exists no adequate history of the United States. When historians began to turn to so-called "sources" they undoubtedly made a step toward accuracy, but it is now evident that most sources offer no more than special pleading, and hence are almost indistinguishable from what are now called press-agents' hand-outs. James Ford Rhodes apparently made a further step when he began to mine contemporary newspapers, but it is hard to believe that anyone forced to read American newspapers during World War

II will ever believe in them again. In all probability it will be eternally impossible to arrive at the precise truth about the majority of salient historical events. At best, only half of the story can ever be known. Worse, there is little indication that historians, as a class, have any actual desire to establish even that half. Those of the academic moiety seldom lift themselves above the level of mere pedagogues, and those outside the fold are commonly highly prejudiced partisans. It would be hard to imagine honest history being written by Woodrow Wilson on the one hand or Henry Cabot Lodge on the other, yet both have respectable places as American historians, and are in fact rather more reliable than most. The best are probably chance bystanders —for example, Gideon Welles. Welles set up his famous diary, I suspect, because he was uncomfortably aware that what was generally believed about the Civil War and its chief actors was not true. But having written it, he began to realize that the truth was not generally relished, so he kept it secret, and it was not published until 1912, a third of a century after his death.

Autobiography, though it always makes interesting reading, is hardly more to be trusted than academic history. It seems to be almost impossible for a man who has had a hand in great events to tell the truth about them. Even the narratives of such realistic and iconoclastic fellows as William T. Sherman and of such dull, unimaginative clods as U. S. Grant are full of palpable evasions. If Woodrow Wilson had written his autobiography it would have been a genuine marvel of false pretenses. Even among the official histories it would have stood out in that respect. Less puissant men sometimes make an effort to tell the truth, but save in a few exceptional cases they do not know what it is.

Gnomes

‹‹‹‹‹‹‹‹‹‹‹‹‹‹‹‹‹‹‹‹‹‹‹‹‹‹‹‹‹‹‹›››››››››››››››››››››››››››››

LOVE is the delusion that one woman differs from another.

Democracy is the theory that the common people know what they want, and deserve to get it good and hard.

It is hard to believe that a man is telling the truth when you know that you would lie if you were in his place.

All men are frauds. The only difference between them is that some admit it. I myself deny it.

During a lull in the uproar of Hell two voices were heard.
"My name," said one, "was Ludwig von Beethoven. I was no ordinary music-master. The Archduke Rudolph used to speak to me on the streets of Vienna."
"And mine," said the other, "was the Archduke Rudolph. I was no ordinary archduke. Ludwig von Beethoven dedicated a trio to me."

Politician: any citizen with influence enough to get his old mother a job as charwoman in the City Hall.

Say what you will about the Ten Commandments, you must always come back to the pleasant fact that there are only ten of them.

From *A Little Book in C Major,* 1916. Copyright 1916 by Alfred A. Knopf, Inc. Renewal copyright 1944 by H. L. Mencken.

One may cherish, perhaps, a profound respect for the Beatitudes, but surely not for the man who believes in them.

Conscience: the inner voice which warns us that someone may be looking.

To an embalmer there are no good men and bad men. There are only dead men and live men.

Democracy is also a form of religion. It is the worship of jackals by jackasses.

Immortality: the condition of a dead man who doesn't believe that he is dead.

No matter how long he lives, no man ever becomes as wise as the average woman of forty-eight.

A gentleman is one who never strikes a woman without provocation.

There was a woman once who was satisfied with her husband, her dress allowance and her complexion. Her name has not been preserved. She died before writing was invented.

A man may be a fool and not know it—but not if he is married.

The great difficulty about keeping the Ten Commandments is that no man can keep them and be a gentleman.

The Shrine of Mnemosyne

<<<<<<<<<<<<<<<<<<<<<<<<<<<<<<<<<<<<<<<<<<<<<<>>>>>>>>>>>>>>>>>>>>>>>>>>>>>

THE little town of Kirkwall, in the Orkney Islands, in a mid-winter mist, flat and charming like a Japanese print. . . . San Francisco and the Golden Gate from the top of Twin Peaks. . . . Gibraltar on a spring day, all in pastel shades, like the backdrop for a musical comedy. . . . My first view of the tropics, the palm trees suddenly bulging out of the darkness of dawn, the tremendous stillness, the sweetly acid smell, the immeasurable strangeness. . . . The Trentino on a glorious morning, up from Verona to the Brenner Pass. . . . Central Germany from Bremen to Munich, all in one day, with the apple trees in bloom. . . . Copenhagen on a wild night, with the *Polizei* combing the town for the American who upset the piano. . . . Christiania in January, with the snow-clad statue of Ibsen looming through the gloom like a ghost in a cellar. . . . The beach at Tybee Island, with the faint, blood-curdling rattle of the land crabs. . . . Jacksonville after the fire in 1902, with the hick militiamen firing their machine guns all night. . . . The first inauguration of Woodrow, and the pretty suffragette who drank beer with me at the Raleigh. . . . A child playing in the yard of a God-forsaken town in the Wyoming desert. . . . Bryan's farewell speech at the St. Louis Convention in 1904. . . . Hampton Court on Chestnut Sunday. . . . A New Year's Eve party on a Danish ship, 500 miles off the coast of Greenland. . . . The little pile of stones on the beach of Watling's Island, marking the place where Columbus landed. . . . The moon of the Caribbees, seen from a 1,000-ton British tramp. . . . A dull night in a Buffalo hotel, reading the American Revised Version of the New Testament. . . . The day I received the proofs of my first book. . . . A goodbye on an Hoboken pier. . . . The Palace Hotel in Madrid.

Three American Immortals

⫷⫷⫷⫷⫷⫷⫷⫷⫷⫷⫷⫷⫷⫷⫷⫷⫷⫷⫷⫷⫷⫷⫷⫷⫷⫷⫷⫷⫷⫷⫸⫸⫸⫸⫸⫸⫸⫸⫸⫸⫸⫸⫸⫸⫸⫸⫸⫸⫸⫸⫸⫸⫸⫸⫸⫸⫸⫸

Aristotelian Obsequies

I TAKE the following from the Boston *Herald* of May 1, 1882:

> A beautiful floral book stood at the left of the pulpit, being
> spread out on a stand. . . . Its last page was composed of white
> carnations, white daisies and light-colored immortelles. On the leaf
> was displayed, in neat letters of purple immortelles, the word
> "Finis." This device was about two feet square, and its border was
> composed of different colored tea-roses. The other portion of the
> book was composed of dark and light-colored flowers. . . . The
> front of the large pulpit was covered with a mass of white pine
> boughs laid on loosely. In the center of this mass of boughs ap-
> peared a large harp composed of yellow jonquils. . . . Above this
> harp was a handsome bouquet of dark pansies. On each side ap-
> peared large clusters of calla lilies.

Well, what have we here? The funeral of a Grand Exalted
Pishposh of the Odd Fellows, of a venerable Tammany leader, of
an aged and much respected brothel-keeper? Nay. What we have
here is the funeral of Ralph Waldo Emerson. It was thus that the
Puritan *Kultur* mourned its philosopher.

From *A Mencken Chrestomathy,* 1949. Included in *Prejudices: First Series,* 1919.
First printed in the *Smart Set,* May 1919. Copyright 1919 by Alfred A. Knopf,
Inc. Renewal copyright 1947 by H. L. Mencken.

<<<<<<<<<<<<<<<<>>>>>>>>>>>>>>

Edgar Allan Poe

THERE are two memorials to Poe in Baltimore, the city where he triumphed, loved, sweated, suffered and died. One is a life-size statue in a public park, showing him in his cups. The other is his cheap and hideous tombstone in the corner of a Presbyterian churchyard—a tombstone quite as bad as the worst in Père La Chaise. For twenty-six years after Poe's death there was not even this: the grave remained wholly unmarked. Poe had surviving relatives in Baltimore, and they were well-to-do. One day one of them ordered a local stonecutter to put a plain stone over the grave. The stonecutter hacked it out and was preparing to haul it to the churchyard when a runaway freight train smashed into his stoneyard and broke the stone to bits. Thereafter the Poes seem to have forgotten Cousin Edgar; at all events, nothing further was done.

The existing tombstone was erected by a committee of Baltimore schoolma'ms, and cost about $1,000. It took the dear girls ten long years to raise the money. They started out with a "literary entertainment" which yielded $380. This was in 1865. Six years later the fund had made such slow progress that, with accumulated interest, it came to but $587.02. Three years more went by: it now reached $627.55. Then some anonymous Poeista came down with $100, two others gave $50 each, one of the devoted schoolma'ms raised $52 in nickels and dimes, and George W. Childs agreed to pay any remaining deficit. During all this time not a single American author of position gave the project any aid. And when, finally, a stone was carved and set up and the time came for the unveiling, the only one who appeared at the ceremony was Walt Whitman. All the other persons present were Baltimore nobodies—chiefly schoolteachers and preachers. There were three set speeches—one by the principal of a local high school, the second by a teacher in the same seminary, and the third by a man who was invited to give his "personal recollections" of Poe, but who announced in his third sentence that "I never saw Poe but once, and our interview did not last an hour."

This was the gaudiest Poe celebration ever held in America. At his actual burial, in 1849, exactly eight persons were present, of whom six were relatives. He was planted, as I have said, in a Presbyterian churchyard, among generations of honest believers in infant damnation, but the officiating clergyman was a Methodist. Two days after his death a Baptist gentleman of God, the illustrious Rufus W. Griswold, printed a defamatory article upon him in the New York *Tribune*, and for years it set the tone of native criticism of him. And so he rests: thrust among Presbyterians by a Methodist and formally damned by a Baptist.

<<<<<<<<<<<<<<<<<>>>>>>>>>>>>

Memorial Service

LET us summon from the shades the immortal soul of James Harlan, born in 1820, entered into rest in 1899. In the year 1865 this Harlan resigned from the United States Senate to enter the Cabinet of Abraham Lincoln as Secretary of the Interior. One of the clerks in that department, at $600 a year, was Walt Whitman, lately emerged from the three years of service as an army nurse during the Civil War. One day, discover-

From *A Mencken Chrestomathy*, 1949. Included in *Prejudices: First Series*, 1919. First printed in the *Smart Set*, June 1919. Copyright 1919 by Alfred A. Knopf, Inc. Renewal copyright 1947 by H. L. Mencken.

ing that Whitman was the author of a book called "Leaves of Grass," Harlan ordered him incontinently kicked out, and it was done forthwith. Let us remember this event and this man; he is too precious to die. Let us repair, once a year, to our accustomed houses of worship and there give thanks to God that one day in 1865 brought together the greatest poet that America has ever produced and the damndest ass.[1]

---

[1] This squib became a fixture in the *Smart Set,* and in some form or other was reprinted at least once a year. It was then taken over into the *American Mercury,* but its first appearance there, in April, 1924, p. 453, seems to have been its last.

BIBLIOGRAPHY

❀ · ❀ · ❀ · ❀ · ❀

The standard bibliography is the admirable *H. L. M.: The Mencken Bibliography,* compiled by Betty Adler with the assistance of Jane Wilhelm (Baltimore: The Johns Hopkins Press; 1961). Miss Adler lists fourteen other bibliographies of Mencken's works, some general and some specialized. Her book covers most phases of his career, including the positive identification of twenty-nine pseudonyms and an indication of fourteen probable ones. "Major Owen Hatteras" became the most celebrated of the pseudonyms, and was used by both Mencken and Nathan. The Major was a frequent contributor to the *Smart Set* and in 1917 published a pamphlet of forty-two pages on Mencken and Nathan under the title *Pistols for Two* (Mencken wrote the sketch of Nathan, and Nathan the sketch of Mencken). The Major served in World War I with distinction and was awarded the D.S.O. When Mencken and Nathan left the *Smart Set* at the end of 1923, the Major's demise was announced and many newspapers carried obituary notices. Miss Adler's volume also contains valuable notes by Mencken written for his bound volumes of typescripts and heretofore unpublished. The book runs to 367 pages, including a complete index.

Following is a list of Mencken's principal works. In most cases, only the date of the first edition is given.

Ventures into Verse. Baltimore: Marshall, Beck & Gordon; 1903.
George Bernard Shaw: His Plays. Boston: J. W. Luce & Co.; 1905.
The Philosophy of Friedrich Nietzsche. Boston: J. W. Luce & Co.; 1908.
The Artist, a Drama Without Words. Boston: J. W. Luce & Co.; 1912.
A Book of Burlesques. New York: John Lane; 1916.

Bibliography

A Little Book in C Major. New York: John Lane; 1916.

A Book of Prefaces. New York: Alfred A. Knopf; 1917.

Damn! A Book of Calumny. New York: Philip Goodman; 1918.

In Defense of Women. New York: Philip Goodman; 1918.

The American Language: a Preliminary Inquiry into the Development of English in the United States. New York: Alfred A. Knopf; 1919. *Supplement I*, 1945. *Supplement II*, 1948. The fourth edition (1936) and the two supplements were abridged and issued in a one-volume edition, with annotations and new material by Raven I. McDavid, Jr., with the assistance of David W. Maurer. New York: Alfred A. Knopf; 1963.

Prejudices: First Series. New York: Alfred A. Knopf; 1919.

Prejudices: Second Series. New York: Alfred A. Knopf; 1920.

Prejudices: Third Series. New York: Alfred A. Knopf; 1922.

Prejudices: Fourth Series. New York: Alfred A. Knopf; 1924.

Notes on Democracy. New York: Alfred A. Knopf; 1926.

Prejudices: Fifth Series. New York: Alfred A. Knopf; 1926.

Prejudices: Sixth Series. New York: Alfred A. Knopf; 1927.

Treatise on the Gods. New York: Alfred A. Knopf; 1930.

Making a President: a Footnote to the Saga of Democracy. New York: Alfred A. Knopf; 1932.

Treatise on Right and Wrong. New York: Alfred A. Knopf; 1934.

Happy Days, 1880–1892. New York: Alfred A. Knopf; 1940.

Newspaper Days, 1899–1906. New York: Alfred A. Knopf; 1941.

Heathen Days, 1890–1936. New York: Alfred A. Knopf; 1943.

A Mencken Chrestomathy, edited and annotated by the author. New York: Alfred A. Knopf; 1949.

The Vintage Mencken, gathered by Alistair Cooke. New York: Vintage Books; 1955.

A Carnival of Buncombe, edited by Malcolm Moos. Baltimore: The Johns Hopkins Press; 1956.

Minority Report: H. L. Mencken's Notebooks. New York: Alfred A. Knopf; 1956.

A Bathtub Hoax and Other Blasts & Bravos from the Chicago Tribune, edited by Robert McHugh. New York: Alfred A. Knopf; 1958.

Prejudices, a selection made by James T. Farrell. New York: Vintage Books; 1958.

H. L. Mencken on Music, a selection by Louis Cheslock. New York: Alfred A. Knopf; 1961.

A Note on the Type

THE TEXT of this book is set in *Caledonia,* a typeface designed by W(ILLIAM) A(DDISON) DWIGGINS for the Mergenthaler Linotype Company in 1939. Dwiggins chose to call his new typeface Caledonia, the Roman name for Scotland, because it was inspired by the Scotch types cast about 1833 by Alexander Wilson & Son, Glasgow type founders. However, there is a calligraphic quality about this face that is totally lacking in the Wilson types. Dwiggins referred to an even earlier typeface for this "liveliness of action"—one cut around 1790 by William Martin for the printer William Bulmer. Caledonia has more weight than the Martin letters, and the bottom finishing strokes (serifs) of the letters are cut straight across, without brackets, to make sharp angles with the upright stems, thus giving a "modern face" appearance.

W. A. Dwiggins (1880–1956) was born in Martinsville, Ohio, and studied art in Chicago. In 1904 he moved to Hingham, Massachusetts, where he built a solid reputation as a designer of advertisements and as a calligrapher. He began an association with the Mergenthaler Linotype Company in 1929, and over the next twenty-seven years designed a number of book types for that firm. Of especial interest are the Metro series, Electra, Caledonia, Eldorado, and Falcon. In 1930, Dwiggins first became interested in marionettes, and through the years made many important contributions to the art of puppetry and the design of marionettes.

COMPOSED, PRINTED, AND BOUND BY
THE HADDON CRAFTSMEN, INC., SCRANTON, PA.
TYPOGRAPHY AND BINDING DESIGN BASED ON
ORIGINALS BY W. A. DWIGGINS